Production/Operations Management

SECOND EDITION

Production/Operations Management
Text and Cases

SECOND EDITION

Terry Hill

Professor of Operations Management
London Business School

Prentice Hall
New York   London   Toronto   Sydney   Tokyo   Singapore

First published 1983 by
Prentice Hall International (UK) Ltd
66 Wood Lane End, Hemel Hempstead
Hertfordshire HP2 4RG
A division of
Simon & Schuster International Group

Second edition published 1991

Typeset in 10½/12pt Plantin
by MHL Typesetters Ltd, Coventry

Printed and bound in Great Britain at the
University Press, Cambridge

Library of Congress Cataloging-in-Publication Data

Hill, Terry, 1940–
    Production & operations management 2E / by Terry Hill.
       p.   cm.
    Includes bibliographical references.
    ISBN 0-13-723727-8
       1. Production management.   I. Title.   II. Title: Production and
    operations management 2E.
    TS155.H463   1991
    658.5—dc20   90-32583
                                                                   CIP

British Library Cataloguing in Publication Data

Hill, Terry, *1940–*
    Production & operations management. — 2nd ed
    1. Production management
    I. Title
    658.5

ISBN 0-13-723727-8

2 3 4 5   94 93 92 91

Contents

Preface to the Second Edition

The area of production/operations management (POM) is often misunderstood by both students of and managers within a business. This misunderstanding is generated partly by the way the subject is presented and taught, and partly by the way the function is perceived and explained by production/operations managers to their fellow executives. There are many reasons why this situation exists and, as with any complex set of activities, there are several approaches to its resolution.

However, part of the problem also lies in the changing field of study. Originally, the conceptual orientation and emphasis within POM was towards the management of the area. Later, specialist developments introduced a set of techniques which made useful, sometimes fundamental, contributions to help in the management of the production/operations task. From this developed a strong, often overriding impetus to teach and develop POM as a series of techniques involving detailed analysis and tactical considerations, and often not discriminating between the usefulness or relevance of one analysis to another. This developed into a technique-oriented approach, with an emphasis towards the quantitative perspective as a way to resolve POM issues. In turn, as this is based on substantial content, the approach usually includes explanations and mathematical derivations of the formulae and solutions proposed.

The outcomes were significant. In the academic world POM became uninteresting and apparently lacked business relevance. Demand fell and growth in faculty resources, research and teaching did not match the general expansion experienced in business education at the undergraduate, postgraduate and post-experience levels. Within the manufacturing and service sectors of the economy the role became devalued. Consequently, the critical perspectives of this large and substantial function were not clearly recognized and were often inadequately presented. Typical results were unbalanced corporate argument, inappropriate allocation of key management resources to POM, and a failure to attract the necessary management talent into the area by matching task, responsibilities and contribution with appropriate status, influence and reward.

However, the importance of the POM function in the growth and prosperity of a business has been re-established. At the same time, it is being increasingly recognized that the nature of the POM's corporate contribution needs to be set within the broader perspective of the management and control of this function rather than the perspectives on which POM has more recently been based. Currently, the emphasis is returning to a managerial focus, and this book is designed to provide part of that focus. It concentrates on providing a management understanding of the important aspects of the production/operations task. In so doing it does the following:

1. Attempts to make the basics of POM more understandable.

2. Provides a conceptual understanding of this area whilst covering in some detail those aspects considered to be essential POM areas.

3. Recognizes and discriminates between the levels of detail within the subjects covered; thus, some chapters present a comprehensive review of the subject matter, and others do not. In addition, there are supplementary technical appendices to some chapters.

4. Stresses the more important areas of the POM task, the controls to be used, and helps the reader to differentiate between the large issues and the small.

5. Introduces non-POM aspects where they are important in the management of the function, but then refers the reader to a detailed coverage provided elsewhere.

6. Deliberately avoids the quantitative/mathematical bias that underlies the treatment of POM in many textbooks, and yet retains the strong analytical approach so essential to the management and control of the POM task.

Lastly, the structure of the book overall and within particular chapters has been chosen to reflect the managerial emphasis on the one hand and to help clarify issues on the other. The book comprises three parts. The first, 'Production/operations: management role and strategic context', sets the scene in two ways. Chapter 1 explains some general background to the production/operations function, the derivation of these titles and the role of the manager of this function. Chapter 2 concerns strategy. The reason it is placed here is to increase the readers' awareness of the fact that the remainder of the book concerns explanations of POM and approaches that may be used in its management and control. But these choices need to be made in the reality of a particular business. Thus, knowing which is the more appropriate approach needs to reflect the relevant strategy for the production/operations function.

Parts II and III then reflect the main split in the POM function — the former concerns process-related issues, and the latter, infrastructure-related issues. Therefore, Chapters 3—7 cover the tangible or 'hard' side of the task and Chapters

8–15 the intangible or 'soft' side. It is important to recognize the subtle mix of these two facets; it is even more important to accomplish it.

By providing a conceptual view of the issues of the POM task and discriminating between the useful and less useful by the extent of topic coverage, it is hoped to serve the needs of those who are or who intend to take on the POM role and those whose roles will relate to this function in a range of businesses. In so doing, it will provide an improved understanding of the POM issues and approaches most suited to different corporate requirements. The book, therefore, is designed to provide for its readers in the following ways:

1. As part of a course study, with explanations and further application through class discussion and the use of appropriate case studies.

2. For managers who can apply the knowledge, concepts and ideas to their own situation to increase their understanding of how to improve their contribution to the overall business performance.

T.J. Hill

Production/operations
Management role and strategic context

Part 1 provides an introduction to production/operations as well as essential context against which the remainder of the book will be set.

Chapter 1 is designed to accomplish a general background to production/operations management (POM) as well as a more detailed review of the manager's role. In this way it provides a range of inputs as a way of interweaving the task of managing the area within a mixed economy typical of the more developed nations.

The basic task is simple, that of converting a range of inputs into required outputs through the operations process. As Figure 1.2 shows, the reality is much more complex. What makes it so is a combination of factors which emanate from the size of the function and the range of its constituent parts. Co-ordinating this aspect of the business is an exciting management role, and the complexity of the task contributes to this excitement. The purpose of the book is to break down the function into its constituent parts whilst bearing in mind that the individual elements need to be placed in some overall context.

Having explained the POM role and introduced relevant background, Chapter 2 explains both the need to place the POM function within an appropriate strategic context and the steps involved in doing this. The position of the chapter at this stage in the book is significant. Agreements and decisions within POM (as within any other area) need to be made within appropriate strategies. Thus, the remainder of the book explains the different ways to develop the various functions and tasks within POM, but the appropriate choice for any organization has to be made to meet the needs of its own business requirements.

Chapter 1

The role of the production/operations manager

Production management and operations management describe the same set of tasks. Both are concerned with managing those resources of an enterprise that are required to produce the goods or services to be sold to consumers or other organizations. The term production management came first, with the emergence of manufacturing industry and the subsequent emphasis placed on the production management task within that sector. The growth of service industries in the industrially developed countries has brought with it the term operations management as a more appropriate, general title. Throughout this book, therefore, the terms production management and operations management will be treated as being synonymous.

The nature of the production/operations manager's role

The production/operations function is that part of an organization responsible for producing the goods or providing the services that it sells in the market-place. Some organizations produce physical items such as furniture, building materials or stationery, whilst others provide services such as medical care, banking facilities or retail sales outlets. In order to produce or provide these items to a required quality level, at an appropriate time and within acceptable financial constraints, organizations create a number of functions that are essential (although often with differing degrees of emphasis due to the varying roles within different segments of the economy) to the buying, producing and selling activities which underpin their existence. One key function is production/operations. Common to all the diverse range of goods and service activities that make up a national economy is the conversion process illustrated in Figure 1.1. The production/operations managements (POM) task is concerned with the transformation process which takes inputs and converts them into outputs, together with the various support functions closely associated with this basic task. The level of complexity within this function will depend upon several factors, including:

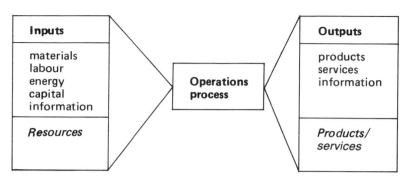

Figure 1.1 Outline of the operations process.

1. The size of the organization.
2. The nature of the products/services involved.
3. The technology levels embodied in both the products/services and processes used within the production/operations function.
4. The extent to which the products/services are made in-house.

The operations system provided in Figure 1.1 is clearly a simplified overview of what is involved. The remainder of the book concerns the features within the POM task necessary to bring this about; they are illustrated in Figure 1.2. Attempting to be both accurate and simple, this overview of the POM task is intended to provide an insight into the whole as well as give some details of the inputs and the transformation process itself. The chapter references at the top left of the blocks will help you to find your way through the book. They also indicate the interrelated nature of these areas: a characteristic which typifies all management subjects. In addition, it offers a base point which may be useful as a reference for each new topic as it is addressed.

Production/operations management in a developing economy

As national economies develop then the balance between different sectors changes. The UK economy, as with other more-developed countries, is a mix of activities from agriculture and mining through to utilities and services provision. Table 1.1 shows the sector groupings in 1987 for selected countries. Reflecting on some of the differences under three headings, it is possible to see that they reflect the general activities associated with the individual countries involved. A review of the primary sector shows the lack of mineral resources in Japan and the natural riches of the USSR, Australia and Canada. The secondary sector reflects the manufacturing might of West Germany and Japan in the free world economies and the USSR in the Eastern Bloc. Although these percentage weightings change over time (for example, the increase in primary activities in the UK with the advent of oil and gas production

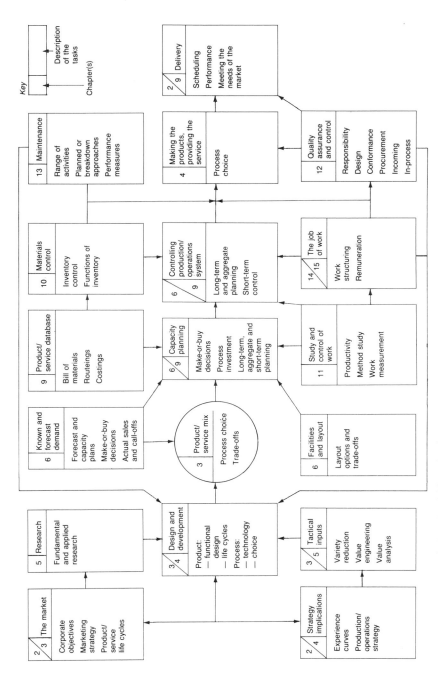

Figure 1.2 The POM task within a business.

Source: adapted from Terry Hill, 'Production/operations management', in *Introducing Management*, eds K. Elliot and P.A. Lawrence (Harmondsworth: Penguin, 1985), chapter 19.

Table 1.1 Percentage of gross domestic product (GDP) by sector grouping for certain more developed economies (1987)

	Percentage of gross domestic product by sector[a]		
	Primary	*Secondary*	*Tertiary*
Australia	10	24	66
Canada	10	25	65
France	5	31	64
Japan	3	37	60
UK	8	28	64
USA	7	27	66
USSR	21	56	24
W. Germany	2	38	60

[a] These sectors include the following activities:

Primary   — agriculture and mining.
Secondary — manufacturing and construction.
Tertiary   — utilities, wholesale/retail trade, transport, services and others. ('Others' are unclassified activities which constitute in all instances a relatively high percentage of the total GDP. This category is included in 'tertiary' since the activities are neither 'primary' nor secondary.)

Source: UN Bulletin of Statistics (1987).

in the North Sea and on the mainland), the shift in emphasis remains small (for example, in 1970 the UK figures were 7, 27 and 66 respectively). This means that in most of the economically more-developed nations the tertiary activities are significant in terms of generating gross domestic product (GDP).

These figures, however, need to be placed in different contexts in order to appreciate their relative importance to trading nations. For instance, further perspectives include:

1. Most services comprise (to varying degrees) an element of product. (The reverse is also true — see Chapter 4).

2. For many nations, trade predominantly comprises products made in the secondary sector. In the UK, manufactured items account for 86 and 83 per cent respectively of the export and import content of visible trade in 1988 (based on figures for January to June 1988).[1]

Thus, the balance of activities not only changes over time but will differ between nations. In the UK, the secondary and tertiary sectors together are significant. Although the activities have been separated to help identify, understand and discuss the whole, in reality they are part of a total economy. For, whereas 'agriculture, mining and manufacturing are the bricks of economic development, the mortar that binds them together is the service industry'.[2] This need for mutual interdependence is acknowledged and attended to by developed countries at both the corporate and national levels — see the next section. Arguments suggesting that developed nations can use the tertiary sector as the means of improving below-average trade performances (as were prevalent in the UK and USA in the early 1980s) are without foundation. The success of countries such as Japan and West Germany and the rapid emergence of countries like South Korea highlight the critical nature of a sound secondary base. Equally, on reflection, it is not surprising that in 1988, eight of the top ten banking institutions in the free world economy were Japanese.

To regain or sustain corporate (and thereby contribute to national) prosperity it is essential to achieve the required level of effectiveness. To do this, it is necessary to manage well those activities responsible for the provision of goods or services. These tasks are therefore critical to the success of an organization and, in turn, of the nation. Operations managers oversee these tasks. They control the inputs and processes which together produce the goods or provide the services. It is the control of these main-thrust activities that is the role of the operations manager, and the one that this book addresses.

The mix of manufactured items and services

Goods are tangible items purchased by individuals or organizations for subsequent use. Services are intangible items that are consumed at the time of provision, with the customer taking away or retaining the benefit of that service. However, in many commercial situations, what is provided or produced by an organization can be a mixture of both goods and services. In some instances there will be a heavy accent on product, and in others, the reverse. Figure 1.3 shows a range of items sold and the mix between product and service content provided. The purchase mix

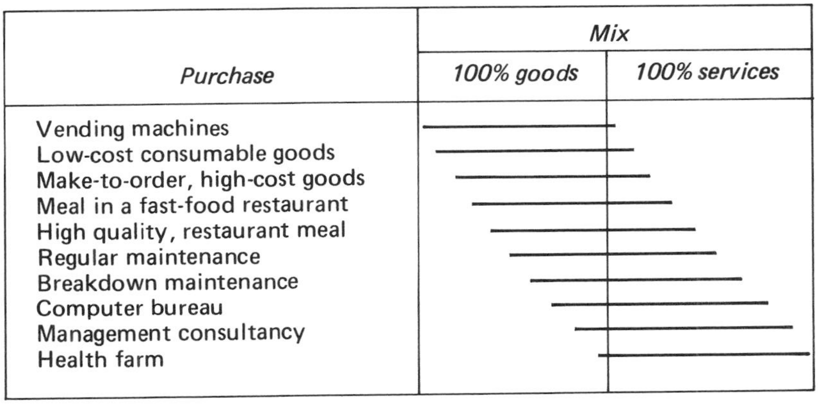

Purchase	Mix	
	100% goods	*100% services*
Vending machines		
Low-cost consumable goods		
Make-to-order, high-cost goods		
Meal in a fast-food restaurant		
High quality, restaurant meal		
Regular maintenance		
Breakdown maintenance		
Computer bureau		
Management consultancy		
Health farm		

Figure 1.3 Different product/service mixes provided in a range of purchases.

represented here is intuitively derived, and others may consider the balance to differ from that shown. It is important, therefore, when considering Figure 1.3, to bear in mind that its purpose is to draw attention to this product/service mix. The question to be answered is: 'Are we a manufacturing organization with an auxiliary service, or a service organization with a facilitating good?[3]

Thus, products and services are packages of explicit and implicit benefits made or provided by a supporting set of processes often using a service or good respectively as part of the package provision. For example, compare a cup of coffee provided by a vending machine and the same item provided in the lounge of a good hotel. The former service offers convenient, twenty-four hour, fast delivery of a product. The production specification itself is largely influenced by the nature of the service, and hence the product range offered is limited both in terms of width and specification: coffee is provided in a number of combinations (e.g. regular or decaffeinated, with or without milk and sugar) and in a disposable cup. On the other hand, coffee provided in the lounge of a good hotel comprises significantly different service factors − choice, presentation, comfort and normally a slower, 'more leisurely' service at a higher price. In the former coffee provision, the ratio of goods in the total package would be considerably higher than in the latter.

In order to compete, some organizations will change this mix to provide a more attractive package. Such a move will bring with it a different operational task, and one that needs to be understood and allowed for in the structure and procedures of the operations function.

The operations manager within the organization

The operations manager is usually responsible for a whole range of functions within an organization. These functions will differ depending upon whether it is a manufacturing or service business, and the nature of the item to be provided. Figures 1 and 2 in the case study 'Too short, the day' at the end of the book show the position of the operations manager within a theatre and the functions reporting to him. Likewise, Figure 1.4 shows the organizational set-up for a production manager within a manufacturing company.

Relating these two illustrations to Figure 1.2 will help to link the functions that form part of the organization to the activities provided by the production/operations function; it also shows the relationship between POM and the other departments within a typical company.

Size of the operations task

Operations management is concerned with the management of physical resources for the production or provision of an item or a service. To accomplish this, the

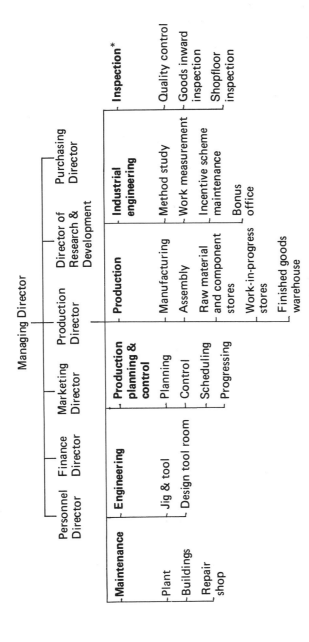

Figure 1.4 Production management functions.

* Quality assurance in this organization reports to the Director of Research and Development.
In many organizations, this task is increasingly being made an integral part of the operator's job.

available facilities need to be managed so as to meet the current market requirements within the cost constraints laid down. In the longer term, it will also be involved in the design or extension of facilities in so far as they affect the operating system.

There are, however, few linear relationships within the operations system. It is dynamic and must be managed effectively in times of economic uncertainty and social change.[4] The size of the operations task is outlined below.

1. The operations task concerns the management of a large number of people. Most employees are usually involved in the main-thrust activities of a business (e.g. direct workers in production). A high percentage of the support staff will also come under the operations manager's control. The total number in this function usually accounts for 70–80 per cent of all those employed by the organization.

2. It is responsible for the effective use of some 70–80 per cent of an organization's total assets. On the fixed assets side, it is usually accountable for land and buildings together with plant and equipment, which together make up a large percentage of the total fixed asset investment. On the current assets side, it is responsible for the inventory holding which, as shown in Chapter 10, is a high percentage of the current assets investment. Since these together constitute a large part of the total investment made, the operations function takes on the responsibility for effectively managing the most significant proportion of an organization's use of funds.

3. Lastly, the operations function accounts for the major proportion of an organization's expenditure. As the majority of the direct costs, such as labour and materials, are incurred in this area, together with much of the overhead costs involved, then it is by far the largest budget area within an organization.

These features mean that the efficient management of the operations process is important to the organization's short- and longer-term success. However, translating the task into the right combination of plant, equipment, people, procedures and processes is a difficult and time consuming job. These areas of activity are not only large in themselves but they are all closely interrelated parts of the whole task. Furthermore, decisions made in this area are difficult to change because of their complicated nature and the high investment cost usually associated with past actions.

The role of the operations manager

As explained above, the size of the POM task is extensive. Furthermore, it comprises a number of internal dimensions which need to be managed within a number of external variables. The former are addressed within the various chapters of the book and overviewed in Figure 1.2. As emphasized throughout, and particularly in Chapter 2, they need to be managed at both the strategic and tactical levels. The latter — the external variables — relate to changes in markets, competition, financial resources and economic trends. The task, therefore, consists of controlling a sizable part of an organization in terms of the effective management of the delivery system regarding customers' needs and corporate targets.

These features of the operations task, their size and their importance, create a situation that is difficult to manage. It is concerned with detail yet must address corporate issues of significant size and importance. To understand more of what is involved, some key aspects of the job are outlined now.

1.   The operations task concerns the management of a cost centre. As explained in the previous section, the function accounts for a large part of the asset investment and has the largest budget within an organization. Therefore, the operations manager is responsible for a large cost centre. If operations budgets and output levels are met, then the cost structure of the business will be sound.

2.   It is necessary for the operations manager to be efficient in both the short and longer term. The task of producing a good or providing a service is a short-term function. A day's lost output will never be recovered without additional costs being incurred. That is the nature of the task. It is essential, therefore, that the day-to-day activities are well controlled, co-ordinated and meet the budgeted output. To meet monthly targets requires that each day's target is met. Other departments, such as sales, work on a different time basis with no one expecting the period sales target to be met *pro rata* each day. As a consequence, there is substantial pressure exerted to meet the operations requirement in the short term.

In fact, POM 'is problem orientated, indeed in this sense its practicability is overwhelming'.[5] 'Pressure is also a distinctive feature'[6] of the job due to the tasks involved, the time contraints imposed and the dependency upon a whole range of activities, some of which are outside the control of the operations function either in terms of the organization's reporting system or in that they are externally sourced.

However, the time pressures on operations managers often result in their having to make as good a decision as possible in any given situation. To think of a better decision at a later date is usually of little value. It would be too late and the consequences of the delay would normally outweigh the improvements involved. It is essential, therefore, that operations managers use their experience to good effect as there is little opportunity for discussion with their colleagues.

It is important, however, that the longer-term requirements do not take a secondary role.[7] In a function controlling such a large portion of revenue expenditure, the longer-term developments of the operations function need to be given the necessary time and attention. For here, small percentage improvements lead to large actual savings.

3.   The operations manager is a manager of technology, both product and process. However, the degree of technology will differ from one industry to the next and from one organization to the next, and in many situations the level is quite low. In most instances, however, the task is the same. The operations manager needs not so much to understand the technology itself as the level of technology involved and how this fits into the total job. (Tables 4.1—4.4 in Chapter 4 illustrate this point in more detail.)

4. Like managers of other departments, the operations manager breaks down the task into subsystems as a way to control the whole task. This is essential in order to cope. However, the manager's role is to control these subsystems whilst trying to control the total system. As the operations task is large, the subsystems will usually be both numerous and interrelated.

In addition, many support and specialist functions will form part of the organizational structure, with much of their activity being concerned with the main-thrust of the organization. Therefore, it is equally important for operations managers to be involved with and contribute to the specialist's tasks and activities as far as they relate to their own area of responsibility.

5. The manager is responsible for both the work-flow and money-flow. The role of controlling the work-flow has been discussed before; it forms an essential part of the job. However, this task is linked to part of the money-flow within the organization as illustrated in Table 1.2, which shows current assets and the relationship to work- and money-flows. The component/material inventory (money

Table 1.2 Work- and money-flows

Money-flow Out	Money-flow In	Current assets	Work- and materials-flow	Activity description
✓	—	Raw materials and components	Materials/components	The necessary materials/components are bought from outside
✓	—	Inventory { Work-in-progress (WIP)[a]	Labour and other materials/components added	The necessary tasks to produce the product or provide the service are completed
✓	—	Finished goods	More labour and materials/components added	Product/service now complete and is or can be sold
—	✓	—	Finished goods/ services are sold	Cash sales
—	—	Debtors	Finished goods/ services are sold	Credit sales
—	✓	Cash	—	Payment made for credit sales

[a] In some cases, payments are made when certain stages have been completed (e.g. stage payments may be made in the building/construction industry) or at the end of a time period (e.g. management consultants usually invoice on a weekly basis).

out) will, in work-flow terms, become work-in-progress with a labour and additional material input (money out), and similarly will eventually become finished goods or services (more money out). Until it is a finished good or service (see the note with Table 1.2), it is not possible to sell the item to create a debtor (except for cash sales). Eventually a payment is made against the invoice (money in) by the customer.

In make-to-order situations, stage payments are often negotiated and, therefore, parts of the loop are circumvented. But the principle still holds (see the note with Table 1.2). Thus the money-flow is tied to the work-flow with collection and payment falling within the accounting function, working on normal commercial rules.

It is for this reason that the 'end of the month rush' takes place in some organizations. Here, the pressure on money-flow to get goods or services completed and submit an invoice before the end of the month, (thus accelerating payment (money in)) will override the efficiency of the process. Thus, improved cash-flow becomes a trade-off with the increased costs which will result from the decrease in efficiency inherent in the 'end of the month rush' activity.

6.   The operations function has to be controlled on both a time and money basis. Time constitutes the common denominator for the control of the process, and money the common denominator for corporate reporting systems. It is essential, therefore, that managers in these functions understand both bases in order to contribute to their design and development, to be able to understand more fully the essential nature of the reporting systems, and to explain the results to others.

7.   One distinguishing feature of this POM task is that it is characterized by tangible outputs. Unlike many other functions, production/operations at each stage in the system can be measured (see Figure 1.1). While this offers intrinsic satisfaction to the incumbents, it may also tend to reinforce other characteristics. For example, as a consequence of this feature many organizations evaluate POM performance by a series of well-specified and objective measures; this often, however, reinforces the incumbents' concern for the short-term aspects of the task (those which are more tangible in nature and, therefore, more specific in application) and the organization's failure to incorporate POM perspectives when determining corporate strategy (an issue addressed at some length in the next chapter).

8.   The operations function forms the interface between the thinking-end and the doing-end of a business. It provides the essential link between the corporate view and the operational task, and the corporate philosophy and the view of working-life held by those who complete the task.

9.   The most important role which embodies the tasks outlined here is that of being a manager of *complexity*. The size and diversity of the tasks involved, the implications of decisions in terms of investment, costs and people are enormous. The challenge in the POM job comes not from the nature of the individual tasks and decisions for which the operations manager is responsible — in themselves they are often quite simple — but from the number of these which have to be completed or made at the same time and the complex interrelationships that exist. As the main-thrust activities constitute the core of the organization, then the work of external specialists will be largely related to the activities of this function. They will be involved not only with improving this function *per se* but also with developing the interrelated activities of this and other departments.

Service features

The similarities and distinctions that characterize the management task in the manufacturing and service environment, and which have been highlighted throughout this chapter, will feature throughout the book. The statistics in Table 1.1 show the importance of each sector within the economies of most industrialized nations. Whilst the POM task has many similarities with manufaturing and service businesses there are features distinctive of the one as opposed to the other. Each

Table 1.3 Distinguishing characteristics and management-related features of a service business

Similarity of service outputs

The similarity of products is built into the product. Services, however, although apparently similar are often significantly varied. The difference in a service stems from:

1. Its intangible nature.
2. The potential for interpretation by those involved in the service delivery system.
3. The presence of the customer at the point of production.

A service is a package of explicit and implicit benefits and/or services built around faeilitating goods (see Figure 1.3). Key management tasks include:

1. A clear understanding of what constitutes the service package.
2. Establishing quality and service levels.
3. Measuring achievement against agreed levels.

Customer participation

In most service firms, customers are an integral part of the service delivery system. They are actively engaged in the process and service transaction. The degree of involvement, however, needs to be determined and carefully evaluated within the context of the system and the agreed quality and service levels. The participation decision will have several implications for and introduce a degree of uncertainty within the operations management task:

1. Design of the service delivery system.
2. Shift/attendance patterns.
3. Capacity provision.
4. Layout.
5. Quality of the service.
6. Length of process time.

chapter highlights these two perspectives and some include a section summarizing any pertinent issues in the service sector. The reason for this is not just to highlight differences but to emphasize the need to distinguish between the two and yet recognize the considerable overlap that exists in terms of the management of the operations function. The chapter layout referred to earlier together with Table 1.3 are provided to illustrate these points. The former lists some of the distinguishing characteristics of a service organization and its operating conditions, and details some of the management issues involved, particularly those relating to the operations function, which will be addressed in the chapters ahead. However, a review of the latter will also highlight both the differences and similarities which exist in POM within the manufacturing and service sectors: a factor which is a feature of the subject area and which needs to be recognized and borne in mind in order to understand this management task.

Conclusion

Few operations managers would consider their role to be other than demanding, challenging, absorbing and satisfying. They would also tell of its frustrations and

---

Barriers to entry

The difficulty of successfully patenting a service involves businesses in a set of strategic responses, including:

1. Achieving market share quickly.
2. Erecting other barriers to entry, as well as market share.
3. Identifying what constitutes the service and establishing quality and service levels to support these distinctive features.
4. Degree of standardization of the service facility and its delivery system provision.
5. Determine the back room/front office relationship in terms of efficiency and personalized service mix:
   (a) automate the back-room-related tasks;
   (b) personalize the front office approach through, for example, extra capacity provision.

Level of competition

Services have different levels of transportability. Some are subject to local competition and local markets (the 'you don't go to Hong Kong for a Chinese take-away' syndrome). Others are subject to national and international market forces — for example, money markets and passenger air travel. This leads to issues concerning:

1. The extent of transportability.
2. Constraints on exporting.
3. The size of delivery system units.
4. Implications of multinational service firms.

Source: based on D.A. Collier, *Service Management: Operating Decisions* (Englewood Cliffs, NJ: Prentice Hall, Inc., 1987), table 1.2.

complexity: this is bound to be so where a function is required to handle a large number of variables and to achieve many, diverse and complicated short- and longer-term objectives.

To manage such a task well requires a range of qualities as indicated in the section outlining the POM role. To this list need to be added hard work and experience. The POM task is, among other things, about hard, physical work. To complete the day-to-day tasks requires much physical effort. However, to perceive the whole and instigate through others appropriate initiatives and developments also requires both intellect and experience. The former to be able to appreciate the issues and perspectives involved and the latter to help alert potential problem areas. The recognition of this need is gaining momentum not least because of the success of industrial nations and the emphasis placed by the more successful upon the management of the production/operations function. By the early 1980s it was becoming clear that Japanese success was not based upon greater investment in processes but in management, particularly manufacturing. Some believe that the managers needed to 'convert manufacturing into a competitive resource may have to be the best rounded and most intellectually able of all corporate managers'.[8] The competences identified included: 'a knowledge of technology ... as well as every business function ... a thinking style that includes the ability to conceptualize as well as analyze complex trade-offs ... [and] managers who are architects of change not house-keepers'.[9]

But, this is not only a prerequisite for managing the production function in manufacturing. Those nations unsuccessful in carrying out this task have stood by and watched their manufacturing sector diminish dramatically in a period of a few years. Next on the list are parts of the service sector. It is essential that the UK (as well as others) at least retains the manufacturing base it still has whilst defending and growing in all relevant sectors. In the past the UK has experienced a major revision in its ratio of goods and services, in part by neglect (see Figure 1.5).

The rest of this book reviews the essential tasks involved and some of the important perspectives that need to be understood by the operations manager. The book attempts both to present the concepts underlying this function and to show which approaches are the most useful to adopt in order to analyse and evaluate each major part of the whole POM task. The emphasis, therefore, is not on covering all existing techniques or mathematical approaches and explanations. As shown in Table 1.4, the higher levels of learning are those concerned with application, analysis, synthesis and evaluation. Knowledge and understanding are the easier, lower levels of learning; the most difficult task is to do the job effectively. This requires the application of relevant knowledge, the analysis of the results of that application, the building back together of the results into an improved form (synthesis) and the evaluation of this in terms of what has to be done. Effective managers are those who are able to do this as a way of continuously developing their own set of responsibilities.

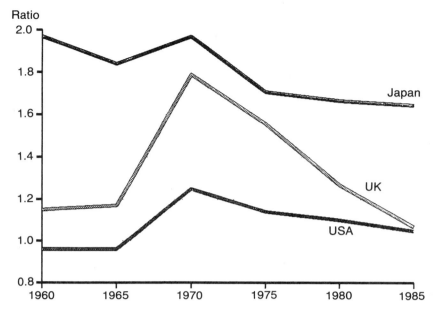

Figure 1.5 Ratio of manufacturing to services (at constant prices).
Source: UN National Accounts Statistics.

Table 1.4 The levels of learning

	Levels of learning	Description
Increasingly higher levels of learning	Evaluation	Appraise, compare, conclude, contrast, interpret and explain
	Synthesis	Classify, compile, design, modify, reorganize, formulate, reconstruct and substitute
	Analysis	Select, discriminate, illustrate, separate and distinguish
	Application	Demonstrate, relate, use, compete and prepare
	Understanding	Explain, extend, generalize, infer, summarize, and estimate
	Knowledge	Know, identify, list, name, outline and state

Source: B.S. Bloom and D.R. Krathwohl, *Taxonomy of Learning Objectives* (Makay, 1956).

Notes and references

1. DTI, *Monthly Review of External Trade Statistics*, 151, (August 1988).
2. R.K. Shelp, J.C. Stephenson, N.S. Truith and B. Wasow, *Service Industries and Economic Developments Case Studies in Technology Transfer*, (New York: Praeger, 1984), p. 1.
3. W.E. Sasser *et al.*, *Management of Service Operations* (Boston: Allyn & Bacon, 1978), p. 10.
4. The fluctuating growth and recession in the economies of many developed countries has been well documented in the last twenty years. On the social side, in the 1970s alone, there were twelve separate Acts of Parliament passed in the UK concerning social changes — details and comments are given in the CRIBA Working Paper no. 94 (July 1981).
5. P.A. Lawrence, *Operations Management: Research and priorities'*, Report to the Social Services Research Council (April 1983), p. 2.
6. Lawrence, *op. cit.*, p. 14.
7. However, the findings in the CRIBA Working Paper no. 94 (University of Warwick) show that the recruitment advertisements in a major national newspaper during the period 1970—79 placed little stress on the corporate role. For appointments at both the manager and board director level, the significance of this is shown in the advertisements for these jobs, where the number of mentions regarding POM's corporate role as a percentage of the total was small in 1970 and did not change throughout the decade (see attachments 7 and 14 of this paper).
8. R. Meyer, 'Wanted: a new breed of manufacturing manager', in *Manufacturing Issues 1987* (New York: Booz Allen, 1987), pp. 26—9.
9. Meyer, *op. cit.*, p. 28.

Chapter 2

Production/operations strategy

Faced with increasing competitive pressures, businesses have a greater need to coordinate the activities of their principal functions within a coherent strategy. However, companies typically fail to do this. They do not embrace all the functional contributions necessary to develop successful corporate responses. One common and glaring omission is that of the production/operations function.

Production/operations' reactive role

When responding to the various outcomes of changing business fortunes, many companies counter these competitive forces from an unnecessarily limited base. This failure to embrace all strategic strengths stems from restricting the number of internal dimensions embodied in their corporate response. In many instances, businesses have neither the way, nor sometimes the will, to incorporate the necessary range of functional inputs essential to determining an appropriate corporate strategy response.

While most companies recognize the need to embrace within their strategy decisions the dimensions of their markets and to identify the financial consequences that ensue or limitations that may constrain, many fail to incorporate the critical perspective of the production/operations implications of the business options that they are considering. For some, the reason is not knowing how to accomplish this facet of strategy development. For others, it offers an easier task. By considering only a limited set of issues the strategy task is made more manageable. Furthermore, by considering only the external features it focuses on the more exciting and apparently more strategic perspectives of the corporate debate. Meanwhile, production/operations bears the label of being uninteresting, strategically unproductive and of little corporate consequence.

However, whilst limiting the number of internal perspectives in strategy formulation makes the task simple, it makes the response simplistic. Manufacturing investments are both large and fixed. A company is thus committed to a corporate direction once it makes these investments. Thus, the results of such a limited approach to strategy formulation are, at best, risky and, at worst, damaging or even disastrous.

Reasons for production/operations strategy's reactive role

The fact that POM has an exacting and critical corporate role to play is undisputed. Why, then, do executives adopt their current reactive role and why does the situation not appear to improve? There are several reasons for this, including the following:

1.   *The production/operations managers' view of themselves*
One of the major contributions to this situation appears to be that production/operations managers also see themselves holding a reactive corporate brief. They define their role as requiring them to react as well as possible to all that is asked of the production or service delivery system. They see their role as the exercise of skill and experience effectively coping with the exacting and varying demands placed on the system and to reconcile the trade-offs as best they can.

Thus, rarely do they adequately contribute to the making of corporate decisions. They do not explain the different sets of implications created by alternative corporate marketing options. They thus fail by default to contribute within the corporate debate.

2.   *The company's view of the production/operations managers' role*
The POM view of its strategic role is reinforced by the company's view of its contribution. Companies also view the operations role as short-term and reactive and, therefore, do not stress the long-term nature of the task. Consequently, companies fail to emphasize the need for and importance of this contribution.

3.   *Too late in the corporate debate*
Production/operations managers are often not involved in corporate policy decisions until the decisions have started to take shape. The result is that executives have less opportunity to contribute to decisions on strategy alternatives and, consequently, always appear to be complaining about the unrealistic demands made of them and the problems that invariably ensue.

4.   *Lack of language*
On the whole, production/operations managers do not have a history of explaining their function clearly and effectively to others within the organization. This is particularly the case in terms of the strategy issues that need to be considered and the POM consequences that will arise from corporate decisions under discussion. Reasons for this failure, however, cannot be wholly placed at the POM door. The knowledge base, concepts and language have not been developed in the same way.

Consequently, shared perspectives within POM, let alone between functions, are not held, adding fuel to the lack of interfunctional understanding.

For many businesses, corporate strategy comprises the independent inputs of different functions. However, this invariably leads to functional conflicts which, without a way of resolving, will result in inappropriate corporate decisions being taken. Where this concerns process and/or infrastructure investments it involves two important characteristics. These investments are large in size and fixed in nature. Consequently they typically take a long time to determine and install, and even longer to change. Thus it is essential that companies understand the relevance of proposed investments in terms of their current and future markets.

The need for strategic difference

Any executive being asked, 'Are all your businesses the same?' or 'Are all parts of one business the same?', would answer 'no' to both questions. Strategy formulation too must acknowledge that reality. Overviewing a company's markets in terms of segments, customers or generic products, is necessary to help understand the whole. To split the production/operations function is, therefore, not only more necessary (as it is more complex) but more essential, as it involves large investments based on change times that are too long to allow errors of judgement — the large and fixed syndrome highlighted earlier.

The need for strategic difference in production/operations is, therefore, a prerequisite on which to build a sound and successful business. To accomplish this, it is necessary for business to recognize relevant issues at two levels:

1. How to develop relevant POM inputs into the corporate strategy debate.
2. To be aware of the different approaches at the operational level within POM so that appropriate consideration can be given to alternatives.

Only when both sets of issues are understood and form part of the total review will appropriate investments be made. Given the large and fixed nature of these decisions, this understanding is essential if businesses wish to avoid committing themselves to inappropriate directions.

This chapter outlines the strategic approach to developing a production/operations strategy.[1] The rest of the book details the alternative approaches relevant at the operational level. It is important, therefore, to review the options detailed in each of the following chapters, both in terms of themselves and within the context of the strategic trade-offs that have to be resolved.

Most parts of a business, however, have an impact upon one another. Production/operations investments are both substantial (about 80 per cent of the corporate total) and embody a set of fixed trade-offs (once a company has made the investments it must live with them for years to come because of the size of these investments and the length of time necessary to make the change).

Similarly, marketing has an impact upon production/operations. Its decisions make demands upon both processes and infrastructure provision. Incremental change, so often the way in which a company's markets move, usually results in a gradual and increasing mismatch between the demands on the production/operations function and its ability to respond. Whilst POM intuitively recognizes the consequences of these changes, it does not, as highlighted earlier, have the concepts and language to argue its case and to alert the company to issues of strategic importance. The result is frustration and an ever-widening gap between the marketing and production/operations functions as essential contributors to the business, its strategy formulation and overall success.

This chapter addresses the need to close the gap by providing approaches to strategy building that bring together marketing and production/operations, facilitate open discussion about the business, and enable sensible resolution of functional differences at the corporate level.

Linking marketing and production/operations

Many current strategy approaches reinforce corporate misunderstanding and promote interfunctional differences. However, there is an urgent need to close the gap, to increase corporate awareness of the tradeoffs involved in the status quo, and to facilitate discussion based on an improved understanding of functional perspectives, business options and overall consequences. For although not all strategy decisions result in a perfect match, company executives do need to keep uppermost in their minds the fact that changes in production/operations are both expensive and time-consuming.

The importance of linking marketing and production/operations is paramount. The question is how? First, however, let us consider a few examples that typify some of the dilemmas resulting from corporate failure to recognize the business dimensions of manufacturing, its inherent complexity and the fixed nature of its responses. The failure to appreciate that, in most situations, the level of differentiation required in manufacturing is greater than in other functions has courted disaster in many companies, as these three examples testify.

Company A

Part of a multinational group, company A faced, like many others, a decline in markets and associated profits. In order to redress these trends, it undertook a major internal review. The key changes concerned its two manufacturing plants. To provide 'orientation to its business' it was decided to manufacture different products at different plants. The 'product orientation' resulted in each plant being allocated particular products and associated volumes. In this period, the number of product types handled by plant 2 was eight times as many as plant 1. As one would expect, product volume changes were reflected in this decision. Whilst in plant 1 individual product average volumes rose by 60 per cent, in plant 2 they decreased by 40 per cent.

The plant and associated infrastructure investments concerned processes, job roles, remuneration and organizational changes. Each plant, however, was deemed to have the same manufacturing change requirements. For plant 1, this was in line with the product allocations and financial targets were met. For plant 2, it led to a significant mismatch between products and manufacturing. Two years on and £17m later, plant 2 had exhausted the goodwill of the workforce, trade unions and local management, had no more investment to allocate, and was turning in a financial performance in steep decline.

Company B

This company produced a range of cartons and other forms of packaging. Eighteen months ago it decided to invest £1.8m in a part of the process producing a range of cartons which, at the time of the decision, accounted for about 30 per cent of total unit sales. On these current sales, the investment would have given a payback of 5½ years. To meet the group's return-on-investment four-year norms, however, it needed to increase throughput in this segment by some 50 per cent, bringing it to a process utilization of 85 per cent.

Increasingly over the years company B had positioned itself in the higher quality end of all its markets. However, to gain the volume increases necessary to justify this process investment, the company had to go for business won on price. The low costs manufacturing requirement thus replaced the delivery speed and customer-support base of its traditional business. The consequences were significant. Not only did the company now have almost 30 per cent of its total orders with distinct low costs needs but it also had to meet the delivery speed needs of the remainder and the willingness to change production schedules and associated disruption that this required. The ramifications were substantial. Almost overnight the process investment had introduced manufacturing conflict in a large part of its total business.

Company C

In a time of increasing competition, company C decided to bring onto one site two separate businesses which were currently sixty miles apart. Whilst one was in high value, low volume, high quality products, the business on the main manufacturing site involved high volume, commodity items. Although some manufacturing processes were unique, most processes were similar in terms of technical provision. In addition to the obvious savings in overheads, part of the rationale for moving onto one site was that the main unit had spare process capacity.

However, the company made two errors of judgement. First it anticipated that whilst few of the skilled operators, supervisors and technical staff would move the sixty miles, the support requirements would be met by existing, main site personnel.

Second, it assumed that all process capacity was the same. In the first instance, not only were the existing main site skills inappropriate to the product and process requirements of the new products but, in terms of production, the move introduced a conflicting set of quality, volume and schedules demands. In the second instance, the company soon became aware of the stark reality that high volume plant capacity is only of use for products with similar order-winning characteristics. Capacity availability does not have a universal application. The question that companies need to address is not only can the process make the product/service in terms of its specification but also can it do so and make acceptable levels of profit.

Differentiating the task: order-winners and qualifiers

The three company examples not only typify the plight of businesses that fail to include the production/operations perspective in the corporate strategy debate but also highlight the failure of companies to differentiate the production/operations task.

Linking production/operations and marketing together, though obvious to all, has proved singularly difficult to bring about. Strategic formulation classically relates marketing strategy to business objectives. As corporate bedfellows they are appropriately involved in the initial steps in corporate decisions. However, in most instances it stops there. The corporate strategy debate ends. The assumption is that production/operations can cope. However, not only is this simplistic in essence but dangerous in application. Production/operations' ability to cope is not an 'all or nothing' issue. It concerns marginality. The extent to which production/ operations cannot support the corporate marketing decision often does not show for a long period, by which time market share has been lost, opportunities have passed by and recovery will take years to effect.

The link between these functions is embodied in a two-fold distinction. The first involves the recognition that companies provide and sell products/services and not markets or market segments. The second is then to determine how products/services win orders in their respective markets today and in the future. In this way, the production/operations task will be differentiated and a recognition of the changes which will take place through relevant product/service life cycles will be highlighted. Separation too has to take place between qualifying and order-winning criteria.[2] Qualifying criteria get a product into the market-place or onto the customer's short list, and keep it there. They do not win orders. Conversely, failure to provide the criteria at appropriate levels will lead to loss of orders. When that happens a company, at best, loses market share or, at worst, loses out altogether. Thus, in such situations competitors do not win orders from a rival, rather the rival loses orders to its competitors. However, having gained entry to a market is only the first step. The problem then is to know how to win orders against competitors who have also qualified to be in the same market. Whilst production/ operations has to provide qualifying criteria (e.g. delivery reliability and quality) to that level required to meet the norms or customer specifications, it has to provide the order-winning criteria (e.g. price and delivery speed) superior to those of its competitors' production/operations functions. This debate clarifies what POM needs to be best at, the time period involved, it signals any anticipated changes, identifies qualifying criteria which have the potential to become order-winning, and signals those qualifiers which are order-losing sensitive. Figure 2.1 illustrates the framework involved and the linkage formed by asking the question, 'How do products win orders in the market-place?'[3]

Achieving the link

Having explained the approach in general terms, it is opportune now to consider in detail how to develop a strategy that embraces the interface between marketing and production/operations. There is no short-cut to production/operations strategy formulation. There are five basic steps to be taken. These provide an analytical and objective structure in which the corporate debate and consequent actions can be taken, and are as follows:

1 Define corporate objectives.
2 Determine marketing strategies to meet these objectives.
3 Assess how different products/services win orders against competitors.
4 Establish the most appropriate mode to manufacture these sets of products or provide these sets of services—process choice.
5 Provide the infrastructure required to support production/operations process.

These are, in one sense, classical steps in corporate planning. The problem is that most corporate planners treat the first three as interactive with 'feedback loops', and the next two as linear and deterministic. Whilst each step has substance in its own right, the critical issue is that each has an impact upon the others — hence the involved nature of strategy formulation. This is further exacerbated by the inherent complexity of production/operations and the general failure to take account of the essential interaction between marketing and production/operations strategies. What is required, therefore, is an approach that recognizes these features, yet provides an ordered and analytical way forward.

The approach suggested to link production/operations with corporate marketing decisions is schematically outlined in Figure 2.1.

How the framework operates

The objective of using this framework is to produce a production/operations strategy for a business (steps 4 and 5). In all instances this will include a review of existing products/services plus a review of proposed product/service introductions. Furthermore, the reviews will be based upon current and future market expectations for the simple reason that production/operations needs to support a product/service

1 Corporate objectives	2 Marketing strategy	3 How do products/services win orders in the market-place?	Production/operations strategy	
			4 Process choice	5 Infrastructure

Growth
Survival
Profit
Return on investment
Other financial measures
	Product markets and segments
	Range
	Mix
	Volumes
	Standardization versus customization
	Level of innovation
	Leader versus follower alternatives
		Price
		Quality
		Delivery:
		  Speed
		  Reliability
		Demand increases
		Colour range
		Product/service range
		Design leadership
		Technical support supplied
			Choice of various processes
			Trade-offs embodied in the process choice
			Process positioning
			Capacity:
			  Size
			  Timing
			  Location
			Role of inventory in the process configuration
				Function support
				Operations/planning and control systems
				Quality assurance and control
				Systems engineering
				Clerical procedures
				Payment systems
				Work structuring
				Organizational structure

Note: Although the steps to be followed are given as finite points in a stated procedure, in reality the process will involve statement and restatement, for several of these aspects will impinge on each other.

Figure 2.1 Framework for reflecting production/operations strategy issues in corporate decisions.

over the *whole* of its life cycle. As product/service requirements change, so will the POM task. Therefore, the range of support requirements will inavariably affect the choice of process (step 4) and infrastructure (step 5) considered appropriate for the business over the whole life cycle of each product or service. (The rationale presented earlier is reinfored by this statement. The following two parts of the book concern both these process- and infrastructure-related choices. Each chapter of Part II outlines the principal features relevant to the process issues of POM, while Part III relates to key aspects of infrastructure and provides details of the important issues within the 'soft side' of POM.)

To reach steps 4 and 5, though, the first three steps need to be taken. With some understanding of what is to be achieved, it is useful now to consider, each step in turn, explaining how the necessary interrelations between these parts come together as a whole to form a corporate strategy for a business.

Step 1: Corporate objectives

Inputs into corporate strategy need to be linked to the objectives of the business. The essential nature of this tie-up is two-fold. It provides the basis for establishing clear strategic direction for the business, and demonstrates the strategic awareness and willingness essential to achieve corporate success. Second, it defines the boundaries and marks the parameters against which the various inputs can be measured and level of consistency established, and thus provides the hallmarks of a coherent corporate plan.

For each company, the objectives will be different in nature and emphasis, reflecting the nature of the economy, markets, opportunity, and preferences of those involved. Typical measures concern profit in relation to sales and investment, together with targets for growth in absolute terms, or with regard to market share. Additionally, businesses may wish to include employee policies and environmental issues as part of their overall sets of objectives.

Step 2: Marketing strategy

Linked closely to the provision of the agreed corporate objectives, a marketing strategy needs to be developed, and will often include the following stages:

1. Market planning and control units need to be selected with the aim of bringing together a number of products with closely related market targets and sharing a common marketing programme.

2. The second stage involves a situational analysis of product markets which comprises:
   (a) current and future volumes;
   (b) end-user characteristics;
   (c) industry practices and trends;

(d) identifying major competitors and a review of the business's relative position.

3. The final stage concerns identifying the target markets and agreeing on objectives for each.

In addition, it will be necessary for the company to agree upon both the level of service support necessary in each market and an assessment of the investments and resources necessary to support these throughout the business.

The outcome will be a declaration to the business of the markets and segments the strategy proposes, while identifying the range, mix and volumes involved. Other issues pertinent to the business will include the degree of standardization/customization within each product/service range, the level of innovation and product/service development it proposes to the business, whether it should be a leader or follower in each of its markets, and the extent and timing of these strategic initiatives.

Step 3: How do products/services win orders in the market-place?

Production/Operations' task is to provide better than the company's competitors those criteria which enable products/services to win orders in the market-place. This step is the essential link between corporate marketing proposals and commitments and the production/operations processes and infrastructure necessary to support them (see Figure 2.1).

Typical order-winning criteria include price, quality, and delivery speed and reliability. However, not only will these be of more or less importance, one to another, but they will also change over time. Furthermore, as explained earlier, products and services will typically have to qualify to gain entry into or retain their position in chosen markets. These qualifiers are an integral part of the production/operations task. However, they are not less important than order-winners but are different. Companies need to support qualifiers to an adequate level, whereas they need to provide order-winners better than the production/operations functions of their competitors.

Step 4: Process choice

Production/operations can choose from a number of alternative processes to make the products/services involved. The key to this choice is volume and the order-winning criteria involved. Therefore, each choice needs to reflect the set of trade-offs involved for the various products or services in current and future terms. The issues embodied in these trade-offs are extensive and important. Chapter 3 has been devoted to the aspect of process choice, where the implications embodied in this fundamental decision will be dealt with in much detail. The remaining chapters in Part II consider the other important process-related aspects listed in Figure 2.1.

Step 5: Production/operations' infrastructure

Production/operations' infrastructure comprises the non-process features within production. It encompasses the procedures, systems, controls, payment schemes, work structuring alternatives, organizational issues and so on involved in the non-process aspects of manufacturing. Part III discusses and illustrates some of the major areas.

Market or Marketing Led?

In many instances, companies do not always keep in sharp focus the critical difference between being market led and being marketing led. To substitute the business (market) perspective with a functional (marketing) perspective will invariably lead to distorted strategies and eventually to corporate disadvantage.

Unfortunately, in many businesses, marketing is increasingly becoming characterized by the perceived role of creating ideas. Where this is manifest, it is invariably indicative of functional indulgence, which at times borders on the irresponsible. Generating ideas becomes an end in itself, with the rigour of testing business fit being left to others. This trend not only trivializes the important functional perspective of marketing, but detracts from its fundamental strategic contribution.

Many companies fail to appreciate the fact that the most critical orders are the ones to which a company says 'no'. For it is this decision that marks the boundaries of the business and declares those segments that fall outside its scope – a prerequisite for developing a production/operations strategy response.

The approach illustrated in Figure 2.1 facilitates these debates. Asking marketing questions of the market requiring production/operations answers takes the strategic discussion away from functional perspectives and places it within a business context. This process helps, therefore, to reorientate the business towards corporate issues, thus facilitating the resolution of interfunctional differences at the business level. It thus sets the scene and prepares the ground for essential corporate strategy resolution.

Conclusion

The heightened nature of competitive pressures within the manufacturing sector was a hallmark of the 1980s. National governments, international companies, the media and various other bodies highlighted this feature and brought it to the attention of everyone concerned. The outcome for many well-established industrial nations has been the stark reality of the erosion of its manufacturing base and the impact on unemployment and balance of trade figures. The UK's £20 billion trade deficit in 1989 bears witness to this.

However, competitive pressure recognizes no boundaries and its impact in the service sector is already being felt. Competition in air travel, hotel provision, tourism, and banking and financial services is already well established — Figure 2.2 provides one example (others appear throughout the book). Unless, therefore, companies encompass all the important functional dimensions within their corporate decisions, they will be seriously disadvantaged in the increasingly competitive world of the 1990s.

In many companies though, strategic developments are still predominantly based on corporate marketing decisions which singularly fail to embrace the production/operations perspectives within these crucial debates. They choose by default, therefore, to ignore the strategic dimension of what is normally the most substantive part of their business when arriving at corporate decisions. In this way the strategic role of production/operations is rendered impotent.

Sound strategy decisions will influence corporate effectiveness more than any other decisions taken in an organization, as illustrated by Figure 2.3. Many

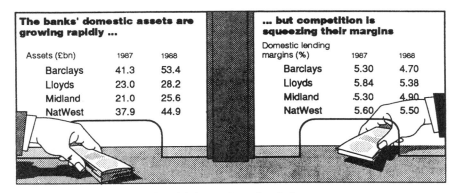

The banks' domestic assets are growing rapidly ...				... but competition is squeezing their margins		
Assets (£bn)	1987	1988		Domestic lending margins (%)	1987	1988
Barclays	41.3	53.4		Barclays	5.30	4.70
Lloyds	23.0	28.2		Lloyds	5.84	5.38
Midland	21.0	25.6		Midland	5.30	4.90
NatWest	37.9	44.9		NatWest	5.60	5.50

Figure 2.2 'Golden era is withdrawn from banks'.
Source: D. Lascelles, *Financial Times* (6 March 1989), p.10. With permission.

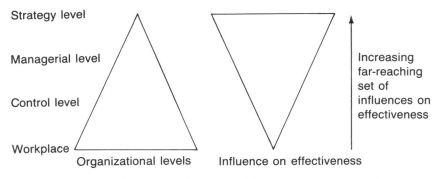

Figure 2.3 Levels in an organization and the influence on effectiveness.

businesses have invested heavily in process-related areas (for example, equipment, other forms of capacity, and manufacturing and service systems — the subject of Part II) and infrastructure-related areas (such as production/operations control, inventory and quality control, and payment systems — the subject of Part III) and this has proved successful over the years. The production/operations strategy perspectives, on the other hand, have been largely ignored. Yet it is these that determine the degree of fit between what markets a business has decided to be in and how well the production/operations function is able to support them. Without this matching procedure, then the activities and investments lower down in the organization are always likely to be out of alignment.

Consider for example, the increasingly open competition between UK High Street banks. The response by banks takes several forms. National Westminster launched a new compensation scheme linked in part to managers' ability to contain costs. Other banks (for example, Barclays) are pursuing cost-cutting reviews.[4] In late 1989 the TSB Group announced a 'blueprint for action' to reduce its twenty-nine thousand staff by five thousand over the next five years as part of an £80 million cost-cutting package. At the same time, however, banks and building societies are expanding their services for private and commercial customers, extending their opening hours, producing more attractive types of account and diversifying their interests.[4] However, unless they have previously determined the implications for the operations function, then issues such as training, availability of skilled staff and the impact upon the service delivery system will militate against its suitable provision. The speed with which clearing banks followed Barclays lead and reopened their doors on a Saturday, left no room to make appropriate decisions about clear objectives, the mix of services to be sold and the implications of staff provision. Lloyds' later decision to reduce its Saturday opening hours is one possible outcome of the lack of adequate strategic debate underpinning its original decision. The cost-cutting initiative by TSB Group mentioned above formed part of its transition from a series of mutual trusts into a serious retail financial group. In addition, the group intends to generate a large amount of new income as part of its overall corporate plan. Whilst it declared its intention to spend £200m on refurbishing up to eight hundred of its branches it needs to recognize that the less tangible features of its operations function will significantly influence its overall success. Whilst tangible facets are readily identified for consideration they are not the core operations issues to be addressed in these circumstances.

The most damaging consequence of this approach is that production/operations is seen to be operational in nature where its strategic response does not apparently have to meet the needs of changing and different markets. Whereas the argument for market differentiation is well understood and supported by most businesses, the production/operations function is invariably not perceived to necessitate any significantly different alignments or to reflect changing and/or different markets. 'One production/operations solution' or 'the scope of existing processes and infrastructures being adequate to meet the range of business needs and their incremental changes', are typical views emanating from the points raised earlier and reinforced by convenience and avoidance in terms of having to implement major strategic decisions with associated large investments.

The impact of competition is the stark reality facing many industrial nations. The closure of plants and premises and loss of traditional markets have grown apace. Initially the impact was most noticeable in the manufacturing sector. However, the late 1980s and early 1990s witnessed similar trends in service industries — and some of these in sectors that had previously been considered traditional and secure. As markets become more global then competition will become more fierce. Landmarks such as 1992 serve only to highlight the fact that the economic world of the 1980s and 1990s is very different from that of previous decades. To convert threat into opportunity will require an appropriate contribution from all parts of a business. And, as the function typically responsible for the largest share of assets, costs and people, POM needs to, and must, adequately and competently fulfil its strategic role.

Notes and references

1.   These approaches and the issues involved are dealt with in greater depth in the following books by Terry Hill: *Manufacturing Strategy: The strategic management of the manufacturing function* (Basingstoke: Macmillan, 1985), and '*Manufacturing Strategy: Text and cases* (Homewood: Irwin, 1989).
2.   Terry Hill, *op. cit.* (1985), pp. 43–51, and Terry Hill, *op. cit.* (1989), pp. 36–46.
3.   Based on Terry Hill, *op. cit.* (1985 and 1989) table 2.2 and figure 2.2, respectively (with permission).
4.   D. Lascelles looks at the growing competition threatening British clearing banks in his article 'Golden era is withdrawn from the banks', *Financial Times* (6 March 1989), p. 10.

Further reading

Buffa, E.S. *Meeting the Competitive Challenge: Manufacturing strategy for US companies* (Homewood: Dow Jones/Irwin, 1984).

Hayes, R.H. and Wheelright, S.C. *Restoring our Competitive Edge: Competing through manufacturing* (Chichester: Wiley, 1984).

Skinner, W. *Manufacturing: The formidable competitive weapon*, (Chichester: Wiley, 1985).

PART II

Process-related issues

As explained in the strategy framework introduced in Chapter 2, the major split of activities within the production/operations function is between process- and infrastructure-related issues. The former concerns the 'hard', tangible decisions within the function, the latter decisions relating to the 'soft', less tangible issues of a business.

Part II comprises Chapters 3–7. Both Parts II and III are similar in that the opening chapter is of a general nature intended to introduce broad issues, some of which are legitimately the province of other subject areas but on which POM issues rest. Hence, introducing these at the beginning provides not only an overview of relevant issues but also introduces perspectives that are essential background to the remaining chapters in each of the two parts. Chapter 3 does this for Part II.

The next four chapters address some of the detailed analyses that have to be made when making decisions about process choice (Chapter 4), product/service investments (Chapter 5) and capacity (Chapter 6).

Chapter 7 concludes Part II by outlining some of the important developments in manufacturing and service systems. Whilst separating them out helps in their understanding, it is critical, however, to remember that these developments need to be placed and understood within the total context of a business and specifically within the issues addressed in the earlier chapters.

Chapter 3

Product/service and process investment decisions
Some general considerations

As explained in Chapter 2, policy decisions give direction to an organization. They identify the broad, longer-term objectives which form the basis for decisions concerning corporate strategies and tactics. This chapter seeks to build on the previous one whilst introducing some pertinent general considerations relating to product/service and process investment decisions. The intention is to provide relevant background perspectives within a business as a prelude to introducing more detailed issues in subsequent chapters.

Objectives, strategies and tactics

Objectives

The overall organizational objectives are statements of intent and are an essential requirement on which to base all subsequent actions at lower levels. As organizations are many and diverse, there will be many different types of objective. Examples can range from the traditional 'maximize long-term profits' through to more nebulous concepts of 'high quality at reasonable cost', to those typical of a non-profit organization, such as 'the best available patient care'. They are the *raison d'être* of the organization. Which ones and how many an organization should have is open to choice. For example, Hanson Trust has an explicit superordinate goal of shareholder wealth maximization; Marks and Spencer's and Sainsbury's goals are quality, value for money and care for staff, and the National Health Service has patient care as one of its principal goals.[1]

Once the objectives are known, then how effectively that organization achieves these can be established. Measures include:

1. *Capacity and capability* How well an organization can produce the goods or provide the services demanded.

2. *Efficiency* Concerns how well the process is managed and controlled. For instance, cost per unit, cost per patient day, profit per employee, sales revenue per employee.

3. *Adaptability* Concerns both the short- and longer-term, and relates to an organization's response to pressure and change, and to the investment in its future through research and development.

As a prime user of resources and the provider of product/service requirement, the operations function will, on the one hand, be affected significantly by the corporate decisions taken while, on the other hand, it will play a major part in achieving them.

Strategies

Strategies are the broad courses of action that an organization needs to follow in order to achieve its objectives. The organization's existing resources will be an important factor in deciding the course of action to adopt in order to achieve a particular objective. Furthermore, the need to invest, modify or develop the operations aspect will be an essential step in the process of determining the link between objectives and strategies. For instance, the capacity and capability measures will directly relate to investment and development policies. Also, the operations infrastructure will need to be developed to provide the best way to meet requirements such as the degree of flexibility and the level of product/service development.

Tactics

Tactics represent the specific courses of action needed to support an organization's strategies. They are the detailed ways in which to carry out a particular, overall course of action, and are devised at the lower levels of an organization. These plans concern the action to be taken, establishing the authority/responsibility links and the time-spans involved. The controls to monitor achievement against a plan or budget, the analysis of variances and the corrective action to be taken will also become part of the tactical decisions to be taken.

Typical operations budgets relate to aspects such as output, capital expenditure, and direct and indirect costs. Also, the use of flexible budgeting to cope with new budgets at different levels of output is an important feature to help control the variable requirements placed on the operations function.

As objectives and strategies are broad statements of intent and method, the approaches used to develop these tend to be less quantitative than those employed in the development of tactics. The remainder of this chapter outlines some of the more important approaches to be used at each of the three levels.

Range of products/services

Strategy issues

Strategic planning has become an important activity for many organizations, and various strategy/policy models have been developed to help in the planning process. Some models are normative, others descriptive. The normative models usually follow from the selection of goals and objectives, to external and internal environmental considerations, strategy formulation, implementation and control. Descriptive models tend to explain specific techniques used by various organizations and whether these have been successful. They also describe different strategic planning routes and how decisions are actually carried out.

Aspects of two descriptive models have been extensively used to aid the strategic planning process. The first of these is the product/service life cycle and the second the product/service portfolio analysis.[2]

Product/service life cycle

The product/service life cycle suggests that products/services progress through a series of stages in the market-place, with each state characterized by a need to modify managerial objectives as shown in Figure 3.1. The concept can be applied to single, or groups of related products/services.

Phase 1. *Introduction and development.* Characterized by uncertain volumes, personal selling, little or no competition, lack of customer knowledge and continued product/service development.

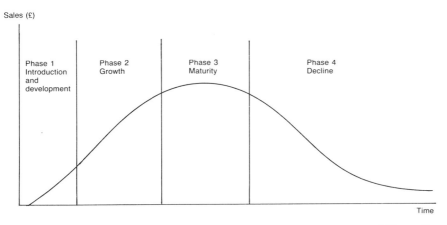

Figure 3.1 Product/service life cycle in terms of sales revenue and illustrating typical phases.

Phase 2. *Growth.*   Market characterized by demand exceeding supply resulting in an order-taking situation requiring little promotion and the entry of competitors.

Phase 3. *Maturity.*   Relatively high volumes characterized by overcapacity, high level of competition, much sales promotion and lower margins.

Phase 4. *Decline.*   Market characterized by high substitution, decreasing demand, competitors leaving the market, uncertain and low volumes attracting higher margins.

The concept of life cycles usually examines sales over time without placing time on a discrete axis. A survey in the late 1970s, however, made 'the time axis explicit such that the perceived product/service profitability over ten years' time was indicated'.[3] Theoretically, it would be expected that new products would increase in perceived importance to profit. 'Unexpectedly, only 54 per cent showed the typical rising then falling profit impact over the ten year period. Another 31 per cent indicated that the profits of the product would be increasingly important, at least, not decrease in importance once it had reached its peak level of importance. An additional 6 per cent indicated that the profit would occur immediately after introduction and diminish over time whilst a further 4 per cent indicated that profit was expected to be constant over time at a given level of performance. The final 5 per cent indicated that the profit impact of their new product would 'wax and wane over the ten years'. (See Figure 3.2.) The report concluded that some of these findings were not totally unexpected since the effect of newly introduced

Type	Curve	Total	%	Type	Curve	Total	%
1	 ⌒\	545	53.91	6	 \/\	10	0.99
2	 /	315	31.16	7	 \/	9	0.89
3	 \	62	6.13	8	 /\/\	16	1.58
4	 —	36	3.56	9	 /\/\	3	0.30
5	 \/\	15	1.48			1,011	100%

Figure 3.2 Shapes of life cycle curves.

Source: J.L. Wall *et al.*, 'An exploratory investigation of the product life cycle and the business matrix: empirical and conceptual considerations' (Working Paper no. 1979–19, Western Illinois University, 1979). With permission.

products may vary significantly by industry. For example, the results indicated that new services for consumers are expected to have a greater impact upon profitability than new introductions in other industries. Conversely, a new product in industries such as construction, mining and oil is least likely to have much impact.[4]

Product/service portfolio analysis

At the level of objectives and strategies, it is of longer-term importance for an organization to determine its total product/service portfolio.[5] Product/service portfolio analysis is one, well-used approach to achieve this. As shown in Figure 3.3, products/services can be separated into four classes with the market share held by the organization being measured horizontally and the growth rate within the market measured vertically.

Products/services are then placed throughout or across two or more of the four segments to illustrate their relative positions against these two dimensions. The resulting 'portfolio' of products/services, investments or businesses (depending upon the particular levels at which the analysis is made) serves as part of the basis by which an organization can determine the appropriate allocation or concentration of corporate resources. The interesting symbols used to describe these quadrants are explained below.

An organization that has analysed its products/services in this way is then able to look at its current or proposed mix in global terms of cash and profits. This will help it to ensure continuity of a suitable product/service mix by determining a series of corporate issues. These include which markets to aim for and the degree of support required, particularly with regard to decisions on operations investment.

Dilemmas   A situation where products/services have a small percentage of a high growth market. In order to maintain or improve its position, the organization will

Growth rate of the market (cash use)	Product/service market share (cash generation)	
	High	Low
High	☆ **Stars** Cash generated is equal to or less than the cash used	? **Dilemmas** Cash generated is less than the cash used
Low	**Cash cows** Cash generated is greater than the cash used	**Pets** Cash generated is less than the cash used

Figure 3.3   Product/service portfolio analysis.

have to allocate more cash than the products/services generate. Although the environment is favourable, current performance is questionable, thus requiring close examination and often remedial action. Consequently, it will be uncertain as to whether the product/service will become a star or a pet.

Stars Products/services with a high market share (typically a market leader) in a high growth market but often in a position where the cash generated is, at best, equal to (and often less than) the cash needed. Stars will eventually become cash cows if they hold their market share; they will become pets if they do not.

Cash cows Products/services with a high percentage of the market, even though the market growth is low, and they are in the latter half of their life (see Figure 3.1). These are the principal generators of funds. The cash cow can be 'milked' to generate more cash than can be profitably reinvested. However, they can in no way be forgotten: they have to be managed efficiently, new developments within that product/service range have to be made and customers have to be carefully tended, with the emphasis on cash-flow rather than building market share.

Pets Also known as cash traps, cash dogs and cash coffins, pets describe products/services where the individual market share is low, market growth is low, and they are cash absorbers, with little or no hope of changing the situation. For many organizations the majority of their products/services fall into this category. They may show an accounting profit but the profit must be reinvested to maintain market share. They leave no cash surplus for investment elsewhere and often absorb cash surpluses created by other products/services. As a rule, they should be disposed of.

The preferred process then is to transfer the funds generated by the cash cows into those products/services at the dilemma stage in order to make them into stars. These, in turn, become the future cash cows as illustrated in Figure 3.4. This cycle

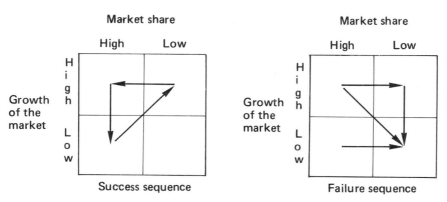

Figure 3.4 Alternative ways to make use of surplus cash.

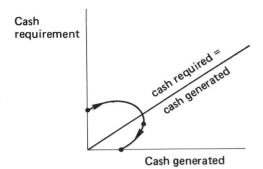

Figure 3.5 Product/service life cycle in terms of cash.

of events is further illustrated in Figures 3.5 and 3.1 which show classical product/service life cycles, both in terms of cash and sales.

Although sweeping in its application and concept, and often criticized for being an approach which is used blindly or to which only lip service is paid, the concept that underpins this analysis has formed part of the basis on which decisions have been made concerning expansion into or phasing out of preferred and undesirable quadrants respectively.

The product/service portfolio analysis is essentially static but is a useful selection technique to help organizations both to understand more fully their current position and to reposition their portfolio (either products/services or investments or businesses, as explained earlier) in the future. Its primary function is to aid resource allocation and cash management by pinpointing those products/services with greatest potential, where cash can be reaped and so on. The product/service life cycle is a dynamic model with associated market-related strategies built in. Thus, combining the portfolio matrix and life cycle models helps to determine/indicate tactical strategies concerning investments and harvesting in terms of cash usage. Figures 3.6 and 3.7 provide a simplified example to illustrate this development. In Figure 3.6, five products/services (A to E) are placed appropriately on the portfolio matrix, using the two dimensions as continuous scales. Showing the relevant life cycle for each product as in Figure 3.7 provides necessary insights into making appropriate current and future investments, together with related product service and production/operations strategies.

Tactical issues

At the strategic level, insights into the appropriate range and mix of products/services can be gained via the life cycle and portfolio models. Strategic decisions are important to the POM task not least because of the bearing they have on capacity and capability investment decisions in terms both of processes and skills.

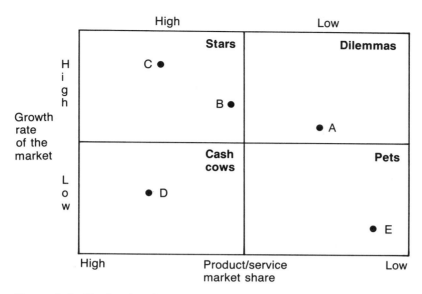

Figure 3.6 Product/service portfolio with continuous axes and the plots for products/services A to E.

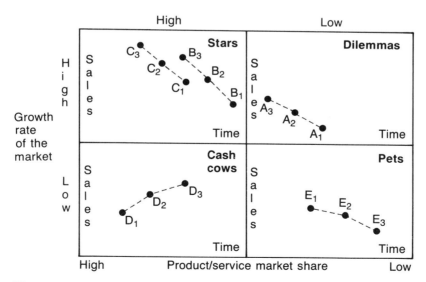

Figure 3.7 Portfolio/life cycle matrix.

Source: adapted from J.L. Wall *et al.*, *op. cit.*, p.10. With permission.

In addition to these approaches there are also insights to be gained at the tactical level which help to refine the corporate-level decisions concerning the product/service range provided. One important approach is now explained.

Variety reduction

At the tactical level a more quantitative appraisal of the range of products/services is offered by the use of variety reduction. In the product/service range provided, some items will generate more sales, or more profit, or contribute more to the fixed costs of the organization than others. Moreover, the costs incurred and efforts involved in providing and selling these lower contributors are disproportionately higher than for other products/services. Consequently, looking closely at the contribution that they make should become part of the tactical approach in order to move towards a reduction in uneconomical variety and to an increased control of variety in the future.

One approach is to list all the products/services into Pareto order of highest total value of sales at the top, and lowest at the bottom. This often reveals that about 20 per cent of items accounts for about 80 per cent of the total sales turnover. This is known as the 80/20 rule (also note its use in Chapter 10). In the example given as Table 3.1, the top 6 of the 24 products account for about 74 per cent of total sales (see note 3 to the table) whereas the bottom 15 products account for only 17 per cent. In addition, these top 6 account for some 76 per cent of the total contribution, whereas the bottom 15 contribute only £187,000, about 13 per cent.

The next step is to check the relative performances over the last three or four years of the items with a low percentage of the sales turnover in order to determine if the individual trend is 'upward—level—downward'. Further checks are then made on the level and downward trend items to see if their contribution can be improved by reducing variable costs and/or increasing the selling price. If this action does not bring about the required changes in terms of percentage contribution to selling price, then phasing out of the range should be considered.

The advantages of variety reduction are many, including:

1. Longer production runs with less down-time through changeovers.
2. Potential savings in plant/equipment requirements.
3. Reduced inventory with the advantages in capital, control, space and costs.
4. More concentrated activity in development and design, sales efforts and after-sales service.
5. Easier operations planning and control.
6. Appropriate reallocation of capacity (particularly scarce resources — see pp. 124—5) to the overall benefit of a business.

The disadvantages of this approach concern the reduction in product/service range in terms of the number of individual items produced or provided, the reduced range available and the danger of cutting out products/services which serve as loss

Table 3.1 Product analysis by annual sales turnover

Product reference number	Sales revenue (£000)	Percentage of total sales	Total variable costs	Total contribution (£000)	Percentage of total contribution
054-19	1,240	19.5	1,064.0	176.0	12.7
303-07	1,067	16.8	842.0	325.0	23.4
691-30	860	13.5	686.0	174.0	12.5
016-10	720	11.3	514.0	206.0	14.8
418-50	490	7.7	338.0	152.0	10.9
402-50	310	4.9	290.0	20.0	1.4
155-29	214	3.8	195.0	46.0	3.4
900-01	180	2.8	120.0	60.0	4.3
308-31	154	2.4	110.0	44.0	3.2
341-17	140	2.2	106.0	34.0	2.4
540-80	130	2.0	100.0	30.0	2.2
701-91	116	1.8	80.0	36.0	2.6
650-27	110	1.7	101.0	9.0	0.6
712-22	96	1.5	70.0	26.0	1.9
137-29	90	1.4	76.0	14.0	1.0
003-54	86	1.4	84.0	2.0	0.1
541-21	70	1.1	61.0	9.0	0.6
543-61	68	1.1	56.0	12.0	0.9
305-04	48	0.8	43.0	5.0	0.4
097-54	44	0.7	43.0	1.0	0.1
323-34	36	0.6	34.0	2.0	0.1
542-93	34	0.5	31.0	3.0	0.2
386-07	22	0.3	18.0	4.0	0.3
440-18	10	0.2	9.8	0.2	—
	6,362	100.0	3,730.8	1,390.2	100.0

Notes
1. Contribution = selling price less variable costs.
2. Further analysis could be completed by grouping like products together and showing the product group totals for columns 'percentage of total sales' to 'percentage of total contribution' inclusive.
3. The 80/20 relationship implied in the rule is only an indication of the size of the actual figures involved. Thus in the example here, 25 per cent of the products accounts for 74 per cent of sales, illustrating clearly the concept of a relatively small number of products accounting for a high percentage of the sales turnover.

leaders. Thus it is variety reduction's net corporate effect which needs to be considered and on which the decision should be based.

The experience curve[6]

So far, the product/service mix within an organization has been looked at in terms of cash-flows and growth. This is necessary to help make decisions at the corporate level regarding a balanced portfolio and the need to invest in new products/services through the dilemma, star and cash cow cycle. However, an examination of the product itself often reveals further sets of analyses which need to be considered in terms of the investment in production/operations.

There is a hypothesis that costs are a function of accumulated operations experience (see Figure 3.8) and it has been shown that real costs decline by some characteristic amount each time accumulated production/provision is doubled.[7] The characteristic decline has been about 15–30% but some measure of reduction can go on in time without limit (ignoring the effects of inflation). However, observed reductions in costs as volume increases are not necessarily automatic.

The important implications of this concept concern recognizing the inherent improvement in any operation (the strategy) and the degree to which that improvement is exploited (the tactics). Normally, the greater the manual content of the work, then the greater is the susceptibility of that work to improvement. This is due to the fact that much of the cost reduction is typically related to investment. However, how much of that improvement is actually realized is usually determined by the ability of the management team to achieve it and to stimulate others to do the same. The improvements critically depend, therefore, upon an able management seeking ways to force costs down as unit volume increases. Production/operations costs are those most likely to decline under this internal pressure. However, in the longer term all relevant costs should decline in order that the organization might remain as profitable as possible. To this extent, the relationship between increases in unit volume/experience and decreases in cost is potential rather than certain. Furthermore, the extent of this potential is also related to growth: the decline in costs will be slow if growth is slow, and fast if growth is fast.

There is an experience curve for each sector of the market and it is important that an organization appreciates in which sector and on which curve it is. There will normally be predominant market sectors, each with their relative experience

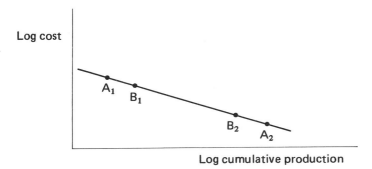

Log cumulative production

Figure 3.8   The experience curve.[8]

curves. Consequently, an organization should either knowingly leave those curves and thus try to compete within a different sector or compete predominantly in its own market sector(s), whichever matches its corporate policy.

Figure 3.8 shows two competitors, A and B, who are on the same market sector experience curve. The initial positions show B with volume/cost advantages (A_1 and B_1). However, in the race down the curve, if A can grow sufficiently faster than B, then the volume/cost advantages can be reversed as shown at B_2 and A_2. The importance and implications of this relationship to production investment decisions are significant. If an organization does not understand its position on the relevant experience curve(s), then the demands it places on production/operations in terms of cost and performance may be unrealistic in terms of the market situation with which it is involved and in relation to its competitors on that same curve. Furthermore, if the objectives of the business have been made clear, the subsequent decisions (strategies) and efforts (tactics) of that organization can then be brought more into line as investment and other decisions support the same set of corporate objectives.

The considerations so far have focused on the activities of individual companies aiming to reduce unit costs as a result of experience. However, it is also important to bear in mind that there are numerous opportunities to benefit from others' experience and learning within an industry.[9] The effects of this for the individual company may be two-fold: a lowering of the entry barriers to a market and declining costs gained more-or-less independently of the company's own efforts and decisions.[10]

Lastly it is important to emphasize again that real cost reductions at the tactical level are not automatic but potential, and depend upon an able management seeking ways of realizing this potential. The fundamental role of process investment has already been emphasized. However, it is equally important to recognize the cost reductions that come from learning. In this regard, organizations need to separate the aspects of learning concerning how to do a task from those aimed to raise a person's skill level to the desired standard in terms of speed and quality. Whilst the former is always addressed, the latter is often ignored and skill-enhancing programmes neglected. These programmes are based on the well-tried approach used in other fields such as sport and learning to play a musical instrument. Here, the required dexterity and skill are developed through special exercises rather than running races or playing the actual scores. This approach leads to a person being able to perform at a higher level in a shorter time. A similar approach involving off-line procedures designed to accelerate the development of experience and skill needs to be devised for production/operations tasks (as well as those completed elsewhere in an organization). Examples from industry include programmes to enhance the motor skills of computer programmers and paint sprayers being trained to control paint density and uniformity by practising on pieces of paper according to a given pattern.[11]

Capacity resources

Capacity decisions

Growth is often a major objective for many organizations and is seen as an indicator of success and a way of measuring an organization's performance. It affords, therefore, a good example of the necessary link between objectives, strategy and tactics discussed earlier in the chapter and the difficulty of building the coherence from one level to the next. For, embodied in this phenomenon is a set of highly complex problems and procedures, all of which have to be handled competently. The wrong move can easily lead to failure.

There are many facets involved in creating or developing growth. The one discussed here is the relationship between the timing of increases in capacity by an organization and the market growth and profitability associated with a product/service. The relationship is far from simple. The decision to invest in additional output capacity can directly influence the rate of growth. Lack of capacity in periods of relatively high demand will lead to a loss of market share to those competitors who do have sufficient capacity. Conversely, the dilemma facing an organization is that excess capacity means higher costs as some part of its investment will give no return.

The life cycle of a new product/service may classically lead to situations of relatively high growth during which period there is insufficient capacity to meet demand. At best, inadequate capacity means long lead times and, at worst, lost sales and lost market share which is often permanent. In turn, and reflecting on the experience curve concept, a change in market share is a change in future output volumes. This means a different position on the relevant experience curve and the related cost postition that this would bring. In addition, a loss in market share always goes to a competitor. The competitor who adds capacity first does not necessarily make a profit. But the competitor that trails on the growth/capacity path will find great difficulty in regaining its future market share position, whether or not it decides to increase its capacity at a later date.

Thus one important strategic consideration in capacity acquisition concerns whether to lead or follow demand. Most organizations opt for the latter, principally because it is less risky. However, the reason that companies select the 'follow' course of action more often stems from the fact that the decision is easy to make and not that it is based on strategy. Companies facing uncertainty often cope by not endeavouring to increase their understanding of those areas of uncertainty. As a consequence, they choose options that postpone the resolution of uncertainty, not for sound strategic reasons but rather because they present an easy way out. The result is that strategic decisions are resolved at the tactical level.

So far, growth and capacity acquisition have been stressed but, equally, the end of the product/service life cycle leads to market saturation, overcapacity and price competition. Plant/equipment capacity, once created, is usually an irreversible investment decision. Labour capacity once created is an expensive decision to change. Growth and its associated decisions present a difficult and challenging task. This is so not only in itself but also considering the interrelated aspects of the total market position and competitors' decisions on capacity and capacity timing.

The process is complex. Organizations are faced with several difficult decisions, such as:

1. Anticipating the end of growth.
2. Avoiding overcapacity.
3. Choosing to plan ahead of growth or to plan to follow growth.
4. What action to take in a situation of overcapacity — divest or diversify.

In analysing the capacity acquisition decision, the factors to be taken into account are:

1. The capacity to make a product or provide a service.
2. Order rate/demand.
3. Unfilled orders or backlog.
4. The lead time on delivery or delivery delay.

An analysis of the capacity acquisition decision must take account of both the interdependence and interrelationship of these factors. The principal set of relationships involved in this decision are:

1. As demand increases (or if organizations only make to order) the result is an increase in order backlog or forward load. Thus, total lead time is greater (see Figure 3.8).

2. The result is a decrease in order rates as customers purchase other products/services or postpone/change their decision.

3. With the decision to purchase additional capacity comes delays, both labour and process related, and a continued slow down in order rate.

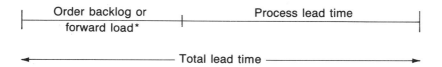

* In some businesses, the time taken for materials to be delivered (material lead time) may be longer than the time taken to complete all orders waiting to enter the process (order backlog or forward load). Where this is so, then the longer lead time for material delivery would be used to calculate total lead time.

Figure 3.9 The components of total lead time.

4. The introduction of additional capacity brings a decrease in order backlog and total lead time.

5. The result is an increase in demand and the cycle restarts.

Service issues and capacity

As all service industries are in a make-to-order situation, they are involved in the order backlog/demand increases cycle described earlier. Thus, when the order backlog becomes too long, customers go elsewhere or delay their purchase, sometimes indefinitely. Some businesses (for example, fast food outlets) adopt strategies designed to minimize the occurrence of this change of events. Restricting product/service range, producing ahead of demand in peak sales periods, and using the customer in capacity provision before the point of sale all help to alleviate the demand/capacity cycle. But it is the use of customer capacity after the point of sale that brings the most significant advantages to keeping queues to acceptable lengths. At this stage, customers are required to resolve any capacity constraints by finding their own solutions to (for example) the lack of seating capacity, which may result in their standing to eat or even having to consume their food outside.

Similarly, large theme parks such as Alton Towers in the UK and Disneyland in the USA need to plan the introduction of additional attractions to keep order backlogs to a reasonable length, especially in times of high growth rates. In the short term, however, these businesses do not restrict customers in order to affect a desired balance. Instead, they develop ways of handling large queues, such as discouraging customers from dawdling in the crowded places and introducing various side shows (normally on an *ad hoc* basis responding to queue length at a given time) as a form of distraction.

In the longer term, then, organizations are concerned with capacity decisions involving labour, processes and facilities as a combination of all three is often used in the service delivery system. In the short term, however, labour is the variable capacity dimension, changed typically by hiring temporary labour when required or pursuing longer-term policies of increasing existing labour flexibility by widening skill levels through training.

It is essential that all factors are considered at the corporate level before making capacity decisions. To decide how much capacity must be added before it is needed is very involved. Adding capacity requires time to plan, acquire and install. Consequently, the decision time must be well in advance of when the increase is needed. Furthermore, available capacity is as important in bringing about market share changes as price competition itself. Moreover, as the market is shared by the competitors within that market, decisions on capacity and the timing of these decisions will help to show up one company's capability against another's. Consequently, an organization's initiative in adding capacity before it is needed is critical in itself and also as a potential inhibitor to competitive investment.

Capability considerations

The concept of product/service portfolio analysis was introduced earlier with regard to cash flow, market share and the need for an organization to develop and maintain a balance in its product/service mix. However, there are other analyses that have to be taken into account when considering the companywide consequences of corporate decisions. Of particular importance is the organization's overall ability to integrate with other work the introduction of new products/services or the modification of existing ones.

Most organizations have only a limited capability to take on, develop and control the support roles necessitated by the changes whilst maintaining the performance requirements of current products/services. The capability needed to complete the tasks range from design and development on the one hand, to controlling on-the-job requirements on the other. Whilst this is necessary in order to complete the development work, it makes heavy demands on the time of people involved. Normally, these people are the more able members of the organization who also have an important role to play in the success of the main-thrust activities. Consequently, an imbalance in the product/service mix can lead to a situation where there is insufficient capability to do all that is required.

Using the product/service portfolio analysis discussed earlier in this chapter, the following analysis considers product/service mix in terms of an organization's capability requirements.

Cash Cows. These are likely to be well-established products/services. The procedures and methods of doing the job are tried and tested with, in the case of products, programmes of an economic length. The need here, however, is to develop or modify the products/services to ensure that their market share is maintained and to continue the investment requirements and management effort to exploit the inherent experience curve advantages.

Pets. These can be at different stages of development but will normally involve short, low priority production/operations programmes which have to be fitted into a schedule dominated by the more important products/services. This often leads to inefficiencies throughout the processes involved.

Dilemmas. These products/services often require development work and, because of inherent uncertainty, will usually lead to a stop−go situation. The resurrection of their importance normally leads to an ineffective use of resources.

Stars. These products/services are usually given high priority throughout the organization. They will make priority demands on all parts of the process from development through to output capacity making heavy inroads into available resources.

The resources and capabilities of an organization are absorbed by both fruitful and less-fruitful activity. The priority of the moment can unduly outweigh the needs of the main-thrust of an organization. Yet, if there is insufficient effort devoted to the cash cow products, then the economics and benefits associated with the experience curve will not be fully achieved and less cash will be available to invest elsewhere. In reality, it is all too easy to assume that the more stable products/services require little capability to maintain or improve. However, both the present and the future performance are necessary to an organization's prosperity. It is critical, therefore, that the organizational impact of product/service decisions is fully understood.

Notes and references

1. The role of goals or mission statements has long been discussed in management literature — see, for instance, Chandler, *Strategy and Structure*, (Cambridge, Mass.: MIT Press, 1962), pp. 1–17, and T.J. Peters and R.H. Waterman *In Search of Excellence: Lessons from America's best-run companies*, (New York: Harper & Row, 1982), A. Campbell, 'Mission statements' (Working Paper, Ashridge Management Centre (UK), 1988), and M.E. Porter, *Competitive Advantage: Techniques for creating and sustaining superior advantage* (Basingstoke: Collier-Macmillan, 1984).
2. The models used are based on the work of the Boston Consulting Group, Boston, Massachusetts.
3. J.L. Wall, B.P. Shin and H.E. Metzner 'An exploratory investigation of the product lifecycle and the business matrix: empirical and conceptual considerations' (Working Paper no. 1979–19, Western Illinois University, 1979), p. 4.
4. Adapted from J.L. Wall *et al.*, *op cit.*, p. 5.
5. In particular, refer to the Boston Consulting Group's Perspective 66, *The Product Portfolio*.
6. As with the product portfolio work, the experience curve is also based on initial work by the Boston Consulting Group.
7. W.B. Hirschmann 'Profit from the learning curve', *Harvard Business Review* (January/February 1964), 116–30; F.J. Andrews, 'The learning curve as a production tool', *Harvard Business Review* (January/February 1954), 1–11; Boston Consulting Group Perspective 149, *The Experience Curve — Reviewed v. Price Stability*; Boston Consulting Group, *Perspective on Experience*, 1972; P. Ghemawat 'Building strategy on the experience curve', *Harvard Business Review* (March/April 1985), 143–9.
8. Changes plotted on a log–log scale have the unique property of showing percentage change as a constant distance along either axis. A straight line on log–log paper means that a given percentage change in one factor results in a corresponding percentage change in the other. In the case of cost–volume slopes, the plotting of observed data about costs and cumulated experience for a product on log–log paper which produces a straight line reflects a consistent relationship between experience and costs.
9. For example, M.B. Zimmerman uncovered significant spillovers of learning in the construction of nuclear power plants, where costs were decreased not only by the individual construction firm's experience to date but also by industrywide experience as reported in his paper 'Learning effects and the commercialization of new energy technologies: the case of nuclear power', *Bell Journal of Economics*, 13 (Autumn 1982), 297–310.

10. P. Ghemawat and A.M. Spence 'Learning curve spillovers and market performance', *Quarterly Journal of Economics*, 100 (1985), 839−52.

11 These examples were taken from A.J. Strauss, 'The new look training programs' (Working Paper MC-WP-87-15, University of Minnesota, 1987).

Further reading

Alchian, A., 'Reliability of progress curves in airframe production', *Econometrica*, 31 (1963), 679−93.

Arrow, K.J., 'The economic implications of learning by doing', *Review of Economic Studies* (June 1963), 155−73.

Dhalla, N.K. and Yuspeth, S., 'Forget the product life cycle concept!', *Harvard Business Review* (January/February 1976), 102−12.

'Hewlett-Packard: where slower growth is smarter management', *Business Week* (9 June 1975).

Lorenz, C., 'Why Boston recanted its doctrine on market leadership', *Financial Times* (20 November 1981).

McInery, A.S. and Geoegan, R.S., 'Variety reduction', *British Productivity Council*, London (Summer 1959).

Spence, A.M., 'Cost reduction, competition and industry performance', *Econometrica* (January 1984), 101−21.

Chapter 4

Production/operations management

The real problems of controlling the operations function are both many and large. As Chapter 1 describes, the features of the role are bound up with size and the inherent complexity of the task. In addition, it is important to recognize the dynamics of operations that arise from the numerous subsystems that exist, the interrelationships between these and the openness of the system to the environment. With changing demands being placed on the operations manager, it is necessary to adjust these systems in order to survive.

This chapter briefly introduces the operations function within an organization. Much of the chapter, however, concerns the choice of operations process made by organizations and the consequences of this decision. In this way, the chapter presents a conceptual view of process choice which provides the reader with a sound base on which to understand better the processes themselves whilst providing insights into the issues of product/service, operations, investment, cost and infrastructure choice that have to be made.

Systems concepts in production/operations management

Systems, in terms of a product/service organization, are sets of interconnected functions designed to produce or provide a predetermined range of products/services. They can be considered at two distinct levels:

1. As part of a large system and hence, a subsystem interconnecting and interacting at its own level.
2. As a set of subsystems, subsubsystems and so on, all of which are interconnected and interact one with another.

It is helpful, therefore, to review the production/operations management (POM) system at these two levels. Essentially, at all levels it is an open system in that it is an integral part of the larger environment (see Figure 4.1). At level 1 POM,

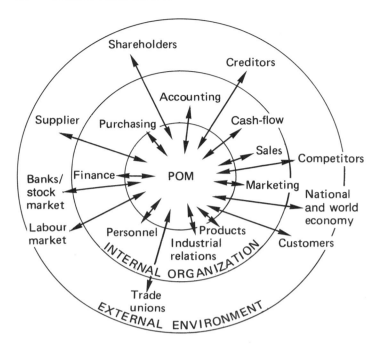

Figure 4.1 POM as an open system with its internal and external environment.

like other major functions, controls its own set of distinct activities but is part of the total organization which, in turn, relates to a larger system. The large investment, expenditure and people features of the POM task mean that it relates to the other major functions within the organization such as marketing, sales, finance, accounting, purchasing, design, personnel and industrial relations. As the activities of these other functions will impinge on the operations manager's role, it is important to clarify the areas of activity which overlap and those where the POM perspectives need to be included in any decisions taken by these other departments. At level 2 it is a structure of subsystems and subsubsystems. In order to control this relatively large system, the POM tasks are broken down into functions, each with its own set of activities. Some of these are directly concerned with the conversion or transformation process, whilst others provide a specialist supporting activity, such as operations planning and control.

This approach to control has developed over the last few centuries. The western culture, in particular, has used analysis as part of its search for new knowledge. The breaking down of data, their classification, rearrangement, systematic re-examination and analysis has led to fresh analysis, further examination, classification and so on. This is often best accomplished through specialization, which is currently used by most organizations as the basis for controlling their activities.

However, this approach has sometimes led to situations where specialist areas have perceived the organization's best interests from their own, too narrow point of view. Thus these areas are in danger of taking the standpoint associated with a closed system[1] with its implied self-containment and defined boundaries.

POM subsystems will, at different times, be analysed in an attempt to improve them and then reassembled in the hope of improving the total system. In many circumstances, such a review will cover two or more subsystems, or even take an overview of several subsystems. The operations manager's task is to build back these functional views into the total system in order to ensure that the overall system's performance is improved. Figure 4.2 illustrates how this relates to the POM system. Here, analyses of parts or wholes are completed, for instance by specialist subfunctions such as design, production engineering, industrial engineering, operations planning and control and operational research. These are then reviewed and built back into the whole function whilst ensuring that full account is taken of the impact upon other relevant subfunctions and on the POM

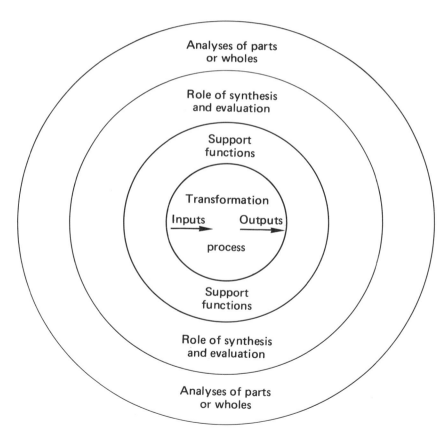

Figure 4.2 The role of synthesis in the POM system.

function as a whole. It is important to recognize that in many POM systems it is likely that a higher level of overall performance will require certain individual subsystems to complete tasks at a suboptimal level.

Whereas analysis is commonplace in most organizations, synthesis and evaluation are not. These latter roles are important tasks of the operations manager at two levels. First, at the level of the POM system as shown in Figure 4.2; the second is in making the corporate contribution where the POM system becomes a subfunction of the corporate whole, as explained in Chapter 3. Here, the operations manager's role is to ensure that the analysis made of POM and other systems which form part of the internal environment (see Figure 4.1) are built back into the whole organization to ensure that the decisions taken are those best for the corporate good. This process, too, will often result in one major subsystem performing in a suboptimal manner (e.g. lower sales but higher profits, or higher operations costs but improved deliveries leading to increased sales and higher overall profit).

Organizations are open systems.[1] They are dynamic and need to respond to new needs in order to survive. They are in constant interaction with their environment at all stages of their activities — inputs, transformation processes, outputs and support functions. To help understand this complexity, the systems approach provides an overview which facilitates the analysis and understanding of complex organizations and complex subsystems. It aids the application of the synthesis necessary to ensure that changes and improvements to the whole or part of an organization, function or subfunction are completed in the way that will provide the most appropriate overall improvement. It reduces duplication, misunderstanding and resistance to change while increasing acceptance, involvement and motivation. Thus by providing a conceptual orientation within which managers may work, it encourages those involved to overcome some of the difficulties inherent in the choice of organizational structures by viewing the whole as well as the parts.

The choice of process

The POM task is concerned with the transformation process which takes inputs and converts them into outputs (see Figure 4.2) and the support functions closely associated with this basic task. This section considers the choice of process or the different methods available to an organization by which it is able to produce the goods or provide the services for the customer.

The transformation process and methods of conversion to produce goods or provide services will actually be an interrelated set of processes feeding into one another as part of the total transformation, as shown in Figure 4.3. Each of these will have its own method of conversion, selected to meet the particular requirements of that stage of the total process (see Figure 4.4). It is the need to help others in the organization to understand these process choices and their implications that is the concern of the operations manager.

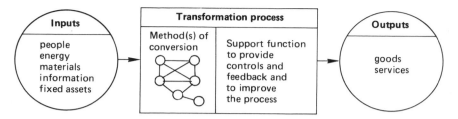

Figure 4.3   The operations function.

There are several perspectives to be taken into account in understanding the choice of processes which can be made. These classifications are useful in the conceptual study of POM. Each choice will bring with it certain implications for investment, control and management and these will be discussed in detail in the next section (p. 60). This section outlines a number of important classifications of the processes to illustrate some basic differences.

Project

Organizations that sell large-scale, complex products or services which cannot be physically moved once completed will normally provide these on a project basis. Product examples include civil engineering contracts and aerospace programmes. Service examples include management consultancy assignments involving corporate policy issues and organizational development, and a large banquet supplied to the customer's own premises. It concerns the provision of a unique product or service which requires large-scale inputs to be co-ordinated to achieve the customer's requirement. The resource inputs will normally be taken to the point where the product is to be built or service provided.

All the activities, including support functions, will normally be controlled in the form of a total system for the duration of the project and under the direction of the co-ordinating team. Similarly, resources will be allocated for the duration of the project and these, like the supporting functions, will be reallocated once their part of the task is complete or at the end of the project.

The operations manager's problem, then, is one of co-ordinating a large number of interrelated activities and resources in such a way as to achieve the customer's requirements whilst minimizing costs through the process.

Jobbing, unit or one-off

The jobbing process is chosen to meet one-off or small order requirements for customers. The product or service involved is of an individual (one-off) nature,

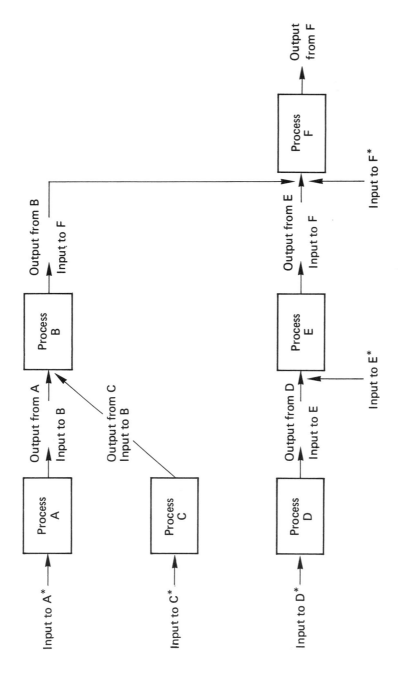

Input* = purchased out goods and services

Figure 4.4 Interrelated processes.

and tends to be of a smaller size (and therefore transportable) and of a simpler nature than in the case of a project process. Product examples include a purpose-built piece of equipment, hand-made, built-in furniture to meet specified customer requirements, a customer designed and specified control unit, and hand-made shoes or clothing. Service examples include a tailor-made management development programme, the design and installation of a computer system, and a banquet at a restaurant's own premises.

Although some of these products and services may be made or provided on-site, usually they are completed in-house and then transported to the customer. The producer, then, often installs and commissions the product or service before it is accepted by the customer. Jobbing, however, requires that the providing organization interprets the design and specification of the job, applying high-level skills in the conversion process. Normally, one or a small group of skilled people will be responsible for completing all or most of the product/service. It is a one-off provision which means that the product or service will usually not again be required in identical form, or, if it is, the demand will tend to be either irregular or with long periods between one sale and the next.

Batch

In a batch process, similar items required in larger volumes than in jobbing will be made/provided. The task is first divided into appropriate stages. Then, each order is processed by setting up the first step of the process to complete the first task. Each order is then completed at this stage, then the next step in the process is made ready and the total order quantity is processed and so on. When one stage of the total task has been completed then, if appropriate, that part of the process is set up for the next stage of the same job or for another order. Thus, capacity at each stage in the process is used and re-used to meet the different requirements of different orders.

Examples in manufacturing include moulding processes where one mould to produce an item is put into a machine. The order for that component is then produced, the mould taken off, the raw material changed, a mould for another product put into the machine and so on. The essential characteristic of batch, therefore, is that to produce another product or provide another service, the process has to be stopped and reset. Product examples include car components, domestic products for the kitchen and bathroom, and items for the office. Other typical batch manufacturing processes include machining metal products, casting and other forming processes. Service examples include a computer bureau that processes the work of several clients on the same piece of hardware. Also, many large clerical functions handle many different tasks. In each case, the job is broken down into different operations and one batch of work completed by one person and so on.

Line

With further increases in volume requirements, investment is made to provide a process that is dedicated to the needs of a single or small range of products. This repetitive process is one, therefore, in which the product(s) or service(s) are processed, with each product/service passing through the same sequence of operations. The essential characteristic of line (compared with batch), therefore, is that to produce another product or provide another service, the process does not have to be stopped and reset. Product examples include domestic appliances and motor vehicles. Service examples are not as widespread as applications for manufactured items. However, they include certain preparatory operations in fast-food restaurants such as McDonald's. A further example is provided by Dr Svyatoslav Fyoderov's Institute of Eye Microsurgery which uses this process in the treatment of myopia.[2] Using laser technology and assembly line methods, surgeons at the institute cure myopia using the classic principles of a line process. The institute is also a world leader in advanced eye surgery.

Continuous processing

With continuous processing, one or several basic materials are processed through successive stages and refined into one or more products, e.g. petrochemicals. Because the costs of starting-up the process are high, the process will have been designed to run all day and every day with minimum shutdowns. The materials are transferred automatically from one part of the process to the next with the labour tasks being predominantly ones of system monitoring. This type of process is not used in the provision of a service.

The implications of process choice

Once the choice of process has been decided or has evolved over time, the consequences will be significant. As the operations task accounts for a very large proportion of both the investment expenditure and workforce, the implications for the business of the chosen process will be correspondingly important. The most significant aspects are outlined in Tables 4.1–4.4 and then discussed under the corresponding headings. Many generalized statements are made in this section to help to both explain the implications of these choices and examine the consequences that normally follow. Note that the analyses contained in each table are intended as general statements relating the usual requirement of one type of process to the other four. Thus, process choices show trends within each of these characteristics that will generally appertain to one type of process relative to the others. In a batch process there will, however, tend to be significant differences between one process and another. This is because this type of process is often the transition between

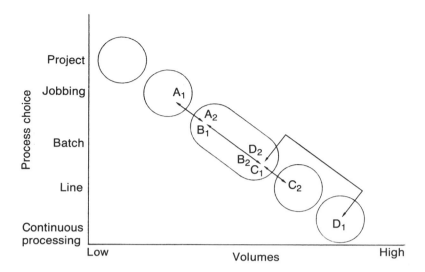

This shows four potential volume transitions which may typically face a business. The first transition shows a move from one-off,* low volume (A_1) to repeat order, low volume demand (A_2) for a product of vice versa and the change in manufacturing process which should ideally accompany this movement. Transitions B_1 to B_2, C_1 to C_2 and D_1 to D_2 show similar demand changes at different points on the volume scale and requiring similar decisions concerning the realignment of the process choice.
* One-off is a description of uniqueness, not order quantity.

Figure 4.5 Potential transitions between the different choices of process.

Source: Terry Hill, *Manufacturing Strategy: The strategic management of the manufacturing function* (Basingstoke: Macmillan, 1985), p. 81.

the lower and higher volume processes and also between the make-to-order and make-to-stock sales patterns.

Furthermore, Tables 4.1−4.4 are presented in such a way as to illustrate the fact that the transition of processes from one to another does not occur. Organizations do not, for instance, choose project and then later replace it with jobbing; similarly, companies rarely move from jobbing to batch then line. Figure 4.5 illustrates this whilst also showing that marginal transitions do take place between jobbing and low volume batch, low volume batch and higher volume batch and high volume batch and line.

Product/service implications

Project/jobbing processes tend, by definition, to be chosen to provide one-off products/services, made-to-order and competing predominantly on aspects such as delivery and quality rather than price. As a provider of one-off, non-standard

Table 4.1 Product/service implications of process choice

Product/serivice aspects		Project	Jobbing, unit or one-off[a]	Batch	Line	Continuous processing
			Typical characteristics of process choice			
Product/service	type	Special	Special ⟶		Standard	Standard
	range	High diversity	Wide ⟶		Narrow	Narrow
Customer order size		One-off	One-off ⟶		Large	Very large
Degree of product/service change required in the process		High	High ⟶		Low	Nil
Make-to-	order[b]	Yes	Yes ⟶		No	No
	stock[b]	No	No ⟶		Yes	Yes
Orientation of innovation-process for product/service		Product/service	Product/service ⟶		Process	Process
What does the organization sell?		Capability	Capability ⟶		Standard products/services	Standard products/services
How does the organization win orders?	Typical order winners	Capability, delivery speed	Capability, delivery speed ⟶		Price	Price
	Typical qualifiers	Delivery reliability, price	Delivery reliability, price ⟶		Delivery reliability, quality	Delivery reliability, quality

[a] One-off is a statement of uniqueness and not order size.
[b] Products/services are either specials (i.e. customized), standards or some combination of the two. However, whereas organizations have by definition to make specials to customer delivery and specification requirements, they may choose to make standards either to stock (i.e. finished goods inventory ahead of demand) or only to customers' orders or in line with customers' schedules (i.e. only when an order or schedule has been placed).

items the organization will offer a diverse range of products/services in order to meet differing customer requirements. For this reason, the company sells a set of capabilities rather than a product/service.

In line and continuous processing, the opposite end of the spectrum prevails. Products and services are highly standardized, made-to-stock with innovation being oriented towards the process rather than the product. Products/services in these markets tend to compete primarily on price. Little accommodation will be provided in the process to meet product change and even where there is (e.g motor vehicles), it tends to be designed to meet the more superficial aspects of product/service change such as colour, trim and extras, and will also be provided only within the supplier's own list of options. A customer requiring an option other than from the approved list will need to arrange this as a retro-fit (i.e. post-delivery) task. The basics will remain standard, for the organization sells its own products/services rather than a set of capabilities.

Batch processes occupy the middle position. With increases in volume, an organization will start to move from low volume to high volume markets. When this happens, competition in the relevant market segments becomes more price oriented. This, in turn, leads to a reduction in the degree of change that can be accommodated and away from small-order markets. Also, the transition from make-to-order to make-to-stock is usually accommodated by a batch process.

Production/operations implications

In project and jobbing situations, the product/service provided is one-off (i.e. unique). Thus, the operations task will be variable (and often in jobbing, unknown) and the operations process will need to be flexible, with many set-ups, using universal equipment and skilled labour. The effective utilization of the skilled labour will, therefore, be the dominant POM task, with relatively low equipment utilization being inherent in this choice of process.

With line and continuous process, the important perspectives change. This choice is made to provide high volume, standard products which are usually competing on price. Operations' tasks will, therefore, be well-defined, using dedicated plant on a large scale. Process times will tend to be short and plant utilization the dominant POM task. Capacity changes will usually require a new, larger-scale facility as only short-term increases to the existing system's capacity will be practical.

Batch process is again the transition between low and high volume activities. It may, therefore, tend towards either jobbing or line and contain a mixture of their characteristics.

The control of operations in terms of activities, quality and capacity will also show marked differences depending upon the choice of process. In project and jobbing, because the operations tasks are variable and the process times are long, capacity will be variable due to the uncertainty of how long tasks will take. The internal span of process (i.e. the extent of the operations process provided within each site) will be wide. This is necessary because the organization needs to have in-house as much of the capability requirement as possible. By doing this it can provide the necessary flexibility, cope more easily with product/service uncertainty, and retain a higher degree of control over the delivery schedule. Also, the large work content of the products/services provided will add to the complexity of both task and control. Quality control will be by the operator plus supplementary spot

Table 4.2 Production/operations implications of process choice

Production/operations implications		Project	Jobbing, unit or one-off	Batch	Line	Continuous processing
Nature of the process technology		Universal	Universal	General-purpose	Dedicated	Dedicated
Process flexibility		Flexible	Flexible	⟶	Inflexible	Inflexible
Ability of the process to cope with	product/ service change	High	High	⟶	Low	Nil
	new development	High	High	⟶	Low	None
Volumes		Low	Low	⟶	High	High
Set-ups/ make-readies	number	Many	Many	⟶	Few	Few
	expense	Variable	Inexpensive	⟶	Expensive	Very expensive
Dominant utilization		Predominantly labour	Labour	⟶	Plant	Plant
Knowledge of the	operations task	Variable	Known but often not well-defined	⟶	Known	Well-defined
	material requirement	Known at the tendering stage	Some uncertainty	⟶	Known	Well-defined
Materials handling provision		Variable	Low	⟶	High	High
Internal span of process		Wide	Wide	⟶	Narrow	Narrow
Control of operations	key feature	Order status	Order status	⟶	Flow of materials	Flow of materials
	basis	System	Person	⟶	System	System
	ease of task	Complex	Complex	Very complex	Easy	Straight-forward
Control of quality		External spot checks	Monitored by the operator	⟶	Off-line inspection	Designed into the process
Process times		Very long	Long	⟶	Short	Short

Table 4.2 *continued*

Production/operations implications		Typical characteristics of process choice				
		Project	*Jobbing, unit or one-off*	*Batch*	*Line*	*Continuous processing*
Capacity	basis for calculation	Labour	Labour	——————→	Process	Process
	scale	Small	Small	——————→	Large	Very large
	definition	Variable	Variable	——————→	Established	Established
	nature of changes	Incremental	Incremental ——————→		Stepped	New facility
	control	Difficult	Difficult	——————→	Easy	Easy
Productivity control		Difficult	Difficult	——————→	Easy	Easy
Bottlenecks	number	Few	Few	Key process(es)	None	None
	position and nature	Random and moveable	Random and moveable	Fixed in the short and medium term	Not relevant	Not relevant
Impact of breakdowns		Variable	Little	——————→	High	Enormous

checks. Lastly, productivity is more difficult to ascertain due to the problem of measuring the inputs to the manufacturing of the product or provision of the service.

The measurement and control of line and continuous processing operations is much easier. The task is shorter and well-defined with quality control designed into the process. Capacity is established due to the standard nature of the process and product/service and hence, easier to control. The internal span of process within a line or continuous processing arrangement will tend to be narrow in terms of the work content of the finished product. However, previous parts of the process will often be provided within the same organization although not necessarily on the same site. For example, volume car manufacturers often have plants for body pressings, castings and engine assembly, with the final assembly completed in a separate plant.

Again, batch processes are the transition between, project/jobbing and line/continuous processing. The increase in volume is catered for by a batch process, one part of which may be dedicated to one product/service for long periods of time. The range of volumes that this process will be able to provide on a competitive basis will depend upon the degree of specialization within its process. But whatever the situation, the range will be very wide. As a consequence, therefore, the level of control complexity will vary depending upon the span of the process involved and the degree of technology embodied in the product/service and the process.

Investment and cost

The typical primary and secondary investment consequences of each process choice will vary. In a project process, the capital (or primary) investment can be low (e.g. the provision of a one-off service such as consultancy or medical specialist), through to high (e.g. civil engineering projects). However, within the other four categories, the relationship between capital investment and process choice will be more uniform.

Table 4.3 Investment and cost implications of process choice

Investment and cost implications		Typical characteristics of process choice				
		Project	*Jobbing, unit or one-off*	*Batch*	*Line*	*Continuous processing*
Amount of capital investment		Variable	Low ——→		High	High
Economies of scale		Few	None ——→		Many	Many
Level of inventory	components and raw material	As required	As required ——→		Planned with buffer inventory	Planned with buffer inventory
	WIP	High	High	Very high	Low	Low
	finished goods	Low	Low ——→		High	High
Percentage of total costs	direct labour	High	High ——→		Low	Low
	direct materials	Variable	Low ——→		High	High
	overheads	Low	Low ——→		High	High
Opportunity to decrease costs		Low	Low ——→		High	High
Basis of cost control		Each contract	Each job ——→		Throughput	Throughput

In jobbing, the capital investment will be quite low because of the universal nature of the process technology and the high level of labour skills required to meet the one-off product/service requirements. With larger volumes, investment in the process will be made in order to reduce process costs, with the process technology deskilling the manual tasks involved. The important secondary investment is made in the form of inventory. Each type of process will require different levels of investment at each of the different stages. In the lower volume areas of project and jobbing, component and finished goods inventory will be low compared to line and continuous processing, where utilization of plant and make-to-stock are the priorities. Work-in-progress (WIP) inventory will, however, be the inverse of this. Because of the long duration and process methods used in project and jobbing, WIP will be high and often need to be so in order to provide sufficient work alternatives to allow for high labour and/or plant utilization. The higher volumes associated with batch processes will usually result in even higher WIP necessary to provide the important decoupling function.[3] With line and continuous processing, since each product/service is added to throughout the process, WIP is minimal, comprising whatever happens to be in the system at any one time. Lastly, finished goods inventory reflects the make-to-order and make-to-stock positions; low in the former, high in the latter.

Organizational implications

In project and jobbing processes, the nature of the task tends to be for unique, variable operations, with a need for flexible operations processes. Sales orders will be low, often by tender and with few formal customer ties. Similarly, supplier relationships will tend to be informal with few long-term agreements. (Note that in the case of some project organizations such as civil engineering, these relationships will often be more established and longer-term.) Thus, the organization more suited to these requirements is one of decentralized control with a more entrepreneurial style and based on the process involved. As a consequence, the predominant managerial input is technological knowledge. Here, the operations manager would be expected to advise in areas of process technology and his or her academic and professional background would therefore be in an appropriate technology. However, the need for specialists to provide supporting advice will tend to be small. On the labour side, the skill level required will be quite high, requiring flexibility to meet a wide range of tasks and to interpret the customer's requirement. The technology involved in the job will also be quite high level and this, together with a wide range of tasks and long cycle of work, will provide the opportunity for an interesting and inherently satisfying job.

With line and continuous processing these characteristics will tend to be reversed. The highly standardized, cost-dominated tasks will be more suited to centralized control and a bureaucratic style. Thus, the process will be designed towards systems developed in line with this concept. The manufacturing infrastructure, however, will change between line and continuous processing. The

Table 4.4 Organizational implications of process choice

Organizational implications		Typical characteristics of process choice				
		Project	Jobbing, unit or one-off	Batch	Line	Continuous processing
Customers	nature of sales	One-off tenders	One-off tenders	→	Defined prices with discounts	Well-established
	degree of co-ordination	Small	Small	→	Highly organized	Highly organized often with forward integration
Suppliers	relationships	Variable	Informal	→	Formal	Long-term contracts
	degree of co-ordination	Variable	Small	→	Highly organized	Highly organized
Type of organizational	control	Decentralized	Decentralized	→	Centralized	Centralized
	style	Entrepreneurial	Entrepreneurial	→	Bureacratic	Bureaucratic
Basis of corporate control		Individual contract	Individual job	→	Systems-based	Systems-based
Production/ operations infrastructure	dominant POM perspective	Technology	Technology	→	People/ business	Technology
	level of skill required	High	High	→	Low	High
	nature of labour skills	Technical	Technical	→	Manual	Technical
	work environment re inherent involvement and motivation	High	High	→	Low	Medium
	level of specialist support	Low	Low	→	High	High

POM skills with a line process will become much more business- and people-oriented because of the high volumes, investments, control requirements and number of people involved.

As far as the POM task is concerned, the technology of both the product/service and process is known. Furthermore, technical support for both the product/service and process will be provided by specialist support services. Thus the investment that has gone into the process will have decreased the technical but increased the business and managerial risks involved in managing the process. Hence labour skill requirements will be low as will the opportunity for a work environment conducive to a meaningful set of tasks. Low skill, large plants and large volumes will tend to give rise to uninteresting jobs in the technological sense, and a lack of opportunity to have other parts of work (e.g. planning) built in as a meaningful part of the task (see Chapter 14).

With continuous processing the trend as seen in a line process will tend to be reversed. The process will be technology-based and the tasks controlled by people with a knowledge of the technology. Labour skills will also be relatively high. In the case of the work environment, there is often the opportunity to traverse the large-scale geography of the plant because the people concerned are no longer tied to the process. However, in the case of both line and continuous processing, there will tend to be a large number of specialist staff to provide technological, planning and control advice and expertise.

Again, the transition comes with the batch process. The lower the volume requirement within the batch process, the more akin the infrastructure requirements will be to those of jobbing. The higher the volume, the more to line.

Product/service profiling

An organization needs to have a comprehensive understanding of the changing implications to its business as different processes are chosen. The earlier sections in this chapter provide these insights.

However, when companies invest in processes they often fail to incorporate these business trade-offs, (and subsequent implications), into that decision. Similarly, as markets change they fail to recognize that the trade-offs embodied in their current processes are fixed and will remain so unless further investment is made (in new processes or modifications to existing ones) or unless the corporate expectations of the extent of one or more trade-offs are changed. The former will provide a new set of trade-offs whilst the latter will enable other trade-offs, relating to other aspects of the business, to be achieved. An example of these alternatives is where a business, in order to help achieve lower inventory levels invests to reduce set-up/make-ready times (the former) or forgoes high machine utilization (the latter).

The concept of product profiling offers the organization an opportunity to test the current or anticipated degree of fit between the characteristics of its market(s) and the characteristics of its existing or proposed processes and infrastructure investments. The principal purposes of this assessment is to provide a method to evaluate and, where necessary, improve the degree of fit between the way in which a company wins orders in its markets and manufacturing's ability to support these criteria.

In many instances, though, companies will be unable or unwilling to provide the degree of fit desired due to the level of investment, executive energy and time scales involved. But, sound strategy concerns not getting the answers right but improving the level of consciousness an organization brings to bear on its corporate decisions. In such circumstances product profiling will increase corporate awareness and allow conscious choice between alternatives.

Inconsistency between the market and an organization's process/infrastructure capability in terms of supporting the business specification of its product/services, can be induced by changes in the market or process investments, or a combination of the two. In all instances, the mismatch is created by the fact that investments within production/operations are both large and fixed in nature. On the other hand, corporate marketing decisions can often be relatively transient in nature. Whilst this allows for change and repositioning, production/operations decisions bind the business for years ahead. Thus, linkage between these two parts of an organization is not just a felt need but a pragmatic necessity.

Procedure

The procedure adopted in product profiling is as follows:

1. Select relevant aspects of products/markets, production/operations, investment/ cost, and infrastructure as outlined in Tables 4.1–4.4. The key at this stage is to base the selection of characteristics on their relevance to the particular organizational issues — listing all the dimensions given in Tables 4.1–4.4 will blur the essential core of the exercise and must be avoided.

2. Display the characteristics of process choice that would be typical for each chosen dimension (as illustrated in the four tables). This provides a statement of the dimensions that would typically be expected for each characteristic and thus creates a backcloth against which the product(s)/service(s) are profiled.

3. Profile the product(s)/service(s) by positioning it on each of the characteristics selected. This tests the level of correlation between the market needs and production/operations' current or proposed response to the provision of those needs.

4. The resulting profile illustrates the degree of consistency between the characteristics of the market and the business specification of the process and chosen features of investment, cost and infrastructure. The higher the level of consistency, the straighter the profile will be. Inconsistencies will be shown by the dog-leg shape of a profile.

Product profiling, therefore, is a way of illustrating the level of fit that exists within an organization or the level that it anticipates as a result of marketing or process/infrastructure investments or as a combination of the two. Figure 4.6 provides one illustration of the use to which product profiling can be put.[4]

It should be noted that organizations often have several processes within the operations function and each may be required to be analysed separately. The example in Figure 4.6, however, concerns one part (albeit the core) of the manufacturing process. Each organization will require its own approach and resolution. The

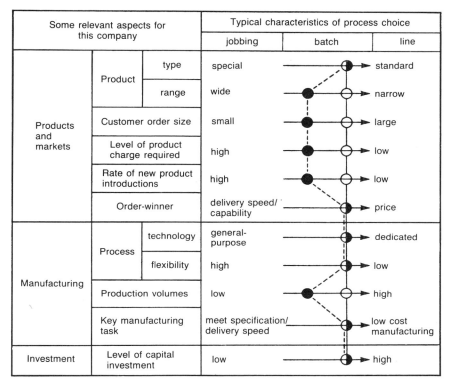

Some relevant aspects for this company			Typical characteristics of process choice		
			jobbing	batch	line
Products and markets	Product	type	special		standard
		range	wide		narrow
	Customer order size		small		large
	Level of product charge required		high		low
	Rate of new product introductions		high		low
	Order-winner		delivery speed/ capability		price
Manufacturing	Process	technology	general-purpose		dedicated
		flexibility	high		low
	Production volumes		low		high
	Key manufacturing task		meet specification/ delivery speed		low cost manufacturing
Investment	Level of capital investment		low		high

○ ◑ Position of plant A on each of the chosen dimensions and the resulting profile

● ◑ Position of plant B on each of the chosen dimensions and the resulting profile

This figure reflects the consistency of products and processes for plant A, and the inconsistencies for plant B reflected by a straight line and dog-leg shape respectively.

Figure 4.6 A profile analysis for two plants of a company illustrating the mismatch between one plant and its market induced by applying the same manufacturing strategy to both plants.

Source: Terry Hill, *Manufacturing Strategy: Text and Cases* (Homewood, Ill.: Irwin, 1989), p. 92. With permission.

example described met the specific needs of the business to which it relates. In no way, therefore, is it intended that the approach described in Figure 4.6 should be considered universally applicable. However, it is the conceptual base on which the analyses rest that can be transferred and used to provide similar insights, where appropriate.

Faced with a decline in markets and profits, the company illustrated in Figure 4.7 undertook a major internal review concerning its two manufacturing plants. To provide orientation to its business it decided to manufacture different products at each of its two sites. This decision resulted in a distinct orientation in each plant in terms of products and associated volumes. Four or five years later the number of product types handled by plant B was eight times as many as plant A, and, as one would expect, product volume changes were reflected in this decision. Whilst in plant A, average volumes for individual product rose by 60 per cent, in plant B they decreased by 40 per cent. In addition, to redress the decline in profits, the company also embarked on major manufacturing investments at each plant, involving identical process investments and infrastructure changes: Figure 4.7 illustrates how these changes fitted plant A's markets whilst they led to a significant mismatch for plant B.

The procedure followed is the one given in the previous section. Again, the first step is to choose the characteristics of product markets, manufacturing, investment cost and infrastructure features pertinent to this business. The dimensions selected for these two plants are detailed in Figure 4.6. First, the characteristics that reflect the change between jobbing, batch and line need to be described. On the one hand, the product range associated with jobbing is wide, and becomes increasingly narrow as it moves through to line. On the other, customer order size is small in jobbing and becomes increasingly large as it moves through to line, and so on. These dimensions represent the classic characteristics of the trade-offs embodied in process choice. Plant A's profile shows a straight line relationship between the product markets and the manufacturing and infrastructure provision. However, when the profile is drawn from plant B it can be seen that a dog-leg occurs because the process and infrastructure investments made in that plant, although similar to those made in plant A, did not relate to the characteristics of its particular market and hence a mismatch occurred.

Conclusion

The POM function is complex both within its own set of subsystems and within its relationship to the organization. When most organizations start to grow, the initial functional division which usually takes place separates the operations task from other functions. With further growth, procedures and systems are developed, and support and specialist functions are introduced to link the marketing/finance dimension with the operations dimension. Figure 4.7 illustrates this development.

The task facing operations is to ensure, through its joint ownership of the links between product/services and processes, between customers and producers, and between quality and attitudes that it makes a contribution towards the improvement of these within the organization. In many instances, operations managers have shed this major responsibility to the detriment of the POM function, their own role and the organization. Figure 4.1 illustrates some of the key areas of responsibility which fall within the POM task, how they interact and how they relate to the organizational system. Therefore, to do the task well, it is essential that the operations manager takes a proactive role within the organizational system.

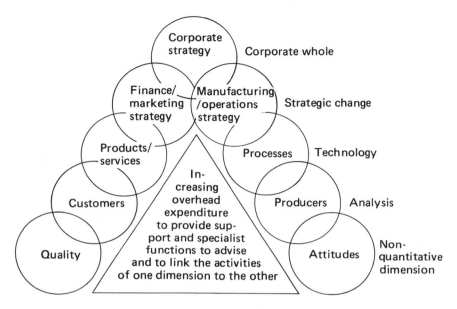

Figure 4.7 Binomial model of an organization.

Source: developed from N. K. Powell, 'Steps towards a definition of operations management', *Management Education and Development*, 9, no. 3 (1979), 162–7. With permission.

The choice of process is similarly complex. It is also essential, therefore, that managers should be aware of the implications involved (see the section on product profiling), take them into account when establishing their objectives and set the standards to be achieved accordingly.

Process choice

The project and continuous process choices are at the two extremes (see Figure 4.8). In most instances, the choice of either project or continuous flow goes hand-in-hand with the product and industry. The process will, therefore, be largely predetermined, and progression from project to jobbing or from line to continuous processing is rare, normally impractical and often irrelevant (see Figures 4.5 and 4.8). Project and continuous processing are, in most situations, isolated from the other three process choices.[5]

However, with jobbing, batch and line processes there is limited transition from one to the other(s) (see Figure 4.5). However, organizations choose an appropriate process based on volumes. Thus, two or more of these three types of process are often found in the same situation providing different products/services with their own distinct characteristics (see Figure 4.9). As in Figure 4.8, batch

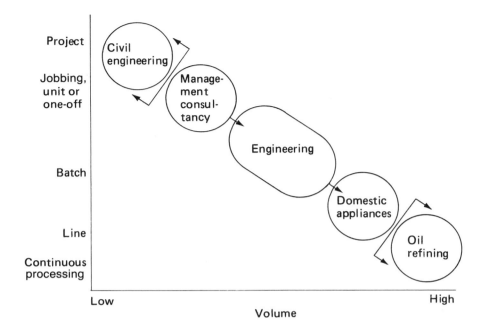

Figure 4.8   Process choices.

Source: developed from R. H. Hayes and S. C. Wheelwright, 'Link manufacturing process and product life cycles', *Harvard Business Review* (January/February 1979), 133–40.

processes are chosen to cope with a very wide range of volumes. Other options at the batch and jobbing stages are now available and include programmable systems such as numerically controlled (NC) machines or machining centres to handle smaller volumes.[6] To cope more efficiently with larger volumes, the decision to dedicate the use of certain processes or the use of group technology may be considered. This can be where one or more processes (not usually specialized) are used exclusively for a product as demand increases, or with the introduction of group technology, which dedicates the use of processes to a small range of similar products. In this way, some of the cost gains inherent in high volume operations can be achieved without investing in dedicated plant (see Figure 4.10). Another option is linked batch process. This is where the operations necessary to complete a number of products are laid out sequentially. However, although the format has the appearance of line, this hybrid in fact has its roots in batch. This is because in order to accommodate a product change the process has to be stopped and reset — the hallmark of batch (see p. 59).

Similarly, a line process can be developed to produce a relatively wide range of products. Such a development is known as mixed mode assembly which, because the product flexibility of the line allows it to produce a given range without stopping

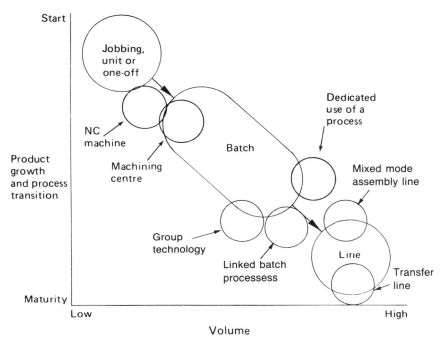

Figure 4.9 Product growth, volume increases and process transition.

the process, has its roots in line. Progressing further down the process continuum reveals a development of line such that it completes some of the operations without manual intervention. These are known as transfer lines and are a hybrid incorporating some aspects of continuous processing. Developments in NC-based processes are discussed in Chapter 7, whilst group technology is discussed in Chapter 6. Both these developments are related in their relevant chapters to the process choice explanations contained in this chapter and illustrated in Figure 4.9.

The discussion so far on types of process implies that these are, to a large extent, distinct types within closely defined parameters. In reality this is not so. Hybrid processes and different subtypes have developed to meet the particular needs of products/services and management philosophies. However, it is important to note that all hybrids have their root stock in one of the five classic processes referred to throughout this chapter. Their position, therefore, in Figure 4.9 illustrates this fact.

The various developments in hybrids and subtypes include:

1. Hybrid process:
    (a) part batch, part line (e.g. linked batch processes shown in Figure 4.9);
    (b) part batch, part continuous process;

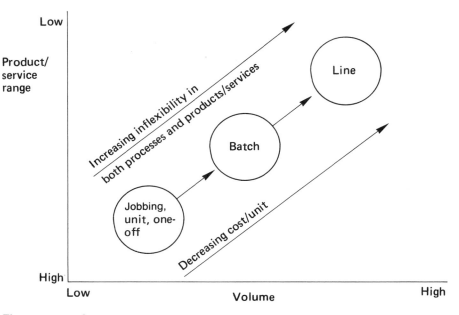

Figure 4.10 Some of the more important trends in product/service features which influence the choice of process.

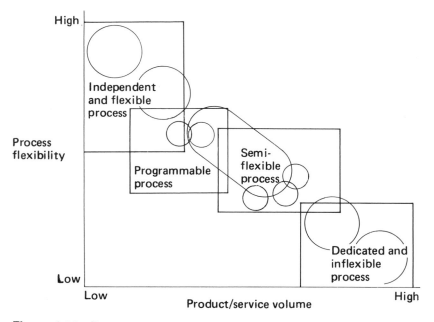

Figure 4.11 Processes by generic type.

(c) part jobbing, part batch;

(d) part line, part continuous process (e.g. transfer line shown in Figure 4.9).

2. Line assembly:

(a) worker-paced;

(b) machine-paced.

In addition, the particular form that each type takes is similarly varied. Figure 4.11, therefore, broadens the view of process types to a higher, conceptual level.

Each of these reviews of operations processes is intended to provide further insights into what is involved when making such a choice. Each operations situation is different and only an analysis of the detail will provide that insight; the framework given here is intended to facilitate this difficult task.

Notes and references

1. A closed system is one that has no environment, that is, no outside systems which significantly impinge on it. An open system is one that has an environment in that there are other systems to which it relates, with which it exchanges information and communicates. All living systems (including organizations) are, therefore, open.

2. Details of this application of a line process within an eye surgery were reported, together with a photograph, in the *Sunday Times Magazine* (8 November 1987), pp. 66–7.

3. WIP inventory provides the function of separating dependent parts of the process by decoupling one operation from the next. It does this by providing inventory into which one operation can feed work and from which the next operation can draw its work. The extent of this inventory will, however, depend upon the degree of certainty in the planning and control operations. Where call-offs are firm and changes in demand are low, WIP inventory requirements will be substantially reduced.

4. The concept of product profiling is more fully explained in two of Terry Hill's books: *Manufacturing Strategy: The strategic management of the manufacturing function* (Basingstoke: Macmillan, 1985), pp. 89–95, and *Manufacturing Strategy: Text and cases* (Homewood, Ill.: Irwin, 1989), chapter 4.

5. The transition between project, jobbing, batch, line and continuous processing is put forward by Hayes and Wheelwright (*op. cit.*). This is, in practice, not the case. Figure 4.9 shows that there is no transition between project and jobbing or line and continuous processing. There is sometimes, however, a transition between jobbing, batch and line and also between batch and continuous processing as shown in Figure 4.6.

6. Numerical control (NC) refers to the operation of machine tools from numerical data stored on paper or magnetic tape, punched cards, computer storage or direct information.

   More advanced NC systems include direct numerical control (DNC), which refers to a system having a computer controlling more than one machine tool, and computer numerical control (CNC) systems using a dedicated minicomputer to perform NC functions.

   The development of the machining centre resulted from NC. In a machining centre a range of operations normally performed by a separate machining process are provided. Tools to perform these operations are stored in the machining centre; each tool can be selected and used as programmed, with some taking place simultaneously.

Chapter 5

Product and service investment decisions

Growth and success is based to a large extent on an organization's ability to introduce new products or services. Whilst a natural market may exist for some essential needs (e.g. food and clothing), for many, a market has to be created. In either case, most organizations have changed from an *ad hoc* approach to the planning of its new products or services to one which is an organized activity involving a procedural cycle from research through to market launch. This chapter examines the procedures involved and some of the important issues to be considered for both new and existing products or services.

Product/service planning

Product/service planning is concerned with establishing the requirements of a product/service in line with given or anticipated market needs. It involves the specification of a product/service prior to its provision and marketing. The idea for the item may come from internal or external stimulus depending upon the organization's allocation of resources internally (e.g. research activities) and its attitude towards the degree of risk it is prepared to take; for example, whether to be a pioneer or follower in its chosen markets.

A product/service idea will often raise certain problems that call for research and which need to be answered before the specification can be defined. The development activity will usually highlight other problems requiring further research. As development work concludes, final design is undertaken and, as with the development phase, this may also lead to more problems requiring more solutions. Throughout all of this procedure, tradeoffs will have to be made between the general specification, process capability and market requirements. In each case, these will have to be resolved before the next stage is undertaken. In POM terms, the most important aspect concerns the capability of the process to meet the technological, cost and other criteria which underpin the viability of the new product/service. In certain instances the process capability will be well able to meet the market requirements and, in others it will not, so making the product/service idea impractical. However, in the marginal cases organizational pressure can often be brought to bear on the operations manager to accept the argument that it is feasible to meet both market and organizational requirements. It is essential in these situations for the operations manager to check thoroughly the cost and other analyses that have been made and on which this decision is being based. These checks will include the level of accuracy involved, how realistic the statements are, and whether alternative plans and decisions have been agreed in the event of actual volumes differing from the forecast.

The research and development process

The objectives of research and development (R&D) activities are to bring about technological change and innovation within both the products and services to be sold by an organization and the process by which these will be produced. The total cycle of events to achieve this embraces programmes both at the strategic and tactical level.

Strategic programmes involve:
1. Fundamental research.
2. Applied research including advanced development work.

Tactical programmes involve:
1. Product/service development.
2. Product/service launch.

Commitment to strategic programmes is an important corporate decision. The degree of commitment will vary. Organizations may decide to adopt either an offensive or a defensive design strategy whilst others fall in between making a moderate R&D commitment by, for instance, contracting research or licensing other organizations' product/service designs.[1]

The offensive strategy brings with it a relatively large research funding with the objective of being a leader in product/service innovation within a given market. The defensive strategy usually limits the amount of research spending to a minimum and will be largely directed towards the development of existing knowledge to enhance product/service roles in the market or in response to customer requirements.

Between these two strategies lie the moderate forms of research commitment. Research contracts are used by governments and other organizations to buy specific research investigations. Research institutes, universities and independent research laboratories are available to take on this work. A second approach is to manufacture under licence or provide a service under a franchise. Marketable products and products manufactured successfully elsewhere are then produced under a licence agreement. Franchising of services (e.g. fast-food restaurants) is similar to licensing except that the products, methods of working and environment are invariably specified and supplies are from a prescribed source.

Strategic programmes

When discussing the strategic and tactical programme it was convenient to separate fundamental and applied research. In reality, the distinction is often blurred.

Fundamental research is not specifically concerned with the practical applications of its results. Its purpose is to study the basic relationships between cause and effect with the aim of increasing knowledge, making discoveries and establishing new applications which may eventually be used on a commercial basis. *Applied research*, on the other hand, is concerned principally with practical applications and solutions to practial problems. Its function concerns classifying and interpreting basic knowledge from fundamental research activities to facilitate problem solving. The return on this research investment is quicker and more assured than for fundamental research. Since applied research is directed towards solving particular problems in the later stages of product/service planning (e.g. advanced development work), the uncertainty is less and the practical usefulness of the results is inherent in the activity. However, an organization may well subcontract some or all of this task until its own research demands can justify employing its own staff.

Impact of technology

The impact of rapid increases in technology that have characterized the last fifty years needs to be carefully assessed and provided for by all organizations. Product/service and process technology advances have become more stepped in nature and more frequent in occurrence. Increasingly, therefore, it is essential that organizations address these opportunities not only in terms of securing or improving their current business base but also in assessing the impact on all corporate functions. This latter need is particularly important in terms of the production/operations function due to the relatively high asset/cost profile that is involved, and the changes in capacity and capability that will ensue. One classic example of this level of technology change is provided by banking:

1960s Cashless payment transactions became technologically feasible. This led to a rapid increase in customers' use of banks initiated by the direct payment of salaries and wages by employer organizations into employees' bank accounts.

1980s Known technology led to increased automation in banking with cash dispensers, multi-functional terminals, point-of-sale systems and video tape systems.

1990s The 1990s will see an increase in self-service and a need to consider the resulting substantial reduction in the functions currently performed by sub-branches of banks. The consequence on the role of advisory *vis à vis* transaction services within banks, and the changing staff requirements will be significant. One development that will undoubtedly follow is home banking supported by video text comparisons, resulting in a greater emphasis on the advice and consultation role of banking staff within the service mix.

With these developments on hand, banks will need to identify those services that lend themselves to automation and those that will be provided (at least in part) by the qualified experts at the identified bank branch. In addition, 'given new technologies such as digital bankwide networks of terminals, many administrative activities could be handled by clerical workstations in the homes of bank staff members. Staff places of work could be set up in their own homes or in separate local or communal working places. The consequences might include a drastic reduction in requirements for and use of office premises; . . . assignment of functions packaged to suit the individual employee'.[2] The ramifications throughout banking, especially in terms of the operations function, would be significant.

Meier-Preschany also identifies the impact of technology on the banks' corporate customers. 'Computer banking, cash management, foreign exchange netting (or "intercompany clearing"), treasury and portfolio management is just the beginning. Is it not inconceivable that banks might become departments of multinational organizations?'[3]

Thus, any organization embracing the new technology needs to recognize the requirement for strategic programmes to assess possible areas of applied research in order to help assess its impact upon all aspect of these organizations, and, not least, upon POM.

Tactical programmes

The steps following these strategic activities concern the tactical considerations involved in the development of a product or service. Although excellent and innovative products/services are continuously being conceived and designed by a whole range of businesses, a feature frequently experienced by many organizations is that the requirements of the production/operations task are not adequately taken into account at the design stage. The result has been higher than necessary costs. The Ford Motor Company's 'effectiveness lever' illustrates the relative impact upon effectiveness that can be achieved at each of the principal stages in the design through to production procedure (Figure 5.1).

Product/service development is concerned with the functional aspects of the design:

1. What will it do?
2. How will it do it?

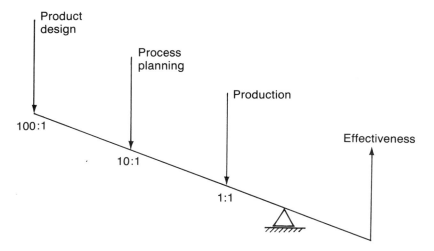

Figure 5.1   The Ford Motor Company 'Effectiveness Lever'.[4]

3. How will it be made or provided?
4. The maintenance and repair requirement.
5. Physical distribution.

The link between technology, development, design, the operations process and the market need is essential to the profitable production of a product or provision of a service,[5] and it is essential that the operations manager plays a prominent role in this procedure. Design concerns the structuring of components or activities so that as a whole they meet customer needs. To do this successfully, however, requires that due consideration is given to the operational capability to make the product or provide the service, the investment requirement necessary to provide adequate capacity/capability or the cost implications embodied in the proposed design if existing capability is insufficient and investment not forthcoming. To ensure that this part of the procedure is adequately completed is one of the prime POM tasks. It is important, therefore, that the operations manager reviews the relevant procedures to ensure that the operations perspectives are embodied throughout each stage of the design to manufacture/provision phase.

The development process concerns defining a product or service by a procedure of checking successive designs until the required specifications are met as economically as possible. This usually involves testing several designs to evaluate their feasibility, for example by prototype testing or laboratory experiments. In addition, computer aided design (CAD) has made an important contribution by integrating computers into the development and design procedure. A CAD system stores, retrieves, manipulates and displays graphical information with great speed and accuracy. It is based on a minicomputer with three dimensional graphical displays. With CAD a common engineering database is developed which is a collection of all the information about related products. Thus, once generated, the information is neither lost nor recreated. In addition, the geometric and non-geometric information stored in the engineering database is then used as the basis for manufacture at a later stage. This then forms part of computer aided manufacturing (CAM) systems of which more will be said in Chapter 7.

A typical CAD system consists of a central processing unit with a large storage facility and a minicomputer plus system software. Linked to this control unit will be a number of design terminals. Through these, the designer interacts with the engineering database to develop a detailed product design whilst monitoring the work on the display terminal. The designer creates, modifies and refines each design without putting pen to paper. Thus the design terminal provides a simple yet powerful interaction between the designer and the computer. The designer instructs the system using an electronic pen or keyboard. Initially, s/he retrieves any completed drawings or other stored information relevant to the design task and the standard design symbols to be used. This on-line library, therefore, eliminates both filing and information retrieval procedures. Then, by using either an electronic pen and drawing tablet or a keyboard, the designer communicates draughting instructions to the system. Graphic displays give designers an imaginary drawing board of some twenty thousand square inches, any portion of which can be viewed through the display in three dimensions with zooming and rotation facilities available to view the design from any angle and allowing for interaction on any basis. In this way, the operator can create and modify the design whilst watching it emerge on the display unit with the system automatically informing him/her of procedural or design rule errors. Also built into the system is the capability for assisting the designer in outline drawings, creating the third dimension at any desired angle, generating views from any side, rotating the part, changing the scale, producing a mirror image and adding the appropriate text all with a sufficient degree of precision to meet the highest engineering standards.

Once the preliminary design is created, the information is stored allowing existing designs to be readily retrieved. At any time, a hard copy of the design can be made in paper form for use outside the CAD system. When the preliminary design has been agreed, various analyses can be applied to test its viability. After making any necessary modifications, the design is ready for the manufacturing stage. Although the costs of creating preliminary three-dimensional geometrical designs are similar to those using conventional methods, the savings when revising and modifying them are substantial. For instance, the operator is able to interrogate the database to help make decisions on designs, whilst further large savings are made on filing, information retrieval and all the error prone, time consuming, handwritten activities necessary with conventional methods.

In addition to new product/service development, the tactical programmes include:

1. Improving, adopting and redesigning existing products/services.

2. Developing new uses for existing materials.
3. Exploring the use of other materials and processes.

These, together with a range of important activities including standardization and value analysis, are discussed later in the chapter.

Research expenditure

The pressure to market more and better products/services has heightened in recent years due to increasing world competition and reducing product/service life cycles. One of the significant factors in achieving the continued growth of an organization or a nation's economy is the rate of technical innovation in terms of the development, design, improvement and application of products, services and processes aimed at increasing their competitiveness in home and world markets. Since 1945 the British research performance overall has been less than the majority of its industrial competitors.[5] Furthermore, Britain's innovative activities have been heavily sponsored by government.

Failure to recognize or to respond to the essential nature of technological change is a critical aspect in the success of industrial nations. McMillan argues that, 'probably no single feature explains the continuing success of Japan's industrial system as the management of knowledge and technology'.[6] Yet for all the success of Japan's technological achievements, there is no doubt of the failure of the UK and some other countries to recognize these areas as an important factor in improving the performance of its industrial base. The need to harness technology (including that imported from other industrial nations) to support economic growth is essential.

In 1985—6, the UK spent a higher percentage of gross national product on government-financed R&D than any other OECD (Organization for Economic Co-operation and Development) country apart from the USA.[7] However, the bias in UK government research spending has been towards defence and away from the industrial productivity and technology category. Table 5.1 shows the major EEC countries' spending as a percentage of total government R&D expenditure for these two categories. In fact, the UK spent twice the EEC average of 25.6 per cent on defence in 1985.

In 1970, however, the UK spent a higher percentage of its budget in the industrial productivity and technology category compared with other countries. By 1980 it was the lowest, and 1985 figures and 1986 budgets confirm this position. This trend is further illustrated in Table 5.2 which shows the percentage increase/decrease of the total R&D budgets which EEC governments allocated to this industrial category. Between 1970 and 1985, the UK and France were the only countries to decrease government R&D allocations to this category — the UK by the substantial markdown of 58 per cent. Furthermore, using an index of technology level as a general measure of activity, Table 5.3 shows the stable level of activity in the UK compared to the increases brought about by some of its major competitors.

Table 5.1 Percentage of government R&D expenditure on the 'defence' and 'industrial productivity and technology' categories for selected years between 1970 and 1986

	Percentages of government R&D expenditure									
	Defence					*Industrial productivity and technology*				
	1970	*1976*	*1980*	*1985*	*1986*[a]	*1970*	*1976*	*1980*	*1985*	*1986*[a]
Belgium	0.4	2.6	0.5	1.5	1.5	9.9	10.6	16.7	17.8	16.2
Denmark	0.3	0.8	0.5	0.6	0.5	8.1	6.6	9.5	21.0	20.6
France	31.8	29.5	37.2	31.3	31.0	15.2	11.2	9.2	12.1	12.5
Eire	0.0	0.0	0.0	0.0	0.0	18.1	20.4	—	28.9	26.1
Italy	3.9	4.5	4.3	9.9	8.4	17.1	10.3	10.4	20.7	19.2
Netherlands	4.9	3.2	3.0	3.0	2.6	6.4	4.8	9.5	10.4	14.8
UK	41.0	47.7	55.6	51.9	51.6	16.0	7.0	4.2	6.7	6.7
W. Germany	17.7	11.4	10.2	11.9	12.4	6.6	6.8	9.9	14.2	14.3

[a] The 1986 figures are based on provisional budgets.

Source: Government Financing of Research and Development (Eurostat Annual Publications, Statistical Office of the European Communities) for relevant years.

Table 5.2 Percentage increase or decrease from 1970 to 1985 in EEC government's allocation of R&D expenditure to the category 'industrial productivity and technology'

	Increase (decrease) on a 1970 base (%)
Belgium	80
Denmark	59
France	(20)
Eire	60
Italy	21
Netherlands	63
UK	(58)
W. Germany	115

The first steps towards redressing this trend include the need for organizations to recognize the trade-off between short-term profit and longer-term growth. In many markets, UK companies are no longer at the forefront of technial design. It is essential, therefore, that not only should the level of R&D expenditure be reviewed but also that the pattern of this expenditure should match the export markets in which the UK has to succeed.

Table 5.3 General index of technology levels

	Late 1960s	Late 1970s
USA	100	200
W. Germany	40	56
France	24	38
UK	25	26
Japan	22	50

Index: using the USA as 100 the average of index positions in patents registered, technological trade balance, value added in manufacturing, and proportion of exports which are technology-intensive.

Source: C.J. McMillan, *The Japanese Industrial System* (Berlin: de Gruyter, 1985), p.113, with permission.

Innovation and product/service life cycles

All organizations have a range of products or services at a given time. To be competitive, it is necessary to have a set that is complementary, relates to the organization's strategic decisions associated with issues such as growth and market share, and takes account of tactical considerations such as completeness of range, process capability and distribution costs. Furthermore, the mix is always undergoing change. New products or services are necessary for survival and growth. However, there are two important factors to be considered:

1. The development and introduction of new products or services is both risky and costly.
2. Successful new products/services tend to follow a life cycle.

Level of innovation, development and new product/service introduction

Organizations are continuously faced with the need to introduce new products/services in a never-ending requirement to keep a mix of products/services which meets the needs of their customers. However, developing and introducing new items is typically expensive, risky and involves a long time horizon. But, it also concerns the very life blood of business.

Attitudes and norms concerning the level of innovation and the introduction of new products/services are affected by both internal and external forces. Decisions to invest in R&D or seek to exploit developments in technology will vary from industry to industry and from company to company, and often markedly so. In product-based companies, the tradition to invest in R&D and to actively seek to introduce new products has noticeably increased over the last few decades. This varies from superficial modifications (for example, in markets such as consumer durables, there is a traditional 'face lift' to existing models/products on a regular basis) to major product changes. Table 5.4 provides a comprehensive example. It outlines the direction of technology planning for the Japanese industrial mechanical equipment and automobile sectors. Although the primary emphasis is on new product development, developments in closely related production processes are both an integral part of the initiative and a source of new product spin-offs — for example, Japanese car makers are now major producers of robot equipment.

A review of service industries also highlights the changes over the last decade in the products/services offered. Protected for a long time by geographical distance, commercial legacies and legal constraints, many service industries remained conservative and insensitive to the needs of their customers. For instance, deregulation and the advances in data processing have made an enormous impact upon the travel industry; the limited competition that UK banks enjoyed from the very beginning changed with the alterations to trading rules for building societies, the opening up of financial markets and particularly investments in data processing. These factors, based on process improvements, have also led at the other end of the scale to significant increases in international banking and corresponding asset growth since the mid 1970s. From being a quite small feature of a typical domestic bank's portfolio, international banking is now substantial (see Table 5.5). A similar example is provided by the link up of financial and investment markets which was also founded on data processing technology improvements. The impact of reciprocal agreements upon competition has been marked and has brought with it a fast pace of change in terms of product/service definitions and operations capacity and capability.

Product/service life cycles[8]

The extent and rate of new product/service introductions can, as illustrated, make a significant impact on a business. However, of equal concern in these decisions is the life cycle pattern anticipated or experienced once the product/service has been introduced. Market-place pressures require that designs are never static and continuous endeavours are made to increase the fit with customer needs whilst scrutinizing the relationships between cost, quality and value. Despite the attention given by most organizations, many products/services enter the market and are then quickly phased out due to the lack of sales.

The process of introduction, initial growth, maturity and eventual decline in sales is referred to as the product/service life cycle (see Figure 5.2). It outlines the phases through which a product or service may go as it moves into and out of the market. New products/services are required to replace those already in the cycle, however extended the time scale may be.

Table 5.4 Direction of product technology developments in Japanese industrial mechanical equipment and automobile industries

Industrial mechanical equipment		*Automobiles*	
Development of new products	*Application and systemization of existing technologies and products*	*Development of new products*	*Application of systemization of existing technologies and products*
• Development of automation machinery for manufacturing processes to increase labour-saving and safety	• Improving labour-saving and work precision by introduction of the computer for individual machines, such as metal working machinery, plastic forming machinery and casting and forging devices (NC-ization, accommodation control, learning control, group technology)	• Development of vehicles with engines which apply new theories, such as gas turbine vehicles, rankine cycle engine vehicles, stirling engine vehicles, electrical automobiles, etc.	• Development of new traffic systems by combining automobile technology with the computer, such as demand-bus systems, and city-car dual mode systems
• Development of unmanned factories		• Development of anti-pollution equipment (such as engine enclosures) and low pollution vehicles	• Development of the automobile comprehensive control system by unifying the automobile and wireless communications
• Application of man–machine systems, promotion of safety improvement by attaching failsafe mechanisms and other measures	• Automation of manufacturing processes such as materials supply, product-conveying, inspecting, working and assembling	• Development of safety in automobiles by adopting, amongst other measures, air bag systems, anti-skid systems, and safety tyres	
• Development of unmanned factories by integrating automation machinery	• Development of unmanned factories		
• Development of biomechanic technology substituting for human functions, such as sensors, artificial organs, molluscan machines, etc.			

- Development of new material technology such as functional materials, function-assisting materials and structural materials in order to expand functions and to improve reliability

- Development of nuclear energy related equipment, cryogenic machinery, etc. by applying technologies adapted to extreme conditions

- Development of resource and energy recycling systems to conserve resources and energy and eliminate pollution

- Development of machinery and apparatus deemed necessary for community systems such as calamity prevention, water supply and sewage, solid waste disposal, new traffic systems, etc., and their systemization

- Development of pollution preventing machinery systems, safety plant systems for solving the problems of pollution and safety

- Application of industrial mechanical systems such as rehabilitation systems and artificial organ systems to life sciences

- Automation and systemization of food production, such as indoor agricultural production systems and cultivated fishing systems

Source: Japan External Trade Organization (JETRO) as quoted in C.J. McMillan, *The Japanese Industrial System* (Berlin: de Gruyter, 1985), pp. 110–11. With permission.

Table 5.5   The presence of international banking, 1980

Home country	*Number of*			
	Banks	*Foreign branches*	*Foreign subsidiaries*	*Associates*
France	19	228	37	126
Japan	23	127	29	93
UK	25	961	86	54
USA	151	800	113	224
W. Germany	21	55	16	115

Source: D. B. Zenoff, Perspectives on the management of international banks', in *International Banking: Management and Strategies*, ed. D. B. Zenoff (Euromoney Publications, 1985), pp. 5–6. With permission.

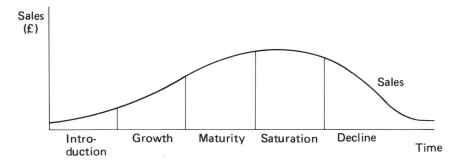

Figure 5.2   The generalized product/service life cycle.

Introduction
The sales pattern of many products/services initially shows a slow growth. Market awareness is low and acceptance has not yet been achieved. The concept is often new, and initial teething troubles are usually experienced. This makes for low sales with slow growth.

Growth
The market has now been conditioned to the product or service. With acceptance comes a rapid growth in sales resulting from promotion, increased dependability, past sales and often a lower selling price.

Maturity
At this stage, competitors have entered the market and the rate of sales increases begins to slow. This is due to the competitors who have entered the market and

the fact that the product/service is now well-known and established within its market segment.

Saturation

In this stage, almost all those who want the product/service have now bought it. Market demand is restricted to replacement demand plus a small quantity of new sales. Product/service promotion is often used more extensively here not to publicize the item but to differentiate it from its competitors.

Decline

In this phase, sales continue to fall off, and invariably at a rapid rate. The introduction of competing products/services either as improvements or as substitutes accelerate the decline to the point where it becomes obsolete. For example, the slide rule had been in the mature/saturation stage for a long time before it was replaced by the hand-held electronic calculator. Similarly, public transport services have in many of the country areas been replaced by private car ownership.

The operations role changes at each stage and follows the lines outlined in Chapter 4. It is important here to stress that at the mature and saturated stages in the life cycle it is often possible to extend the life cycle by introducing refinements so that the original single form is developed into several different forms.[9]

Analyses of products and services

The need at the tactical level to appraise the range of products/services offered by an organization and to reduce variety where appropriate is examined in Chapter 4. It is important however, to introduce and maintain further tactical analyses as a way of helping to reduce costs.

Standardization

In addition to its application to finished products/services, the concept of standardization can be applied to components, materials and process choice to great effect.

Components

Standardized components and subassemblies can be used to make finished items that are different in appearance and performance. This approach can be formalized into providing modular designs such that a variety of final products use only a few basic components. This approach results in economies due to component inventory reduction, longer production runs, increased opportunity to automate, purchasing advantages and improved delivery performance.

Materials

In a similar way to components, standardization can be applied to both direct and indirect materials. In this case, both the variety of material sizes and types can be simplified through close examination. It is important, however, to seek a balance between the cost gains due to reduced inventory, easier control and bulk purchasing, and the overspecification and lower utilization of material which will increase the materials bill.

Processes

The standardization of equipment choice, assuming that there is no requirement to increase flexibility, will lead to a reduction in spare parts inventory and will simplify the maintenance requirement. Where it is feasible in terms of capability to choose equipment of the same type and size, then standardization of equipment choice will also lead to increased flexibility (e.g. tool changes in manufacturing or compatible computer hardware and software in operations).

However, to make standardization work effectively requires the formulation of a corporate policy together with the establishment of agreed criteria that will be applied to all the products produced or services provided.

Service issues

A product tends to be highly specified. This is due in part to its tangible nature and in part to the fact that product specifications have traditionally been an integral feature of manufacturing industry, and the engineering/technical perspectives developed as part of the professional dimensions within relevant disciplines. The same is not true in most service industries.

However, specifying the dimensions of a service and including appropriate levels of standardization are equally critical to the successful business. Where, however, the service is highly customized then, as with a product, the specification needs to be developed in line with the customer need and not as the outcome of applying previously agreed parameters. In a service business it is necessary to identify the levels of:

1. Customer contact.
2. Discretion to be used by the server.
3. Amount of service provided on-line and off-line.

By eliminating 'personal' discretion outside that agreed, a business can standardize on the service(s) offered and secure different levels of appropriate standardization.

A fast-food restaurant, for instance, establishes a high level of product and service standardization and then trains its staff to provide only what has been agreed. By establishing this high degree of standardization and taking away 'server discretion', these outlets can maintain essential qualities of the product/service package (particularly service speed) which they offer. A good quality restaurant, on the other hand, allows and even encourages 'server discretion'. The desirability of a server to introduce features to reflect customer needs and the opportunity to do so in the service delivery system creates a customized product/service package that contains distinctly different features reflected in delivery speed and price.

Value engineering and value analysis

The price of materials, components and services is the concern of the purchasing function. To a large extent, it will be influenced by world markets, competition and usage volumes. However, the other important factor determining an organization's material costs is how well it utilizes these materials. The significance of a reduction in these costs is substantial. In 1986, the cost of purchases made by all UK manufacturing industries totalled £132,112m. A small percentage reduction, therefore, would reveal a considerable amount overall. However, it is the incidence of labour costs which concerns most UK companies and where most organizations put their resources in an attempt to reduce costs. However, the *Census of Production* revealed that in 1986, the purchases of all UK manufacturing industries was 5.6 times higher than the cost of operatives (at £26,566m), 7.7 times higher than the cost of other wage and salary categories (at £17,201m) and 3 times higher than all wages and salaries. For the period 1970–86, this also applies to a cross-section of industries (see Table 5.6), and, as the figures illustrate, the ratios show a consistent, marked and upward trend of these patterns. For the UK to be competitive, it is essential that not only should productivity gains be sought in labour terms, but also that effective, material cost management is introduced and maintained on a corporate basis.

An important, but often under-used, technique to help provide this systematic approach to reducing the cost of a product or service but without impairing its function is *value analysis*. It is concerned with the methodical examination of each product, component or service with the purpose of minimizing its cost without reducing its functional value.[10] Although value analysis was applied initially to existing manufactured products, it is now applied with equal success to service and overhead costs within the organization. The term *value engineering* is often used synonymously with value analysis but, strictly speaking, it refers to the use of this technique in the initial stages of product/service design.

Value analysis, like method study, aims at reducing costs. However, its orientation is different. *Method study* (discussed in detail in Chapter 11) tends to accept the product/service as determined and concentrates on the way it is made or provided. Thus, the principal aim is to reduce labour costs in the process. Value

Table 5.6 Ratio of purchases to costs of wages and salaries for selected industries and for all manufacturing industries

| Industry | Ratio of purchases to wages and salaries | | | | | |
| | 1986 | | 1979 | | 1970 | |
	Operatives	All	Operatives	All	Operatives	All
Food, drink, tobacco	9.6	6.8	8,3	6.0	7.6	5.5
Chemical	9.6	4.5	8.9	4.8	6.6	3.5
Metal manufacture:	6.6	4.5	4.9	3.5	4.7	3.5
Mechanical	3.2	1.8	3.0	1.8	2.7	1.8
Instrument	3.1	1.6	3.1	1.6	2.6	1.4
Engineering (electrical and electronic)	4.1	2.1	3.7	2.1	3.6	2.1
Shipbuilding	1.7	1.2	1.5	1.1	1.5	1.1
Motor vehicles	5.2	3.4	3.9	2.7	4.3	3.1
Textile	3.3	2.4	3.5	2.6	3.5	2.6
Clothing, hats, gloves	2.4	1.8	2.6	2.0	2.3	1.8
Footwear	1.9	1.5	2.6	2.0	2.1	1.7
Furniture	3.6	2.5	2.6	2.0	2.1	1.7
Rubber products	3.2	2.0	3.4	2.2	2.8	1.9
Sports goods	4.1	2.4	3.2	2.1	2.9	1.9
Processing of plastics	3.8	2.5	3.6	2.5	2.9	2.0
Bolts, nuts, screws, rivets	1.9	1.3	2.4	1.6	2.4	1.8
All manufacturing industries	5.0	3.0	4.6	3.0	3.9	2.6

Notes
1. Industry categories were revised in 1986.
2. Purchases include materials for use in production, and packing and fuel: these include the cost of raw materials, components, semi-manufactured goods and workshop materials, replacement parts and consumable tools not charged to capital account, packaging materials of all types, stationery and printed matter, fuel, electricity and water materials.

Source: HMSO Business Statistics Office, PA 1002 *Business Monitor Report on the Census of Production.* Summary tables for the relevant years.

analysis, however, considers the functions which the components, products or services are intended to perform. It then reviews the present design in order to provide these functions at a lower material and labour cost, without reducing the value. However, as illustrated in Table 5.6 the potential gains by reducing material costs average five times the value of equivalent reductions in direct labour costs.

The need for value analysis to be introduced and maintained throughout an organization is an essential part of any corporate strategy for systematically reducing costs. As Lawrence Miles, who developed these concepts in the immediate post-war period, said: 'On average, one fourth of manufacturing cost is unecessary. The extra cost continues because of patterns and habits of thought, because of personal limitations, because of difficulties in promptly disseminating ideas and because today's thinking is based on yesterday's knowledge.'[11]

Value can be classified under two headings:[12]

Use value. The properties and qualities that accomplish the function of the product or service.

Esteem value. The properties, features or attractiveness that cause people to want to own it.

Value, therefore, constitutes the combination of use and esteem properties related to the cost of providing them.

The analysis of value

In attempting to analyse value, three aspects of operations are reviewed:

1. Design of the product or service.
2. Purchase of materials or services.
3. Process methods.

Design

Too often design decisions are made without due consideration of the effects on product or service costs. This is because:

1. Designers are often preoccupied with the initial task of designing to meet the functional requirement involved.
2. Traditional designs are often concerned with reliability and quality without asking value-for-money questions.
3. Designers often adopt a safety-first policy and thereby overspecify against the necessary requirement.
4. Too often there is a lack of current information available to designers. Therefore they design too much from yesterday's principles and information sources.
5. The functional specialisms that exist help to create barriers between design, purchasing, operations and sales.
6. In the case of services, too often the specification is not clearly determined as explained in an earlier section.

Purchasing

In many organizations too little attention is given to the need to obtain materials and services that meet design requirements at lowest cost. This is because:

1. Purchasing in most organizations is still seen largely as a paper-processing task. For this reason, the executive staff attracted to this critical role tend to be of insufficient quality to provide the essential cost and value-oriented approach.
2. It is too easy to: (a) rely on previous or known suppliers, or allow other functions

to specify the source for items; (b) avoid investigation and questioning as an integral part of the purchasing procedure, and (c) be reactive in this role.
3.   Purchasing, too suffers from the barriers created by functional specialisms.

Operations
Many organizations have an established clerical work measurement, industrial engineering or work study section. However, what tends to happen is:

1.   The staff do not spend much of their time on method study.
2.   When they are involved in establishing the time to do a job (one of their major tasks), the work study staff tend to accept the present method of working without detailed questioning.
3.   Even where method studies have been made, they have been limited in the following ways:
      (a) the investigation has been based on an operation or department rather than the service or product through all its stages including design;
      (b) method study has usually concentrated all its attention on the process, the way the work is completed. In so doing, it has failed to ask essential questions regarding design and materials.

Lastly, the operations function also incurs the problems brought about by the lack of co-ordination mentioned in both the other aspects.

Thus the source of savings associated with value analysis comes principally from materials and, because of the size of purchases compared to direct labour and total wage and salary costs (see Table 5.6), small percentage reductions will lead to sizable total reductions. Typical savings include:

1.   Eliminate a component, transaction, etc. without reducing the functional qualities involved.
2.   Combine the functions of two or more components or services by redesign.
3.   Use cheaper materials or services as a direct substitute, without reducing quality.
4.   Reduce tolerances which are unnecessarily tight and make for higher operations costs.
5.   Extend the concept of standardization (see pp. 91–2).
6.   In conjunction with many of these savings, it will be possible to simplify the process task and consequently reduce labour costs.

The value analysis procedure is in two parts: (1) those responsible for completing the analysis, and (2) the procedure to be followed.

The make-up of those responsible for completing the analysis work is quite wide-ranging. The classic structure is to have a group comprising a full-time specialist (the value analyst) and representatives from design, purchasing, costing and operations. However, other forms have proved equally successful and, in the case of many Japanese companies, includes the groups constituted under quality circles (described in Chapter 12). In each instance, however, prerequisites to the successful application of value analysis are that those concerned are trained in the procedures involved, and that corporate goodwill is demonstrated at all points throughout, including time to complete the tasks, access to cost and other data, and liaison with outside suppliers. The steps involved are:

1. Select the item.
2. Gather information about it.
3. Analyse its function and its value for money.
4. Generate alternative ways to provide the same function through speculation and brainstorming. [13]
5. Assess the worth of these ideas.
6. Decide what is to be done.
7. Implement the decisions.
8. Evaluate the results.

The items selected are usually known to be of high cost and the use of the 80/20 rule will help in the procedure. [14] However, it is important not to select a product/service that is nearing the end of its life cycle. Value analysis is not a prop to help non-viable products/services become viable. It can, however, form a legitimate part of extending the product life cycle as explained earlier in this chapter (p. 91).

When introducing value analysis, it is important to ensure that the procedure in no way brings with it an air of recrimination. It is essential that those concerned contribute to the procedure in an objective way without implying criticism of any department's or person's previous work. The following series of questions will help when applying value analysis to each item or part of the product or service:

1. Does it contribute to the esteem or use value of the product/service? If so, how?
2. What is its cost? Does the cost appear to be in proportion to its function?
3. Are all the features essential? Which ones are questionable?
4. If it is necessary, what else could provide the same function:
   (a) Standard part?
   (b) Alternative part?
5. Is the way in which the product/service is currently made or provided in line with current volumes? Often volumes change, but the process does not.
6. Has anyone asked the supplier if an alternative is available to provide the same function?
7. Have alternative supplies been sought recently in terms of current volumes and prices?

Value analysis consists of taking each part of the product/service and looking in detail at its function. Every feature, tolerance, hole, degree of finish, piece of material, part of the service is vetted to ensure that none of these is adding to the total cost without providing a useful function.

The application of value analysis principles to products can be readily visualized. However, these principles are increasingly, and appropriately, being applied within service industries. One example is provided in a review of the Paul Revere Life

Insurance Companies application of value analysis in the mid-1980s as part of achieving their corporate strategic objective of improved quality.[15] As part of this drive, management groups formed value analysis workshops to address the question, 'Are we doing the right thing?'[16] resulting in recommendations to improve basic work functions and processes. The responsibility for implementing these orgnizational and work process changes was delegated to those running the individual sections, with department managers themselves eventually taking part in the value analysis workshops. Having identified the more important departments and the functions within a department, standard value analysis procedures were applied. Annual savings in the first part year were $6m.

Service strategies

Service organizations need to develop appropriate strategies by identifying what they are, the choices open to them, and what they wish to be. Without this, a company will find difficulty in providing the necessary level of orientation on which to base service delivery system decisions. The several aspects needed to form part of this resolution are now discussed.

Identifying segments and different types of business

An initial step concerns identifying different segments within a market as a way of recognizing difference not only in terms of marketing, but also when establishing the operations task involved within a service delivery system. An illustration of this is the approach adopted by Handels Bank NW (HBNW) of Zurich.[17] HBNW adopts a differentiated approach, based on the following market segments:

1. Institutional investors.
2. Portfolio management clients.
3. Large investors.
4. Standard investors.
5. Medium investors.
6. Small investors.

These segments reflect the needs of its investors, the appropariate investment tools to be used, and the differential costs the bank applies in providing its different services. In this way, the bank more clearly identifies the type and level of service to be provided and the operations support required in that provision.

In addition to segmentation, services can also be separated by type. One split concerns those services based principally on equipment and those principally on people.[18] Within these two broad divisions, subdivisions concerning skill requirements can be identified, as illustrated in Table 5.7.

Table 5.7 Types of service showing the range of operations requirements within the service delivery system

Predominant base	*Level of automation and labour skills*	*Examples*
	Automated	Cash dispensing Photocopying Vending machines Car wash
Equipment	Monitored by unskilled/ semi-skilled people	Photocopying Dry-cleaning Gardening Tree surgery Taxis
	Operated by skilled people	Airlines Computer time-sharing Word processing
	Unskilled	Cleaning services Security guards
People	Skilled	Catering Vehicle maintenance Appliance repairs
	Professional	Lawyers Management consultants Accountancy

Customer Expectations

Customers have different expectations within service industries, and they are becoming more demanding as this sector of the economy expands. Examples illustrating this are to be found in several industries: e.g. the expectations of the holiday and business traveller have changed noticeably over the last two decades and the products on offer have evolved accordingly. Services, therefore, win orders in different ways, a factor not only critical in itself but also in its implication for operations function investments − see Chapter 2.

Also, because of the customers' involvement in the delivery system, the service takes on a more personalized nature than in the product/sales domain. Companies, therefore, need to assess expectations and modify the service delivery system both in terms of these and to minimize occasions where customers' perceptions of the system detract from the quality image projected by advertising and marketing.

Strategies to reduce cost

Companies in various service systems have pursued strategies to reduce costs in several ways, including the following:

1. *Seeking out low-cost customers.* Some customers cost less to serve than others, without any deterioration in the perceived level of service provided. Non-smokers are eligible for lower life insurance rates, and accident-free customers for lower insurance premiums. Shouldice's Hernia Hospital near Toronto carefully screens patients and only accepts those in good physical condition with forms of hernia on which it specializes. This contributed to rapid recovery rates and early discharge, which are reflected in the hospital's prices and costs.
2. *Standardize a customer service.* Developments in mortgage lending illustrate the gains to be secured by standardizing the service within appropriate parameters.
3. *'Do-it-yourself' customization.* Numerous examples exist in the service sector to illustrate this growing phenomenon – telephone subscriber dialling, self-service salad bar provision in restaurants, hot drink and mini-bar facilities in hotel bedrooms all illustrate the provision of an acceptable level (and often preferred type) of service whilst reducing customer complaints and, at the same time, conserving costs.

Strategies to enhance service

Companies basing their approach on service differentiation have employed several strategies to bring this about, including the following:

1. *Making the intangible tangible.* One way to bring the intangible facets of a service to the attention of a customer is to make them tangible. In this way, parts of a service package which would often go unnoticed are now a visible part of the provision. For example:
   (a) Maid service in a hotel bedroom to include collars placed on toilets with words similar to 'sanitized for your personal use', end-folding toilet roll paper, folding down the bed in the evening with a personalized note and guest room checklist duly completed and signed (see Figure 5.3).
   (b) The recent water conservation drive in parts of the USA has led to many restaurants withdrawing their automatic cold water provision and replacing it with a 'by request' service. Many restaurants, however, made sure that customers appreciate that this provision is still part of the service. The example in Figure 5.4 not only signals this but also makes it an item of interest by providing information on water conservation on the reverse side of the table card.
   (c) Some hotels are increasingly making in-room hot drink provision a feature, as illustrated by Figure 5.5. Moreover, most hotels provide the highest quality amenities such as French-milled and smooth facial soaps, shampoo, conditioner, bath foam, hand lotion and shower caps; aftershave for male

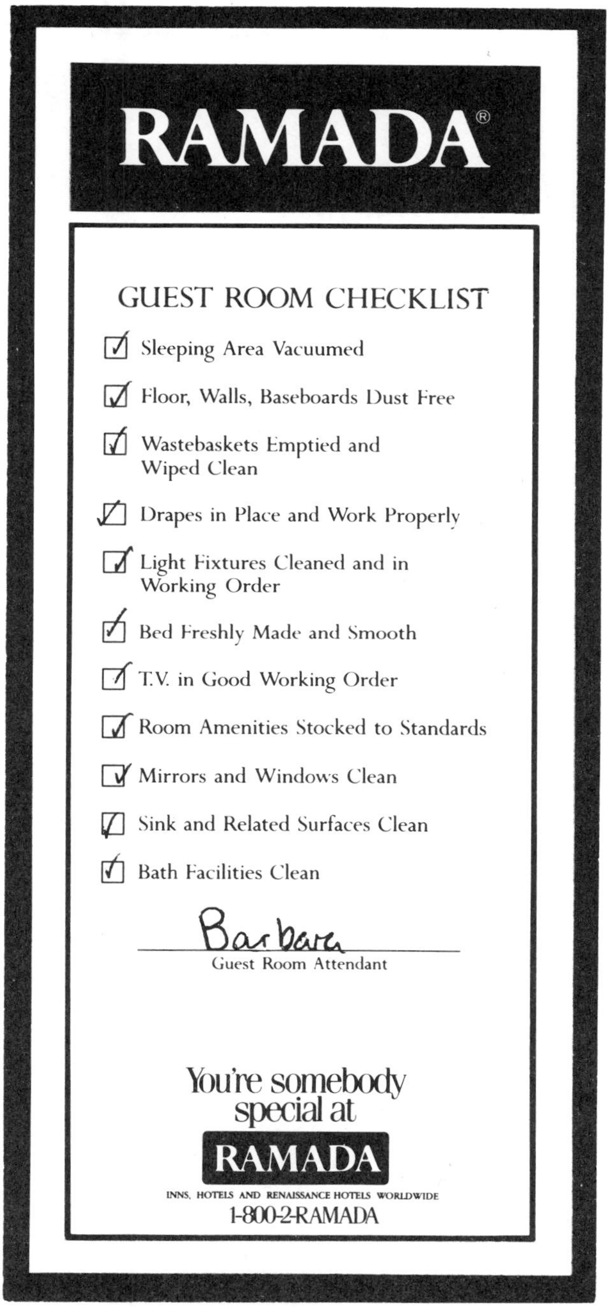

RAMADA®

GUEST ROOM CHECKLIST

- ☑ Sleeping Area Vacuumed
- ☑ Floor, Walls, Baseboards Dust Free
- ☑ Wastebaskets Emptied and Wiped Clean
- ☑ Drapes in Place and Work Properly
- ☑ Light Fixtures Cleaned and in Working Order
- ☑ Bed Freshly Made and Smooth
- ☑ T.V. in Good Working Order
- ☑ Room Amenities Stocked to Standards
- ☑ Mirrors and Windows Clean
- ☑ Sink and Related Surfaces Clean
- ☑ Bath Facilities Clean

Barbara

Guest Room Attendant

You're somebody special at

RAMADA

INNS, HOTELS AND RENAISSANCE HOTELS WORLDWIDE

1-800-2-RAMADA

Figure 5.3 A typical checklist left for the guest to see and which helps visualize an otherwise less tangible part of the hotel's service. With permission.

A cold glass of water?

Yours for the asking...

By serving water only upon request, our restaurant, in cooperation with the San Diego County Water Authority and its 24 member agencies, is doing its part to help conserve San Diego's most valuable resource.

WATER CONSERVATION: SAN DIEGO'S WAY OF LIFE

SAN DIEGO COUNTY WATER AUTHORITY
2750 4TH AVE., SAN DIEGO, CA 92103 (619) 297-3218

The San Diego County Water Authority imports up to 90% of the water used in San Diego County from as far east as the Rocky Mountains and as far north as the Sierras.

In an effort to help conserve San Diego's limited water supply, here are some points of interest to remember when using water.

- Each glass of water served requires another 2 to 3 more to ice, wash and rinse.
- A dripping faucet can waste more than 25 gallons of water a day or about 9,000 gallons a year.
- You can save 3 gallons of water a day by not letting the water run while brushing your teeth.

San Diego County needs your help in conserving our limited water supply. Let's all do our part and **HELP CONSERVE OUR MOST VALUABLE RESOURCE.**

Design/Gregory Starmack

Thank you for your cooperation!

Figure 5.4 A note to each customer advising them of the continued 'cold water' provision. With permission.

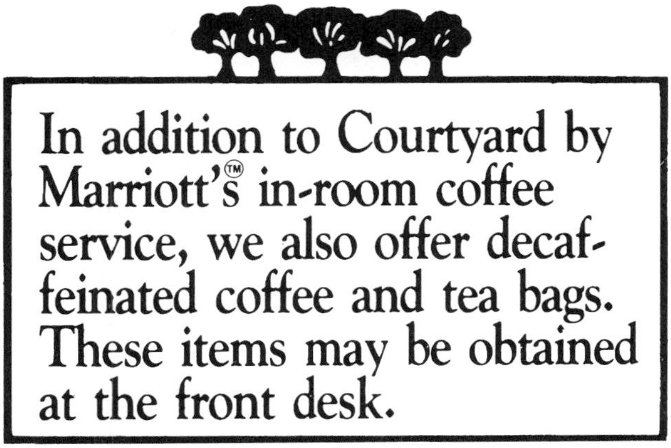

In addition to Courtyard by Marriott's® in-room coffee service, we also offer decaffeinated coffee and tea bags. These items may be obtained at the front desk.

Figure 5.5 In-room hot drink service — advising the guest of the wider product range available. With permission.

travellers and make up remover; and styling preparations for their female counterparts. And, all in keeping with the hotel's standards of service provided elsewhere (see Figure 5.6).

(d) In a similar vein, hotels now display notices in the guests' bathrooms informing guests that, should they have forgotten any essential toiletry item then just to telephone reception for complimentary provision (see Figure 5.7).

(e) Prompt service is also made tangible in one of several ways — many hotels guarantee an in-room breakfast delivery within ten minutes of the requested period or it will be provided free of charge. Domino's Pizzas promise to deliver an order to your home within thirty minutes or $3 will be taken off the cost of the meal. Also, the latter company guarantees quality with an 'if not satisfied, then the pizzas will be replaced or money refunded' promise.

(f) In maintenance work, cleaning up after completion provides a 'reverse' example of this same perspective. Similarly, a car-wash given free with a routine service or paper covers left inside the vehicle demonstrate to the customer the level of care taken by the company.

2. *Customizing a standard product.* Hotel telephone receptionists addressing a guest by name, Burger King's policy to increase the level of customization in its food service provision to help differentiate it from McDonald's strategy of a low price, standard menu.

3. *Influencing quality expectations.* The definition of what constitutes good service varies by customer and transaction, 'but it is influenced as much by customer expectation as by a customer's experience of the services actually delivered'.[19]

Figure 5.6 Some of the complimentary toiletry items provided by Trusthouse Forte hotels.

Approaches that influence expectations include identifying customer expectations and aligning these with service delivery systems capabilities or vice versa.

Developing a service specification

In addition to the points raised earlier in the chapter, there are other important perspectives pertinent to service specification development which need to be recognized by an organization. For example, the following service characteristics have an important bearing on their provision by an organization; both concern service definition:

1. By their very nature, services are less tangible than products. Thus, whilst the physical dimensions of a product require specification, services lack these characteristics and hence are intrinsically less defined. It is necessary, therefore, for an organization to ensure that the task of determining the service specification is undertaken.

2. In manufacturing, the products and customers are invariably decoupled in the system, for example through inventory and the wholesale/retail stages in the total process. In services, however, the provider and customer are invariably

Avez-vous oublié quelque chose?

Si un article de toilette vous manque, n'hésitez pas à contacter la réception. Nous serons heureux de vous le fournir gracieusement.

Forget Something?

If you have forgotten any essential toiletry item, please call Reception. We will be pleased to deliver it to you with our compliments.

Was vergessen?

Haben Sie notwendige Toilettenartikel nicht eingepackt? Bitte wenden Sie sich an den Empfang. Wir helfen Ihnen gerne kostenlos mit vergessenen Toilettenartikeln aus.

Figure 5.7 Complimentary provision notice where guests may have forgotten an essential toiletry item. With permission of Holiday Inns International.

linked at the point of provision. The result is that the opportunity to interpret what is meant by 'service' is at the point of provision. It is necessary, therefore, for organizations to determine the level of discretion to be allowed in the service delivery system concerning the interpretation of what each service should comprise.

Within the context of the characteristics described above, organizations need to address the elements of service specification in order to determine the operations issues involved within the delivery system. To help in this task, the following perspectives should be taken into account:

1. It is important to determine the product/service mix (see Figure 1.3) that best reflects the nature of the services provided. This will reflect the market segment(s) in which the organization wishes to compete, influenced at least in part by competitive pressure. For example, McDonald outlets in the USA offer a breakfast menu in line with competing businesses. The result is an increased product range, some of which is only available before mid-morning. In addition, compared with the UK, the overall range offered is more extensive in part reflecting the competitive pressure in the different fast-food markets.

2. Within this context, a service can be expressed as a combination of the following:[20]

(a) *a service within which there is a facilitating good;*
(b) *a good which also involves a facilitating service;*
(c) *the explicit services provided;*
(d) *the implicit services provided;*
(e) *the supporting structural facilities.*

(a) *A service within which there is a facilitating good.* A look back at Figure 1.3 is a reminder that most of what is purchased is a combination of goods and services. Where the mix is predominantly service, then the goods element of the package is known to be facilitating in nature.

(b) *A good which also involves a facilitating service.* Many purchases of goods contain an element of service. The extent of the service content within the total package will vary, for example, the purchasing of a television set as compared with tailored kitchen units requiring installation; or a meal provided by a high-class restaurant as compared with a fast-food outlet.

(c) *The explicit services provided.* When services are purchased, customers perceive that they are receiving one or more explicit service. For example, a bank provides the explicit service of money transactions; a hotel provides food and accommodation; and a hairdresser the styling of hair. Customers may choose from a range of quality levels concerning the provision of a service and this will typically influence their selection of the providing organization.

(d) *The implicit services provided.* In many markets the implicit services may well be as, if not more, important a factor in customer selection as the explicit service that is at the core of the purchase. For example, security and privacy within a banking system; level of attention, promptness and recognition of a regular customer by hotel staff; magazine and hot/soft drink provision and levels of cleanliness within a hairdressing salon.

(e) *The supporting structural facilities.* This aspect concerns a recognition of the need to determine support facilities that reflect the nature and customers' perceptions of the services provided. The quality of buildings, furniture, fittings and equipment, appropriate decor, level of maintenance and general up-keep are typical examples.

Establishing the level of contact with a customer

'A few manufacturing firms use the customer for do-it-yourself assembly, but basically the customer buying a product is decoupled from the factory. Service managers must decide exactly what the customer should experience and how the customer will or will not participate in the creation of the service. The degree of self-service desired in a service delivery system affects many factors including capacity provision, service levels, training requirements for company employees, and cost control.'[21]

Companies need to determine the extent of customer participation. Increases will lead to the gains mentioned whilst reductions decrease the levels of contact and the opportunities to personalize service and encourage customer loyalty. The trade-offs need to be understood and the operations implications for supporting the service delivery system need full assessment. For example: whilst banks in the UK are increasingly standardizing procedures in bank loan applications, in Japan the procedure has already progressed to the use of a score sheet. Answers to several questions are graded and if the customer's score is above a certain level, the loan application is handled quickly. The impact upon operations provision is significant.

The concept of do-it-yourself approaches was addressed earlier in this section. It also relates directly to the issue here. Example of service industries increasingly using this approach include:

1. *Supermarkets*: these control over 80 per cent of the gross retail market and sell principally on a self-service basis.
2. *Fast-food outlets*: these form a growing part of overall restaurant provision.
3. *Telephone services*: the introduction of subscriber dialling has led to the majority of telephone calls being made by the customer.
4. *Garages*: self-service petrol provision is now the norm as well as screen washing and oil, water and tyre pressure checks.
5. *Catalogue showrooms*: these are a rapidly growing sector of the retail industry. They require the customer to complete the selection and application part of the procedure, with the business providing a fast delivery service once the transaction is fed into the service system.

The reasons for the growth in these sectors vary. Table 5.8 summarizes some factors that relate to their success.

Table 5.8 Factors for success embracing products and services brought about by do-it-yourself approaches in selected service sectors

Factors for success	Selected service sectors				
	Supermarkets	Fast-food outlets	Telephone services	Garages	Catalogue showrooms
Faster service	✓	✓	✓	✓	✓
Lower price	✓	✓	✓	✓	✓
Improved product quality	✓	✓			
Increased product variety	✓				✓

The scheduling of customers' labour is less critical since they help themselves at the time as well as undertaking any pre- and post-service activities. However, for this to be successful companies must assess the total operations requirement of the service delivery system and carefully complement the customer inputs by well-trained staff and reliable equipment.

As service industries develop, the considerations of customer-based capacity provision need to be revised. One example concerns the differential pricing arrangements in petrol stations in the USA. As Figure 5.8 shows, the price per gallon of fuel varies depending upon whether it is a self-service or full service provision. A similar price differential (and in this instance it is financially-based) also exists between cash and credit sales (see Figure 5.9).

Figure 5.8 Price differentials reflecting the level of service and degree of customer participation. With permission.

Figure 5.8 *continued*

Figure 5.9 Price differentials reflecting cash and credit sales. With permission.

Level of server discretion

As explained earlier, the server/customer interface allows for discretion. It is important, therefore, for organizations to establish the appropriate level of discretion to be exercised within each service category. Issues already addressed concerning service standardization, levels of customer contact and automation all have an impact upon server discretion levels. Thus, firms need to recognize these factors as ways of reducing or increasing customization and to use them to develop a service delivery system that supports the level of customization desired. In so doing, organizations can improve their control of quality within the service delivery system with given levels of customer contact and staff skills.

Off-line versus on-line

Some services are inherently on-line and do not allow the server to be separated from the customer (for example, hairdressing and passenger transport). However, other service businesses do allow for a measure of server/customer decoupling. Where this is so, on-line services can be done off-line if desired.

Furthermore, once parts of a service are off-line they can also be transferred from the front office to the back room. This not only allows them to be completed using different methods and at different times (thus enabling for instance, low cost opportunities to be exploited) but it also allows firms to improve customer perceptions of the service itself.

The Royal Bank (Canada), for instance, believes that customers' perceptions are a critical factor in service provision. The bank considers that when queues form, customers' attitudes to waiting are affected by both the server's attitude when they are eventually attended to, and the fact that when waiting, customers judge service by the level of attendance shown in the front office. Thus, if bank staff are doing jobs other than attending to customers, and the queues are long, customers' attitudes to the bank's overall regard for service quality are affected. Thus, the bank's aim is to transfer as much paperwork to head office or to the back room as possible (also refer to p. 124).

Customer interface: front office or back room

Connected to the last section is the need for a company to determine where the customer interface will take place — the front office or back room. The reasons for separating the service delivery system in this way is to orientate activities within the system thus allowing decisions to be based on appropriate pragmatic (and often) strategic perspectives — for example, the provision of facilities. One set of disadvantages with this arrangement concerns the decoupling of part of the service provision from the customer. It is vital, therefore, that organizations both ensure that their front office/back room arrangements provide the preferred mix of advantages and disadvantages and recognize the need to reassess these over time.

One small electrical repair shop recently changed the customer/supplier point in the delivery system. Whereas previously the customer explained the repair needs to those in the front office, the customer now takes the repair to the back room and discusses the problem with the person who will complete the repair. Everyone gains. The repair person can now ensure that all pertinent questions are covered and the customer is able to discuss the repair both before and after the service is completed. This, of course, has long been the arrangement in many good quality dressmakers and tailors.

Using limited capabilities

Businesses offering a wide range of services may well find that by carefully analysing tasks in terms of skill requirements and checking these against servers' actual skills they can realign needs to provision and ensure that the capacity of skilled servers is maximized in terms of the total services provided. Some companies employ this approach to gain the maximum leverage of its scarce resources. For example, the auditing divisions of large accounting firms employ large numbers of junior or associate staff on relatively low salaries. With little opportunity for advancement, the levels of labour turnover are high, which helps support the leverage ratios on which these activities are based.

Conclusion

Product/service investment decisions and their strategic and tactical implications need increasingly to be taken at the corporate level. Investment by companies in R&D activities leads to both a growth in technology and the ability to use this new knowledge in the design and provision of its products/services. Recognition of the production/operations task within the production process or service delivery system is equally critical in terms of product/service provision and the effect on current and future sales. Its importance is possibly best illustrated by the national and corporate strategic decisions undertaken in Japan. As part of the catching up process with the West, Japan's main emphasis has been in the core industries (e.g. iron, steel and petrochemicals) and in their engineering-based off-shoots (e.g. cars and ship-building). Research by MITI has argued for new technologies for the 1990s. The basic thrust of this re-ordering of its industrial priorities is illustrated in Figure 5.10. Up to 20 per cent of Japan's GNP will be directed towards new high technology industries.

   In the immediate post-war period, Japanese productivity in comparison with the USA was very low: 5 per cent, for example, in coal mining and chemicals, 10 per cent in rubber, 20 per cent in rayon. Within a quite short period of time this position has been reversed. Japan now rivals the USA and the leading European industrial nations in most of the major industries. At the same time it has been widening its industrial base, moving from a predominance in industries with low

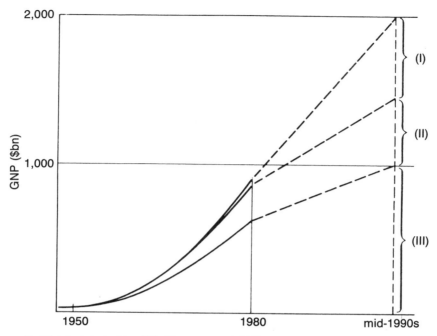

(I)   High-tech industries (15–20 per cent of GNP):
      Aircraft/space, data processing, electronics, new energy, life sciences, new basic materials, etc.
(II) Key industries (15–20 per cent of GNP):
      Steel, automotive, electric machinery, chemical, etc.
(III) Other industries:
      Agriculture and fishery, construction, electric power and gas, wholesale and retail, finance and
      insurance, services, etc.

Figure 5.10   Forecast shift in Japan's industrial structure.

Source: C. J. McMillan, *The Japanese Industrial System* (Berlin: de Gruyter, 1985), p. 106. With permission.

R&D in the 1960s (e.g. textiles, steel and cars) to high R&D sectors (e.g. electronics and production processes) in the 1980s and 1990s. Nor is this technology plan based principally on imitating or buying foreign technology as in the past. As Table 5.9 shows, Japan now registers more than 1.5 times the number of patents than the USA and over 4.5 times the rate of the UK. 'The seeds of Japan's technology future lie in these investments. Technology is a central element of Japan's general approach to industrial planning and highlights the priorities for new products, materials and production systems. In Japan this approach is called knowledge intensification of the industrial structure and forms the basis of management strategies in the 1980s and 1990s.'[22]

However, it is also important to consider other forms of R&D investment. Besides the well-argued, and well-founded case for changes in education and the

Table 5.9 Comparative patent registration, 1980

	Total patent applications	Resident	Non-resident	Patents per 100,000 people
Japan	191,020	165,730	25,290	147.0
Australia	15,936	6,582	9,354	48.0
Canada	24,974	1,785	23,189	7.7
Sweden	9,192	4,106	5,086	50.0
USA	104,329	62,098	42,231	28.8
UK	41,640	9,612	22,028	35.0

Source: C.J. McMillan, *The Japanese Industrial System* (Berlin: de Gruyter, 1985), p. 94. With permission.

Table 5.10 Technological balance of payments in selected countries, 1975–87

		1975	1980	1985	1987
Japan	Receipt	233	644	982	1,490
	Payment	592	966	1,229	1,958
USA	Receipt	4,008	6,617	16,669	22,281
	Payment	473	762	6,215	8,877
UK	Receipt	589	779	848	980
	Payment	578	672	692	908
W. Germany	Receipt	264	430	614	1,081
	Payment	679	1,025	1,206	2,443
France	Receipt	394	688	894	1,348
	Payment	472	823	1,064	1,732
Italy	Receipt	90	233	144	301
	Payment	480	662	546	788
Canada	Receipt	53	n.a.	393	425
	Payment	190	n.a.	534	541

Notes
1. All figures are US$ million.
2. n.a. indicates not available.
3. The figures for the UK and Canada are for 1986 and not 1987.

Source: OECD, *Main Science and Technology Indicators*, 1989–1.

status and contribution of scientists, engineers and other technically qualified personnel, it is also important for companies to consider adopting an industrial strategy of using imported technology. Table 5.10 shows that several countries (for example, West Germany, Japan, and Italy) have for a number of years imported far more technology than they have sold. The reverse is true of, for example the USA and the UK. The sale of technology must be recognized by a company as part of its overall R&D decision making and to ensure that it maximizes the return on its technology investment.[23]

The corporate level

The impact of R&D expenditure and industrial success at the corporate level is exemplified by the motor industry. In 1970 the USA spent six times and western Europe four times as much in this field as Japan. By 1985 Japan was spending more than western Europe and 75 per cent of that by the USA.

At the tactical level, an understanding of the nature of the product/service provision is equally important to the success of a business. Firms need to know what elements of a product/service are important to the customer. The Retail Council of Canada commissioned a survey in 1986 to identify the factors determining what made customers shop where.[24] It revealed the following priorities:

1. Quality of merchandise.
2. Refund policies.
3. Guarantee policies.
4. Friendly staff.
5. Price.

According to those interviewed, the product/service mix was significant and the low rating of price a reflection of the importance of the role of operations in the service delivery system.

The decision to go ahead with a new item rests on many issues. For the operations manager, two of these are critical. The first concerns the technology of the product and process, and the second the detailed costings that underpin the financial justification for its introduction. The technology of the product has been the subject of this chapter and the technology of the process is dealt with in Chapter 6. The aspect of costings, however, warrants highlighting here, and particularly the operations manager's role within this procedure.

All cost calculations concern: (1) a definition of the costs involved, and (2) a forecast of sales volume. It is essential, therefore, that the operations manager is involved in the determination of these and argues for a realistic assessment of both. Too often accountants have prepared costs statements based on ideal circumstances and volumes. In addition, when actual demand is known, it is necessary both to prepare standards of performance in line with known demand and that the new items are assessed in the light of these (see Chapter 4).

Notes and references

1. This explanation of the design strategies was first put forward by R.J. Schonberger in *Operations Management*, (Plane, Texas: Business Publications, 1981).

2. M. Meier-Preschany, 'Perspectives on banking in the 1990s', in *International Banking: Management and Strategies*, ed. D.B. Zenoff (Euromoney Publications, 1985), p. 72.
3. *Ibid.*, p. 74.
4. The graphical representation of the relationship between the frontier in the design—production procedure and its effect on effectiveness is a product of the Ford Motor Company.
5. Detailed studies of British industrial levels of innovation and comparisons with its major competitors have been made in *Technical Innovation and British Economic Performance*, ed. Keith Pavitt, (Basingstoke: Macmillan, 1980).
6. C.J. McMillan, *The Japanese Industrial System*, (Berlin: de Gruyter, 1985), p. 93.
7. Percentage of gross national product spent on government-financed research in OECD countries 1975—6.

	%
France	1.2
Italy	0.4
Japan	0.5
The Netherlands	0.9
UK	1.3
USA	1.4
W. Germany	1.2

Source: OECD.

8. For further information refer to: T. Levitt, 'Exploit the product life cycle' *Harvard Business Review* (November/December 1965), 81—4; R. Polli and V. Cook, 'Validity of the product life cycle', *The Journal of Business*, vol. 4 (October 1969), 385—400; N.K. Dhalla and S. Yuspeh, 'Forget the product life cycle concept', *Harvard Business Review*, (January/February 1976), 102—12.
9. This idea is enlarged in B.M. Enis *et al.*, 'Extending the product life cycle', *Business Horizons* (June 1977), 45—56.
10. Value analysis is defined in BS 3138 1979 *Glossary of Terms used in Work Study and Organisation and Methods* 33006 as: 'a systematic interdisciplinary examination of factors affecting the cost of a product or service, in order to devise means of achieving the specified purpose most economically at the required standard of quality and reliability.'
11. L.D. Miles, *Techniques of Value Analysis and Engineering* (Maidenhead: McGraw-Hill, 1961)
12. In chapter 4 of *The Four Kinds of Economic Value* (Harvard Business Press, 1926), C.M. Walsh describes four kinds of value: 'Use-value is a thing's power to serve our ends. Esteem-value is its power to make us desire to possess it. Cost-value is its power to impose upon us effort to acquire it. Exchange-value is its power to procure other things in its place.'
13. It is important with brainstorming techniques to use someone with experience and to select carefully the group involved. The selection should avoid the potential problems of seniority and be designed to give a wide range of disciplines within the group. This stage is essential to the successful application of this technique and needs to be used with care.
14. The 80/20 rule concerns the phenomenon that, for example, 80 per cent of costs will be incurred by 20 per cent of the items. Chapter 10 provides another example of its application
15. *The Paul Revere Life Insurance Company*, Case Study no. 42, (Houston: American Productivity Center, February 1984).
16. *Ibid.*, p.1.
17. H.B. Meier, 'Moving towards a more customer-focused organisational structure', in *International Banking: Management and Strategies* ed. D.B. Zenoff (Euromoney Publications, 1985), p. 140.

18. D.R.E. Thomas, 'Strategy is different in service businesses', *Harvard Business Review* (July/August 1978), 158–65.
19. J.L. Heskett, *Managing the Service Economy* (Boston: Harvard Business School Press, 1984), p. 59.
20. These concepts were first introduced by W.E. Sasser *et. al.*, in *Management of Service Operations: Text, Cases and Readings* (Boston: Allyn & Bacon, 1978), pp 10–11.
21. D.A. Collier, *Service Management: Operating Decisions* (Englewood Cliffs, NJ: Prentice-Hall Inc., 1987), p. 43.
22. C.J. McMillan, *op. cit.*, p. 95.
23. D. Ford and C. Ryan, in their article 'Taking technology to market', *Harvard Business Review*, (March/April 1981), provide some useful insights into the corporate decisions of when, how and whether organizations should sell their technologies.
24. This report was summarized in R. Maynard, 'Satisfaction guaranteed, *Report on Business*, (January 1988), 58–64.

Chapter 6

Capacity investment decisions

When organizations develop their longer- or short-term business objectives, one important consideration will concern the provision of appropriate capacity to provide the products/services that they sell or envisage selling in the market-place. In turn, these decisions will need to relate both to the aspect of process capability and to throughput: capability involving considerations of design and cost, and throughput involving considerations of volume. The capability provision will vary depending upon the nature of the product/service design. Similarly, the extent of sales volume forecasts will underpin the extent of the capacity requirements to be considered. However, the uncertainty of forecasts and the certainty of reality will continue to create situations of false starts, underutilization of capacity and an inability to cope with demand. Furthermore, capacity considerations in service industries and the perishable nature of service capacity creates its own set of difficulties.

Additionally, on the one hand, the costs involved by investing forward when increased sales do not materialize and, on the other hand, the lost sales involved in not being able to meet demand, support both argument and counter-argument for alternative business strategies. The residues of past strategies have made their mark on all aspects of the operations function. Even successful strategies place substantial strain on organizations as they attempt to change direction. It requires departmental responses both at the strategic and tactical levels. However, to be successful, this in turn calls for fresh insights and a high level of co-ordination to fit the parts into a related whole. The initial stimulus leading to the decision necessitating the capacity investment will command attention. As such, this prime task is approached with thoroughness and care because of the external vetting and control and internal self-interest that normally accompany investment proposals. However, it is equally essential that an analysis of the other important functions is linked into this rigorous approach, especially as the self-generated interest will not be present.[1] Too often organizations fail to appreciate fully the impact of uplifts in capacity upon other functions within the business. This may be due to a failure to understand, overoptimism or a desire to minimize the apparent total investment involved in the corporate decision in an effort to improve the financial attractiveness of the proposal. However, the outcome is often an underprovision of the required support for the growth initiative which, when later corrected through necessity, will often prove to be more costly and time-consuming than it would have been had it formed an integral part of a total investment package.

This chapter addresses the important POM perspectives of capacity investment decisions that are to be considered by the organization. However, it is recognized that other aspects (outside the scope of this book) need to be taken into account before making these decisions. Noticeable amongst these is investment appraisal. This covers the various ways in which the necessary financial appraisal of a particular investment can be made.[2]

General definitions

Before discussing specific aspects of capacity investment decisions, it is important to clarify some important concepts on which these decisions are based, and to recognize the degree of relevance that each concept has to different types of organization and business activity.

Costs

Much has been written on costs and it is not intended here to discuss them in detail. However, there are certain issues on which operations managers ought to ensure that there has been adequate discussion and that appropriate decisions have been made.

In many situations, the costs considered to be variable may well contain substantial elements of costs that are fixed. For example, in a restaurant the cost of food may be thought a variable cost. However, this is not so. Food costs due, for instance, to waste and theft are not incurred *pro rata* with increases in volume. Similarly, certain labour functions (e.g. the chef) are not strictly related to volume.

In addition, at a level higher or lower than the 'normal' volume of operations, variable costs often show marked differences from those experienced near the 'normal' level of operations. This is because:

1. When volume levels are below normal, 'variable' capacity is difficult to shed quickly or utilize effectively elsewhere in the business.

2. When volume levels are above normal, capacity will tend to be overloaded, and ineffective ways of boosting throughputs will be used in an attempt to meet sales 'at all costs'. These are known as *congestion costs*. Typical of these are the temporary deployment of people without sufficient training and the

inefficiencies that accrue, and the increasing levels of complexity brought about by significant increases in activity together with their associated costs.

Lastly, the operations manager should understand the basis adopted by the accounting function for absorbing overhead costs. As these are usually a significant percentage of total costs, then a swing either way can, on paper, show whether an investment is acceptable or not. These dangers arise from two principal sources. First, the basis for absorbing overheads may be inappropriate for the products/services involved. Second, in many organizations, the arbitrary loading of overheads is, at best, a crude accounting device to make the books balance. Hence, a product/service may have an under- or over-overhead loading which, in turn, will have important consequences in terms of corporate attitudes towards investment, apparent costs involved and pricing policies adopted. Part of the POM role, therefore, is to challenge the accounting base in order to understand it, check that it is appropriate and ensure that it is updated so that it becomes more able to reflect the reality of this sizable set of costs.

Economies of scale

The argument to build facilities of increasing size has to a large extent been based on the argument of economies of scale. This view, concerning output volumes and unit cost, has enjoyed a marked appeal in facilities investment decisions. The gains due to scale are derived from several sources:

1. Throughput volumes and the opportunity to spread fixed costs over a greater number of units.

2. Economies of capacity size. Where sales volumes warrant investment in capacity dedicated to a given range of products/services then non-productive costs (e.g. set-up costs) will decrease and investment in finished goods or WIP inventory is potentially lower.

3. Higher volumes will justify investment in the process which, in turn, will reduce costs.

However, it is essential to recognize that there are additional perspectives to be included. One concerns the earlier comments on variable and overhead costs. Another is that the financial argument often suppresses two, less tangible aspects of an investment proposal. The first of these is the adequacy of manning and infrastructure levels that form an integral part of each investment. The second is the lack of attention given to the work environment, industrial relations and managing the task issues that are also an integral part of the proposal but, because of their intangible nature, are not easily put into figures. It is an important POM role to ensure that these issues are quantified and form part of the necessary detail on which all investments need to be judged.

This last point, in fact, now forms a fundamental part of the strategic arguments developed within POM. Expressed under the title 'focus', it concerns structuring the production/operations function to undertake a set of tasks that are homogeneous in nature thus allowing the processes and support activity to be orientated towards a consistent set of market needs. It is the homogeneity of tasks and the repetition and experience within the production/operations function of completing these that is the basis of focus. Thus, focusing the demands on POM will enable resources, efforts and attention to be concentrated on a defined and homogeneous set of activities, so allowing management to identify the major tasks and priorities necessary to achieve a better performance.[3]

However, as many businesses are in established facilities then the opportunity for 'green field' solutions is slight. The approach adopted for existing business, therefore, is to split the production/operations function on the basis of focus and to manage these 'multi-businesses' separately, each with their required overhead. Such a solution is directly opposed to the principle of economies of scale, arguing instead that the increased levels of complexity and inherent lack of orientation that accrue with traditional approaches outweigh the gains.[4]

Capacity

The final set of general definitions concerns capacity.

1. Capacity in planning terms will be measured by either labour or plant. Reflecting on the issues raised in Chapter 4, in most project, jobbing and batch processes capacity will be governed by the number of people employed in a process or part of a process. With line and continuous processing methods of operations, the factor governing capacity will be plant.

2. Capacity in service industries presents its own unique traits:
   (a) Large parts of services are perishable and cannot be turned into inventory.
   (b) Because of the inherent producer/consumer interaction in a service business, the consumer becomes a potential source of capacity. The extent of this consumer-generated capacity will vary according to the design of the service.
   (c) What constitutes a service in many businesses is open to individual definition. Consequently, it is difficult to measure throughput (refer to the analyses in Chapter 4).
   (d) In most cases, a service is provided and consumed in the same time span. Thus, either the customer comes to where the service capacity is situated, or the service capacity goes to the consumer.

3. In project, jobbing and batch processes, thre is often excess plant/equipment

capacity. However, with a growth in sales, some processes will reach their capacity limit in plant or equipment terms. These are then known as 'key processes' and need to be reviewed in detail to ensure that additional capacity is provided when future growth takes place. With increased sales demand, these or other processes will eventually become the next key processes and so on.

4. Keeping capacity in balance is essential to ensure that future growth can be sustained.

5. Different process technologies will change levels of capacity within a particular part of the process. Each process will have different throughput and changeover times resulting in different process and downtime combinations.

6. Higher order volumes (in both make-to-order and make-to-stock situations) will themselves lead to reduced downtimes due to fewer changeovers, and hence lead to an increase in productive capacity.

Process design

The design of a process reflects throughput volumes, the product/service mix and many other features discussed in Chapter 4.

However, there are other perspectives giving insights into process design and these will be discussed now, prior to describing the procedure to be used in determining capacity and the layout of facilities. The aforementioned other perspectives fall into two categories:

1. Issues concerning the process/equipment used in making the product or providing the service. The hardware and process chosen will bring a set of trade-offs which need to be taken into account when making capacity decisions. Similarly, the inherent features embodied in the technology of a process need to be appreciated and form part of these sets of decisions.

2. Issues affecting the definition of capacity. It is important to recognize that capacity has different characteristics affected by aspects such as performance, relevance to the products/services on hand and the use of the outcomes.

Issues concerning the process/equipment used

Technology and the manager

Operations managers need to understand the technology of the process. The extent to which they will need to appreciate the engineering/technology base in order to contribute to it will vary (see Table 4.4). However, it is essential in all situations that the manager should understand the processes in terms of the following:

1. The relationship between set-up time and process time so as to help choose between options by using the break-even concept:

$$\text{Break-even} = \frac{\text{Additional setting-up time for a process}}{\text{Reduction in process time per unit of product/service}}$$

2. The operating requirements of each process including loading, unloading, maintenance, and waste by-products created.

3. The different dimensions of flexibility including the ability to:
   (a) produce part or all of the current/anticipated range of products/services;
   (b) respond to increases in demand on a time scale that cannot be met by the purchase of additional process capacity;
   (c) meet delivery promises leading to a high level of both delivery speed and reliability;
   (d) cope with customer specification changes during the process;
   (e) choose between different sets of processes/equipment to achieve a high level of compatibility in facilities, tools, dies and other auxiliary equipment.

4. The possible impact upon the definition of a product/service by the technical capability of the process. For example, direct access by computers within the travel industry allows for parts of the booking-in procedure to be completed before the day (e.g. seat reservations) and affords the opportunity to list options in parts of the services such as alternative routes.

5. The introduction of technology into all facets of the operations function will lead to changes in terms of skill requirements and staff mix.

6. Technology creates the opportunity for change, but if the basis of a business is to change fundamentally it must be driven by customer need and not by technology.

7. The process has to be able to meet the product/service specification. Furthermore, when evaluating process investments, companies need to distinguish between process capability features accruing from the fact that the process under review will be new whereas the one it replaces may be old and unable to meet the specification demands due to wear and tear and those features accruing from the fact that it is state of the art offering new and relevant capabilities.

8. Technology may result in both barriers to entry on the one hand and ease of access on the other. The investment (£)/skills support requirements are well understood. However, it offers access to others — for example airlines are increasingly moving into the 'booking' phase of their business as telephone/computer access obviates the need for a high street presence.

The link between product/service and process

There exists an inherent link between decisions made concerning the product/service to be provided and the design of the process to make that provision. Consequently, aspects such as design features and choice of materials will influence the process options that may be considered.

Process characteristics

In Chapter 4 the implications of process choice were described in detail. It is important, therefore, to group together the sets of characteristics that appertain to each process to ensure that a complete picture is drawn of the product/service, operations, investment and cost, and infrastructure implications and to ensure that these are taken into account when choosing and designing the process for each stage of the total POM task.

Process innovation

The characteristics of innovation in the earlier stages of the product/service life cycle are directed towards the product/service itself. As the product/service technology is perfected and starts to stabilize then the rate of major product/service innovation begins to slow and the rate of process innovation, increases. As markets develop, demand increases and, as a consequence, the low price, high volume requirements of the growing market-place become more important under the pressure of growing price competition. Investment in the process follows, designed to make it more efficient.

Issues affecting the definition of capacity

Product/service specification

Although a product lends itself more naturally to a precise and tangible set of definitions than does a service, all businesses need to decide how reactive or proactive they should be in terms of customization policy. Varying degrees of customization will have an impact upon the process capability and flexibility dimensions addressed earlier, while decisions on make-to-order, assemble-to-order and make-to-stock responses to the market will also affect many aspects of a business including capacity and delivery times.

Decisions on service interpretation will involve like issues. At the higher level they will affect major allocations of capacity and expertise as well as all areas from recruitment through to the strategic direction of the business. At the operator level they concern the specification of the service itself in all its detailed forms including set-up norms (a polite welcome) and subsequent process responses. These details will affect aspects of short-term capacity requirements, performance and customer service.

Back room and front office

Within service businesses a distinction needs to be made between the two basic parts of the process (the back room and front office — see pp. 110–11). Capacity requirements, the opportunity to spread demand and the differing impacts of technology are some of the perspectives involved.

Back room.   This will usually offer more opportunity to spread demand fluctuations. The impact of technology is more likely to be in the form of productivity and data processing throughput gains.

Front office.   Improvements will normally be more qualitative in this part of the process. Some productivity gains will accrue in their own right and others may be achieved in conjunction with back room improvements, as technology offers the opportunity to enhance or substitute knowledge skills by providing quick and easy access to data. Increasingly, too, decision-making skills are being enhanced by or substituted for expert systems, which are becoming more advanced and more readily available.

Use of the customer

The unique opportunities in service industries to incorporate the customer into the total process capacity provision needs to be recognized and form part of this decision-making process. Customers have proved willing to take part in the service delivery system if it can be shown to be profitable, supportive of customers' needs, convenient or enhances the sociable nature of the total process. Examples include self-service facilities of all kinds, direct telephone dialling, purchases by television links, investment brokerage services and travel arrangements.[5] The impact upon the provision and type of capacity is considerable.

Similarly, manufacturing companies need to recognize that what they also sell invariably involves a service element (see Figure 1.3), and then determine the customer's role within this element. For example, a small company offering specialized material finishing capability experienced difficulties in keeping pace with the growth in demand. It recognized that one loss of capacity resulted from its earlier decision to collect and deliver the items from/to customers. Not only was this time-consuming in itself but invariably involved wasting time at the customers' premises. A policy change requiring customers to deliver and collect enabled the company to improve its delivery turnaround, this being a major aspect of the total service and one which most of its customers wished to purchase.

Capacity in short supply

Companies need to adopt a considered approach in their use of capacity in short supply. Many service companies aim to increase the leverage of their senior people by providing them with many junior support staff. Audit divisions of large public accountancy practices and legal firms are examples of this arrangement.

In manufacturing companies process constraints should be reviewed in terms of determining the actual contribution per hour for different products. Known as contribution by limiting factor (i.e. that process capacity which is a bottleneck) this analysis enables a company to maximize the contribution it can earn from a given, finite capacity by recognizing the differences between the actual contribution per hour achieved and the percentage contribution for different products. Thus, the more a product uses a limited process capacity then the less contribution per hour will be generated.

These analyses should also take into account the opportunity to consider switching one element of a service from one part of the system to another. Thus, back room activities could be switched to the front office and vice versa based upon scarce resource principles. Furthermore, where demand fluctuates then companies need to capitalize on the opportunity to transfer parts of a task from one part of the system to another where short-term demand changes are experienced.

Effective performance

Effective performance measures actual standard hours produced against attendance hours (see p. 346 for details). It is a major factor in the calculation of capacity for it is part of the way to assess the amount of work produced in a given time period. Furthermore, managers need to recognize that where capacity is labour controlled (i.e. operators are the determining factor in making a product or providing a service, see p. 63) then potential uplifts in throughput are more possible in the short-term than in businesses that are process controlled.

Load and capacity

Load is the portion of the resource which has been committed to complete product/services and is normally based on standard or estimated times (see Chapter 11). On the other hand, capacity is a statement of the capability of a business to produce the products/provide the services and is expressed in an appropriate common denominator (e.g. units of time). The statement on capacity will need to take into account the issues already addressed in this section as well as adjustments for appropriate levels of non-productive time, rework and customer changes in the process.

Waiting as a by-product of the service delivery system

The role of the consumer in the service delivery system is central to the task of determining the required service capacity. Fluctuations in demand for services are handled by the system in the form of queues (order-backlog — see p. 48). Consumers typically arrive at random and place immediate demands on the available service. If the service capacity is fully utilized at the time (and as the service delivery system is typically batch, it is a planned trade-off that the consumer waits for the process) then the consumer is expected to wait. Varying arrival rates and different service time requirements result in queues. Thus, unless a business holds one of these two dimensions steady (for example, by requiring a customer to pay more as in the case of private medicine or keeping the service time to a minimum whilst under tight control as in fast-food establishments and then emphasizing the speed of customer throughput) the queuing phenomenon will be a central feature of service delivery systems.

Determining capacity

Capacity management is one of the most important responsibilities of operations managers, for all other planning activities take place within the constraints imposed by decisions on capacity. The objective of capacity is to match the level of operations to the level of demand. What makes the task difficult is the uncertainty of demand and the consequences that this has in terms of size and type of capacity.

In Chapter 9 aggregate planning and operations control will be dealt with in some detail. To facilitate the presentation of the concepts, *long-term capacity planning* will be dealt with in this chapter although, more often than not, it forms an integral part of the operations planning procedure. Consequently, Figure 6.1 would in reality form the top part of a diagram to include the operational steps in capacity management concerning the links to aggregate planning and operations control.

Forecast demand for products/services

Demand forecasting is difficult. No matter which method is used, it will not be accurate. However, despite this inaccuracy, when planning ahead it is necessary to forecast demand, for the alternative is no forecast at all.

A prerequisite for capacity planning is a statement of demand. The demand itself may take the form of an expression, estimation or expectation. Businesses making standard products may need (or decide) to anticipate demand and make to finished goods inventory. Other businesses, through their policy on design, may be able to make part of the product (i.e. investing in WIP inventory) and then assemble to order. Lastly, businesses making-to-order (which includes most service organizations) will only be able to make on an order backlog basis. However, in all instances organizations need to forecast demand in order to anticipate future capacity requirements as well as the other resources in a business (e.g. buildings and facilities).

All businesses have capacity planning horizons. These will differ depending upon lead times. Where capacity is in the form of labour (e.g. in a jobbing and

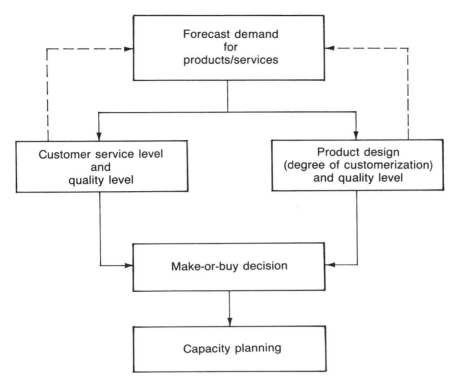

Figure 6.1 Procedure involved in capacity planning for a manufacturing or service business.

many service businesses), the relevant time horizon will normally be shorter than where investment in plant and equipment is involved. However, where labour is a scarce resource, this may not be so. Similarly, where uplifts in capacity are of a stepped nature (for example, arranging a second shift for a batch or line process — see Table 4.4) then the lead times involved can also be considerable.

Where plant or equipment is essential to the operations process then purchase, installation and commissioning lead times can be a major delay in bringing about changes in capacity. Manufacturing examples come readily to mind — machinery processes, assembly lines and petrochemical plants. However, service industries with a similar dependency upon equipment will also experience long lead times — most elements of the transport industry, for example.

Thus, forecasting demand for products/services is critical in planning capacity. Without the passenger projections illustrated in Figure 6.2, for instance, plans for aircraft production and purchase would probably not be anywhere near the actual requirement for the next two decades.

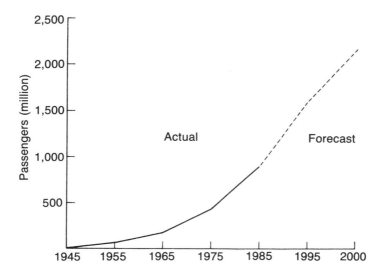

Figure 6.2   Air traffic growth: total ICAO scheduled passengers. With permission.

There are many books explaining the options for demand forecasting. It is not intended to cover these here, but for those who wish to study them a list of suitable material is given at the end of this chapter.[6]

Whilst demand forecasts are often completed elsewhere in a business, it is necessary for those involved in capacity planning to understand the procedures used, the assumptions made and the implications for the production/operations function. To help appreciate these issues some of the features involved in forecasting are now described. First, key aspects of forecasting procedures are highlighted, partly from a POM perspective. Next a list of features concerned with the POM part of the procedure is presented, highlighting key perspectives in general and service features in particular.

Forecasting procedures

What follows is a short review of the steps to be taken in capacity planning within the air travel industry to illustrate the general issues/perspectives that may be involved.[7] It is not, of course, intended to be comprehensive, merely illustrative.

The level of growth depicted in Figure 6.2 is significant. Couple this with aircraft replacement requirements in terms of investment costs, lead times and known aircraft developments (e.g. Boeing and the European Airbus products) then the time-frames are uncertain yet crucial. Put this within a framework of airline profitability trends as given in Figure 6.3, and the need not only to plan capacity

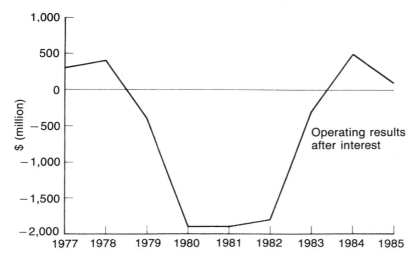

Figure 6.3 Airline profitability: IATA scheduled results 1977–85.
Source: IATA. With permission.

but also to be accurate in terms of amount and phasing (in whatever terms are relevant) is critical.

Within this scenario there are also current trends to be assessed in terms of deregulation and its impact upon increased competition, customers who will become more demanding (through familiarity and being offered greater choice), and the need to achieve adequate returns on investment. The impact upon capacity forecasts and provision, and the role of POM within the process are and will remain significant. Issues to be addressed include:

1. Capacity provision in terms of airports, aircraft, operations and support staff.

2. The role of operations staff in terms of meeting customers' expectations.

3. The level of vertical integration (addressed under make or buy decisions in the next section) and its impact on operations capacity.

4. The control of costs and improved cost effectiveness.

5. The efficient running of the operations process in terms of customer service levels and capacity provision.

Consequently, although for reasons of clarity the issue of capacity planning has been separated from other issues in the management of the production/operations function, in reality they all interrelate (see p. 203 where this aspect of POM is discussed under point 4). In the longer-term, major decisions concerning aircraft capacity, routes and the impact of deregulation will underpin the growth potential of an airline. Similarly, unless issues are resolved concerning product/service design and specification, the quality level to be achieved, delivery performance levels to be attained, then issues of costs, efficiency and overall performance will be affected.

POM issues in forecasting

Some general and specific issues relevant to the forecasting process are listed below and discussed from a POM perspective in order to highlight those that need to be recognized and addressed by this function.

General issues

The nature of accuracy within forecasts
It is important to recognize that the degree of accuracy within forecasting will increase in the following circumstances:

1. The more general the statement, the more accurate the forecast. Thus, the forecast for all sales in a period will usually be more accurate as a statement of total period sales ($£$) than as a statement of forecast sales for each individual product/service that forms the statement of total demand.

2. The longer the time period to which the forecast refers the more accurate will be that statement. Thus, the total forecast sales for a year will usually be more accurate than the fifty-two weekly sales forecasts of which it is composed.

At the end of the day the accuracy of a sales forecast will be judged on its aggregate cumulative total to date. However, an operations function has to work on a much shorter time scale. Thus, POM performance will be measured on a part-daily, daily or, at best, weekly basis. The reason is that whereas a sales function is not expected to sell one-fifth of weekly sales each day or one-quarter of monthly sales each week (in total let alone by product/service mix), POM will need to produce or provide to target. Time lost in the operations function will normally not be recovered as capacity provision is continuously adjusted in line with requirement. How the operations function manages these shorter time-scales effectively whilst meeting delivery requirements and minimizing inventory investment is the subject of Chapter 9.

Costs of a stockout
Stockouts can have a range of costs from uneasiness due to poor service through to results with major consequences. Responses include substitution by the customer or accelerating priorities within the process. The effect on customer allegiance/behaviour is unique to each corporate situation. However, whereas short-

term responses can minimize the impact of short-term problems, failure to plan capacity in the future can lead to lost market opportunity or even losing out altogether.

Considerations in choosing a forecasting method
The inherent difficulties of forecasting have led to the development of many forecasting models in the past fifty years, latter-day ones making use of developments in computer-based information systems. Choice of model is often difficult and several factors need to be considered:

1. The total development and operating costs. The former concern constructing the model, validation, debugging and training. The latter concern the costs of computation time and those associated with collecting the input data.

2. The required level of accuracy of predictions and the trade-offs involved.

3. The extent to which a model assumes that past behavioural patterns and relationships will continue in the future. A continuous check on presumed levels of stability between the past and future need to be embodied in the forecasting procedure in order to evaluate this feature of a model.

4. Establishing the appropriate forecasting horizon that reflects the capacity time horizons currently experienced.

5. The need to establish a match between the selected forecasting model and the data patterns that are present in a particular business. The most common patterns are constant, trend, seasonal and cyclical. A business needs to ascertain its own data patterns to ensure that the model chosen reflects them appropriately.

Specific issues

The nature of forecasts
Whilst all forecasts concern predicting behaviour, the simultaneous provision and consumption in a service delivery system means that the operations process is more frequently exposed to the uncertainty of the market-place. The opportunity to cushion the service system (see Figure 9.1) is, therefore, less available and thus customers' immediate behaviour introduces a higher level of uncertainty into the demand forecasts available.

Planning horizons
Although planning horizons need to vary depending upon the different perspectives under review (e.g. capacity planning/material planning/time-scales), they tend to be shorter in respect of service industries. The opportunity to postpone process response to customer demand is less available and hence planning service capacity on short notice is a more typical feature of service businesses.

Process customer links

Customers normally either need to be present (e.g. a restaurant, hair cut, hospital appointment) or in contact (e.g. hotel, travel reservations, video shopping) with the service delivery system in order to use or experience the service. Thus the process and customer are coupled to a much higher degree than in manufacturing which, in turn, means that the provision of capacity at the appropriate time is at a premium in the capacity planning procedure.

Cost of stockouts

The cost of a stockout in some service industries can be too high to risk (for example, in emergency services). In these situations capacity planning has to be a level of acceptable service speed which does not reflect average forecast demand.

Building and retaining a client base

Forecasts partly reflect the customer relationships established through the nature of the transaction. However, the type of relationship will vary depending upon the nature of product/service itself. Some services are discrete transactions, such as the purchase of insurance for a one-off requirement. Others involve the regular delivery of a service over varying periods of time — for example, the provision of a personal pension fund. Some may not be based on a formal relationship, whilst others are of a continuous nature. The potential to build and retain a client base will, therefore, be related to this feature, as illustrated in Table 6.1 which reflects key differences within service businesses. One outcome concerns the prediction of future sales.

Table 6.1 Service delivery and type of relationship matrix and its relation to the building and retention of a client base

Service delivery	Type of relationship	
	Continuing	*One-off*

Continuous delivery of a service	Personal pension plan
	Banking services
	Medical and dental
	  services
	Automobile Association
	Garage services
		Mail service
		Police protection
		Fire service
		Hospital accident
		  unit

Discrete transaction	Theatre-going through subscription Commuter travel	Toll bridge Pay phone Public transport Cinema Car wash Car rental

Source: based on C.H. Lovelock, 'Classifying services to gain strategic marketing insights', *Journal of Marketing* (Summer 1983), 13.

Make or buy decision

Theoretically, every item, process or service currently purchased from an outside supplier is a candidate for in-house provision, and vice versa. In reality, however, the choice is not so extensive, but often the decision to make or buy is taken with insufficient forethought. Organizations addressing this issue need to recognize that there are both strategic and tactical considerations.

At the *strategic level*, issues such as process/infrastructure capability and the nature of the process provision need to be recognized:

1. Many organizations in the pursuit of short-term improvements in financial performance have decided to subcontract tasks that have traditionally been completed within their own operations function. In some instances it may make sense, but there are various levels of arrangements to be considered. Although in the short term improvements may accrue, organizations need to be aware that the decision may in fact be one of avoiding a managerial problem with its short-term trade-offs. Similarly, some companies have painted themselves into the 'hollow corporation syndrome'[8] with the long-term consequences of an eroded production/operations base (both process and infrastructure) from which it will normally be more difficult to initiate change.[9]

2. The choice of process, reflecting the type of business in which an organization is involved, will also impinge on make or buy decisions. As explained in the section on 'product/service profiling' in Chapter 4 (p. 69), a business will need to assess the fit between current and future products/service and the processes in which it has already invested. A company making household products, for example, used subcontract capability in the early stages of the life-cycle of a new product until it was able to ascertain the volumes involved. On the basis of this assessment it could then allocate a new product range to a different part of its own manufacturing facility in keeping with the anticipated volume requirements or leave it with the existing supplier or switch the contract to another supplier, again based on volume fit. Failure to recognize the need to establish the product/process fit may lead to a degree of mismatch similar to that illustrated in Figure 4.6 on p. 71.

Lastly, an organization that develops products/services involving a stepped increase in technology often has to buy-in that technology. Decisions on this and future make or buy options, however, must be recognized and form part of the decision-making process.

Once strategic issues like these have been considered, the *tactical aspects* of this problem can be considered. They include:

1. The organization's internal capability to do the job or provide the service at the required levels of quality together with the space and other non-technical considerations involved.

2. The position of the item in the process and the degree of dependence that the final product or service has on the subcontracted item, process or service.

3. The availability of suitable suppliers at the volume and quality levels involved.

4. Comparative costings are usually an important consideration in this decision. However, it is most important that internal costings reflect the true costs involved.

5. The provision of an item or service internally increases aggregate volumes, and consequently: (a) contributes to overhead recovery, and (b) facilitates the balancing of demand and operations capacity over time.

6. A business may decide against purchasing from an outside supplier in order to protect product, process or service ideas.

7. The decision to make or provide internally is often subjective, e.g. the belief that no one can do it as well or as cheaply.

The provision of capacity

Capacity refers to the productive capacity of the operations facilities to provide the range of goods or services to be sold in the market-place. It is usually expressed as the volume of throughput within a given time period. Operations managers are concerned with the provision of capacity for the following reasons:

1. Sufficient capacity has to be provided to meet the throughput volumes required by the organization.

2. The size of available capacity (including short-term adjustments) will lay down the constants for operations scheduling.

3. The acquisition of additional capacity (excluding short-term adjustments) is a long-term investment decision which reflects corporate marketing decisions, underpins the future success of the organization and needs to reflect the capacity planning time horizon (see Figure 6.4).

Having determined forecast demand requirements including fluctuations over time, the provision of capacity may now seem straightforward. But, as capacity plans are developed, hidden complexities become apparent. For example, throughput rates are dependent upon the process technology employed and the type of product/service mix being provided. In addition, it is necessary to decide first upon a number of issues before being able to identify the level and type of capacity required:

1. *Choice of process.* As explained in Chapter 4, the choice of process will be made,

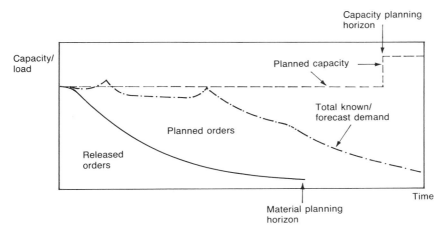

Figure 6.4 Provision of capacity in terms of load, and material and capacity planning horizons.

amongst other things, on the basis of anticipated volumes. The unit quantities and work content involved will determine throughput and hence capacity requirements to meet forecast sales. However, the implications of process choice are complex and it is important to judge the trade-offs involved when taking this decision.

2. *Process technology.* The degree of investment in the process will also affect the rate of throughput and hence the capacity and labour requirements.

3. *Size of plants.* A further consideration is to establish the size of plants. Earlier analysis based upon economies of scale considerations tended to support large plant decisions. Later arguments based upon the inherent complexities of running large plants questioned the relative simplicity of earlier views and analyses. This issue was addressed in Chapters 4 and 6.

4. *Chase demand, level capacity or a mixed plan.* The determination of capacity will also be affected by the way an organization decides to meet demand. Although this is an issue relevant to longer-term capacity decisions, it is used more frequently in the development of aggregate plans (see Chapter 9).

Facilities layout

Facilities layout means planning the arrangement of productive facilities. This includes machines, equipment, work-places, customer service areas, material storage areas, supporting functions and the flow of materials and people through the buildings. It does this in such a way that all aspects of the business are integrated and feasible operating schedules can be formulated. These factors, in turn, affect the operating costs, the orderly and efficient use of space, plant, equipment and manpower and the level of customer satisfaction.

Facilities layout can only begin when important decisions have been made concerning the product/service mix to be provided, the make or buy decision, the process to be used, expected level of demand and materials handling. In addition, constraints concerning the physical restrictions of the building and the need to re-use existing plant and space will have to be accounted for.

Every organization encounters a layout or relayout requirement over time. Facilities layout determines the operating configuration of a process. This is true when determining future requirements, but it is more often used to relayout part or all of an existing set of facilities. Since change is a common requirement for many businesses, because of shortening product life cycles and the consequent change in product mix, layout changes to meet new product and process designs and work methods will have to be resolved. The scope of these changes will vary from minor adjustments to the complete redesign of existing facilities.

Changing requirements reduce the efficiency of existing layouts. It is necessary, therefore, to include maximum flexibility in layout design so as to reduce the need for the relayout of facilities (thereby minimizing the total costs involved over time).

Layout related to the choice of process

The choice of process will have a fundamental influence on the design of the layout. This is simply due to the dependence of the layout upon the operations flow — the flow may be materials in a manufacturing plant, people in a service system or paperwork in an administrative function. There are three broad types of layout.

Fixed position layout

Some businesses use a layout that locates the product in a fixed position due to either its bulk/weight/fragile nature (e.g. shipbuilding, missile and large aircraft assembly) or the impossibility of moving it once it has been built. In these situations, the resources needed to complete the task must be transported to it. Such is the normal layout for the choice of process entitled *project* in Chapter 4.

Process layout

A layout by process or function is characterized by the physical bringing together of similar process capacities. Process layouts are typically used in *jobbing* and *batch* processes (see Chapter 4). The reason is that such a business offers a wide product/service range in the market-place, the sales volumes (quantity × work content) for which are not sufficiently large to justify a process being dedicated to one or a small range of products/services. Consequently, different orders follow different paths through the sets of processes provided in the business so as to comply with the different processing requirements of the wide range of items sold.

Facilities and equipment are grouped together according to the function performed in order to encourage forms of specialization, provide a geographical orientation within the operations function, improve the utilization of capacity, and make the more specialized processes readily available to all products/services (see Figure 6.5). Similarly, in service organizations, a functional layout is appropriate to meet the needs of the product or customer. For example, in a hospital, the specialized units such as radiology, operating rooms and intensive care are functionally based. Also, a retail shop or chain store is set out functionally with foods and drinks of similar types being placed together and checkouts, empty trolley collection and other functions each within their own area.

The advantage of being able to route different orders through functionally-based work areas is gained at the cost of increased complexity in the movement of a product (see Figure 6.6). To help in the evaluation of different process layouts use is made of distance, load and trip-frequency charts. With a matrix format similar to those shown in Figure 6.7, the various departments can be displayed to represent the origin and destination of actual or simulated movements within the process. In addition, a relationship chart (see Figure 6.8) can be used to identify how close one department needs to be to another. Also known as *systematic layout planning*,

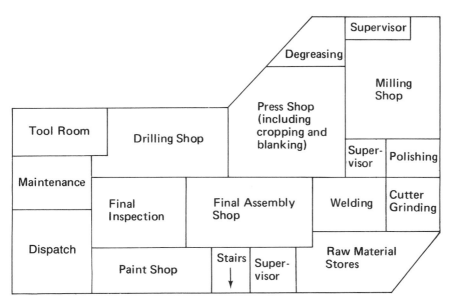

Figure 6.5   Process (or functional) layout for an automotive component manufacturer.

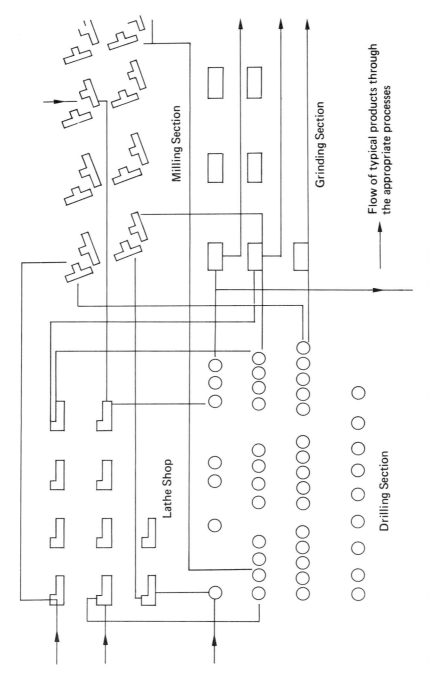

Figure 6.6 Typical product movement in a simplified process (or functional) layout situation.

To From		1	2	3	4	Departments 5	6	7	8	TOTAL
	1		28	—	—	16	43	5	9	101
	2			19	—	6	2	—	18	45
Departments	3				2	12	7	—	28	49
	4					—	15	58	—	73
	5						13	21	17	51
	6							6	38	44
	7								—	—
	8									
TOTAL		—	28	19	2	34	80	90	110	363

Note: The bottom segment of the matrix is blank because in this instance the movements from, for example, departments 1 to 6 have been added to those movements from departments 6 to 1. If, for any reason it was necessary to distinguish between these movements then the chart can accommodate this.

Figure 6.7 Load or trip frequency chart showing simulated movements between departments.

this approach makes use of a priority code to show the preferred proximity of two departments and a justification code specifying the reason for the desired proximity.

As the complexity of the task increases, however, these approaches to layout will be unable to cope with the increasing occurrence of multiple flow patterns and constraints. Several computerized methods are available to overcome these limitations. Like manual methods, they use logical rules to list variations and then evaluate them. Computerized systems, however, can handle a greater refinement and variety of data and offer more layout variations. Three of these are: ALDEP (automatic layout design program), CORELAP (computerized relationship layout planning) and CRAFT (computerized relative allocation of facilities technique). For those who wish to study these further, suitable references are given at the end of this chapter.[10]

Product layout

With high product/service volumes, the choice of process moves towards *line* or *continuous processing* (see Chapter 4). The high volumes involved warrant the dedication of facilities to a small range of items. As a consequence, all units follow the sequence of operations specified by the route sheets, equipment must be arranged accordingly. Hence the flow of materials through the operations sequence becomes the basis for product layout. Examples of product layout in the manufacturing

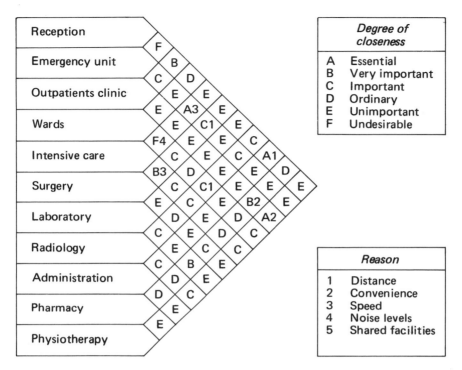

Figure 6.8 A relationship chart.

sector are domestic appliances, cars, food processing and oil refining. In service industries, this is not as widespread. Examples here are some fast-food restaurants, certain banking activities, large administrative/clerical procedures and selected aspects of hospital activities.[11]

For a given product/service, the task consists of arranging the required set of operations in the correct sequence. The specific form of an operation will depend upon the throughput rate required from the group of operations. For example, if the desired throughput is 900 units per 7½ hour shift, then each operation must consist of sufficient work to be completed in 0.5 standard minutes (0–100 BSI scale).[12] The objective would be to have each operation of that length or some multiple of that length which would allow single, one and a half, double, etc. manning at each particular workstation. This is known as line-balancing.[13]

Group technology

The underlying difference between batch and line processes is one of volume. What group technology does is attempt to gain for a batch process some of the advantages inherent in the higher volume, line situation. Hence, it changes a typical *process layout* associated with batch operations, into a *product layout* associated with dedicated process such as line (see Figure 6.9). It does this in the following way:[14]

1. The major manufacturing divisions, which have usually already been identified and exist (e.g. forging, fabrication, machining, finishing and assembly), are separated.

2. Families of like products are grouped together. The total volumes for each of these families now justify the dedication of the use of certain processes to their manufacture. The basis for determining families of products include:
    (a) production criteria — components requiring similar operations; similar component shapes requiring similar machining processes;

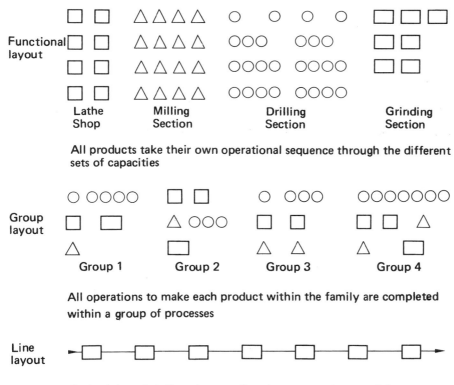

Figure 6.9 Group layout, its relationship to process (functional) and product (line) layouts to illustrate the transition from the former to the latter.

(b) particular features — each component in a family has a particular feature requiring the use of specialized machines; components requiring high machining tolerances which necessitate the use of certain machines; components of a particular size needing certain plant.

However, some major manufacturing processes (e.g. forging and finishing) do not normally lend themselves to the application of group technology because of the cost of duplicating plant and the low cost effectiveness of smaller processes.

3. The next step is to bring together the process capabilities required to manufacture the forecast volumes of those components within the family (see Figure 6.10).

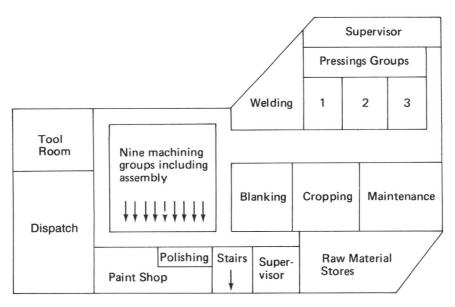

By comparison with Figure 6.5, changes in raw material specification, and the incorporation of material treatment plant eliminated the need for degreasing. Material would be cropped, blanked and pierced and then onto the Pressings Groups (some via Welding). Each pressing group would take the blank parts and complete all operations including assembly and inspection. The parts would then go to the Paint Shop or Dispatch. In a similar way, the machining groups consisted of presses, milling machines, drills and broaching machines. Assembly and inspection of products were built into each group. When completed, the products would go to the Paint Shop or Dispatch.

Figure 6.10 The group layout revision of the automotive component manufacturer as shown in Figure 6.5.

4. The location of each of these processes is then determined by establishing the component routes between the processes in order to offer the best layout. The configuration is usually cellular but a straight-line arrangement is not uncommon.

5. The final stage is to complete a tooling analysis within each family. The aim of this analysis is two-fold. The first is to group together parts within each family of components which can use the same tooling. The loading of jobs is then sequenced to reduce total setting times by completing all the order quantities of components using the same tooling before resetting. The second is to record these set-ups and then add to tooling subfamilies by designing new parts to use appropriate existing tooling. To achieve these gains redesign to provide a common tooling facility will be necessary.

The advantages that group technology provides are gained partly by process relocation and partly by improved control and redesign (see Table 6.2). Some examples are listed below;[15] others are to be found in the literature.[16]

Table 6.2   Advantages associated with the introduction of group technology

Advantages of group technology			*Brought about by*	
			Group layout	*Improved control and redesign*
Reduced	↓	Manufacturing lead times	***	*
delays	↑	Work-in-progress inventory	***	*
Reduced indirect	↓	Materials handling	***	
costs	↓	Setting-up costs		***
Increased	↑	Machine	**	**
utilization	↑	Floor space	***	
	↓	Storage requirement	***	*
Simplified	↓	Paperwork system	***	
control requirement	↓	Production control task	***	*
Improved	↑	Group identity	***	
job satisfaction	↑	Group autonomy over work schedules	***	
	↑	Opportunity to involve people in the non-doing tasks (e.g. quality control)	***	

The number of asterisks reflects the degree to which an advantage is brought about by each of the two aspects.

Type of manufacturer	Some advantages gained
Control valves	Manufacturing lead times down from 43 to 17 days
Gauges	Average delivery from one cell down from 14 to 2 weeks
	Inspection now undertaken by operators
General engineers	Productivity increased by 25 per cent
	Stock turnover ratio up by 30 per cent
	Cycle time reduced by 40 per cent
Small tools	Waiting and setting times reduced by 25 per cent
Valves	Set-up times reduced by 60 per cent
	Productivity increased by 15 per cent
Instruments	Inspection costs down by 75 per cent
	Throughput time decreased by 75–90 per cent
Gears	Throughput time down from 10 to 3 weeks
	Reduced paperwork
	Reduced scrap

However, there is one significant limitation to the appropriate application of group technology. The underlying justification for the dedication of processes to a family of products is combined volumes. Therefore, a business needs a stable product mix and stable sales to ensure that the volume base for this decision is sustained. Group technology is an expensive investment even if it involves only the relayout of processes and the reorientation of activities. If the basis of this decision is eroded by changes in product mix and volumes then many of the advantages listed in Table 6.2 will decrease, whilst also incurring other disadvantages. There are, however, two further perspectives to take into account. First, the combination of several sequential operations within one geographical location (the essence of group layout) is also provided by NC machining and particularly by machining centres. In that way they should be viewed as alternative investments especially with lower product volumes (see Figure 4.9). The advantage offered is one of increased flexibility as opposed to group technology which falls into the semi-flexible category near to the border with dedicated and inflexible processes (see Figure 4.11). Group technology is not within the inflexible process category because, if needs be, the plant can be moved elsewhere or deployed for other uses. It does tend, however, to border this category because the re-use of those semi-dedicated processes can normally be achieved only with further investment. To mitigate this problem, a method that uses group technology without group layout was developed. This still allocates the use of certain processes to a range of products but does not change the physical location of those processes. Hence, the group technology concept would be applied but the concept of group layout would not. However, this too raises problems as certain of the advantages brought about by group layout (Table 6.2) would be more difficult to achieve (the physical relocation of the relevant processes into a group facilitates — or is often the prime reason for — the achievement of many of these gains). In addition, a group technology revision without the group layout concept would quite likely fail unless the infrastructure supporting the change was fairly sophisticated and well able to develop and maintain this less compact arrangement.

Service issues

Some issues (in part already covered in this chapter) relate more specifically to service industries.

Level of customer involvement

As mentioned earlier (p. 120), because of the inherent producer/consumer interaction within the service delivery system, the consumer becomes a potential source of capacity. The extent of that provision within the different service and delivery systems is an important decision in terms of the overall source of capacity provisions, for the following reasons:

1. It is itself a source of capacity and has an impact upon costs.

2. It affects the provision of capacity at 'peak' points in the system where all or part of the service is consumed. For example, in a self-service restaurant, the role of the waiter is provided partly by the customer. In turn, this requires that a definition of the movement of a customer to the service capacity or vice versa be resolved.

3. It allows service definitions (within agreed parameters) to be refined with the customer.

4. It provides a good opportunity to personalize the process and influence the extent to which customers will select a service delivery system to meet similar sets of customer needs.

Demand/capacity imbalance

Service capacity is perishable: it cannot be transferred to a future time period and if not used it will be wasted. One major task of the operations function, therefore, concerns adjusting capacity provision and/or attempting to modify demand to improve the trade-offs involved within a background of requiring to respond to random customer needs. The opportunity to adjust capacity provision and/or modify demand will differ depending on whether the changes relate to the back room or front office.

1. *Back room.* In many organizations the backroom activities are decoupled from the customer interface, so the adjustments tend to be inherently easier. The work involved can be cumulated and then completed (with the improved

effectiveness which will ensue), averaged out within the same time period by delay/arranging additional short-term capacity on a formal (pre-planned)/ informal basis or spread over into another time period (e.g. computer updating overnight or tasks left until the next day). Part of the TSB Group's £200m cost-cutting initiative (see p. 31) announced in late 1989 was to close all the backroom operations in its branches and move them to eighty customer-service centres. The Group had clearly identified the opportunities available in different parts of its service delivery system.

2. *Front office.* As this involves interface with the customer responses, different from those suggested for the back room, will normally have to be considered. They take two basic forms:

   (a) Long-term: to develop complementary services which may be undertaken in periods of low demand for core, front office tasks;
   to arrange for the transfer of appropriate work from the back room in similar periods of low demand in the front office;
   to create flexibility through training in order to widen the range of skills thus increasing the opportunity to transfer some parts of the service capacity to and from the back room and front office in line with short-term fluctuations in demand.
   (b) Short-term: where demand is temporarily higher than capacity then an organization can remove some of the overload caused by the queuing that inevitably results. For example, to eliminate unfairness a single queue feeding several counters (as in many banks and post offices) or the dispensing of numbered tickets to customers who can then await their turn in a more relaxed manner.

With the high cost associated with lost revenue related to the perishable nature of service capacity, some industries have adopted a policy of overbooking to ensure that capacity is used as much as possible. A classic example of this is passenger airlines that overbook an average of between 10 and 30 per cent to counter the no-show factor — passengers who fail to turn up for a flight. Airline seats are perishable and at a cost of something between £70 on a domestic flight and more than £2,000 on a London/New York concorde, lost revenue can be of a high order. British Airways experiences an average no-show rate of between 15 and 25 per cent: 'It varies enormously depending on the route, time of year, the type of passenger and the fare paid. Concorde for example, has a 20 per cent no-show rate. If we didn't overbook, we'd go out with empty seats and that's not good news either for BA or the customers. Not only could passengers be refused the flights of their choice, but empty seats spell higher costs and hence higher fares.'[17] In 1989, BA admits that it 'bumped' (known as involuntary boarding denial) some 10,000 passengers (including volunteers) out of the 23 million it carried. How airlines cope with customers' inconvenience, and the time-consuming and expensive outcome varies. Only with the USA are both local and foreign airlines legally obliged to offer 'denied boarding compensation'. No doubt this is, to some extent, a reflection of the level of US service sector development in general and the degree of competition within passenger airlines in particular. As deregulation increases then compensation in these circumstances will become more regularized and sensitive to customer levels of inconvenience.

Location

There are no traditional product distribution channels (i.e. factory to warehouse to wholesaler to retailer) in the service delivery system. Instead, either the consumer travels to the service or the service moves to the customer.

Similar services provide examples of both: for example, libraries and mobile library services; school-based education and individual tutoring/distance learning; retail shopping and door-to-door sales approaches. Others are unique — the fire service provides an example of the server moving to the customer both in terms of its basic service and its help in unusual situations (e.g. pet dogs/cats in difficult and precarious positions). The medical services, on the other hand, provides a mix in terms of ordinary patients making their own way to the hospital as opposed to accident call outs and its home collection provision.

The necessity of bringing the consumer and provider together typically results in a facility serving a small geographical area with the trade-off between the number and cost of facilities and the costs of bringing together the server and consumer being exercised within a competitive market environment.

However, in all instances the location of the facility with respect to its market is critical for success. Facility location defines the potential market within the overall context of the different rules that apply in the case of public and private services. Service market expansion is accomplished by adding new facilities at geographically dispersed locations with organizations choosing different expansion rationales depending partly on the nature of the business. For example, Sainsbury plc adopted a gradual northward expansion based on the need to support the turnover of food with an adequate and cost-effective distribution service. Boots plc expanded its pharmaceutical/retail network in a more widespread manner because the support requirements were not tied to perishable products.

The steps to be taken when deciding upon facility location include:

1. Determine the target customer profile and the services that each facility should provide. For example, a review of the role of the travel agent highlights the changes brought about by the increasing demands of the customer and the corresponding segmentation of the market.[18]

    The time is over when a travel agent could simply sell an air ticket, catering for any type of customer, through one outlet. The seats may be on the same flight and to the same destination, but individual customers' demands may be radically different. The business traveller needs one type of service, the family holidaymaker another: both expect a different service. . . . Segmentation has been a centrepiece of developments throughout all retailing in the 1980s, and travel is no exception. A single outlet or image can no longer appeal across the total range of potential customers. The travel agency sector is splitting into different businesses, at one level into business travel, group travel and incentive travel: but beyond that into outlets reflecting different lifestyles and cultures.[18]

The larger travel companies have reflected this in their organizational structure (for example, the UK-based Hogg Robinson has formed different businesses to handle the requirement of different market segments).

2. Decide on the number of facilities required and the capacity of each facility.

3. Decide on the characteristics of the location.

4. Select a site. This choice needs to take into account three sets of criteria:
    (a) Market-related factors including:
        • demand factors (current and future);
        • survey of local businesses to include distinguishing between supportive and competitive categories, the degree of sales seasonality within each local business, and the growth/decline and level of prosperity enjoyed;
        • population (income distribution, age profile, daily inflow/outflow, growth/decline)
        • premises.
    (b) Cost-related factors including:
        • transportation;
        • level and availability of labour;
        • site, utilities, rents and rates, and any government-related inducements.
    (c) Socially-related factors including:
        • housing availability;
        • car parking;
        • degree of technical support within the local business infrastructure.

Layout

Approaches to determining the appropriate layout for a business were discussed earlier (pp. 135–40). Examples of approaches to meet the requirements of different businesses are now provided as Figures 6.11 to 6.13, together with a brief comment on each.

Figure 6.11 comprises five photographs illustrating 'old' and 'new' exteriors and interiors of a high street outlet of Thomas Cook Travel. These types of change and their impact upon the service delivery system is further illustrated by the layout diagrams of the Cheltenham and Gloucester Building Society branch at Solihull (Figure 6.12). When additional space became available upstairs, the opportunity arose to reshape the back room/front office provision. With the revised layout, customers not only find that they can tap into the service delivery system more

(a)

(b)

Figure 6.11   A high street outlet of Thomas Cook Travel. (a) Old exterior. (b) New exterior. (c) Old interior. (d), (e) New interiors showing the reshaping of the back room and front office space allocations and associated tasks. With permission.

(c)

(d)

Figure 6.11   *continued*

(e)

Figure 6.11 *continued*

easily but they also consider the system more approachable and responsive. Where a business aims to increase its service range, as did many building societies in the late 1980s, then this redesignation of the front office facilitates the accomplishment of these revised tasks by creating an air of greater informality, efficiency and customer responsiveness. It is no longer necessary for a customer consciously to leave the informality of the front office and enter the apparent, formal 'domain' of the back room, so traditionally embodied in previous layouts.

Lastly, the layout at McDonalds (Figure 6.13) is classic of its type and also provided much of the stimulus for the reshaping of back room/front office provision in service outlets that has taken place since the 1970s.

Conclusion

There are several variables which form part of the plant/equipment investment decision-making procedure. Some fall outside the principal set of POM responsibilities for capacity planning (e.g. product mix, product development requirements and volumes) whilst some fall within (e.g. longer-term capacity

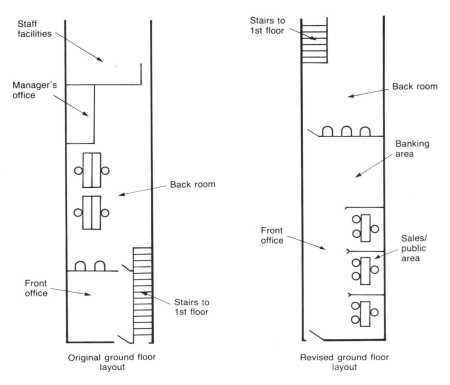

Figure 6.12 The Cheltenham and Gloucester Building Society's Solihull office (not to scale).

acquisition, and plant layout) — see Figure 6.14. The aspects of capacity concerning products/services and their provision are discussed in Chapters 4 and 5. It is stressed that the essential POM role is to analyse the impact of these alternatives and ensure that the full implications for each proposal are presented, understood, discussed and taken into account in both the decision and later performance reviews within the business.

More within the POM role and area of decisions are longer- and short-term capacity provisions (discussed in Chapter 9) and the configuration of those processes to meet the required cost and delivery performances. Each will have a different time base and degree of ease with which it can be both arranged and implemented.

If the longer-term capacity decisions are adequate then in most organizations the short-term decisions concerning capacity levels can be planned and implemented quickly, will incur few major costs (little capital investment but usually some increase in direct labour costs), and can be analysed and agreed at the tactical level. It is the fundamental decisions on longer-term capacity acquisition, its flexibility requirement and layout arrangement that are the more difficult both to make and

Figure 6.13 Layout of McDonalds — now a typical format for fast-food outlets. With permission.

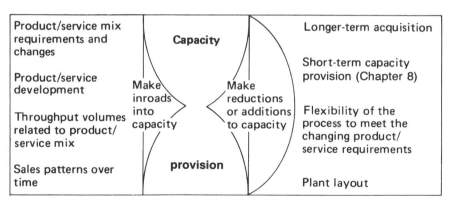

Figure 6.14 Capacity and some of the debilitating inroads into reductions and additions to the initial provision.

to change. These decisions, falling within the province of the operations manager, are based on volume and cost configurations. It is essential (both as part of the longer-term capacity decision itself and for providing the basis of the principal measure of operations performance) that flexible production budgeting accommodates both volume and cost differences.

Also, it is important to recognize that the ease of defining and controlling capacity, whether in product or service organizations, will change depending upon the process choice. Where organizations make-to-order using project, jobbing or batch processes, then capacity will vary both between parts of the process and in terms of aggregate throughput. This is due, respectively, to the wide range of requirements of the process and of the capacity as a whole. In addition, as each item is made-to-order, then there will always be a measure of uncertainty surrounding the size of the task. In make-to-stock situations, however, capacity definitions and control become easier because the level of uncertainty is reduced (see Table 4.2). However, although the degrees of definition and control do change, neither should be ignored. Exactness is not essential for the definition and control of capacity to be soundly based. As with all POM activities, the critical task is to determine the suitable degree of exactness and then control it accordingly.

Lastly, the corporate choice of processes and the implications embodied in those choices are just as fundamental to the organization's success since investment in the process technology itself is necessary and may provide a competitive market edge. Process technology investment requires additional infrastructure and systems investment to be made if the potential returns of the initial technology investment are to be gained. The need to invest in the hardware of the process, once agreed, is never in dispute. Too often, however, the software investments (both in terms of initial capital requirements and their subsequent, on-going costs) are underestimated or undergo pressure to be reduced to the short- and longer-term detriment of the plant investment decision involved. The POM task is to construct appropriate argument or to record the effects of inadequate investment (if that is the decision made) in order to turn the opinionated reasoning into factual evidence on which to base and influence decisions in the future.

Notes and references

1. In their article 'Coupling strategy to operating plans' (*Harvard Business Review*, May/June 1977), J.M. Hobbs and D.F. Heany discuss problems concerning the gap between strategic plans and those prepared at the operating or functional level, and offer some practical steps to help improve this situation.
2. Books that cover the subject of investment appraisal include: J.C. Van Horne, *Financial Management and Policy* (Englewood Cliffs, NJ: Prentice Hall, Inc., 1977); M.G. Wright, *Discontinued Cash Flow* (Maidenhead: McGraw-Hill, 1967); H. Bierman and S. Schmidt, *The Capital Budgeting Decision* (Basingstoke: Collier Macmillan, 1975); and J.R. Franks and J.E. Broyles, *Modern Managerial Finance* (Chichester: Wiley, 1978).
3. These issues are covered in detail in Terry Hill, *Manufacturing Strategy: The Strategic Management of the Manufacturing Function* (Basingstoke: Macmillan, 1985), pp. 100–1.
4. The concept of focus is covered in Terry Hill, *op. cit.*, chapter 4, and Terry Hill, *Manufacturing Strategy: Text and Cases* (Homewood, Ill.: Irwin, 1989), chapter 5.
5. However, if involvement in all or part of the delivery system does not meet expectations, then customers fail to participate in or do not complete their perceived involvement. For example, supermarket shopping trolleys (an integral part of the self-service provision) are

often left abandoned after use because of the long distances involved in returning them to their designated areas. The resulting inconvenience and added costs have stimulated most large supermarket chains to introduce a deposit system, thus penalizing uncooperative shoppers.

6. Other ways of forecasting demand are covered in the following: R.G. Brown, *Smoothing, Forecasting and Prediction of Discrete Time Series* (Englewood Cliffs, NJ: Prentice Hall, Inc., 1963); J. Heizer and B. Render, *Production and Operations Management* (Boston: Allyn & Bacon, 1988), chapter 4 and readings 4.1–4.3; and C.D. Lewis, *Industrial and Business Forecasting Methods* (London: Butterworth, 1982).

7. A. Wheeler, 'The role of the air carrier', in *The Travel and Tourism Industry: Strategies for the Future*, ed. A. Hodgson (Oxford: Pergamon Press, 1987), pp. 37–48.

8. See, for example, 'The hollow corporation', special report, *Business Week* (3 March 1986).

9. These strategic aspects of the issue are dealt with in some detail in Terry Hill, *op. cit.* (1985), pp. 144–5, and similar in Terry Hill, *op. cit.* (1989), pp. 139–41.

10. A comprehensive description of these and other computerized methods is given in R.L. Francis and J.A. White, *Facility Layout and Location* (Englewood Cliffs, NJ: Prentice Hall, Inc., 1974).

11. One example is provided on p. 60 which illustrates the use of laser technology and assembly line methods to cure myopia at Dr Svyatoslav Fyoderov's Institute of Eye Microsurgery as reported in *The Sunday Times Magazine* (8 November 1987), pp. 66–7.

12. 0–100 BSI scale is the rating scale most commonly used in the UK to establish a standard time. It is explained fully in Chapter 11.

13. A useful description of line balancing is provided in E.S. Buffa, *Operations Management: The Management of Productive Systems* (Chichester: Wiley/Hamilton Series in Management and Administration, 1976).

14. For a more detailed look at group technology together with practical examples refer to: G.A.B. Edwards, *Readings in Group Technology* (The Machinery Publishing Co., 1971); J.L. Burbidge, *The Introduction of Group Technology* (London: Heinemann, 1975); 'Group technology: more teamwork, fewer bottlenecks', *Works Management* (February 1976), 28–33; R. Leonard and K. Rathmill, 'The group technology myths', *Management Today* (January 1977), 66–9; and N.L. Hyer, 'Management's guide to group technology', *Operations Management Review* (Winter 1984), 36–42; G.C. Gallagher and W.A. Knight, *Group Technology Methods in Manufacture* (Chichester: Ellis Horwood, 1986).

15. These examples are from a Mechanical Engineering EDC publication, *Why Group Technology?* (1976), appendix C.

16. Mechanical Engineering EDC publications *Production Planning and Control* (1966), and *Better Delivery* (1989); G.A.B. Edwards, *Readings in Group Technology*, and M. Page, in *Works Management* (February 1978), 92–5.

17. Comments by BA's capacity control manager reported in A. McWhirter, 'Feeling the squeeze', *Business Traveller* (February 1990), 16–21.

18. Provided by L. Mayhew, 'The travel agent — rise or fall?', in *The Travel and Tourism Industry*, ed. A. Hodgson (Oxford: Pergamon Press, 1987), pp. 51–7.

Further reading

Amstead, B.H., Ostwald, P.F. and Begeman, M.L. *Manufacturing Processes*, 7th edn (Chichester: Wiley, 1979).

de la Mare, R.F., *Manufacturing Systems Economics* (New York: Holt, Rinehart & Winston, 1982).

Goldhar, J.D. and Jelinek, M., 'Plan for economies of scope', *Harvard Business Review*, 61 (November/December 1983), 141–8.

Hawthorne, E.P, *The Mangement of Technology* (Maidenhead: McGraw-Hill, 1978).

Levy, H. and Sarnat, M. *Capital Investment and Financial Decisions*, 2nd edn (Hemel Hempstead: Prentice Hall International, 1982).

Malpas, R., 'The plant after next', *Harvard Business Review*, 61, (July–August 1983).

Schilling, D.A., 'Strategic facility planning: the analysis of options', *Decision Sciences*, 13 (1987), 1–14.

Vollman, T.E., Berry, W.L. and Whybark, D.C., *Manufacturing Planning and Control Systems*, 2nd edn (Homewood, Ill.: Irwin, 1988).

Chapter 7

Developments in manufacturing and service systems

The period since 1950 has witnessed substantial developments in the systems used by companies in the provision of products and services. Many of these involve improved computer applications to the fundamental tasks within the operations process and have taken the form of hardware and software improvements and the essential links between the two.

Although several of these developments have been referred to elsewhere in the book the purpose of this chapter is to provide an outline of the more important ones as a way of offering an overview of these changes both in themselves and in the way they link to one another. Whereas the initial sections will be oriented towards manufacturing, at the end of the chapter developments within service systems are reviewed.

Computer aided design

Product design embraces a range of activities which comprise the following:

1. Innovation including preliminary product feasibility assessment together with technical and economic evaluation.
2. Engineering analysis, including structural and functional dimensions.
3. Product design, including modelling and design simulation.
4. Detailed draughting.
5. Product specification, including bill of materials.

Computers were first used to mechanize the draughting phase within the design cycle. Since then, developments include interactive graphics with full three-dimensional capabilities and, with the advent of 32 bit microcomputer architectures and large data storage facilities, an increasing use in design engineering in both engineering analysis and automated draughting.

The central hardware of any CAD system is the graphics workstation, the

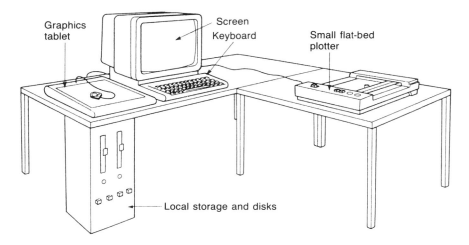

Graphics tablet

Screen

Keyboard

Small flat-bed plotter

Local storage and disks

Figure 7.1   Graphics workstation for a CAD system.

Source: N. Schofield, 'Strategies for acquiring and building integrated CAD/CAM/CAE systems' (unpublished).

important elements of which are illustrated in Figure 7.1. This is supported by a range of software which includes design/draughting and design engineering/analysis applications.

Design/draughting

Available as two- and three-dimensional systems, CAD software is able to fulfil the physical production of drawings based on corporate standards established within the database.

With three-dimensional systems, wire frame or solid modelling systems are available with spin-off advantages in marketing, training and other general purposes. The advantages include:

1. Improved response time to customers' initial and modified requirements.

2. Reduced costs for creating and maintaining drawings.

3. It supports the need for simplification, the use of standard components, and forms an integral and important part of value engineering/value analysis initiatives.

4. The elimination of the more mundane facets of the draughting task.

5. It facilitates adherence to corporate norms and procedures.

6. It provides accurate and easily accessible records to support future requirements.

Engineering analysis

Product development in the past has been a lengthy and often expensive phase in the design process. In addition, designers having to cope with the unknown have reduced uncertainty by modelling, analysis, prototype building and the overspecification of component and material requirements to address the range of possibilities introduced at this phase. In addition, typical modifications have also led to a lengthy and often expensive phase within the total design process.

The use of engineering analysis software has led to cost and lead time reductions as it is possible to undertake 'what if' studies as an integral part of the procedure. This relates to fundamental questions of form, fit and function and involves assessments on aspects such as strength, stress, material content, and weight. (To provide a further link between the customer and the sale, Caterpillar, the American construction machinery and heavy equipment maker, has introduced a software package with extensive colour graphics and 'exploded' shots to give customers a close-up of the working parts of the equipment that they buy.)

With the increasing need to respond quickly to consumer demand changes, the key advantages derived from CAD concern reductions in cost and response time. In fact, in many organizations it is the latter which can often be the more relevant gain and which should be given equal weight when evaluating investments in this area of a business.

Computer aided manufacturing

As CAD concerns the use of computerized processes in designing and testing new products or modifications to existing products, computer aided manufacturing (CAM) is the application of computerized processes to help integrate the production of parts through computer-controlled automatic processes. In both CAD and CAM, computerized processes relate to both individual stages within the total design or manufacturing process and the link between the stages themselves. As with the previous section on CAD, this section on CAM describes the parts (the developed applications) while recognizing that the link between the parts will typically offer a greater set of benefits (a fact highlighted by the section on computer integrated manufacturing).

Automation

Automation is nothing new. Improvements in manufacturing based on increasing levels of automation (from the use of gravity to sophisticated robotics) have been a feature of engineering activity and have underpinned many of the substantial productivity improvements made since the Industrial Revolution. Thus, the use of appropriate forms and levels of automation is and always has been a critical feature when designing a process.

What is new, however, is the fusion of computing with control and machine technologies to produce systems that are both highly productive and flexible. Some of the different forms in which machines or other mechanisms can do the work conventionally performed by people are now described. Although all these applications fall within the generic description 'automation', under that umbrella is a distinct set based on the use of computerized processes known as CAM. The emphasis here will be on the latter.[1]

Transfer mechanisms

The introduction of transfer mechanisms into processes has developed from the traditional, power-driven conveyor and gravity roller concepts into a range of machines that transfer a product from step to step at each end of which operations are performed automatically.

Mechanization

Varying forms of mechanized aid have been developed and designed into processes. These involve power-driven fastening devices with magazine feeds, quick-locating and grasping devices for machines, strip feeders into stamping or punching machines, vibrating/rotating hoppers to feed components into automated machines, automated welding and jointing, assembly of products, automated product finishing, testing and materials handling which includes the use of automated guided vehicles (AGVs).[2] All replace human effort either in part or in whole. Normally, they are specially designed to provide one or a few operations at the most.

Numerical control

The use of computers has led to a number of major improvements within the field of automation and the move towards the complete, automatic control of a process. This progression is described in Figure 7.2 which shows three levels of automation culminating in the integration of a large number of machines or processes.

The move towards the automatic control of a process has been provided in the form of a series of coded instructions, and because mathematical information is the base used, the concept is called numerical control (NC). An NC machine refers to the operation of machine tools from numerical data stored on paper or magnetic tape, tabulating cards, computer storage or direct information. Thus, NC is the operation of machine tools and other processing machines by a series of coded instructions.

It was first developed in the 1950s by the Massachusetts Institute of Technology whose work was sponsored by the US Air Force to find ways of improving the

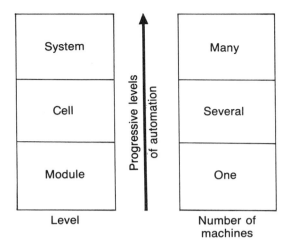

Figure 7.2   Different levels of automation.
Source: based on the Open University Manufacturing Systems Engineering Programme (1988).

methods used to manufacture jet aircraft. The principal objectives concerned costs and the repeatability of work requiring very close tolerances. The original NC machines used cards or punched tape with semi-skilled labour to load and unload the machine.

Recent NC machines no longer receive their instructions from a punched tape or card but from a computer. A system which has a computer controlling more than one machine tool is known as *direct numerical control* (DNC). The NC machine tools are linked to a common computer memory with access to all data being provided on request. *Computer numerical control* (CNC) systems, on the other hand, use a minicomputer to perform NC operations which are stored in a computer memory. This minicomputer may be used as a terminal to accept information from another computer source or by direct input. For example, dial control may be used to input dimensions for each work-piece.

An NC program is a means of machine control which initially (and most importantly) defines the relative position of the tool to the work-piece. The list of instructions which forms the program establishes feeds and speeds and normally includes adaptive control to sense operational variables such as torque, heat, vibration, material condition, tool wear or breakage and other machining conditions, and then to adjust the speeds and feeds accordingly.

A further development from the NC concept is the machining centre. This has a magazine storage for up to over a hundred tools on a permanent or semi-permanent basis which can be selected and used as programmed. Centres can start and stop machines, select and return tools to the magazine, insert them into a spindle, mill, drill, bore, ream, tap and contour (with some operations being completed at the same time) and index the table to a programmed position.

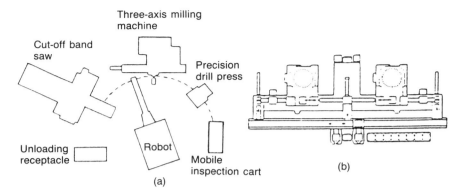

Figure 7.3   Examples of cell configurations. (a) Semi-circular. (b) Linear.
Source: Open University.

In all the NC developments one important feature is the link with the CAD engineering database referred to earlier. The transfer of the design and processing information into the CAM procedure will further enhance the growing advantages of NC applications.

Within the context of Figure 7.2, an NC-based machine would be an example of a module. On the other hand, a cell would typically contain a small number of interconnected NC-based machines often with some level of automated loading and unloading. In some instances, the machines are in a semi-circular arrangement to facilitate a robot to perform the materials handling function (see Figure 7.3). Other configurations may be linear with the transfer of parts from one machine to another provided in a number of ways (see Figure 7.3). The growth in the application of NC is illustrated by the increase in Japanese CNC machine tool orders (Japan supplies about 75 per cent of all CNC systems manufactured in the world) from 40.3 billion yen in 1976 to an estimated 560 billion yen in 1986.[3]

Co-ordinating measuring machines

Automating to reduce costs is one facet of the drive to increase market share. However, an equally important part of this automation initiative concerns quality. NC-based equipment offers an important step in this direction. However, direct applications to improve the level and reduce the costs of quality control are also increasing and one estimate suggests that by 1992 more than 40 per cent of inspection systems in manufacturing will have vision capabilities.[4] Cameras are currently used to check joints and welds and to take measurements. However, where accurate manufacture is essential then co-ordinate measuring machines (CMM) are available.

CMMs are computer-controlled machines that can be programmed to go through a routine set of measurements for solid objects. Using a probe at the end of an

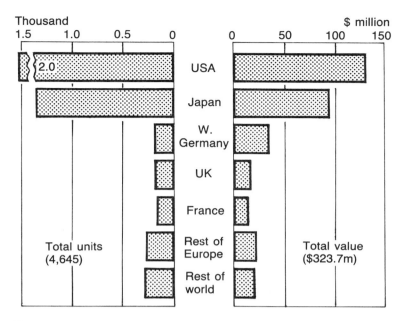

Figure 7.4   Markets for CMMs in 1985.

Source: J. Dwyer, 'Machines get the measure of quality', *Financial Times* (3 February 1986), p. v.

arm which registers when it touches an object's surface the machine switches to the next dimensional check and thus, by following a programmed path, can undertake the measurement of complicated parts machined to close tolerances.[5]

Companies have developed ways to use CMMs in flexible manufacturing system (FMS) cells and to link them to CAD systems to generate CMM programs as a by-product of the computer-based design system. Such applications are increasing the demand for CMMs with a world market in 1985 of $324m comprising over 4,500 machines (see Figure 7.4).

Flexible manufacturing systems

A flexible manufacturing system (FMS) links the work of a number of cells and/or individual modules (see Figure 7.2). It is a larger version of a cell and hence will typically require some form of automated transport to link the parts of the system together. These often include a combination of automated guided vehicles (AGVs) and conveyors (see Figure 7.5).

The first FMS was developed in the 1960s by Molins, but it was not until the advent of inexpensive and powerful programmable control that the growth in applications took place as illustrated in Figures 7.6 and 7.7. As with other forms

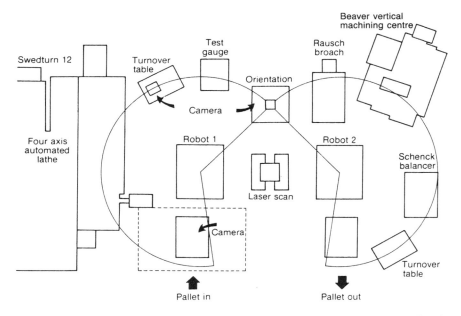

Figure 7.5   Layout and general view of the flexible manufacturing system at R.A. Lister.

Source: M. Dooner and J. Hughes, *Structure and Design of Manufacturing Systems*, Unit 2, Flexible Automation (Milton Keynes: Open University Press, 1986). With permission.

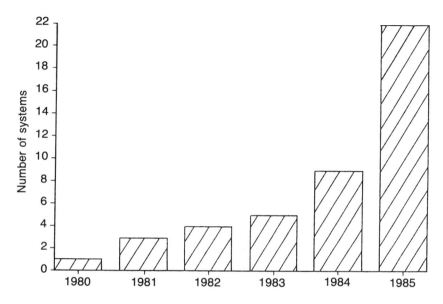

Figure 7.6 Growth in FMS installations in the UK.

Source: J. Bessant and B. Haywood, 'Experiences with FMS in the UK', *Int. J. Personnel Management*, 6, no. 5. With permission.

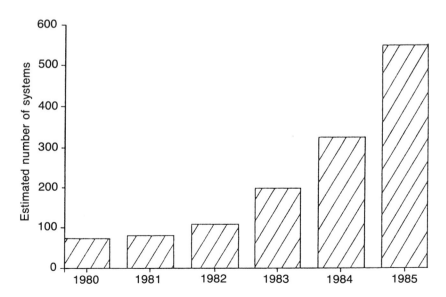

Figure 7.7 Worldwide growth in the use of FMS.

Source: Bessant and Haywood, *op. cit.* With permission.

Table 7.1   Changes in systems applications in W. Germany, 1982—5

Number of machines in cells or systems installed	1982	1985
1	9	23
2	7	14
3—5	9	12
6+	7	3

Source: B. Haywood and J. Bessant, 'The Swedish approach to the use of flexible manufacturing systems', Occasional Paper 3 (Brighton Polytechnic, 1987), figure 3.

of NC-based applications, the gains inherent in these developments come from linking different operations with built-in tool change capability supported by automated work-piece transfer. Thus, aspects of the manufacturing task such as inventory levels and production control are reduced in size and complexity respectively as many operations on a product are now completed within the module, cell or system before the work-piece is transferred to the next stage.

On the other hand, FMS installations are expensive and complex systems which require adequate utilization levels and appropriate manufacturing infrastructure provision and developments in order to be successful.

Two factors which affect the sophistication levels of the applications of these systems are the difficulties that suppliers are experiencing in working at the forefront of technology, and in determining customer requirements.[7] The result is a shift away from complex, multi-machine systems to simpler alternatives. Research in West Germany revealed the trend towards single machine cells and away from multi-machine applications as shown in Table 7.1, a feature supported by figures from the UK and Scandinavia which revealed that between 50 and 60 per cent of all installations were for single machine cells.[8]

Robotics

Robots are machines that can perform human-type operations. They are a form of programmable automation designed to undertake highly repetitive tasks. Initial applications were often to undertake heavy, dangerous or unpleasant work where the financial benefits for such investments were of secondary importance.

Robots, as with other forms of programmable automation, do as they are told and, as yet, are not sufficiently intelligent to make judgements. The absence of sensory data, adequate control mechanisms and sophisticated programs incorporating artificial intelligence have limited the principal use of robots to repetitive tasks such as welding, paint spraying, palletizing, the loading/unloading of machines and assembly-related operations. Improvements in the areas of path control, sensing devices and manipulative dexterity are increasing the opportunities for robot applications. However, as shown in Table 7.2, there is a marked difference in the number and growth rate of applications from one country to the next.

A computer-controlled robot system has three major components (see also Figure 7.8):

1. The mechanical structure (linkage or manipulator).
2. An actuating or drive system to power the manipulation.
3. A control system.

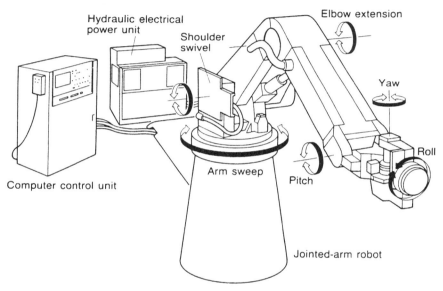

Figure 7.8 Major components of a robot system.

Source: Dooner and Hughes, *op. cit.*, p. 27. With permission.

Table 7.2 Industrial robots in selected countries, 1981−8

	1981	*1985*	*1988*
Japan	21,000	93,000	176,000
USA	6,000	20,000	32,600
W. Germany	2,300	8,800	17,700
Italy	450	4,000	8,300
France	790	4,150	8,026
UK	713	3,208	5,034
Sweden	1,125	2,046	3,042

Source: International Federation of Robotics.

The degree of sophistication within a system can be defined as being at two levels. A level I robot is one where the system cannot be modified through the result of a feedback and control process that senses the external environment. Thus, all aspects of the task must be explicitly specified in advance. On the other hand, level II robots are systems which can be modified based on adaptive feedback and a control process which senses the external environment through some type of transducer. The result is a robot that can perform some tasks without having to specify explicitly all aspects in advance. Thus, in Table 7.3, the ability to transport and manipulate an object falls within level I robotics, a factor which is reflected in the major areas of application (i.e. material handling, machine loading, spraying and welding). The ability to use external sensing for feedback control relates to level II robotics and allow applications in the areas of machining (involving tool positioning), assembly and inspection tasks especially where visual information

Table 7.3 Major categories of robot applications in manufacturing and the capabilities generally required within each application

Major application area	Examples within area	Capabilities required to perform application		
		Transport	Manipulation	Sensing
Material handling	Parts handling	✔		
	Palletizing	✔		
	Transporting	✔		
	Heat treating	✔		
Machine loading	Die cast machines	✔	✔	
	Automatic presses	✔	✔	
	NC milling machines	✔	✔	
	Lathes	✔	✔	
Spraying	Spray painting		✔	
	Resin application		✔	
Welding	Spot welding		✔	
	Arc welding		✔	
Machining	Drilling		✔	✔
	Deburring		✔	✔
	Grinding		✔	✔
	Routing		✔	✔
	Cutting		✔	✔
	Forming		✔	✔
Assembly	Mating parts		✔	✔
	Acquiring parts		✔	✔
Inspection	Position control			✔
	Tolerance			✔

Source: Tech Tran Corporation, *Industrial Robots: A summary and forecast* (1983), p. 63.

Table 7.4 Some principal types of hand applications for level I robots

Hand types	Built-in applications
Magnetic	Photo cell detectors
Vacuum	Television cameras for inspection
Spray gun	Microswitch sensors
Welding gun	
Hook(s) for heavy objects	
Extra-long finger(s)	

is used to identify the part, to determine its location and to have the robot move into position and grip the part appropriately.

As expected, level I robots are more limited in their application but nonetheless have many uses within manufacturing. By building-in attachments to provide the equivalent of the manual function, the use of robots has shown a marked increase in the 1980s (see Table 7.2). Many versions exist and some of the principal types of hand application are given in Table 7.4.

As future sales will need to be justified on investment grounds, then several things need to happen:[9]

1. Continued price reduction, including the development of fixed price kits of parts for add-on conveyors and feeders to allow appropriate configurations to meet new needs at low costs.

2. Improved robot simulation, with easier built-in, off-line programming. This enables a user to reprogram a robot for a new application without taking it out of commission.

3. The need for suppliers to abandon systems work. The ideal would be for suppliers to sell the equipment in modular form and so allow a company to organize the application to meet its own requirements without the added costs associated with current levels of systems support.

As labour costs continue to rise at a faster rate than the costs of robots, and as the flexibility of robots is improved and simplified, then the viability of robotic applications will increase. Even in 1984, one estimate had payback periods for a playback robot on a two-shift basis down to one year.[10]

Automated warehousing

The application of computers in warehousing has been undertaken for many years with the number of fully-automated warehouses in the UK estimated at about 150. It is based on an automatic storage and retrieval system using automatic stacker cranes under computer control. The system identifies each arriving pallet using bar code technology; the operators need only to key in the details and the system does the rest. For example, Frigoscandia's fully-automated cold storage distribution warehouse in Bristol was built with 5,600 spaces, uses stacker cranes fitted with microprocessors which are controlled by the warehouse's supervisory computer. The computer also operates a stock control system and uses critical path analysis to minimize crane movements.

Automated warehouses in a production set-up are based on principles similar to those in distribution though often linked to the automated guided vehicle (AGV) system used in the plant. Thus an AGV will deliver goods for storage to a load station from where a stacker crane will automatically pick up and transfer them to a given location. All instructions come from a warehousing control system which, in turn, is linked to its counterpart in manufacturing. The benefits include reduced labour costs, the elimination of paperwork, improved utilization of floor space, highly accurate inventory records, reduced damage and controlled stock turnover.

Developments in control systems

Chapter 9 provides details of the principal manufacturing planning and control system developments all of which have contributed to the improved integration of manufacturing. The recognition of reduced set-up times, in part accomplished through automation and other forms of process investment, is at the forefront of many current improvement initiatives as an appropriate response to changing market demands. However, the different manufacturing needs require, in turn, different planning and control systems to provide part of the necessary integration within manufacturing.

Computer integrated manufacturing[11]

Computer integrated manufacturing (CIM) is an umbrella term that refers to a total interpretation of design, engineering, manufacturing and the planning and control procedures used within an organization through the application of complex systems. In many continuous processing industries this level of integration has already been achieved because of the nature of the product and process involved. CIM seeks to move the manufacture of discrete parts (rather than homogeneous parts as in, say, oil refining) towards this level of integration.

Typically, investments in computer applications are one-off, designed in isolation of one another and resulting in 'islands' of automation. The need to link these is an essential step in order both to reduce the directly resulting problems and to harness the potential benefits of interfacing these with each other and within a total system. CIM involves the interpretation of the various piecemeal applications into a coherent whole.

In the early 1960s some experts predicted that most manufacturing would be computer-integrated by the 1990s: still often referred to as the 'factory of the future'. That forecast has not been met. CIM is an industry-driven technology, with each sector conditioned by its own particular needs, experiences and circumstances. For all sectors, however, adapting computerized technology takes time, investment and a commitment by everyone. It often involves fundamental changes to existing systems, controls and skill requirements. The financial investment and time-consuming nature of these decisions brings its own level of risk and often results in a cautious approach. This is clearly identified by the level of developments undertaken, the integrating factor provided by CIM is often the feature that is overlooked: a fact which reduces the inherent gain from a given single investment whilst contributing to the existing reluctance to invest and tendency for caution.

Services applications

The application of automation in service businesses is part of the progression which has followed the growth of this sector. In a labour intensive industry the opportunities to increase productivity through timely and appropriate investments are widespread. Some of these are of a general nature whilst others are specific to one or more types of service business as explained below.

General technology applications

Clerical, administrative and secretarial services support all types of business and are not unique to one sector. The application of microtechnology to the transmission of data and speech has introduced significant opportunities to improve the efficiency of all businesses. The basic tasks within this wide group of activities relate to:

1. Collecting, processing, analysing, storing and retrieving information.
2. Transmitting spoken and written messages.
3. Presenting, discussing and assimilating information.
4. Composing, preparing and distributing documents.
5. Co-ordinating activities within agreed timescales.

These activities have always formed the basic tasks within clerical, administrative and secretarial activities, but the application of technology to some of them has changed their nature, the role of those providing these services, and enabled quicker and more accurate support to be available.

Collecting, processing, analysing, storing and retrieving data

Computers that store data in a way that facilitates access whilst reducing the time required at each step of the procedure (collecting, processing, etc.) have been used increasingly in all sectors. Although one principal benefit is the cost reductions involved, there are other significant advantages such as the space needed and speed of retrieval. For many companies, the problem is paper. In 1988, 1.3 trillion (million million) documents were created in the USA alone — enough to wallpaper the Grand Canyon 107 times. About 95 per cent of company information is stored on paper — and it takes up space. With quick access required, this normally requires storage on site which is expensive.[12]

However, there is a technological solution known as documentation image processing (DIP). The theory of DIP is simple: information is stored and transmitted electronically; the advantages are significant. At Western Provident Association, the Bristol-based private medical insurance company, central filing took up 25 per cent of floor space whilst between 25 and 35 per cent of all salary costs was dedicated to managing records. The introduction of DIP has begun to yield significant benefits.[12]

Transmitting spoken and written messages

The application of solid state electronics to telephone systems has enabled a range of developments to take place which have reduced the inconvenience of being unable to make contact with the person concerned and the task of redialling, as well as providing the opportunity to redirect calls, hold discussions with several people at one time, to receive a signal when another call is waiting, and to leave and receive recorded messages. In addition, message exchange systems allow users to call their own numbers and receive any recorded message thus facilitating communication between people on the move who do not have a high level of administrative support.

Managers' use of tape recording machines to dictate memos, letters and to draft reports eliminates the need for dictation and the corresponding duplication of effort. Audio facilities also mean that the taped material can be transposed to a hard copy format with little error whilst decoupling the manager and support staff thus allowing each to work more effectively and efficiently.

Composing, preparing and distributing documents

Mailing lists can be stored on computer and, linked to a capability to prepare standard letters with customized changes, can offer personalized letters and mailing shots as a by-product of the system.

The ability to transmit written messages using the telephone sytem in the form of a telex has been supplemented by the capability to transmit facsimiles of written documents quickly and accurately down telephone lines to locations throughout the world. The 'fax' system scans a document, converts the images to electronic impulses, and sends them across telephone lines to the receiving facsimile machine which converts the impulses back to an identical hard copy of the original. The receiving machine prints the copy on thermally treated paper which is stored in the unit. In 1980, fewer than 20,000 facsimile machines were operating in the USA.

By 1989 there were two million and by 1992 experts predict that the number will double.[13]

Presenting, discussing and assimilating information

A growing number of proprietary on-line databases are available which subscribers can access. British Telecom offers a range of services from a daily recipe to weather reports and the up-to-date position on selected sporting events. In the USA there are more than two thousand commercial databases offering a range of professional services. These include, stock price quotations, full texts of major foreign newspapers, and local regulations and legal opinions for the needs of solicitors and lawyers. April 1989 also saw the introduction in New York and Philadelphia of the facility to search for homes using a television programme and telephoning system to seek further detailed information including mortgage arrangements.[14]

Specific technology applications

Besides the general technology applications described above, different levels of automation have been taking place in several parts of the service sector. Some of these are specific to or predominantly developed for one part of the sector, whilst others have more universal application. Driven principally by productivity gains, these developments have also allowed decisions to be made about the location of back room and front office tasks within a business's service delivery system. The main applications within a part of the service sector are described below. There are, however, overlaps which in many instances have not been highlighted.

Education

The introduction of automated equipment into the process of learning has provided a new range of options for those involved. For children it offers the opportunity to pace the speed of learning to their own capabilities whilst freeing a teacher to attend to individuals needing assistance. For adults it presents similar opportunities allowing them, for instance, to use journey time constructively by listening to taped lessons. Furthermore, it enhances the learning process by extending the use of visual aids: a medium which is generally acknowledged to increase levels of knowledge retention.

In some areas of learning, sounds can be pre-recorded ensuring the highest quality reproduction. Language learning provides a classic example where the use of audio material can help in developing correct intonation and accent. In addition, recording the learner's own correct version of a particular item of learning (e.g. to improve spelling or to increase a person's foreign language vocabulary) has been found to increase the progress of those with learning difficulties.

Financial services

The introduction in the 1930s of cheque sorting machines was the first example of automation within the banking industry. Since then, banks have been automating increasingly throughout their operations. In the back room, electronic funds transfer systems (EFTSs) move monies electronically between different bank accounts. Direct payroll deposits, instant credit analysis and automatic teller transactions are all services made available through an EFTS.

In the front office, automatic teller machines (ATMs) enable customers to withdraw cash, make deposits and check their account balances without the help of bank employees. This not only improves the speed of service and reduces the administrative support within the back room and front office but it also enables these basic services to be provided twenty-four hours a day throughout the year.

Financial services are also using computer-based support to help automate several tasks. Trust administration and portfolio management are examples where automation is helping to improve the level of service whilst reducing administrative costs. The transfer of stock exchange dealings throughout the world's major finance cities was a well-publicized event in the late 1980s. This now enables share price quotations to be given on demand, has lengthened the period of stock dealings within a centre whilst in effect linking the markets to form the equivalent of a globally-based activity.

Health care

Rosenthal identified different types of medical technology applications in the field of health care.[15] These are given below together with examples, and illustrate the wide range of uses within this growing part of the service sector.

1. Diagnostic — scanners, endoscopes, clinical test analyses, fetal monitoring and electrocardiography. For example, at Kochi Hospital (Japan) computerization produces results of tests from the pathology department within a maximum of twenty-six minutes, whilst laboratory staffing costs have been cut by 50 per cent.[15]

2. Survival — intensive care and coronary care units.

3. Illness management — pacemakers and renal dialyses.

4. Prevention and cure — organ transplants, diet and computerized instruments to measure health risks, and the use of probes and lasers in surgery.

5. System management — hospital and medical records, access to biomedical data for research and teaching and to financial records. In El Camino Hospital near San Francisco a computerized operational care system enables doctors to access patients' medical records upon referral and to write up the necessary orders even before admission. The results include shortening the average patient stay

by a full day and an estimated saving on record-keeping time of eight hours per 34-bed ward per nursing shift.[16]

Between 1980 and 1985 the increase in information systems support in US hospitals rose from $0.9bn to $2.5bn and was split as follows:[17]

	%
Financial	64
Patient care	22
Laboratory	7
Pharmacy	2
Other	5
	100

Hotel and catering

The use of automation within the hotel industry is increasing. The provision of lifts and escalators to move people and materials have long been in place. Back room applications now include food preparation, dishwashers, automatic laundry and ironing machines, and automatic clean-up, vacuum, washing and waxing machines. In the front office, investments are increasingly being made in automated reservation and message and morning-call systems as well as electronic key and lock systems.

In addition, a range of information-based systems are apparent in this growing part of the service industry. The applications relate to both the back room and front office and are described as evolving through four stages:[18]

1. Clerical computer applications used for accounting, payroll and to maintain reservation records.

2. Administrative computer applications, including food and beverage control, inventory control, guest histories, reservations and planned maintenance procedures.

3. The provision of information to assist tactical decision-making. This will enable managers to include in their decisions information on consumer tastes, tour operator schedules and link-ups, and money market fluctuations.

4. Strategic decision-making is the final phase: a feature which is expected to increase in the 1990s. At this stage, 'the computer will be used to identify markets, plan products, schedule capital requirements, recommend manpower needs, allocate resources optimally to different business activities and suggest what kind of production processes should be used in the highly automated kitchens.[19]

Table 7.5 Computer system applications — Holiday Inn
(Glasgow)

Computer system	Application
Micos	For front desk operations and hotel accounts
Remanco	For customer orders and bills in restaurants and bars
Telectron	Which monitored private 'Minibars' in each room
Innfax	Free and automatic in-house teletext service
Holidex	Worldwide computerized Holiday Inns reservations system
Transtel	Telephone call logging system
Bytex	Monitoring charges for use of television video service
Uniqey	Computerized system of reprogrammable door locks
Black boxes	Two microcomputers for accounting, cost control, market analysis personnel, payroll and word processing
Ercos	Programmable remote control system for heating and air conditioning equipment

A typical computer application is described for the Holiday Inn, Glasgow.[20] By
1985 this hotel had the range of computer systems shown in Table 7.5 which
illustrates the mix of back room and front office applications developed over time.

Leisure

The use of electronics within audio-visual products has partly been behind the
growth in certain aspects of the leisure industry. Television games, stereo systems,
home movie projectors, video-cassette recorders, compact disc audio-visual systems
and gambling machines are some of the common applications.

Restaurant/food services

Automation is increasingly being brought into the area of food preparation.
Automatic ovens, food processors, drink dispensing machines and disposal systems

are illustrative of back room applications. The increasing versatility of vending machines has offered improved service to the general public, whilst frozen food/microwave systems enable hot food choice at all times of the day.

Transportation

The principal forms of transportation are air, rail, road, water and pipeline. Automation in air transport includes baggage conveyance, air ticketing machines, security surveillance systems, and auto-pilot capability.

Switching terminals, signalling systems, computerized rail car tracking systems and ticket booking are examples of automation in the rail industry, whilst automatic motorway toll systems and swing bridges are examples on roads. Automated loading and unloading equipment, automated locks on rivers and canals handling ocean-going vessels, and the electronic navigational devices and electric power systems on ships illustrate the wide range of applications in water transport.

Pipeline technology is highly sophisticated. Instrumentation, pumping systems, control units and valve-based distribution systems combine to provide a highly automated form of transportation.

Wholesale/retail trade

Bar coding is having widespread implications for the wholesale and retail trade. A bar code is a set of bars and spaces of various widths which are unique to a product and that are read by an optical scanner. The information contained includes a product's name, lot number, location and price. The bar code system facilitates changes to variable data such as location and price by simply changing the information file for that product: a quick low cost operation. A bar code can be printed directly onto a product or its packaging or can be printed onto a label for fixing at an appropriate stage in the manufacturing process.

At a supermarket checkout, the sales assistant uses an optical scanner to read the bar code on the product. The price is automatically recorded on the sales till whilst inventory records are updated. Similar applications are used in library and credit card systems.

Other examples of automation include computer aided vehicle repairs, dry-cleaning equipment, car-wash facilities, automatic fire sprinklers and newspaper dispensers.

Utilities and public services

Utilities and public services describe a diverse group of activities including electricity, gas, communications, refuse collection, armed forces, libraries, social security departments, hospitals, fire service, legal system, tax offices, customs and excise, and postal delivery services. In addition to the clerical and secretarial applications described earlier, automation takes many forms within this varied sector. Examples include ERNIE to select premium bond winners, library lending services with electronic-based checking, disposing and recording procedures, military warning systems, computer-based missile systems, automatic incinerary facilities, electronic fighting equipment, heat sensoring devices and power generation stations.

Developments in telephone systems have already been mentioned. The late 1980s saw the introduction of advanced systems enabling data, voice and graphics to be sent over ordinary telephone equipment and the resulting impact upon investment and user costs. When pictures supplement the already available group-based calls, the need for many centralized meetings will be obviated, with savings in travel costs and management travel load.

Conclusion

Computer-based applications have underpinned many of the recent developments in manufacturing and service systems. The intention is to incorporate production/operations technology with management/business technology.[21] Production/operations technology is concerned with the process that makes products or provides services. Management/business technology deals mainly with the flow of information essential to the effective planning, control and management of the conversion process. Their increasing integration is helping to bring about vital co-ordination within an organization and the benefits which accrue.

It is essential, however, to recognize the key features underpinning these initiatives and to ensure that they characterize the nature of the activities within the organization. These include:[22]

1. *The need for the initiatives to be business-led.* System developments are not an end in themselves. Both the stimulus for and the specification of these initiatives must be business-led. The business objectives, as translated through an appropriate production/operations strategy, need to provide the parameters in which the developments should take place (see Figure 2.1).

2. *The initiatives should be multi-disciplinary in nature.* The opportunities offered by system improvements and the mix of hardware and software developments require an integrated response best provided by a multi-disciplinary approach. A combination of line executives and relevant specialists ensures that not only are the technical knowledge inputs provided but also that rigorous testing takes place in terms of the complex nature of reality. Unless solutions embody the application/evaluation loop (see Figure 1.4) then the constraints and needs of reality will not be adequately recognized. Furthermore, it is essential that the proposals form a coherent whole in order to avoid the serious limitations and potential inadequacies of piecemeal developments.

3. *The initiatives should be action and change orientated.* The success of systems development needs to be measured by the resolution of problems or realization

of opportunities. Implementation should be made on a continuous basis and the practicality of improvements needs to form the ultimate test. A report, no matter how comprehensive, is not a measure of success. Action and change need to be the sole goals of these initiatives.

It is most important that organizations place systems improvements within the context of their business needs. Major changes have too often been specialist-led and panacea-driven.[23] Organizations need to develop business-based strategies which can then provide the direction for developments. As emphasized in Chapter 2, investments in the production/operations function are both large and fixed by nature; it is essential, therefore, that a business understands what it is buying to ensure that the opportunity for systems development is maximized.

Notes and references

1. Chapter 11 provides basic approaches to improving productivity and thus overlaps the non-computer-based applications referred to briefly here.
2. J. Dwyer, 'AGVs set free to wander', *Financial Times Survey of Manufacturing Automation* (3 February 1986), p. iv provides references to current applications of AGVs.
3. C. Rapoport, 'Fanuc: young company far ahead of the pack', *Financial Times Survey of Manufacturing Automation* (3 February 1986), p. ii.
4. I. Rodger, 'Manufacturing automation', *Financial Times Survey of Manufacturing Automation* (3 February 1986), p. i.
5. BS 6808 *Co-ordinate Measuring Machines*, giving users the measurements they should take, the directions of travel to use and the readings at the probe tip they should obtain if they follow the guidance.
6. Also refer to G. Charlish, 'Machine vision ends tedium', *Financial Times Survey of Manufacturing Automation* (5 February 1985), p. 21.
7. I. Rodger, 'Hitachi Seiki: flexible system profits demand intensive use', *Financial Times Survey of Manufacturing Automation* (3 February 1986), p. vii.
8. B. Haywood and J. Bessant, 'The Swedish approach to the use of flexible manufacturing systems', Occasional Paper 3, (Brighton Polytechnic (UK), 1987).
9. J. Dwyer 'Robotics: tough for the adolescent industry', *Financial Times Survey of Manufacturing Automation* (3 February 1986), p. ii.
10. K. Ohmae, 'Japan: from stereotypes to specifier', *McKinsey Quarterly* (Spring 1982), 2–33.
11. A CIM update is included in *Control*, 14 (August/September 1988).
12. P. Abrahams 'Throwing away the paper-based system', *Financial Times* (26 April 1989), p. 18.
13. L. Whitley, 'Facts about fax', *Sky* (May 1989), pp. 24–30.
14. A. Kates, 'TV brings homes to shoppers', *USA Today* (20 April 1989).
15. 'Medical technology: the culprit behind heath care costs?', *Proceedings of the 1977 Sun Valley Forum on National Health*, US Department of Health Education and Welfare Publication no. (PHS) 79–3216 (1977).
16. 'Computers streamline care in hospitals', *Sunday Times* (7 May 1989), p. F5.
17. From O. Eralp and B.B. Rucker, *The Hospital Information System Industry* (San Francisco: Hambrecht & Quist, 1984). The breakdown by activity is based on 1982 information.
18. P.R. Gamble puts forward these four evolutionary stages in *Small Computers and Hospitality Management* (London: Hutchinson, 1984), p. 211.

19. *Ibid.*, p. 24.
20. D.A. Buchanan and J. McCalman, 'Confidence, visibility and pressure: the effects of shared information in computer-aided hotel management', *New Technology, Work and Employment*, 3, no. 1 (1988), 38–46.
21. An idea mooted by K. Hitomi in *Manufacturing Systems Engineering* (London: Taylor & Francis, 1979).
22. These ideas form part of the Open University's 'Manufacturing Systems Engineering Course' (1989).
23. Discussed in more detail in Terry Hill, *Manufacturing Strategy: The strategic management of the manufacturing function* (Basingstoke: Macmillan, 1985), p. 103, and Terry Hill *Manufacturing Strategy: Text and cases* (Homewood, Ill.: Irwin, 1989), p. 101–2.

PART III

Infrastructure-related issues

The third section concerns infrastructure. Whilst it is widely appreciated that process-related decisions normally incur high investment and consequently warrant careful consideration, decisions concerning infrastructure do not generally attract the same high profile. But, this can (and does) lead to significant misunderstandings and the inadequate allocation of management energy and attention both in terms of level and time. However, many of the decisions within this part of the POM task are not only expensive in themselves but will equally bind organizations for years to come.

As with Part II, the opening chapter introduces the background to this aspect of POM. In so doing, it explains the key differences between the production/operations task and two other functions which are often mistakenly seen to be similar in content and coverage. Chapter 8 also helps to bridge Parts II and III by reviewing parts of the total POM task and restating the areas of linkage.

Chapters 9–15 then provide a detailed review of the important facets of this aspect of the production/operations function. Chapters 9–12 concern major areas of control — the need to plan and control the production/operations system (Chapter 9), the materials within the system (Chapter 10), and the essential quality of the product and service (Chapter 12). In between, Chapter 11 looks at the study and control of work. The two common denominators in a business are time and money. Production/operations (unlike any other function) uses time as its base currency for the management and control of and within the system. This chapter explains the different ways used to help provide the common denominator of time as well as the systematic review of operations as a way to reduce costs.

Chapter 13 concerns the maintenance of the processes within the system. As a key resource, the importance of a well-maintained process is an essential feature of the POM task and its coverage here explains some of the different approaches of managing this important function.

The final two chapters concern people. The way in which companies structure work and reward employees is a critical dimension of a successful business.

Moreover, with responsibility for typically some 80 per cent of the organization's staff, it is vital that production/operations managers be articulate in those areas. Chapters 14 ('The job of work') and 15 ('Remuneration') address the various aspects of work structure and reward that need to be taken into consideration by production/operations managers and also demonstrate their importance to the POM task.

Chapter 8

The task

The 1980s proved to be more challenging and difficult for the operations manager than any other time since the Industrial Revolution. The 1990s may prove even more so. The traditional manufacturing problems of archaic work rules, out-of-date technologies, underdeveloped infrastructures, inefficient work methods and manning arrangements, inappropriate payment systems and effective scheduling and control systems have been coupled with a whole set of new challenges — increasing world competition, decreasing product life cycles, stringent regulations concerning employee and environmental protection, safety, quality and the scarcity and rising costs of energy and raw materials. Furthermore, the linked world economy has resulted in a more complex business environment, with new and different competitive situations, legal and tax issues and political, social and business characteristics.

Similar pressures have started to unfold in the service sector. Although many service industries are protected to varying degrees by geography, many major services have increasingly been subjected to national and international competition. Deregulation in US airlines, the growth in the hotel chain concept and the interrelation between share and money markets through the world's stock and financial centres have brought similar demands on related businesses and highlighted the importance of the operations manager's role. Although the phenomenon of international (and for some services, even, national) competition will be less widespread than in the manufacturing sector, it will show similar increases, if not at the same overall level. The continued and significant improvements in data storage and transmission will open up many areas to competition and spawn services new in themselves or in their application.

As a consequence, the operations manager will need increasingly to provide the support essential to the success of the wide range of goods and services involved, different in themselves, and changing in nature over time with life cycles which will continue to become shorter. New efforts to increase productivity, create technological advantage and to find additional methods to increase the return on assets will be part of the challenge facing those in charge of these functions.

Misunderstandings of the POM task

Before discussing some of the basic characteristics of the POM task it will be helpful to examine a fundamental misunderstanding concerning POM in general and two specific misunderstandings in particular.

As explained in Chapter 1, the production/operations function comprises a wide cluster of subfunctions, each significant in its own right and sizable within an organization. For a number of reasons, not least the fact that the production/operations manager too often fails to provide the necessary direction and co-ordination to this complex set of activities which form part of the total function, the area is incorrectly perceived to be a number of different and separate functions/activities bound together, if at all, as a loose federation. When organizations grow this process of separation increases. The result is that the essential co-ordination is not recognized as a critical activity let alone emphasized as a key task in the evaluation of POM performance. In teaching and textbooks a similar disparity arises. Teachers too often present the area as a set of distinct activities/techniques.[1] Textbooks on POM address the subject in similar fashion with little emphasis on the management of the task and ignoring that it is, like other management topics, an applied subject area. The consequence is that POM is perceived to be uninteresting and concerned with day-to-day issues characterized by detail and dull routines. Nothing could be further from the truth.

Specific misunderstandings

The lack of understanding of POM is exemplified by two examples. These concern its relationship with both production engineering and operations research. However, whereas a review of any business will show a clear separation between production/operations and these other functions, the same clarity is present neither in the approach typified by the business in terms of responsibility for developing the subfunctions within the area nor in the approaches used to research, describe or teach this area within the educational system.

Production engineering

Production engineering is often confused with production management. But the tasks, qualities and skills associated with each are not the same. The degree of dissimilarity will depend upon factors such as the products being manufactured, the span of processes involved, production volumes, the method(s) of production or types of process used and the degree of technology associated with the product and the process.

Tables 4.1–4.4 (pp. 62–8) compare the types of production process and indicate the characteristics associated with each. An important feature which these illustrate is the movement away from a technology contribution associated with jobbing towards a need to handle the large numbers of people associated with line operations together with the management controls, high level costs, fixed asset utilization and other non-technical, management aspects of the job which come with the necessary investment in the process to meet the competitive, low-price criterion of a high-volume market.

Furthermore, over the last forty years, and particularly during the 1970s, the social and legislative changes which have taken place, and their impact on organizations has been considerable. The pace and size of these changes have placed a still greater emphasis on the people aspects of the POM task.

The misunderstandings which exist between POM and engineering emanate to some extent from the perception of the role and importance of technology in manufacturing. Table 4.4 first addressed these issues within the question concerning the relative importance of technology or business/people within the POM role. In most businesses, the product and process technologies are given. Similarly, where service industries concern high volume businesses, then the relevant technologies will also be given. The POM task in such manufacturing and service organizations is to manage the transformation process and inherent complexity which follows, with specialists providing the necessary product/service and process support. The confusion, however, typically remains and, as a consequence, inappropriate attributes are called for and the wrong performance measures applied within POM, thus reinforcing the problem and failing to contribute to the changes which need to be brought about.

Operations research

The second specific example of misunderstanding comes in the shape of the area known as operations research (OR). In part, the confusion comes from the word 'operations' and, in part, from the fact that the majority of applications of the techniques embodied in OR are in POM areas. In the 1960s and 1970s, scholars and businesspeople were optimistic about the future role of OR, model-building and computers in organizations. It was implied, if not explicitly argued, that these developments would make routine many of the traditional functions of middle management typically in production/operations resulting in the elimination of many of these positions and the creation of a quantitative élite corporate management.

Many universities responded with the prediction that future managers would need quantitative tools of analysis and, as a result, developed courses which included subjects such as

Quantitative methods	Computer simulation
Model-building	Linear programming
Queueing theory	Regression analysis
Network models	Dynamic programming
Game theory	

During the 1960s, the consensus was that OR should hold a dominant position in the teaching of POM. Textbooks followed suit to reflect this view, and displayed the use of these subjects, their application and the mathematical derivations of the formulae which underpinned the approach.

Only now is this view being seriously contested. However, it is a difficult and lengthy process to turn the ship around and even more so without the necessary and weighty counter-arguments in business and academia. Developing fresh and pertinent concepts to stress the management of complexity rather than its resolution (if only the dynamics of reality did not exist!) is starting to take shape and gain a foothold.

One key distinction rests in the recognition that the essence of management concerns knowing which pictures to draw, not how to draw pictures. Whereas OR concerns the latter, the management of production/operations requires knowing which pictures will give the necessary and incisive insights on which to build appropriate courses of action.

Since the early 1980s a more pragmatic review has prevailed and OR's practical limitations have been recognized. A change in attitudes, however, will take longer as vested interests run deep for two important reasons:

1. The OR approach is attractive in itself due to the apparent and intrinsic solutions it offers.

2. The OR approach is teachable (and examinable) without production/operations management experience.

This allows specialists within the broad area of POM to stress non-managerial topics while giving inadequate coverage to the essential perspective on which POM rests — the management of this area.

The first step, however, concerns understanding that within an organization, the operations task is concerned with the management of complexity. The factors of complexity are size, the level of detail and the inter-related nature of the activities both within POM and also with the other functions of the business. Whilst every POM system is different and has its own history, it is important to review the particular characteristics of each system within some general set of principles. This acts as a check against anticipated 'norms' which in turn helps in reviewing parts of the system and also provides a framework to facilitate the understanding of both the parts and the whole.

Trade-offs between some of the essential functions of a business have to be made. The reconciliation is difficult. To do this well requires a detailed practical understanding of the activities of the operations process.

The confusion that exists between production engineering and production management needs to be clarified. Whilst both are associated with the manufacturing process, production engineering concerns the design of resources whilst production management concerns the organization and use of resources.

Production engineering, therefore, largely concerns the technological aspects of the design, manufacture, use and development of the processes involved, the tools, equipment and machinery necessary to make the products. Production

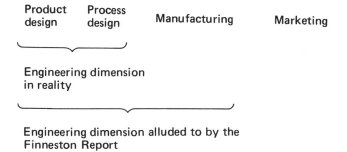

Figure 8.1   Production engineering and production management.

management, on the other hand, is concerned with the development of all production resources within the firm, of which the technical input is usually relatively small. An important aspect of this role is to apply the results of other disciplines (including the technical output of production engineering) to the production function. As part of this procedure, it has to fit the parts of the whole together and evaluate the consequences of each part within the whole. Some typical operations management areas of responsibility are operations strategy, work structuring, payment systems, industrial relations, labour standards and the control of work, the selection of operations processes and their development, operations planning and control, inventory control and the control and reduction of cost throughout the process.

There is no question that process technology is essential for efficient operations. It is in the choice of the technology of the process that these two functions overlap. Both need to contribute to that decision. But, the choice having been made, it is the ability of operations management that determines the level of effectiveness achieved in the use of the process technology investment.

However, these distinct roles are confused by many. Examples of this confusion range from the Finneston Report[1] on the one hand through to the layman's view, on the other. The Finneston Report regards engineering as synonymous with manufacturing, leading to suggestions that the 'engineering dimension'[2] includes the manufacturing task (Figure 8.1).

It is most important for organizations to distinguish between these tasks. Failure to do so can result in the wrong attributes being called for and high level talent being applied to the wrong job.

Components and characteristics of a process

As explained in Chapter 4, the process is a collection of tasks connected by a flow of goods and information that transforms various inputs into useful outputs, with the capability to store both the goods and information during the transformation.

Every operations system is unique. It has its own detailed components, which reflect the technology and infrastructure choices that have been made, and its own characteristics, which are descriptions of aspects such as capacity and flexibility. In this section, ways of looking at processes to help understand them are discussed. Being able to review a process conceptually not only helps to gain insights into what is happening, but also reduces the chances of being overawed by the enormous level of detail involved. Often when faced with the daunting task of separating the wood from the trees it is all too easy to take the issues one at a time and ignore the essential task of reviewing the whole before reaching some decision concerning a change in one part of the process.

Components of the process

The essential components of a process concern handling the requirements placed upon it and the use of the capacity within that process. To complete this analysis it is necessary to determine:

1. The range of products/services to be provided.
2. The process capabilities available.
3. The control of the process to meet the longer- and short-term demands placed upon it.
4. The measurement of capacity and its control.

The remainder of this section considers these aspects in detail. Suffice it at this stage to outline some of the issues and perspectives to be considered in the POM task as a way of illustrating the wide-ranging and interrelated nature of the responsibilities involved.

1   The range of products/services

The specification defines the function and form of a product/service. The products/services to be provided and the degree of similarity within each range will determine the nature and extent of the basic POM task.

This aspect links with the design function of the business. With specials, design clarity will be critical in establishing the essence of the POM task in providing the product/service. With standards, the POM task will be concerned with providing the range of products/services in the light of capacity, inventory and flexibility constraints whilst conforming to agreed levels of quality. Some of these issues have already been discussed in Chapter 5.

2   The process capabilities available

Products are made and services are provided by the process. The process itself is a combination of equipment and labour capacities and capabilities. The impact of the demands placed upon the process (see 1 above) is obvious. Other aspects which also impinge significantly on the process capabilities include changes in quality requirements, the maintenance of quality over time and the introduction of new technologies (see Chapter 7).

The first two components of the process concern its definition and the specification of the product to be made or service to be provided. The next two components concern the control of the task, linking back to these first two components where appropriate.

3   The control of the process to meet the longer- and short-term demands placed upon it

This involves forward planning to meet anticipated demand as well as controlling the short-term and current requirements placed on the system. Longer-term considerations include investment in capacity to meet peaks, investment in inventory to allow level output, the planning of future capacities to meet current or new markets and the introduction of new technologies for reasons of quality, cost or provision of new product/service features. In the short-term, the need to meet delivery requirements, quality levels and cost budgets are part of the POM task. In addition, new product/service developments, scheduled launches and the introduction of new technologies will be superimposed on the day-to-day task of the operations function.

4   The measurement of the effective use of the process

The final component is to measure the effective use of the process as a control in itself and also as an input into calculations of future capacity. Therefore, the way in which the system is measured must relate to how the operations function is required to support the performance criteria in the market-place. It is not possible for the system to compete on every yardstick.

Once these four major steps have been reviewed, it is possible to record product/service flows through the process from task to task, from task to storage, storage to task and so on. In the same way, information flows can be traced to indicate the records, documents and instructions that are issued and how these fit the process.

Characteristics of the process

In addition to the 'vertical' look at the process provided by 'components' it is also important for the operations manager to review the process by taking a 'horizontal' slice through the system to illustrate some important insights. Such analyses will reflect particular characteristics which include the following.

Capacity

Capacity concerns the output from the process. The dimensions of the output in this context include rate of throughput and what constitutes an effective maximum. To measure either of these requires a detailed understanding of the process. Neither are fixed. The throughput rate and maximum output level can change depending upon inputs such as raw materials and labour, but more importantly upon product/service mix, product/service development requirements and volumes.

Flexibility

Flexibility concerns the extent to which a process can be changed to meet customer requirements in terms of specification changes, product development and delivery requirements. Within this broad definition the operations manager needs not only to understand the extent of the change but also factors such as throughput rate, degree of process adaptability, similarity/interchangeability of processes, and inflexibility due to the constraints of meeting sales demands.

Productivity

Productivity is the measure relating the output of the process to the value or volume of input which has been made to achieve that output (see Chapter 11). Any form of productivity measurement meets with difficulties of definition; however, global statements relating output to a general input base (e.g. man-hours, number of direct or total employees) are useful ways to summarize, over time, the performance of the operations system in itself or in relation to the business as a whole.

As large increases in productivity often result from investments in the process, it is important to segregate the source of productivity improvements especially in terms of payment and other reward systems.

Efficiency

As with productivity, efficiency is also covered in greater detail in Chapter 11. Efficiency concerns the measure of actual output to the predetermined standard set for output against a time/money base. Operations managers need to be involved in determining standards as these classically form part of the set of measures against which their own performance is judged.

Trade-offs

An operations process inevitably involves trade-offs and compromises.[3] All gains have some costs. One critical feature of the POM task is to apply this concept to the process. This analysis will have consequences both at the operating level within the process and at the corporate level between the operating process and the rest of the organization.

Corporate level

The importance of understanding the interrelationship between operations and corporate strategy is not in dispute. Certain corporate marketing strategies place different demands on the POM system and, conversely, the system should be designed to support the strategic requirements of the business. The difficult task is to determine this fit as part of the corporate strategy procedure. Chapter 2 discusses approaches to help resolve this fit, outlining a framework to be used whilst addressing some of the issues to be taken into account.

Operating level

Instead of first considering the operations strategy in line with the corporate requirements and then defining the operations task, organizations usually employ some less effective resolution. They strive to provide a system based on the premise of being 'all things to all men'. In this way, a system is provided and evaluated in terms of low costs, high quality, acceptable delivery promises and adequate response to meet customers' needs. The measures chosen reflect an organization's view of achieving the optimum balance between conflicting demands.

This perspective is to some extent based on a simplistic view that given the materials, labour and equipment, the operations process will perform effectively and efficiently. What is missing from this analysis is that it fails to recognize the important trade-offs within the POM process. In Chapter 4 some of the important decisions necessary in the provision of an operations process were discussed, and the different aspects which, in general, appertain to each choice of process were illustrated. Other important trade-off decisions in POM are outlined in Table 8.1.

The issues raised are not new. The importance of highlighting them, however, concerns the need to recognize that trade-offs are an inherent part of the POM task. The operations manager needs to recognize, explain and discuss them with the other functions' managers when relevant issues arise. Only in this way will an informed decision be reached and the consequences of the eventual choice be understood by all concerned. When this understanding has been achieved, it is then possible to agree the way in which the POM system will be structured and the yardsticks on which it should be measured.

Conclusion

POM is seen by most managers as a complex, technology-oriented area with long working days involving detail and aggravation and resolving low-level, day-to-day issues in a situation of pressure from all sides.

However, operations managers have failed to explain the complexity they control in a way that helps others to understand the issues and trade-offs involved. As a consequence, they attempt to strike a balance as best they can between the options

Table 8.1 Some important trade-off decisions in POM

Aspect	Issue	Some alternative decisions
Capacity provision	Span of process	Make or buy
	Plant size	One large plant or plants of a maximum size
	Providing a range of products/services	Common capacity used for all products/services or the separation of capacity to serve a limited range of products/services
	Coping with changing demand over time	Order backlog, excess capacity held in the process or finished goods inventory
	Layout	Functional, line or group technology
Flexibility in the process	Meeting the delivery speed requirements of the market place	Excess capacity, fast changeover capability or component/WIP/finished goods inventory
	Process interchangeability	Degree of conformity in terms of the process itself and/or support tools, equipment or software programs
	Product/service development	Product/service development within the existing process or by setting-up a separate function
	Degree of product/ service change	Customerization or standardization
Controls in the process	Measurement of the process	Controls designed to achieve a high utilization of the equipment or labour, or to meet sales demands or quick deliveries
	Quality control	The extent of quality control re incoming materials, in-process provision and finished goods or services
	Inventory size	High or low inventory in terms of raw materials, WIP and finished items
Infrastructure	Type of organization	Control by specialists or building specialists into the line functions
	Wage payment system	Job or skill base; hourly paid or incentive schemes; individual, group or companywide bonus schemes
	Executive and supervisory style	Autocratic or democratic
	Corporate control	Centralized or decentralized
	Participation	Consultation or negotiation; trade union or employee representation; board-, plant- or shopfloor-level participation

This table has been developed from Exhibit 1 of W. Skinner's article 'Manufacturing — missing link in corporate strategy', *Harvard Business Review* (May/June 1969).

presented by the different pressures in the organization. This neither makes for a sound decision-making process nor allows the operations task to be understood by other departments. Consequently, the necessary insights are often not focused on the demands being placed on the process and the trade-offs implied by the decisions which are taken.

The approach to POM in the past has emphasized the use of techniques to resolve parts of the whole. In addition, over the last thirty years there has been an increase in the use of quantitative analysis (linear programming, simulation, queuing theory and other aspects of operations research). These have failed to bring the results they promised. In order to cope with the complexity and dynamics of POM, the simplistic approach of applying a technique-based solution to one area has tended to be used. The result has been numerous failures, always expensive and always absorbing on-the-spot, expedient measures to keep the process going. In most cases, the problem has been delegated to specialists who, without appreciating the considerable trade-offs involved, developed a simplistic approach designed, to a significant extent, on their own judgements about what is important whilst pursuing the refinements of their own particular specialism.

Who is at fault is not the question. What is essential to appreciate is that solutions are not easy to come by and the simplistic premise on which most techniques are developed has to be broadened to check its suitability, both in terms of the present and its ability to provide for future development. The complexity of the area can be awesome. The belief that an optimum blend between major choices in the POM system will set the POM task for all time is held by many. This approach invariably leads to a series of conflicting decisions in the short-term, with each new decision attempting to redress the results of the last. For instance, squeezing inventory as a quick, short-term measure will affect POM efficiency, customer service and profit: for inventory investment has its trade-offs. It is essential, therefore, to revive concern for the operating side of the business and to increase the understanding within an organization of the essential details of the process so that more informed decisions can be made in that part of the business where the substantial percentage of costs are incurred.

Notes and references

1. 'Engineering our future', *Report of the Committee of Inquiry into the Engineering Profession*, Chairman Sir Montague Finneston. HMS Cmnd 7794 (January 1980), pp. 7—8.
2. Finneston Report, p. 21.
3. The concept of trade-offs within the POM system was first put forward by W. Skinner in 'Manufacturing — missing link in corporate strategy', *Harvard Business Review* (May/June 1969).

Chapter 9

Production/operations planning and control

The task of a business is to sell its goods/services in the market-place and then provide them through its operations function. To do this, it invests in the primary facilities of buildings, processes, people and procedures. However, the problem confronting most organizations is meeting both the needs of the market-place and the performance targets (e.g. output and efficiency) that a business places on its operations function. On the one hand, they form the basis of the sale, whilst on the other they underpin the very success of the organization.

One cause of this conflict arises from differences in the nature of the two activities. Whilst the market-place is inherently unstable, the operations function needs to be kept as stable as possible in order to achieve the performance levels essential to the success of the business. To cope with these differences organizations invest in a number of ways to cushion the core from the instability of the market (see Figure 9.1). One such investment is on appropriate production/operations planning and control systems, the subject of this chapter.

To provide goods and services, organizations invest in the necessary processes. However, investment is represented by not just process hardware. It consists of any change to the operations system which improves an organization's capability to meet customer requirements. Thus, as illustrated by Figure 9.1, investments to cushion the demands that an unstable market places on the stability of the operations core take several forms. Long-term capacity change was discussed in Chapter 6. Inventory is the subject of Chapter 10.

Another important area of investment is in the operations planning and control procedures to help reflect forecast and actual demand in terms of forecast and actual capacity and capability. These procedures cover a wide planning horizon which spans the strategic through to the tactical decision-making levels:

1. *Long-term operations planning* is a strategic business issue, generally looking five or more years ahead and was dealt with in some detail in Chapter 6. It aims to provide for the long-term capacity requirements and resource allocations

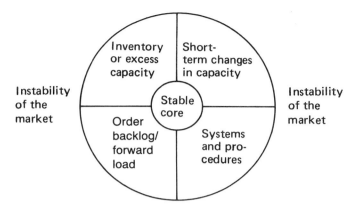

Figure 9.1 Cushioning the production/operations core.

to meet the future organizational objectives by planning for capacity changes in line with major shifts in existing products/services and to meet plans for new products/services, technologies and markets.

2. *Medium-term or aggregate planning* is for periods up to two years ahead and details how demand will be met from available facilities which, in principle, are considered to be at a fixed level.

3. *Short-term, production control* is responsible for monitoring day-to-day operations activities to ensure that customer demand is met and resources are used effectively.

This chapter is concerned with medium- and short-term planning and control. Some of the relevant underlying concepts involved in control systems are explained and then some management perspectives of planning and operations control are reviewed. In the discussions on control, the systems appropriate to each choice of process form the basis of the analysis. A section highlighting some of the aspects particular to service provision is also provided. The final part of the chapter is concerned with the managerial control statements which may be used to provide the necessary statements to help examine and monitor this important POM task.

Underlying concepts

Before discussing the more detailed aspects of operations planning and control systems, it is important first to address several issues, decisions and design structures which form the basis on which these systems need to be built.

Aspects of control and information design

Essential design principles

The first step in designing a control system is to specify the objectives of the operations function as they relate to the strategy requirements of the business. It is then possible to establish the purpose of the system and to agree how performance within operations is to be measured, what information is required and the measures that best reflect this performance in line with a company's business strategy.

Information and decision systems

The factors affecting the structure of information and decision systems include:

1. The type of manufacturing or service organization which determines the primary function of the business.
2. The organizational style and structure, e.g. decentralized/centralized, and degree of autonomy at different levels within the system.
3. The type of decisions that need to be taken, e.g. the extent of programmed and non-programmed decisions, and the levels at which decisions are made.
4. The size of the organization in terms of departments, branches, transactions and other forms of activity.
5. The management style within the organization in terms of degree of participation, and the authority/responsibility links.
6. The nature of the business in terms of business fluctuations, degree of demand certainty, level of responsiveness required in the market-place and whether it is a special or standard product/service.[1]

The system and the user

A system has no intrinsic value. It is essential at all times to relate the system to its users and not to its designers or to the producers of the information.

The nature of information

Information is data that has been processed into a form that is meaningful to the user and which contributes to the task on hand. The tasks themselves have also to be differentiated so that they are clearly understood in terms of their information requirements.

However, many organizations decide to produce a standard product or provide a standard service only on receipt of a customer's order or schedule (i.e. on a make-to-order basis). In most service industries it is impossible to produce a service ahead of demand. Also, in many manufacturing businesses the decision is made not to

Table 9.1   The different requirements of planning and control information

Aspect	Planning	Control
Purpose	Forward-looking and providing the basis for long-term decisions	Statements of past results against targets and the use of variances to adjust future targets or on which to base short-term actions
Basis	Broad and organizationally based	More specific, with a departmental or functional orientation
Timescale	Relating to long time periods and showing trends	Shorter time periods and related to specific sets of responsibilities
Level of detail	Broad, corporate, or divisional statements reflecting substantial parts of the business and showing trends over time	Detailed department or section statements within a business unit showing specific results and performance trends

produce ahead of demand but to use order backlog/forward load as the mechanism for handling fluctuations in orders.

1. Information for planning is different from that for control. Some of the important differences are summarized in Table 9.1.
2. Information can be provided for the following reasons:
   (a) to help decision-making by establishing choices between options;
   (b) to measure performance;
   (c) to provide the basis for administrative actions.

Aspects of operations

Make-to-order or make-to-stock

The essential requirements of an operations control system will differ between make-to-order and make-to-stock situations. This is due to the following factors:

1. Certainty of the order.
2. Certainty of the volumes.
3. Level of knowledge of the task.
4. Degree of product/service modification to be accommodated within the process.
5. Lead time.
6. The different order-winning and qualifying criteria in the market-place.

Choice of process

As discussed in Chapter 4 and as described above, the operations planning and control task will contain different variables and requirements depending upon the choice of process. Because of these changes, it is essential that the chosen control systems meet the differing needs of each process and that all embracing systems and procedures are avoided.

Lead time

Total lead time is the time which elapses between the moment a product/service is ordered (make-to-order or make-to-stock) and the time it is available for use. Depending upon the process, lead time will have some or all of the following elements:

$$\text{lead time} = \text{generating paperwork} + \text{purchasing} + \text{setting-up} + \text{processing} + \text{waiting to be moved} + \text{movement} + \text{queuing}$$

Table 9.2 The unproductive elements of lead time related to the choice of process

Unproductive elements of lead time	*Process*				
	Project	*Jobbing*	*Batch*	*Line*	*Continuous processing*
Generating paperwork	Usually extensive but often most of it is completed as part of the order quotation		Make-to-order situations will be high, but make-to-stock often much lower	High	High
Purchasing	High	High but may be supplied by the customer	Will be related to make-to-order (higher) or make-to-stock (lower)	Low and scheduled	Low and scheduled
Waiting to be moved Movement Queuing	All related to those sets of activities which form the critical path[a]	Low Low Low[b]	Medium High Very high	Built into the process	Built into the process

[a] The critical path through a network is explained fully later in this chapter.
[b] Where queuing for a process does occur in jobbing, the skilled operators will decide priorities between themselves and reorganize their own activities accordingly until the process is available for use.

However, measurement of part(s) of this total are used in most organizations. 'Generating paperwork' includes determining requirements, linking into the control systems and ordering; 'purchasing' is the time it takes for a product/service to be delivered from a supplier; 'setting up' is the time involved in setting up the process for completing the particular operations(s) or the preparation time involved before completing the particular operation(s) or the preparation time involved before completing part or all of a service; 'processing' is the actual time that the job/service is being worked on; 'waiting to be moved' is the time that a job/service waits before being moved to the next part of the process; 'movement' is the time that a job/service spends in transit from one process to the next; and 'queuing' is the time that a job/service is waiting to be worked on because another job/service is already being worked on in that part of the process. Several of these elements of lead time (particularly the last five) may be repeated in the provision of a typical product/service.

Elapsed lead times are always far greater than actual setting-up and processing times. The unproductive elements of lead time will vary in terms of aspect and content depending upon the process chosen; they are summarized in Table 9.2. Ways of assessing and controlling the ratio of the time taken to complete the operations to the lead times involved are detailed later in this chapter.

Control system design

Types of decision

An operations system requires many decisions to be made in order to achieve its intended purpose. These decisions can be classified into three types:

1. *Planning* decisions concerning the future and made on an infrequent and often irregular basis.

2. *Operating* decisions involving routine decisions made on a frequent and regular basis.

3. *Predetermined responses* to situations (e.g. reordering inventory or the calculation of material requirements from forecast finished items).

Types of information

There are two broad types of information:

1. *Parameters* describing relatively constant information such as labour standards (see Chapter 11), overhead recovery rates, process times and reorder levels.

2. *Variables* describing changeable information. These comprise data that reflect the current status of the operating system (e.g. current inventory levels, actual

processing times, new orders and performance levels) and the results of other decisions.

The decision process

A decision process consists of three basic elements:

1. Information into the decision process which may be new information, previous decisions, parameters and variables.

2. The decision required.

3. The decision function which takes the information and converts it into a decision. The functions which do this include:
    (a) mathematical equations;
    (b) statistical procedures;
    (c) sets of rules;
    (d) a manager's judgement;
    (e) simulation or other computer models.

The control system

The control system consists of the decision process elements; the basic format is shown in Figure 9.2.

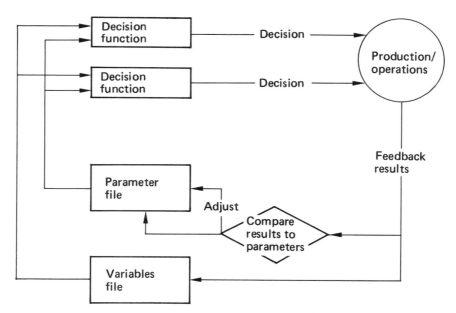

Figure 9.2 The basic format of an operations control system.

User requirements

There are inherent delays in control systems due to the time involved in making, implementing and getting feedback from decisions. It is critical, however, that the time requirements of the user are recognized to ensure that the timing of controls and reporting statements is in line with user needs. Too often information with one set of time requirements is presented at the same time and with the same frequency as others with different sets of time requirements. To be of use in the decision making process, therefore, information needs to be not only relevant but also timely.

Production/operations planning

Although in many organizations the planning and control aspects of the operations function are embodied in the same department, the functions themselves are different although entirely interdependent. Planning is concerned with all the pre-operations activities whereas control is responsible for all the tasks and decisions to be made during the operations process.

Operations planning, therefore, is concerned with determining and arranging all the facilities necessary to meet the future plan. Appropriately referred to as the 'front end',[2] operations planning embraces the aspects of capacity and resources planning along with that of demand management. It not only encompasses these basic dimensions of a business but also exposes constraints and limitations. In so doing it provides the production/operations inputs into the overall business plan within the agreed corporate strategy whilst highlighting areas of future mismatch within the business which need to be realigned at the strategic level and ahead of time, rather than at the operational level when the problem has occurred and necessitating short-term responses with the adverse effect on corporate performance overall and customer support in particular.

Chapter 6 concerns capacity investment decisions. It shows how demand forecasts enable managers to improve their ability to plan future operations levels. The further role of the planning function is to convert these forecasts into product/service, process and labour requirements. Chapter 6 also discusses the critical nature of the make-or-buy decision which together with demand forecasts form the initial capacity-related activities inherent in the operations planning role. Further planning activities contributing to these capacity considerations are:

1. Designs, whether provided by the customer or internally.

2. Material specification and quantities involved.

3. Processes to be used, bearing in mind existing skills, plant and capacity constraints, other processes available and investment implications.

4. Process sequence, including specifications, job routes, skills and equipment requirements.

5. Additional support equipment (e.g. jigs and tools) or software (e.g. program developments) necessary to complete the task.

6. Internal or external movements (e.g. outside plating or specialist services).

7. Quality and inspection requirements in the process (see Chapter 12).

As well as being responsible for their determination, the pre-planning task includes requisitioning and scheduling all these requirements in line with the plan. Furthermore, it is essential that the needs of an organization's competitive strategy are related to these activities as this will determine the overall structure of the operations provision in the business. Decisions at the planning phase will commit resources and investments for the future and will, by their very nature, debilitate an organization's response to change because of time and capital investment considerations.

Aggregate planning

Medium-term or aggregate planning for periods up to about two years ahead is used within the overall framework of the long-term plan. It consists of establishing feasible medium-term plans to meet agreed output levels in a situation where capacity is considered to be relatively fixed.[3] It does this by adjusting demand and capacity variables within the control of the organization in order to adjust throughput to demand fluctuations. Examples of these variables include workforce levels, overtime, a reduced working week, inventories, order backlog (forward load) and subcontracting.

An aggregate plan determines the sales requirement for monthly forecasts of demand during the relevant period and, assuming that capacity is relatively fixed, it calculates capacity availability from existing known resources. This activity sets the overall planned levels of output from period to period.

As sales orders are received, detailed schedules of the products/services to be provided are developed and the aggregate plans adjusted upwards or downwards to accommodate the actual as against forecast sales position. It is at this stage that the short-term operations control activity takes over.

Small adjustments to sales patterns can be accommodated from one sales period to another. However, it is necessary to develop aggregate plans in order to cope with an overloading or unloading of facilities in the longer-term. In this way, an orderly and systematic adjustment of capacity can be made to meet any significant changes in aggregate demand and sales mix whilst facilitating the achievement of delivery commitments to customers and internal operating efficiency.

Thus, aggregate planning helps to control medium-term changes whilst allowing the short-term, fine-tuning of the system to remain within manageable proportions.[4]

Steps in aggregate planning

In Chapter 6 the initial steps in the aggregate planning procedure are discussed when dealing with longer-term capacity planning. These also apply when developing the aggregate plan and are listed here as a reminder. The other steps are then dealt with in more detail.

1   *Forecast sales*

Forecast sales for each product/service within each time period. The initial forecasts will be adjusted by the known trends in actual sales and, in some organizations, the opportunity to differentiate between estimated or forecast sales and expected and expressed (or actual) sales, thereby hardening the information on future sales patterns.

2   *Make-or-buy decision*

The make-or-buy decisions based on both the strategic and tactical perspective will be under review. Changes in these decisions will require to be measured in capacity terms, initially through the aggregate plans and, where major shifts occur, against the long-term plan.

3   *Select common measures of aggregate demand*

The next step is to aggregate demand for all products or services into statements of common or like capacity groups. For single product/service organizations this is often not difficult. For the brewer it could be gallons of beer; the doctor, patient visits; a coal mine, tons of coal. For multi-product or service organizations great care has to be used in arriving at appropriate measures.

4   *Develop aggregate plans*

Aggregate plans need to be developed to achieve agreed corporate objectives. The primary objective is usually to meet demand at lowest cost. However, it is essential to agree secondary objectives such as providing continuity of employment as they are also part of the base on which the decisions may be made.

5   *Select the planning horizon*

For each business, it is necessary to select an appropriate planning horizon for the aggregate plan. Whilst this will cover several time periods (normally six to twelve months), the plans will typically be used on a month by month basis. This is because of the interrelated nature of the operations decisions which need to be made from one month to the next. Decisions made in one time period will often limit the decisions which can be made in the next time period(s). In addition, many operations decisions are actually part of a composite set of decisions which need to form a consistent whole. Decisions made which ignore future consequences will often prove costly.

6 *Smooth out capacity*

Within each planning horizon the anticipated sales generated by the earlier forecasts will be measured against the resource assessment. The task is to smooth out capacity utilization by attempting either to influence demand or by changing capacity in the shorter-term. The fundamental task concerns the decision on which way an organization will meet demand. The basic options are *chase demand, level capacity* or a *mixed plan.*

Chase demand involves linking throughput rates to demand. In this way capacity adjustments would need to be made quickly to respond to sales changes. However, many companies prefer to couple the production and demand rates. In make-to-stock situations, this allows throughput levels to be smoothed by using capacity in low demand periods to make work-in-progress and finished goods inventories to be sold in higher demand periods (see Figure 9.3). In make-to-order situations, the backlog of orders (also known as forward load) can be adjusted to take account of fluctuating demand.

Whereas production situations can take advantage of a level or mixed plan, service organizations usually cannot. Because most services cannot be stored, then either chase demand or order backlog/forward load adjustments are the only options open to these organizations.

It is also feasible to choose a mixed plan where some smoothing is used to create stability in the capacity requirements (especially regarding people's continuity of employment). Here, some inventory is accumulated to make effective use of existing capacity and some capacity changes are made to reflect changes in demand.

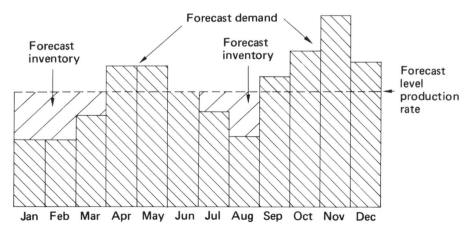

Figure 9.3 Level production plan and its effect on capacity.

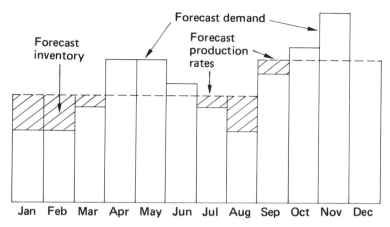

Figure 9.4 A mixed plan involving level production, inventory and an increase in capacity from September to December inclusive.

For example, Figure 9.4 shows an increase in capacity during September to December. This has been based upon the introduction of a temporary evening shift (18.30−22.00 hrs) to help reduce inventory holdings throughout the twelve month period.

7 Short-term changes to meet demand fluctuations

After existing capacity has been measured and future requirements determined, it is important to identify other ways of modifying capacity in the short-term. The extent to which these options apply will depend upon the process selected by the organization (see Table 4.2) and the working arrangements within the organization. The short-term opportunities can usefully be divided into changes in demand and changes in capacity.

Changes in demand
The changes in demand which can be used fall into three categories. The first is to reduce demand by actions such as refusing business or increasing overall price levels to bring demand more in line with capacity. The second is to change the pattern of demand, for example, by altering price levels to differentiate between peak and off-peak business periods or by advertising. An alternative to this is to introduce complementary products/services, the demand for which will be in the periods of lower sales for current products or services. Examples include the use of hotels in the winter for conferences, and coach tour operators providing school bus services. The third way is to use scheduling as a way of accommodating demand fluctuations. This can be achieved by either improved scheduling to help spread demand over time or to accommodate the excess in demand over capacity by either work-in-progress (WIP) or finished goods inventory holdings (in make-to-stock

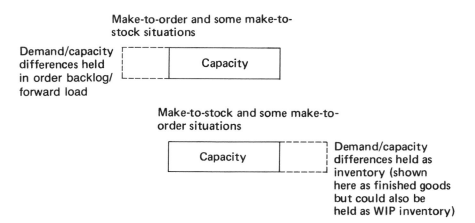

Figure 9.5 The use of order backlog/forward load and finished goods inventory holdings to help in the adjustment of demand/capacity differences.

situations) by extending or reducing the order backlog/forward load (in make-to-order situations) or by a combination of both methods (see Figure 9.5).

The use of finished goods inventory is discussed earlier in this chapter. In a similar way, an organization may decide to make to a part-finished stage (WIP) so that in periods of high demand the capacity requirements will be reduced accordingly. Although this option is available primarily only in make-to-stock situations, it is also possible in some make-to-order businesses where components or subassemblies are known to be required, irrespective of the detailed customer requirement.

The use of order backlog/forward load is used mainly in make-to-order situations. However, this approach is likely also to be used by organizations making and selling their own products, potentially falling, therefore, into the make-to-stock category. An example of this is the furniture industry where companies will often put an order quantity of work through the manufacturing process only when it has been sold or part-sold with the remainder being designated before the time the order quantity reaches the finishing stage of the process.

Lastly, a business may use both alternatives. For instance, a make-to-stock company may have a policy of producing an item only when, say, four weeks' outstanding sales have accumulated (the backlog). If it takes two weeks to produce the equivalent of twelve weeks of sales, then by the time this quantity is made the company will, on average, have sold half the order quantity with the other half going into finished goods inventory (see Figure 9.6). When this inventory has been sold, the cycle is repeated.

Changes in capacity
The alternative method that an organization can use to meet short-term capacity changes is to change capacity itself. These changes fall into the two broad categories:

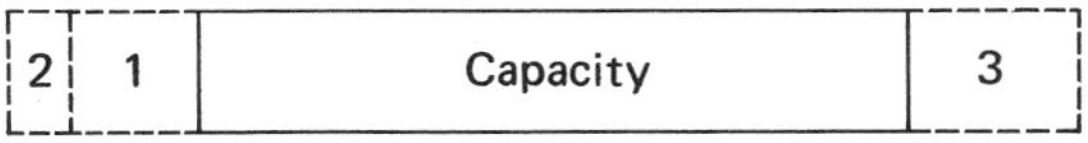

2	1	Capacity	3

1 Four-week backlog of orders — initiate production order for the equivalent of 12 weeks of sales
2 During the production lead time, two further weeks of order backlog/forward load accumulate
3 The equivalent of 12 weeks of sales is completed, the 6 weeks of backlog orders are met and the balance is finished goods inventory to meet future sales

Figure 9.6 The use of both order backlog/forward load and finished goods inventory to provide adjustment between demand/capacity differences.

1. Short-term adjustments to capacity. Choices here include the transfer of people from one area to another, engaging part-time or full-time employees on a temporary basis, overtime working, working a reduced week or agreeing to postpone or pull forward holiday entitlement.

2. Absorb or release capacity in the short-term. This can be achieved by actions such as subcontracting work or calling-in work from subcontractors in periods of high and low demand respectively, deferring or bringing-forward maintenance work and scheduling programmes of work with a high labour content so as to achieve labour efficiency levels whilst keeping inventory investment to a minimum.

8 *Select the aggregate plan*

The final step is to select the most suitable aggregate plan to meet the corporate objectives determined earlier in the procedure.

Operations control

Operations control concerns meeting the short-term, specific plans. Its principal activities, therefore, are to authorize instructions to complete the tasks necessary to meet customer orders, to ensure that all the requirements to make the products or provide the services are available as and when they are needed, and to complete these within the corporate objectives specified in the aggregate plan.

Not all organizations require the same operations control system; apart from the choice of process there are two general points to consider.

1. There are other factors besides the choice of process which will make the operations control task different from one organization to another:

    (a) it is essential to relate the operations control system to the strategic requirements of the business which have to be provided by the operations function;

(b) the internal span of process within the business inherent in the make or buy decision;

(c) the nature, range and volume of the products/services to be provided;

(d) the decisions that have been reached on the capacity demand reconciliations.

2. An operations control system has three phases:

(a) *loading*—the initial assignment of a job to a part of the process (e.g. work centre or person);

(b) *sequencing*—determining the order in which jobs will be completed at each stage in the process;

(c) *scheduling*—involves the allocation of a start and finish time to each particular order.

The remainder of the chapter is devoted to describing the types of operations control system appropriate to the choice of process, together with a detailed synopsis of different planning and control systems currently used in many organizations.

In many sites there will often be two or more types of process used and more than one example of each of these processes to cope with the range of product/service requirements. It is important, therefore, that operations control developments do not lead to single systems being designed to cope with this wide-ranging task. The development of a basic system designed around the principal or most common process may save on investment but will lead to inadequate overall control. The increasing use of microcomputer facilities has led to the opportunity for systems development to meet the requirements of different processes. The differences are now explained.

Project

The project process is usually the one adopted by businesses involved in providing products/services of considerable magnitude (which, when completed, cannot normally be transported) and usually, but not always, carried out on a one-off basis. If the project contains only a few activities, an informal scheduling and control approach can be adopted. However, most projects are complex and involve many inter-related activities necessitating the development of a formal plan.

The one-off or infrequent nature of these tasks, however, militates against the use of the more traditional scheduling and progressing methods that are described later. As a result, network analysis has developed, the principles of which technique are described below.

General aspects of network analysis

The first task is to determine the level of detail on which the activities to complete the task will be based. Often in large projects an overall network will be developed with subnetworks being provided to give control at a more detailed level. When this has been agreed, the activities which have to be completed will be listed. *Activities* are tasks which have a time duration. At the start and finish of each activity will be, in network language, an *event* which occurs instantaneously and says that the preceding activity or activities are now complete and other activities which depend upon their completion can now start. These are the two principal building blocks for networks and use the symbols shown in Figure 9.7. In addition there is one further symbol, that of a dummy activity, which will be explained later.

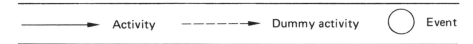

Figure 9.7   The symbols used in the construction of networks.

All the activities listed represent the total task. By building a network, the task is stated as a series of activities all of which have to be completed for the task to be finished. The key, however, is to build so that the activities are shown in the order in which they have to occur. To do this it is necessary to establish for each activity, the other activity or activities that have to be completed before it can start. This is called dependency. One or more activities will, however, be independent and these are obviously the ones that are completed at the beginning (although in complex networks some independent activities may not be started at the beginning). When these have been completed (an event) then other activities can start and so on. In this way the network is developed. Those activities which follow others are said to be sequential, whilst those which can be completed at the same time as others (i.e. they are independent) are said to be parallel (see Appendix A to this chapter which looks in more detail at network analysis).

Intermittent systems—jobbing and batch

Both jobbing and batch processes are designed to provide a wide range of product/services often in small quantities and on general purpose equipment. They are classified as intermittent because the product/service does not flow through the system but rather goes through a series of stops and starts (particularly in batch). However, whilst there are some similarities between them in terms of the operations control task, there are sufficient differences that it makes sense to discuss them separately.

Jobbing

The jobbing process supplies orders that will not be repeated or where the time interval between identical orders will be long. Thus, the situation is a make-to-order provision of goods or services. The operations control task, consequently, is to load, sequence and schedule a customer's requirement consisting of a large variable product/service order mix, through a wide series of processes normally based on people skills and independent of one another. The control system will be based on the customer order, with the purchaser determining the product/service specification. The objective of the control system will be to ensure that the operations are done in the correct sequence, the jobs are scheduled without conflict and to meet operations criteria such as customer deliveries whilst keeping WIP inventory and the utilization of labour to agreed levels.

The factors which will influence the complexity of the control task will be the range of jobs, the number of jobs outstanding (quantity × work content), the process capacity provision and the order arrival pattern.

Loading

In a jobbing situation, all or most of the task is likely to be performed by one person. It is the capability of these skilled people, together with that of the support and managerial staff, that a business sells. When orders arrive, therefore, they will be allocated to appropriate people. Factors influencing this choice include the current and future workloads of the people in the process, the recognition of key processes (those on which demand is normally high),[5] current order backlog and the delivery requirements of known orders. Although the known backlog position provides the element of certainty which facilitates the loading task, in make-to-order situations there will still be the uncertainty about which orders a business will win and hence the overall demand requirements to be met. Similarly, but to a much lesser extent, as all jobs are unknown, then the length of time necessary to complete the tasks will also be uncertain. This factor, however, typically reduces nearer the end of the task. Normally, quotations for jobs will be based upon a delivery promise from receipt of the order, but where accepted quotations are higher or lower than anticipated this will, in turn, make loading more difficult.

In a make-to-order situation, a job will be assessed in terms of the skill levels and experience of the people available and their current workload. A loading choice will then be made according to the delivery requirements of the order and shuffling orders to accommodate new demands is not uncommon.

Sequencing

The next step is to determine the sequence in which the jobs are to be completed. This is particularly important in terms of delivery and its affect on WIP levels.

Some of the rules to be considered in helping to determine the sequencing of jobs are given below. Although no one selection rule will be best for all situations, most jobbing businesses attempt to perform well against a dominant objective such as improving some aspect of customer service. Common rules include:

1. First come, first served.

2. The job requiring the shortest operation time is completed first, the next, second and so on.

3. The job requiring the longest operation time, is completed first and so on.

4. The job with the shortest average slack time (days until order due less outstanding processing time) is completed first and so on.

5. The job with the shortest slack time per operation remaining is completed first where

$$\text{Average slack time per operation} = \frac{\text{Total slack remaining}}{\text{Number of outstanding operations}}$$

6. To ensure that major labour or plant processes (those which are normally fully loaded) are scheduled to achieve a high utilization of that process.

Scheduling

The scheduling task concerns allocating start and finish times to tasks. In a make-to-order situation, however, there will usually be an element of uncertainty as to how long a task will take because no previous knowledge is available. An estimate, therefore, will usually be made. A bar chart represents the simplest way of scheduling the various activities to be completed.

In jobbing the principal capacity is represented by skilled people, as tasks are completed by them and the role of equipment is to support the skilled person in doing the job. Therefore, orders will typically be loaded against a person and against a time dimension (Figure 9.8). In businesses where the jobbing process is used, it is normal for the skilled person to determine the more detailed aspects of the

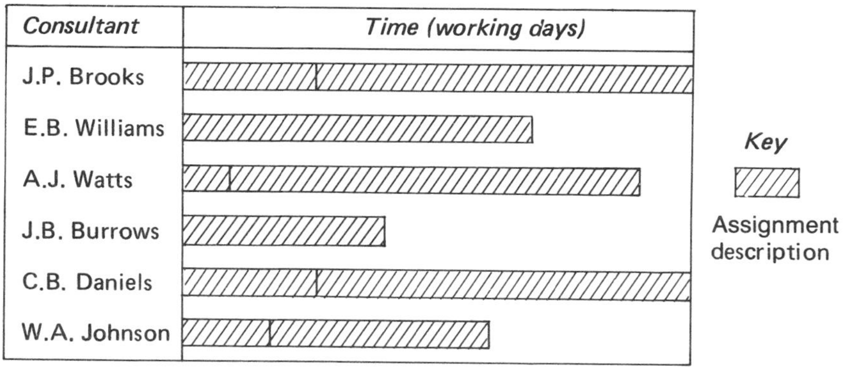

Figure 9.8 Bar chart representing assignment allocations to management consultants.

task and to control them throughout. Thus, where two or more skilled people require the same process at the same time then priorities will be settled between them in the full knowledge of the other productive tasks which can be completed in the meantime and the relevant delivery schedules. Thus, a manually-based system would normally suffice to control the production of goods or provision of services in these types of organization.

Batch

The production control task for a batch process usually concerns the loading, sequencing and scheduling of a wide range of products/services often involving a large number of operations. This task is made more difficult by the varying and often large volume requirements of an order. Sales may be for standard or special items. In the same way as a jobbing business, the processes to complete the task are shared by other work, with different orders having different priorities. This has a significant effect on the production/operations control task as the scheduling decisions will affect the delivery requirements of the customer and the level of WIP inventory in the system. Often, the final stage of the process is assembling the product or bringing the different facets of the service together for the customer. Therefore, there is a need to co-ordinate the different parts of the job to make them available for that final stage.

All these features result in a large number of loading, sequencing and scheduling combinations. The task of identifying and evaluating possible sequences and then controlling the outstanding operations is formidable. Factors determining the size of this task are:

1. The internal span of process provided by the organization.

2. The number and size of jobs (quantity × work content).

3. The pattern of sales and whether they are internally (i.e. from within the same organization) or are externally generated.

4. Sales of special (not known) or standard (known) products/services.

Loading

Whether an organization provides special or standard products/services will alter its operations control requirements. For specials the approach to control will be similar to a jobbing business. The differences are that an order will normally be for two or more similar items and, more significantly, that order will be loaded against different processes (see Figure 9.9) rather than skilled people as in jobbing. This signals the change which takes place when organizations choose batch. Increasingly it is the process which makes the product or provides the service and, therefore, becomes the resource on which the control system needs to be based.

Where products/services are standard, the operations control requirements are based on a process which is known and established. The repetitive nature of demand will have cost implications in the market-place, and investment in process aids to reduce the overall time taken will be warranted (e.g. jigs, tools, outline solutions to similar problems, and past records). Other ways of completing the task should be available and should be costed to provide the base for consideration when the occasion demands. As with specials, tasks will normally be loaded against processes and not people as shown in Figure 9.9.

For standard products/services, a route or master card is prepared for each job to specify the operations and their preferred sequences through the process. It will also specify materials, set-up and process times, particular job features, packaging requirements and any other details relevant to completing the task. This information is compiled from experience and updated over time.

In addition, with most batch situations, certain processes will invariably have a heavy workload. These *key processes* will need to be monitored carefully at the loading stage to reflect overload situations (process hour requirements versus available hours of capacity) especially in terms of delivery dates and the cost implications of any necessary short-term capacity changes or the selection of less-preferred routings. It is important, therefore, that the operations system provides relevant and timely information for these processes to facilitate making decisions on incoming orders. This need will be of paramount importance where an organization has a mixed specials/standards business and knowledge of the impact of product/service mix changes upon process loadings will be critical to the operations control function.

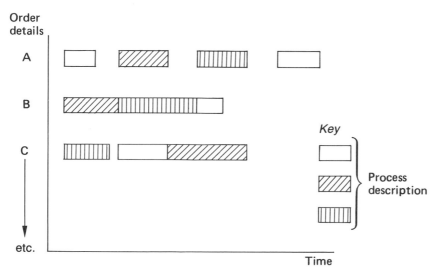

Figure 9.9 Orders shown against process sequence on a time scale: a more typical form of bar chart in batch.

Sequencing

In most batch systems, the principal method of sequencing jobs through the process entails breaking the job down into its different operations, determining from the delivery requirement the dates at which these operations need to be completed and then allocating each operation to the relevant part of the process. As new orders are received, the loading on each process needs to be monitored for periods when demand is greater than available capacity so that decisions to reconcile this imbalance can be made. This is particularly important for those *key processes* which exist in the business.

In addition, where a product is required to meet forecast demand then an analysis to aid sequencing decisions is to calculate the run-out time for an item in the next production period. This will be expressed in terms of the rate of usage for an item:

$$\text{Run-out time} = \frac{\text{Opening inventory} + \text{Scheduled output} - \text{Forecast demand for this period}}{\text{Forecast demand for the following period}}$$

Scheduling

Attempts have been made to determine the start and finish times for each operation at each process at the time of issuing work. However, not only is this far too complicated but also the frequent changes in terms of capacity and requirement (e.g. substandard materials, process scrap, absenteeism and process breakdown) are such that the system is too slow to obtain the feedback and provide the new information. For this reason, the allocation of work to the supervisor for a time period (e.g. a week) with information on delivery requirements and priorities will provide a system which can respond to capacity and customer order changes in a much more sensible way. Further, the increasing use of microcomputers will enable those who use operations controls to tap into the system and, using the database, to evaluate other options and scheduling changes in the light of the new information. Chapter 11 discusses these points in more detail.

However, in many organizations using batch processes the scheduling task is enormous. This is particularly the case for jobs with a large work content requiring many operations. In situations like these, scheduling by target dates at suitable points in the total process is a useful way of monitoring potential lateness well before it is impossible to rectify the position.

Continuous systems—line and continuous processing

Continuous systems are designed to handle large volume requirements of a single or small range of products/services on dedicated processes;[7] using either line or continuous processing plant and equipment.[8] The entire range of items is completed on the same plant using the same materials and components, going through the same processes at a predetermined rate.

Both the loading of jobs to the process and the sequencing to be completed at each stage are built into the process. The routeing of the job is incorporated into the line or continuous processing plant and each item flows through the predetermined operations which incorporate the agreed modifications within a product range. Scheduling, on the other hand, consists principally of establishing a production rate, whether the process is machine or operator controlled. Orders are triggered by an authority to produce and the process is monitored by the rate of acceptable items recorded.

The basis of production control for continuous systems is one of flow control, as opposed to order control in intermittent systems. Thus the emphasis is on controlling the rate of flow of raw materials, components and subassemblies to the line and the shipment of final products off the line.

In many manufacturing companies there will be more than one production process in a plant. Typically, the continuous system developed for final assemblies will not be used for manufacturing the numerous subassemblies and components that go into this assembly. These will more normally be produced by batch or even a jobbing process and controlled accordingly.

Accommodating the predetermined variety of the final assembly of high volume items made on a line (e.g. the motor vehicle industry) is a difficult production control task. Component and subassembly variety then become the key to successfully supplying the array of customer demands on a single line process.

In continuous processing production situations (e.g. oil refining) the in-process controls are built into the system and monitored from the outside. Much less product variety is provided and the key production control tasks concern the flow control problems mentioned earlier. The in-process controls are computer-based and provide constant monitoring of instruments, equipment and the product status whilst measuring and checking the process variables against predetermined limits.

Developments in planning and control systems

The previous sections consider the aspects of planning and control more in principle than related to specific systems. This section details two developments in planning and control systems that illustrate fundamentally different approaches to meeting the needs of different situations. In addition, it reviews a futher approach and places this in the broader context of these overall system developments.

Material requirements planning

The system known as material requirements planning (MRP) looks at future requirements for finished products and uses this and other information to generate statements on the subassemblies, components and raw materials necessary to complete the end-products. It is often known as a 'push' system (as opposed to a 'pull' system, such as just-in-time, described in the next section) in that statements of requirements are made in line with agreed delivery dates and these are stimulated at the start of the process in line with relevant schedules. In this way, the appropriate subassemblies, components and raw materials are pushed into the process. Thus, in order to keep inventory low and the task associated with its control as simple as possible, the dates on which orders fall due (referred to as 'due dates') are checked first (via the master production schedule) to agree 'rough capacity' which is then fine-tuned via capacity requirements planning (explained on pp. 126–30). Materials are then 'pushed' through the system to meet due date requirements. However, there is an argument that this is, in fact, a pulling action which leads to mixed views over the term 'push' system. But, through this chapter the two basic systems will be distinguished in this way.

MRP is a time-phased, materials ordering system which has been used under different names for many years, for example in jobbing processes. However, the advent of low-cost computing has enabled the application of MRP to the planning and control of the manufacture of multi-components assemblies. Before this time, the systems that were used to meet these latter needs often included a combination of systems typically supplemented by an expediting function whose role was to identify current requirements and prioritize the behind-schedule parts on the basis of a 'pull' demand. Low-cost computing offered companies the opportunity to plan and control the manufacture of their complex businesses in an orderly way using MRP principles.

MRP relies on the fact that the demands for all sub-assemblies, components and raw materials are dependent upon the demand for the finished product itself. They are said to have *dependent demands*. Some items, however, have independent demands in that the demand for them does not depend on the demand for any other item. Examples include finished products and also components and subassemblies in the form of spare parts sales requirements.

Thus a dependent item is one that goes into the manufacture of another item or is converted into a 'higher level' product. For such items only one forecast is necessary. It must be made at the highest level (i.e. where the item has an independent demand pattern), from which all other demands can be calculated. The principle on which this information system is based is one of planned requirement, hence its name. The method is to calculate requirements for components (this term includes all inventory items other than products or end-items, i.e. either bought-out or manufactured subassemblies and parts) based on the forecast demand of the higher-level assemblies (e.g. finished goods) in which they are used. As independent items, finished goods demand is determined from forecasts and/or order backlog (from customers or within the company) modified by existing inventories, and forms a schedule of manufacturing requirements or *master schedule* normally over one or more production time periods. This, then, is the input to MRP which, by means of a parts explosion, calculates the requirements for all dependent items.

In an MRP system, the master schedule equates to the order book translated into production requirements. When the parts explosion has been completed the system collates similar parts, thus often creating 'anonymous' order quantities to be completed by the relevant processes, as a way of reducing the number of set-ups within the overall system. When the parts have been completed MRP 'reassembles' the constituent elements of particular products to meet assembly requirements. In this way, the system is designed to help ensure minimum WIP inventory.

Anonymous batching, however, hampers programme management as it makes the monitoring of a particular customer's requirement difficult. As batches do not carry sufficient identity, reporting structures are based on part numbers rather than customer-order information. Thus, urgent jobs are put together with less urgent jobs, with the details separating this urgency being released only when a complete batch is finished. The consequence is that progress can often only be monitored in the system when the batch is complete.

This synopsis is designed to give an overview of MRP both in itself and as a way of providing a comparison with the other systems described in the following sections. Appendix B at the end of the chapter provides considerably more detail for those who wish to gain greater understanding of this basic approach to production/operations control.

Just-in-time

The advent of low-cost computing enabled the widespread use of MRP systems in the planning and control of different processes and manufacturing conditions. Compared with the confusion and disorder associated with systems supported by expediting and constantly changing priorities, MRP offers a well-ordered system reducing the need to reschedule frequently. However, an alternative approach to the planning and control task is widely used in the Japanese automobile industry, and has now gained much support in other industrial countries. It is known as the just-in-time (JIT) production system. Whereas MRP is a plan-push system, JIT is demand-pull (see Figure 9.10)

The JIT production system is relatively simple, requires little use of computers,

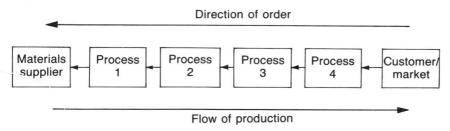

Figure 9.10 The flow of orders and production in a just-in-time control system.

and in some industries can offer far tighter controls than computer-based alternatives. The idea is to produce and deliver goods just in time to be sold, subassemblies just in time to be assembled into finished goods, fabricated parts just in time to go into subassemblies, and purchased materials just in time to be transformed into fabricated parts.[9] The purpose is for all materials to be in active use within the total process; in this way they are a productive element within the manufacturing system which avoids incurring costs without corresponding benefits. Thus the JIT system is based upon the concept of producing small quantities just in time as opposed to many current philosophies which are based on making inventory 'just in case' it is required.

With the continued spread of JIT systems through the industrialized world, many varieties or hybrids of the system are being developed. Unfortunately many of these developments purport to be something that they are not, mainly because those involved have not recognized the concepts on which JIT is based, and, consequently, have introduced apparent JIT initiatives without understanding, examining and explaining the often significant modifications introduced and the different mix of trade-offs which have resulted. In some instances the concept has been so changed that the potential advantages of JIT are not forthcoming. In order to explain the concept of JIT, this section outlines the principles involved and against which JIT proposals should be measured.

JIT systems are based on two principles. The first is the development of a series of small factory units (typically employing less than three hundred) each delivering to one another in successive stages of production and eventually to the final assembly plant. The second development is to have a system in which each factory unit works to a lead time of one day. What happens is that on one day each unit delivers to the next unit the exact quantity it needs for the following day's production. To allow this to happen, the scheduling system used (called Tacto by Toyota) sets the monthly production rates by quantity and type for all its products and hence creates a uniform daily demand throughout the entire production system.[10]

The main features of these systems are:

1. To reverse the flow of information concerning parts and subassemblies, so that the assembly line calls off the parts it needs. The widely quoted Kanban system of inventory control is typical of the card system used. At Nissan the similar card system is called 'action plate' and at Honda 'DOPS'[10]—see Figure 9.10.

2. To reduce WIP inventory to a minimum.

3. To eliminate bottlenecks and reduce machine downtimes.

4. To reduce changeover times such that the smaller batch sizes become practical. For example, the set-up time for a hood and fender stamping operation was estimated by Toyota for typical plants as follows: USA 6 hours, Sweden and West Germany 4 hours, and Toyota's time 0.2 hours.[10]

5. As a consequence of 4, the production systems handle smaller amounts of parts and materials on a more frequent basis (two to ten deliveries per day is typical).

The concept is very appealing. However, there are several prerequisites if it is to be achieved.[11]

1. It is most suited to high volume manufacturing situations.

2. It must be end-user driven. The business making the final products must take responsibility for instigating this development and liaise with its suppliers accordingly.

3. Production schedules must be firm. If the material is not available in the system then production schedules cannot be increased.

4. Suppliers must be geographically close to the customers thereby enabling regular deliveries to be made.

The essence of this system is stability of call-offs and developing close relationships with suppliers. In many UK companies, however, the impact of the inherent instability of the market-place (see Figure 9.1) and a lack of close liaison with suppliers tend more to be the manufacturing situations that production control systems have to handle.

This section provides relevant background for JIT systems. As with MRP, there is important detail that needs to be appreciated if a JIT initiative is to be considered. Appendix C provides additional insights for those who wish to deepen their understanding of these control system developments.

Optimized production technology

Much attention has been given recently to a proprietary system called optimized production technology (OPT). The development comprises two facets. The first is the conceptual base of the system and the second is the software package (OPT/SERVE) which supports the system. As this book addresses the management of the production/operation function, then OPT will be discussed only in terms of its conceptual base.

OPT's main impact concerns the shopfloor control system. In essence (although OPT does possess other inherent contributions)[12] it is a sophisticated control system based on finite loading procedures and which concentrates on a subset of work centres (the bottlenecks).[13] The software package uses an algorithm developed by Eliyahu Goldratt to accomplish the finite loading.

The basic philosophy underpinning OPT is not only important in itself but also in helping to understand some major issues in the management of a production/operations function. OPT stresses several fundamental insights which are briefly described here:[14]

1. To achieve the most profit from a given set of resources, it is necessary to maximize the flow through and not the utilization of these resources. Throughput is limited by the capacity constraints (or bottlenecks) which exist within the system. Thus, it is necessary to control the inputs into the manufacturing process in line with these constraints, for it is only this level of throughput which can be sold. By adopting a policy of maximizing resource utilization a business will generate work at some stages of the process which cannot be worked on at other stages (i.e. bottlenecks) because of lack of capacity. The result is WIP inventory. Thus, whereas additional scarce resource capacity is 'useful' (i.e. it can be used), additional non-bottleneck capacity is 'surplus' (i.e. it cannot be used except to make WIP inventory).

2. From 1 it is clear that bottlenecks are the limiting factor governing the level of work through the total manufacturing processes. Thus, bottlenecks govern both throughput and inventory levels in the system. The aim, therefore, is to reduce bottlenecks.

3. Derived from 2 is the recognition that the level of utilization of a non-bottleneck process is determined not by its own potential but by some other constraint in the system.

4. Thus, the aim of a company should be to balance flow and not capacity. Reducing bottlenecks will increase total flow through the system thus releasing the potential capacity of other non-bottleneck processes.

5. As a consequence of the above, an hour lost at a bottleneck is an hour lost forever but an hour saved at a non-bottleneck is a mirage. Thus, saving set-ups at a bottleneck increase throughput, while additional set-ups at a non-bottleneck do not affect throughput but do minimize WIP inventory.

6. Activating the use of a resource is not synonymous with utilizing a resource. Utilizing a resource concerns generating schedules to maximize throughput, minimize inventory and protect the schedule from disruption. Activating the use of a resource is simply what it says.

7. The transfer order quantity may not and often should not be equal to the order quantity processed. This recognizes the fact that a company needs to determine order quantities at a bottleneck process with a view to both reducing the number of set-ups and hence increasing available capacity (the concept of cycle inventory—see chapter 10) and then reducing the order quantity it transfers to the next process in line with demand rather than the utilization of subsequent

processes. Thus, the process order quantity should be recognized to be variable not fixed.

8. When determining schedules, capacity and priority need to be considered at the same time and not separately.

The principles underlying OPT philosophy have universal applicability. Consequently they can be used to enhance many existing control systems as well as providing useful insights into the more effective management of the production/operations function.

Service system

Service capacity is perishable and not transferable: therefore, when demand falls short of capacity, the result is idle capacity. However, the variability in service demand is pronounced because the work content of a service cannot be stored: it is provided and consumed more-or-less simultaneously. Hence a nation's work culture and its domestic and social habits create a situation where peaks and troughs of demand are most pronounced. The majority of people sleep, eat out, work, partake in leisure activities and take holidays at similar times of the day or year which contributes greatly to the high and low demand phenomenon in much of the service industry. The operations control activities, therefore, concern attempting to alter demand and capacity provisions so that they are more in balance whilst responding to random customer orders.

Lastly, there are three further dimensions in a service system which affect the planning and control task—the choice of process, the phenomenon of 'front office' and 'back room', and the use of customer capacity in the service delivery system. With this brief overview established, some of the important perspectives are outlined.

Defining customer service and quality levels

A service comprises a package of explicit and implicit benefits usually supported by a facilitating good. As discussed in Chapter 5, a service can possess tangible (high goods content) and intangible (high service content) attributes. Whereas with a manufactured item the specification of the product is well-defined, this is not necessarily so in the case of the service content. In part, difficulties arise from the fact that in the front office the customer and provider are interlinked in this service provision. The result is a potential discrepancy in the levels of specification and quality being provided and those defined by the company as desirable. In the back room, this is less of a problem because the system is normally cushioned from the delivery point.

In all parts of the service delivery system it is most important to define both service and quality levels. This will, however, differ depending on the choice of process involved. In jobbing, for instance, an organization sells capability which includes high levels of customization which is reflected in the price. In a fast-food restaurant, the business sells standard products within set options.

Reshaping demand

The first step concerned defining the service and quality levels. With these parameters now established, an organization is able to consider ways of facilitating this control task, one of which is reshaping demand.

1. In the provision of most services, demand can be separated into planned and random. Although the proportions will change from one situation to another, total demand can be made smoother by separating these two perspectives of demand and analysing the pattern of 'random' demand. Once this has been established, then planned demand can be arranged to fill in the troughs as much as possible and so smooth demand. Figure 9.11 shows an application of these tactics in a health care, outpatients clinic.

2. Because of the demand fluctuations, many service organizations have found that they could sell more capacity than they have in peak demand times, but grossly undersell capacity in off-peak times. For this reason it is important to promote off-peak demand. One way to do this is to offer reduced prices to encourage people to use the service in off-peak times. For example, off-peak telephone calls, electricity

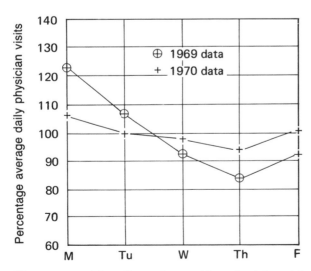

Figure 9.11 The effect of smoothing physician visits by day of week.

Source: E.J. Rising *et al.*, 'A systems analysis of a university health service outpatient clinic', *Operations Research*, 21, no. 5 (1973). With permission.

and passenger train fares and out-of season offers at resort hotels. Another way is to encourage the voluntary spreading of activity away from annual peaks such as 'shop early for Christmas'.

3. A further development open to some service organizations is to offer complementary, secondary services which can be bought whilst waiting for the primary service to become available. For example, many restaurants have created a bar lounge to accommodate customers waiting for a table. Also, video games are often to be found in take-away restaurants for similar reasons.

4. The demand problems facing many service organizations are caused not only by the random nature of customer's orders but also by the variable service times involved (e.g. a doctor's consultation). These difficulties can be reduced by the following ploys:

(a) An appointment service (for example, at a doctor's or dentist's surgery and at a hairdresser). This often improves control over the timing of arrivals, minimizes customer waiting and improves the utilization of capacity.
(b) Similarly, a reservation system helps an organization to formulate a better estimate of demand (the expressed or stated sale as opposed to estimated sales referred to earlier in the chapter) and will also reduce customer disappointment (e.g. hotels and airline bookings).

However, with all these problems, late arrivals and people who do not keep their appointments will disrupt the system.

Controlling capacity

In addition to reshaping demand, it is also necessary to adjust capacity so as to reflect the service needs. There are two aspects to this task.

1. The need to arrange the basic or core capacity required to meet the service needs. This involves forecasting demand, converting demand into service capacity requirements, scheduling the shift coverage to meet the demand patterns through the operations period and then assigning operators to shifts. Where organizations need to provide coverage for twenty-four hours a day, every day of the year, then the choice of shift pattern needs to be made with care. Over the last decade, various solutions to this problem have been developed.[15]

2. The second aspect is to devise ways of altering the provision of capacity so as to overcome some of the demand fluctuations referred to earlier. Options to consider include:

(a) Increasing consumer participation in the service provision wherever possible, for two reasons. The first is to use the capacity inherent within the customer and thereby reduce the overall capacity provision. For example, in fast-food establishments, the consumer orders direct, collects the meal, takes the meal to the table, is encouraged to put the waste in appropriate containers and to return the tray. The second reason, and often the more important, is that the customer's capacity provision has a key resource advantage in that it provides capacity at the exact moment it is required thereby helping to eliminate the provision of capacity additional to the net needs of the actual service requirement.

(b) A second way is to separate capacity into core and secondary provision. Core capacity is geared to meeting the essential or basic needs of the service demands and is normally highly stable in its provision. However, the level of secondary capacity is often adjustable, for example, through part-time staff, and temporary shifts.

(c) Also, it is important to create flexible capacity so as to accommodate demand and service-mix changes. For example, training people to widen their range of skills so as to be able to increase capacity on peak-demand jobs when required (e.g. bank tellers and supermarket checkout staff) and then to switch to non-peak jobs at other times.

Control systems and the choice of process

Once these arrangements have been made then the appropriate operations control system is adopted. For example, large system developments or organizational developments are often best handled by a project process. Tailor-made services or large consultancy assignments are typical of a jobbing requirement. Hospitals and educational institutions are classical batch process situations where different people or groups of people use the same facilities or processes and the need is to schedule effectively the multiple use of resources. Administrative procedures in large organizations are also arranged as a batch process in order to perform different tasks in separate procedures (e.g. order processing and the payment of sales invoices). Some services have moved to a line process (e.g. fast-food restaurants) but these are still quite the exception, whereas continuous processing does not avail itself as a suitable process choice.

Systems similar to those detailed earlier in this chapter could be appropriate ways of handling the requirements of the operations control task involved. However, as might be expected, it is important for organizations to review the appropriateness of their operations control procedures in relation to changes in the overall size of the operations function, in the operations tasks themselves and/or in customer needs. An illustration of this is provided by the Loews Anatole Hotel, Dallas. In the early 1980s this hotel expanded from a 900-room establishment to the largest hotel in the American South West with 1,620 guest rooms, 58 meeting rooms, 8 boardrooms and 6 major ballrooms. Two thousand employees oversee 1.8 million square feet of interior space as well as seven acres of parkland. The operations task involves handling 0.25 million pieces of linen each week in its own laundry, with over 2 million meals a year created by its 14 kitchens. Its other facilities include 19 major restaurants and lounges, two night clubs and its $12 million spa and sports centre.

Initially, the hotel continued with the same operations control system as before to support the day-to-day activities. Not until it recognized that the old system could not support the significant increases in complexity which resulted did the hotel management regain control over the essential support activities for its guests. One major change involved updating the internal communications network which allowed a floor co-ordinator radio contact with one of four houseman teams to service immediately the overall demands on the system. The RUSH network enabled the hotel to re-establish the level of co-ordination essential to supporting the quality levels at the core of the Anatole's service delivery system.[16]

Conclusion

The relationship between an organization's corporate strategy and its operations planning and control is both critical and complex. Critical in that the planning and control function is an essential prerequisite for the effective and efficient provision of the products/services that the business sells. Complex in that the inputs, decisions and time spans which relate to the strategy, planning and control phases differ widely.[17]

Operations planning and control is not solely an operations activity. Its role is to link an organization's market demands with the resultant capacity and supply requirements and to contribute to both the control and flow of products and services through the system. For this critical function to meet the very demanding planning and control requirements of the POM task the means of producing the goods or providing the services must not be separated from either the markets they serve or the way they are controlled through the process. It is essential that the products/services, the process for providing them and the system to plan and control them are developed as integrated facets or parts of the one task. The software provision can no longer be viewed as piecemeal additions to help tune the process. The inherent weakness of inadequate systems can be reduced by adaptation, sound implementation and good management. However, they will continue to be inadequate if the requisite planning and control needs (relevance of information, or timing of its provision) are not available.

In the same way, systems design is frequently developed as a response to a particular problem with little understanding of the interrelated nature of the total system. Systems design and development is too often powered by one perspective of the planning and control issues involved. As a result, the development of operations planning and control systems is often handled in a fragmented way by reviewing one problem at a time and treating it as independent of the other perspectives involved. Similarly, many organizations have attempted to control with a single operations planning and control system a situation with combinations of the different processes described in Chapter 4. The decision to do this has usually been made without adequate appreciation of the different requirements and tasks to be fulfilled in each situation. For as Table 9.3 illustrates, the features of production planning and control differ substantially from one process to another.[18]

At the strategic level, the operations plan represents management's grip on

Table 9.3 A summary of some of the production planning and control features as related to different processes

Process	Key task		Capacity adjustment		Other control features	
	Longer- or medium-term planning	*Short-term control*	*Short-term*	*Longer-term*	*Orientation*	*Information required and provision*
Project	Develop the overall network and any subnetworks for major phases of the task	Organizationally, need to determine the release of capacity to go to other project sites particularly key people and plant. For each project, control linked to critical sets of activities	Very flexible arrangements normally through overtime. Usually used to bring an order back onto schedule or to correct an overcapacity problem in one or more parts of the process	Incremental increases in capacity in line with product/service mix and volume forecasts	Focused on the contract as a whole or through the control of composite parts of the operations involved	The sequence and job times are an integral part of the network analysis. The analysis also distinguishes between critical tasks, and sequential and parallel operations. Control normally exercised by the site manager
Intermittent systems Jobbing	Establish capacity requirements to facilitate realistic planning and delivery estimates	Controlling the orders through the process to meet customer delivery dates and co-ordinate different sets of activities where necessary		Incremental increases through additional labour. In most situations, process investment will be for cost or technology rather than capacity reasons	Order control. Normally, each order is controlled throughout the process	Paperwork includes a route sheet, with estimates against each operation. The supervisor normally controls the work issued for a period against known priorities

Batch	Plan the operations in correct sequence (with alternative routeings) and any investments in the process including inventory levels and hardware and software requirements	Co-ordinating the progress of all parts through the process to come together for the final assembly or compilation	Less flexible arrangements as often the more interrelated process requires these problems to be resolved within the constraints of the capacity balance	Need to adjust or increase capacity in both labour and key processes in line with forecast	The prime concern is order control; however, this necessitates a strong, secondary emphasis on the control of process capacity and process scheduling	Paperwork for each step in the process with details of the operations, standard times (or estimates if not a repetitive order), process alternatives, special instructions and equipment. Work controlled by supervisors and issued to them for a period against known priorities
Continuous systems — Line	To determine the layout configuration in line with capital investment cost and process needs and to establish the materials flow through the system, (including buffer inventory) and total space requirements to meet volume forecasts	To control the rate of flow of all items necessary to meet the assembly requirements of the line. Need all parts for some items, not some parts for all items	Some options may be open. However, requires organizing the group of people necessary to run the process. Therefore has to be planned more ahead of time	Necessitates the provision of a new facility, although some opportunity may be available for marginal increases in capacity	The emphasis is towards flow control. Order control is inherent within the flow process and the concern therefore, is with production levels and scheduling the necessary parts	The work is determined by the line sequence. Jobs well-known by all concerned. Labour standards known or set by the pace of the line. Centralized control
Continuous systems — Continuous processing	To control the rate of flow of raw materials to the process and the shipment of end-products	The process concept is based on continuous running, therefore short-term capacity adjustment is not a consideration	Necessitates the provision of a new facility			The work sequence follows the process layout. Throughputs are pre-set within the process. Centralized control

the business. It forms the policy statement on how the operations function should provide the forecast requirements of the business in terms of output, throughput levels, capacity levels, inventory levels and so forth. In this way it forms the basis of the rough-cut statements of capacity.

The planning task itself, however, is characterized by four major factors:

1. The complexity of the link between products/services and processes in terms of the data parameters. Features within this include volume, product/service range, the task complexity itself, whether the product/service is repeated or not, and the process chosen to complete the tasks.

2. The level of certainty in demand forecasts, capacity provision, product/service supply and the knowledge of the task.

3. The organizational decision on how to cope with the imbalance between demand and capacity and the amount and timing of their provision.

4. The final aspect which compounds or simplifies the other features is the overriding organizational style, level of development in the system and the degree of maintenance or development of the planning and control system over time.

At the control end of the operations task, the real opportunities for development lie in the application of computers to improve the tactical, operational information systems. The creation of the database to store the basic task information not only eliminates storage needs but also reduces the risk of errors in data correction and update, and simplifies the procedure for preparing clear, accurate instructions on what tasks to complete.

However, these control systems should also provide essential management control statements on the process and how well it is providing the essential features of the business.

Control statements and reports

Some of these statements and reports include:

1. *Order turnround* to provide information on delivery performance in general:

   (a) Number of customer complaints.

   (b) Delivery index $= \dfrac{\text{Order required date } - \text{ Order delivered date}}{\text{Average number of orders per month}}$

   (c) Throughput efficiency $= \dfrac{\text{Actual process lead times}}{\text{Planned process lead times}}$

2. *Order backlog (forward load)* to provide an overall review of the demand and capacity situation for the process as a whole or by work-centre:

   (a) Frequency of order backlog $= \dfrac{\text{Average order backlog per month}}{\text{Average number of orders per month}}$

   (b) Rate of order backlog $= \dfrac{\text{Units in order backlog per month}}{\text{Average number of units ordered per month}}$

   (c) Number of backlog orders per month.

3. *Order status and work-centre management* to provide current information on the status of individual orders or about overall operations activity:

   (a) Work-centre efficiency $= \dfrac{\text{Standard hours produced}}{\text{Clocked hours}}$

   (b) Work-centre utilization[19] $= \dfrac{\text{Standard hours produced}}{\text{Available hours}}$

   (c) An order status report showing — the current location of each order; the operations completed and remaining for each order; the expected completion date.

   (d) A report showing the profit or loss for each order.

   (e) A work sequence report showing — orders being worked on; queue orders; arriving orders.

4. *Costs* to provide information on cost performance:

   (a) Cost variance reports showing the actual labour, material or total costs incurred compared with the labour, material or total costs planned for all jobs or only those where the variance is above a specified percentage of planned costs.

   (b) Cost simulation reports to show the effect of material or labour price increases, material substitution and different routeings of a job through the process and the effect these would have on job costs.

5. *Scrap* to monitor scrap levels in the process:

   (a) Scrap rates $= \dfrac{\text{Number of rejects}}{\text{Number of units produced}}$

6. *Inventory* to report the work-in progress (WIP) levels throughout the process:

(a) WIP valuation report to monitor the investment and trends in this inventory category.

(b) Order release rate to record the orders released against planned capacity and reviewed against trends in WIP inventory.

(c) A review of the overall WIP situation to include analyses such as: all WIP orders; overdue orders only.

The choice of what a business decides to control and how it reports and measures those features is important not only in control terms but also in the way that it will shape behaviour and effort towards maintaining and achieving those criteria which make it successful in the market-place. For the key objective of any business organization is not just to make the sale but also to ensure that it retains that customer's future business.

Appendix A: Network analysis

Following on from pp. 208–9, more detailed information on how to draw networks and understand their use is now provided. In addition, this section will be most important when analysing relevant case studies at the end of the book.

Constructing a network

The steps to follow in network construction are:

1. *Planning.* Establish all the activities or steps to be completed, determine the dependency between these activities and draw the network.
2. *Scheduling.* Apply to the network any limiting factors such as time, cost and the availability of materials, equipment and labour. These factors will often necessitate the redrawing of parts of the network to accommodate the constraints they impose.
3. *Controlling.* The task of obtaining feedback during the project to ensure adherence to the plan, and to update the plan in the light of any changes which occur.

1 Planning

The first task is to establish and list all the activities necessary to complete the project and at the level of detail already agreed (see p. 209). This step will be invaluable as part of the overall control of the project. Following this, it is necessary to determine which activities depend upon which other activities being completed before they can start; this is described as dependency. The final task is to draw the network. Several examples of these tasks are provided later. However, the following general guidelines will prove useful when setting about the task of drawing a network. The symbols used throughout are explained on p. 209.

1. All activities start and end with an event.
2. An activity is a time-consuming task.
3. An event is instantaneous. Its occurrence means that all activities entering that event sign have now been completed and therefore all activities leaving that event sign can now be started.
4. Any number of activities can go into and out of an event.
5. Activities, wherever possible, should go from left to right.
6. Activities occurring on the same path are sequential and are thus directly dependent upon each other.
7. Activities on different paths are termed parallel activities, are independent of other sets of parallel activities and can, therefore, take place at the same time.
8. Dummy activities are used in two ways:

    (a) as an aid to drawing the network. As such they form part of the set of conventions to be followed; thus, two or more activities cannot leave one event sign and enter the same end event sign (see Figures 9A.1 and 9A.2);
    (b) as the way of extending the dependency of one or more activities to other activities (see Figure 9A.3).

The role of the dummy activity is, therefore, to facilitate the presentation of networks and to extend the dependency function to other, relevant activities which is the essence of the network concept. Dummy activities, therefore, are not time-consuming (this is already covered by the original activity) and hence their name.

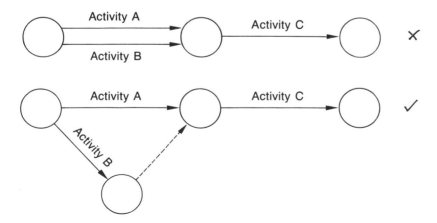

Figure 9A.1   Introducing the use of a dummy activity.

To explain, the following example lists the activities to be undertaken to complete a task and indicates those activities on which an activity is dependent. Therefore, activity B cannot start until activity A has been completed and so on.

Activity	Activities on which it is dependent
A	—
B	A
E	A
C	B
D	B
F	C, D
G	E
H	F, G

The resulting network is shown as Figure 9A.2. It starts with activity A as the only activity which does not depend upon any other activity before it can start. Then the rest of the activities are built into the network to represent the statement of the task.

2 Scheduling

The next step is to schedule the network. This involves applying the limiting factors of time, cost and so on. In the example detailed in Table 9A.1 the activities are given for the production of an educational cassette with the number of days it takes

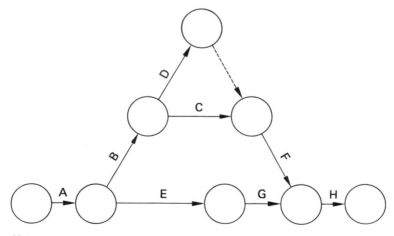

Notes
Activities A, E, G and H are examples of sequential activities.
Activities B, C and F are parallel to activities E and G.

Figure 9A.2 Network representing the task above.

Table 9A.1 The activities involved in preparing an educational cassette

Activity		Duration (working days)
1	Client briefing	4
2	Write draft 1	7
3	Await client approval of draft 1	5
4	Write draft 2	6
5	Await client approval of draft 2	5
6	Create the production script (PS)	3
7	Await client approval of the PS	2
8	Produce the cassette tape of the PS	5
9	Book studios	1
10	Confirm studio booking	1
11	Send script to the actors	1
12	Actors prepare the scripts	2
13	Complete artwork roughs	1
14	Await client approval of artwork roughs	5
15	Send artwork roughs to artist	1
16	Fine artwork and typesetting by artist	10
17	Check fine artwork and photocopy	2
18	Send copy of artwork to three printers	1
19	Await quotations of printers re artwork	3
20	Accept printer's quotation	1
21	Send artwork and confirmation to the printer	1
22	Artwork printed	10
23	Send artwork prints and cassette tapes to a duplicating house	1
24	Tapes duplicated and matched to artwork prints	10
25	Deliver to client	1

Notes
1. This list describes the sequence of tasks involved in the production of an educational cassette for a client. The consultant engaged in this work was able to vary his working week by working the odd Saturday or Sunday in order to meet any necessary deadlines, but this is to be regarded as the exception rather than the rule. However, for the purpose of this task, any parallel activities requiring the consultant's time should be regarded as not being able to be completed at the same time. All times are given in whole days even though some activities may only take a few minutes.
2. The numbering of the activities is for reference purposes only.
3. The earliest the studios can be booked is following activity 3.
4. Once activity 6 is complete, activities 10 and 11 can start.
5. Artwork roughs can be completed after activity 3 is complete.

to complete an activity. All the tasks, unless specified, are completed by the consultant running the business. Note that the time units in which duration is expressed must be common for activities, should reflect the task on hand and can be in hours, days, weeks or even months. From this information the resulting network is shown as Figure 9A.3. There are three further points to note from this figure:

(a) Activity descriptions, often abbreviated, are written above the line of the arrow

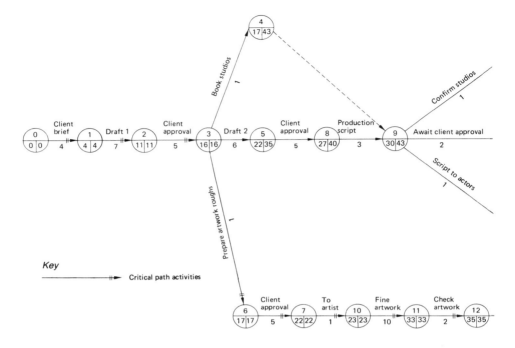

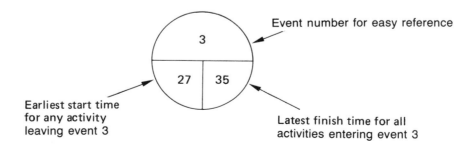

Figure 9A.3 Network for the activities given in Table 9A.1 for preparing an educational cassette.

symbol. It is important to avoid using references where possible (often difficult with a computer program) because it makes the reading of the network laboured and may lead to mistakes being made.

(b) The time duration for an activity is written below the line of the arrow.
(c) The event signs (known as nodes) have been used to provide additional information. This is explained in Figure 9A.4.[20,21]

Figure 9A.4 Explanation of the information contained in an event node.

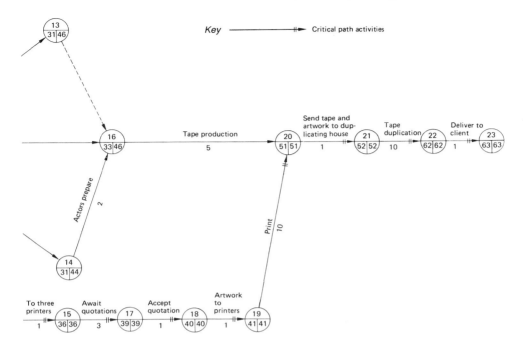

Earliest start time is calculated from the beginning of the network by cumulating the time units for all sequential activities. It expresses the earliest time by which any activity leaving the particular event can start. Where two or more activities enter an event then the activity to finish last will be that which establishes the earliest start time for any subsequent activities. The final event sign contains the planned finish time for the project.

Latest finish time is calculated from the finish of the network. The same cumulative time as that entered in the earliest start time segment of the final event node is entered in the latest finish time segment of that node. Then the duration of activities is successively subtracted from this finish date and entered into the appropriate event sign. Where two or more activities back into one event, then the earliest of the cumulative times will determine the latest finish time for all previous activities in order that time additional to the planned time is not added to the task in hand.

Of essential interest in project scheduling is the minimum length of time it will take to complete the project. This is determined by *critical path analysis*. To do this it is necessary to find the longest path through the network. Each task on the critical path, moreover, is called a critical activity. The path and activities are called critical because delays on any of these activities will increase the overall length of the project. The critical nature of these tasks is also shown by the fact that the earliest start and latest finish times recorded in the series of events on the critical path are the same. For these activities there is no flexibility; if the start is delayed, the project will be delayed. The critical path is then marked in one of several ways, see Figure 9A.3 for example.

However, when activities do not fall on the critical path, some delay will have no effect on the completion time for the project. The extent of the delay before the overall time is affected is the difference between the earliest start time and the latest finish time less the activity duration. This is known as total float or slack[22] and is usually entered on the network diagram as part of the information necessary for the controlling phase of the project.[21]

3 Controlling

A network is a control mechanism. Therefore, information on the tasks completed and delays anticipated or incurred need to be fed back so that the network can be updated. Knowledge of these changes and the impact they have on the project as a whole are essential for three important reasons:

(a) It is a prerequisite for the control to be effective.
(b) It allows decisions to be made throughout the life of the project on the best course of action to take in the light of changing circumstances. The network readily helps managers to appreciate the impact of delays. This then allows them to consider in advance what action to take (with knowledge of the consequences) on aspects such as cost and completion dates, rather than in a crisis with insufficient time to evaluate alternative courses of action.
(c) Out-of-date networks will soon fall into disrepute and managers will stop using them.

The details discussed so far form the basis for network analysis and have introduced the concepts of scheduling the limiting factors and the task of controlling the project as it progresses. It is not intended here to go into further detail. However, there are some important points of which the operations manager should be aware:

1. The examples provided are intentionally simple. Network analysis is normally used for complex tasks consisting of many interrelated activities.
2. Although one-off projects are the most frequent tasks for which network analysis is used, it is also applied to tasks which will be repeated. Its purpose in these situations is to establish the best way to complete the interrelated activities involved, and this is then used on future occasions. The production of an educational cassette is an example of this application (see Table 9A.1 and Figure 9A.3).
3. In complex project applications, there are usually several sets of constraints that need to be accounted for within the network. This chapter refers to the use of critical path analysis (CPA). However, there are many more applications which provide for the more sophisticated requirements of complex one-off projects. These include PERT (programme evaluation review techniques), resource levelling and precedence diagrams.[21]

4. One important safeguard to incorporate into any network is the concept of target or key dates. This provides phases within the project at which reviews can take place and, more importantly, helps to prevent float or slack from one phase in the project being used up at an earlier stage. If this is not carefully controlled then projects can use up float prematurely and create a situation in which the end phases have little or no float and hence several sets of activities become unnecessarily critical.

Appendix B: Material requirements planning

Within the body of this chapter a synopsis of material requirements planning (MRP) was given both as an overview and to help provide the basis for comparing this with other production/operations control systems. This appendix provides a more detailed coverage of this important system.

Figure 9B.1 is a general model of a planning and control system depicting MRP as the control function on which it is based and providing details of the inputs and outputs of the system. As shown in the figure, the total MRP system consists of several elements — the inputs, the package itself which carries out the calculations, and the output reports. The general model depicted here may differ in details of content and the descriptions used, depending upon the organization and the products in question, but it is important to appreciate the purpose of these elements in order to understand the basis on which MRP is structured. The principal components are now explained.

Master production schedule

The master production schedule (MPS) is a management commitment to produce certain quantities of finished products in particular time periods. To do this it takes statements of demand (both forecast sales and known orders) and tests them against statements of capacity and resources (aggregate plans and short-term elements of capacity). The result is an anticipated schedule of finished products. As such, it is a statement of production and not of market demand:[23] that is, the MPS is not a forecast and should not be confused with such. Sales forecasts are a major input into the master production scheduling function. However, by taking into account capacity limitations as well as the desire to utilize capacity fully, the master production schedule will optimize these requirements when forming its statement of what is to be produced. Thus, the system highlights problems but the master production schedule resets levels to match capacity; in this way the MPS forms the basic communication link with manufacturing. It is a schedule and thus states requirements in terms of product specifications (e.g. part numbers) for which bills of materials exist. Thus, the detailed schedule produced by the MPS drives the MRP systems, the shopfloor and purchasing records and systems.

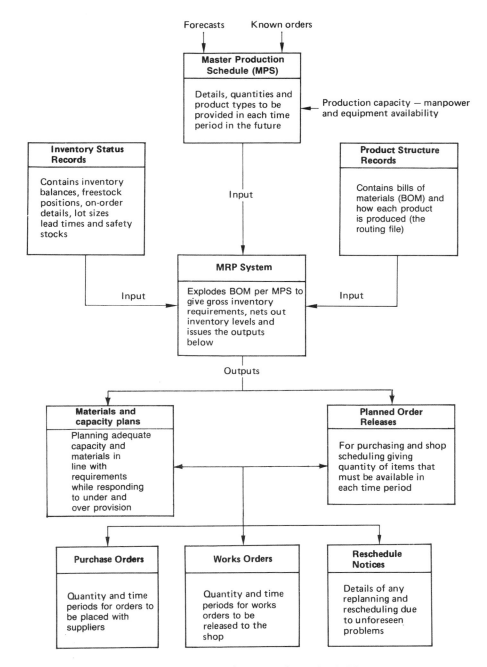

Figure 9B.1   Details of inputs to and outputs from the MRP system.

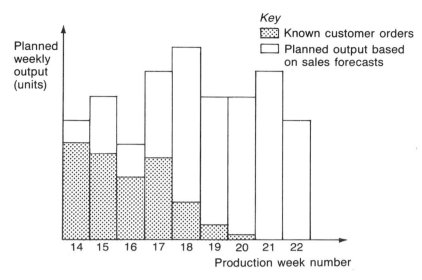

Figure 9B.2 Master production schedule for a given product at a given point in time.

An MPS is created for each finished product using known customer orders, sales forecasts and a knowledge of manufacturing capacity. It is likely that the schedule will contain a major proportion of firm customer orders in the more immediate time periods and will be based mostly on forecasts in the later periods of the planning horizon as shown in Figure 9B.2. The length of the planning horizon is determined by calculating the total lead time for the product (material lead time plus process lead time — see p. 48 and pp. 198–9) and adding a period of time to allow the purchasing function visibility over the future so that price and delivery advantages can be secured (see Figure 9B.3).

For many companies, the resultant planning horizon will be several months. It will, therefore, be impractical not to allow changes to an MPS, particularly for time periods well into the future. One method of controlling changes to the MPS is to split the planning horizon into time zones, each of which has different rules concerning acceptable levels of change (see Figure 9B.3).

Material requirements planning system

The MPS formed the 'front end' of the planning and control system; material requirements planning (MRP) is at the centre of, or is the 'engine' phase of the system.[24] MRP's primary purpose is to take the period-by-period (time-phased) statements of specific products required from the MPS and produce a time-phase set of subassembly, components and raw material requirements. The MRP package

Current period   Future periods

Level of change allowed

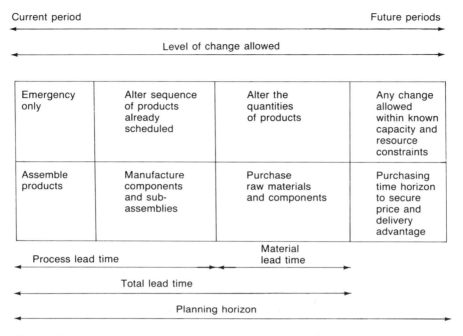

Emergency only	Alter sequence of products already scheduled	Alter the quantities of products	Any change allowed within known capacity and resource constraints
Assemble products	Manufacture components and sub-assemblies	Purchase raw materials and components	Purchasing time horizon to secure price and delivery advantage

Process lead time   Material lead time

Total lead time

Planning horizon

Figure 9B.3 MPS planning horizons and rules concerning the level of allowed change.
Source: adapted from the Open University Manufacturing Systems Engineering Programme, Materials Requirement Planning (MRP) module (1988), figure 5.

completes these calculations on a level by level basis thus converting the MPS of independent demand statements of finished products into planned or suggested orders for dependent demand parts. To do this it requires 'bill of materials' information (including relevant engineering change data) for relevant products, together with 'inventory status data' in order to make the necessary adjustments. Therefore, it acts as a translator of the overall plans for production into the detailed individual steps necessary to accomplish those plans. It thus provides the link between the 'front end' of the business and the necessary outputs on which the planning and control system within manufacturing works.

In an MRP system, therefore, the MPS equates to the order-book translated into production requirements. Thus, the MRP system often creates 'anonymous' order quantities within the overall system in order to reduce the number of set-ups or make-readies required. It then segregates orders into constituent elements and reassembles the total order requirement (known or forecast) as aggregate shopfloor order quantities of detailed parts, suitably scheduled to meet assembly requirements.

The system is designed to ensure minimum WIP inventory, whilst providing a significant reduction in set-ups by order quantity aggregation. However, anonymous batching of requirements hampers programme management as it makes the monitoring of a particular customer's requirements more difficult to accomplish. As shopfloor order quantities do not carry sufficient identity, reporting structures are based on part numbers rather than customer order information. Thus urgent jobs are put together with less urgent jobs, with details identifying this urgency being released only when a complete order quantity is finished.

Product structure records

The product structure records provide information on materials/components (the bill of materials) and how each product is made (the routeing file). The bill of material (BOM) is a file or set of files which contains the 'recipe' for each finished product. The recipe consists of information regarding the materials, components and subassemblies which make up each finished product and is held on what is often known as a product structure file. It, therefore, constitutes the specification or formula for relevant products (see Figure 9B.4). In addition, a parts master file contains all the standard information about each item including part number, description, unit of measure, process lead time, materials lead time, purchase order quantities, buffer stock holding and inventory data.

Depending upon the complexity of the product structure, there will be a number of levels within a bill of materials. The end-item itself is usually level 0. The components (subassemblies, parts and raw materials) which together make the end-item will be listed in the parts explosion and designated level 1. Any level 1 components which have themselves a components list will, in turn, be exploded as level 2 and so on. In some organizations certain item categories (e.g. bought-in components and raw materials) will all have the same level designation. This explosion would then be completed for all components across all products. The requirements for each component would be accumulated plus any independent demand (e.g. for spare parts) and these would then be batched to provide delivery

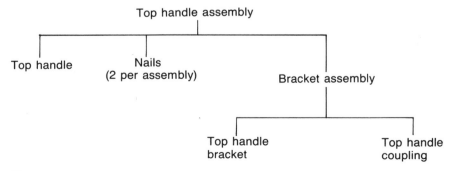

Figure 9B.4　The bill of materials for a 'top handle assembly' which forms part of a snow shovel.

plans. Using the delivery times and product lead time, a release schedule for each order to meet final assembly is then determined.

In addition, it is frequently preferable to identify a component requirement with the higher-level component or end-item for which it is to be used. This is known as *pegging* and provides a partial listing which identifies, at a desired level of detail, where requirements come from and are to be used. This can often be of help when rescheduling.

The routing file provides information on the preferred sequence of operations to be undertaken to complete the components and subassemblies together with other possible routings.

Inventory status records

The inventory status file keeps a record of all transactions and balance of inventory throughout the organization. The transactions are mainly receipts, issues, and adjustments as a result of inspection reports or physical inventory checks. As the degree of control required will vary, the level at which inventory records are kept will also vary. Where greater control is required then the WIP inventory condition may be separated into a number of different stages within the total process. This enables relevant components and subassemblies to be monitored from one predetermined stage (or even operation) to the next.

As with product structures, the main requirements of inventory status information are accuracy and timeliness as they are critical to the running of the MRP system and their absence would undermine the very usefulness of the output reports which form the basis of the manufacturing and purchasing plans.

For organizations with diversified product lines MRP is practical only with some form of data processing. Without this aid it would normally be difficult to calculate requirements for complex assemblies with each change in the schedule. MRP provides a control and information system in the co-ordination of all the manufacturing decisions from finished goods, raw material/component and WIP inventory levels and the scheduling and rescheduling of raw materials and components through manufacturing to final assembly and inspection. It does this by time-phasing requirements by quantity, based on a due-date planning system for higher-level items.

There are two approaches to MRP — *regeneration* and *net change*. With regeneration, previous plans are discarded and a new master schedule is calculated at the beginning of each time period. Each time, the master schedule of forecast requirements for the independent items is exploded into the gross component requirements, available inventories are deducted and net requirements form the new planned orders for dependent items. With net change,[25] only changes from the last master schedule are exploded down through the bill of materials until a component is reached that is unaffected by the change.

Basic MRP records

The basic MRP record is a representation of the status and plans for each item. This is shown as a time-phased record giving anticipated future usage, available balances, scheduled receipts at the beginning of the period, planned orders and planned inventory at the end of the period — see Figure 9B.5.

A key element of the MRP system is the gross to net explosion. This is the procedure for translating product requirements into component part requirements whilst taking existing inventories and scheduled receipts into account. Only the requirements net of any inventory or scheduled receipts are considered, as shown in Figure 9B.6. Thus, the gross net relationship is not only the basis for calculating appropriate quantities but also the communication link between part numbers.

Period			1	2	3	4	5
Gross requirements				10		40	10
Scheduled receipts			50				
Projected available balance		4	54	44	44	4	44
Planned order	releases				50		
	receipts					50	

Lead time = 1 period
Shopfloor order quantity
or lot size = 50
Minimum balance = 4

Figure 9B.5   The basic MRP record.

Source: based on T.E. Vollman, W.L. Berry and D.C. Whybark, *Manufacturing Planning and Control Systems*, 2nd edn (Homewood, Ill.: Irwin, 1988), figure 2.2.

Part description	Part number	Inventory	Scheduled receipts	Gross requirements	Net requirements
Top handle assembly	13122	25	—	100	75
Top handle	457	22	25	75	28
Nail (2 required)	082	4	50	150	96
Bracket assembly	11495	27	—	75	48
Top handle bracket	129	15	—	48	33
Top handle coupling	1118	39	15	48	—

Figure 9B.6   Gross and net requirement for the top handle assembly of a snow shovel.

Source: Vollman, Berry and Whymark, *op. cit.*, figure 2.5. With permission.

Therefore, it underpins the concept of dependent demand. To calculate the latter, bills of materials, inventory status and scheduled receipts are all necessary. The concept of dependent demand is often called the fundamental principle of MRP as it provides the way to remove uncertainty from the requirement calculations.[26]

Output reports of MRP systems

The principal outputs of an MRP system are the executive instructions, in the form of different levels of reports, to make or purchase items. The initial phase concerns statements, both in terms of materials and capacity, of planned order releases in terms of manufacture and purchased parts. As shown in Figure 9B.1, the MRP outputs at this point form plans and not committed actions. Thus they are easy to change (and need to be so as account has to be taken of known material and capacity provision) which is one important reason for not converting plans into actions any earlier than necessary.

The next phase, however, is to convert these plans into commitments. These take the form of scheduled receipts (see the entry in Figure 9B.5) which commits material and capacity to the manufacture of relevant parts and/or authorizes the purchase of appropriate bought-out items, work orders and purchase orders respectively.

Appendix C: Just-in-time

Some of the important issues to be taken into account when considering the introduction of JIT were provided earlier in the chapter. This appendix addresses the more detailed aspects of these systems.

Achieving JIT

Just-in-time advantages concern the pursuit of zero inventories. However, equal to this objective is the resulting reduction in costs associated with the control not only of inventories but also of manufacturing.

The most important feature of JIT applications is replacing discrete order quantities with production rates. Thus it replaces the time-based principle of MRP with a rate-based one. To achieve this switch, and the advantages which go with it, the programme of change has several elements.

1. *Physical changes.* There are several physical changes which need to be accomplished in the system, including:

(a) The fundamental aim of JIT is to create a manufacturing requirement which moves towards the characteristics of a line process (see Chapter 4). To achieve this requires the development of a manufacturing task which has the basic volume requirements necessary to underpin the investments involved and which allows the creation of a series of processes which are as near to the coupled nature of line as is appropriate. The extent to which this is feasible will be determined by process choice arguments similar to those explained in Chapter 4. The facets of the development include:

— product simplification in terms of range and degree of standardization (see Chapter 3);
— mixed mode assembly to allow the concurrent manufacture of different products on the same process (see Chapter 4, p. 75).

(b) Set-up time reduction and a drive to reduce order quantities to one. This is necessary to enable components, subassemblies and final assemblies to be made in line with demand and to be unaffected by the length of time it takes to prepare the process.

— layout changes are arranged so that the flow of products follows a consistent pattern in terms of the preferred product billed routeing (see Figure 9C.1);
— the manufacturing arrangements are often based on autonomous cells, each being responsible for its own manufacturing tasks and the supply to and from adjacent cells;
— smoothed line billed rate to achieve consistency with the characteristics of available process capacity;
— preventive maintenance programmes (see Chapter 13) normally support JIT initiatives in order to help remove the causes of uncertainty and waste, especially in a manufacturing arrangement with minimum WIP inventory;
— standard containers to hold predetermined quantities are used in order to fix material levels, and as part substitute for a control/paperwork system.

(c) Improved quality through the process. The pursuit of improved quality and the use of statistical control techniques (see Chapter 12) results in lower costs and the elimination of both process stoppages and the need to hold inventories.

2. *Worker involvement.* The role of the worker within the process is also radically changed in the following ways:

(a) Their day-to-day role is broader in terms of the job content. Often working in a manufacturing cell (see above) each worker is trained to complete all relevant tasks. In addition, the depth of the job is increased by including aspects of planning and evaluation (see Chapter 14). This not only improves the quality of the task but also means that when there is no active work to complete (in JIT the authority to make an order quantity must be received before work can commence) then workers can do planning and evaluating tasks which are now forms of 'legitimate' work. However, in more traditional systems, when there is no scheduled work to do then the choice is between making inventory and recording 'excess' labour.

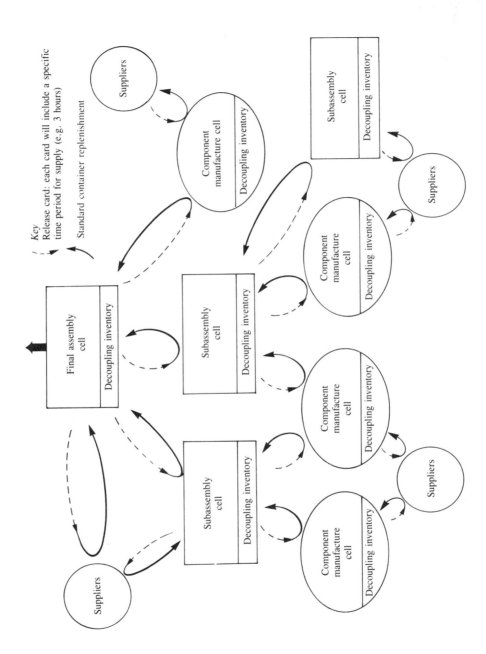

Figure 9C.1   Simplified manufacturing unit controlled by a JIT system.

(b) As part of (a), the worker assumes responsibility for quality checks completed during the process (see Chapter 12). This includes responsibility for stopping the process if a quality defect is discovered.

(c) The increased involvement of workers is also designed to use their knowledge to improve the system as part of the drive for continuous improvement.

3. *Control system changes*. JIT has an impact upon all areas of planning and control systems, but principally within the shopfloor and purchasing systems. The objective of a JIT system is to ensure that all materials in the process are active, and in order to do this, steady schedules need to be supported by a drive towards shorter set-up times so that appropriate quantities of components/sub-assemblies can be delivered to each stage of the process. To enhance the basic quantity factor, standard containers designed to hold agreed quantities are introduced. Lastly, a card-type system (Kanban, action plate and DOPS were mentioned earlier, p. 218) is the basis of all transactions. This document is the authority to produce, and only on receipt of it can work be started. Figure 9C.1 provides an outline chart illustrating materials flow in a simplified manufacturing business. The last module in this illustration is the final assembly cell which makes the end product. As a demand-pull type material flow system, the final assembly will withdraw a standard container of work from a small quantity of decoupling inventory (see Chapter 10). Part of this transaction includes sending the release card to the previous appropriate cell. In turn, this latter cell is now authorized to make a standard quantity of components or subassemblies. To do this, it withdraws from its own small quantity of decoupling inventory a standard container of components/subassemblies. Again as part of this transaction, this cell also releases a card to its 'supplying' cell and so on. Similar arrangements are also developed with suppliers as illustrated in Figure 9C.1.

By striving continuously to reduce set-ups and WIP inventory, the production system is simplified in control terms and requires less inventory material to support transactions and process dependencies. As a result, inventory levels continue to decline and the basis of control is simplified still further.

However, given the instability of the market-place described in Figure 9.1, in order to achieve the high level of stability necessary to underpin a JIT system the 'core' has to be effectively cushioned. This is achieved in two principal ways:

(a) Schedules are fixed. This justifies one of the prerequisites listed earlier that such a system needs to be end-user drive.

(b) Finished goods inventory is held. Thus, when demand is lower than output, inventory will be created to sell in a later period (known as capacity-related inventory — see Chapter 10). Figure 9C.2 shows the inventory holding at a Mitsubishi sales outlet in California. The finished goods inventory at the time totalled 284, 2-cwt vans of standard design over a given range of colours. Similar finished goods inventory is also illustrated in Figure 9C.3.

From these general requirements it can be deduced that JIT applications are suitable to the regular schedules of repetitive manufacturing and not to

Figure 9C.2 Finished goods inventory at a Mitsubishi outlet in California.

Figure 9C.3 Finished goods inventory at a Nissan outlet across the street from the Mitsubishi outlet shown in Figure 9C.2.

the irregular work demands associated with one-off, low volume batch processes providing the needs of markets with uncertain and intermittent demands: a matter to be addressed when considering which control system reflects the characteristics of a particular business. It is equally important to recognize that a manufacturing company may require more than one type of planning and control system to meet the differing business needs within one plant.

At a more detailed level, there are a number of shopfloor prerequisites to be met in order to support the conceptual base of a JIT system, including:

(a) The schedule must be level, which means not only that every day's workload must be equal, but also that the sequence of items to be assembled must be nearly identical for an extended period.

(b) Schedules must be frozen for a period of time, typically four weeks. To do this, a company should be able to use the final assembly schedule as the master production schedule. This, in turn, necessitates getting the cumulative process lead times sufficiently short to eliminate the need for parts holdings at an intermediate level.

(c) Routings must be fixed to allow all fabrication or parts manufacture schedules to follow closely the final assembly schedule.

(d) A large number of set-ups will be completed each day in order to support the basis of making only as required. Consequently, set-ups must be very short.

(e) Order quantities must be small and fixed: a rule of thumb is to have them equivalent to one-tenth of the daily requirement.

(f) The plant must run according to the level schedule over a weekly period, although ± 10 per cent deviation may be accommodated on a given day.

(g) Quality levels must be high to reduce rework and to increase the certainty of both capacity provision and schedules.

(h) Equipment must function which necessitates diligent preventive maintenance.

(i) Non-standard products are scheduled at the end/beginning of an appropriate time slot (e.g. day/week).

(j) The principle of labour utilization should not be the basis on which the schedule is determined. This, in turn, requires that those involved are trained to cope with a wide range of tasks in order to provide the necessary capacity requirements demanded by a changing product mix.

(k) The workforce must participate in making improvements in order to monitor the existing system to ensure that quality levels are maintained in the short-term and to achieve continuous improvements in the future. The goal is, therefore, correct rather than hurried work.

Notes and references

1. Special implies that the product/service will not be repeated or the time interval between orders will be lengthy. Standard implies that the product/service will be repeated. However, many organizations decide to produce a standard product or provide a standard service only on receipt of a customer's order or schedule (i.e. on a make-to-order basis). In most service industries it is impossible to produce a service ahead of demand. Also, in many manufacturing businesses the decision is made not to produce ahead of demand but to use order backlog (forward load) as the mechanism for handling fluctuations in orders.

2. See T.E. Vollman, W.L. Berry and D.C. Whybark, *Manufacturing Planning and Control Systems*, 2nd edn (Homewood, Ill.: Irwin, 1988) for a comprehensive statement and explanation of approaches to the planning and control task. Their general model of a manufacturing planning and control system is drawn upon throughout this chapter and is used specifically in the later section on material requirements planning.

3. The effects on aggregate planning on the learning curve are discussed in R.J. Ebert, 'Aggregate planning with learning curve productivity', *Management Science*, 23, no. 2 (1976).

4. More information on aggregate planning is available in many of the articles and standard textbooks on production/operations management. For example: E.E. Adam and R.J. Ebert, *Production and Operations Management*, 4th edn (Englewood Cliffs, NJ: Prentice Hall, Inc., 1989); R.B. Chase and N.J. Aquilano, *Production and Operations Management: A life cycle approach*, 5th edn (Homewood, Ill.: Irwin, 1989); L.J. Krajewski and L.P. Ritzman, *Operations Management: Strategy and analysis*, 2nd edn (Reading, Mass.: Addison-Wesley, 1990); S. Eilon, 'Five approaches to aggregate production planning', *AIIE Transactions* (June 1975), 118–31, and T.E. Vollman, W.L. Berry and D.C. Whybark, *op. cit.*, and A.N. Moore, 'Aggregate planning in health care foodservice systems with varying technologies', *Journal of Operations Management*, 5, no. 1 (1985).

5. However, this is not normally an important factor in jobbing, as the purpose of the process investment here is mainly a combination of support for the product/service range offered and to facilitate the skilled worker in completing the task.

6. For further information refer to B.M. Worrall and M.M. Sivaresan, 'A production scheduling technique for a job shop system, paper presented at the Fourth Conference on Production Research, Tokyo, 1977.

7. The range of items made on a line may sometimes be quite wide. For example, with mixed and multi-model products.

8. As explained in Chapter 4, the use of a line process in a service organization is limited whilst continuous processing is never used.

9. One of the earliest statements providing this definition comes from R.J. Schonberger, *Japanese Manufacturing Techniques: Nine Hidden Lessons in Simplicity* (New York: Free Press, 1982) p. 16.

10. For further information refer to D.O. Nellmann and L.F. Smith, 'Just-in-time vs just-in-case production/inventory systems', *Production and Inventory Management*, 23, no. 2: 12–21; R.H. Hayes, 'Why Japanese factories work', *Harvard Business Review* (July/August 1981), 56–66; K. Ackerman, 'Just-in-time manufacturing', *Corporate Board*, 9 (May/June, 1988), 18–22; L. Krajawski, *et al.*, 'Kanban, MRP and shaping the manufacturing environment', *Management Science*, 33, no. 1 (1987), 39–57; A.T. Sadhwani and M.H. Sarhan, 'Putting JIT manufacturing systems to work' (Just-in-time manufacturing and operating systems), *Business* 37, (April/June, 1987), 30–7; R.J. Schonberger, 'Just-in-time production systems: replacing complexity with simplicity in manufacturing management', *Industrial Engineering*, 16, no. 10 (1984), 52–63.

11. This list is taken from Terry Hill, *Small Business: Production/operations management* (London: Macmillan Education, 1987), p. 148.

12. A comprehensive summary of OPT and its contributions to all parts of a manufacturing planning and control system is provided in Vollman, Berry and Whybark, *op. cit.*, pp. 844–56.
13. Vollman, Berry and Whybark, *op. cit.*, p. 845.
14. OPT principles are well described in E.M. Goldrate and J. Cox, *The Goal: Excellence in Manufacturing* (New York: North River Press, 1984) as well as a four-part series of articles by Bob Fox entitled 'OPT — an answer for America', *Inventories and Production*, 2 and 3 (1982, 1983).
15. K.R. Baker and M.J. Magazine, 'Workforce scheduling with cyclic demands and day-off constraints', *Management Service*, 24, no. 2 (1977).
16. Further details of the Anatole's response to the increase in service complexity is given in the American Productivity Center's *Productivity Letter*, 5, no. 13 (1986), 1–2.
17. R. Van Dierdonck and J.G. Miller's 'Designing production planning and control systems', *Harvard Business School Working Paper Series HBS 79–74* (revised April 1980) presents a contingency model designed to explain differences in production planning and control systems as related to a firm's competitive strategy.
18. J.L.J. Machin and L.S. Wilson 'Closing the gap between planning and control', *Long Range Planning*, 12 (April 1979), 16–32 gives a list of the 'more obvious and critical attributes' of both planning and control.
19. Work-centre utilization relates normally to the equipment provision in a work-centre.
20. In more complex networks the event node often contains more information.
21. The following books treat network analysis in depth and provide the more detailed information and analyses often used in the control of complex projects: A. Battersby, *Network Analysis for Planning and Scheduling* (Basingstoke: Macmillan, 1978); P.J. Burman, *Precedence Networks for Project Planning and Control* (Maidenhead: McGraw-Hill, 1982); J.D. Wiest and F.K. Levy, *A Management Guide to PERT/CPM* (Englewood Cliffs, NJ: Prentice Hall, Inc., 1977).
22. Strictly speaking these are not the same, and in complex networks it may be important to distinguish between them. In many instances, though, this would not be a worthwhile exercise.
23. Several ideas and illustrations in this section are taken from T.E. Vollman, W.L. Berry and D.C. Whybark, *Manufacturing Planning and Control Systems*, 2nd edn (Homewood, Ill.: Irwin, 1988). It offers detailed insights into the concepts and working of these systems. This particular reference in on p. 297.
24. Vollman, Berry, Whybark, *op. cit.*, p. 35.
25. Net change may also be required to accommodate changes due to amending item master record data, any unplanned inventory movement or alterations to minimum inventory records, lead times or purchase order quantities.
26. Vollman, Berry and Whybark, *op. cit.*, p. 43.

Further reading

Anderson, J.C. *et al.*, 'Material requirements planning systems: the state of the art', Operations Management Program Working Paper (Graduate School of Business Administration, University of Minnesota, 1980).

Anderson, J.C. *et al.*, *Material Requirements Planning: A study of implementation and practice* (American Production and Inventory Control Society, 1981).

Berry, W.L., Tallow, W.J. and Boe, W.J., 'Product structure analysis: a key element in the design of manufacturing planning and control systems', Working Paper 3-30-87 (College of Business Administration, University of Iowa, 1987).

Collins, R.S. and Vollman, T.E., 'Improved productivity through manufacturing planning and control (MPC) systems', paper presented at the Second International Working Seminar on Production Economics, Lans/Innsbruck, Austria, 16–20 February 1981.

Edwards, J.N., 'Integrating MRPII with JIT', *Control* (October/November 1988), 45–53.

Hall, R.E. and Vollman, T.E., 'Planning your material requirements', *Harvard Business Review* (September/October 1978), 105–12.

Lofti, V. and Pegels, C.C., *Decision Support Systems for Production and Operations Management* (Homewood, Ill.: Irwin, 1986).

Morris, B. and Johnson, R., 'Dealing with inherent variability: the difference between manufacturing and service?', *IJOPM*, 7, no. 4 (1987), 13–22.

Nicholson, T.A.J., 'Regaining understanding of the production and inventory control system', *BIPCS Proceedings 17–20 November 1987*, 89–101.

Northcraft, G.B. and Chase, R.B., 'A model for managing service organisation demand at the point of delivery', Working Paper (Department of Management and Policy, University of Arizona).

Plossl, G.W., *Manufacturing Control, the Last Frontier for Profits* (Reston, Virginia: Reston, 1973).

Plossl, G.W. and Wight, O.W., *Production and Inventory Control* (Englewood Cliffs, NJ: Prentice Hall Inc., 1967).

Shingo, W., *Study of Toyota Production System from Industrial Engineering Viewpoint* (Japan Management Association, 1981).

Sugawara, K. *et al.*, 'An advanced MRP programme based on parts demand/supply characteristics', paper presented at the Fourth Conference on Production Research, Tokyo, 1977.

Tallon, W.J. and Berry, W.L., 'An experimental comparison of master production scheduling techniques for assemble-to-order products', Working Paper (College of Business Administration, University of Iowa, 1987).

Wallace, T.F., *MRPII: Making it happen* (Brattleboro, Vt: Oliver Wight Publications, 1985).

Waterlow, J.G. and F.J. Clouder Richards, *Report on the CAPM Workshop and Tutorial, Bristol 6–7 September 1988* (ACME, Science and Engineering Research Council, 1988).

Chapter 10

Materials control

Inventory as a current asset

The way that an organization uses its funds and then controls and monitors these investments is a critical management function. Table 10.1 gives extracts from the balance sheets of eight UK companies. The largest single investment for each is inventory: large both in itself and in relation to other uses of funds. The data are summarized in Table 10.2. It makes sense, then, that companies should both analyse inventory investment in terms such as its return and how it relates to sales, and ensure that the degree of control exercised matches the high investment involved.

However, inventory management, although important, is not usually allocated sufficient resources or given adequate attention. Whilst decisions to use funds for plant and equipment purchases are usually carefully judged and monitored, the effort normally put into controlling inventory is relatively low and usually comes too late. Increases in inventory invariably happen first and a company becomes concerned about controlling them later. There are several reasons for this inverse degree of control:

1. Inventory is an inherent part of a company's operations. When production exceeds sales, or purchases exceed production, inventory increases. Thus it is a consequence of a company's day-to-day activities. With equipment purchases, however, the investment is invariably made following a conscious decision.

2. Inventory all looks the same and there are normally large but acceptable quantities of it; more of the same is not easy to detect. However, new equipment, no matter how small, draws attention, questions and control.

3. The control of inventory investment needs to be on-going. Plant investment on the other hand is a one-off decision and often, therefore, is not so demanding over a period of time.

Table 10.1   Extracts from 1988 balance sheets

Company	Inventory	Plant and equipment (less depreciation)[a]	Total current assets	Total assets
General Electric Company	1,251.7	353.9	4,115.2	5,255.0
Lucas Industries	355.9	324.1	937.2	1,436.3
TI Group	115.5	82.7	443.3	616.8
Tootal Group	114.3	59.5	211.6	306.0
Portals Holdings	45.4	19.4	146.2	229.1
Hestair	24.9	8.2	69.8	89.0
Ferguson Industrial Holdings	20.9	20.4	49.2	79.4
Volex Group[b]	14.1	9.3	35.5	50.6

All figures in £m.
[a] Not including leasehold plant and equipment.
[b] Previously Ward and Goldstone.

Table 10.2   Analysis of the 1988 balance sheet extracts given in Table 10.1

Company	Inventory			
	£m	Percentage of current assets	Percentage of total assets	Ratio to plant
General Electric Company	1,252	30	23	3.5
Lucas Industries	356	38	25	1.1
TI Group	116	26	19	1.4
Tootal Group	114	54	37	2.0
Portals Holdings	45	31	20	2.3
Hestair	25	36	28	3.0
Ferguson Industrial Holdings	21	42	26	1.0
Volex Group	14	40	28	1.5
Average	—	37	26	2.0

4. Inventory control is often not seen as part of the task of senior executives. It has no qualities which give it inherent attraction or bring it to the attention of top management. It is not dynamic. It is a task of day-to-day detail seen by most as mundane. The content issues and discussions on inventory all appear to be the same. As a consequence it is not normally an agenda item for a management meeting (unless the horse has bolted) whereas fixed asset investment usually is. However, in the Japanese automobile industry, one result of companies allocating corporate-level resources and sufficient effort to the control of inventory has been to achieve low levels of inventory with little adverse

effect on the manufacturing efficiency. The just-in-time production systems referred to earlier have enabled inventory to be minimized.

5.   Companies fail to distinguish between records and controls. Consequently, the inventory information provided is typically in the form of a record — a statement of the past often for historical, financial purposes. However, companies mistakenly interpret this as control data whereas in fact it merely expresses the value of inventory in a format required for financial statements. The result is that on-going controls necessitated by the size of this asset are not developed, invariably leading to unnecessary investment of a high order.

In this chapter, the types of inventory, their functions, an analysis and understanding of inventory and the actual controls which may be used to monitor this significant investment are outlined.

Types of inventory

The types and amount of inventory that an organization should hold will depend upon several aspects including the products manufactured or services provided, product/service range, type of process and span of process. The principal types (see Figure 10.1) are:

1.   Raw materials, bought-out parts and components to be used in making the products.
2.   Partly finished WIP items awaiting the next stage in the process.
3.   Finished goods consisting of products ready for sale.

In addition to these, others are used in the process itself or to keep the plant and equipment going. These include supplies, consumables, spare parts, tools, jigs and fixtures.

Generally, organizations whose activities are centred around products or manufacturing processes have more tangible inventory systems than do service organizations. In a service organization, such as a bank, the operation is the service

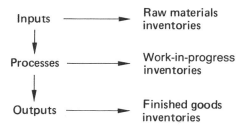

Figure 10.1   Principal types of inventory.

that is consumed as it is generated. The forms and other paperwork used in this process are similar to supplies in the production situation. Whilst in both situations the control of supplies is an important feature of the process, greater emphasis on materials control will exist in a manufacturing organization because of its greater importance to the business both in terms of activity and value.

However, in those service organizations that are less labour-intensive, inventories may be much more significant. Retail shops, for instance, have substantial inventories essential to their business. Similarly, hospitals may carry stocks of plasma to supplies of linen and cleaning materials.

Why inventories exist

Why does an organization invest so heavily in inventory? What is the return? Although there are common reasons for holding inventories, there are also advantages which are particularly important and which relate more to one type of inventory than another. These are outlined for the principal inventory types given in Figure 10.1.

1. Raw materials and bought-out parts inventory will allow the organization to:
    (a) cater for the variability of supply;
    (b) take advantage of quantity discounts or market prices;
    (c) provide strategic stocks of items which could be in short supply due, for instance, to strikes or other supply problems;
    (d) to guard against inflation;
    (e) as a form of investment when price increases are anticipated.

2. Work-in-progress inventory helps maintain the independence of stages in the process by decoupling the production steps involved. This leads to:
    (a) greater flexibility in production scheduling especially at times of machine breakdown;
    (b) stabilizing the different output rates at each part in the process;
    (c) improving the utilization of plant, processes and labour.

3. Finished goods inventory with which the organization can:
    (a) provide off-the-shelf customer service;
    (b) achieve a steady supply of goods in the face of intermittent production or supply;
    (c) cope with fluctuations in demand, particularly in the case of seasonal products;
    (d) provide an insurance against plant or equipment breakdowns and, in some instances, against internal or suppliers' strikes.

Thus 'Why hold inventory?' is easily answered. It is more difficult or even impossible to measure return. Some hold the view that the costs of not holding inventories are usually greater than the costs of holding them. But it is more that they are necessary in order to do business. Whichever view is taken, only the costs of holding inventory are measurable in the corporate sense. However, the low inventory levels achieved in the just-in-time manufacturing systems described in the previous chapter question these views, especially in high volume, standard product organizations.

Recognizing that an organization needs inventory and that this investment is costly, the more pertinent question is, therefore: 'Is the amount of inventory necessary?' Some inventory may be unnecessary and will have no return. For example:

1. The inventory holding of an item may be in excess of the level necessary to provide the return associated with holding that item in stock. The 'excess' thus provides no return.[1]

2. An item may be readily available from a reliable supplier who holds stock. The level of inventory may not, however, allow for this situation.

3. One standardized item could replace the inventory holdings of a number of other items.

How an organization balances the investment/return relationship thus becomes an important feature in the control of inventory.

The functions provided by inventories

Regardless of their form, inventories may be further described as one or more of decoupling, cycle, pipeline, capacity-related and buffer inventories. Each of these fulfils a specific function. Figures 10.2 and 10.3 illustrate the inventory functions and how they relate to both the category of inventory and the particular choice of process. An explanation of these two figures is now provided.

1. *Decoupling inventory* separates one process from another. In jobbing there is no decoupling as the skilled person will progress a job on a continuous basis. Similarly, in line process there is no need as the line itself is a set of coupled processes. An exception to this is where inventory is used to decouple the dependency of one part of the process from the preceding part by providing an inventory holding which can be used in the case of machine breakdowns or yield uncertainty. However, this is not usual and should not be a permanent feature of a line process, a factor which is illustrated by the absence of a tick in Figure 10.3. Thus, where this exists it should be recognized as corporate inventory with the category 'process or yield uncertainty' (see pp. 263 and 265).

Decoupling inventory is predominantly found in batch. Inventory in this category decouples one process from the next, allowing them to work independently

Inventory function	Inventory category		
	raw materials	work-in-progress	finished goods
Decoupling		✔ ✔ ✔	
Cycle		✔ ✔ ✔	
Pipeline		✔ ✔ ✔	
Capacity-related		✔ ✔	✔ ✔ ✔
Buffer*	✔ ✔	✔ ✔	✔ ✔ ✔

✔ Degree of function typically provided.
* Buffer concerns variation in demand which could be provided by holding inventory at any stage. However, where it is held because of reasons such as supplier uncertainty, then it should be identified under a relevant category within corporate inventory.

Figure 10.2 Inventory functions related to different categories of inventory.

Inventory function		Type of process		
		jobbing	batch	line
Decoupling			✔ ✔ ✔	
Cycle			✔ ✔ ✔	
Pipeline		✔ ✔	✔ ✔	
Capacity-related	work-in-progress		✔	
	finished goods		✔ ✔	✔ ✔ ✔
Buffer	raw materials		✔	✔ ✔
	finished goods		✔ ✔	✔ ✔ ✔

✔ Degree of function typically provided.

Figure 10.3 Inventory functions in relation to jobbing, batch and line processes.

and separating otherwise dependent parts of the total operation. The emphasis is, therefore, on the material waiting for the process so that the process itself is most 'efficiently' used.

2. *Cycle inventory* relates to the decision to manufacture a quantity of products (sometimes referred to as a lot/batch size) which reflects criteria such as set-up to production run length time and customer order size). The rationale is to reduce set-up costs and avoid the loss of process capacity.[2] In jobbing there is little need for this function as the skilled person will set up for each job individually and is often making an order quantity of one. Similarly, cycle inventory is a function which line does not require as it is continually set up to manufacture an agreed range of products.

3. *Pipeline inventory* concerns the inventory support where companies decide to subcontract one process to an outside supplier at some time during the total process lead time. All the inventory associated with this decision is classed as pipeline. A decision to subcontract one operation within line processing would be infeasible and therefore does not happen. However, in both jobbing and batch many companies decide to subcontract a particular process and, in so doing, create pipeline inventory in support of that decision.

4. *Capacity-related inventory.* One way to cope with anticipated sales is to plan production in line with sales forecasts. This, however, often leads to a situation of peak capacity requirements involving overtime, recruitment of additional labour and the holding of spare process capacity. Another way is to plan some sort of level production programme, stock-piling inventories in the low sales periods for selling in the high sales periods. Capacity-related inventory concerns transferring work from one time period to the next in the form of inventory, and provides one way of stabilizing production capacity in an environment of fluctuating sales levels (see Figure 10.3).

5. *Buffer inventory* concerns the basic problem that average demand, by definition, varies around the average — as explained in more detail later in the chapter. In order to cope with this, companies may hold higher levels of inventory — see Figure 10.3. Buffer inventory's function, therefore, is to help protect the process core (see Figure 9.1) against the unpredictable variations in demand levels or supply availability. The higher the service level or the lower the level of stockout risk set by the business, then the greater the quantities of buffer inventory required.

Lastly, raw material inventory can also provide the function (see Figure 10.2) of supporting process flexibility investments concerned with the ability of the process to respond to the demands of a wide range of products. Only with this inventory support is a company able to exploit fully the flexibility advantages inherent in the process investment involved by eliminating material lead time.

It is important to make two comments at this point:

1. At any one time certain parts of inventory are performing all or some of these functions simultaneously.

2. It is necessary to distinguish between the separate functions of inventory (as well as having highlighted earlier the particular advantages associated with its different forms) for the following reasons:
   (a) To understand the degree to which each type of inventory is controllable. Although it may be difficult to measure the results accruing from inventory holdings, it is relatively easy to establish the level of inventory holding which provides these advantages. An important management task in this procedure is to determine that level of inventory, often different at different times of the year, which provides an acceptable return and then to keep inventory levels within those bounds.
   (b) To help distinguish between inventory that provides these functions and inventory that does not. This, in turn, requires that inventory is viewed not only in terms of the main types recognized within an organization but is also analysed and recorded in functional terms as well.
   (c) To form the starting point for looking at inventory from the corporate perspective in terms of acceptable levels, reasons for providing inventory, inventory review and inventory control.

Attitudes towards inventory levels

A factor influencing the size of inventory investment is the pressure applied by the various departments within an organization, each of which will have a different idea of what is a desirable inventory level (see Table 10.3). The result is a conflict of views over where the company's funds should or should not be invested.

Table 10.3 General preferences of three departments towards the level of inventory holding

Type of inventory	*General preference*		
	Accounting	*Production/ operations*	*Sales*
Raw materials	Low	High	Indifferent
Work-in-progress	Low	High	Indifferent
Finished goods	Low	Indifferent	High

Inventory and profits

So far this chapter has looked at inventory as a part of working capital investment. However, it is not just in this form that pressure is applied to inventory levels. Consider the situation facing managers where a company is going through a period of reduced sales. It is difficult to shed costs quickly in the short-term by reducing either variable or fixed costs. Such a course of action would normally be expensive. However, if all the costs were carried by a level of production equal to current sales, the profits for the period would be considerably reduced. Instead, management often decides to carry some of the costs over by using spare capacity to produce for stock. Thus, a legitimate proportion of the costs can be absorbed into inventory. The result of this action will be that profit will not fall as much as it would otherwise have done and the value of the company will be held more in check. The rationale is further extended to the hope that there will be an upturn in sales. When this happens, the inventory will be sold and the investment recovered.

If the upturn in sales does not come about, then a company will be reluctant to sell the excess inventory at a low price in order to recover at least some of the investment. Such action would usually lead to further reduced profits and a further reduction in the value of the company. This aspect of inventory can, therefore, frequently result in organizations operating with too much inventory and yet being reluctant to remedy the situation.

Control of inventories

Two approaches are used to help determine the types of control and their level of application. The first deals with the corporate perspective of control and the second considers control at the detailed level. Throughout, the discussion concentrates on the management aspects of control as opposed to exploring the mathematical derivations of particular models.[3]

Before considering these in detail it is important to recognize the following perspectives which form part of the essential context in which the control of inventory needs to be placed before appropriate decisions can be taken:

1. Many initiatives concerning the control of the production/operations process (for example, MRP, JIT and OPT described in Chapter 9) cite inventory reduction as one of the substantial advantages accruing from these applications. As a result, these savings frequently form part of the overall financial justification.

    However, when inventory reduction is presented as a principal component of such proposals, it typically fails to highlight the fact that the quoted gains compare current practice (which is typically far from adequate) to the proposed system which is based on 'best practice'. Such an appraisal leads to a false comparison, as illustrated in Figure 10.4. This shows the different types of benefits which need to be distinguished. The 'real benefit' which is a direct result of the proposed investment, is often substantially less than the total savings quoted and on which the new procedures are partly justified.

2. The planning and control systems described in the last chapter are a proven and recognized source of initial inventory reduction and its improved control from thereon. It is not intended in this section to discuss these systems again. However, several of the principles (e.g. independent/dependent demand) embodied in them are universally applicable in themselves. They stand alone and can be used outside the context of the particular system of which they form an integral part. The individual principles will be discussed here, as they offer approaches to helping improve the control of inventory with or without being embodied in a relevant planning and control system.

3. Companies, therefore, need first to reduce inventory levels to those which reflect good practice by applying selected approaches to their existing systems and procedures. Further benefits gained, for instance from the application of a new planning and control system, can then be judged in a relevant context as far as inventory savings are concerned. Only by making decisions based on inherent benefits can companies ensure that infrastructure investment is appropriately made.

However, this does not mean that planning and control systems are not stand-alone developments. On the contrary, in most businesses the rationale for these is (and should be) to secure planning and control improvements. It is important, therefore, not to obscure the argument with secondary advantages, especially where they may be overstated.

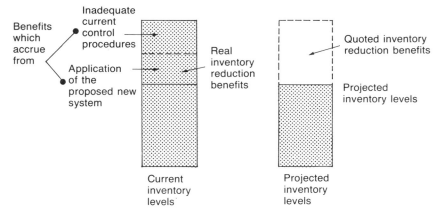

Figure 10.4 An illustration of the different components of inventory reduction relating to proposed investments.

Corporate perspectives

There is great need for organizations to consider more carefully how and what to control and then to control the larger investments. To illustrate, consider the inventory and plant balance sheet entries from 1977 to 1988 for the eight companies referred to in Table 10.1. In each case the figures have been indexed on 1977 to allow easier comparisons (see Table 10.4).

For four of the companies, the actual increase in inventory investment (£m) exceeded that made in plant over the same period (although in only one instance was there a *pro rata* increase). In fact, the aggregate inventory increase for the eight companies was £807m against a £470m increase for plant. However, it is very likely that all the companies' investment decisions regarding fixed assets would come under the normal close and sophisticated scrutiny of investment appraisal methods. An organization would require the fixed asset investment to be compatible with its corporate objectives, and that it be more acceptable than other options in terms of return and risk. Yet in the case of inventory it is quite conceivable that these very large investments could be undertaken without such careful evaluation. It is, therefore, important that some effective inventory control system should exist not only at the detailed level but also at the corporate level; these are now considered.

Corporate level control

1. The initial step in corporate-level control is to recognize that inventory is held for many reasons. In manufacturing and the less labour-intensive service companies, the main categories involve raw material and components, WIP and finished goods. In the labour-intensive service organizations, the main type of inventory is supplies. However, only inventory which genuinely fulfils the production/operations, sales or process needs described earlier (p. 256) should be included in the inventory category which provides the production/operations-related functions also described earlier (pp. 257–9). There is much inventory that does not fall into this description and must be categorized separately. Without this separation, the controls used to monitor actuals against budgets will show a distorted picture without a clear view of why the excess exists. Without knowledge of the reasons why, meaningful control becomes difficult to achieve.

Thus, inventory that is not production/operations-related needs to be segregated and separately accounted for and controlled. This category of stock is known as *corporate inventory*. Having recognized that this inventory exists, the next step is to decide what types of corporate inventory are involved. Some of these categories are:

(a) Service level — customer service parts or repaired items being held until requested by the customer.

Table 10.4 Further balance sheet analyses of the companies introduced in Table 10.1 to show increases in plant and equipment, and inventory for the years 1977–88

Company	Aspect[a]	1977 £m	1977 Index	1979 £m	1979 Index	1981 £m	1981 Index	1985 £m	1985 Index	1986 £m	1986 Index	1988 £m	1988 Index	Actual increase (decrease) between 1977 and 1988 £m
General Electric Company	Inventory	548.5	100	621.4	113	903.6	165	1265.1	231	1274.8	232	1251.7	228	703.2
	Plant	167.0	100	254.4	152	387.8	232	350.3	210	359.3	215	353.9	212	186.9
Lucas Industries	Inventory	225.5	100	275.3	122	298.8	133	300.2	133	314.3	139	355.9	158	130.4
	Plant	98.0	100	130.9	134	200.4	204	220.4	225	297.2	303	324.1	331	226.1
TI Group	Inventory	227.2	100	319.2	140	282.3	124	176.5	78	144.7	64	115.5	51	(111.7)
	Plant	80.4	100	158.3	197	169.4	211	114.3	142	92.2	115	82.7	103	(2.3)
Tootal Group	Inventory	94.6	100	118.3	125	101.0	107	96.9	102	98.3	104	114.3	121	19.7
	Plant	44.6	100	43.0	96	54.1	121	58.0	130	53.2	119	57.5	129	12.9
Portals Holdings	Inventory	10.7	100	14.5	136	31.7	296	31.3	293	30.6	286	45.4	424	34.7
	Plant	5.8	100	9.2	159	10.2	176	23.7	409	24.3	419	19.4	334	13.6
Hestair	Inventory	11.4	100	16.5	145	17.0	149	25.7	225	22.7	199	24.9	218	13.5
	Plant	1.9	100	3.4	179	3.5	184	6.2	326	6.8	358	8.2	432	6.3
Ferguson Industrial Holdings	Inventory	3.8	100	8.5	224	12.2	321	19.2	505	11.6	305	20.8	547	17.0
	Plant	0.2	100	2.7	1,350	4.1	2,050	7.8	3,900	8.7	4,350	20.4	10,200	20.2
Volex Group	Inventory	14.0	100	18.9	135	17.4	124	11.1	79	10.5	75	14.1	101	0.1
	Plant	5.8	100	7.8	134	9.0	155	3.8	66	6.2	105	7.9	136	2.1

To allow comparisons to be drawn, all costs are based on historical costs since current costs were only available for later years.
[a] Plant refers to plant and equipment net of depreciation.

(b) Customer banks — inventory held at a customer's request, normally as a safeguard for that customer's supply.

(c) Design and development labour — labour that is charged to inventory for a part-completed (often non-standard) item.

(d) Safety supplies — resulting from a corporate decision to hold raw material and component inventory as a safeguard against future supplies.

(e) Foreign supplies — the amount of above-normal inventory purchased in large quantities because of, for example, changing lead times and transportation costs associated with imports.

(f) Discount stock — inventory held at above-normal levels which has been acquired to gain the purchasing discounts involved.

(g) Export holding — inventory packed and awaiting export.

(h) Customer delay — inventory held due to the customer delaying the delivery date.

(i) Credit holds — inventory ready for delivery but held for reasons of customer credit.

(j) Marketing — inventory holdings above the normal level as part of a marketing strategy (e.g. promotions).

(k) Sales — inventory holding above forecast due to production having been made to budget but actual sales having been below forecasts.

(l) Phased-out parts — inventory holding of a phased-out part, including spare parts to service previous sales.

(m) Prototype inventory — inventory supporting the R&D function of the business.

(n) Slow-moving — that inventory which falls within an organization's definition of this category.

(o) Policy inventory — inventory over and above normal levels which has been caused as a direct consequence of a policy decision: for example, to make certain items due to low sales or material unavailability.

Which of these categories (and there will be many others) relate to a particular organization will be clearly recognizable in each situation.

2.   The next step is to develop a master plan (in terms of a forecast manufacturing or assembly schedule over an appropriate planning period) needed to achieve that required production level. The compiling of this plan will obviously reflect the product lines produced and include present inventory, existing order backlog, forecast production requirements during the period, and end-of-period inventory. Inventory here relates only to the three main categories given earlier of raw materials, WIP and finished goods.

3.   The organization then needs to establish an inventory standard. Initially this might prove an arduous task. It has to be completed for the large inventory categories of raw material, WIP and finished goods and also for the corporate categories of inventory similar to those listed earlier.

4. The final stage is to compare actuals to forecast and to analyse variances. These can be attributed to sales or production volume variances, price variances or purchasing variances. To simplify this task an acceptable variance on a particular inventory category should be agreed at the corporate level. Reports on all other variances are essential for this system to be effective. It is also important that the standards set and non-reportable variances allowed are reviewed regularly.

The adoption of this procedure will provide the organization with a broad plan, one that aggregates inventory as a way of controlling the total investment in this significant asset.

Detailed control

Corporate inventories

Inventories in this category may arise for many reasons. The recognition, categorization and separation of these is the first step in their control. The procedure for their individual control then takes a similar form to the aggregate control as described in (3) above. Each category should be analysed, and on the basis of what is currently held and what is anticipated in the future, realistic standards should be set. The control loop is closed when actuals are compared to forecasts and the variances analysed.

In addition, it is equally important here to engage in a planned reduction of each category with the ultimate aim of eliminating them wherever possible.

Mainstream inventories

For the *mainstream* or *principal* forms of inventory (raw materials and components, WIP, finished goods and where relevant, supplies) it is necessary to review these using the dependent/independent demand principle.

The inventory control system ultimately initiates the order for each item. There are, however, two basic methods for determining when to issue this replenishment order, and they relate to the assumption underlying the demand pattern of each particular item.

1 The dependent/independent demand principle
Where the rate of use for an item does not relate directly to the use of any other item then it should be treated as an item with an independent pattern of demand. Examples include finished goods, factored items and supplies such as paying-in and withdrawal slips at a bank. Conversely, items for which demand is linked to the use of other items are said to have a dependent pattern of demand. For example, subassemblies which go into a higher-level component or finished item, standardized parts for several subassemblies and/or assemblies and the ingredients necessary

in the preparation of a range of drugs or other pharmaceutical products. The choice of inventory system depends upon whether the items have a dependent or independent pattern of demand. As an organization will tend to have items which fall into each category then it will need to employ both sytems. It is, however, a mistake to use an independent system for a dependent item and vice versa. It is not a case of choosing one or the other type of system for all inventory. The systems should be used side by side, complementing each other.

2 Inventory control for independent items
The basis for inventory control of independent items is that of past demand as a guide to future requirements. The control is concerned with establishing a mechanism for initiating the order to replenish inventory.

To determine the nature of the controls to use here, however, it is necessary to understand the relative values of inventory. When this is known it is then possible to decide the type of control to apply to each item of inventory in order to maximize the return (i.e. reduced inventory investment against the control costs involved). Organizations have to keep track of a large number of items, all of which vary in terms of their annual usage and unit cost. It is, however, in the area of high cost and high usage where most of the effort in inventory control should be concentrated in order to maximize the control exercised.

The problem of where to direct this major effort is easily derived from a Pareto curve of annual requirement value. For each item of inventory two facts are needed: unit value and annual usage. The product of these two figures is known as the annual requirement value (ARV).

The inventory items are then placed in the order, largest ARV first, then the next largest and so on. Table 10.5 lists a representative sample of thirty items in order of decreasing ARV. Such a list would be typical in many organizations. Because of the wide range of ARVs it would not make sense to spread the effort of inventory control equally over each part. Pareto's 'vital few' and 'trivial many' idea or the '80/20 rule' (in general it can be said that about 20 per cent of the items in inventory will account for 80 per cent of the total ARV) applies here. Table 10.6 illustrates this.

From this summary it can be seen that 74 per cent of the total ARV is accounted for by as little as 22 per cent of the total items held in inventory. (Note that the 80/20 relationship implied in the rule is only an indication of the size of the actual figures involved.) This approach to inventory control is further extended into the ABC analysis. Here the high ARV items are classed as A items, the middle range as B items and the low ARV as C items (Figure 10.5). Once this has been accomplished (bearing in mind that the ARV for an item may change over time and so, therefore, would its classification) the approach used to control items in each of these categories is summarized in Table 10.7.

It stands to reason that A items should be controlled and checked. The requirements for these need to be calculated in order to keep inventory levels in line with forecast usage. In addition, it is worth the clerical and management costs

Table 10.5 A representative sample of thirty inventory items listed in order of decreasing annual requirement value (ARV)

Part number	Unit value (£)	Annual usage (units)	Annual requirement value (£) Actual	Annual requirement value (£) Cumulative
303-07	58.50	6,000	351,000	351,000
650-27	2.46	80,000	196,800	547,800
541-21	210.00	500	105,000	652,800
260-81	164.11	450	73,850	726,850
712-22	2.39	25,000	59,750	786,400
054-09	5.86	10,000	58,600	845,000
097-54	136.36	300	40,908	885,908
440-18	17.30	2,000	34,600	920,508
440-01	337.35	100	33,735	954,243
308-31	136.20	200	27,240	981,483
016-01	12.89	2,000	25,780	1,007,263
305-04	45.30	475	21,518	1,028,781
155-29	38.02	500	19,010	1,047,791
542-93	62.91	300	18,837	1,066,664
582-34	32.08	500	16,040	1,082,704
323-34	71.30	200	14,260	1,096,964
412-27	23.01	600	13,806	1,110,770
540-80	24.76	500	12,380	1,123,150
137-29	12.31	1,000	12,310	1,135,460
401-53	30.64	400	12,256	1,147,716
418-51	168.86	65	10,976	1,158,692
418-50	168.80	65	10,972	1,169,664
390-02	17.47	500	8,735	1,178,399
037-41	24.05	200	4,810	1,183,209
402-50	22.00	600	4,400	1,187,609
900-01	41.64	100	4,164	1,191,773
543-61	15.10	200	3,020	1,194,793
900-11	46.80	50	2,340	1,197,133
003-54	11.41	200	2,282	1,199,415
691-30	0.41	5,000	2,050	1,201,465

Table 10.6 Summary of the items given in Table 10.5

	Percentage of total items	Percentage of total ARV
	22	74
	43	21
	35	5
Total	100	100

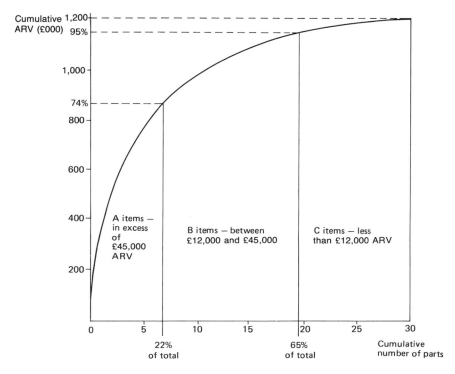

Figure 10.5 Pareto curve of the cumulative ARV for the thirty items listed in Table 10.5 and analysed into ABC categories.

Table 10.7 General approaches to be used for A, B and C items

Aspect	A	B	C
Degree of control	High	Moderate	Low
Basis of control	Calculated	Past records	When needed
Records required	Exact	Global	None
Checks necessary to revise the schedule	Close	Some	None
Expediting	Continual	Only regarding shortages	None
Level of buffer inventory	Low — less than 2 weeks, sometimes 1 or 2 days	Medium — 1 to 3 months	Large — in excess of 3 months

involved to keep the buffer inventory low with small, frequent orders being made as required.

At the other end of the scale, C items require loose controls and little checking. What should happen is that relatively large buffer inventories are held which will absorb all the possible fluctuations in usage and lead times. For example, in Table 10.5 item 691-30 has an annual usage of 5,000 units with a unit value of £0.41. If this item had a lead time of one month then the reorder level should be set at say four months inventory (i.e. with a buffer inventory of three months). But this relatively high buffer inventory only amounts to 1,250 units @ £0.41, totalling a little over £500. Whereas part number 303-07, having a similar annual usage (6,000 units in this instance) has, on the other hand a unit value of £58.50. Consequently every 9 units of this item more than necessarily held in stock equates to holding 3 months inventory of item 691-30.

The ABC classification is arbitrary and depends upon the shape of the curve obtained. There will be borderline items. For example, items just in the A category which may be better treated as B items and vice versa. Having set rough divisions by this form of analysis, consideration can now be given to what specific methods can be used to control inventory levels.

Reorder levels and buffer inventory.   The first question to deal with is, 'When should an order be placed to replenish inventory?' Assuming that a company does not wish to run out of inventory then the level at which it must reorder is calculated by multiplying the time it takes to get an order into the company from an outside supplier (the lead time) by the number of units used of this particular item during the same period. Thus, if the lead time for an item is one week and the weekly usage is 100 units then the reorder level (ROL) is $1 \times 100 = 100$ units. Ideally, the time to place the order is such that the last item of inventory is used as delivery of the next order is made.

Variable demand.   Usage of a particular item, will tend to vary considerably. While it is not possible to forecast exact usage it is possible to relate usage to forecast sales where a production plan is made, and to determine the average usage expected from past figures. To avoid a stockout it will be necessary to carry extra inventory to cater for the higher-than-average demand during a lead time. This extra quantity is called buffer inventory. Hence the ROL calculation can now be modified:

ROL = average usage in a lead time + buffer inventory

It is important to realize that this basic inventory model rests on the following assumptions:

1.   Inventories arrive all at one time, and all go into store before any are used.
2.   Demand for inventories is known for certain to occur at a constant rate.
3.   The lead time between placing an order and receiving the inventories is known for certain and is constant.

Buffer inventory. When there is sufficient information, buffer inventories can be calculated using basic statistics. This should normally apply only to A items and possibly some of the B items. In these instances it is worth the time and cost involved. For other B and all C items, buffer inventory levels would be determined using much cruder methods (see Table 10.7, 'level of buffer inventory').

Returning to the basic statistical method, the first step is to calculate average usage for an item and the standard deviation of usage around that average. For example, assume that an item has an average weekly usage of 100 and is normally distributed with a standard deviation of 12 units. By applying normal curve theory (see Figure 10.6) the individual weekly usage would be within two standard deviations either side of the average for 95 per cent of the time (the mathematical explanation of this is not given here, for those interested it will normally be available in any textbook on inventory control). Of the 5 per cent of the time that usage does not fall within two standard deviations, half can be expected to be less than average and half to be more than average. Now, the organization is concerned only with instances of above-average uses, therefore it can expect that only for 2½ per cent of the time would usage exceed the average + two standard deviations. That is 100 + 2(12) = 124. In this situation, if the reorder level was set at 124 then a stockout would not be expected more than 2½ per cent of the time or one time in 40 occasions.

A company can, however, determine the risk of a stockout that it is prepared to accept. This probability can be expressed as a percentage and is called the *protection level*. It is equivalent to 100 × (1 − probability of a stockout). Protection levels can thus be established and the buffer inventory calculated.

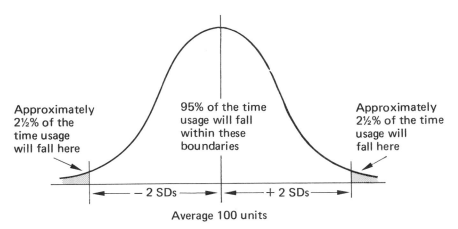

The shaded areas under the left and right tails represent the 5% of the time when actual usage would exceed average usage plus and minus 2 standard deviations (SDs)

Figure 10.6 Normal distribution curve showing the average weekly usage of 100 units and two standard deviations (SDs) either side of this average.

A further measure which may be used to gauge the level of customer treatment is the *service level*. When there are stockouts, the level of service which an organization wishes to maintain can be established as a ratio of customers served without delay to the total demand, or equally, as a ratio of units supplied without delay to total orders received.

$$\text{Service level percentage} = \frac{\text{Customers served}}{\text{Total customer demand}}$$

or

$$\frac{\text{Customers supplied without delay}}{\text{Total orders received}}$$

Economic order quantity (EOQ) and economic lot size (ELS).   The formulae given here minimize the total variable costs.[4]

$$\text{EOQ} = \sqrt{\frac{2zC_s}{cC}} \quad \text{for instantaneous replenishment}$$

or

$$\text{ELS} = \sqrt{\frac{2zC_s}{cC}} \times \frac{p}{p-d} \quad \text{for replenishment at rate } p$$

where z = total annual usage
C_s = cost of placing an order
c = unit cost of the item
C = carrying cost rate per year
p = production rate (units) per day
d = demand rate (units) per day

This calculation would normally only be used for A and possibly some B items. However, on the whole EOQs have not worked in every situation. This is for several reasons including:

1. EOQs relate to cycle inventories and ignore the potential pipeline, capacity and decoupling benefits.

2. The gains of price discounts may outweigh EOQ considerations.

3. Practical problems such as large product size often determine the amount to be produced rather than the economic order quantity.

Capacity-related inventory — labour/inventory value ratios

Where companies use capacity-related inventory as one way of balancing fluctuating demand levels with the decision to maintain level production output, it is important for them to establish the different ratios between the standard hour content of inventory and its overall value. Listing the ratio between inventory value and standard hour content will enable a company to elect to produce for stock those items with the most favourable ratios. In this way it will be able to absorb 'spare capacity' for the lowest inventory value increases. Table 10.8 provides an example of this approach. Representative items from a company show the different rates of absorbing 'spare capacity' in terms of the costs of increased inventory holdings. Thus, whilst E180 has a unit inventory value of £25.80 it in effect uses 6.3 standard labour hours to produce each item. Consequently its labour/inventory ratio is only 4.1. On the other hand, E150 and WD162 both have unit values less than E180 at £13.50 and £18.65 respectively. However, their labour/inventory ratios are significantly higher than that for E180 at 19.3 and 23.3 respectively. Thus, using this criterion as one factor in planning inventory at times when capacity is greater

Table 10.8 Labour/inventory ratio: Establishing the ratio between the value of inventory (WIP and/or finished goods) and its work content (standard hours) as a means of setting priorities in times when available capacity exceeds sales

Product		Standard labour hour content	Inventory value (£)	Inventory per standard labour hour used	Product rankings — to minimize inventory value (£) increases per standard labour hour used	
Reference	Inventory category	Per unit			WIP/finished goods	Overall
WB674		13.2	66.05	5.00	2	3
WA321		2.6	35.50	13.70	8	13
WC193		3.2	32.85	10.30	5	10
WB280		4.1	21.15	5.20	3	4
WB055		1.4	19.00	13.60	7	12
WD162	Work-in-progress	0.8	18.65	23.30	10	18
WD610		0.4	6.35	15.90	9	16
WB405		0.9	4.25	4.70	1	2
WE350		0.4	3.54	8.90	4	8
WC184		0.1	1.15	11.50	6	11
G163		10.1	150.10	14.90	7	15
D114		8.0	122.50	14.20	6	14
A195		3.2	93.75	29.30	9	19
B680		12.5	65.00	5.20	2	4
B008		5.5	33.60	6.10	3	6
D710	Finished goods	2.9	28.00	9.70	5	9
E180		6.3	25.80	4.10	1	1
E150		0.7	13.50	19.30	8	17
B160		1.3	11.50	8.80	4	7
D109		0.2	6.75	33.75	10	20

than sales will enable companies to keep inventory increases to a minimum whilst using effectively the capacity on hand.

Inventory control and its relation to planning and control system developments

In the previous chapter several developments in planning and control systems were outlined and their impact upon and role within the level and control of inventory was stressed. This section adds to those observations and links related issues raised in this chapter to the relevant points made in Chapter 9.

Order point

The logic of an order point system is to trigger the reorder for a part every time the inventory level of that part falls to a predetermined level. As illustrated by Figure 10.7, the timing and quantity of the reorder takes into account the usage in the lead time plus the agreed buffer inventory to take account of above-average usage, as explained on p. 259. Using the example from p. 270 as the basis for this illustration, then the reorder level is the sum of the average usage in the lead time (1 × 100 = 100 units) and the extra inventory to cater for the above-average demand during a lead time (estimated here as 25 units). Figure 10.7 illustrates the control of an individual part through an order point system. The three cycles in this example show different levels of usage during the lead time, although the pattern of usage has been simplified (it would not normally be so regular) and the actual lead times are shown as being more consistent than experienced in reality. However, this illustration shows the importance of recognizing that only usage patterns after the reorder level is reached are of consequence in terms of stockouts and for this reason the period following an order point is known as 'being at risk'.

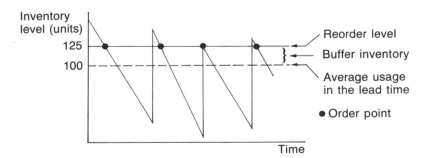

Figure 10.7 The control of an individual part through an order point system.

An order-point, MRP comparison

Order point is not normally the most appropriate way to control all parts. The principle underlying the independent/dependent demand states that inventories of finished goods items, service parts and other independent items should be replenished using reorder levels or reorder points. However, MRP should be used for all components going into higher-level components. Demand should not be forecast when it can be calculated. Thus, for dependent items, the forecast is made only for the end-item. It is much more efficient to order components from schedule product requirements and reduce component inventory between these requirements to the lowest practical level. Independent demand inventory models when used for dependent demand items are still, compared with MRP, clerically more expensive and cause more instances of excessive inventory on the one hand and shortages on the other. A comparison of these two systems is given in Table 10.9, whilst Table 10.10 illustrates the extent of these and other improvements following the

Table 10.9 Comparison of reorder and MRP systems

Aspect	Order point system for independent demand items	MRP system for dependent demand items
Orientation	Every item	End-products only
Item demand pattern	Independent	Dependent
Ordering signal	Reorder level/point	Time period
Basis of calculation	Historic usage	Future production
Degree of forecasting	All items	End-items only
Amount of buffer stock	All items	End-items only with some exceptions

Table 10.10 Data survey of 326 companies on the improvements achieved and expected with the introduction of MRP

Aspect	Material requirements planning		
	Pre	Current improvement	Reported improvement
Annual inventory turns	3.5	4.7	5.6
Delivery promises met (%)	64	81	93
Split orders due to shortages (%)	32	21	13
Number of expeditors required	9.5	5.6	3.8
Lead time from order to delivery (days)	64	57	42

Source: J. Anderson and R. Schroeder, survey in *Business Week* (6 August 1979).

introduction of an MRP system. However, it can often be far from easy to achieve such results.[5]

Thus, using MRP for dependent items will help reduce some of the following disadvantages inherent in the fixed reorder point system:

1. The large inventory investment, made up of buffer stock and inventory holdings held awaiting usage within the production process.

2. The unreliability associated with items having a highly variable rate of demand.

3. The factor of obsolesence.

4. The administrative task of forecasting demand for all items.

The disadvantages of MRP lie primarily in the assumption underlying its use. Product structures must be assembly-oriented and bills of material and inventory status prepared and available for use in the data processing system. Lastly, the master production schedule has to be accurate and assumes that what is planned will take place. It is essential that inventory data from the shopfloor are reliable, for otherwise a well planned MRP system can be made a nonsense. Whilst training people to keep accurate inventory records is not easy, it is critical to the success of an MRP application.

Just-in-time

Organizations which provide the investment and ensure that the prerequisites for just-in-time (JIT) are in place will create a significant advantage, not only in terms of low inventories themselves but the overhead reduction which results from removing the need for inventory control. Details of these factors were given in the previous chapter (pp. 244–9) which also drew attention to the resultant element of finished goods inventory — depicted in Figures 9C.2 and 9C.3. However, it is important to reinforce the underlying message of JIT approaches and applications which concerns the pursuit of zero inventories. Even where JIT initiatives cannot be pursued, some of the precepts on which they are based are equally and appropriately applicable in many forms of business and these need to be pursued.

The key, therefore, is to recognize that the first task in the management of inventory is to determine the level of complexity to be controlled. The second is then to select the appropriate form of control to be used. JIT provides a classic illustration of this philosophy and one which POM needs increasingly to follow.

Optimized production technology

As with JIT, but on a more limited base, optimized production technology (OPT), as explained in Chapter 9 (pp. 219–21), is designed to maximize the flow of resources through an organization and not their utilization. By controlling the inputs into the manufacturing process in line with its known capacity constraints (or bottlenecks) a business will reduce inventory (together with associated elements of complexity) by not generating work at some stages of the process which cannot be worked on at subsequent stages because of capacity limitations. Thus, bottlenecks govern both throughput and inventory levels in the system.

Companies, therefore, need to balance the flow of materials (in terms of standard hour content) and not capacity. One result of this will be to reduce inventory with its attendant problems of investment and control costs. As with JIT, therefore, using appropriate planning and control systems will offer companies the opportunity to effect inventory levels and hence undertake the appropriate first step of determining the size and nature of the control problem before addressing the question of which system to develop.

Management control systems

Increases in inventory tend to lack the level of control that should be accorded to them. Equally, management directives to reduce total inventories are often insensitive to their nature. As inventories are the result of many decisions and policies, a typical broad course of action ignores the interrelated features of this investment. Existing purchasing, operations and marketing policies and the prior commitment, inflexibility and time dimensions of inventory make the orderly and sensible execution of global cuts difficult. To act on such directives would usually result in the elimination of important functions such as those provided by buffer and decoupling inventories. The unwillingness to make decisions until the last moment and the lack of understanding of interrelationships are typical underlying features of corporate inventory decisions. It is most important, therefore, that the responsibilities associated with inventory investment and control are assumed at the corporate level. Policy decisions taking account of all the important perspectives need first to be made so that the control at lower levels in the organization can work in accord.

Corporate rules of thumb

Acceptable levels of inventory often exist but usually without sufficient understanding as to their origins and how they should work. For example, inventory turnover as the ratio between cost of sales and average inventory. Let us assume that an acceptable turnover is five times, so that on £10m sales the average inventory level would be £2m. If sales increased to £15m should average inventory then rise to £3m?

The key to answering that question lies in a comparison between the composition of the £10m and £15m of sales and between the £2m and £3m of inventory. The types of inventory which exist do not all vary directly with sales volume and so this rule of thumb can be misleading. For example:

1. *Pipeline inventories.* If the increase in sales is achieved by selling more of the same products then inventory levels need not normally change *pro rata* to the increase in sales as much as if the sales increase was achieved partly or totally by the production of different products.

2. *Cycle inventories.* Cycle EOQ inventories vary as the square root of demand so that they should rise proportionately less than sales (e.g. if sales rose by 50 per cent then cycle inventories would need to increase only by the square root of 1.5, which is 1.2).

3. *Buffer inventories.* The requirement for these inventories will depend upon several factors but is principally to protect against the uncertainty of demand or supply. Thus the service and protection levels specified by management will affect this inventory holding which will not necessarily be volume-related.

4. *Capacity-related inventories.* Decisions concerning capacity and inventory will often change at different sales volume levels. Consequently, if sales turnover increases by 50 per cent, the capacity/inventory mix will rarely move in corresponding proportions.

5. *Decoupling inventories.* In situations of sales growth, these inventories will tend (more) to change by a stepped function rather than gradually over time. Also, it is common for the function of these inventories to be provided on a reducing scale.

Although an acceptable turnover level has at some time been established, it does not mean that this is achievable or desirable at different sales volumes. Consequently, executives never know if the guidelines presented by these rules are the best and on what basis they have been established. It is important, therefore, to re-evaluate them over time or when significant changes take place such as in sales volumes, product mix and material supplies.

On reviewing the relationship between inventory and sales for the eight companies introduced in Table 10.1, both items have been indexed on 1977 so as to facilitate comparisons. It can be seen from Tables 10.11 and 10.12 that there has been a gradual overall improvement in the relationship between inventory and sales revenue in the period reviewed. No doubt the increased and appropriate attention given to inventory during the 1980s has stimulated companies to get the total levels of inventory under control.

This analysis has been made to focus attention on how easily inventory can increase, how new rules of thumb can be created and how important it is for a company to concern itself with the effective control of inventory at the corporate level. It is of paramount importance that with changes in sales revenue levels, these companies continue to exercise the same level of control.

Table 10.11 Analyses of inventory and sales changes for the companies introduced in Table 10.1, 1977–88

Company	Aspect	1977 £m	Index	1979 £m	Index	1981 £m	Index	1985 £m	Index	1986 £m	Index	1988 £m	Index
General Electric Company	Inventory	548.5	100	621.4	113	903.6	165	1,265.1	231	1,274.8	232	1,251.7	225
	Sales	2,054.6	100	2,500.5	122	3,462.0	168	5,222.4	254	5,252.6	256	5,552.5	270
Lucas Industries	Inventory	225.5	100	275.3	122	298.8	133	300.2	133	314.3	139	355.9	158
	Sales	886.1	100	1,071.2	121	1,186.2	134	1,498.9	169	1,619.2	183	1,833.1	207
TI Group	Inventory	227.2	100	319.2	140	282.3	124	176.5	78	144.7	64	115.5	51
	Sales	791.8	100	1,213.8	153	1,122.0	142	997.1	126	1,043.6	132	958.9	121
Tootal Group	Inventory	94.6	100	118.3	125	101.0	107	96.9	102	98.3	104	114.3	121
	Sales	324.6	100	401.4	124	377.1	116	435.4	134	388.0	120	503.8	155
Portals Holdings	Inventory	10.7	100	14.5	136	31.7	296	31.3	293	30.6	286	45.4	424
	Sales	77.4	100	100.6	130	143.4	185	240.0	310	212.8	275	243.8	315
Hestair	Inventory	11.4	100	16.5	145	17.0	149	25.7	225	22.7	199	24.9	218
	Sales	53.4	100	59.0	110	59.0	110	116.0	217	135.2	253	216.8	406
Ferguson Industrial Holdings	Inventory	3.8	100	8.5	224	12.2	321	19.2	505	11.6	305	20.8	547
	Sales	31.5	100	56.5	179	78.9	250	141.5	449	150.2	478	127.6	405
Volex Group	Inventory	4.0	100	18.9	135	17.4	124	11.1	79	10.5	75	14.1	101
	Sales	57.0	100	62.6	110	73.2	128	54.3	95	67.8	119	83.4	146

Table 10.12   An analysis of the information given in Table 10.11

Year related to the base year 1977	Number of companies where the inventory/sales ratio was		
	Worse	*About the same*	*Better*
1979	4	2	2
1981	3	3	2
1985	2	—	6
1986	1	—	7
1988	2	—	6

Management inventory systems

In order to control inventory effectively companies need to be able to assess the reality of their own business in order to determine the appropriate production planning and control systems to be used and to choose from the range of inventory control options described throughout this chapter. However, a prerequisite for determining the most suitable mix of approaches is to determine the level of complexity with which a control system has to cope. Until managers break down the size of the task, then it is not possible for this critical step to be completed. In most instances, therefore, the control of this large asset comes from a mix of corporate decisions, as an integral part of an inventory control system and a range of other procedures oriented towards this task. The basic requirements which should be reflected or understood in any practical system are:

1. The model should describe the most important variables which operate in the system (e.g. the appropriate costs involved).

2. Recognition of the inherent variability of demand and supply lead times and to include this within the model (see also the assumptions listed under 'variable demand' on p. 270).

3. Recognition that a rational system will involve some shortages and lost sales unless an infinite shortage cost can somehow be justified.

There are two main approaches to the control of inventory. These are based on the dependent/independent demand function explained earlier.

1 Dependent items

These will be controlled through the basic production/operations control system which are described in Chapter 9. This will state what is needed and when. The question of what is ordered and when is then determined on the basis of order quantity, call-offs and other purchasing criteria.

2 Independent items

These can be controlled by one of two basic approaches:

(a) *Fixed reorder quantity system.* When inventory falls to a predetermined level (the reorder level described earlier) an order of a specified size is issued.

(b) *Fixed reorder cycle system.* Here inventory is checked on a periodic basis, say every two weeks. If there has been usage at the time of checking then an order is issued for that quantity which has been used. This is also called the replenishment cycle.

In addition to these there is a third approach which combines features of the two systems.

(c) *Optimal replenishment system.* In this system inventory is checked both on a quantity and a time basis. Either of these will highlight the inventory item for review but an order is placed only if the fixed reorder quantity has been used.

All three systems are used with minor variations. The choice of system will depend upon the features of inventory involved, some of which are listed in Table 10.13.

Referring back to the ABC stock classification, most B and all C items will normally be controlled by the fixed reorder quantity system. In its simplest form it is known as the two-bin system. Here, the inventory holding is separated into two or three portions and when one portion is used then an order is placed for the fixed reorder quantity. Such systems use visual reminders to reorder; as explained earlier, this visual reorder level includes a very high element of buffer inventory. Two examples are:

(a) Two bins of inventory are kept; when one is used an order is placed.
(b) A painted line inside a bin signals the need to reorder.

Table 10.13 Aspects of inventory and the suitable control system to be used

Aspect of the inventory items	Most suitable type of system		
	Fixed reorder		Optimal replenishment
	quantity	cycle	
Low activity	✓		
Low value	✓		
Need for quick response to demand changes		✓	✓
High activity		✓	✓
High value		✓	
Buffer inventory required		✓	

Because the items are of relatively low annual requirement value the key to their control is to ensure continuity of supply and yet keep clerical costs to a minimum.

For all A and some B items one of the other two systems would be used. The guiding principle for these high annual requirement value items is to keep buffer inventory low. Because of this, regular checking is necessary as an item is at risk of a stockout once the reorder level is reached. Consequently, because the buffer is low, assessment of usage pattern and known future demands for these items needs to be taken into account in the reordering decisions. The frequent, small replenishment orders, though clerically costly, keep the total costs to a minimum.

Conclusion

Inventory control involves a complex set of decisions because of the many forms and functions of inventories. In addition, inventories are the result of functional policies within an organization as well as short- and longer-term decisions in the buying, making and selling functions of the business. There is, therefore, a need for the corporate perspectives of inventory investment to be taken at the highest level as well as detailed controls being used in an aggregate form lower down. Furthermore, the all-embracing nature of this investment requires that this responsibility is understood and resolved not only vertically but between departments at the same level in the organization. The interrelated nature of this significant investment needs to be shared by all concerned. Lastly, it is necessary for most companies to undertake some radical thinking regarding inventory functions and levels. The consistently high performance of Japanese manufacturing companies brought with it in the 1980s an appropriate series of the approaches developed within these organizations. High on that list was inventory reduction. In fact, the contrast in views is possibly nowhere more stark than over this critical facet of a business. In his article on Japanese factories, R.H. Hayes quotes one senior Japanese manager's view of inventory:

> We feel that inventory is the root of all evil. You would be surprised how much you simplify problems and reduce costs when there are no inventories. For example, you don't need any inventory managers or sophisticated inventory control systems. Nor do you need expediters, because you can't expedite. And finally, when something goes wrong, the system stops. Immediately the whole organization becomes aware of the problem and works quickly to resolve it. If you have buffer inventories, these potential problems stay hidden and may never get corrected.[6]

Although these comments refer to high volume, repetitive manufacturing processes, this philosophy towards inventory could well be used to help reduce inventory levels in all types of organization. However, for this to be achieved, corporate attitudes towards inventory must be changed and rigorous planning and discipline implemented from design through to the market-place as befits investment levels of this size.

Notes and references

1. The arbitrary approach to what the levels of inventory should be often leads to carrying larger stocks than necessary. For instance this approach may lead to overcompensation for changes in demand, commonly known as the theory of cascading inventories — see J.W. Forrester, 'Industrial dynamics', *Harvard Business Review* (July/August 1958), 37–66.
2. The principal gains from cycle inventory are reductions in costs and, often more importantly, avoidance of process capacity losses. Refer to p. 220 where 'useful' and 'surplus' capacity are distinguished by the identification of bottleneck processes.
3. Mathematical derivations are covered in several textbooks. For example, R.J. Schonberger, *Operations Management: Productivity and quality* (Plane, Texas: Business Publications, 1985); E.S. Buffa and R.K. Sarin, *Modern Production/Operations Management*, 8th edn (New York: Wiley, 1987), and L.J. Krajewski and L.P. Ritzman, *Operations Management: Strategy and analysis* (Reading, Mass.: Addison-Wesley, 1987).
4. The mathematical derivation for these formulae is to be found, amongst other sources, in Schonberger, *op. cit.*, pp. 243–54; R. Wild, *Production and Operations Management: Principles and techniques*, 3rd edn (London: Holt, Rinehart and Winston, 1984), pp. 412–13 and Krajawski and Ritzman, *op. cit.*, pp. 450–6.
5. R.W. Hall and T.E. Vollman, 'Planning your material requirements', *Harvard Business Review* (September/October 1978), 105–12.
6. R.H. Hayes, 'Why Japanese factories work', *Harvard Business Review*, (July/August 1981), 56–66. Also refer to J.W. Rice and T. Yoshikawa, 'A comparison of Kanban and MRP concepts for the control of repetitive manufacturing systems', *Production and Inventory Management*, 23, no. 1 (1982) 1–14.

Further reading

Cavinato, J.L., *Purchasing and Materials Management: Integrative strategies* (St Paul, Minn.: West, 1984).

Johnson, L.A. and Montgomery, D.C., *Operational Research in Production Planning, Scheduling and Inventory Control* (Chichester: Wiley, 1974).

Orlicky, J., *Materials Requirement Planning* (New York: McGraw-Hill, 1975).

Schonberger, R.L. *Japanese Manufacturing Techniques: Nine hidden lessons in simplicity* (New York: Macmillan, 1982).

van Hees, R.N. and Monhemius, W., *An Introduction to Production and Inventory Control*, (Basingstoke: Macmillan, 1972).

van Hees, R.N. and Monhemius, W., *Production and Inventory Control: Theory and practice* (Basingstoke: Macmillan, 1972).

Wallace, T.F. *MRP II: Making it happen* (Essex Junction, Vt: Oliver Wright Publications, 1985).

Chapter 11

The study and control of work

Operations managers, whether in control of a manufacturing or service activity, are responsible for the conversion process which transforms the necessary material, labour and capital inputs into the required outputs of goods and services. To do this, they need to establish the processes involved, the facilities to be used and the procedures to be followed. This will cover many detailed aspects including product/service range, the determination and co-ordination of capital investment, utilization of materials, labour and capacity, and the expectation of productivity at all levels in the system. This chapter is concerned with aspects similar to the latter. Section A reviews the critical nature of productivity performance and concentrates on the understanding and measurement of productivity. Section B turns its attention to the study of work as an important aspect of productivity improvement. Section C discusses the control of work and the systems which may be used to effect that control whilst Section D introduces appropriate controls to be exercised and procedures to be followed in a management services function.

The two dimensions used by a business to control its activities are time and money. Time is the basis for tasks such as planning, estimating, costing and payment systems, and money is the basis for trading, accounting and financial reporting. The operations manager, as the person responsible for the main-thrust activities of the organization, must understand both these dimensions in themselves and ensure that the translation from one to another is both accurate and appropriate.

Whereas the money dimension is primarily explained through accounting and finance, it is through operations management that an understanding of the time dimension may be gained. It is essential, therefore, that operations managers fully understand how work may be measured and are able to choose the most appropriate method of measurement in any given situation. This chapter explains these aspects of the task in great depth.

Section A: Productivity

The prosperity of nations and organizations alike is recognized as being dependent upon their comparative productivity. In times of increasing competition, this has been brought sharply into focus. For example, the relationship between national productivity performance (illustrated by Table 11.1) and the overall performance of nations (illustrated by Table 11.2) is clearly visible. However, the impact is not confined to within a sector. Competing effectively in one sector has noticeable and understandable knock-on effects elsewhere. For instance, it is not surprising that Japan's manufacturing performance underpins the fact that eight of the top ten banks in the world are also Japanese.

At the corporate level, a similar picture of marked differences in productivity levels might be between companies in various countries. Table 11.3 compares selected measures relating to the performance of two companies manufacturing similar products for a range of industries.

Table 11.4 provides further evidence. This table compares the productivity and performance in four UK factories, two of which were Japanese, one American-owned and the fourth British. All four plants were similar (except that the British plant was much bigger in size), producing large volumes of colour television sets. A glance at the data shows that while quality, labour productivity and absenteeism were lower in the Japanese-owned plants than the other two it did not rest on the notion of employee satisfaction, better working conditions or more holidays. Takamiya argues that the reason for the differences stemmed from three factors: production management, interdepartmental communication and industrial relations.[1] Key features within these included responsibility for quality (the British-owned plant relied on a high investment, sophisticated test machine, whereas the Japanese plants placed the responsibility for quality with the operator who employed visual checking and constant feedback), regular daily meetings, less job demarcation, higher training and higher levels of discipline were also apparent in both Japanese plants. Other differences highlighted the fact that the British plant handled significantly more models (sixty as against eight or less in the other three plants), experienced less communication between sales and manufacturing regarding customer promises, and managed more poorly the co-ordination between design and manufacturing. Lastly, the Japanese plants adopted a 'hands on' approach to co-ordination whereas the other two firms (particularly the American plant) relied heavily on formal manuals, standard operating procedures and laid down methods.

However, productivity differences are not confined to comparisons between nations and manufacturing companies, they show marked variance between sectors within one economy, components within each sector and between one country and another. Table 11.5 shows the performance trends between segments and sectors within the USA and Japan from 1970 to 1983. It is interesting to note the comparative performance of manufacturing within both economies, overall trends

Table 11.1   Trends in gross domestic product per employee, 1973−85

	Relative level				Annual growth	
	1960	*1977*	*1985*	*1986*	*1973−85*	*1981−5*
USA	100	100	100.0	100.0	0.4	1.0
Canada	86	92	99.8	101.9	1.1	1.6
France	57	85	93.6	93.2	2.1	1.7
Japan	25	63	75.5	75.2	2.9	2.9
Korea	n/a	n/a	n/a	33.9	4.9	6.0
UK	53	56	76.1	76.5	1.6	2.6
W. Germany	53	79	93.4	93.0	2.2	2.1

Source: American Productivity Center, *Productivity Perspectives* (1987), with supporting information supplied by the Center for 1973.

Table 11.2   Main manufacturing countries' percentage share of the total exported manufactured goods from these countries[a]

	Percentage share of total						
	USA	*Canada*	*France*	*Italy*	*Japan*	*UK*	*W. Germany*
1969	19.2	6.3	8.2	7.3	11.2	11.2	19.1
1974	17.0	4.5	9.2	6.8	14.4	8.8	21.6
1979	16.0	4.2	10.5	8.4	13.7	9.1	20.8
1980	17.0	4.0	10.0	7.9	14.9	9.7	19.9
1981	18.6	4.6	9.2	7.7	17.9	8.5	18.4
1982	17.7	4.9	9.2	8.0	17.4	8.5	19.5
1983	16.9	5.5	8.9	8.1	18.5	7.9	19.0
1984	17.2	6.3	8.6	7.7	20.1	7.6	18.1
1985	16.5	6.2	8.5	7.8	19.7	7.9	18.7
1986	14.0	5.4	8.8	8.2	19.4	7.6	20.7
1987[b]	13.7	4.9	9.1	8.2	17.9	7.9	21.5
Percentage change[c]	−28.6	−22.2	11.0	12.3	59.8	−29.5	9.7

[a] Included in the definition of main manufacturing countries, but not listed here, are Belgium, Luxembourg, Netherlands, Sweden and Switzerland.

[b] The figures for 1987 are based on quarters 1 and 2 only.

[c] Percentage change is the difference between 1969 and 1987 as a percentage of 1969.

Source: Department of Trade and Industry, *Monthly Review of External Trade Statistics*, 145 (January 1988), Table E2.

in the period and the comparison between 'goods producing' and 'service' industry trends. During the period 1970−83, whereas output per hour increased in US manufacturing by over 40 per cent, the increase in Japanese manufacturing was over 150 per cent. The improvements in service industries were substantially lower in both countries at 13 and 49 per cent respectively, thus providing an interesting

Table 11.3 Comparative performance of two companies making similar products for a range of industries, 1987

Performance measure	Corporate base	
	UK	Japan
Ratio of indirect to direct staff	1.4	0.5
Delivery lead time (UK index)	100	70
Sales (£000) per employee	36	70
Inventory as percentage of sales (%)	15	4
Product cost (UK index)	100	70
Percentage of deliveries made on time	75	95

Table 11.4 Productivity and performance in four UK colour television plants

	Japan A	Japan B	USA	Great Britain
Number of employees	700	300	700	2,000
Labour productivity[a]	0.83	1.07	0.71	0.56
Quality record[b]	4–5%	10%	14–15%	85%
Employee satisfaction[c]	15.6	12.71	13.20	11.32
Labour turnover	30%	25–30%	30%	30%
Absenteeism	4%	5%	8%	8%
Hourly paid employees:				
Sick pay	Nil	Nil	2–28 weeks	8–40 weeks
Holidays	1 yr–17 days	1 yr–17 days	20 days	20–25 days
Unionization rate	98%	98%	—	100%
Number of trade unions	1 (Operators)	1 (Operators)	—	7
	1 (Technicians)	1 (Technicians)		

[a] Colour television sets produced per day.
[b] Rejection rate of printed circuit boards assembled.
[c] Employee Survey index.

Source: adapted from C.J. McMillan, *The Japanese Industrial System* (Berlin: de Gruyter, 1985), p. 275.

four-way comparison. The increased drive in the US to improve manufacturing productivity compared with that in the service sector is further marked in Figure 11.1 which reveals trends over a longer and more up-to-date period. This reveals that in the period 1979–85 the level of productivity in the service sector declined.

For many decades the importance of productivity has been witnessed at the business level by the level of corporate resources allocated to the improvement

Table 11.5 Levels of output per hour 1970–83 for the USA and Japan in 1975 at constant US dollar and yen equivalents

Sector		USA				Japan			
		1970	1975	1979	1983	1970	1975	1979	1983
Manufacturing	Food and tobacco	9.51	11.86	12.56	13.72	3.81	6.39	6.23	7.23
	Textiles	5.12	5.66	7.30	8.74	1.57	2.54	2.76	3.50
	Paper and pulp	8.28	10.25	11.59	13.26	5.11	7.55	9.90	10.79
	Chemicals	10.26	13.32	15.33	16.41	6.54	10.56	18.82	25.50
	Metals: primary	11.51	11.96	12.42	13.11	8.61	13.74	21.52	17.37
	fabricated	8.55	8.80	10.03	11.37	3.32	3.73	5.14	5.43
	Machinery: electrical	6.90	8.11	10.02	11.78	2.78	5.41	10.79	20.42
	other	8.54	9.20	10.11	11.75	4.03	5.26	7.60	10.43
	Transportation equipment	8.47	11.07	11.60	11.57	5.19	7.02	9.37	12.17
	Other	6.56	7.84	8.04	8.69	3.83	4.42	4.98	5.67
	All	7.91	9.35	10.16	11.17	3.91	5.54	7.50	9.82
Service	Transport and communications	9.29	11.33	12.61	13.79	3.86	4.76	4.90	5.64
	Utilities	21.98	25.50	25.45	24.64	14.01	16.32	18.31	21.40
	Trade	6.88	7.66	8.16	8.77	2.88	3.99	4.48	4.81
	Finance and insurance	8.21	8.49	8.28	8.29	6.69	10.18	11.88	14.72
	Business services	7.50	7.77	6.70	7.03	3.39	3.53	3.44	3.49
	All	8.62	9.39	9.44	9.73	4.20	5.35	5.74	6.26

Source: derived from G.E. Sadler, *International Productivity Comparisons* (American Productivity Center, 1986), appendix tables 2 and 3.

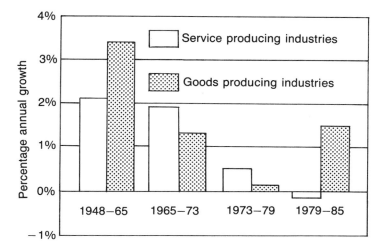

Figure 11.1 Productivity trends: 'goods producing' and 'service producing' industries, USA, 1984—5.

Source: American Productivity Center (1987).

and control of this performance measure. However, much of this activity has been directed at one relatively small and declining facet of many businesses — direct labour. The decline in these related costs within the total and the continued trend towards service industries' contribution to a nation's gross domestic product have not been matched by corporate response. However, organizations of all forms are redirecting their attention to the issues of productivity throughout the whole organization. This chapter attempts to reflect this in its coverage and reference provision.

Productivity overview

Productivity, in general terms, expresses a relationship between outputs from a system and the inputs which go into their creation. However, to use productivity as a means of measuring actual operations, it is important that the concept is clearly understood so that it can be used effectively as a way of analysing and evaluating performance.

Productivity is the relationship of output to input:

$$\text{Productivity} = \frac{\text{Output}}{\text{Input}}$$

An increase in productivity, therefore, can result from either an increase in output (whilst input remains the same) or a decrease in input (whilst output remains the same), or some combination of the two. However, an increase in output itself does not necessarily mean an increase in productivity unless there has been a more than *pro rata* reduction in the inputs.

Productivity and efficiency

It is important to the difference between productivity and efficiency. Whilst productivity measures the amount of input required to achieve a given output and thus concentrates on that relationship, *efficiency* shows how well the input resources have been utilized. Thus it compares actual output achieved with the expected or standard output that should have resulted from the use of the resources involved:

$$\text{Efficiency} = \frac{\text{Actual output}}{\text{Expected or standard output}}$$

Productivity measurement

A basic problem in productivity improvement is the difficulty of measuring it. Labour productivity (relating output to the input of labour) has been the most common form to be used. One reason for this is that labour inputs are more easily measured than other inputs. This is especially so when productivity is expressed in the form of output per employee, per labour hour or per £ wage and whether on a direct, indirect or total labour employed basis. However, the choice of labour as an expression of an organization's productivity is a gross oversimplification. For, just as the operations process is complex then so is the measurement of productivity within that process, and the mix of inputs, resources and outputs will each have a profound effect on the input/output ratio.

General concepts

The first step in deciding how best to measure productivity is to clarify the reasons for wanting to measure it. By agreeing these, guidelines on what and how to measure productivity may become apparent. Although these purposes will differ from level to level in an organization, it is useful to consider some general concepts at each level which will help in the formulation of relevant measures. For example:

1. *Objectives level* — to help form and then measure organizational effectiveness. For instance, as a measure of some part of the company's performance such as return on investment, revenue per patient or net profit per £ or $ sale of goods/services.

2. *Strategic level* — to analyse the current performance of an organization as a way of assessing its internal strengths and weaknesses, to help provide an appreciation of its internal position so as to allow the necessary monitoring and changes to take place. In addition, it may draw a comparison with competitors or similar organizations to provide a limited measure of its performance. Once an organization has completed this exercise, it is then able to develop its marketing, financial, operating, organizational and personnel strategies.

3. *Tactical level* — these involve the specific decision options that may be considered. For instance, to allow a comparison between the benefits arising from the use of different inputs, processes or output mixes. Alternatively, the productivity measures may be required to form the basis of a pay agreement in wage negotiations.

However, it is important to recognize the difficulties that exist when using these measures and especially when drawing comparisons with other organizations:

1. *Inputs* — it is difficult to compare the inputs used in these calculations. The materials, facilities, labour and management skills will change over time and are difficult to measure in themselves and their influence on productivity.

2. *Outputs* — in the same way aspects such as product/service mix and product/service volumes will have an important influence on the input/output comparisons.

3. *Input/output comparison* — it will not be easy to choose which input/output comparisons are the most relevant in evaluating performance.

4. *Interpretation* — to understand what the findings show will prove difficult not only because of the factors listed above but also because of the influence of external constraints or a changing environment.

Approaches to productivity measurement

Two types of productivity measure are commonly used: single-factor and total factor (or multi-factor) productivity. As an example of single-factor measurement, labour productivity typically measures output per hour (based on hours worked or paid for) in a plant, business unit, industry or some national aggregate (e.g. the banking and financial sector). Total factor productivity includes not only labour but also the inputs from plant and equipment, energy and materials. When output is measured on a value-added basis (as explained later) only capital (i.e. plant and equipment) and labour inputs are included in the measure. All intermediate inputs are netted out.

Each type of measure has its advantages and limitations. In each instance, the output measure includes the effects of improvements throughout the transformation process including technological change, higher-quality capital goods and the increasing 'skills' and know-how of the people, together with other indirectly-acquired sources of productivity improvements.

Single-factor productivity measures

Labour productivity
Labour productivity is the most commonly used measure of productivity, relating output to hours worked (see below). Its universal application derives from several factors:

1. It is easy to calculate.

2. Labour was a significant factor of production when the concept of productivity first received attention.

3. The labour cost element was seen to be a more variable factor in the total costs mix than other factors such as material and capital.

$$\text{Labour productivity} = \frac{\text{Output ($£$ value)}}{\text{Hours worked}}$$

Whilst still a useful measure, labour productivity has to be reviewed in the total costs picture of an organization.

Material productivity
This measures the material cost in terms of output. With the significant increase in the percentage of material costs to total costs it is important to monitor this carefully (see 'Value analysis', Chapter 5). This measure should reflect the sourcing of raw materials and their substitution in the process. However, the efficiency of their use should be measured as:

$$\frac{\text{Actual output per tonne or square metre of material}}{\text{Standard/expected output per tonne or square metre of material}} \times 100$$

Each time that a productivity improvement is made that concerns the expected output per tonne, then revised standards need to form the new denominator in the efficiency calculation given above (for example, increased output per tonne due to the use of reinforcing additives which allow wall sections to be thinned without impairing a product's strength).

Plant productivity
A typical measure of plant productivity is

$$\frac{\text{Output (£ value)}}{\text{Machine hours}}$$

More general methods of plant productivity would compare the value of goods sold (£) to the fixed asset investment in plant and equipment. Measures of efficiency would reflect actual output per machine hour to standard output per machine hour thus reflecting downtime, output rates and other aspects affecting throughput.

It is important to remember when using measures of productivity based on some form of cost that the effect of changes in productivity depends upon both the rate of the change and the rate of utilization of the particular factor of production. Thus:

1. Labour productivity reflects man-hours and wage rates.

2. Material productivity reflects materials used and material costs.

3. Plant productivity reflects capacity used and investment costs.

Multi-factor productivity measures

The labour, material and plant measures of productivity provide one view of a total picture and, in using them, it is important to guard against the problems described earlier. However, in taking a total productivity measure, such as total costs (£ or $) as an expression of total output, certain of these problems will be overcome.

Total factor productivity
Total (or multi-) factor productivity includes not only labour inputs but also capital, energy, materials and other purchased services, using the common denominator of cost:

$$\frac{\text{Output (£ value)}}{\text{Cost of labour, capital, energy, materials and other purchased services}}$$

This measure is appropriate when assessing the structure of production/operations and provides an improved framework for the analysis of productivity changes involving the substitution of single factors.

Added value
One useful measure is that of added value. This is calculated as the difference between sales revenue and all material and service costs incurred in making those sales. Material and service costs include raw materials, energy, stationery, cleaning materials and outwork costs (see Figure 11.2):

Added value = Sales revenue − Material and outside service costs

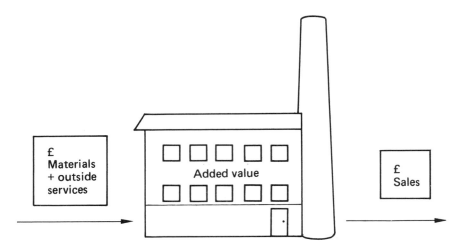

Figure 11.2   Added value in relation to bought-out materials/services and to sales.

Thus, added value measures the wealth produced by the unit or plant in financial terms, over the period being reviewed. The added value index (AVI) is also a useful overall measure because it relates the added value to total employment costs (e.g. wages, salaries, pensions and national insurance contributions). It is calculated as follows and is often expressed as a percentage:

$$\text{Added value index} = \frac{\text{Total employment costs}}{\text{Added value}}$$

This ratio is a valuable measure of management performance because unlike profit it is less affected by factors outside a manager's control (e.g. inflation) and because it focuses on a fundamental aspect of mangement's task: the responsibility for employee productivity.

AVI measures operations by relating the current AVI against a previously agreed standard, with a lower figure indicating an improvement in this ratio. Added value bonus schemes are also being used by some organizations.[2]

Relationships between productivity measures

It is possible to use the single and multi-factor measures to enhance understanding of productivity changes. For instance, labour productivity can be studied in a total factor framework. This enables labour productivity growth to be shown as deriving from growth in the ratios of capital, energy and materials to labour as well as the growth in overall (i.e. total) productivity. Table 11.6 demonstrates the important insights that may be gained into the sources of the total 11 per cent growth in

Table 11.6 Sources of Japanese productivity growth, 1965—73

Sources	*Percentage contribution*
Capital/labour ratio	3.9
Energy/labour ratio	0.2
Materials/labour ratio	6.1
Total factor productivity	0.8
Total growth in labour productivity	11.0

Source: Productivity Policy: Key to The Nation's Economic Future (Washington D.C.: Committee for Economic Development, 1983), p. 11.

labour productivity in Japan from 1965 to 1973. Of this total, all but 0.8 per cent a year resulted from an increase in capital, energy and materials used per hour of labour input. Consequently, labour productivity grew rapidly while total-factor productivity grew rather slowly.

Approaches to improving productivity

There are three basic levels at which productivity improvements can be made:

1. Scientific, involving research activities which result in new knowledge of materials and processes, etc.

2. Technical, which involves the adaptation or application of new scientific knowledge to replace existing ideas or provide new ways of completing tasks.

3. Operational, where the aim is to develop procedures that make the best use of the technical developments.

In terms of productivity improvements, the activities at the scientific and technical levels provide the principal increases. However, they will also be more expensive to fund, and take much longer to bring to fruition than activities at the operational level (see Figure 11.3). For this reason, many organizations decide not to invest at these two levels. At the operational level, the investment is relatively inexpensive and yields quick, though less significant, results. Consequently, many organizations have pursued productivity improvements at the operational level: the methods adopted, however, vary. Some improvements come through experience, trial and error, or ingenuity. Other ways of studying work have been developed which provide a systematic approach to the investigations of existing methods and to the development and implementation of improved methods as ways of increasing the productivity of existing resources.

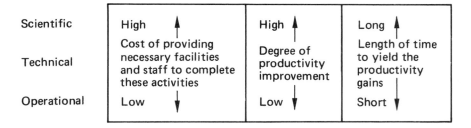

Figure 11.3   Approaches to higher productivity.

Service applications

Measuring white-collar productivity is difficult but not impossible. The assessment techniques for measuring the contribution of these workers to the goods of an organization have not been adequately developed. This is partly because productivity measures for goods-producing sectors have evolved over time, are understood and their use in terms of comparative trends are established. Consequently, there has been a tendency to transfer this approach (at least in part) to service industries, which has meant that the development of measures pertinent to this sector has been retarded. However, there are also specific obstacles to be development of measures. These fall into a number of categories:

1. It is difficult to define the output or contribution made by certain white-collar workers. In a manufacturing firm, output in the productivity equation is the goods produced and sold. Similarly, in the service organization, output comprises the services provided and sold. However, in neither situation are white-collar workers or their equivalent likely to be directly responsible for this output. Generally, they contribute to the output by providing support services to the goods-producing and service-producing activities. Defining the nature, value and unit measure of this contribution to output has proved difficult.

2. A factor which increases the difficulties outlined in 1 above is the less definable nature of a service. The basis of productivity analysis is to measure activity rather than results. Countable units are easy to put into a productivity ratio and to monitor. However, although a countable product can embrace the necessary features of the specification (e.g. quality), this is difficult to accomplish in a service. Consequently, maximizing this ratio may not be the preferred route to follow to the point of being counter-productive.

3. It is difficult to match inputs and outputs within an acceptable time-frame. Today's efforts may not show in the foreseeable future whilst they will undoubtedly affect tomorrow's performance. The development of new

products/services, client support and the drive to improve productivity are examples.

4. The quality of a product/service is inseparable from the item/activity itself. However, the nature of service provision makes the measurement of quality more difficult to define, rejects more difficult to ascertain and the delivery of a substandard service more difficult to prevent. The result is that quantifying both output and quality levels is difficult to establish.

5. People working in a service business (as is the case with white-collar workers in goods-producing firms) are not accustomed to being measured. They view measurement as an inappropriate means of assessing their contribution and a reduction in the status of their work. The result is resistance to introducing measurement based partly on a fear of the outcome.

However, the need to improve and measure productivity in service industries (and their white-collar equivalent in goods-producing firms) is a significant and necessary task. It is important, therefore, to accomplish this in an effective and participative way. In so doing, companies should both remember lessons from the past and also consider those factors which are pertinent to the nature of the work and the organization.

Involve those concerned
The failure of companies to involve blue-collar workers in the past led to resentment and resistance at the time, an attitude which purveys even today. The success achieved by other nations (e.g. Japan) has in part been based upon appropriate high levels of involvement. Involving people in the process needs to be undertaken as early as possible particularly in service industries where the procedures are less rigid and the outputs less tangible. Discussions on the purposes of the measures and their ultimate use will allay fears, reduce resistance and match the expectations of incumbents concerning levels of responsibility and their role in the interpretation of the service and the delivery system.

Establish the purpose
Starting with the goals of the organization, measures should be developed to fit these needs. Congruency between the measure and objectives ensures relevance of effort, and consistency and coherence of purpose. In service industries this linkage is normally inherently less defined than its goods-producing counterpart.

Determine the measures
Starting with existing output/input ratios in mind often incurs the problem of trying to modify a measure which is inappropriate for the purpose. The approach to be followed is to determine first the outputs, then the inputs and lastly the ratios. This will enable the different factors to be assessed independently of one another initially then later in their related form.

This procedure allows each part to be defined separately thus simplifying the task. Furthermore, by electing to define outputs first, the more difficult and important factor in the equation is addressed without introducing further complexities. Since output measures are often difficult to determine directly, surrogate measures are often used. It is most important, therefore, to involve those concerned in this decision in order to ensure that what the measure is intended to accomplish is understood. This avoids undue emphasis being placed on non-critical factors which, if achieved, would result in an apparently high, overall business performance. Group consensus not only reduces this possible outcome but also creates the opportunity to refine the measure over time.

Input measures should be chosen to reflect the task. Choices between single- and multi-factor measures are discussed earlier and some illustrations are given in Figure 11.4. When choosing which measures to use, the need to relate them to the output measures must also be appreciated. One aspect to consider here is the appropriate time base of the input compared to the output(s) involved. Thus, clerical staff inputs may be measured in hours or days whereas the research department would be more appropriately described in numbers of people or the salary bill.

The last step in defining the measures concerns selecting the ratios. The multiples on hand will be many, so some factors to consider, in general terms as well as to do particularly with service applications, include:

1. Avoid second measures: keep the number of measures small and focused.

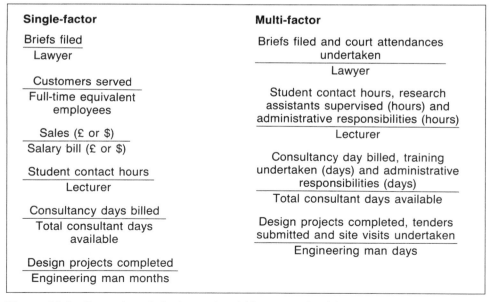

Figure 11.4 Examples of single- and multi-factor productivity measures relating to service businesses.

2.　Select measures with the following characteristics:
　　(a)　data are readily available;
　　(b)　reflected performance is understood by all concerned;
　　(c)　some control is exercised by those being measured.

3.　Measures for one function are compatible not only with other parts of the organization but also with the corporate measures in use.

Revise
Implementing a productivity measurement system is not a one-off project. In service industries in particular, changes in mix, continuous reinterpretation of the task, the application of technology and changes in organizational goals will bring about short- and long-term implications for the business and the measures used to evaluate performance and improvement. Periodic revision needs to be built into the system both in relation to productivity measurement in particular and as part of an on-going, corporate review in general.

Section B: The study of work

This section will concentrate on some of the systematic approaches to work at the operational level, and the term *work study* will be used to embrace these approaches. Many organizations employ qualified people to study work; these people normally work extensively in the operations area and report to the operations manager. It is essential on these two counts, that the latter understands the activities involved, how these should be applied, how to evaluate their use and can measure and control this function's contribution to the improvement of his area of responsibility. Consequently, this chapter deals in depth with the important aspects embodied in the study and control of work.

Defining work study

The term work study was defined in British Standard 3138 as:

> The systematic examination of activities in order to improve the effective use of human and other material resources.[3]

Work study is an analytical and systematic technique. *Analytical* in that it requires factual answers to questions, so enabling decisions to be taken which are based on facts. Guesses and trial-and-error have no part in this procedure. *Systematic* in that it follows step-by-step procedures as part of the fact-finding investigation.

Until the early 1950s, work study was applied almost exclusively on the factory floor in industry. Today, however, it is being used in all functions of profit and non-profit organizations whether making a product or providing a service.

Work study leads to higher productivity and lower costs. The facts established in the investigation lead to better use being made of the inputs. Controls then compare what has happened with what should have happened according to the plan and highlights the area(s) in which corrective action should be taken.

There are two broad aspects of work study:

1. Method study — to find the best way of doing a task.
2. Work measurement — to find how long the job should take.

As shown in Figure 11.5, the facts derived from these two aspects of work study are used in various ways to improve productivity at the operational level. What do these two techniques embrace and how do they relate to one another? Both are defined in BS3138[3] as follows:

> Method study is the systematic and critical examination of the ways of doing things in order to make improvements.

> Work measurement is the application of techniques designed to establish the time for a qualified worker to carry out a task at a defined level of performance.

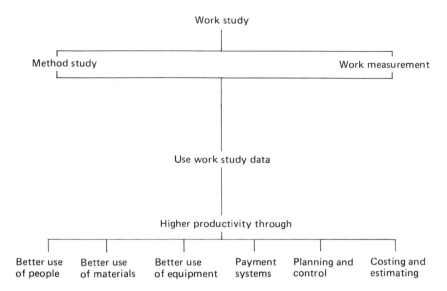

Figure 11.5 Work study.

These two techniques are, therefore, closely linked and used in conjunction with each other. Method study is used to reduce the work content of a procedure or job, whilst work measurement is used to determine how long the task should take.

As a general rule, method study should precede work measurement when time standards for output are being set, for there is no point in measuring the time taken until the improved method has been established. However, there are occasions when information on how long operations take is an important aid to a method study investigation. For example:

1. To assess the present method by highlighting where most time is being spent and, therefore, where the potential savings are greatest.

2. To allow comparison between various method improvements.

3. To indicate the extent and causes of ineffective time so that action can be taken to reduce or eliminate these before method improvements on existing procedures take place.

Method study

Method study is still often only applied to manual, repetitive tasks. As such, it limits itself to the study of operations and handling methods, the more traditional domain of motion study.[4] However, as any procedure is open to improvement, method study should be concerned with the process from product design to dispatch, service request to delivery or prime data creation to management report.

The main objectives of method study are:

1. To improve productivity by achieving either a lower cost for the same end result; or an improvement in the value of the end result.
2. Better working conditions.

In turn, these can be attained by:

1. Improved design or specification of the product/service.
2. Improved use of resources (people, materials and equipment).
3. Improved layout of premises and workplace.
4. Improved design of equipment.
5. Economy in human effort and the reduction of unnecessary fatigue.
6. Full utilization of existing skills and the development of new skills.
7. The development of better physical working conditions.

A systematic and critical approach

The key words in the earlier definition of method study are *systematic* and *critical examination*. Whilst substantial improvements can be made as a result of undisciplined ingenuity or trial-and-error methods, a systematic approach has the following advantages.

1. All the activities are considered, and not just the more obvious inefficiencies.
2. It will avoid situations where minor changes are later superseded by more global improvements.
3. It provides a basis for choosing between different options.
4. It helps to get nearer to the ideal method of working.
5. Recording the present method provides a reference point which can be used when necessary.

Sequence of analysis

The systematic procedure to be applied to an existing task, procedure or process is given below. It is important in any method study application that this procedural analysis is applied in the following sequence:

1. **Select** the work to be studied.
2. **Record** all the relevant facts about the present work method.

3. **Examine** the facts critically, in sequence, and using the techniques best suited to the purpose.
4. **Develop** the most practical and efficient method of doing the work, bearing in mind any contingencies.
5. **Record and re-examine** the new method to ensure that it is practicable in all aspects, and to seek comment from those involved.
6. **Train** those doing the task in the new skills required.
7. **Install** the new method as standard practice.
8. **Maintain** this practice by regular checks.

It is necessary not to be misled by the apparent simplicity of this procedure into thinking that method study is easy and routine. Method study is often extremely complex and requires the person(s) involved to possess the determination to see the process through, the ability to produce results, and an understanding of the human factors involved.

In addition, there are other important aspects to method study:

1. A questioning mind is essential — facts and not opinions are required, and nothing should be taken for granted.

2. A small percentage improvement of something large is usually better than a large percentage improvement of something small.

3. Always review the work in its total context, and keep the study and possible improvements in perspective.

Select

Selecting the work is one of the most important steps in the method study procedure, for where and on what the time is spent will be the basis for the gains that follow. It is essential, therefore, that the work will be of lasting benefit and that the return is sufficient for the time investment involved. Some symptoms which may prove useful as a guide in this selection are given in Table 11.7.

Record

Recording all the facts relating to the existing method is the next step. It is essential that the record is concise, clear and accurate because it provides the basis for the critical examination and the development of the improved method. Particular advantages accruing from the recording process are that it:

1. Aids systematic approach, and leads normally to a fuller investigation.
2. Is an aid to memory.
3. Promotes detailed examination.

To help in this detailed procedure, techniques have been designed to facilitate

Table 11.7 Some symptoms and their causes as a guide to the selection of 'profitable' areas of method study investigation

Symptom		Possible causes	
		Production organization	*Service organization*
Materials	High scrap Excessive usage	Product design; insufficient utilization; training; material quality; product/process design	Damage in store; pilferage; turnover of inventory to prevent obsolescence
Staff	Low staff performance Excessive lost time Excessive setting up time Low output Decreasing staff/ output (service) ratio	Inadequate skill levels; work scheduling; supervision; lack of work; short production runs; excessive, non-productive times; bottlenecks; high fatigue; poor working conditions	Inadequate skill levels; work scheduling; supervision; need to redevelop the current procedures; engaged on tasks outside the job scope; bottlenecks, poor working conditions
Equipment	Low output High costs	High setting up times; short production runs; breakdowns/maintenance; skills	Skills; frequent adaptations in order to keep the procedure going; breakdowns
Transport	Low utilization Excessive handling High costs	Plant layout; double handling; inadequate equipment; small batches	Layout; waiting; part loads; choice of various options; scheduling

recording all the relevant facts of a situation. The type of chart or diagram used depends upon the particular aspects of work being looked at and the level of detail required.

1 Charts indicating process sequence
These charts record the process used and the sequence followed for different levels of detail, and show different aspects of the task. The recording of this work is facilitated by classifying activities under five headings, each represented by a symbol (see Table 11.8). This form of shorthand is used almost universally; it not only saves time but also adds clarity and allows easier comparisons to be made between existing and proposed methods of working.[5]

Table 11.8 Summary of the symbols used to complete process charts, and their different meanings

Symbol	Activity	*Used to represent*		
		Material/document	*Person doing the task*	*Hand movements*
◯	Operation	Material, product, or document is modified or acted upon during the operation	Person completes an operation or task. This may include preparation for the next activity	Hand completing a task at one position
▢	Inspection	Materials, product or document is checked and quality, quantity or accuracy is verified	Person checks and verifies for quality, quantity or accuracy at this stage in the process or procedure	Inspection or checking procedure
⇨	Transport	The material, product or document is moved to another location without being part of an operation or inspection	Person moves from one position to another as part of the process or procedure without being part of an operation or inspection	Hand movement to another position
◗	Delay	Temporary storage or filing of an item. Not recorded as 'in store' or filed and not requiring authorization for its withdrawal	Person unable to complete the next part of the task	Waiting
▽	Storage	Controlled storage, governed by authorized receipt and issue; document filed and retained for future reference	Not used	Holding an object or document
⬡	Combined activities	To show activities performed at the same time or a person completing two tasks at the same time.		

Outline process chart. The two principal activities in a process or procedure are operations and inspections. This chart gives a valuable overview of the work being studied, with the minimum of recording effort, by showing the sequence of only the main operations and inspections involved. It is usually completed at the start of an investigation into a department or function to help decide the further areas for study. Against each main operation and inspection, a brief description is shown together with the time taken if available (see Figure 11.6).

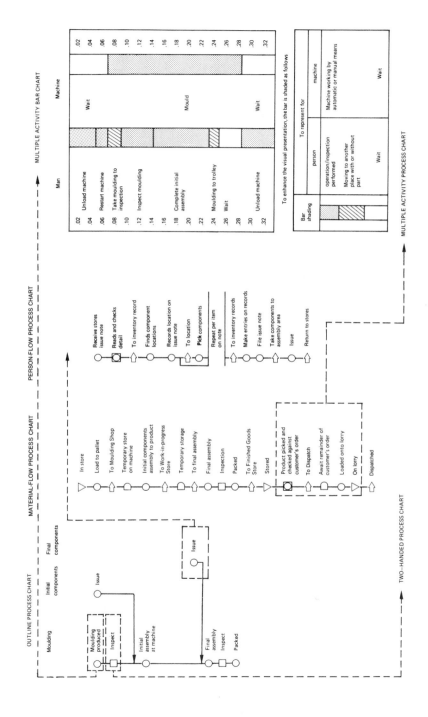

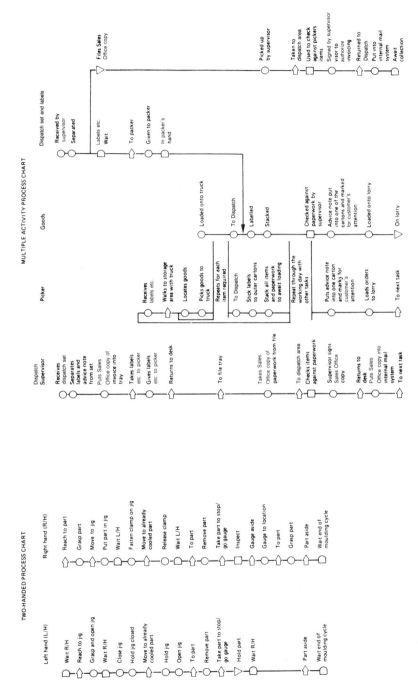

Figure 11.6 Relationship of charting techniques showing the relative level of detail and illustrating their differences.

Materials flow process chart.   A materials flow process chart records what happens to materials or documents in the process or procedure being studied. It amplifies an outline process chart by showing all operations and inspections as well as the movement, delay and storage/filing of the materials or documents involved (see Figure 11.6).

Person flow process chart.   This chart shows the movement of a person who has to move from place to place to carry out the task. As with the materials flow process chart, it shows all the operations and inspections which take place together with any movements and delays (see Figure 11.6).

Multiple activity process chart.   A multiple activity process chart shows the interrelated activities of persons, equipment, materials or documents with the latter particularly relating to clerical and administrative activities. It records, on a common scale, all the activities completed in the task and how they relate to one another within the process or procedure (see Figure 11.6).

Two-handed process chart.   The two-handed process chart is used to record the synchronized movement of a person's hands when carrying out a task, at one location (see Figure 11.6). The information recorded may be extended to other parts of the body (e.g. the legs), where relevant. The meaning behind the symbols used are those given in Table 11.8.

It is usual when completing this chart to note the need for any particular skills necessary to complete an operation.

In addition to these charts there is also an equipment flow process chart. This shows the flow of equipment through the process. It is not described more fully here as it is not in common use.

As the example in Figure 11.6 shows, the level of detail is significantly greater for some charts. For the operations manager, the most useful is often the outline process chart which gives an overview of the main activities. This can then be used to agree a work programme for future investigations and also provide a framework to guard against situations where a change in detail will cause problems elsewhere in the processes or procedures.

2 Charts using a time scale
The multiple activity bar chart is used to record simultaneously the activities of a group of persons or of one or more persons controlling two or more machines. It is a bar chart with separate bars for each person and/or each machine; the length of the bar is to scale and represents the time to complete an activity (see Figure 11.6). It is used to examine team or man and machine operations where the tasks are interrelated.

Other charts using a time scale are:

(a) Simo charts — simultaneous motion cycle charts which show (often based on film analysis) the activities of a person's hands, legs and other body movements on a common time scale.

(b) PMTS charts — charts to record the movements of an operation based on one of the predetermined motion time standard (PMTS) codes (see p. 322).

Both these are examples of micromotion analysis. They are concerned with the most detailed aspects of method improvements, are expensive and should be undertaken only in very short-cycle, high volume activities.

3 Diagrams indicating movement

Flow diagram.   The flow diagram is a two- or three-dimensional outline, drawn to scale, of the relevant area (e.g. plant, building or department) on which are traced the paths followed by people, equipment, materials or documents when completing the task. It is best used to illustrate either the flow of a component or product, or the movement of a person(s) repeating the same task.

String diagrams.   String diagrams are used chiefly to show the paths or movements of people, equipment, materials or documents, in a work situation. A scale outline of the work area is constructed, and pins are fixed at each work position visited. A piece of thread is then used to trace the movements in the actual sequence followed. The length of the thread, related to the scale used, gives the total distance travelled. The density of the string shows concentration of movement and highlights possible areas for improvement.

Neither of these diagrams is often used, having limited application. They can help to improve existing layouts, but it is essential to measure the constraints of other activities not being studied, and the effects of the proposed improvements on the overall layout.

4 Video

Improvements in video recording equipment have not only simplified its use but also led to significant reductions in cost, both in terms of initial investment and subsequent applications. Its advantages over methods of charting include:

(a) Level of accuracy — it provides a complete record of the activities that take place, especially where the task itself is complex.

(b) Facilitates analysis — the medium of a picture record facilitates subsequent analysis, both in terms of access and skill/experience levels of those involved. A visual record of events can be reviewed by all concerned and on any number of subsequent occasions. In addition, it allows all concerned to participate in the examination of activities.

(c) Acceptability — by taking away the element of human interpretation and presenting a more neutral approach to the activities under review, those involved more readily accept the record of events and acknowledge their participation in the procedure, leading to improved ways of working.

Examine

Critical examination is the essence of the method study procedure. The objectives of this step are to establish the exact reasons for each part of the procedure and to list ideas which will form the basis for developing the improved method.

The results achieved will be influenced by the attitude and skills of the person undertaking the investigation. Earlier (p. 303) some important aspects were given and it will prove worthwhile to bear these in mind throughout any such study.

To facilitate the investigation leading to these improvements, a procedure has been developed which helps to concentrate attention, in a logical way, on each set of activities. Before considering this in detail, however, it is necessary to be aware of the means available for improving the present method and the preferred order in which they should be used. The most fruitful step is either to *eliminate* or to *simplify* the products, components, procedures or any of the principal activities listed in Table 11.8. Either of these steps necessarily reduces the cost of the work involved. Other means of improvement are by *combining* or *changing* the materials, components, procedures, the sequencing of operations undertaken, where the work is completed, the equipment to do the task or any of the activities listed earlier. However, these options should be adopted only if they result in reduced costs.

Process examination

The examination of products and components is the subject of value analysis and value engineering and is covered in Chapter 5. However, the possible modifications to component/product design and materials should be borne in mind when undertaking a process investigation. Such an investigation is intended not only to identify areas of improvement but also to review the interrelationship of product and process in order to consider possible reductions in total costs.

The examination is designed to achieve the two objectives stated earlier: to establish the exact reasons for each part of the procedure, and then to generate ideas which will form the basis for developing the improved method. There are three steps involved:

1. The first aspect to be examined is *purpose*. Here, the aim is to determine the present method being used and the exact reason for doing the task(s). The crux of this review is to determine whether the task(s) can be *eliminated*.

2. If the task cannot be eliminated then the second step is to determine how the task is currently performed, why it is done that way and to generate ideas on how else it can be done. The aim here is to *simplify* the process.

3. This establishes where, when and who does the task(s) and why it is completed as at present. The aim is to improve the method by *combining* or *changing* any or all of these three aspects providing that the decision results in reduced costs.

Develop

Examining the existing methods is intended to form the basis of the development stage in the procedure. It does so by highlighting alternatives to the present method which then form the initial guidelines for an improved way of completing the task. However, there are still certain basic principles to be followed:

1. Build up the improved method in the following way:
    (a) outline the principal 'doing operations' in the best possible sequence;
    (b) add to these the minimum 'auxiliary operations' such as preparation, and putting aside;
    (c) agree on the points of inspection necessary to ensure the level of quality, and related to the costs involved in rectification at a later stage;
    (d) build up the transportation requirements essential to combine these activities with the minimum distances involved;
    (e) determine the delays which are necessary in the process to provide the WIP inventory functions; also, add in any necessary delays, for instance in two-handed operations, to balance out the cycle;
    (f) insert into the process the storage points necessary to serve functions such as rebatching, subassembly stores, cleanliness and to prevent pilferage; also, add holding functions which cannot be replaced by the use of jigs and fixtures.

2. Take into account known or proposed changes in the future and make allowances for these when developing the new methods.

3. Aim to make the new methods as simple as possible.

4. Adapt the job environment to the person's needs and capabilities to achieve efficiency, safety and comfort. Under the collective name of ergonomics or human engineering, this body of knowledge is concerned with the design of normal tasks, non-machine systems and manually operated equipment for the most effective accomplishment of the job.[6]

Record and re-examine

This step involves recording the new method and then checking and rechecking to ensure that the procedure is practical. Recording the proposals offers a visual description of the improvements and facilitates the checks that need to be made. In addition, recording allows the existing and proposed methods to be compared and improvements to be summarized (see Figure 11.7).

In this respect, the use of video again offers similar advantages to those listed earlier (p. 309). In addition, however, it also provides an excellent medium for transferring method improvements and best practice from one site to another. Organizations undertaking similar tasks and using similar equipment and machines can more easily transfer improved approaches and current best methods from one part of the business to another, thus maximizing benefits to be gained from these

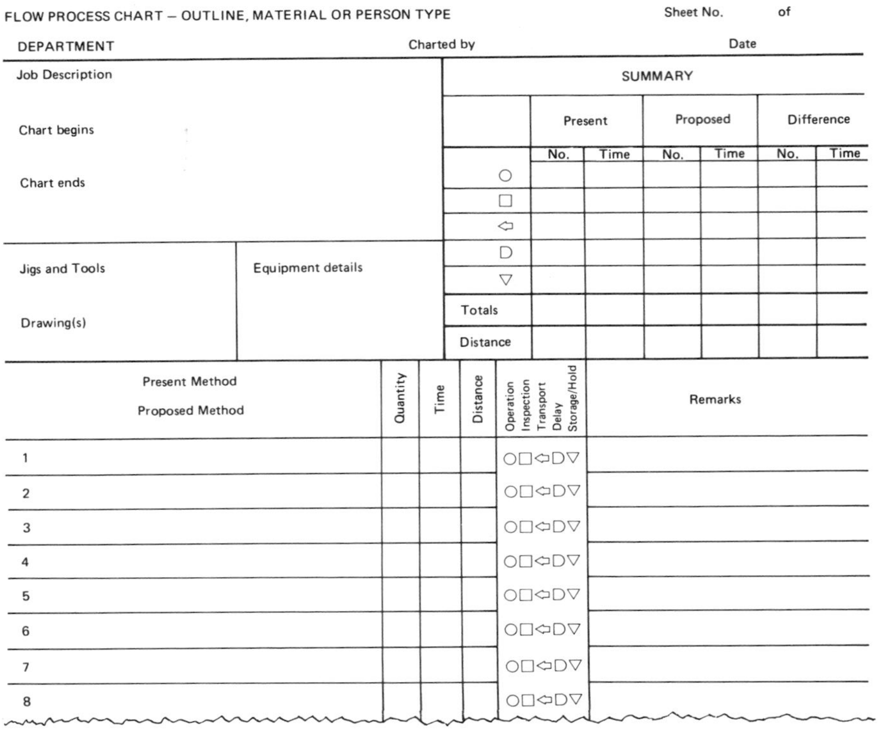

FLOW PROCESS CHART — OUTLINE, MATERIAL OR PERSON TYPE   Sheet No.   of

DEPARTMENT   Charted by   Date

Job Description		SUMMARY						
Chart begins			Present		Proposed		Difference	
			No.	Time	No.	Time	No.	Time
Chart ends		○						
		□						
		◁						
Jigs and Tools	Equipment details	D						
		▽						
Drawing(s)		Totals						
		Distance						

	Quantity	Time	Distance	Operation Inspection Transport Delay Storage/Hold	Remarks
Present Method / Proposed Method					
1				○□◁D▽	
2				○□◁D▽	
3				○□◁D▽	
4				○□◁D▽	
5				○□◁D▽	
6				○□◁D▽	
7				○□◁D▽	
8				○□◁D▽	

Figure 11.7 Typical flow process charting paper.

improvements. These inherent qualities also contribute to the next step in the procedure, which concerns installing and maintaining the improvements that have been identified. A permanent visual record facilitates the reinforcement of earlier training, thus providing a practical way of helping to maintain best practice.

Where proposed method improvements need to be considered by higher management, then the case for the change will need to be submitted to those concerned. The report should include statements on the existing situation, the relevant details of the proposals, the reasons for these changes and the results expected from the recommendations. Details such as the training required and the course of action to be followed in implementing these changes should also be included.

Install and maintain

Before effective installation of an improved method can be made, the following stages have to be undertaken:

1. *Gaining acceptance by supervision.* Supervisors generally have the greatest knowledge of existing methods. It is important, therefore, to consult them at

an early stage so they can contribute ideas and later help test the practicality of the proposed changes.

2. *Approval by management.* Top management will usually need to approve all major changes together with any minor changes involving capital expenditure. Changes need to be discussed at an early stage to sound out opinions, incorporate any ideas and keep management abreast of developments.

These first two steps are part of the earlier steps in the procedure. Unless they have been accomplished then there is little point in going further.

3. *Gaining acceptance by the persons doing the work and by their representatives.* People are often suspicious of investigations and new methods. It is important to work with them to allay these fears and, particularly, to incorporate their suggestions. It is important to tap the source of knowledge and ideas which exists in the place of work for the benefit of all concerned. They should always be kept in the picture — it is their livelihood.

4. *Training and retraining the people concerned in the new methods.* In many instances, the new method will not be very different from the existing one and the training requirements, therefore, will be small. However, where the new method involves either new or extensive skill changes, it is essential that adequate training is given to ensure that a satisfactory performance is reached as early as possible. Aspects to consider here are:

   (a) development of skills — where possible, this should initially be done away from the production area itself, following skills analysis; later, training will be completed on-the-job;
   (b) the learning curve — after developing the required skills it is necessary to build up a person's stamina and recognize that progress towards the measured output levels of the new system will only be achieved over time;
   (c) retraining and reverting to previous methods — if the differences between the existing and proposed methods are mainly to do with the methods used by the person doing the job then there are real dangers of the person reverting to the previous methods; in such circumstances this factor must be taken into account.

5. *Monitor the tasks in order to maintain the new method* — it is important, following installation, that periodic checks are made to monitor the progress being achieved and to ensure that the job is running as intended. In addition, this procedure allows adjustments to be made in order to overcome any snags which have come to light.

It is not always easy to gain co-operation from the people involved, but concern, interest and action after the event, when the excitement has died down, is an important way of demonstrating continued interest in the people and also of ensuring that the organization gains the most return from the investment it has made.

Service applications

The opening paragraph of this Section B highlighted the need to recognize the potential opportunities of using these approaches within service industries. The increasing proportion of costs incurred by overheads and the increasing willingness of companies to confront the need to increase productivity in white-collar areas in all sectors has brought about a growth in these applications. A survey in 1985 by the American Productivity Center[7] revealed the leading areas where white-collar productivity improvement had already started in the respondents' organizations — see Table 11.9.

The delay in addressing the productivity in these areas had been prolonged for many reasons. One concerns the inherent nature of the tasks involved. Typically, a white-collar workforce functions in a complex system, providing services which are difficult to count and measure. Procedures are hard to specify and track, and the work is highly discretionary and non-routine. However, productivity improvements in the rapidly growing service sector are critical to a nation's economy and in the increasingly competitive nature of the market-place.

Service redesign

Service redesign offers an opportunity to examine or review the service delivery system; and according to the 1985 survey, is used by 46 per cent of companies as one way to increase white-collar productivity.[7] It helps ensure that the system and its outcomes are consistent with its objectives and quality services are provided in an efficient manner. In so doing, the service redesign approach focuses on the whole work unit with the aim of identifying work-flow obstacles to increasing

Table 11.9   Areas where white-collar productivity improvement is underway

Areas where programmes were underway	Percentage of respondents
Operations/facilities management	62
Human resources/personnel	53
Accounting/finance	52
Management information systems	50
Clerical staff	49
Engineering and design	46
Customer services	41
Marketing	29
Research and development	28
Legal	10
Other	10

Source: American Productivity Center, *Productivity Letter*, 5 (December 1985), figure 2. With permission.

productivity and efficiency, to do a better job of meeting customer and/or user expectations, to improve the timeliness of the service and identify suitable current and future technology applications.

The first step is to prepare a flowchart outlining the service. The diagram is used to help understand the service delivery system so improvements can be made. The major elements to be highlighted are:

1. The steps in the service delivery system.
2. Information inputs from outside the work unit.
3. Key decision points.
4. Interface with the customer which can affect the perceived level of service.

A review of the flowchart should be completed by a cross-sectional group who, having checked the accuracy of the information, should develop an ideal system. When preparing the latter, constraints (e.g. current job descriptions) should be ignored. A comparison of the current with the ideal helps identify areas for improvement which may concern specific aspects or major parts of the service delivery system.

Action plans need to be developed which embody certain critical characteristics to help increase the success rate. These include that each plan should:

1. Lead to substantial change.
2. Be consistent with the ideal system.
3. Be identifiable with the service delivery system's objectives.
4. Be of reasonable time-frame.
5. Attract wide support.

Other points similar to those highlighted in this section need to be incorporated at each stage. Certainly, drawing up explicit responsibilities for implementation, addressing an implementation schedule, identifying and allocating the necessary resources, and following up during the post-implementation period are critical to successful developments.

Job restructuring
The increasing need to change the context of work in line with changing markets and the need to respond to demand requirements is well recognized as an on-going task. The approaches differ depending upon whether the job has a back room or front office location, due to the different levels of customer contact inherent in the two parts of the service delivery system.

1. *Back room.* Approaches similar to those applied in manufacturing companies have been used successfully to improve backroom procedures in service organizations. Part of this involves redesignating work to a lower level thereby reducing costs and also releasing what is often scarce capacity. Some service firms are using technology applications to bring together a number of individual parts of the process. The result is that it increases service awareness, it often transcends the back room/front office arrangements, reduces lead times and error rates in the system and encourages those involved to improve the system further.

2.   *Front office.* Restructuring jobs involving high customer contact is more difficult because of the perceptions that customers may have of roles and tasks. Thus, having the one person handle both 'low' and 'high' level work in the same organization may have sound corporate reasons but may be difficult for customers to reconcile in terms of business image. Expectations and appearances need to be carefully matched and the reconstruction of jobs needs to take this factor into account if it is to be achieved successfully. In addition, the expectations of those working in the service delivery system need also to be part of this resolution.

Some service businesses lend themselves more than others to opportunities of job restructuring. The chef in a restaurant creates interest and atmosphere by preparing dishes at the guests' tables, thereby combining several roles in one and bringing the back room to the customer. Electrical service businesses are increasingly linking the customer to the repairman rather than involving the potential misinterpretations of the front office interface. However, the hairdresser needs to take care on how much of the total task is performed by trainee staff. Similarly, although house conveyancing in the UK is completed largely by back room clerical staff, the professional solicitor still links with the client in the front office part of the system in order to provide the necessary assurances for a customer who is undertaking a significant and special transaction.

Applications of technology
The paperless office was much heralded in the early 1980s but it is only in recent years that developments in electronic equipment and office systems are helping to bring this about. Installation is being stimulated by a recognition that technology can offer both competitive advantage as well as the productivity gains so vital in achieving the necessary improvements in increasingly competitive service and industrial markets.

Whilst many of these technology applications are new, others are replacing existing low-technology investments of the past. For example, sales of typewriters in the UK were stagnant in 1988 but forecasts for 1989 and 1990 showed a fall of 30 and 50 per cent respectively compared with the 1988 total of 269,000 units. Personal computers (PCs) are taking their place. In 1988 there were 18 million PCs in the US, in the UK there was one PC for every 3.5 office workers, and by 1993 that will be a one for two ratio.[8]

The change in attitudes towards applications in technology is in part attributable to a growing recognition that they are an investment not an expense. The office equipment automation market is buoyant and is the fastest growing sector within the $340bn worldwide market for business equipment; as Figure 11.8 illustrates, forecasts show a continued rise in sales.

The applications which make up this market are several although computer systems at 41 per cent of 1988 sales is by far the largest (see Figure 11.9) with

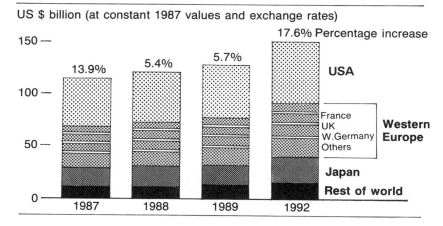

Figure 11.8 Actual and projected growth in the office automation equipment market.
Source: 'Office equipment', *Financial Times Survey* (19 October 1988), section 3, p.i. With permission.

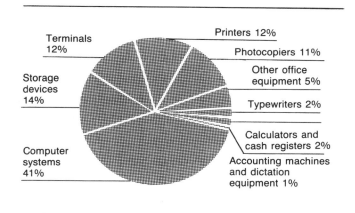

Figure 11.9 UK office automation market by product, 1988.
Source: Financial Times Survey, op. cit. With permission.

electronic equipment accounting for $115bn of the $340bn market. The impact that this is having is at two levels. At the general level it offers new ways of organizing and undertaking work whilst at the specific level it offers particular applications of some significance.

General opportunities   To illustrate the opportunities, two developments have been chosen. The first is the move towards a digital era. Traditional methods of text generation are expensive — for instance, an average of the findings of different organizations estimates the cost of producing an average business letter at £13.00.[9] Not only does the use of dictating machines reduce these costs but it also reduces errors caused by forgetfulness and omission. However, current research is centred on voice transmission. A voice messaging system comprises a sophisticated telephone answering machine allowing extension users to access facilities. Sales worth $20m in 1985 are expected to increase eleven-fold by 1994.[10] The second, and more radical, opportunity concerns the use of new technology enabling people to work from an office at home — in the UK it is estimated that by 1995 as many as four million people could be involved in this work-base transfer. 'Telecommuting'[11] is seen by many as heralding a new way of working. Shrinking microcomputers, portable/desktop options and telephone linkage make all this practicable. The opportunities in service industries and for office activities are significant. If the product is data transmittable then geographical location is unimportant where access is as short as a telephone call or quicker than a walk to another part of the building. The impact upon productivity and use of resources is of a high order of magnitude.

Specific opportunities   There are many specific applications of technology of note within the service sector. There follows just a few to illustrate the extent and importance of these opportunities to improve productivity within organizations.

The use of bar coding systems is now widespread throughout the retail industry as well as the basis for public lending library systems and the user-end of pharmaceutical products. The impact on inventory levels, especially with regard to perishable items (food, books and drugs), and the simplification of tracking and researching systems have been significant contributions to productivity improvements. The ability to provide up-to-date sales information from retail stores to either the parent company or wholesalers has enabled companies to reflect consumer trends. The Italian-based company, Benetton, developed an approach to retailing that makes effective use of small spaces. The typical Benetton outlet is no more than six hundred square feet, compared with the four thousand square feet of its traditional competitors. The key is the company's electronic communications system support by a manufacturing process which allows for a dyeing-to-order system and the rapid replenishment of items in greatest demand during a particular selling period. The result is low inventory and the reduction in necessary floor space where floor selling and inventory holding is kept to a minimum.

The impact of cash dispensing facilities in banks not only reduces demands on the system but also provides a 24-hour per day service. Direct access to general and personal information has also reduced demands on the enquiry service which leads to smaller queues and higher productivity.

A final example to illustrate the significant advantages which may be derived from technology applications is provided by computer aided design (CAD). Discussed more fully in Chapter 7, it offers not only substantial gains in terms of data storage and retrieval but also improves the ability to consider options, to cope with design changes, to provide a practical interface between the specialist and the user and to offer an organization the wherewithal to respond faster to market demands for change.

Involving the customer
Chapter 5 discusses the opportunity for involving the customer within the service delivery system. Customers have proved willing to carry out part of the task. The principal reasons include:

1. *Price reductions.* Supermarkets can offer lower priced (and often higher quality) products than other retail outlets partly because of the self-service principle. Petrol stations too are predominantly self-service due mainly to price benefits but also to the extra control it affords customers over the filling operation. In the USA, there is now a stated price differential between self-service and attended service as depicted earlier in Figure 5.8.

2. *Convenience.* Many self-service applications offer increased convenience to the customer. Subscriber telephone dialling (STD) has, for many telephone users, made operator-assisted calls troublesome and time-consuming. Cash dispensing facilities at banks and building societies have eased the customer's busy daily schedule. In some countries (e.g. Denmark) these facilities are increasingly being located at main shopping centres and in large department stores.

Back room versus front office
The final service issue concerns the need to distinguish between back room and front office activities. The section on job restructuring identified this, and similar distinctions need to be made throughout the service delivery system. Some points of which to take account include:

1. When jobs are reviewed it is essential to distinguish those tasks which are exclusively front office or back room from those which can be completed in either part of the system. Where manning levels permit, it is preferable to complete back room tasks in that part of the system.

2. The range of method study techniques described earlier in this chapter are in common use in many service organizations as part of the way to improve productivity and maintain acceptable levels of efficiency. This is particularly so in the back room activities of banks, building societies and supermarkets which handle high volume transactions, normally supported by batch (with some line) processes.

3. Front office transactions typically involve higher levels of discretion than their back room counterparts and necessarily need to provide for the uncertainties in the process, and the varying and unpredictable levels of customization

associated with a low-volume batch/jobbing process. Those involved need to embrace most aspects of the task and systematically look for improvements based upon experience. Identifying opportunities to review methods as volumes increase (because of demand or because there is duplication of effort within the system) is an essential part of the drive to improve productivity.

4. As organizations grow, communications become more difficult. Although procedures become departmentalized for reasons of efficiency, it is important to recognize that the trade-offs in achieving these gains often include problems which show up as delays in the system and an increase in time-consuming activities necessary to resolve the higher number of instances which are not resolved by the current procedures.

It is important, therefore, to review the service delivery sytem as a whole in order to secure the necessary improvements. Restructuring large parts of the system is a common source of significant gain. These may emanate from switching front office and backroom tasks, or creating approaches which transcend the departmentalization of activities thus reducing the disadvantages of this latter approach to service delivery system arrangements whilst maintaining the basic structures required by more specialized roles.

One example concerns TRW Inc.'s[12] attempts to improve the variance analysis reports (VARs) procedure as it related to a classified programme to develop software for a military satellite. Before work started, half the forty VARs each month were rejected. At the end, this number had dropped to one-quarter of the original rejection rate (i.e. one-eighth of the VARs). The VAR procedure for reporting deviations brought tensions between the design and business reporting groups. Changes resulted in joint meetings to discuss the format and content of a VAR before it was processed. Not only did the reject rate drop but a modified VAR was produced in one day rather than the two weeks taken under the previous approach.

Identifying problems and solutions

An important part of the study of work concerns the identifying of problems and potential solutions. To help in this task it is important to recognize two different kinds of thinking.

1. Convergent thinking, which concerns logical deduction from known facts. Also known as analytical thinking.

2. Divergent thinking, which is required where the facts do not facilitate or permit logical thinking, imagination is called for, often leading to several possible answers. Also known as creative or lateral thinking.

In practice, most applications call for a mixture of both. The analysis of known facts is followed by some divergent/creative thinking to find other possibilities. These, in turn, are analysed to find answers which stimulate more creative thinking, and so on.

Convergent thinking

The approaches detailed throughout this chapter and elsewhere in the book have been principally analytical in nature. One important addition to these, of particular use in identifying the source of problems, is the technique known as fishbone analysis. As illustrated in Figure 11.10, the result is fishbone in shape, hence the name. (A further example is provided by Figure 12.6 on p. 408.) This illustration is the outcome of an investigation into a company's problem of being unable to supply quality product to meet the requirements of the high speed production lines of one of its customers. Excess processing waste was clearly identified, involving a minimum loss of about $40,000 in addition to the serious problem of failing to achieve acceptable levels of delivery reliability. The detailed analysis and systematic review provided by the fishbone diagram enabled the company to review the causes and identify the several areas where improvements were needed and were made.

Divergent thinking

Most people, because of their training and background, are good at analytical thinking. On the other hand, few are good at divergent or creative thinking, either on its own or in combination with analytical approaches. Barriers are set up, either consciously or unconsciously, which prevent the growth of ideas. These restrictions come from a number of sources:

1. Self-imposed limits to possible solutions.
2. An inherent belief that there is one right answer.
3. Fear of being wrong.
4. Conformity to behaviour norms.
5. Unwillingness to challenge the obvious.

Analytical approaches restrict imagination, and continuous evaluation puts the brake on ideas outside apparent norms or perceived boundaries. Creative thinking, on the other hand, is the process of relating ideas or things which were previously unrelated. By consciously suspending judgement and evaluating ideas at a later stage, the mind is given the opportunity to think laterally rather than being constrained within the vertical dimension associated with analytical approaches.

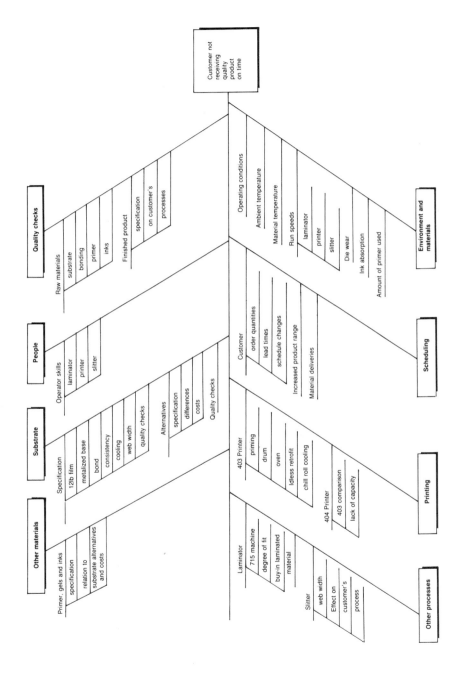

Figure 11.10 An example of fishbone analysis.

The stages involved in creative thinking are:

1. *Preparation* — collecting the known facts, defining the problem in different ways, and restating/clarifying the problem.

2. *Generation* — concerns the need to generate ideas, both in themselves and as a stimulus to creating other perspectives.

3. *Incubation* — leaving the problem in the subconscious state as a way of creating new thoughts, the process of bisociation.

4. *Insights* — linking ideas to possible solutions.

5. *Evaluation* — analysing all the facts on which to base evaluations of the possible solutions.

Stages 1 and 5 are based on analytical approaches, whereas the other three are based on creative thinking. The key in this procedure, therefore, is the deliberate separation of the creation and evaluation of ideas phases. Completing stages 2, 3 and 4 is best done in groups and with the aim of creating quantity not quality of ideas: by creating large numbers of ideas, new ideas are sparked off. To help achieve this, the following rules apply:

1. *Suspend judgement* — criticism of ideas is not permitted. Evaluation comes after the creative stage. Bringing these two phases together will lead to implied criticism and a reluctance to contribute. The key is to discourage self-evaluation from entering the process.

2. *Freewheel* — wild ideas are deliberately fostered as they lead to better results.

3. *Cross-fertilize* — at set stages, give participants the task of combining and improving on the ideas of others.

To help in the generation of ideas a number of techniques may be used including:

1. *Brainstorming* — six to twenty people take a problem and, working under the rules 1–3 above, seek solutions. All ideas are written so as to remain visible throughout. Typically, the five stages listed earlier form the basis for using this technique.

2. *Reverse brainstorming* — this asks, of an idea which is being considered, 'In how many ways can this idea fail?'

3. *Attribute listening* — this technique lists the main attributes of the idea or object and then examines how it can be changed.

4. *Forced relationships* — this approach seeks to list the ways in which ideas or objects can be combined.

Often a combination of two or more of the above techniques may be used as one way of increasing the total number of ideas.

Set-up reductions

The traditional method of coping with long machine set-ups or make-readies has been long production runs. However, the concept of just-in-time (JIT) has highlighted the need to review and systematically reduce set-ups. JIT insists that companies aim to produce a product when the customer wants it, and so the outcome is typically that more frequent and smaller order quantities are produced. However, order size and length of set-up is an important relationship, and companies need to reduce set-ups in line with lower order quantities at least to maintain the balance between them. Furthermore, outside the context of JIT, set-up reduction is intuitively a sound approach to improving productivity. The key is to simplify set-ups thus reducing the:

1. Direct costs incurred.
2. Capacity losses involved.
3. Level of inventory which results.

Depending upon the particular situation, companies will strike a balance between these advantages. For example, producing smaller order quantities will mean more set-ups for a given output, which will lead to lower inventory levels but not necessarily lowering associated total direct costs, as more set-ups will be required, even though the time per set-up has been reduced. Similarly, if current demand for a product does not require overtime working, then the gains associated with reducing losses in capacity stemming from set-ups, although available, will not be relevant.

Lastly, it is most important to recognize the contribution to be made in set-up reductions by those involved in completing the tasks. They are the experts, and ownership is vital to the actual level of improvement achieved and of its effective installation and maintenance. Supporting these people, though, are the technical experts offering a range of appropriate inputs and ideas. With shopfloor and support personnel working together, all set-up reduction ideas can be implemented following sound engineering, and tool and equipment design principles.

Procedure

Set-up reduction starts with selecting a team of people comprising two or three of those responsible for set-ups, one or two technical support staff and a group leader. In addition, the area supervisor may be included, depending upon availability and personality.

The next step is to record the actual set-up operation from start to finish. The most suitable medium for this is a video tape embodying a digital clock in the corner to facilitate timing the different aspects of the set-up. The video recording need not be a professional production: the objective is simply to capture the organization and choreography of the set-up, with essential detail being provided at a later stage.

The team then reviews the recording to identify the activities involved, separating these into four classifications:

1. Internal/external
2. Clamping
3. Adjustments
4. Problems.

Listing the activities by category and prioritizing them by frequency and duration enables the team to separate the important from the less important, and gives clues to the questions which should be addressed.

Internal/external

This question seeks to identify those elements of a set-up which can be completed when the process is running (external elements) and those which can be completed only when the process is stopped (internal elements). The outcome is a two-fold task:

1. All set-up elements which can be undertaken when the process is running must be completed at that time.
2. Convert as many internal tasks to the external category.

This is built on the premise that many elements of a set-up can be completed before the machine stops. These instances, therefore, normally require duplicate investments where tooling and equipment is involved.

Clamping

Threaded fasteners (e.g. nuts, bolts and screws) have the advantages of enormous holding power and are space saving as a method of clamping. They are ideal clamping mechanisms for permanent positions.

However, where changeovers are involved, the disadvantages are significant. In particular, a level of precision is demanded which is not only time consuming but also needs care to ensure that further difficulties and problems are avoided (e.g. cross-threading). Moreover, it is only the last or first half turn which actually provides the holding or releasing function. All the activity before or after this final or initial step is not critical and only necessary because of the chosen method of fastening. Threads are also prone to damage, necessitating replacement, adjustment or additional time. Lastly, tools are needed to complete clamping mechanisms based on threads and this adds uncertainty and time through possible loss or the available tool being unsuitable for some applications and it creates a need for additional motor skills in order to complete the task satisfactorily.

The aim, therefore, is to:

1. Eliminate tools.

2. Reduce the essential motions to secure/release the clamping function to one or, at the most, two.

Linked to this is the need to determine the amount of force which the clamp has to overcome and then consider alternatives to threads to provide this — for example, levers, pins, wedges, levers and cam-action clamps.

Adjustments
The time taken to get the equipment running correctly, once the set-up is complete, is adjustment time. The goal is to eliminate all adjustments during set-up, including the practice of testing the set-up for potential adjustments. Sources of adjustments include:

1. Most equipment is designed for a wider range of applications than that on which it is being currently used. Building on this knowledge, mechanical stops replace graded adjustments performed by experience and measured by eye.

2. Often, several adjustment methods are used. The task is to select the exact position for different parts, thereby eliminating the need for adjustments on these products.

3. The steps to complete adjustments need to be reduced by introducing self-positioning mechanisms where possible. The aim is to arrive at a situation where the first method of positioning fixtures is sufficient. If the current method involves much time on clamping, unclamping and adjustments, then the clamping methods need reviewing.

Problems
Frequently a high percentage of the set-up time is taken up with problems. This category includes any event which prevents a perfect, trouble-free set-up from being completed. It is essential that the root of these problems is uncovered. The aim is not to devise a procedure which facilitates the set-up despite the problems, but to eliminate the problems altogether.

Work measurement

It is worthwhile repeating here the definition of work measurement given earlier:

> Work measurement is the application of techniques designed to establish the time for a qualified worker to carry out a specified job at a defined level of performance.[3]

In other words, work measurement sets out to answer, 'How long should this job take to complete?'

Before describing the techniques used to provide this information it is important to understand the objectives of measuring work. These are:

1. With method study:
   (a) to eliminate ineffective time, with work measurement determining the extent of the possible improvement(s);
   (b) to allow comparisons of alternative methods to be made;
   (c) to balance work members in a team;
   (d) to determine an adequate workload for a person.

2. As a basis for:
   (a) planning and scheduling work;
   (b) estimating and costing;
   (c) labour and labour-cost control;
   (d) incentive schemes;
   (e) estimating future labour requirements;
   (f) establishing delivery promises.

Measuring work

The simplest way to measure work is to time how long a task takes. However, human work, being a complex mixture of manual and mental skills, does not lend itself to such a simple method. When calculating the time to complete a task, three major difficulties have to be accounted for:

1. Different methods may be used.

2. The time taken relates directly to the speed and effort of the person doing the task.

3. Some jobs are more strenuous than others, and this will affect the time taken to complete them.

Briefly, these three points are overcome in the following ways:

1. All work measurement techniques give a time for one particular method of doing a job. This time is, therefore, invalid for other methods.

2. Variations in speed and effort are accounted for by arranging for the observer to assess these aspects — this is known as *rating* and relates to a numerical scale which the observer is trained to use in this assessment process.

3. During a study, all rest is excluded from the time to complete the task. This 'net' time is later increased uniformly to include an allowance for rest and personal needs. How much the allowance should be is stipulated by a set of tables based upon the results of experiments conducted into aspects of fatigue.

Procedure

The steps to be followed in this procedure are outlined here:

1. **Select** the operation to be studied. The reasons behind the selection will tend to relate to the two sets of objectives given on p. 327.

2. **Record** all relevant details of the operation — space is usually provided at the top of the sheet used in the analysis.

3. **Analyse** — break down the work into smaller elements. How small these should be will depend upon the chosen work measurement technique.

4. **Measure** — establish the basic time for each element.

5. **Establish a standard time** — add to the basic time the allowances for rest and personal needs and those covering general aspects of work which have to be completed but are not directly part of the specific work cycle.

6. **Production studies** to check the time established by testing it under working conditions.

There are four basic principles to be considered when deciding on the most appropriate technique of work measurement:

1. Total tasks may be regarded as repetitive or non-repetitive. The appropriate technique for measuring work should reflect this.

2. The work embodied in completing the task may also be regarded as being repetitive or non-repetitive. Repetitive means that a series of steps or a stage in the operation to complete one task is the same as that required to complete other tasks.

3. The more accurate the level of measurement chosen, then the more time-consuming and costly it will be.

4. The expression of the time taken will vary with the length of the overall job. Completion of short repetitive tasks will normally be expressed in minutes and parts of a minute. On the other hand, completion of an oil tanker will probably be expressed in weeks and parts of a week.

Select

As in method study, the first step in work measurement is to select the job to be studied. There is often a reason why a job needs to be measured: usually, it relates to the objectives of work measurement given previously. However, there are sometimes other reasons which are equally valid and important in terms of the total work task. Some of these reasons are:

1. It is a new job, therefore basic information is required in terms of production planning and scheduling, costing, incentive schemes and so on.

2. A change in the materials used, operations involved or method of working which require a revised time standard.
3. A complaint or query has been made by the person doing the task.
4. To investigate plant or equipment utilization especially where output is lower or downtime higher than expected.
5. As an input to a method's investigation.
6. Where the labour cost of a job appears to be excessive.

Which person is selected for study is also very important. Returning to the definition of work study given earlier in this chapter, it specifically states the need to 'establish the time for a qualified worker to carry out a specified job'. Consequently, when establishing the time to do a job it is necessary to study the performance of a skilled person who has received the training to do the task in the method laid down.

Similarly, a procedure should be agreed on how to approach the person involved or that person's representative which is both practical and courteous. If a choice of qualified workers is available then it is good practice to study more than one and to ask the supervisor and staff representative for their advice on which persons they would consider suitable.

Record

All relevant details should be recorded about the study and filed with it when the study is completed. Standard analysis sheets carry the usual information which should be recorded (see Figure 11A.1 of the appendix to this chapter).

Analyse

The first step is to check the method. Where the job has been studied before, both the specified method of completing the task and the elements used in previous studies should be noted. The method currently being used by the person doing the task should then be checked (bearing in mind that the time previously established relates only to the method being used at the time the work was measured) and the work elements timed should be used to provide later comparisons.

Where the task is new, the method being used should be checked against the agreed method if it has been established. If there is no agreed method, then this has to be established before measurement can take place. The next step is to determine the elements of work within the task, which will facilitate the measuring process. The length of these work elements will, however, relate to the length of the job. In short cycle, repetitive work the preferred length of an element is between 0.1 and 0.5 of a minute (usually a minute is expressed in decimals to facilitate calculations). This is to avoid situations of difficulty in recording when the duration is too short, and difficulty in noting the speed and effectiveness applied during an element of work when that element is too long.

However, in certain methods of work measurement (e.g. estimating) the work is not broken down into elements and the points made here do not apply.

Measure

Techniques to measure short, repetitive tasks

As a general rule, the techniques which should be used to measure short, repetitive tasks will be chosen to provide accurate information expressed in minutes and parts of a minute. The reason for this is fundamental to the task itself — as it only takes a short time to complete, but will be completed on numerous occasions, the measurement needs to be accurate.

The techniques most commonly used to provide this level of accuracy are time study and predetermined motion time standards. The first of these will be described in detail and the complete procedure to establish what is known as a 'standard time' will be shown. The reason for providing such detail is that time study can be regarded as a basis for understanding work measurement and how 'standard times' are calculated.[13] It will, therefore, provide a sound basis for understanding the measurement of work. The other techniques which can be used for measuring work will be described in less detail.

Time study. Before describing the procedure to be followed in measuring work when using time study, it will be useful to outline three general points on which the concepts of establishing the time to do a job are based: types of element, rating and units of work.

The work cycle or total task must first be broken down into separate elements selected for convenience of observation, measurement and analysis. The three most important elements are:

1. Repetitive elements — these occur at least once in every work cycle.
2. Occasional elements of regular frequency — these occur at regular intervals and relate to the work cycle (e.g. once in every ten cycles).
3. Occasional elements of irregular frequency — those aspects of work which, though related to the work cycle, occur irregularly and usually infrequently.

In addition to the work elements, other periods of time will be recorded during a study. These are:

1. Contingencies — those aspects of work which occur at irregular intervals and, though not related directly to the task in hand, are part of the general working conditions. In these situations, the person is 'legitimately' prevented from carrying on with the task being studied.

2. Ineffective time — those times when the person is either relaxing or doing something entirely unconnected with the job in hand (e.g. part of another task). It is important here to recognize that there will be situations in which a person is required to pay attention to the process even though it requires no human input (e.g. during a machining process, inspection process or print-out sequence). If this is essential to the task, then it is regarded as productive work and part of the work cycle (see the comments on repetitive and occasional elements above).

The need to be able to assess the speed and effectiveness of the person doing the task is discussed earlier in the chapter. The way to accomplish this is by *rating*. This is the process of assessing a person's speed and effectiveness of working relative to a predetermined standard, in order to determine the amount of work done. It is a judgement of the effective rate of working, to account for a person's speed of movement, dexterity and consistency of application.

When the assessment is made it is based on a numerical scale. There are three such scales in use, known as the 60−80, 0−133 and 0−100 scales. They each serve the same purpose. The most commonly used are the latter two, and of these the 0−100 scale is preferred and has been adopted as the British Standards Institution (BSI) scale. In this book, only the BSI 0−100 scale will be used in the text and examples. There are two fixed points on the BSI 0−100 scale:

    0 = No work
  100 = Incentive performance (called standard performance)

Other points are also referenced to help gauge performance and these are given in Table 11.10. In each instance, the person being observed must have attained the required level of quality and accuracy when completing the task.

Table 11.10   Some points on the 0−100 rating scale, with descriptions

Rating (0−100)	Description	Comparable walking speed (mph)
150	Exceptionally fast; requires intense effort and concentration. Usually able to maintain this over short periods only	6
125	Very fast; well above the average performance. Shows high degree of skill, co-ordination and speed	5
100	Brisk performance — the average performance of a person paid on an incentive scheme. Known as *standard* performance	4
75	Steady, deliberate performance. Known as *day rate* to imply the speed and effectiveness of someone not working on an incentive scheme	3
50	Very slow with fumbling movements. Person shows distinct lack of speed and effectiveness or appears to have no interest in the task on hand	2
0	No activity	0

A unit of work comprises:

The basic time required to do the task[14]
+ An allowance to cover necessary work outside the particular task under review
+ An allowance for rest and personal needs, dependent upon the nature of the task.

Work measurement, therefore, establishes the basic time to do a task. The calculation of allowances for other work and for rest and personal needs is a separate exercise relating to each task. The end-result is to provide a percentage uplift on the basic time to provide for the allowances inherent in completing the task in question.

The appendix to this chapter gives a worked example of the procedures involved in taking a time study. The method used is based on the use of a decimal stopwatch. The person completing the study measures the elements of the task over a period of time. The total time for the job is established by calculating the average basic minutes (i.e. actual time taken adjusted by the rating observed — see Figure 11.10) for each element as provided by a number of studies, building in other parts of the total task (occasionals and contingencies) and giving due allowance for rest. When this is completed, the standard time for a job has been established — see pp. 363–6.

Predetermined motion time standards (PMTS). The essence of time study is to time and rate the task by direct observation. However, from the genesis of work study the concept of having predetermined times for operations was considered. Several effective systems have been devised which replace observations by highly detailed method study in order to analyse and classify the motions used. Tables of predetermined times for each classified motion are drawn up, and thus the total time for an operation can be calculated by adding together the predetermined times of its constituent parts.

The tables have been established through research and analysis and are given in the form of basic minutes. The most widely used system in the UK is Methods Time Measurement (MTM). Within this, and the other systems used, about twenty different elementary motions covering all body, limb and eye movements have been identified and times for each provided. Rules regulating the application of PMTS systems are in force, and training courses are provided.

The application of these systems follows detailed method study with basic motion patterns such as reach, grasp, move and position, having to be identified within the study. The appropriate times for each movement, depending upon its degree of difficulty and the distance moved, are then applied to give a time for the task. However, the amount of detailed work involved means that basic PMTS systems were only suitable for short-cycle, repetitive work. For instance, it takes, on average, 150 minutes to complete an MTM analysis of an operation taking 1 minute.

An important refinement, therefore, has been the development of a second

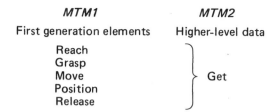

Figure 11.11 An example to illustrate the concept of higher-level data by comparison with first generation data.

generation PMTS system (see Figure 11.11). This development is based on the fact that certain motions always follow one another (e.g. if a person reaches for something then a grasp will follow and a move will follow that). Consequently, 'higher-level' data have been developed (e.g. MTM2) which have reduced the application times for PMTS systems by a half or more. The advantages of using these systems are:

1. They remove the need to time someone doing the task.
2. They have increased trade union support because of 1 above.
3. Accurate estimating of new work is possible.
4. The effect of method changes can be predicted.
5. Standards can be set in advance.
6. Consistency between time standards established for different tasks is potentially greater.

The disadvantages are:

1. They are costly — where work has a cycle time greater than two minutes then time study is quicker.
2. A high calibre of observer is necessary.

Note that in using PMTS systems to establish a standard time for a task, it is essential to know if relaxation allowances have already been included in the times given.

Synthetics. In the same way that PMTS systems provide predetermined times for basic operations, synthetic times can be built up from previous time studies carried out in an organization. In this way, times for completing part or all of a task can be calculated from numerous past studies, and used to build up the time to complete a range of similar work at a defined level of performance.

Normally, these times would embody higher-level data and cover much longer parts of a task than basic human movement. For example, dust a chair, paint one running metre of window frame or make an outer carton (type 5) (see Figure 11A.1 in the appendix to this chapter).

Increasingly, synthetic times are being used as a substitute for individual time studies in instances where tasks are made up of elements of work which have recurred a sufficient number of times in jobs previously studied. Synthetics have, therefore, many of the advantages and fewer of the disadvantages associated with PMTS systems.

Techniques to measure long, non-repetitive tasks
Many tasks have a long work cycle and will often occur infrequently. For such, time study and PMTS are not economic means of measurement. It is more appropriate to use one of three forms of estimating. (Note that synthetics may be based on times derived from any source of work measurement — see below).

Estimating. This form of measurement involves an 'assessment of the time required to carry out work, based on a knowledge and experience of similar types of work'.[3] This assessment is made on the total job without a breakdown into elements — see Table 11.11 — and is thus dependent upon the knowledge and experience of the evaluator. In making an assessment, the evaluator will often use historical times in an informal way.

Analytical estimating. This is a refined form of estimating, in which 'the time to carry out elements at a defined rate of working is estimated partially from knowledge and practical experience of the work concerned and partially from synthetic data'.[3] When using this technique the work is broken down into suitable elements and the times for these are either estimated or taken from synthetic data — see Table 11.11. Although more time consuming to apply than estimating, it is normally more accurate.

Comparative estimating. This is a further development of estimating in which the time for a task is evaluated by comparing the work involved with the work in a series of similar tasks. This method is based on the principles of using categories of work, where jobs are not given precise times but are placed in a time band (e.g. 2–3 hours), and the use of benchmark jobs — see Table 11.11. These latter jobs are chosen as being representative of a time band, and their times are based on a primary method of work measurement (e.g. time study). The use of benchmarks makes for speedy evaluation by slotting tasks into broad bands of time. Because a job is being measured against another job and not against a time, the process eliminates variables (such as skill, effort expected and unforeseen problems) that can obscure an evaluator's judgement. The comparison, therefore, can be made to allow for the same degree of skill and effort and for the same incidence of trouble.

In the same way that synthetics can be compiled from time study data, then synthetics can be established using the data generated from the estimating methods of work measurement. In fact, synthetics based on a combination of time study and estimating are often used for a wide range of work (see the comments under 'Analytical estimating'). The important prerequisite here, as elsewhere, is to be aware of the opportunity to build synthetic data and then ensure that all work measurement activity takes this into consideration when recording the basic information in order to facilitate its collection.

Table 11.11 Types of estimating which may be used to determine the time to be allocated to completing a particular task

Task	Estimating	Analytical estimating	Comparative estimating
Office cleaning	**An estimate of the time it would take** to empty all the ashtrays and waste bins, vacuum clean and dust the office under review would be made. This would be based on the estimator's own past experience of similar work.	The tasks involved in cleaning the office under review would be broken down into smaller parts, for example: Emptying 10 ashtrays Emptying 10 waste bins Dusting 10 desks Dusting 10 chairs Dusting 20 filing cabinets Dusting 50 metres of skirting board Dusting 10 window ledges Dusting 5 doors Vacuum cleaning 150 square metres of carpet with a high level of furniture congestion The next step is to complete an estimate for each of these parts. The individual estimates would be added to give an **overall time to complete the cleaning of this office**. Again, the times should be based on the estimator's own past experience of similar work.	From past experience of cleaning offices, a number of job categories would be compiled by the estimator. These would be chosen to reflect the **different timebands of the work undertaken** (see below), and one or more **benchmark jobs** would be selected as being representative of each band. When selected, each benchmark job would then be analysed in greater depth, and a detailed study would be completed to check that the timeband to which each job had been allocated was **appropriate**. A full description of the individual tasks involved for each job would also be recorded, and filed for later use: Timeband (hr) Benchmark job(s) $0-\frac{1}{2}$ Partner's office, 8 Southall Gardens $\frac{1}{2}-1$ Purchasing Department, AB Imports, Floor 4, Bradley House $1-1\frac{1}{2}$ Drawing office, Markham, Roberts & Co. $1\frac{1}{2}-2$ General office, Housing Department, Bursley DC $2-3$ Main open plan office, British Energy, West Midlands And so on. All future jobs would then be compared to each benchmark job and, usually, the midpoint of the timeband for the job to which it was most similar would be allocated and used in all the appropriate calculations.

Source: Terry Hill, *Small Business: Production/operations management* (Basingstoke: Macmillan Educational, 1987), pp. 162–3. With permission.

Techniques to measure capacity utilization and requirements
In many situations it is important both to measure the extent to which existing capacity is being used and to be able to monitor utilization in the future. The techniques available to provide this information are described here.

Activity sampling. Activity sampling is defined as:

> A technique in which a number of successive observations are made over a period of time of one or a group of machine(s), process(es) or worker(s). Each observation records what is happening at that instant and the percentage of observations recorded for a particular activity or delay is a measure of the percentage of time during which that activity or delay occurs.[3]

An extension of this technique is to rate when making the observations. This enables the time involved to be established at a known level of performance (e.g. 100 performance) as opposed to the observed proportion of time occupied by activities or delays (i.e. actual time).

Activity sampling involves making random observations over a representative period of time to provide information on: (1) capacity utilization of the facilities or persons employed on a task or in an area, and (2) the average time taken to complete a common task. Applications of this technique include: production areas with several pieces of equipment; warehousing, and administrative, clerical or typing units. In each, an assessment of utilization or an average time taken can be established.

The overall time spent on the specified activity is deduced from a number of random observations. Owing to the limitations inherent in sampling, an error is introduced. The size of this error can be calculated statistically. For this purpose, a 95 per cent confidence limit is considered to give sufficient accuracy, and is built into the following formula:

$$N = \frac{4P\,(100-P)}{L^2}$$

where N = number of random observations; P = percentage occurrence of the particular activity being reviewed; and L = the level of accuracy required. For example, if it is necessary to know the number of observations required to determine the unused time of a piece of equipment estimated at 35 per cent (this can be an estimate or the observed unused time from a pilot study) to an accuracy of ± 5 per cent, with 95 per cent confidence in the answer, the calculation would be:

$$N = \frac{4(35)\,(65)}{5^2} = 364$$

Conversely, it may be that a study has been completed, and the level of accuracy obtained at 95 per cent confidence limits needs to be ascertained. The following equation would be used:

$$L = 2 \times \sqrt{\frac{P(100-P)}{N}}$$

For example, if the percentage of time that warehousemen were not working was 10.1 per cent of the time observed and the number of observations totalled 6,500 the level of accuracy at 95 per cent confidence limit would be

$$L = 2 \times \sqrt{\frac{10.1(89.9)}{6,500}}$$

$$= 0.7$$

So, the warehouse staff were not working between 9.4 and 10.8 per cent of the time. If there were 20 staff observed then the capacity needed to cope with present throughputs could be reduced by some 10 per cent.

So far, the activity sampling study has revealed the percentage of time an activity has happened during the period of observation. To assess how long on average a task took, the percentage of time observed when staff were doing the task is first established in the way described. A period of time (e.g. day or week) is then studied to determine on how many occasions the task was completed (e.g. orders dispatched, letters typed, units produced). If during an 8 hour day, four staff were employed 65 per cent of their time on dispatches and completed in that period 180 dispatches, then the average dispatch time can be calculated as follows

$$\frac{65\% \times 4 \times 8 \text{ hours}}{180 \text{ dispatches}} = \frac{1,248 \text{ minutes}}{180} = 6.9 \text{ minutes per dispatch}$$

Information provided in this way enables management to establish the capacity required to handle the throughput observed during the period studied. Whether this is a normal load can be checked by comparing, say, the number of dispatches completed within the observed period with the number of dispatches completed in a reference period in the past. This reference period is chosen to represent a period of normal working over a period of time (e.g. three months).

When the capacity required to handle a normal workload has been established, then monitoring throughput against capacity levels on a regular basis can be put into effect. This is achieved by comparing, say, the weekly net hours available (i.e. total hours less rest and personal time) in a finished goods warehouse with the amount of work completed in the same period, e.g. the number of dispatches made, deliveries received, stock checks made and paperwork processed, the times for these activities having been established through activity sampling. Where work was not seen during the sample (e.g. tasks completed on a monthly basis only) then estimates for these are established.

This comparison enables management to monitor any throughput changes and their effect on, in this instance, the warehouse, and enables them to come to better decisions on whether to increase or decrease capacity on a temporary (through overtime or by making an internal transfer) or permanent (adding staff or natural wastage) basis.

Variable factor programming. Variable factor programming (VFP) is the name used by the American-based WOFAC Corporation for a labour, cost-reduction approach in indirect areas (e.g. maintenance, clerical, warehousing and administrative functions). The first task is to establish times (that a trained person is expected to achieve on a day work basis without allowance for rest) for all the major tasks in a particular department. This is accomplished through the use of:

1. Predetermined times for the common tasks which have been built up by WOFAC. These are called work factor times, and are then verified for each local operation by determining the number of tasks completed during, say, an hour. A simple calculation is then made to determine an average time, and this is checked against the work factor time to ensure no major discrepancies exist.
2. For tasks not covered by work factor times, a time is usually established in the same way as the checks on predetermined times described above. Normally, a longer period is chosen and more than one person is checked, where possible.
3. Times for other tasks are estimated.

While this information is being generated, the number of tasks completed in the department each day is being recorded. The average number of tasks completed in this period is calculated and extended by the time allowed. The number of people required (making due allowance for rest and personal needs) is then established.

As in activity sampling, the capacity required is agreed, and changes are monitored in the future. This is done by totalling the number of tasks completed each day, extending these by the agreed time and calculating the total labour content of the work done that day. This is compared to the hours worked during that day, and an 'efficiency percentage' is calculated. These daily controls are monitored at departmental level, with weekly controls for each department being provided for the next level of management.

Group capacity assessment. In a similar way to VFP, group capacity assessment (GCA) provides a basis for controlling staffing levels in indirect areas where more rigorous forms of work measurement are more difficult and expensive to apply. As with VFP, incentives are not recommended and so the times established are those that a trained person is expected to achieve on a day work basis, with an allowance for rest. This would be the equivalent of a 75 performance on the BSI 0–100 scale where rating was used. To establish the times for each task, any appropriate form of work measurement is used. For example, time study, synthetics, activity sampling and analytical estimating. In sensitive situations, a running wristwatch check (similar to that described for VFP) is made, and the number of completed work cycles counted in that period. An average time is then established.

The remainder of the GCA procedure is the same as for VFP. It is important, when using either of these methods, that synthetic data become a prime objective for the organization. This reduces the time for installing these controls in the future, and brings with it greater consistency between one area and another.

Clerical work improvement programme. Since its introduction in 1976, Barclays Bank plc has been monitoring the staff requirements within its branches through a clerical work improvement programme (CWIP). Centrally administered, CWIP measures the staff requirements for each branch based primarily upon the volume of tasks which are undertaken. The initial database of synthetic times was established by filming the range of activities undertaken to give times for basic movements (for example, opening a drawer and filing a document) similar to those of a higher level of MTM (see p. 333). Thousands of individual elements of work were identified in this way. Standard times (16.5 per cent is added to the synthetic times to allow for contingencies and rest) were then built up from these data for existing jobs, new jobs and to allow for changes to existing work. All times are later verified by observing the tasks being completed on a number of sample sites. Signed agreement on a new time forms part of the procedure.

The assessment of staff needs is primarily based on the number of transactions completed. Daily volumes are recorded (normally as an automatic by-product of the system) and continuously reviewed over a twenty day period. The assessment also covers other elements of work classified as follows:

1. Constant — parts of the procedure carried out regularly irrespective of the number of items processed.
2. Variable constant — regular operations readily tailored to a branch's circumstances (e.g. distance walked).
3. Other (e.g. non-standard, special jobs) and allowances for queries depending on the size of the customer base.
4. Unmeasured.

The four-weekly reports form the basis by which the company is able to monitor capacity and help in the control of this large area of cost.

Establishing a standard time

The previous phase of this procedure establishes the basic time for each element of work, or for the whole task by using some form of work measurement (e.g. estimating). However, an intrinsic part of work includes other tasks which can be directly related to the job being studied or form part of the broader context of work. As these are legitimate facets of the total job then account of them needs to be taken. Lastly, due allowance has to be made for rest and personal needs of those completing the work. The inclusion of these adjustments leads to the establishment of a standard time. This procedure and the steps leading up to a standard time are summarized in Figure 11.12. This shows that the basic times for all repetitive and regular, occasional elements having been totalled, are increased by allowances for the other elements of work (namely irregular, occasional elements and contingencies) and for rest and personal needs. The specific procedure used to establish a standard time will vary depending upon the type of work measurement used. The principal differences in measuring the time taken are described in the previous section. Below is a summary of the more usual approaches adopted under the steps which follow the measurement phase (see Figure 11.12).

Basic time. If an assessment of speed and effectiveness is made concurrently with the recording of actual times then the adjustment shown in Table 11.11 can be

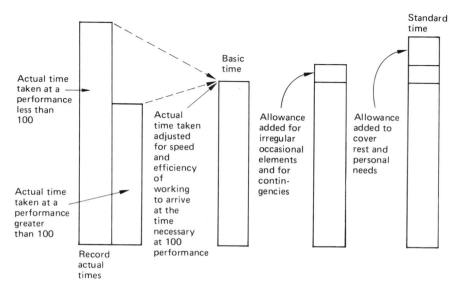

Figure 11.12 The main steps in the establishment of a standard time.

made (also see the appendix at the end of this chapter for further details and a worked example of a time study). Where this has not been completed then the issued time (i.e. the time to be used within the organization) would need to clarify this, as would the expected performance levels for those completing the various tasks involved. Normally in these circumstances, the time base would be established at a 75 performance. Alternatively, an estimated (by observation based on some agreed form of sampling) average rating could be introduced in order to allow the necessary adjustment to be made between actual/observed time and basic time. However, the latter alternative would need to be completed in a most rigorous fashion especially to guard against basing the findings on an unrepresentative sample of activities. Frequent checks over a period of time should also be completed to test the validity of the original sampling procedure.

Irregular occasional elements and contingencies. When observing work, the analyst records the different elements of work (and associated times), later separating them into their various categories, of which irregular occasional elements and contingencies are two (see p. 330). When the relevant studies are summarized all work in these two categories is separated out and used to establish a percentage which is then added back into the calculation (see Figure 11.12 and Figure 11A.5 in the appendix). In some circumstances an overall percentage can be agreed and this figure would be used in these calculations.

Rest allowances. Standard, universal tables providing the necessary allowances for rest and personal needs are available.[15] These are used to establish the relevant percentage allowance for each element of a task, the time for which is adjusted accordingly (see Figure 11.12 and also Figure 11A.5 in the appendix).

In the case of synthetics and techniques to measure capacity utilization and requirements, just as the times provided may be either those at 100 or 75 rating then they may or may not also include a rest allowance. Establishing the ingredients for the times provided is, therefore, an essential prerequisite to their various uses.

Production studies

Before work values can be used, it is essential to carry out production studies to ensure that the calculations have been correctly made and that the people working to the values can achieve a reasonable performance. The minimum length of such a study is half a day or half a shift, and the details, results and conclusions should be filed with the set-up (see p. 350).

Service applications

Some of the particular difficulties concerning the measurement of work in service organizations are covered on p. 314. Whilst it is necessary to bear these in mind, the previous section on work measurement examined some of the approaches which have been used successfully within the service sector. Table 11.12 provides a

Table 11.12   Typical applications of the different categories of work measurement techniques

Work measurement		Typical applications
Category	Technique	
1	Time-study, PMTS and synthetics	Schedules maintenance tasks (e.g. vehicles, aircraft and equipment) Cleaning services Secretarial, typing and clerical tasks Administrative activities
2	Estimating, analytical estimating and comparative estimating	Scheduled maintenance tasks, often using data derived from category 1 techniques Restaurant — back room and front office operations Hotel — back room and front office support services Consulting assignments Design services
4	Activity sampling	Warehousing and stores provision Equipment utilization Telephone exchange Supermarket — back room and front office activities
5	Variable factor programming and group capacity assessment	Banking and financial services Administration Typing and secretarial services Warehousing and stores provision Estimating function

summary of likely applications to illustrate the widespread nature of these opportunities and to help identify others within different functions and organizations. (When reviewing Table 11.12 it is important to bear in mind the category of work measurement technique under which the 'typical applications' are given, that different techniques can be used for similar applications, and that different work measurement techniques can be used in conjunction with one another.)

Section C: The control of work

There are three important aspects to controlling work:

1. A plan to show management where it ought to be going.
2. Information to show management where they are going and enabling comparisons to be made.
3. Corrective action by management, if required, to get back to the plan.

As the objective of controls is to enable management to take any necessary corrective action then the controls must:

1. Be prompt with the minimum time between the event and the control being applied.
2. Be relevant to each level of management and reporting only those aspects of performance for which that level of management is responsible and for which it has the authority to take the necessary action.
3. Be significant to the level of management receiving the information. This is achieved by being selective, and differentiating between the important and less important control information.
4. Stimulate prompt action by comparing actual to budget.

Collection of control data

Data for the controls described in this section are from two main sources: hours and output data from the daily worksheets and pay details from the pay office. When the controls are envisaged, the retrieval system for providing these data must be established in terms of content and timing.

Daily controls

Controls resulting from work measurement based on activity sampling, variable factor programming (VFP) and group capacity assessment (GCA) have already been discussed. A typical daily control sheet for this type of system is in Figure 11.13.

The daily worksheet to provide this information would be prepared by each individual or group of individuals as appropriate. The number of hours worked would be collected probably within the department, including any authorized overtime working. To facilitate counting the number of times a task was completed, the supervisor will often issue the work in batches or count the end-products by some readily available source of information. For example, the number of invoices or letters typed can be ascertained by counting the copies in a tray at the end of

Goods Receiving Stores

Day
Date

Tasks	Allowed time		Total	
	minutes	per	items	time spent
Deliveries received		delivery		
Requisitions processed		requisition		
Stock record entry (in)		delivery		
Stock record entry (out)		requisition		
Stock-taking		tray of record cards		
Rest and relaxation allowance		person		
Other (please specify)		actual		

Total earned minutes

Clocked time for the day   (hours)

Efficiency % $\dfrac{\text{Total earned minutes}}{\text{Clocked time x 60}}$ x 100 = $\dfrac{\qquad}{\qquad \text{x 60} \qquad}$ x 100 =   %

Note The allowed times (minutes) would also be pre-printed on this type of form.

Figure 11.13 Typical daily control sheet for an indirect function using data derived from activity sampling, VFP or GCA methods of work measurement.

each day. Similarly, the number of parcels dispatched can be calculated by counting the total parcels given on despatch notes. The important point here is to arrange the data collection so that wherever possible, it becomes a by-product of another system. This minimizes the administrative and clerical work and makes the control quicker to compile.

In the case of direct workers, the control data are often more detailed. This is because this information often provides the basis for incentive bonus payments to each person/group, or monitors the amount of work that has been completed where individuals/groups are paid on a high day rate on the basis that agreed output performances are maintained over each working period. A completed daily worksheet in these circumstances will need to show:

1. The work done including description, quantity completed and maybe the time on or off the job.
2. Any lost time, waiting time, unmeasured work or temporary allowances. It will normally show the reason and the time involved.
3. The standard minute value for the operation from which the total standard minutes for each task and the total for the day are calculated.

4. The calculation of bonus and performance. This section also provides space for control data to be calculated which will, in turn, be transferred to the daily control sheet.

Daily worksheets are completed by all people within the department and the information is summarized as a daily control sheet (see Figure 11.14). This control sheet would normally be provided for each section or department and run for four weeks. This is an important working document for the section or departmental supervisor. As such, the information must be relevant, highlight the significant measures and be available as early as possible in order for corrective action to be taken quickly. For each category, an initial budget figure is agreed and the actuals each day are compared with this. As in all controls, trends are important. More detailed information is normally only given on request.

Weekly controls

This control is provided for middle management. It summarizes the information and adds details of pay and costs (see Figure 11.15). In addition, this information is summarized for each section either on a weekly or period basis to provide an overview of the total operations activity. Again, the essence of this control goes back to the points listed on p. 343: it must be prompt, relevant, significant and designed to stimulate quick action. Trends are once more important.

Service applications

Controls which can be and are used in service businesses are referred to in the previous section (e.g. Figure 11.12). This section extends these illustrations by providing examples of specific applications in different parts of the service sector.

Insurances: Continental Insurance, based in New York, undertook an internal analysis designed to provide a control system for the forty branch offices and seven thousand staff operating across the USA.

A branch office comprises some fourteen departments which handles insurance policy transactions in one of four ways: new business, renewal, change or cancellation. Since Continental offers twenty different kinds of personal and commercial policy, transactions in a branch office are numerous and varied.

The resulting system (known as the productivity indicator) reflects each department's task in each transaction, the different legal requirements in each state and any other branch-specific factors. The sum of all transactions completed multiplied by the assigned departmental weight was divided by the number of workers in each department. The tenth-best department of all forty branches was chosen as the benchmark against which poorer performers could measure

Daily Control

Department

Date	Controls		Productive hours		Hours worked		Non-productive hours					Allowances		Performance	
	output	eff	meas'd	un-meas'd	direct	in-direct	meas'd	wait	rectif.	m/c b'down	total	PSHs	non-PSHs	EP	PP
Budget															
	A	B	C	D	E	F	G	H	J	K	L	M	N	P	Q	R	S
Total															

Column

A Date each day and a weekly total; also budget is inserted in the top line

B Output index $= \dfrac{\text{Actual D}+\text{E}}{\text{Budget D}+\text{E}} \times 100$

C Efficiency index $= \dfrac{\text{Actual R}}{\text{Budget R}} \times 100$

D Measured output, expressed in productive, standard hours

E Unmeasured output, expressed in productive, standard hours

F Actual clocked hours of direct employees

G Actual clocked hours of indirect employees

H Non-productive tasks inherent in the process which have been measured (e.g. machine setting)

J–L Non-productive hours in each category

M Non-productive hours general category to be specified

N Total non-productive hours

P Temporary allowances given which concern productive work (e.g. material difficulties)

Q Temporary allowances given which concern non-productive work (e.g. additional set-up time)

R Effective performance $= \dfrac{\text{D}+\text{E}}{\text{F}} \times 100$

S Pay performance $= \dfrac{\text{D}+\text{E}+\text{N}}{\text{F}} \times 100$

Figure 11.14 An example of a daily control sheet.

Weekly Control

Department

Week ended	Controls		Output			Unmsd non-PSHs	Allowances		Direct		Indirect		Bonus %		£ PSH	Performance	
	output	cost	units	PSHs meas'd	PSHs unmsd		PSHs	non-PSHs	hrs	pay	hrs	pay	dir	indir		EP	PP
Budget																	
A	B	C	D	E	F	G	H	J	K	L	M	N	P	Q	R	S	T

Column

A Week ended; budget; period total (4 weeks)

B Output index = $\dfrac{\text{Actual E+F}}{\text{Budget E+F}} \times 100$

C Cost index = $\dfrac{\text{Actual P}}{\text{Budget P}} \times 100$

D Output in units (where applicable)

E Output in measured productive standard hours

F Output in unmeasured productive standard hours

G Total unmeasured non-productive standard hours

H Temporary allowances given which concern productive work (e.g. material difficulties)

J Temporary allowances given which concern non-productive work (e.g. additional set-up time)

K Total direct clocked hours

L Total gross pay for directs

M Total indirect clocked hours

N Total gross pay for indirects

P $\dfrac{\text{Total direct bonus} \times 100}{\text{Total direct basic pay (including overtime)}}$

Q $\dfrac{\text{Total indirect bonus} \times 100}{\text{Total indirect basic pay (including overtime)}}$

R $\dfrac{\text{E+F}}{\text{L+N}}$

S Effective performance = $\dfrac{\text{E+F+H}}{\text{K}} \times 100$

T Pay performance = $\dfrac{\text{E+F+G+H+J}}{\text{K}} \times 100$

Figure 11.15 An example of a weekly control sheet.

themselves. This difference was converted into a headcount figure and the combined departmental rankings into an overall rating for each branch.

Building on this, Continental then introduced an indicator to assess the level of service to agents and policyholders (a computerized service report called 'Branch Office Service Measurement'). Using this, the productivity indicator and the branch expense ratio (transaction-related expenses to dollars received in premiums), Continental devised an overall branch office performance measurement dubbed the productivity performance index (PPI).

The opportunity to compare overall internal performance, to identify inconsistencies in performance between the PPI and its components and to check its individual standing against other branch offices enabled local management to identify areas for improvement and to measure current and future performance within the context of its own organization. In 1982, productivity and services rose 18.4 and 12.5 per cent respectively, whilst branch office expenses dropped by about 5 per cent.

Hospitals. The two hundred districts within the UK National Health Service use a wide range of control statements to help measure trends. A report in the *Sunday Times* included some of these used which illustrate trends against set objectives.[16] One such is shown in Figure 11.16.

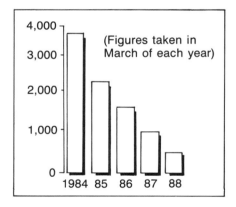

Figure 11.16 Patients waiting for more than one year for operations in the Coventry Health Authority area.

Source: B. Dear, 'Perking up on the medicine of competition', *Sunday Times* (3 July 1988), p. A.11. With permission.

Section D: Control of the management services function

It is important for management to know how and what to control in the management services department. Although the attitudes and views held by others in the organization towards this, and any other function, will be an important indicator of their ability and standing, these are too general to be useful as a means of measuring its effectiveness. It is important, therefore, to know how the effectiveness of this resource can be more specifically measured, for the establishment of sound work standards and the development of effective methods of working underpins many of the activities in the operations area.

The procedure followed within a management services function

As in many departments, a sound, professional approach is often the hallmark of a competent and capable function. This does not apply to the surface view of the department but refers, more importantly, to the procedures followed: in this instance to the study of methods and the measurement of work. In order to gauge this aspect of the function the following points will prove useful.

A forward plan of work

Although, as in many departments, a large part of the work carried out is in response to short-term needs, a plan covering both future methods study and work measurement activities should be available for discussion and agreement.

An up-to-date study register

A study register showing, by function, the studies completed should be available in the department. One should be kept for both method study and work measurement. The detail kept in the register should include reference, date, description of work and, in the case of work measurement, net study time and total BMs per study.

Filing

The appropriate study data should be available for each assignment and referenced accordingly.

Set-ups

This is a technical document describing in detail how the standard minute values (SMVs) in a particular section were established. If an incentive bonus scheme has been applied as a result of work measurement, the basic concepts of the scheme will be included. The set-up is in three parts:

1. Narrative explaining the work of the section and the basis of the establishment of SMVs.
2. The sheets on which the establishment of SMVs have been made (see the appendix to this chapter).
3. A copy of the work specifications (documents containing tables of the SMVs and details on how the scheme operates).

It is essential that set-ups are carefully prepared in the first instance, and then up-dated as required.

Production studies

It is important that production studies (see p. 341) have been and are being carried out as a check on the standard times being issued.

Developing synthetics

For reasons of cost, consistency and availability, synthetics should, wherever possible, be developed from the work measurement activities undertaken. Details of this development and progress made, as well as the increasing use of synthetics, should be in evidence. Management should request a statement on the function's intention of developing towards this resource and receive regular (possibly quarterly) statements of the cumulative progress that has been made.

Changing times

There is normally pressure to change times, especially when they form the basis of incentive schemes. Inconsistency in the time issued will fuel such requests. It is important, therefore, that the function is prepared to both loosen (i.e. increase) and tighten (i.e. reduce) an SMV (see the comments on production studies — p. 341).

In addition, a quarterly review of the reduction of irregular occasional and contingency elements and the corresponding adjustments to the relevant SMVs should be made by the management services function.

Other aspects that reflect the activities of the management services function

Rating

The application of a rating assessment to the speed and effectiveness of a person undertaking a task requires the judgement to be both accurate and consistent. It is important, therefore, for the work study practitioners to undergo regular checks in order to ensure accuracy and consistency within the study office. The practitioners' results can be graphed and filed to show progress and for reference.

Amount of study work undertaken

A regular monitoring of the amount of study work completed by the section is an important check on the level and direction of the function's activity. The study register will give the total amount of net study time completed in the period under review. On the basis that extending and 'working-up' a study away from the task takes as long as the net study time involved, then twice the net study time recorded in the study register is an accurate enough guide to the amount of time spent on measuring work.

Similarly, the amount of time spent on method study exercises should be included in the study register; this would allow a cumulative time to be provided.

Other necessary tasks have to be completed by a work study function, but an analysis similar to the one described here provides a useful insight into the function's current activities.

Level of work measurement updating

Ways that reveal situations where there is insufficient updating of the work measurement are also useful guides in assessing the activities of this function. These include:

1. The number of provisional and estimated times which exist for tasks carried out in the organization. It is important that these show a decreasing trend over time in order to maintain accurate work standards throughout the control, costing and pay systems.
2. Similarly, the amount of unmeasured work which exists in the system should be monitored and controlled. The aim here is to keep this below 5 per cent of the total output of a department as measured in standard hours of work (see Figures 11.14 and 11.15). The consequence of a high level of unmeasured work is obvious — it reduces the incentive in any bonus system and results in control and costing systems falling back on guesswork.
3. Finally, a simple check is to compare the effective and pay performance levels within a department. The gap between these two figures shows the extent of the unproductive work (both measured and unmeasured) in that section — see Figures 11.14 and 11.15. As a guide, this performance should never be greater than five points. If it is, then the causes need to be investigated and remedies sought.

Conclusion

The study and control of work within operations is of paramount importance. As time is the common denominator used to plan, control and evaluate these activities, then understanding what constitutes the different forms of time (e.g. actual, basic and standard) is an essential base for effective management.

However, the application of these techniques has a sorry history in many organizations. This has been caused partly by management's objectives in using these techniques, and partly by the way in which these approaches have been introduced. In some organizations this has led to a situation where its use has been restricted and its full potential largely untapped. On top of this, operations managers have too often not understood the fundamental need to study and control work, what these approaches have to offer how they should be used and how the outcomes need to be controlled. In the past, for instance, it has been used primarily to generate information on which to develop incentive schemes. Where this has been the overriding consideration, management has often failed to avail itself of the more important uses of these data. Similarly, the introduction of these approaches has caused considerable aggravation and created situations of lasting mistrust. This, in turn, has led to instances of stop/go applications and changes in emphasis and direction which have seriously undermined the credibility and use of this important source of data.

The future use of these invaluable analytical techniques must, in many organizations, be changed in the following ways:

1. The importance of studying the methods and work content of operations activities must be fully understood by those responsible for their execution. What needs to be done, how to do it and the ways to control these approaches are a key operations manager's task.
2. These work analyses must be fully maintained by an adequate and competent staff which increasingly includes those involved. Methods, procedures and labour standards will only be as good as they are maintained. Without maintenance the systems, which are based on these data, will degenerate and become meaningless. As this may include costings, delivery schedules and pay systems, the consequences could be traumatic.
3. The involvement of the people being studied is becoming increasingly common. Some European countries (e.g. Norway, Sweden and Denmark) have agreement at national level between employers and trade unions on the training of workers' representatives in these techniques and approaches including secondment to that department. Wherever it has been adopted it has proved to lead to substantial benefit. The need to develop a situation where this joint involvement takes place will not only improve the mutual understanding and trust in the organization when these techniques are used, but will also offer the opportunity to utilize the considerable talents and abilities which exist in the workplace.

An example of the benefits to be gained from attention to detail and adopting a philosophy of continuous improvement is provided by Japan, which over the last forty years has consistently outperformed other countries with strong industrial traditions. The lessons to be learned are simple in nature and are divorced from the culture and attitude dimensions often linked to the cause of Japanese corporate success. What follows is provided as a brief summary of some of the important dimensions that companies need to consider, and also to emphasize the need to review the production/operations function as a whole in which all the activities addressed in this book contribute to the improvement and successful management of the production of goods and the provision of services.

Improved productivity through continuous improvement

The success of Japanese companies in many industrial sectors has been a feature of world competition since the early 1950s. A review of the production/operations contribution to this success reveals a number of approaches, some new, but most of which have been widely known and publicised throughout the world. The latter point is, in fact, well supported by the content of books published in the field of production/operations management since the end of the Second World War.

What is new, however, is that the approaches form part of an overall philosophy rather than a piecemeal list of alternatives. The result brings two major differences. First, the approaches adopted build on one another as part of a coherent way to bring about improvement. Second, improvement does not end with implementation. The hallmark is one of continuous improvement. The aim is to move closer all the time towards an absolute ideal by making small improvements throughout the processes and infrastructure of the operations function.

Many chapters of this book address ways of achieving improvements. What follows is a summary placed within the context of some of the important features of the Japanese approaches to improving productivity. It is an outline, not complete in itself, but intended to provide linkage, with more extensive coverage provided elsewhere in the book.

1   The manufacturing sector

(a) *Eliminating waste*
A key item within Japanese practice is the elimination of waste, in all its forms. F. Cho (Toyota Motor Company) provides a concise definition of waste as 'anything other than the minimum amount of equipment, materials, parts and workers which are absolutely essential to production'. The aim is to strive to achieve this ideal by introducing continuous improvement throughout a range of activities.

(b) *Improved product design*
Linked to a policy of increasing volumes with the additional potential to decrease costs, product design is based on two fundamental principles. Standardized parts with their inherent advantages (see pp. 91–2) and the reduction in consumer choice (or options provided) by improving the specification, thereby making more features

a standard part of the product. Both induce higher component volumes and thereby help to reduce overall costs.

In addition, early involvement in the design procedure is secured for process engineering, manufacturing and other relevant functions in order to simplify production, minimize engineering changes, reduce warranty claims and keep maintenance costs to a minimum.

(c) *Jidoka — quality at source*
Introduced in the early 1950s by Taiichi Ohno (Toyota Motor Company), jidoka is based on the philosophy that all individuals should be personally responsible for the quality of the products they make (see Chapter 12 which addresses these aspects of quality control). In the line process of Toyota, jidoka push-buttons were introduced and all employees are authorized to stop the line by pressing one of these devices. Such action is taken for reasons of quality, safety or pace of the line. With the process at a standstill, all attention is placed on correcting the fault for, until the problem is solved, all production is stopped. Similar responsibilities are typically an integral part of people's roles in many Japanese firms. Here, the making and evaluation of products are clearly and firmly the responsibility of the same person (see pp. 447–8).

(d) *Process re-design*
Where volumes allow, the re-design of processes on a cellular basis (see pp. 140–5) or to accommodate JIT production is important in Japanese companies as part of reducing waste with the attendant costs of control (see pp. 217–19).

(e) *Set-up reduction*
As illustrated earlier in this chapter, set-up reduction not only eliminates waste in its own right but is also a prerequisite for process re-design and JIT production approaches.

(f) *JIT production control systems*
Chapter 9 offers a comprehensive explanation of JIT production control systems and the benefits that accrue in terms of work-in-progress inventory reduction and control of costs throughout the manufacturing process.

(g) *Involving people*
To support these approaches, Japanese companies extensively involve people both within and outside the organization. Work, therefore, is structured in terms of increased participation, involvement, responsibility/authority and job interest. This leads to a situation where continuous improvement can flourish as an integral part of the way an organization works.

The companies adhere to the principle of employing people for their heads as well as their hands. This is in stark contrast to the West. As Mr Konosuke Matsushita explains 'Your firms are built on the Taylor model; even worse, so are your heads. With your bosses doing the thinking, while the workers wield the screwdrivers, you are convinced deep down that this is the right way to run a business. For you, the essence of management is getting the ideas out of the heads of the bosses into the hands of labour.'[17]

Similar differences in approach are to be found in supplier relations. Many US and European customers still manage their suppliers by threat in terms of contract placement — the you-need-us-more-than-we-need-you syndrome. They fail to appreciate that win/lose situations are a poor base on which to build mutually beneficial relations. Japanese companies, on the other hand, have for decades viewed their suppliers as partners in terms of design, quality, cost and delivery improvements.[18] As customers (depending on relative company size) generally hold the power, then they must initiate sound and mutually beneficial relations with suppliers. As a partnership, both sides need to contribute. For them, win/win situations need to be developed in order successfully to compete in global markets.

2   The service sector

The need continuously to improve performance within the service sector is sizable and, in many organizations, well overdue. In order, however, to avail themselves of these opportunities it is first necessary to review service provision in a more positive way. Part of this change lies in the need clearly to separate the dimension of customer contact from that of customization. The former is an inherent feature of the service delivery system, while the latter is a distinct feature of customer requirement. The need to reflect this in relevant approaches within operations is the first step. Opportunities to progress improvements are then set against these basic differences but include general approaches, some of which are outlined below.

(a) *Eliminating waste*
Excesses in all forms are unnecessary and costly. Because services tend to be labour-intensive, many of the improvements concern changing the activities and roles of people. However, other key areas of waste reduction come from activities such as improving housekeeping and the immediate environment in general.

(b) *Improved service design*
Related in part to the customization issue discussed above, it is important to review a service in terms of the opportunity to standardize as part of an overall aim to simplify overall design. Eliminating unnecessary features, limiting server interpretation or simplying facets of a service often lead to significant cost reductions.

(c) *Jidoka — quality at source*
The inbuilt link between the providing and evaluating tasks within a service system has not usually been separated in terms of its provision. The relatively simple operations involved and the fact that a service is provided and consumed at the

same time have militated against this separation in service firms, unlike developments in manufacturing. Quality at source is, therefore, an integral part of the structure of a service delivery system. However, although it is more an inherent feature of service provision than when making a product the opportunity still needs to be realized.

(d) *Process re-design*

As explained in Chapter 4, it is essential to recognize that the choice of process to provide services as well as to make products relates to volume. However, as with manufacturing, the opportunity to simplify processes as well as to rearrange them in order to improve service provision is available. Rigorous re-examinations of service delivery need to be made in order to re-align process choice in terms of meeting customer requirements and system trade-offs. Opportunities for process investment with high volume on the one hand, and cellular approaches (e.g. client groups) reflected in teams to handle specific customer needs are examples of more common rearrangements.

(e) *Involving people*

Because the customer interface is an inherent feature of the delivery system does not imply that involving people in service firms will automatically exist. However, the opportunity to and benefits from adopting the hiring-head-as-well-as-hands philosophy within service organizations presents an overhwelming argument here as in other sectors of the economy. Work sharing and other part-time employment policies more typical of service businesses place even greater need for involvement if corporate goals of quality, cost and meeting customer needs are to be maintained, let alone improved. Similarly, though often overlooked, the recognition of supplier networks as part of the total service delivery system needs to be made and comprehensively developed as an integral part of the total provision.

As the service sector becomes more important it is essential that organizations in their quest for better performance not only recognize the benefits but also the opportunity to realize these by adopting a philosophy of continuous improvement. As product quality and manufacturing productivity was a central feature of the 1980s, then service quality and productivity will be a major theme of the 1990s. Attitudes to improvement, however, need to be developed. Without this core activity many firms will, at best, underperform while, at worst, will miss out altogether.

Appendix A: Taking a time study and developing a standard time

The method described in Figure 11A.1 is based on the use of a decimal stopwatch. The person completing the study measures the elements of the task over a period of time and thus establishes a total time for the job. The time study procedure is now explained with the aid of a worked example.

To provide overall verification of a time study, a check is made against another clock. The stopwatch is started by synchronizing it with this other clock. The time that elapses before the study starts (TEBS) is recorded (see the first entry in Figure 11A.1) and similarly the time elapsed after the study (TEAS) is recorded when the observer clocks off, again using the independent clock. In clocking on and off the seconds hand at the 60 seconds point is used. All the times recorded throughout the study including TEBS and TEAS are totalled. This total is then compared with the elapsed time (the difference between the actual time of the day the study was started and finished). Agreement within ±1 per cent should be attained: where the error exceed ±2 per cent the study should be discarded. It is important to establish this policy with all concerned.

When the observer has 'clocked on', the information on the study sheet is completed, including a study number and the start time which is entered at the top of the study sheet. Below the top of the study sheet are a number of columns each containing figures. These are now explained.

Column 1 A symbol (here A–G) for the repetitive elements which are used in column 2 at different times during the study.

Column 2 The description of the element of work.

Column 3 Rating judgement made by the observer for that element.

Column 4 Observed time (or actual minutes) recorded by the observer.

Column 5 Normalized or basic time.

The observer now undertakes the study by timing and rating the work under review. All elements of work (see p. 330) are timed and the study illustrates those differences which are shown in Figure 11A.2.

On returning to the study office, the observer clocks off and makes the overall time check as explained. Next the actual times are converted into basic times. This is known as normalizing the times or extending the study. Here, all the times for the elements of work are calculated to show what they would have been if the person doing the task was working at standard performance (i.e. 100 on the 0–100 scale):

$$\text{Basic time} = \frac{\text{Observed time (i.e. actual minutes)} \times \text{Observed rating}}{\text{Standard rating (i.e. 100)}}$$

Dept _Assembly and Packing_ Section ____   No. ___ A 64
Name _Ann Dixon_ No. _104_ Taken by _WMP_   Date _10 JUN_
Operation _Examine and pack 6" bowl into a_   Start _2.15 pm_
polythene bag and six per outer carton (type 5) specification   Finish _2.53 pm_
_6016_   Elapsed _38.00_
Working conditions _Normal_   Ineffective _16.68_
    Net time _21.32_

	TEBS		1.81					
A	Walk to stack, empty tote				C	80	·20	·16
	tray aside, pick up tote				B	80	·17	·14
	tray of 24 bowls and place				C	80	·21	·17
	on bench (Break point, hands				B	85	·15	·13
	leave tote tray)	100	·18	·18	C	90	·18	·16
B	Pick up 1 bowl, remove from				B	85	·15	·13
	polythene bag and inspect				C	90	·16	·14
	(Break point, hands leave				D	95	·20	·19
	bowl to get label)	100	·12	·12	E	95	·36	·34
C	Get label and stick on bottom				F	100	·17	·17
	of bowl. Pack bowl into new				G	95	·10	·10
	polythene bag and aside (Break				B	95	·12	·11
	point, hands leave bowl)				C	95	·16	·15
		95	·16	·15	B	95	·14	·13
D	make outer carton (Break point,				C	90	·18	·16
	hands leave formed carton)				B	100	·14	·14
		—	—	—	C	100	·15	·15
E	Position vertical separator and				B	105	·11	·12
	horizontal pads in packing 6"				C	105	·14	·15
	bowls to outer (Break point,				B	95	·14	·13
	hands to tape gun)				C	95	·16	·15
		—	—	—	B	90	·15	·14
F	Seal outer with 3" tape from				C	90	·17	·15
	gun dispenser, stamp with				D	90	·21	·19
	packers code, colour code and				E	95	·39	·37
	aside (Break point, hands				F	95	·15	·14
	leave outer)	—	—	—	B	100	·12	·12
G	Take 2 outer boxes and load				C	100	·15	·15
	to trolley (Break point, packer				B	105	·10	·11
	at bench)	—	—	—	C	105	·15	·16
	B	85	·14	·12	B	85	·14	·12
	C	90	·18	·16	C	90	·19	·17
	B	95	·12	·11	Talk to Supervisor	100	1·25	1·25

No. __A 64__

Description				Description			
B	85	.14	.12	B	85	.16	.14
C	90	.18	.16	C	85	.18	.17
B	90	.12	.11	D	90	.26	.23
C	90	.18	.16	E	95	.39	.37
B	100	.11	.11	F	95	.16	.13
C	100	.17	.17	G	90	.14	.13
D	100	.24	.24	B	95	.14	.13
E	100	.38	.38	C	90	.18	.16
F	100	.17	.17	B	90	.15	.14
G	100	.12	.12	C	85	.19	.16
Aside faulty bowl – repack into used polythene bag and into tote tray	95	.36	.34	Tea break			11.46
				B	90	.13	.12
B	90	.14	.13	C	90	.19	.17
C	95	.17	.16	B	90	.14	.13
B	85	.15	.13	C	85	.20	.17
C	95	.16	.15	B	95	.12	.11
B	95	.12	.11	C	90	.18	.16
Discuss faulty products with inspector	100	.67	.67	B	90	.14	.13
				C	95	.16	.15
C	100	.16	.16	D	95	.21	.20
B	90	.14	.13	E	100	.33	.33
C	90	.17	.15	F	95	.18	.17
B	95	.12	.11	B	95	.12	.11
C	95	.16	.15	C	90	.17	.15
B	95	.13	.12	B	85	.16	.14
C	105	.14	.14	C	85	.18	.15
D	100	.26	.26	B	90	.14	.13
E	100	.36	.36	C	90	.16	.14
F	100	.17	.17	B	95	.13	.12
A	95	.24	.23	C	90	.18	.16
A	100	.21	.21	B	95	.12	.11
B	95	.11	.10	C	95	.17	.16
C	90	.16	.14	B	90	.15	.14
B	100	.10	.10	C	90	.16	.14
C	100	.15	.15	D	95	.24	.23
B	95	.12	.11	E	95	.34	.31
C	90	.18	.16	F	95	.15	.14
B	95	.13	.12	G	95	.11	.10
C	95	.16	.15	TEAS			3.41
B	90	.14	.13	—	21.42		
C	90	.16	.14				

Figure 11A.1 An example of a time study.

WORKING SHEET

Element										Total BMs	Occ.	BMs/Occ
A	·18	·23	·21							0.62	3	·21
B	·12	·12	·11	·14	·13	·13	·11	·13	·14			
	·12	·13	·14	·12	·11	·12	·12	·11	·11			
	·13	·13	·11	·13	·11	·12	·13	·10	·10			
	·11	·12	·14	·13	·14	·12	·13	·11	·13			
	·11	·14	·13	·12	·11	·14				5.15	42	·12
C	·15	·16	·16	·17	·16	·14	·15	·16	·15			
	·15	·15	·15	·15	·16	·17	·16	·16	·17			
	·16	·15	·16	·15	·15	·14	·14	·15	·16			
	·15	·14	·17	·16	·16	·17	·17	·16	·15			
	·15	·15	·14	·16	·16	·14				6.51	42	·16
D	·19	·19	·24	·26	·23	·20	·23			1·54	7	·22
E	·34	·37	·38	·36	·37	·33	·32			2·47	7	·35
F	·17	·14	·17	·17	·15	·17	·14			1·11	7	·16
G	·10	·12	·13	·10						0.45	4	·11

Total repetitive BMS   17.85

Talk to Supervisor   1.25
Aside faulty bowl   ·34
Discuss faulty products with inspector   ·67   2.26
            Total BMs   20.11

Tea break   11.46
TEBS + TEAS   1.81 + 3.41   5.22
Total ineffective   16.68

Figure 11A.2   The working sheet for the time study in Figure 11A.1.

This is done because all times under this rating scale are issued as standard time (i.e. the time when working at 100 performance). If over the work period the person is faster, then the performance will be above 100, if slower, then below 100. How many points above or below will reflect the actual time taken over the whole working period.

The effect of this calculation on the actual minutes observed when completing the task (i.e. the observed time) is illustrated below. In this example, the actual minutes vary as shown due to the actual speed and effectiveness of the person doing the job. When these are normalized, however, they all have similar basic minutes for the task, as expected.

Example

		Actual minutes	$\times$	$\dfrac{\text{Observed rating}}{\text{Standard rating}}$	$=$	Basic minutes
Rating below standard (say 90)	$=$	8.90	$\times$	$\dfrac{90}{100}$	$=$	8.01
Rating at standard (i.e. 100)	$=$	8.00	$\times$	$\dfrac{100}{100}$	$=$	8.00
Rating at above standard (say 110)	$=$	7.28	$\times$	$\dfrac{110}{100}$	$=$	8.01

Thus, referring to Figure 11A.1, the entries in column 5 are the result of applying this equation to the rating assessment and actual time observed, as recorded in columns 3 and 4.

The next task is to complete a working sheet (see Figure 11A.2), to calculate the average basic minutes recorded throughout the study for each repetitive element, to summarize the irregular occasional elements and contingencies observed, and to list the ineffective time.

The final task is to complete a study summary sheet (Figure 11A.3). The information is from Figures 11A.1 and 11A.2 with the exception of the overall time check, in this instance shown as 'accuracy 0.5 per cent'. This has been calculated by comparing the net time of 21.32 minutes from the summary block in Figure 11A.1 with the recorded actual minutes of 21.42 which is the last entry on page 2 of Figure 11A.1.

In the bottom half of the summary sheet the following information is provided:

Column 1 Element reference.
Column 2 Element description.
Column 3 Total basic minutes (BMs) recorded in the study for each element.
Column 4 Number of occasions the element was observed.

Dept. _Assembly and Packing_ Section _____ No. _A64_

Name _Ann Dixon_____ No. _104_ Taken by _WMP_ Date _10 JUNE_

Operation _Examine and pack 6" bowl into a_ Start _2.15 pm_
polythene bag and six per outer carton (type 5) Finish _2.53 pm_
— see specification 6016 Elapsed _38.00_

Working conditions _____ _Normal_ Ineffective _16.68_

_____ Net time _21.32_

		Average rating 94			Accuracy 0.5%					
A	Walk to stack, aside empty tote tray, pick up tote tray of 24 bowls and place on bench			Frequency for a carton of 6 bowls						
		·62	3	·21	1 in 4	Average rating = $\frac{\text{Total Study BMs}}{\text{Total Study AMs}}$ × 100				
B	Pick one bowl, remove from polythene bag and inspect	5.15	42	·12	6 in 1	= $\frac{20.11 \times 100}{21.32}$ = 94				
C	Get label and stick on bottom of bowl. Pack bowl into a new polythene bag and aside	6.51	42	·16	6 in 1					
D	Make outer carton (type 5)	1.54	7	·22	1 in 1					
E	Position vertical separator and horizontal pads in packing 6" bowl to outer	2.47	7	·35	1 in 1					
F	Seal outer with 3" tape from gun dispenser, stamp with packer's code, colour code and aside	1.11	7	·16	1 in 1					
G	Take two outer boxes and load to trolley	·45	4	·11	1 in 2					
	Talk to Supervisor	1.25								
	Aside faulty bowl	·34								
	Discuss faulty product with inspector	·67								

Figure 11A.3 The study summary sheet for the time study in Figure 11A.1.

Column 5 Average BMs per occasion calculated, thus:

$$\frac{\text{Column } 3}{\text{Column } 4} = \text{Column } 5$$

Column 6 Frequency of the regular, occasional elements within the cycle.

At the bottom, the irregular, occasional elements and the contingencies observed during the study are listed.

This study is now complete. The next stage would be to use these data to establish a standard time.

Establishing a standard time

When the basic times for each element of the job under review have been established, the next stop is to calculate the standard time for that task.

Analysis of study summaries

More than one study must be made before a time for a task can be considered representative. How many studies will depend upon several factors, including the frequency of the task and the volume of the total work in the department that the task represents. As a general guide, a task should be studied at least three times, preferably taken by three different observers on three different persons performing that task. Where this is not possible, provisional standard times should be issued where at least one study has been calculated, and estimated times issued where no study information at all is available.

When studies of the same task have been completed then 'an analysis of study summaries' is compiled (see Figure 11A.4). When a similarity in average basic minutes (BMs) per element has emerged, then no more studies should be undertaken. The completed studies are now totalled as in the final three columns on the right of Figure 11A.4. An average for all the studies is then calculated for all elements. The sheet showing the estabishment of a standard minute value is now compiled (see Figure 11A.5).

The information in the first six columns of Figure 11A.5 is provided by Figure 11A.4. Columns 7–9, however, need further explanation.

Column 7 This shows the percentage increase to the BMs for each repetitive and regular occasional element necessary to cover the time involved in completing the irregular, occasional elements, and contingency work as observed throughout these studies. The calculation of this is shown at the foot of the example. In some situations, departmental percentage to cover this type of work is established and agreed. It is important, however, that the basis for this agreement is study work and that all future studies still record these elements and

Study number		A64	A67	A75	A82	Total BMs	Number of occasions	BMs per occasion	Frequency	
Date		10 Jun	14 Jun	20 Jun	26 Jun					
Study person		WMP	AJ	DMA	AJ					
Operator		A Dixon	B Jones	F Corne	P Burn					
Average rating		94	96	91	93					

REPETITIVE ELEMENTS

			A64	A67	A75	A82	Total BMs	Number of occasions	BMs per occasion	Frequency
A	To stack, aside empty tote tray, pick up tote tray with 24 bowls and to bench	TBMs	·62	·93	·72	·61	2·98	13	·23	1 in 4
		Occs	3	4	3	3				
		BMs/Occ	·21	·23	·24	·20				
B	Pick up one bowl, remove from polythene bag and inspect	TBMs	5·15	8·96	7·41	7·84	29·36	228	·13	6 in 1
		Occs	42	72	54	60				
		BMs/Occ	·12	·12	·14	·13				
C	Get label and stick on bottom of bowl. Pack bowl into new polythene bag.	TBMs	6·51	12·36	10·27	11·21	40·35	228	·18	6 in 1
		Occs	42	72	54	60				
		BMs/Occ	·16	·17	·19	·19				
D	Make outer carton	TBMs	1·54	2·41	2·10	2·12	8·17	38	·22	1 in 1
		Occs	7	12	9	10				
		BMs/Occ	·22	·20	·23	·21				
E	Position vertical separator and horizontal pads in packing 6" bowl to outer carton	TBMs	2·47	4·45	3·11	3·61	13·64	38	·36	1 in 1
		Occs	7	12	9	10				
		BMs/Occ	·35	·37	·35	·36				
F	Seal outer carton with 3" tape from gum dispenser, stamp with packers code & colour mark	TBMs	1·11	1·13	1·40	1·72	5·96	38	·16	1 in 1
		Occs	7	12	9	10				
		BMs/Occ	·16	·14	·16	·17				
G	Take two outer boxes and load to trolley	TBMs	·45	·74	·56	·65	2·40	20	·12	1 in 2
		Occs	4	6	5	5				
		BMs/Occ	·11	·12	·11	·13				

OCCASIONALS & CONTINGENCIES

			A64	A67	A75	A82	Total BMs
	Talk to supervisor	TBMs	1·25				1·25
		Occs	1				
		BMs/Occ	1·25				
	Aside faulty bowl	TBMs	·34			·61	0·95
		Occs	1			2	
		BMs/Occ	·34			·30	
	Talk to inspector re quality	TBMs	·67			1·12	1·79
		Occs	1			1	
		BMs/Occ	·67			1·12	
	Stop for fork lift	TBMs		·67			0·67
		Occs		1			
		BMs/Occ		·67			

Figure 11A.4   An analysis of study summaries for the time study in Figure 11A.1.

	Element	Total BMs	Number of occasions	BMs per occasion	Frequency per outer carton	BMS per outer pack	Irregular occasional and contingencies %	Rest Allowance %	SMs per outer carton of 6 bowls
A	To stack, aside empty tote tray, pick up tote tray with 24 bowls and to bench	2.98	13	·23	1 in 4	0.058	5	14	·07
B	Pick up one bowl, remove from polythene bag and inspect	29.36	228	·13	6 in 1	0.780	5	13	0.93
C	Get label and stick on bottom of bowl. Pack bowl into new polythene bag	40.35	228	·18	6 in 1	1.080	5	13	1.28
D	Make outer carton	8.17	38	·22	1 in 1	0.220	5	13	0.26
E	Position vertical separator and horizontal pads in packing 6" bowl to outer carton	13.64	38	·36	1 in 1	0.360	5	13	0.43
F	Seal outer carton with 3" tape from gun dispenser, stamp with packers code and colour mark	5.96	38	·16	1 in 1	0.160	5	13	0.19
G	Take two outer cartons and load to trolley	2.40	20	·12	1 in 2	0.060	5	14	0.07
	Total	102.86							3.23

IRREGULAR OCCASIONAL ELEMENTS & CONTINGENCIES

Talk to supervisor   1.25
Aside faulty bowl   0.95
Talk to inspector re quality   1.79
Stop for fork lift truck   ·67
TOTAL   4.66

STANDARD MINUTE VALUE PER 10
OUTER CARTONS OF 6 X 6" BOWLS
= 32 SMs

Irregular occasional elements and contingencies % = $\frac{\text{Total BMs for irregular occasionals \& contingencies}}{\text{Total BMs for repetitive elements}} \times 100$

= $\frac{4.66}{102.86} \times 100$ = 4.5% say 5%

Figure 11A.5 An establishment of a standard minute value for the time study in Figure 11A.1.

calculate the percentage allowances. This acts as a check on the agreed figure. Where this type of work is reduced through better procedures and work routines, then the percentage allowance should be reduced accordingly.

Column 8 This represents the percentage uplift to the BMs for each repetitive and regular, occasional element to compensate for fatigue, and to allow adequate time for rest and personal needs. Standard tables providing the necessary allowances are available.[19] Detail on the make-up of these percentages is not given here.

Column 9 This represents the standard minutes (SMs) for each element and is calculated by:

$$\text{Column } 6 \times \text{Column } 7 \times \text{Column } 8 = \text{Column } 9$$

Lastly, the figures in column 9 are totalled to give the SMs for the task as shown at the bottom of Figure 11A.5.

Notes and references

1. Adapted from M. Takamiya, 'Japanese multinationals in Europe: international operations and their public policy implications', *Columbia Journal of World Business*, 16 (Summer 1981), 5–17, and as used by C.J. McMillan in *The Japanese Industrial System*, (Berlin: de Gruyter 1985), p.275.
2. A British Institute of Management Survey, *Added Value: An introduction to productivity schemes*, MSO 40 (1978) by M. Woodmansey examines current schemes operating in fourteen companies and summarizes the benefits gained and problems encountered.
3. British Standard 3138 (British Standards Institution, 1979).
4. Motion study, is the term used by Frank and Lilian Gilbreth to cover their research into the facet of human motion and motion economy. As such, their work relates to manual tasks and breaking these down into a few fundamental motions. These are then analysed and the most efficient methods built up.
5. These symbols are those recommended by the American Society of Mechanical Engineers (ASME) and developed from originals introduced by Gilbreth (see above).
6. Two basic textbooks on this subject are K.F.H. Murrell, *Ergonomics: Man in his working environment* (London: Chapman and Hall, 1979); and E.J. McCormick, *Human Factors in Engineering and Design*, 4th edn. (Maidenhead: McGraw-Hill, 1976).
7. The American Productivity Centre conducted a survey at its conference, entitled 'Improving White Collar Productivity' 30–31 October 1985. The results were published in its *Productivity Letter*, 5, no. 7 (1985).
8. 'Office equipment', *Financial Times Survey* (19 October 1988), section 3, p. i.
9. *Financial Times Survey* (1988), pp. vi and vii.
10. *Financial Times Survey* (1988), p. vi.
11. See F. Kinsman, *The Telecommuters* (Chichester: Wiley, 1987). Also, *Financial Times Survey* (1988), p. viii.
12. American Productivity Center, *Productivity Letter*, 5, no. 8. (1986).
13. Time study is also one of the most commonly used ways of measuring work. For instance, an Institution of Production Engineers booklet, *A Management Guide to Incentive Payment Schemes* (1982) revealed that from a survey of 153 companies, the methods used to measure work were as follows:

Work measurement methods used	Percentage use by category of employee		
	Direct	*Indirect*	*Staff*
Time study	56	21	2
Synthetics	36	17	7
PMTS	10	3	0
Rate fixing	12	3	0

Notes
1. The percentages may exceed 100% as companies used more than one method.
2. The term standard data and not synthetics is used in the booklet.

14. The term 'basic time' has a distinct meaning in work measurement. A fuller explanation is given on p. 339.
15. See, for example, International Labour Office, *Introduction to Work Study*, 2nd edn (Geneva, 1969), pp. 292–7, and R.M. Currie, *Work Study*, 4th edn, (London: Pitman, 1977), chapter 12.
16. B. Deer, 'Perking up on the medicine of competition', *Sunday Times* (3 July 1988), p. A.11.
17. K. Matsushita 'Why the West will lose', *Industrial Participation*, Spring1985, p. 8.
18. See, for example, the actions taken by Honda as long ago as 1974 in terms of working with suppliers and as reported in *Strategic Alternatives for the British Motor Cycle Industry*, Report prepared for the Secretary of State for Industry by the Boston Consulting Group, HMSO, July 1977, p. 34.
19. See Terry Hill, *Small Business: Production/operations management* (Basingstoke: Macmillan Educational, 1987), pp. 162–3.

Chapter 12

Quality control

The quality of products/services provided by a business is an important concern to both the organization and its customers. Whilst the cost of quality calamities can be high in themselves,[1] customers' confidence in the level of quality is also an important factor because of its effect on future demand and, in its turn, the longer-term success of the organization. To ensure that quality levels meet the market requirements, policy issues concerning quality need to be resolved at the corporate level and be seen to form an integral part of the organization's objectives, strategies and tactics. This is not easy to achieve, but unless addressed at the corporate level it will, as in many organizations, be decided at the operational level because of the necessity to achieve output levels, efficiency and other yardsticks, and to meet delivery promises.

The determination of corporate objectives will need to be based, in part, on an analysis at different quality levels of market demand for goods and services. At the strategic and tactical levels, the organization will need to assess the trade-offs involved in the quality choices before them, establish appropriate quality levels, determine the methods of providing the product/service, and design quality control procedures to ensure that these levels are met.

This chapter covers the issues considered to be important in this aspect of POM. The approach used is to look first at some of the concepts involved. Then, with these in mind, the quality control aspects appertaining to each part of the process are reviewed; this part of the chapter goes into more detail and introduces suitable approaches to each of these situations.

Quality assurance and quality control

The concept of quality concerns how well and for how long a product/service meets the requirements of the customer. BS 4778 (1987) defines quality as, 'the totality of features and characteristics of a product or service that bear on its ability to

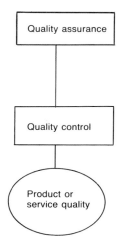

| Quality assurance | All those planned and systematic actions necessary to provide adequate confidence that a product/service will satisfy given requirements for quality. For effectiveness, it usually requires a continuing evaluation of factors that affect the adequacy of the design or specification for intended applications as well as verifications and audits of production installation and inspection operations |

| Quality control | The operational techniques and activities that are used to fulfil requirements for quality. It involves operational techniques and activities aimed both at monitoring a process and at eliminating causes of unsatisfactory performance at relevant stages of the quality loop |

| Product or service quality | The totality of features and characteristics of a product/service that bear on its ability to satisfy stated or implied needs |

Figure 12.1 The relationship between quality assurance, quality control and product/service quality.
Source: BS 4778 (1987), part 1, 3.6–3.7.

satisfy stated or implied needs.'[2] However, providing a precise definition of quality can reinforce one view which is all too prevalent — that quality is often bolted onto the conversion process afterwards (or even as an afterthought) rather than being incorporated into the system as an integral part of the whole. Emphasizing this feature of quality provision early on in the chapter has been done for a reason. If the conversion process does not embrace quality from the outset then achieving and maintaining appropriate quality levels will always prove to be difficult.

However, to establish an appropriate approach to quality first requires an understanding of its constituent parts and the relevant approaches which may be adopted. The first step is to distinguish between quality assurance and control. These two interrelated aspects of quality need clarification immediately. Figure 12.1 shows the relationship diagrammatically together with relevant definitions. The quality of a product/service is the result of two separate activities: product/service design and the operations system that makes the product or provides the service. How well the design meets the market needs and the process meets the design specification determines the quality level of the particular product/service.

Development of approaches to the control of quality

The concept on which the control of quality is based depends upon the nature of the business and the type of process chosen. Table 12.1 illustrates the range of development which has taken place in some businesses. In organizations largely

Table 12.1 Responsibility for quality control and the type of process

Type of process	The task	Responsibility for quality
Project and jobbing	The task and quality are normally integrated in the skills of the person	Usually vested largely in the performance of the task or provision of the service. Primarily the person responsible for this part of the process plus supervisory support
Batch and line	Work has been deskilled to reduce amongst other things, labour costs. Inspection and later quality control introduced	Theoretically the responsibility is still vested in the person providing the task with supervisory, quality control and inspection support. In reality, quality control and inspection are seen as being responsible for quality
Continuous processing	Quality is determined by the process and, therefore, reintegrates quality into the task	Usually built into the process as an integral part of the design. The facilities to monitor the quality are usually controlled by the same person who is responsible for other aspects of the task

at the project or jobbing end of the process spectrum the person responsible for doing the task or providing the service still identifies strongly with the product/service and its quality. Jobbing companies in manufacturing industry, large parts of the construction industry and the greater part of the service industry are examples of this. The change in many manufacturing companies to deskilled work has brought with it the quality problems experienced and reported on a regular basis. In continuous processing situations, on the other hand, the inability of the technician/operator to affect the quality level has resulted in the need to build the control of quality into the process.

Where the deskilling of work has taken place, the approach to the control of quality has changed over time. Initially, inspection departments were established as a necessary support to the operations process. However, in many organizations they served to divorce the responsibility for performing the task still further from the achievement of desired quality levels. By the 1960s a statistical approach to quality control was being developed as part of the way to regulate the achievement of quality (see Table 12.2). However, it tended to widen further the gap between those responsible for completing the work and those seen as the custodians of quality. More recently, the view as to how best to control quality has favoured the concept of quality assurance, which recognizes the need to look at all the activities impinging

Table 12.2   Developments in the control of quality

Initial work arrangement	→	Work progressively deskilled	→	Continuous processing
		Inspection		
Quality embodied in the craft/work process		Statistical quality control		Quality embodied in the work process
		Quality assurance		

on the control of quality. Quality assurance tries to build the responsibility for quality back into the operations task. Hence inspection and quality control have often reverted to being part of the operations function and the inspection task reverted to being part of the doing task. Lastly, where the choice of process has led an organization to a more continuous process, then the embodiment of task and quality has come full circle.

However, organizations have in recent years recognized the illogical nature of separating the responsibility for doing the task from that of ensuring it is done to the agreed level of quality. Based on the economies of scale argument, specialization of tasks took root and separation of responsibilities became the norm. In recent years, both sense and sensibility have been brought to bear on this issue and appropriate changes are being made. This need for change is more a requirement in manufacturing than in service companies, as in the latter the division of labour and the separation of responsibilities described above is often less advanced and less appropriate.

People such as Denning, Juran, Crosby and Taguchi have provided both the impetus and insights into the approaches to be used to improve quality.[3] They stress three aspects which organizations must adopt:

1. Top management commitment.
2. Involvement throughout an organization.
3. The use of appropriate statistical tools to plan, control and improve quality.

To achieve improvements in quality throughout an organization it is essential for these features to be an integral part of the corporate commitment. The rest of the chapter reflects this and outlines the concepts underlying these factors together with a detailed review of the issues involved and the approaches to follow. The quality of design, the need to attain quality in the products made or services provided (quality of conformance), the ways to control quality, and where the responsibility for quality should lie are all dealt with here. The approach which should be adopted by the operations manager is first to determine the responsibility issue and the way in which quality is to be controlled. Not until these have been resolved can the aspects of quality control be determined, as they will affect later decisions.

Policy issues relating to quality control

The role of management in quality control is to demonstrate a total commitment to the achievement of adequate quality throughout the system, where adequate implies providing a product/service which meets the specification.

The key to good quality lies in good management and not how well the activities in the process or delivery system are undertaken. In Denning's view, as management is responsible for 95 per cent of the quality problems, management has to give the lead in changing the systems and processes that create the problems.[4] However, 'everyone doing his/her best is not the answer. It is necessary that people know what to do. . . . The responsibility for change rests on management. The first step is to learn how to change.'[5] But, before this, it is necessary to address important policy issues which need to be resolved.

Reactive or proactive approach to quality

The first issue is for an organization to determine whether its basic philosophy is to adopt a reactive or proactive approach to quality control. In the former the emphasis is towards detection with the objective being to prevent faulty work being passed onto subsequent processes, and so minimize the costs involved in rectification, scrap, returned or rejected products/services and non-repeat business. The latter is a prevention-oriented approach to quality control, allocating resources to make products/services right the first time. The two essentials of quality — design and operations — are analysed to identify the important factors affecting them. Consequently, attention is paid to the achievement of these factors. This results in more products/services being right the first time.

Reactive or detection-oriented approach

The objective of this approach is to inspect completed work from one part of the process to prevent it from being passed onto the next stage of the process. The inspection is carried out by staff outside the operations function and takes place between process stages or after a sequence of stages to filter out substandard work. This is then either scrapped or is reworked to bring it to standard. Inspection stages are expensive and time-consuming. Faulty items, although detected, are costly. Only when faulty items are discovered at the stage in the process where the fault first occurs can corrective action be taken to prevent further faulty items being made or provided.

Proactive or prevention-oriented approach

This approach aims to allocate resources so as more often to make products or provide services right first time. This is achieved by reviewing the quality of both design and conformance in order to identify the factors affecting these two qualities. Quality control is then designed around this analysis.

Control system design

The design of an individual control system will depend upon the level of predictability between the process and the product/service. The choice exists between open-loop and closed-loop control. Open loop control works as follows. Where the control of a process has a predictable relationship with the quality of the output, it may not be necessary to measure the output: instead, reliance is placed on setting the controls. If the process setting is achieved and monitored, then the output will always be as expected. With closed-loop control the objective is to control the process so that it does not produce substandard items. Any deviation in quality signals an adjustment to be made in the process before it produces substandard items (see Figure 12.2).

Some processes have been designed which incorporate automatic feedback and are self-adjusting (e.g. in-process gauging or forms of continuous processing). Others signal the fault or provide readings to allow adjustments to be made.

Responsibility for quality

The measurement of quality is just one part of the control procedure which reviews how well quality is being achieved either in terms of design or the level of design conformance. The prerequisite of this is to define clearly departmental responsibilities throughout the process. The prime set of responsibilities concerns that of the quality function itself. This function usually parallels the structure of operations since its basic role is to establish control procedures, and to measure and then report on the quality performance of the operations departments.

The quality control philosophy that underpins the way in which the procedures are arranged, measurements are taken and reported, and where the responsibility

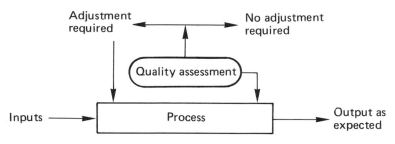

Figure 12.2 Closed-loop control.

is held for quality, will differ from one organization to the next. In recent years, these differences have become more marked. Quality assurance has become the function responsible for developing the quality structure and the responsibilities and activities within that structure, together with establishing procedures to ensure the organization meets the agreed quality levels. In some organizations, the responsibility for quality has always been an integral part of the work of the person responsible for making the product/providing the service. In some, work responsibilities have been enlarged to incorporate part of the quality checking function more associated with inspection. However, in others the role of operations is kept separate from quality control, based on the premise that control is enhanced by this separation.

There exists in every business, however, some overall method of controlling quality even if it is only to monitor customers' views and reactions to the quality of the product/service. If management superimposes checks and controls on quality outside the scope of the person completing the task, then the sense of participation in the total work is taken away from that person. In addition, the procedure to inspect the quality of the process cannot help but raise the costs of operations. This is because:

1. The discovery of a quality fault is normally made some time after it has occurred.
2. It reinforces the attitude held by the operators that whilst the doing task is their responsibility, the detection of quality lies elsewhere in the organization.
3. Inspection is an overhead and much of the work could be done more effectively at the time the product is made or service provided.

In fact, in many service organizations, the larger job content still prevails because of the nature of the task and the fact that the breakdown of the task to provide the service has not been engineered into the process. The responsibility, therefore, for providing the service at the specified level of quality is still with the same person. This participative role tends to make people care more about the quality of service they provide and for which they are accountable.

Quality circles

Perhaps the most important way to illustrate the impact of participation on quality and other aspects of a business is to refer to the Japanese experience which over the last few years has received considerable attention. In the last decade, the Japanese have achieved increases in output per man-hour consistently higher than in other leading industrial nations. This has been accomplished from a similar level of per capita gross national product and despite difficulties of the rapidly rising costs of energy and other resources. The main reason for this has been Japan's relatively high level of capital investment in technology and manufacturing facilities. However, another set of factors which has been acknowledged as a probable reason for productivity increases, is the quality control activity known as quality circles widely employed at plant level. By the mid-1960s, several major Japanese companies had begun to introduce quality circles. The effectiveness of this approach led to its widespread adoption in Japanese industry. By the early 1980s the estimate was over one million circles involving some ten million employees. Under guidance from supervisors and middle managers, a quality circle (usually of 5−20 employees) chooses a problem related to quality control, productivity and similar aspects of its operation. Discussion centres on the reasons and extent of the problem, and how improvements can be made.

The results of these activities are demonstrated in the quality achievements of Japanese companies and have been reported extensively.[6] A report published in 1981 which reviewed interviews with seven Japanese firms using quality circles, reported the following major findings:[7]

1. All seven companies could demonstrate with specific examples how quality circles had contributed to improvements in productivity, quality control, prompt deliveries, safety, communications and employee morale.
2. The introduction of quality circles necessitates the introduction of an appropriate employee/supervisory structure and the introduction of employees to these techniques and to other relevant activities.
3. The main steps in quality circles are to:
    (a) identify the problem;
    (b) establish specific goals for the company;
    (c) establish plant and individual circles;
    (d) prepare a plan for solving the assigned problems;
    (e) conduct a statistical survey of current conditions;
    (f) analyse the causes and develop ways to remedy various problems;
    (g) put the solutions into practice;
    (h) carefully test the results;
    (i) select the final solution;
    (j) report and disseminate the results.
4. Some difficulties were experienced. In most companies an initial year of training was necessary to introduce quality circle activities. Trade unions were also kept in the picture and potential interlevel conflicts between technical personnel and operators were recognized and avoided.
5. After extensive use of quality circles, the reasons for their effectiveness were attributed to:
    (a) reduced compartmentalization and increased awareness of the interrelated nature of the activities involved;
    (b) the importance of choosing appropriate problems by middle management;
    (c) the persons responsible for doing the work were able to make invaluable contributions to the solution of important problems, and their suggestions were found to be indispensable.
6. The introduction of quality circles into Japan appeared to be facilitated by:
    (a) greater emphasis on group working;

    (b) lower emphasis on individual accomplishments especially through individual rewards;

    (c) corporate commitment to lifetime employment;

    (d) the system of job rotation helping to break down compartmentalization.

The application of quality circles within service businesses has also met with success. In 1983, the Paul Revere Life Insurance Companies (part of Avco Corporation, an American-based conglomerate) determined that quality was to be the corporate goal. Under a quality steering committee, two approaches were chosen to complete the drive to top quality status: the use of quality teams (modified quality circles) and value analysis workshops. With the selection of these structural elements came several significant policy decisions:

1. Quality improvement would involve all employees on a non-voluntary basis.
2. Quality teams would have the authority to implement their suggestions.
3. Responsibility for implementing organizational or procedural changes would be pushed down through the organization to those managing the units.
4. No matter what the outcome of these activities, continued employment was assured.
5. The activities of the quality teams and value analysis workshops would proceed simultaneously.
6. Quality team formation was to use the following guidelines:

    (a) everyone (including all managers) had to be on at least one team;

    (b) team size should average 10 to 15 members;

    (c) teams were to meet weekly;

    (d) although not mandatory, the 'natural' leader of a work unit should become the team leader;

    (e) the team leader was to be a member of the quality team at the next corporate level.

7. Besides the quality steering commitee, a quality team control and quality team tracking programme were introduced to handle the administrative and systematic reporting activities respectively.

The results were apparent in three ways

1. The involvement of those concerned brought a regular stream of 'certified' suggestions from the company's 127 quality teams. In the first year 7,100 ideas were generated of which 4,100 were implemented completely.
2. Savings were running at the rate of $3.25m on an annualized basis.[8]
3. The initiative of the Paul Revere companies encouraged Avco to adopt quality improvement as a major emphasis amongst all its subsidiaries.

Although the successful introduction of quality circles is widespread, it is important to be realistic about their deployment. The danger of using this initiative as a panacea can be overwhelming, and organizations must ensure that quality circles form only part of a total organizational development, are an appropriate means of intervention, and are based on realistic expectations. The costs are high and should be monitored; moreover, there will often be failures and some circles will be short-lived.[9] A most sobering observation is provided by Robert Cole, a leading authority on the Japanese labour force:

> The fact is that the circles do not work very well in many Japanese companies. Even in those plants recognized as having the best operating programs, management knows that perhaps only one-third of the circles are working well, with another third borderline and one-third simply making no contribution at all. For all the rhetoric of voluntarism, in a number of companies the workers clearly perceive circle activity as coercive. Japanese companies face a continuing struggle to revitalize circle activity to ensure that it does not degenerate into ritualistic behavior.[10]

As with all successful developments, the key is top management support and hard work. Introducing initiatives without this recognition degrades them to the level of techniques and results in premature failure. Controlling these important developments needs managerial attention, energy and perseverence. Much of management comprises establishing the direction, and supporting it with hard work. Quality initiatives are critical but the POM task is complex. There are, therefore, no short cuts to success.

Quality assurance, control and costs

The role of quality assurance and quality control outlined here is developed from the premise that the control of quality is best vested in the producer rather than an inspection department. Although inspection will still exist within a quality control department, the main task of this section would be to participate in the establishment and on-going development of quality functions within the organization, to verify that the quality functions of all other departments are being carried out adequately and to stimulate adherence to existing procedures and their appropriate development. In addition, it may often perform inspection tasks on parts of the process such as incoming materials and the completed product/service. Thus, quality would provide an auditing function with information to both management and the departments concerned on the performance of individuals, facilities, processes and procedures within the organization. However, this change in role must be agreed by management, and management must have a clear understanding of the complications involved in terms of the new responsibility/authority links which will then exist.

With the resolution of these policy issues, the organization is then able to evaluate the economies of quality assurance. This entails two sets of costs. The first is the cost of quality assurance, whose total will increase as the activities and functions concerned with the attainment of quality increase.

The second concerns those costs associated with internal failures (e.g. spoilage and rework of defective items) and external failures (e.g. warranty claims, including repair and replacement, warranty service costs and reduced future sales). The management task here is to strike a balance between the cost and value of quality assurance. Figure 12.3 shows the economics of quality assurance relating the total costs involved (assuming a constant operations cost), with the value of the quality level provided.

It is important when reviewing quality to recognize, as with other investments, the difference between costs and return. The 'quality is free' argument is designed to emphasize the significant corporate gains embodied in the decision to improve quality. It does not imply that there are not costs associated with this decision, but that the return on the investment is considerable. Growing customer and user awareness of quality levels needs to be at the forefront of an organization's quality stance. Failure to understand its markets or to recognize the opportunity to exploit the characteristics of relevant segments can result in an organization underperforming. Quality is here to stay in terms both of costs and dividends. What is also relevant is that the costs of maintaining higher quality may not necessarily be *pro rata* to the costs incurred in achieving that higher level. Doing it right first time most of the time is not a cost-related issue. It concerns appropriate attitudes at all levels in an organization. The benefits, however, will remain the same and the impact upon the success of a business will remain significant — a factor which forms the basis for total quality management initiatives outlined in the next section.

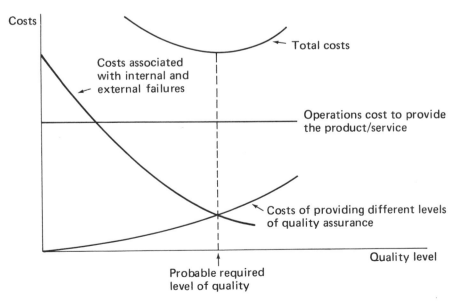

Figure 12.3 The economics of quality assurance.

Total quality management

Besides embodying many of the policy issues addressed in the previous section, this section on total quality management also highlights points of detail covered in the later sections of the chapter. In that way, therefore, it provides part of the link between the policy and operational dimensions of this essential feature of the current competitive environment.

In the increasingly competitive world of the 1990s, quality is no longer an optional extra, it needs to be an integral part of business strategy. The generation of quality products/services demands total commitment by the entire organization, and one approach which has been developed to highlight this need and to provide the direction necessary to achieve these goals is that of total quality management (TQM). Many of the policy issues addressed in the previous section have been brought under this single umbrella.

Background

The 1980s witnessed rapid growth in emphasis upon quality. Data on customer preferences for the year 1986 indicated that eight out of ten buyers within international, industrial and consumer markets made quality equal to, or more important than, price in their purchase value decisions — an increase of over 50 per cent on a similar survey conducted in 1979.[11] This change has had a major, and often volatile, influence on the business results of organizations: a factor which has stimulated a recognition of the need to increase quality and to develop it as an integral part of a business.

Characteristics of TQM

Some of the world's largest companies have recognized the need to build a clear strategy around the principle of quality and that to achieve this they need to build it into the management of the business through total quality management. This level of commitment has a number of essential characteristics, some of which have been addressed in the section on policy issues but brought together here under the TQM banner.

1. Quality is neither a technical function nor a department but a systemic process extending through an organization.
2. Quality is the concern of everyone and must be correctly structured within an organization to create these conditions.
3. The emphasis on improved quality must take place throughout all phases of the business and not just in the operations process. Marketing, design, development, engineering, purchasing, production/operations and service support need to be involved to ensure quality provision.

4. Quality achievement must be externally/customer and not internally/company driven. It needs to be based on the buyer's wants and not on internal perspectives such as efficiency.
5. Quality provision needs to be supported by appropriate new technology, from quality design to computer aided quality measurement and control.
6. Achieving widespread quality improvement needs to be based on the participation and contribution of the workforce and not a group of specialists.
7. Organizations have to establish a clear, customer-oriented quality management system, the understanding, ownership and development of which is vested in everyone concerned.

Steps in the introduction of TQM[12]

1 Leadership
The first step to achieving quality excellence is the decision to make quality leadership a fundamental strategic goal. Unless this clear statement is made, the financial resources are allocated and management energy is committed to the resulting tasks, then the required results will not be achieved. Quality leadership requires a commitment through the organization in all facets of its activities.

To achieve leadership, organizations need to replace the traditional approach to quality — establishing a 'right' level and then aiming to attain that — with a recognition that quality levels are not permanent. The positioning and repositioning of the competitive stance of organizations and the changing customer perception of quality creates a moving target which is upward in direction.

2 Corporatewide introduction
Quality needs to be defined in terms of all the dimensions of a product/service package, including implicit and explicit benefits and supporting facilities — see pp. 104–6. With this defined, the next step is to implement all the necessary actions throughout the entire organization and not just in existing or new quality functions/departments. It is for this reason that some Japanese organizations have used the phrase companywide quality control (CWQC) to emphasize the all-embracing nature of the commitment and activities.

3 Changing corporate orientation
Moving towards TQM involves a reorientation of the corporate approach to quality which involves a number of familiar phases:

(a) Product/service orientation. This relates to the traditional form of quality control involving specialists undertaking quality assurance tasks, and the inspection function after the event. This defect-correction way of thinking has been dominant and stems from a belief that solving problems will improve quality. In reality, problem solving not only fails to guarantee but often militates against improvement as it sets 'quality failure' as being an acceptable performance and correction without improvement an acceptable practice.

(b) Process orientation. Quality control during the process is based primarily on statistical process control (SPC — discussed later in the chapter). This provides the opportunity for significant gains, but the achivement of these depends upon the correct use of SPC methods and adequate knowledge in product/service and process design optimization.

A key feature supporting SPC is the need for organizations to orientate the emphasis of their quality effort towards the downstream activities of customer needs and development, as illustrated in Table 12.3. In addition, within the scope of each activity, a clear recognition of the full extent of SPC's role in quality improvement needs to be recognized. For example, it is often employed as a way of reducing the number of substandard operations completed. However, such an interpretation emphasizes the reactive element of this approach and fails to incorporate the opportunity to use the increased understanding of the cause of variability as a way of reducing the extent of variability by appropriate improvements, a factor which is discussed more fully on p. 401.

(c) Systems orientation. The next stage is to achieve a quality structure which moves the level of integration from involving only those functions which are a direct part of the production process or service delivery system to one which embraces all parts of a business. Ishikawa has likened this approach to the weaving of cloth.[13] The strong vertical weave, so characteristic of traditional approaches, needs to have a horizontal weave of equal strength. Often, however, the former tends to weaken the equally necessary horizontal interaction. The essence of the Japanese approach is to deploy the customer needs horizontally and not vertically throughout the organization.

4 Motivation, education and training

The next step is to create continuous motivation to achieve quality improvements supported by appropriate education and training. Continuous motivation is generated in a number of ways, some of which have their roots in the steps previously

Table 12.3 Required change in current emphasis in the quality effort, by activity

Predominant orientation	*Quality effort by activity*			
	Customer needs	*Functional specification*	*Process*	*Reactive problem-solving*
Current	Low	⟶		High
Future	High	⟶		Low

identified. However, coupled to this is the need to place greater emphasis on education. It is through education that people's attitudes and motivation to achieving quality improvements will be most affected. Training, on the other hand, is merely to improve skills. The key, therefore, is to build on the basis provided by formal education in order to ensure that people's contributions increase.

Lastly, companies must support suggested improvements with adequate resources to ensure that they are achieved within appropriate timescales. There is no greater motivator than action leading to improvement. And, conversely, there is no greater demotivator than the lack of action and a failure to move forward.

5 *The robust function*

Emanating from the systems orientation is a recognition of the need to build quality into the product/service at the design stage. The work of Genichi Taguchi has highlighted this aspect by identifying the features which will most influence customer choice:[14]

1. Not only is choice to do with the initial wish to own or purchase, but also that a customer's desire increases with ownership or experience.
2. The product/service must be functional and robust against the environment (changes in temperature, road conditions and environments that cause functional variation), deterioration (changes due to wear and tear) and variation (differences in the product/service due to specification variability).
3. Being better than competing products/services' features and style and in terms of price and ownership costs.

6 *Cost orientation*

The objectives underpinning customer choice are achieved through:

1. Optimizing product/service and process/delivery system design for improved quality and lower costs.
2. Use of the quality loss function to quantify quality improvements in terms of cost and for use in tolerance design. Known as the Taguchi loss function, it alters the perspective on the most appropriate way to measure quality by linking it to a cost base:

   Quality loss is the financial loss imparted to society after a product is shipped... . It is measured in monetary units and is related to quantifiable product characteristics. Two products that are designed to perform the same function may both meet specifications, but can impart different losses to society. Therefore, merely meeting specifications is a poor measure of quality.[14]

7 *Customer orientation*

The final step is to apply quality control principles to design, thereby formalizing the mechanism for ensuring that customer requirements are incorporated into the design and development phases of provision. This orientation process is facilitated by a recognition of different levels of requirement.

If the customer is a manufacturer of industrial goods, that manufacturer can generally identify its own primary required quality characteristics. The buying public, however, often mentions second- or third-level requirements when asked what it wants. For example, airline passengers might say that they want to arrive on time or to eat well prepared food (second- or third-level requirements) and say nothing about the safety of the flight (obviously a primary requirement). Because consumers' requirements are incomplete, companies must fill in the gaps revealed by the required quality matrix. The companies often must work back from second- or third-level requirements to primary ones.[16]

The remainder of this chapter concerns some of the important operational features within quality provision, the details of which need to be related to the issues of policy which have been covered so far.

Quality of design

Products are made or services provided in response to a market need. The task is to:

1. Ascertain the exact requirements of the customer or user in a make-to-order situation, whilst determining customers' perception of quality in make-to-stock products or off-the-shelf service situations.
2. Embody these requirements into the design and development of the product/service.
3. Fix the product/service design by detailing all the features and characteristics in the specification.
4. Prove the specification by testing the adequacy of the design itself and the capability of the process to provide the product/service at the required level of quality.

Figure 12.4 outlines the procedure involved. Although the quality of a product/service is determined by the market need, management is responsible for establishing the appropriate quality levels for its products/services and ensuring the attainment of these through appropriate functions and procedures.

In make-to-order situations, the quality requirements will usually be either specified by the customers from their own analysis (as a result of discussion with the suppliers) of what they require from the product/service, or be implicit in the customers' choice of an organization as one able, by reputation or past performance, to provide the quality levels required. Thus, if the food is not to the customers' liking, then they will not return to eat at the restaurant. For make-to-stock products or off-the-shelf provisions of services, the determination of quality will involve questions of how the quality of a product/service is perceived by the customer and then how well the supplier matches this level of quality.

Figure 12.5 illustrates the relationship between the cost and value of various quality levels as far as the customer is concerned. The higher level of quality will increase the value of the product/service to the customer but also increase the costs.

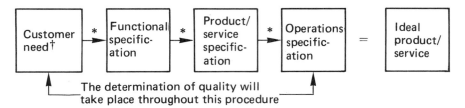

The determination of quality will
take place throughout this procedure

* Points at which there is a potential loss in the interpretation of the original stated or
interpreted customer need.

† In a contractual environment, needs are specified, whereas in other environments,
implied needs should be identified and determined. Needs are usually translated into
features and characteristics with specified criteria. Needs, as defined in BS 4778,
may include aspects of usability, safety, availability, reliability, maintainability,
economics and environment.

Figure 12.4   Quality of design.

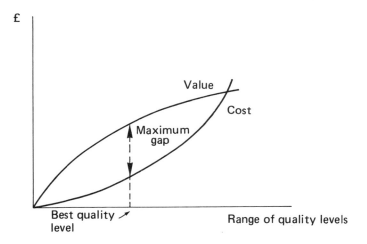

Figure 12.5   The cost and value of quality.

However, for any particular product/service the rate of increase in value to the
customer will decrease as the quality level increases, whilst the rate of cost increases
will accelerate in the same circumstances. The best implied quality level for the
customer is the point where the value/cost relationship has the maximum gap.

The design function translates stated needs into a form which can then be
produced or provided. To do this economically the designer has to have a good
working knowledge of the capabilities of the process and then, as far as possible,
design the product/service within these constraints. The formal nature of this
procedure will vary from one organization to the next, depending upon the size

of the organization, the product complexity, whether it is a product or service and the way in which the organization works. However, no matter what the organization provides or the organizational philosophy involved, the time spent at this stage in the process will seldom be wasted. The BIM report concerning quality calamities, reported that 16 per cent of all these errors were due to a 'lack of/wrong specification' — the cost of playing blind man's bluff.[17]

One of the advantages of high technology activities, such as aerospace and Formula 1 motor racing, is that the demanding nature of these tasks helps push the boundaries of technology in terms of product, process and procedures. One example of the latter is the failure mode and effects analysis (FMEA) originally developed in the American space industry. It seeks to identify all potential weak points at the development stage of a product, so that they can be removed as cheaply as possible (see Figure 5.1). By aiming to identify problems in advance, design effort is focused on aspects which could be the source of post-development quality problems and costs. One company adopting this development within its own organizational approach is Bosch. In its use of FMEA, 'teams from design, preproduction and quality assurance thrash out all possible defects according to a regulated procedure'.[18] However, working ahead of problems is more difficult than being reactive and changing attitudes is part of the difficulty. For improvements to be secured, organizations need to recognize that their approach has to be more integrated and stringent and that preventive quality assurance is a tough and systematic activity, requiring much hard work and willpower. However, the rewards are significant.

The next step is to fix the product/service design through the specification. The tendency to specify services verbally rather than in writing should be avoided. The process of writing down a specification will help to achieve a more complete design statement. BS 4778 defines a specification as 'the document that prescribes the requirements with which the product or service has to conform'.[19] The specification may cover many details and BS 4778 lists twelve types. What is covered will vary not only from product to product but also from product to service. Table 12.4 shows some typical aspects covered by a specification.

The final step in this part of the procedure is proving the specification. This is to enable the design, materials and processes of a product/service to be tested and later modified as necessary. Similarly, it allows for the procedures to be followed and facilities offered to be checked in terms of features such as conformity and timing to ensure the adequacy, feasibility and degree of proficiency that can be provided by the system. Although this appears to be an obvious measure, the BIM paper concluded that the largest single source of the quality problems reviewed was at the pre-production stage.[20] In fact, the results revealed that the largest single reason for failure, at 36 per cent of the total, was found to be the lack of proving new designs, materials and processes. This final step is critical to the eventual quality level of the product/service, not only in its role as a step in the procedure but also as the means of double-checking the earlier stages whilst providing a review of the overall design itself.

Table 12.4 Some typical aspects covered by a specification

Aspect	Specification by	
	Product	*Service*
Function	Functional specification stating what the product is designed to do and the performance characteristics involved	A statement of what the service entails and is designed to provide. Less tangible statements of performance will often be provided
Product/service characteristics	Will include statements of the physical characteristics involved. These are separated into variables which can be measured on a finite scale (e.g. dimensional characteristics) and attributes which embrace those characteristics which are assessed on a subjective basis and not on a scale of measurement (e.g. surface finish)	A description of what constitutes the service with individual aspects differentiated in terms of their importance in the total service concept. As with products these can be separated into variables and attributes with the latter, in many instances, being the most important set of characteristics.
Performance	A statement of the functional and performance requirements of a product.	This will specify the regularity and level of attainment to be achieved by the service
Reliability	The reliability of a product to provide these performance requirements under certain conditions over a period of time	The reliability with which the service is provided, e.g. timetables, hours of opening and service range offered

Quality of conformance

The next step concerns the control of quality in the process to ensure that the goods and services conform to the agreed design. This involves the following stages:

1. Determine the responsibility for complying with the specified requirements at each level in the organization.
2. Control quality at the point of purchase to ensure that the bought-out materials, components and services comply with the specification.
3. Process quality control to ensure that the goods or services being produced or provided meet with the specification, including final inspection, delivery and installation.
4. After-sales service control to provide service-level commitments as specified at the time of sale.

General aspects of quality control

Before addressing the particular issues of purchasing and process quality control, it will help first to consider some important general issues relating to quality control.

Where to inspect

In establishing quality control it is important to consider just where to inspect in the process. The answer is based on *process*, *technical* and *cost* considerations.

Within the operations process, there are a number of possible points where quality activities and functions could be provided. Decisions concerning the points chosen and the extent of the functions and activities to be provided need to be related to each operations situation. The scope of these is outlined in Figure 12.6.

The *technical considerations* include aspects such as importance and process timing. Importance concerns recognizing which parts of the process are responsible for the essential function of the product or substantive feature of the service and to ensure that adequate quality checks are made at these points. Process timing

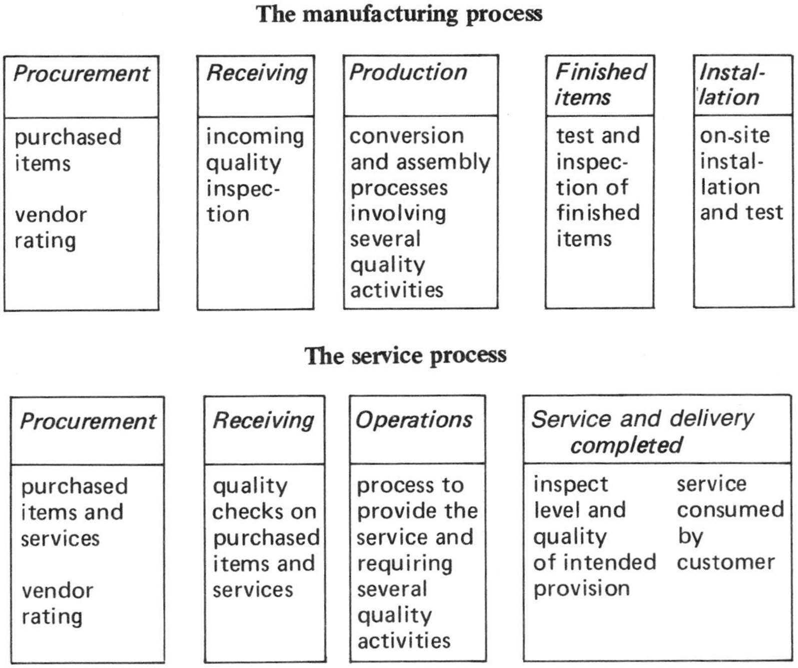

The manufacturing process

Procurement	*Receiving*	*Production*	*Finished items*	*Instal- lation*
purchased items vendor rating	incoming quality inspec- tion	conversion and assembly processes involving several quality activities	test and inspec- tion of finished items	on-site instal- lation and test

The service process

Procurement	*Receiving*	*Operations*	*Service and delivery completed*	
purchased items and services vendor rating	quality checks on purchased items and services	process to provide the service and requiring several quality activities	inspect level and quality of intended provision	service consumed by customer

Figure 12.6 The scope of quality functions and activities in the manufacturing and service process.

refers to aspects such as ensuring accessibility to perform the inspection task for products or the recognition of the point where the provision and consumption of the service takes place and the need to check close to that point. Other considerations include inspection prior to irreversible processes or those which would cover defects made in earlier processes.

The *cost considerations* fall into two sets. The first is the inspection costs involved and the second is the cost of allowing defective items (production) or errors (service) to pass on through the process. The optimal number and location of these points is achieved when the total of these two sets of costs is at a minimum. The assessment of these costs, especially the latter, is not easy and tends largely to be one of judgement. The costs involved are those at each stage in the process plus those for correcting errors and defective items. Thus, selecting inspection points before relatively high cost parts of the process are started or where error correction would become substantially more expensive or not cost-effective, become important factors in this choice.

How to inspect

If we wished to ensure that the quality level was being attained in the process, then a first reaction would be to say 'let us inspect everything'. A 100 per cent inspection procedure should, in theory, ensure that no substandard product/service is allowed to proceed through the process. In practice, however, this procedure has major limitations:

1. It does not guarantee that all substandard products/services will be found. Where the inspection involves people, this plan will create a monotonous task and does not eliminate human error.
2. The costs involved are high and could result in an organization not adopting the best position (see Figures 12.3 and 12.5).
3. Unacceptable delays may be introduced into the process.
4. Deterioration may take place, for example through excessive handling.

These limitations give rise to the concept of acceptance sampling. Most acceptance inspection procedures are based on the principles of statistical inference by which conclusions are drawn about the characteristics of a large batch of products or standard services provided, by inspecting very carefully a small sample from that batch. Any acceptance sampling plan, however, may lead to a wrong judgement — this is known as sampling risk and is discussed later in the chapter.

There has been much written about the subject of sampling and the methods are so well refined that it is not necessary to understand the mathematical principles involved. Also, tables are available that show the inferences which can be drawn from the different samples that have been chosen. When the concept of sampling is used the following principles must, however, apply:

1. The sample has to be either truly random or stratified (i.e. the samples are chosen so as to be representative of the production/service provision over the time period involved).
2. The sample size needs to relate to the size of the batch involved to ensure that what is checked is sufficiently representative of the whole.
3. The identity of the bulk lot from which the sample has been taken should, where possible, be preserved. After all, a sample has no meaning in itself; it is the bulk lot that is important.

Acceptance sampling plans

There are several types of acceptance sampling plan which may be used. In each case, the plan is designed to ensure that items or parts of a service do not pass to the next stage in the process if an unacceptably high proportion of the batch is outside the quality limit. Some of these different plans call for a single sample to be taken, others for double or multiple sampling from a batch. The plans may also differ in the way the items in the sample are checked. Some of the more important differences are examined here. In practice the plans used are rarely designed from first principles but more frequently are based on one of several already published.[21]

Acceptable quality level (AQL)

BS 4778 defines AQL as 'the maximum per cent defective (or the maximum number of defects per 100 units) that, for purposes of acceptance sampling, can be considered satisfactory as a process average'.[22] Thus, when a value of AQL is determined for the quality characteristic being checked, providing the average number of defective items is not greater than the agreed AQL, then the great majority of the lots inspected will be accepted.

Sampling risk

The phrase 'great majority' was used above because no sampling scheme is perfect. There will be the risk that an unacceptable batch will satisfy the AQL and therefore be accepted (known as the consumer's risk) and, similarly, that an acceptable batch fails to meet the AQL and therefore, is rejected (known as the producer's risk). The way to reduce this risk is to take a larger sample, with the 100 per cent sample plans being the upper limit where, theoretically, no risk is taken.

Economics of sampling

The consumer's and producer's risks referred to above both incur costs. In the former they are the costs associated with passing defective items or part services through the process. In the latter, they are the unnecessary checking, rework and administrative costs involved as the batch is, in fact, acceptable. Thus two sets of costs are involved at each inspection point in the process: those associated with making the check and those relating to the sampling risk. Clearly, the level of inspection to apply is that at which the sum of these two sets of costs is at a minimum. However, in practice it is difficult to assess these costs and so what constitutes the minimum sum is judgemental. It is important, though, that the concepts described here are appreciated and form the basis of that decision.

Sampling scheme

The sampling scheme contains a range of sampling plans and procedures whereby the results of inspecting one or more samples are used to assess the quality of a lot and help determine whether or not to accept it.

Each sampling plan states the sample size to be taken in relation to different batch sizes and the decision criteria (e.g. acceptance or rejection number) to be used for accepting or rejecting a batch. The sample sizes are based on the mathematical theory of probability and will not be covered here.[23]

Earlier, the limitations surrounding a 100 per cent inspection procedure were discussed. While the concept of sampling holds true in most situations, there are times when 100 per cent inspection is necessary, for example where safety is of the utmost importance.

Single sampling plan

This plan is essentially a go/no go procedure. The sampling size related to the batch is determined and the acceptable quality level is applied. Only if the number of defective items (products) or errors (services) meets the AQL criteria is the batch accepted.

Double sampling plan

A double sampling plan introduces another option to the single plan above. The example shown in Figure 12.7 requires a sample of 100 to be taken from a batch of a known size. If on the first sample of 100 the number of defectives or errors

Sample number	size	Number of defective items or errors	
		acceptable quality level	unacceptable quality level
first	100	$\leqslant 2$	$\geqslant 7$
second	100	$\leqslant 7$	$\geqslant 8$

Figure 12.7 Double sampling plan.

is two or less then the whole batch is accepted on the first sample. Conversely, if the number of defective items or errors is seven or more, then the whole batch is rejected on the the first sample. If, however, the number of defective items or errors is between three and six then a second sample of 100 is taken. If the cumulative number of defective items or errors from both batches is seven or less then accept it, if eight or more then reject it.

Multiple sampling plan
The principle of the double sampling plan can be extended into a multiple sampling plan. This too uses not only the AQL concept but also the unacceptable quality level (UQL) concept. This latter relates to the percentage defective level at which the batch would be rejected. As in the case of double sampling plans, there is a yes, no and don't know situation. A first sample is taken which is usually smaller than in a single sampling plan. If the number of defective items or errors is between the accept and reject areas then further samples are taken until the cumulative results of the multiple samples fall into either the accept or reject category (see Figure 12.8).

Sequential sampling plan
A sequential sampling plan is similar to the multiple plan. The sample size is one, with the results normally plotted on a graph. The sampling is repeated until the graph contains sufficient information on which to reach a decision.

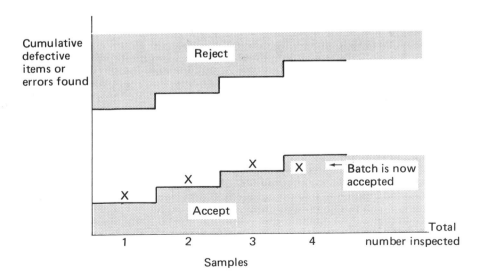

Figure 12.8 Multiple sampling plan.

Variables and attributes
A product or service is made up of many individual qualities. However, these are grouped into two sets of characteristics:

1. *Variables* — those characteristics which can be measured on a numerical scale (e.g. weight, dimensions).
2. *Attributes* — those characteristics which are assessed either by judgements without measurement (e.g. surface finish) or checked without detailed measurement (e.g. with a go/no go gauge which indicates that an item falls within the specification but not its exact measurement).

Normal, tightened and reduced inspection
Normal inspection is defined as that used where there is no reason to think that the quality of a product differs from that specified.[24] Inspection is tightened or reduced when the results of normal inspection indicate that the quality of the lot is worse or better than specified.

Quality control aspects at stages in the total process

Having explained the important general aspects of quality, the next step is to consider the major stages in the process or procedure and the types of quality check to apply. Figures 12.9 and 12.10 outline the conversion process for products and services and the important areas where the nature of these quality activities have to be considered. These are now discussed in more detail.

Purchasing

Stock phrases often used in the past on purchase requisitions and purchase orders of 'as sample' or 'as before' are inappropriate for most situations. As materials form an even higher percentage of total costs, this increases the need to control their quality.

In a production situation, machines, equipment or people convert material from one form to a more developed form. In machining processes, the process is subject to variation. In non-machining processes, adjustment by the operator can be made only within certain limits. Thus, the material being fed into the process must fall within certain limits of variability to enable the machining or non-machining process to convert the material into the required new state. Thus the level of quality must be predictable and the levels of variance assessed and agreed. However, for this to happen the supplier must first be told what is wanted. If he does not know then he will not be able to supply at the necessary level of quality. Hence a precise specification is needed, and to do this the first step is to explain what is required in terms of variables and attributes, as outlined above. The use of a purchasing specification is most essential where the items or services:

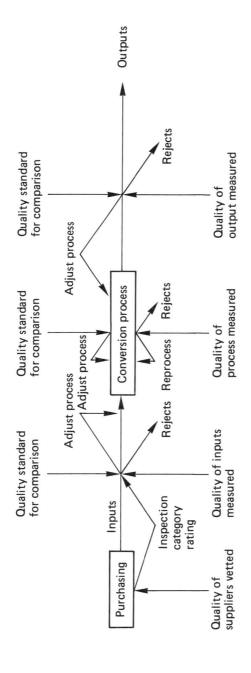

Figure 12.9 The production system — purchasing, input, process and finished product aspects of quality control.

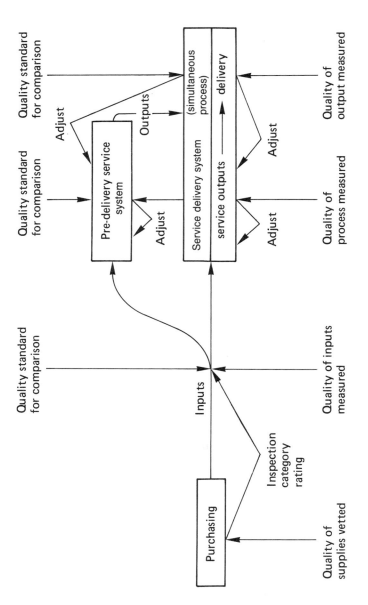

Figure 12.10 The service delivery system in relation to quality control.

1. Are expensive in themselves or are bought in large quantities.
2. Relate to the essential function (product) or essential attribute (service) to be provided by what is to be sold.
3. Will cause difficulties and expense in the process if they are below the quality requirement.

For products/services that do not fall within these categories, the decision whether to prepare a specification is one of cost.

To help maintain desired quality levels it is essential to buy materials or services from reliable suppliers. There are other important considerations such as cost and delivery which will form part of this choice, but are not discussed in this section.

The quality of purchased components and materials is rooted in the process of suppliers. A company will not get the required quality if the methods used by its suppliers are not capable of consistently meeting the agreed specification. It is, therefore, important that an evaluation of procedures is established for suppliers who provide materials or services that are critical to the process and end-product/service. This will usually contain three distinct phases. The first is vendor appraisal which is completed before placing an order and is designed to assess the ability of the supplier to supply goods/services at the required level of quality.[25] The second concerns supplier evaluation which is designed to vet a supplier's control of quality when an order has been given, and the goods/services supplied. The final phase is that of supplier rating which monitors the actual performance of a supplier.

Checking purchased items or services

In situations where the maintenance of quality levels is critical to the internal process, then an organization would have to insist on monitoring a supplier's processes and quality control procedures. The classic example of this is the Ministry of Defence which has developed sophisticated quality assurance procedures to meet the high safety requirements of many of its component and equipment purchases.[26] Similarly, a company wishing to purchase the services of another company (say a management consultant) will now more often interview one or more consultants and select the one who appears most suitable. However, most organizations limit themselves to checking items or services once they have been purchased. Understandably, as the item becomes more complex, then so do the inspection procedures. But in many instances this may be no more than a quantity count as, for example, with office supplies. Yet even where an organization wishes to check the characteristics of a product it will not usually check each one: the costs of doing so are just too high. Thus the inspection agreed with the supplier has to contain not only what is intended to be the quality level but also how it is to be judged and measured and the level of imperfection that is acceptable (see earlier in the chapter). Where some level of imperfection is permitted, then sampling is the basis on which to proceed.

Consequently, the principle of acceptance sampling will be applied in this situation (see p. 389). The design of any sampling plan is a trade-off between sampling cost and risk. To help in this choice, a useful way of depicting the relationship is provided by plotting an operating characteristic (OC) curve (see Figure 12.11). Each OC curve is associated with a particular sampling plan and it shows how well an acceptance plan discriminates between good and bad batches. Figure 12.11 explains how a particular acceptance plan operates, but as each acceptance plan relates to a particular situation, then each OC curve will usually be uniquely designed, offering different choices between sample size and the acceptable number of defectives — see Figure 12.12.

In Figure 12.11 the OC curve must meet the following conditions:

Acceptable quality level (AQL)	2%
Lot tolerance percentage defective (LTPD)	15%
Producer's risk	5%
Consumer's risk	10%

Let us remind ourselves of what these factors mean:

1. AQL is the desired quality level at which the probability of acceptance would be high.
2. LTPD is the rejection quality level at which the probability of acceptance would be low.
3. Producer's and consumer's risk are the probabilities of good order quantities

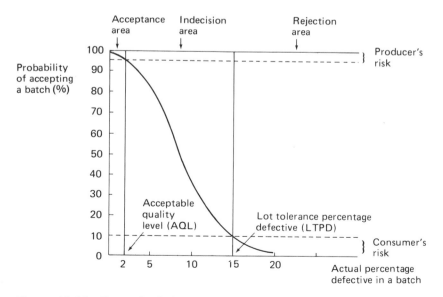

Figure 12.11   General relationships of an operating characteristic (OC) curve.

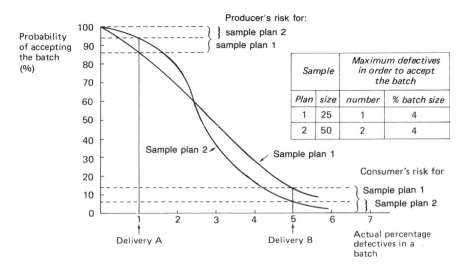

Figure 12.12 Operating characteristic (OC) curves for different sampling sizes.

(at AQL) being rejected or substandard order quantities (at LTPD) being accepted.

A curve that passes through the two specified points AQL and LTPD can be found by trial-and-error or by using tables.[27] This example shows not only the power of the plan to discriminate between good and bad batches but also the extent of the risk of accepting bad batches and rejecting good ones. The question now is, 'How can managers modify acceptance plans in order to minimize this risk?' The most obvious way is to increase the sample size. Figure 12.12 shows the effect of this and the larger discriminatory power of the sample size, as shown by comparing sample plans 1 and 2 against two deliveries, delivery A with 1 per cent actual defects and delivery B with 5 per cent actual defects. It can be seen clearly from the figure that sample plan 2 reduces both the consumer's risk and producer's risk. As it is consumers who are most concerned about the degree of acceptable risk inherent in the application of sampling plans to incoming inspection, then it is they who not only set the AQL but also the steepness of the OC curve. As illustrated in Figure 12.12, this is related to the sample size, for although the maximum percentage allowable batch acceptance was the same at 4 per cent of the sample, the increase in sample size resulted in a steeper curve. Figure 12.12 also illustrates the probabilities of accepting a delivery if sample plan 1 or 2 were adopted. Where the actual percentage defective in a batch was only 1 per cent (as in delivery A), then the probability of accepting the batch increases; where the actual percentage defective in a batch was 5 per cent (as in delivery B) then the probability of accepting this batch decreases.

An OC curve, therefore, is a graph showing what any particular sampling plan will be expected to do in terms of accepting or rejecting batches. Although any sampling plan can be used without understanding its operating characteristics, it makes sense that the quality assurance function of any organization should be able to compare one sampling plan with another to help establish appropriate quality controls. As the selected AQL is the dividing line between good and bad batches, the ideal system would be one in which all batches whose quality was better than the AQL were accepted, and all whose quality was worse, rejected. This, of course, is only possible with 100 per cent inspection (see Figure 12.13). Sampling, being the alternative to this method, will not provide this level of discrimination and means that the vertical line shown in Figure 12.13 will have to run at a slope as shown in Figures 12.11 and 12.12. Which OC curve to choose returns to deciding between risk and cost. The closer the OC curve fits the slope of the curve in Figure 12.13 then the lower the risk but the nearer to 100 per cent inspection and the costs associated with this form of checking.

The AQL system has been adopted by most western countries, including the UK, and is now in common use. The British Standards Institution, for instance, issues standards which fully explain this system and provide sampling plans to suit the everyday needs of most inspection requirements. In addition to the single sampling plans discussed in this section, there are also details on double and multiple plans at different levels of inspection.[21] For most situations, these are adequate to meet normal inspection needs.

Process inspection

The way a process or person performs is independent of the product/service. To control quality, therefore, it is necessary to know what the process will do, is likely to do or, better still, what it is doing. Furthermore, processes do not make identical products: merely similar. Variability is inherent in the process and the need to appreciate this is an important first step in considering process quality control.

In process control, information is received on what is happening in the process and so distinguishes between those quality changes resulting from the natural

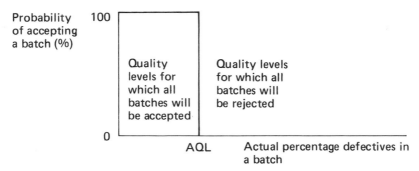

Figure 12.13 The operating characteristic (OC) curve for 100 per cent inspection.

variation of the process (referred to as an assignable cause) and those caused by some new, persistent influence on the process (referred to as a random cause). This distinction is fundamental to controlling quality in the process and allows corrective action to be taken only where it is necessary. To do this effectively, it is necessary to:

1. Use the knowledge of what has been happening in the process.
2. Differentiate between assignable and random changes in the quality characteristic in the process.
3. Determine the cause of the random change and rectify it.

Whilst acceptance sampling of a completed batch is an important part of inspection, other forms of control are necessary to help prevent worsening quality going undetected. Typical inspection methods to achieve this require an inspector to take one or more items from the process and compare them with the appropriate requirements. Typical views of carrying out the inspection function include in-process inspection which is carried out at predetermined points in the process or procedure, and patrolling inspection which involves routine and/or random visits to several stages in the process.

The drawback of inspection is that it is based on the use of people (with their potential inconsistency) and is less effective than a systematic statistically-based procedure. It is important, therefore, to agree a specification detailing an organized system for checking the process, an acceptable quality level and the consequent action if rejects are found.

This form of control system is designed so that the person performing the task hands over the quality aspects of that task to others or to a system. However, as stated earlier, quality control works best where the person responsible for the doing aspects is also responsible for the quality of those aspects. In this way quality control then becomes quality measurement and the person responsible for the process is able to measure the process, monitor quality movements and rectify any abnormal changes.

Two of the more important ways to achieve quality measurement are control charts and cumulative sum (cu sum) charts. Whereas inspection is often used simply to sort good and bad items and usually after the process is completed,[28] control charts control the process while it is taking place. They can be used to control both variables and attributes of, for the most part, repetitive processes.

Control chart for variables
Typically, the process mean is established and acceptable levels of deviation agreed. These have two sets of limits: warning limits which form the band of usual variation, and action limits which form the band of unusual variation (see Figure 12.14).

Control chart for attributes
As attribute measures of quality are obtained by an acceptable or unacceptable classification, then an exact measure of the process is not taken. Consequently,

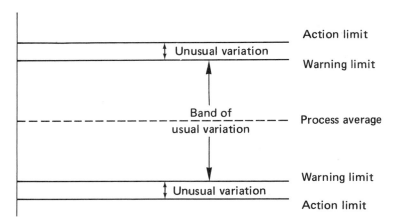

Figure 12.14   Control chart for variables.

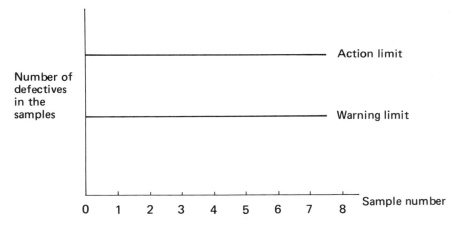

Figure 12.15   Control chart for attributes.

to control attributes through the use of control charts, sampling is used as shown in Figure 12.15. The control chart measures the actual item or number of defectives in the sample and, when plotted, shows any variation in the process of which corrective action needs to be taken.

Cumulative sum charts
The control chart is a clear way of presenting data. However, it is based on checking specific observations independently from one another. Cumulative sum (cu sum) charts on the other hand, take into account past data and, by incorporating these into the chart, allow trends to be more clearly shown than in control charts.

The cu sum chart is devised by establishing a reference value for the process which is usually the process mean. The actual reading is then made and is subtracted from the reference value. This result is then plotted. The next reading is similarly calculated but is then added to the previous result and then plotted. In this way, slight changes in the process can be detected, for if the mean value increases there will be a rise in the cumulative sum level. Similarly, a downward slope will mean a decrease in cumulative sum, while a horizontal graph will show stability in the data.

Statistical process control
The increasing competitive pressure to produce higher quality products or provide higher quality services has brought about changes in attitude and expectations. This is illustrated by the succession of terms used to express what is an acceptable and achievable goal for quality.[29]

1. *Yield.* Up to about 1970 the expression of quality was embodied in the term 'yield'. The focus was on the good parts produced with acceptable levels of around 90 per cent.
2. *Scrap.* During the 1970s the focus turned to scrap as an expression of the material and work created in the system and the aim to reduce this loss over time.
3. *Quality is job 1.* By the 1980s, previous levels of quality were recognized as not being competitive so slogans like 'quality is job 1' were used to highlight the prime importance of the quality task and the need to reduce losses to below 1 per cent.
4. *Parts per million.* By the mid-1980s the resolve became firm to reduce scrap still further embodied by the Japanese use of the term 'zero defects'.

Coupled with these changing attitudes and targets, the use of statistical process control, incorporated within the responsibilities of those completing the task, became a key factor in achieving these significant improvements. Only through monitoring the process on a continuous basis (e.g. using charts similar to Figures 12.14 and 12.15) can quality levels be systematically improved by checking the outputs from the process or system and making any necessary adjustments on an on-going basis.

However, it is important to recognize that the purpose is not to achieve a position where all sample points are within limits and close to the average. If this prevails, it is usually a sign that the proactive use of this approach has not been recognized. The Shewhart rule for a process in control is to have two-thirds of the points within one-third of the limits and some points outside the limits.[30] The dual purpose of SPC includes the need to change the sampling scheme in such a way as to achieve the Shewhart result. The next steps would then be to change the process, thereby bringing all the points within limits, and then resample to show some points out of limits. The overriding aim, therefore, is to reduce variability by improving the process capability.

Restructuring work (see Chapter 14), supporting new responsibilities with appropriate training and providing top management's active and continued support are essential to achieving and maintaining quality improvements. As emphasized earlier, quality is not free but the return on investment is most attractive. Furthermore, organizations which are not proactive in these initiatives not only miss an opportunity but may miss out altogether.

Output control

The final stage is concerned with the control of quality at the end of the process, including delivery and installation where appropriate. In make-to-stock situations, inspection of finished items will usually form an integral part of the system. For products of high value, there will usually be a 100 per cent inspection on certain functional aspects of the item. As with on-going inspection, the first step will be to prepare a specification based on appropriate variables and attributes and then to detail the inspection procedures to be followed. With less expensive items, a sampling plan would be more appropriate and will be based on the same factors as those discussed earlier under purchased items and services (p. 392).

In make-to-order organizations, decisions similar to those described in the last paragraph will obtain. In addition, however, with large items or in the case of particular organizations (e.g. British Telecom and the Ministry of Defence), strict procedures concerning quality checks will form part of the contract and will be conducted by the customer.

With the appropriate role changes, since at this final stage the organization is the supplier to its customers, the points raised earlier concerning the purchasing of items and services are again pertinent.

BS 5750

The British Standards Institution (BSI) has been in the product certification business for many years. However, product certification has its limitations and to meet the expressed needs of industry, the BSI introduced in 1979 the System for the Registration of Firms of Assessed Capability in those situations where product certification is impracticable. The current system document for assessing firms in manufacturing and process industries is BS 5750 (1987). Where a firm's design capability is to be included in the assessment, BS 5750, part 1 is used. Where a firm manufactures to a published or the customer's specification, then BS 5750, part 2 or part 3 is used.

BS 5750 is a practical national standard for quality systems which can be used by companies of all sizes. It does not set out special requirements with which only a very few firms can comply. On the contrary, it identifies the basic disciplines and specifies the procedures and criteria to ensure that a firm's products meet the customers' requirements. It does this by building in quality at every stage, and sets out how to establish an effective quality system with appropriate documentation.

BS 5750 comprises nineteen sections to facilitate its implementation which, when completed, entitles a company to appear in the Department of Trade and

Industry's *Register of Quality-assessed UK Companies*. The principal requirements to be met as regards design, manufacture and installation are given below.

General provisions
1. Good organization — identify and assign responsibility for all quality-related functions, with one designated manager with appropriate ability and authority to co-ordinate, monitor and manage the quality system.
2. Periodic and systematic reviews to include internal audits and which need to accommodate the purchaser's representative where appointed. These reviews need to list system defects, identify problem areas, suggest improvements, verify that corrective action is effective and the desired results are being achieved.
3. The quality system must be planned and developed to take into account other relevant functions, such as design, development, manufacturing, subcontracting and installation.
4. Quality planning needs to be undertaken to identify new testing and inspection techniques as well as completing process assessments.
5. Documentation and records need to be installed to cover test and measuring equipment monitoring.

Specific provisions
1. Design functions to be specified and controlled include a design and development programme; provision of a code of design practice and procedures; investigation of new techniques; identification and control of design interfaces; preparation and maintenance of drawings, specifications, procedures and instructions; demonstrated consideration of statutory requirements; evaluation of new material; control of the reliability and value engineering tasks; establishment of design review procedures, and appropriate use of data feedback from previous designs.
2. Well designed system to evaluate subcontractors and suppliers of material. These should cover written controls for purchased materials, components and services, purchasing data, inspection and verification procedures.
3. All manufacturing operations (including written work instructions) must be carried out under controlled conditions. On the factory floor, similar desciplined control is mandated. Procedures and work instructions should cover every phase and BS 5750 details what these work instructions should contain.
4. In-process quality plans are specified and details include sampling, rules for acceptance and the segregation and screening of rejected lots.
5. In addition to in-process inspection, it is customary to perform a final test. Test procedures, personnel, test equipment capability assessments and environmental conditions are all covered by the standard.

The initial assessment is followed by regular, (normally four times a year) unannounced surveillance visits to ensure that standards are maintained. Registration is increasingly being required by many (especially large) companies and a supplier's need to comply with BS 5750 not only makes sense in itself but is a prerequisite to entering many markets.

Service issues

In the past, many companies have placed significant emphasis on the control of costs. More recently, however, there has been a growing recognition that it is essential both to emphasize a range of performance measures which are relevant to corporate objectives and also to relate one to another within the assessment of total performance. One measure of growing importance is quality.

However, in many service organizations the control of quality is inadequately undertaken as it is often difficult to accomplish because of the following:

1. The intangible nature of services which involve dealing with something that is primarily delivered to people by people.
2. Setting standards requires a careful measurement of both the provider's and customers' perception of quality.
3. Controlling quality during the process must be completed in such a way as not to interfere with the provision of the service within the delivery system.

As the control of quality is a significant factor in the success of a service organization (and often directly linked to productivity), it is important to overcome these inherent characteristics. To help in this, companies need to understand what the service does and of what it should comprise, the separate parts of the delivery system and how they relate one to another and the way to establish aspects of service quality which need to be improved and controlled. Each of these is now considered in more detail. However, although the approach put forward embraces the whole of the service delivery system, it is important in this section of the book to place these factors within a quality context. Therefore, the principal aim of the following analysis is to help an organization understand the service package, the way it is delivered and the points at which quality can be improved and controlled.

Determining the different facets of the service package

A service comprises four distinct facets which are different from one another and the combination of which comprises the total.[31] Whilst the make-up of individual services will differ, this analysis helps to explain the whole by first understanding the parts. Thus it enables companies to reconstitute the service package and to understand which elements have the greatest impact on the quality provided.

1. *Supporting facilities involved.* This comprises the physical resources which must be in place before a service can be offered. For example, a restaurant, aeroplane, hospital or retail premises. To evaluate this aspect of the service package the relevant perspectives to be taken into account include:
    (a) exterior design — architecture, materials and state of repair;

(b) interior appointment — design, decoration and choice of furniture and equipment;

(c) layout — space, adequacy of provision and suitability;

(d) supporting equipment — level of technology, age of equipment and the level of maintenance and up-keep.

2. *Facilitating goods*. This part of the package concerns the materials and goods purchased or consumed by the customer. Examples include food consumed, equipment used (e.g. the rental car provided) or professional advice/opinion given. Criteria for assessing this aspect of the service package include:

(a) quality — consistency from one purchase to the next, presentation and relevance/accuracy of the information provided or advice given;

(b) quantity — portion control and total size of the offering (e.g. replenishment of coffee);

(c) selection — the range and variety of items on offer.

3. *Explicit services*. This refers to the readily perceivable benefits which consist of the essential or intrinsic features of the service. For example, quality of the server's service (level and speed of attention, degree of interpretation of the mood of the event in terms of a speedy or leisurely requirement), and quality of the instruction (including an instructor's level of understanding, ability to teach and the apparent interest and level of customization shown). The factors for assessing this feature include:

(a) availability — comprising aspects such as level of on-call provision, proximity of the service to customers, and access to public transport/parking facilities;

(b) consistency of provision — punctual flights, and built in assessment of the service delivery system provision;

(c) comprehensive nature of the service — for example, range and choice provided.

4. *Implicit services*. These refer to the psychological benefits which a customer may perceive or experience and which are ancillary to the service itself. Examples include, level of privacy, punctual nature of the service, trouble-free nature of the repair and level of assurance engendered. The criteria relevant to this feature of the service package include:

(a) attitude of the service personnel — level of interest shown and the personal disposition of the server;

(b) convenience/service level embodied at the point of entry to the service delivery system — use of an appointments system, free-parking provision, being placed on 'hold' during a telephone enquiry and waiting in queues;

(c) atmosphere and status — level of differentiation within the service, customized/standardized aspects of the package and size of the vehicle (e.g. the aircraft used).

The service package is a combination of these features, all of which are experienced by the customer and form the basis of the service itself. However, to assist in achieving the necessary quality levels, it is now necessary to separate those features of the service which are substantive and those which are peripheral in nature. By differentiating in this way, the relative importance of each facet of the service and the appropriate standards and emphasis to be made can be established.

Reviewing the service delivery system

The next step is to review the service delivery system in order to establish the following:

1. The back room/front office mix.
2. The position of each facet of the service package within the delivery system and broken down into type (supporting facility, facilitating goods, explicit services and implicit services) and importance (substantive or peripheral).
3. The existing points of customer contact.

Establishing the aspects of service quality which need to be improved and controlled

The purpose of this part of the analysis is to review each of the above three aspects in order to revise them within the context of the total service delivery system and so ensure that the service package is appropriate and that the quality levels and subsequent controls can be agreed. In this way, the mix within the service package can be reviewed, new emphasis of what is important can be agreed, appropriate quality levels at each stage can be established and suitable controls can be used to monitor the system. In particular, it is important to:

1. Identify and optimize the number of points of contact with the customer. Before trying to measure and set quality standards attention must be given to defining service transactions that take place throughout the delivery system. When the current system is understood, it is opportune to consider the number of points of contact with the customer and to assess their potential contribution to achieving the required level of quality. In addition, reviewing the system with the intention of improving the server/customer interface enables an organization to optimize the influence it brings to bear on establishing and achieving desired levels of quality.
2. Develop appropriate measures and criteria to assess the level of quality achieved within the delivery system. Information should be both quantitative (e.g. rating scales and percentages) and qualitative (e.g. customer complaints and management impressions when observing the system). It is essential within the quality provision that the attributes of the organization's services are defined and then quantified and measured. Some attributes simply cannot be quantified, whilst others may be measured on an appropriate scale — for instance binary yes/no, numerical (for example, 1, 2, 3, 4) or using relevant ratios.
3. Monitor and evaluate actual performance — the quality of the service package

and the service delivery system must be constantly evaluated to ensure that the actual performance meets the standards laid down and expected. This monitoring can be achieved in one of several ways:

(a) through the constant communication and checking by management as a way of motivating employees to excel at service provision;
(b) measure and constantly revise the service and check the mix of attributes involved;
(c) measure the service delivery system against agreed standards to assess the level at which the service is provided.

Within this evaluation it is also helpful to separate the service delivery system into its major parts as a way of distinguishing the appropriate mix of a service package (goods and attributes), placing each part of the package within the appropriate phase of the delivery system (back room versus front office) and, lastly, ensuring that quality standards reflect the importance and impact of each facet within the total service package.

Some service examples

To improve service quality, it is necessary to analyse the quality problem carefully to provide insights as to possible causes and to pinpoint areas where remedial action is most needed. Figure 12.16 illustrates an approach to analysis and Table 12.5 a set of results. Identifying cause and importance provides the first step.

Management's use of these insights is two-fold. The first concerns undertaking quality improvement projects, ideally based on employee involvement mechanisms such as quality circles. This will include a critical assessment of broader issues (e.g. location of tasks between back room and front office) as well as the more detailed activities necessary to effect improvement. For example, in shops that undertake repairs on site, there is a move to link the customer to the back-room in order to reduce the incidence of misunderstanding and to improve the level of technical advice to the customer in both the pre- and post-repair stages of the system.

To maintain and improve quality levels it is also necessary to establish standards against which performance can be measured and on which improvements and developments can be focused. Within the service delivery system, the controls need to be well defined and understood if they are to be effective. Figure 12.17 is an example of the level of detail which underpins both the necessary understanding of the constituents of quality and the insights necessary to control quality within the system.

With standards established, quality levels can be monitored. Distinguishing explicit from implicit measures also helps tune the sensitivity of the control system. Explicit measures may include trend analyses against corporate norms (see Figure 12.18) or involving comparisons with competitors as well as customer evaluations based on surveys and other forms of feedback (see Figure 12.19).

Implicit measures can also be introduced which, for instance, reflect the quality of service provided within the system. For example, the North Carolina National

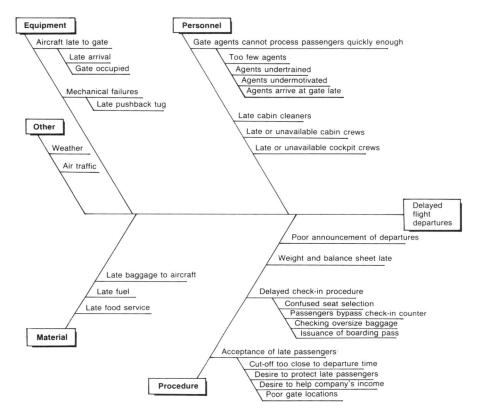

Figure 12.16 A portion of Midway Airlines' fishbone analysis — causes of flight departure delays.

Source: D. Wyckoff, 'New tools for achieving service quality', *The Cornell HRA Quarterly* (November 1984), p. 89. With permission.

Bank (NCNB) uses a star achiever system comprising four levels embodied in a name-plate with the heading 'Expect the Best'. Stars are awarded to an employee in the following ways:

1. Customers receive every month a total of four stars which they are entitled to send in, at their own discretion, as recognition of having been provided with good service by a nominated employee.
2. Similarly, bank employees receive eight stars every month which they are able to award to other employees (within any part of the NCNB banking network) in recognition of receiving good support in terms of serving customers.

For each ten of these customer or employee stars received, the employee concerned is given a star to a maximum of four. Besides the motivation of becoming a full-grade 'star achiever', employees receiving a recommendation have their name

Table 12.5 Pareto analysis of flight departure delays

	All stations, except hub			Newark				Washington (National)		
	Percentage of incidences	*Cumulative percentage*			*Percentage of incidences*	*Cumulative percentage*			*Percentage of incidences*	*Cumulative percentage*
Late passengers	53.3	53.3	Late passengers		23.1	23.1	Late passengers		33.3	33.3
Waiting for pushback	15.0	68.3	Waiting for fuelling		23.1	46.2	Waiting for pushback		33.3	66.6
Waiting for fuelling	11.3	79.6	Waiting for pushback		23.1	69.3	Late weight and balance sheet		19.0	85.6
Late weight and balance sheet	8.7	88.3	Cabin cleaning and supplies		15.4	84.7	Waiting for fuelling		9.5	95.1

Source: D.D. Wyckoff, 'New tools for achieving service quality', *The Cornell HRA Quarterly* (November, 1984), p. 89. With permission.

1. **First contact** — cocktail server speaks to customer within two minutes of customer seating.
2. **Cocktails delivered** — beverage service at table within four minutes of order. If no beverage order, request for food order within four minutes of first greeting.
3. **Request for order** — within four minutes after beverage service, customer should be asked whether he or she cares to order.
4. **Appetizers delivered** — salad, chowder, or wine delivered within five minutes.

5. **Entree delivered** — entree served within 16 minutes of order.
6. **Dessert delivered** — dessert and coffee or after-dinner drinks served within five minutes after plates are cleared.
7. **Check delivered** — check presented within four minutes after dessert course or after plates are cleared if no dessert.
8. **Money picked up** — cash or credit cards picked up within two minutes of being placed by customer on table.

Cocktail-service standards

1. **First contact** — greeting given and cocktail order taken, seafood bar, happy-hour specials and wine-by-glass menus presented within two minutes.
2. **Cocktails delivered** — cocktails delivered within five minutes after first contact.

3. **Seafood bar delivered** — seafood bar and happy-hour specials delivered within seven minutes of first contact, ten minutes for cooked items.
4. **Next contact** — check for reorder of cocktail, seafood bar, customer satisfaction, and table maintenance within five minutes from delivery of first cocktail.

Figure 12.17 Rusty Pelican food-service standards.

Source: D. Wyckoff, 'New tools for achieving service quality', *The Cornell HRA Quarterly* (November 1984), p. 89. With permission.

entered into the bank's monthly lottery. Lottery winners receive prizes including a week's holiday, an additional day's holiday leading to a long-weekend (with and without a hotel holiday thrown in) down to a range of smaller prizes.

In addition, companies can review the service delivery system and identify areas where they can improve the customers' view of quality levels by addressing perception as well as monitoring and improving the system, as outlined in this section. For example, Prontaprint offer free coffee to customers who decide to wait for the printing services to be completed, while Prestage Garages have established a television facility in their Birmingham (UK) outlet. Both developments are designed to reduce the customer's perception of the length of waiting time in the queue.

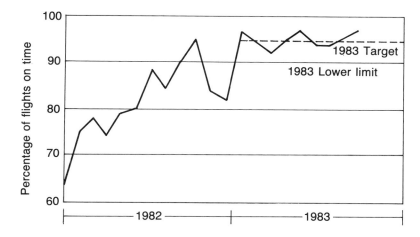

Figure 12.18 Control chart showing trends in Midway Airlines' departure delays.
Source: Wyckoff, *op. cit.*, p. 87. With permission.

	International members (%)*		UK members (%)*	
	Top 10		*Top 5*	
1.	Swissair	37.9	British Airways	38.4
2.	Lufthansa	25.0	Swissair	28.3
3.	Singapore Airlines	25.0	British Caledonian Airways	26.4
4.	British Airways	18.9	Singapore Airlines	20.2
5.	KLM — Royal Dutch		Cathay Pacific Airways	17.3
	Airlines	17.2		
6.	Cathay Pacific Airways	16.1		
7.	SAS — Scandinavian			
	Airlines	15.4		
8.	Air France	10.6		
9.	Thai Airways			
	International	10.6		
10.	British Caledonian			
	Airways	10.5		

* Members were allowed to nominate up to four airlines

Figure 12.19 The airlines judged to provide the best in-flight service.
Source: C. Evans, 'Airline performance as rated by frequent passengers', in *Are They Being Served?*, ed. B. Moores (Oxford: Philip Allan, 1986), p. 71. With permission.

Conclusion

The growth in buyer emphasis on quality since the late 1970s is one of the major market-place changes in industrial memory. It has become a core requirement for success not only for manufacturing and service companies but also for trading nations. Without doubt, it is a factor that will continue to increase in the future.

Quality is becoming an integral part of the successful management of an organization — an appropriate way of meeting the differing marketing needs. Although certain departments have specific responsibilities, quality is the concern of everyone in the business. Customers choose which product/service to buy by making judgements about the essential criteria of the market-place: quality is one of these. Many organizations have in the past reviewed quality in a piecemeal way. They have made decisions in some areas but have failed to realize how much they may impinge upon the establishment and maintenance of quality throughout the organization. In the provision of both products and services, the UK will increasingly be competing with other industrial nations. Moreover, customers and users are nowadays more aware of the quality of goods and services. As a result, the quality of what is provided will be an essential selling feature. To compete, therefore, the corporate policy issues must first be resolved. In recent years, as with many areas of business, there has been an over-concern with the application of techniques to resolve problems. Promises of how quality will improve with the application of these techniques have been made now for some years. In the UK the promise has never been realized because techniques, in themselves, are not adequate.

Until the issues of responsibility and the approach to the quality control are resolved as a statement of corporate philosophy then the problems which beset many businesses will remain. For, it is these policy issues that are the key to bringing about major changes in the achievement of sustained quality improvement.

Notes and References

1. R.M. Belbin, in the British Institute of Management Occasional Paper OPN8 'Quality calamities and their management implications' (1970), outlines the minimum cost associated with 121 quality calamities reported in nine BIM seminars in the period 1968–70. These totalled in excess of £3.5m.
2. *Glossary of International Terms* BS 4778 (British Standards Institution, 1987), part 1, 3.1.
3. W.E. Denning, *Quality, Productivity and Competitive Position*, (Cambridge, Mass: MIT Press, 1982); J.M. Juran, *Quality Control Handbook* (Maidenhead: McGraw-Hill, 1974); P.B. Crosby, *Quality is Free* (New York: McGraw-Hill, 1979); and G. Taguchi, *Designing Quality into Products and Processes* (Asian Productivity Organization, 1986).
4. A view also endorsed by the West German company, Bosch, in A. Fisher, 'Bosch: reducing human error to a minimum', *Financial Times* (19 September 1988), p. 18.
5. W.E. Denning, *op. cit.*, p. ii.
6. For example, 'Why does Britain want quality circles', *The Production Engineer* (February 1980), 45–6; H.R. Ferguson, 'Quality circles — an idea whose time is now', (Manager Quality Circles, Westinghouse Defense and Electronics Systems Center, Baltimore); J.D.

Blair and J.V. Hurwitz, 'Quality circles for American firms? some unanswered questions and their implications for managers', in J.M. Lee and G. Schwendiman (eds), *Management by Japanese Systems* (New York: Praeger, 1983); and D.L. Dewar, *The Quality Circle Guide to Participation Management* (Englewood Cliffs, NJ: Prentice Hall, Inc., 1982).

7. Report by JETRO, *Productivity and Quality Control: The Japanese experience*. Now in Japan Series, no. 30/1981.
8. Examples of the ideas implemented, together with further details of this initiative, are given in the American Productivity and Quality Center, *Case Study 42: The Paul Revere Life Insurance Companies* (February 1984).
9. A useful resumé of the use of quality circles is provided by J.D. Blair and K.D. Ramsing, 'Quality circles and production/operations management: concerns and caveats', *Journal of Operations Management*, no. 1 (1983), 1–10.
10. R.E. Cole, 'Will QC circles work in the US?' *Quality Progress* (July 1980), 30–3.
11. A.V. Feigenbaum, 'Total quality developments in the 1990s: an international perspective', in R.L. Chase (ed.), *Total Quality Management* (Bedford: IFS/Springer-Verlag, 1988), p. 3.
12. Based on L.P. Sullivan, 'The seven stages in company-wide quality control', in R.L. Chase (ed.), *op. cit.*, pp. 11–19.
13. K. Ishikawa, 'What is company-wide quality control?', paper presented to Ford executives (May 1983).
14. G. Taguchi, *op. cit.*
15. L.P. Sullivan, *op. cit.*, p. 17.
16. *Ibid*, p. 18.
17. BIM Occasional Paper OPN8, *op. cit.*, p. 3.
18. *Financial Times* (19 September 1988), p. 3.
19. BS 4778. Also note the twelve types of specification recognized and listed in BS 4778 (1979), 6.1.
20. BIM Occasional Paper OPN8, *op. cit.*, p. 4.
21. For example, see BS 6001 (1984), part 2.
22. BS 4778 (1979) 23.1.1.
23. Books which outline the application of statistical methods to quality control include: E.L. Grant and R.S. Leavenworth, *Statistical Quality Control* (New York: McGraw-Hill, 1974); G.B. Wetherill, *Sampling Inspection and Quality Control* (London: Chapman and Hall, 1977); A.V. Feigenbaum, *Total Quality Control* (New York: McGraw-Hill, 1983); M.N. Sinha and W.O. Willborn, *The Management of Quality Assurance* (New York: Wiley, 1985); and W.S. Messina, *Statistical Quality Control for Manufacturing Managers* (New York: Wiley, 1987).
24. BS 4778 (1979), 21.16.
25. As throughout this chapter, the definitions in this paragraph relate to those given in BS 4778 (1979).
26. For example, the revised Defence Standards series 05-20 to 05-29, issued in 1973/4 to cover: (1) an assessment of the capability of a supplier, leading to registration (or refusal) of that supplier. Unless registered, a supplier would not be able to tender for defence contracts, and (2) contract surveillance.
27. BS 6001 (1972, 1984 and 1986) and BS 6002 (1979) provides a range of suitable sampling plans, with explanations on how to use them. They include OC curves, AQLs, single, double and multiple sampling plans and cover both attributes and variables.
28. Information collected by inspection can also be used to control the process. Unless, however, the gathering and feedback of this information is structured to achieve this then such control is unlikely to happen.
29. These trends are based on E.M. Goldratt and R.E. Fox, 'The drive for quality', in *The Race* (New York: North River Press, 1986), section 2, pp. 4–5.
30. W. Shewhart, *Economic Control of Quality of Manufactured Product* (New York: Van Nostrand, 1931).

31. These ideas are based on the work of W.E. Sasser, R.P. Olsen and D.D. Wyckoff, *Management of Service Operations* (Boston: Allyn & Bacon, 1978) and J.A. Fitzsimmons and R.S. Sullivan, *Service Operations Management* (New York: McGraw-Hill, 1982).

Further reading

Adams, Jr, E.E. and Barker, E.M. 'Achieving quality products and services', *Operations Management Review* (Winter 1987), 1–8.

Caplan, R., *A Practical Approach to Quality Control* (London: Business Books, 1971).

Czepiel, J.A., Solomon, M.R. and Surprenant, C.F. (eds), *The Service Encounter: Managing employee/customer interaction in service business* (Lexington Books, 1985).

Feigenbaum, A.V., *Total Quality Control: Engineering and management*, 3rd edn (Maidenhead: McGraw-Hill, 1983).

Juran, J.M., 'Japanese and western quality — A contrast', *Quality Progress* (December 1978), 10–18.

Juran, J.M. and Gryna, F.M. *Quality Planning and Analysis*, New York: McGraw-Hill, 1980.

Murdoch, J., *Control Charts* (Basingstoke: Macmillan, 1979).

Peters, T., *Thriving on Chaos*, (Basingstoke: Macmillan, 1988).

Price, F., *Right First Time: Using quality control for profit*, Aldershot: Wildwood House, 1986).

Sinha, M.N. and Wilborn, W.O., *The Management of Quality Assurance* (New York: Wiley, 1985).

Woodward, R.H. and Goldsmith, P.L., *Cumulative Sum Techniques* (Oliver Boyd, 1964).

Chapter 13

Maintenance

As part of the need to reduce costs, investment in the process will continue to be made and is likely to increase in the future. Rapid advances in technology have led to more opportunity to invest in both the hardware and software parts of the operations process. The technology dependence, however, may change in form (e.g. microchips), thereby altering the concept of maintenance provision. For example, stand-by processes will tend not to be financially viable through reasons of investment and obsolescence, but not so a stand-by control or other type of process support unit. This pattern of investment, however, has led to a growing need in most organizations to establish an appropriate maintenance strategy. This chapter outlines important maintenance decisions and illustrates the types of control and task which maintenance managers, as part of the overall operations function, should address.

Maintenance and terotechnology

The increasing importance of reviewing physical assets in terms of investment and cost has led to the concept of *terotechnology*, defined in BS 3811 (1984) as:

> A combination of management, financial, engineering, building and other practices applied to physical assets in pursuit of economic life cycle costs.[1] Its practice is concerned with the specification and design for reliability and maintainability of plant, machinery, equipment, buildings and structures, with their installation, commissioning, operation, maintenance, modification and replacement and with feedback of information on design, performance and costs.[2]

Although there is little that is new about each of these activities and ideas, there is a need to focus attention on the gains to be made by co-ordinating their interrelated functions. How these important aspects relate to one another needs to be understood. The introduction of terotechnology (from the Greek *terin* meaning to watch over) was designed to concentrate awareness on this important concept and to help to promote and apply it appropriately throughout an organization.

Whereas maintenance is the largest aspect of terotechnology, and that on which this chapter concentrates, many activities at earlier parts of the business cycle, such as design and purchasing, can significantly affect maintenance costs and effectiveness. For example, the co-ordination necessary to determine that a modified design may lead to reductions in maintenance costs is typical of the gains to be made by reviewing activities on a wider perspective and in a co-ordinated way. When reading this and other chapters it is important, therefore, to consider the parts and wholes as discussed in Chapter 1.

The nature of the maintenance problem

All physical facilities are susceptible to failure through breakdown, deterioration in performance through age and use, and to obsolescence due to improvements in technology. Each of these features affects output costs in the following ways:

1. Failure results in unplanned losses in the output of products or services.
2. Deterioration usually results in an increase in both the instances of failure and unacceptable levels of quality.
3. Obsolescence results in a situation where competitors can achieve a lower unit process cost.

However, reducing the likelihood of these features occurring involves considerable expense. If the only objective was to reduce the instances of failure, deterioration or obsolescence, then the investment and expense involved would eventually exceed the actual costs of allowing the status quo to exist. Achieving the balance between the levels of expenditure and investment, and the added costs of failure and obsolescence has to be determined. Each situation, however, is different. Some processes will require a more sophisticated maintenance function than others, whilst with an increase in investment in the process, the importance of achieving a high plant utilization will increase (see Table 4.2 in Chapter 4).

The range of maintenance activities

The maintenance function encompasses a wide range of responsibilities in different organizations.[3] Although the prime task usually concerns keeping the operations system in good working order, there are other important responsibilities which fall within its total function (see Table 13.1). The list given in the table is not exhaustive but is typical of the set of tasks frequently placed under the control of this function, if only as a matter of convenience.

Table 13.1 Typical maintenance activities

Area of responsibility		*Typical activities*
Buildings and structures		To provide extensions, modifications and repairs to all building and structures, including grounds
Support-function provision		To arrange the re-layout, modification, and non-equipment provision and repair in office and administrative functions
Utilities		To maintain and provide supplies of all utilities including power, light, gas, water, steam, heating, air conditioning, pollution, sewage, refuse disposal and general housekeeping
Plant and equipment	Repair	To maintain (including relayout) all items of plant and equipment both in the operations process and in the support functions
	Essential work	To design and manufacture, complete major modifications and to install equipment. To manufacture auxiliary equipment (e.g. tools and jigs) for new or existing equipment
Safety		To ensure that the necessary safety requirements are met, including the provision of mechanisms to reduce the likelihood of accidents

Maintenance policy issues

Although maintenance involves a range of responsibilities referred to in Table 13.1, the rest of this chapter will concentrate on those functions directly concerned with the operations process. At times other areas will be referred to, but it is not intended to address comprehensively the management issues involved in these.

In order to determine maintenance policies, there are four areas to be considered:

1. To determine which parts of the process are to be maintained.
2. To decide between the different types of maintenance which could be employed and agree when maintenance should take place.
3. To consider the various policies available to the organization, including repair or replacement, use of internal or external personnel and a centralized or decentralized maintenance function.
4. To assess the cost effectiveness of the maintenance policy which has been chosen.

Which parts of the process to maintain

A prerequisite of maintenance activities is a list of all items which need maintaining. The list should include not only equipment in the process but also other equipment, transport, building and structures in line with the range of activities set out in

Table 13.1. This list will comprise the physical asset register and provide details of each item including:

1. A unique reference number for identification and often coded to show location and function.
2. Description — make, model, age and modifications.
3. Location.
4. Details of major components or parts to include any items common to other equipment, and inventory holdings.
5. Comments upon the critical nature of the equipment to the process.

Different types of maintenance and timing

A company may, of course, undertake its maintenance function as an unplanned response.[4] However, the concern here is planned maintenance. An important maintenance policy decision is to select the forms of maintenance which will be provided and the extent of that provision:

> [Maintenance concerns] the combination of all technical and associated administration actions intended to retain an item in, or restore it to, a state in which it can perform its required function.[5]

The most effective method will vary depending upon the item concerned and its importance in the operations process. There are several elements which may comprise the planned response to the range of process-related maintenance activities and a mix of these results in the formulation of a maintenance strategy.[6] This mix varies from one facility to another and depends upon the goals of maintenance, the nature of the facility, and the type and age of the processes involved. However, what makes them a co-ordinated strategy is the fact that they are planned, an approach which may include reactive as well as different forms of preventive maintenance.

Reactive maintenance

Reactive maintenance repairs equipment as needed and undertakes emergency maintenance as required. The systematic identification of parts of the process which need, or may need, to be replaced or maintained is not a feature of this approach. However, the reactive approach is planned in nature. When breakdowns occur maintenance teams are allocated to the problem and their role is to respond quickly and make the necessary decisions to minimize the effect of the breakdown on the operations system. In many instances, temporary repairs may be made so that the process can function again as soon as possible. Permanent repairs would be made at a later and more convenient time.

Preventive maintenance

Preventive maintenance is 'carried out at predetermined intervals or corresponding to prescribed criteria (e.g. equipment hours worked) and intended to reduce the probability of failure or the performance degradation of an item.'[7] Its objective is to reduce the probability of breakdown by replacing worn components at set intervals. The replacement interval is usually based on the mean failure time of certain components. However, in critical areas such as aircraft maintenance, replacement and maintenance, schedules are typically specified by a legal or government body.

A common misconception about preventive maintenance is that it is a high cost alternative. In fact, this approach has two inherent characteristics which may reduce the total cost of maintenance by minimizing the overall cost of breakdowns:

1. Breakdowns (and the potential additional costs directly related to in-process failure) due to worn-out parts occur less frequently.
2. Maintenance tends to be scheduled so that planned operations time is not interrupted.

Condition-based maintenance

'Condition-based maintenance concerns preventive maintenance initiated as a result of knowledge of the condition of an item from routine or continuous monitoring'.[8] It often involves a procedure of systematic inspection (especially of key parts or those which are expensive in themselves or to replace) and can be undertaken to identify instances where maintenance could be performed either earlier or later than the regular preventive maintenance schedule dictates.

In addition, this planned procedure can also enable on-going checks to be made on the effectiveness of a preventive maintenance schedule and thus enable it to be fine-tuned where necessary but without incurring the disadvantages which would accrue from the original schedules.

Stand-by equipment

The provision of stand-by equipment for all or part of a process is another potential element of an appropriate maintenance strategy. It will typically be used where the cost or risk of breakdown is extremely high. Thus it offers an alternative to paying for a high level of maintenance in order to reduce the impact of breakdowns. In addition, back-up equipment can be an effective policy to use where time constraints demand that planned maintenance is undertaken in normal working hours. However, as mentioned at the beginning of the chapter, it is less likely to be a viable alternative for core processes on account of the high investment involved. Its use is more likely to be as a cover for support services such as compressed air, water, other utilities and control units.

Stand-by equipment does not take the place of regular maintenance but serves as an insurance policy for equipment that can seriously disrupt the process if it breaks down. However, if stand-by equipment is provided it is important to ensure that it is fully operational. Where possible it is advisable to run the equipment on a regular basis.

Lastly, it is important to recognize that equipment standardization can significantly lower the investment in this form of planned maintenance provision.

If several pieces of equipment are identical, then one stand-by unit can serve this function for all on-line processes and result in a substantially lower-cost provision.

Equipment upgrades

Upgrading equipment can form part of a planned strategy to provide higher levels of maintenance. In these circumstances, existing equipment is redesigned or modified in order to achieve one or both of the following:

1. To increase process reliability.
2. To facilitate repair.

In many instances, these upgrades form part of a larger decision which embraces enhancing a process in terms of technical capability or throughput speeds.

Planned maintenance

The previous section reviewed the various components of a strategy based on the concept of planned maintenance. This does not, therefore, advocate one approach but does stress the need to determine the maintenance provision so that it is organized and carried out in a conscious manner. Thus, reactive and preventive maintenance are two ends of the maintenance continuum but can both constitute appropriate planned responses to this important task. This section details still further some of the considerations embodied in planned maintenance and thus provides necessary insights into the POM issues involved.

Important management decisions concern the extent to which planned maintenance is to be applied and the depth of the planning decisions which are to be made. To do this, management needs to: (1) make a reasoned decision rather than allow the situation to exist through default, and (2) monitor the relationship between benefits and costs as a basis for confirming or changing the previous balance between planned and unplanned maintenance activities.

Planned maintenanced programmes yield a range of benefits, though not all will be realized in every situation. They include:

1. Minimized maintenance costs — plans can be made and material and spare parts ordered in line with the plan.
2. Maintenance can be completed when it is convenient to the operations process.
3. Reduced loss of capacity as the maintenance tasks can be planned with the minimum of time lost.
4. Minimum material and spare parts inventory can be achieved, with levels of inventory in line with planned requirements rather than in anticipation of possible breakdowns.
5. Increased opportunity to use contract maintenance more effectively. Work of a similar or specialized nature can be planned thus reducing the higher costs associated with one-off jobs.

6. A reduction in overtime following the reduction in emergency repairs associated with planning.
7. The disruption which accompanies emergency work will be less extensive.
8. The need for stand-by equipment can be reviewed and the trade-off between the reduced incidence of emergency breakdown and the costs associated with stand-by equipment can be assessed.

The disadvantages of planned maintenance include:

1. Planned maintenance may not be applied on a discerning basis. It is not necessarily the best way to control every maintenance problem. It is essential, therefore, to review regularly the cost/benefit relationship discussed earlier.
2. As a result of 1 above the estimated gains may not be realized and consequently, may not always exceed the increased costs.
3. The most serious breakdowns are often not detected through a planned maintenance scheme (e.g. metal fatigue or component failure).

The objective of any planned maintenance programme is to reduce the total cost of providing maintenance. To determine whether this is so it is necessary to compare the costs of planned maintenance with those which would have been incurred if other programme mixes had been implemented. A useful approach is to consider the total costs of running a maintenance function which normally comprises the sum of the individual costs for:

1. Preventive maintenance (see Figure 13.1).
2. Corrective and emergency maintenance (see Figure 13.1).
3. Indirect maintenance (costs incurred through loss of output and excess production costs).

The optimum level will be when the total maintenance cost is the lowest (see Figure 13.2). Figure 13.2 illustrates some important points:

1. There is a non-linear relationship between preventive maintenance costs and the other sets of costs.
2. The total maintenance cost is significantly higher than the preventive and corrective/emergency costs and, therefore, becomes the important cost consideration when making a decision on maintenance provision.
3. The total cost curve is relatively flat around its minimum and hence some deviation around this point (the optimum level of preventive maintenance provision) has no significant consequence in terms of total costs. This is fortunate because the determination of costs, particularly indirect maintenance costs, is far from precise. However, it is most realistic to use the total maintenance cost approach to establish a level of preventive maintenance provision.
4. The purpose of this graph, therefore, is to show that there is a preferred level of preventive maintenance provision within any organization.

A series of case studies published by the Department of Industry examines the

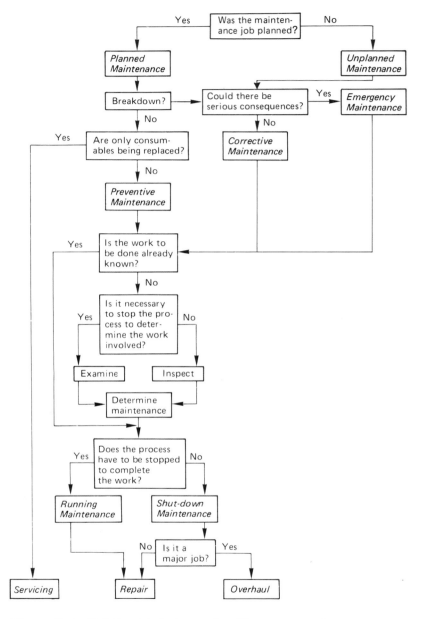

Figure 13.1 Relationship between the different types of maintenance.

Source: Department of Industry, Committee for Terotechnology, *Planned Maintenance*, no. 1 in the Maintenance Aspects of Terotechnology series (London: HMSO, 1978), p. 5. With permission.

* The terms used in Fig. 13.1 are based on *BS 3811*:

Planned Maintenance — maintenance organized and carried out with forethought, control and the use of records to a predetermined plan. *Note*: preventive maintenance is normally planned; corrective maintenance may or may not be planned.

Emergency Maintenance — maintenance carried out to restore (including adjustment and repair) an item which has ceased to meet an acceptable condition.

Preventive Maintenance — maintenance carried out at predetermined intervals or to other prescribed criteria, and intended to reduce the likelihood of an item not meeting an acceptable condition.

Running Maintenance — maintenance which can be carried out whilst the item is in service.

Shut-down Maintenance — maintenance which can only be carried out when the item is out of service.

Servicing — the replenishment of consumables needed to keep an item in operating condition.

Repair — to restore an item to an acceptable condition by the renewal, replacement or mending of decayed or damaged parts.

Overhaul — a comprehensive examination and restoration of an item, or a major part thereof, to an acceptable condition.

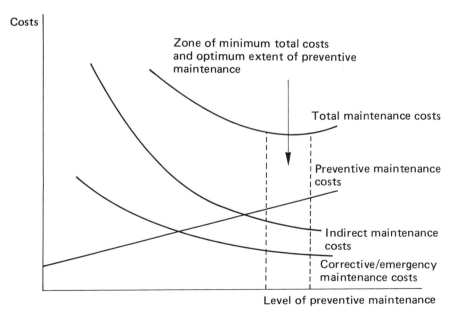

Figure 13.2 Relationship between total cost and the level of preventive maintenance.

successful implementation of planned maintenance and are summarized in Table 13.2.[9]

Establishing planned maintenance
Step 1 has already been discussed and involves the compilation of a plant register (see pp. 417–18).

Step 2 is to produce a schedule for each item on the register. The schedule details the maintenance work required and its frequency. What work is to be done will be determined from a range of options, such as for example:

1. Replace the item only when it has failed.
2. When the equipment reaches a point where it no longer meets acceptable levels of performance (output and/or quality), then replace.
3. Replace after so many operating hours or a period of time whichever is the sooner.
4. Inspect at regular predetermined intervals.
5. Build up a history of failure over time and then in the future replace the item when the failure trends are seen.

Step 3 is to establish a programme of planned maintenance work with each task being allocated to a particular period of time. It is easy to let planned maintenance work slide because of pressures from the operations function, emergencies and other work of a high priority. Inevitably, if this slide is not checked then the benefits of planning are lost and total costs will rise. It is necessary to agree a sensible schedule and then to adhere to it. However a regular review of

Table 13.2 Summary of the principal benefits gained in four companies where planned maintenance was introduced

Type of organization	Summary of principal benefits gained on the introduction of planned maintenance
Foundry	Downtime reduced by about 75 per cent during a period when output increased by 77 per cent. After four years of operating planned maintenance, the annual cost of maintenance had not increased despite a substantial increase in production
Spade manufacturer	Emergency repairs now account for less than 6 per cent of the maintenance work. In two production areas, lost production time was less than 4 per cent and 1 per cent respectively
Food factory	Downtime reduced by about 40 per cent. Engineering department hours down by 9 per cent and net engineering material costs down 17 per cent despite increases in output
Containerbase	Direct maintenance costs fell by 16 per cent per ton handled. With no increase in equipment, the base handled double the tonnage

the programme content is necessary. This often leads, in the light of experience, to some decrease or exclusion of parts of the programme whilst introducing or increasing the frequency of others.

In establishing the maintenance programme, short- and longer-term plans will be determined with each task allocated throughout the period. A planned approach will not only ensure that all items are included but also provide for a fairly even workload across the maintenance function on both a short- and longer-term basis. This evenness will aid capacity, overtime, purchasing and costs.

Other policy issues

In addition to the decisions concerning the nature and extent of the planned maintenance activities, there are other issues of policy which concern the maintenance provision.

Internal or external personnel

The decision whether to provide the necessary maintenance personnel or facilities internally or externally is based primarily on cost and technical know-how. Often a combination of the two will be the most suitable arrangement. When the needs are irregular or require very high technical know-how, maintenance will usually be contracted to outside firms. For instance, organizations frequently contract out their maintenance requirements on elevators and computers whilst for other specialist equipment, such as photocopying and telephones, maintenance forms part of the rental agreement. These decisions are straightforward.

The more difficult decisions on provision are associated with the mainstream maintenance tasks — the operations processes. Where the technical know-how is not available within an organization (for example, when new equipment is purchased) then external maintenance services are often used initially. However, an organization will normally wish to build up its internal skills because of the high downtime costs associated with these processes. It will do this through training courses supported by sound documentation, the development, where possible, of self-diagnostic facilities into the equipment and the use of diagnostic tools and instruments to enhance visual checks (e.g. vibration monitoring equipment). In situations where the internal maintenance expertise is available, problems of demand peaks for these capabilities will be eased through planned maintenance and other forms of forward planning, and will be supplemented by overtime working or buying-in from outside.

Centralized or decentralized maintenance

Maintenance may be organized on a centralized or decentralized basis. With centralization, all the workers are in one location with work being allocated as the need arises. In a decentralized set-up, the workers are located in different geographical areas and with responsibilities more-or-less confined to those areas.

Advantages of centralization include:

1. Improved utilization of the workforce (especially specialists) and equipment.
2. More able to balance maintenance capacity to fluctuating workload demands.
3. Allows more centralized control (e.g. one manager, centralized systems, and more control over capital work).
4. Better training and the employment of specialists can be justified.

Advantages of decentralization include:

1. Faster service, with travelling time reduced.
2. Improved continuity from shift to shift.
3. Greater knowledge of the particular processes.
4. Improved supervision with reduced geographical area of working.

Group or individual replacement policies

Some components are increasingly prone to failure as they age. Sudden failure creates more difficulty than wear and tear. Therefore, where a large number of identical low-cost items fall into this category, then a group replacement policy becomes feasible. At the other end of the scale, individual replacement applies to a single item that is replaced when it fails. Several types of policy are possible, for example:

1. Replace only failed units as they fail.
2. Replace only failed units periodically.
3. Replace all units (both good and failed) periodically.
4. Replace failed units as they fail and all units periodically.

Which method is chosen will be determined by the critical nature of the item. For instance, policy (3) may be feasible for certain light bulbs in a building but not for electronic components or relays in a critical part of the process. To help in making this decision, three zones in the operating life of a item need to be identified and then used to determine which policy should be followed:

1. 'Infant mortality', the initial failure period.
2. Normal operating life — if a component survives the initial failure period, then the chances of failure tend to be low for a time.
3. Lastly, the wear-out zone, where the probability of failure rises sharply, peaks and then falls. The shape of the curve must be discovered by testing.[10]

Replacement parts inventory

Replacement parts carry the same costs as those outlined in Chapter 10. On the other hand, the costs of failing to have a part available when needed can be considerable. As a first step, it is important to classify the parts to be stored.

Spare materials and parts

1. *Critical parts.* Spare parts are held for a number of reasons, including:
   (a) essential to the process, in that shutdowns would occur if they were not available;
   (b) the purchasing lead times are long;
   (c) there may be safety or pollution hazards if the part is not replaced quickly.
2. *Normal parts.* Normal parts refers to items used frequently in maintaining the process.

Equipment and tools

Equipment and tools refer to portable plant used by maintenance personnel in carrying out their tasks.

An analysis of spare materials and parts and equipment and tools will normally reveal a sizable investment. However, a check needs to be made on the purpose and importance of these items and then an ABC analysis established to distinguish the level of control to be used for the various categories of parts. These steps will ensure that a distinction is made between those items needing to be held in stock, and those that do not. Of those that do, the large cost items are to be controlled as described in Chapter 10.

Computerization of records

As part of the drive to reduce costs and improve the accuracy of records, computers are increasingly being used in this function as elsewhere in organizations. Particular applications include asset registers and recording systems, such as for costs and spares. Companies changing to computerized procedures, however, need to be aware of the problems associated with these conversions:

1. The inaccuracy of existing records.
2. As maintenance needs to be available throughout the working day, there will often be times when the administrative support is unavailable. All staff, therefore, will need to be conversant with the proposed system.

Energy management

A significant part of the broad maintenance task concerns the aspect of energy management. This comprises 'the management of the storage, conversion, distribution and utilization of energy directed to the economic provision of required services and the elimination of avoidable costs'.[11] In 1989, it was estimated that British businesses would spend £10bn on energy to run their heating, lighting and process requirements.[12] However, their concern for improving the management of these costs represents a much lower response to this task than witnessed in the USA, which has been increasingly active in energy management since the 1970s.

Energy management comprises three parts:

1. *Assessment and targets.* The first task is to undertake an energy audit to determine the actual amount of energy used in each part of an installation. Once completed, targets can be set which establish the desired levels of energy demanded within the different parts of a building or process.

2. *Energy use.* The second aspect concerns the level of efficiency at which energy is used and includes aspects of reclaiming and recovering heat. These lead to heat gains which concern 'the flow of heat into an enclosure from all sources other than by space heating means.'[13]

3. *Energy management systems.* There are four main components of an energy management system:
   (a) sensors to monitor inside and outside temperatures and lighting and humidity levels;
   (b) direct digital controllers which activate or shut down the system depending upon the information received from the sensors;
   (c) a network to link the digital controllers;
   (d) supervisory terminals to inspect the information, including the automatic display of faults.

The installation of energy management systems in the USA was worth £1.7bn in 1989, whereas in Europe estimated sales will only be 50 per cent of this total by 1992. In part, this is because of the different perspectives held by businesses. In Europe these developments are judged primarily on the basis of cost savings, whereas in the USA they are also recognized to be an integral part of employee comfort.[14]

The effectiveness of the chosen maintenance policy

The management task in maintenance is similar to that for other functions — the manager must plan and control the work against realistic standards of performance both in terms of man-hours and cost. This section is concerned with the control aspects of the maintenance function.

Capacity requirements and utilization

In Chapter 11 three ways of measuring the capacity requirements and utilization of a function were outlined. Two of these, variable factor programming (VFP) and group capacity assessment (GCA), are well suited to the task of determining maintenance capacity requirements compared with the function's current workload. It also enables management to monitor workload fluctuations and to adjust capacity accordingly.

In addition to the VFP and GCA methods of establishing times for maintenance tasks, the universal maintenance standards (UMS) scheme is available. This is similar to analytical and comparative estimating as described in Chapter 11. In UMS, a large number (200–300) of benchmark jobs are chosen as being representative of the maintenance work involved. Each of these is directly observed and the method checked. An analysis is then completed for each element using methods time motion (MTM) values, and times for completing each element are determined.[15] Time is expressed as a range of values to reflect the varying conditions observed.

From this analysis, a table of about twenty to thirty elements is constructed. All other work is then analysed, using the agreed method for completing the task. The elements of each job are then matched to this table of elements with the aid of the benchmark jobs, and time standards established.[16]

Maintenance performance indices

The costs of maintenance are, for many organizations, significant. It is essential, therefore, to use measures which reflect performance. Some such indices measuring trends in key maintenance tasks and features of the service are now outlined.

Some corporate ratios

The ratios described in this section are part of a pyramid of ratios derived by the Centre for Interfirm Comparison under contract to the Department of Industry's Committee for Terotechnology.[17] Those given here are useful both as a comparison between similar organizations and as a way of monitoring trends within a particular business. The examples given in the Department of Industry's booklet relate to an engineering and general group and to a commercial vehicle group.[17] Similar ratios could be used for other manufacturing and non-manufacturing categories of business using the same logic and approach.

(1) $\dfrac{\text{Maintenance costs}}{\text{Maintenance assets}}$

This relates maintenance costs in terms of the value of the assets that are being maintained and helps to put maintenance costs in perspective. Maintainable assets for the general and engineering group includes plant, machinery and buildings but exclude vehicles, office furniture and equipment. For the commercial vehicles group, they include all assets for which maintenance was responsible.

(2a) $\dfrac{\text{Maintenance costs}}{\text{Value added}}$

(2b) $\dfrac{\text{Maintenance costs}}{\text{Own haulage revenue}}$

Often maintenance costs are related to total production costs or to total production value based on the selling price. However, by relating these costs to value added (ratio (2a)), distortions which arise from the inclusion of material costs and which can change with product/service mix or market price are avoided.

In the case of the commercial vehicles group (ratio (2b)), maintenance costs are related to 'own haulage revenue' which avoids the effect of changing revenues from non-haulage activities (e.g. warehouse rentals).

The next group of ratios break down the total maintenance cost into its major segments in order to identify which aspects of costs are responsible for any movements in ratio (2a) or (2b).

(3a) $\dfrac{\text{Maintenance materials}}{\text{Value added}}$

or

(3b) $\dfrac{\text{Maintenance materials}}{\text{Own haulage revenue}}$

(3c) $\dfrac{\text{Maintenance employee costs}}{\text{Value added}}$

or

(3d) $\dfrac{\text{Maintenance employee costs}}{\text{Own haulage revenue}}$

(3e) $\dfrac{\text{Maintenance overheads}}{\text{Value added}}$

or

(3f) $\dfrac{\text{Maintenance overheads}}{\text{Own haulage revenue}}$

(3g) $\dfrac{\text{Maintenance work subcontracted}}{\text{Value added}}$

or

(3h) $\dfrac{\text{Maintenance work subcontracted}}{\text{Own haulage revenue}}$

Maintenance ratios related to production/operations
Ratios (4a) and (4b) relate the hours of maintenance to the hours that the process or vehicles are being used.

(4a) $\dfrac{\text{Total direct man-hours of maintenance labour } (+\text{subcontract equivalent})}{\text{Total production/operations direct hours}}$

or

$$(4b) \quad \frac{\text{Total direct man-hours of maintenance labour } (+\text{subcontract equivalent})}{\text{Total hours vehicles on road}}$$

A deterioration in this will be due to a decrease in one or the other. Although initially this may not affect ratio 5, the longer-term picture needs to be checked before a judgement can be made.

$$(5a) \quad \frac{\text{Production operating time}}{\text{Production operating time} + \text{downtime}}$$

or

$$(5b) \quad \frac{\text{Vehicle on road time}}{\text{Vehicle on road time} + \text{off road time due to all types of maintenance}}$$

This ratio is most useful to calculate availability of all equipment (5a) and all vehicles (5b), or for key processes (5a) or for individual vehicles (5b).

$$(6) \quad \frac{\text{Number of operating hours}}{\text{Number of breakdowns}}$$

Operating hours refer to production or vehicle hours and this ratio is useful to assess any chages in the failure rate of plant or vehicles.

Departmental maintenance ratios

$$(7) \quad \frac{\text{Total cost of maintenance (including subcontract work)}}{\text{Total hours worked (including subcontract equivalent)}}$$

This gives a total maintenance cost per hour worked which, allowing for inflation, provides an overall measure.

The next three ratios show changes in the relative use of different forms of maintenance both as a global measure and to ensure that policy decisions are being adhered to. In each case, the equivalent hours on subcontract work are to be included.

$$(8a) \quad \frac{\text{Maintenance hours on preventive maintenance}}{\text{Total maintenance hours}}$$

$$(8b) \quad \frac{\text{Maintenance hours on emergency maintenance}}{\text{Total maintenance hours}}$$

$$(8c) \quad \frac{\text{Maintenance hours on corrective maintenance}}{\text{Total maintenance hours}}$$

The next ratio is to assess the level of inventory held and the materials being used and is the equivalent of a stock turnover ratio. Inventory holdings need to be well controlled and any excess investment should be reduced.

$$(9) \quad \frac{\text{Cost of maintenance materials used}}{\text{Maintenance inventory value}}$$

The last set of ratios concern the control of work and will be usefully used with the capacity requirement and utilization section earlier in this chapter.

$$(10a) \frac{\text{Total hours of maintenance work produced}}{\text{Total maintenance clocked hours}}$$

This is equivalent to the measure of efficiency as described in Chapter 11 and is usually expressed as a percentage.

$$(10b) \frac{\text{Number of maintenance work orders on hand}}{\text{Number of maintenance work orders completed in a given period}}$$
$$\text{(e.g. a week)}$$

This would give a guide to the number of weeks of work outstanding for a maintenance function at a moment in time, and also show changes in workload over a longer period. A more precise loading for the whole department or by trade could be achieved where times for jobs were determined. The total outstanding time could then be compared with average working hours to give a more accurate assessment of future workload.

An annual report
It is important that maintenance management provides information on the appropriate assessment of their contribution and shows how suggested investments, technology changes and other factors would affect their function.

An annual report provides the opportunity to outline some of these factors and should include the aspects given here. The fact that an annual report is compiled indicates that forethought and plans have been made by maintenance management to provide a co-ordinated and comprehensive review of this important support function.

Cost evaluation. By using the indices described on p. 429, an evaluation of maintenance performance can be made in cost terms. In this way, and by using the common denominator of money, performance can be reviewed from one period to another.

Workload. Workload trends can be shown and reviews made by again using the indices. Information needs to be provided on any mix-of-work changes especially those linked to known or proposed capital investments or changes in technology. Statements on the flexibility of the workforce and the training completed and planned in the light of these needs should be included here.

The use of internal and contract maintenance. This section would review the use of internal and contract labour showing costs and flexibility related to known or anticipated future workloads.

Capital investments. The involvement of maintenance should begin at the point where capital investments are being considered. It is at this early stage that the demands on maintenance and the extent of the maintenance costs involved need to be assessed as part of the investment appraisal. Investment decisions need to be made with a complete understanding of their maintenance implications. To ensure that this happens, it is necessary for maintenance to be proactive in the organization and particularly in capital appraisal development.

Changes in technology. Linked to the capital investment part of the annual report should be a section on changes in technology. This would reveal the changes in skills, show the need to build up certain skill areas and also discuss the flexibility and contract versus internal resource questions raised earlier.

Capital proposals by maintenance. In addition to providing the essential support service, it is equally necessary that the maintenance department should be concerned with capital projects both to improve the ability of maintenance to perform the work required and to reduce the demands on maintenance by changes in plant, equipment, materials handling systems and other areas. These proposals would come under the normal investment appraisal requirements.

Conclusion

For organizations to achieve the necessary productivity increases requires the efforts of all functions. Maintenance is no exception. As a result, the role and activities within this function have changed to meet those new requirements:

1. To help reduce the growing cost of maintenance, organizations are increasingly considering the maintenance dimension much earlier in investment decisions in recognition of the importance of post-installation costs as a factor within this appraisal procedure.

2. As part of the importance to support delivery needs, whilst keeping inventories low, process support becomes a vital role. Quick and effective response to process problems and breakdowns is an increasingly important task. On site, well-trained staff are needed to support core processes, whilst those companies using control systems often supplement their own in-house capability by establishing computer links to outside specialists to help diagnose problems through the use of computer-based control systems.

3. The need to reduce costs has also led companies to reduce total manning levels within maintenance and to compensate for the loss of skill areas by increased training of staff and changes in working practices through teamwork approaches based on multi-skilling principles and the increased uses of operators to take on appropriate routine maintenance tasks (refer also to Chapter 14).

   As part of this development, companies are also increasingly involving the maintenance function in the later stages of installation and throughout the commissioning phase of process plant as the first stage of training and also to provide the opportunity to identify possible modifications to help simplify process support in the future.

All organizations will continue to invest in the process at an increasing rate in order to reduce costs. In addition, the changes and developments in technology will add a further dimension to the increasing maintenance requirement. It is important for organizations to recognize this. Maintenance managers have increasingly to plan and control the effective use of their resources and be able to bring top management's attention to these important perspectives before the technology and investment decisions are made. Furthermore, with increased investment, the need for supporting specialists will also increase. It is essential, therefore, that the management of the company's physical resources is at the appropriate level and that the controls to ensure that this is so are installed and developed.

Notes and references

1. Life cycle costs are defined as the total costs of an item throughout its life including initial, maintenance and support costs.
2. *Glossary of Maintenance Terms in Terotechnology*, BS 3811 (British Standards Institution, 1984), no. 101.
3. The maintenance function is usually either an engineering or a POM responsibility. This will depend on aspects such as the size of the organization and the nature of its products/services. Figure 1.4 illustrates this function as part of the operations task. In other organizations it may report to the research and development director or, more normally, to the engineering director.
4. BS 3811 (1984), no. 219.
5. BS 3811 (1984), no. 102.
6. Additional relevant terms needing to be distinguished are listed in the footnote to Figure 13.1.
7. BS 3811 (1984), no. 220.
8. BS 3811 (1984), no. 221.
9. Department of Industry, Committee for Terotechnology, *Terotechnology of Case History*, nos 1–5 (1975).
10. The concept of an operating life cycle is explained more fully in several books. For example R.J. Schonberger, *Operations Management* (New York: Business Publications, 1981).
11. BS 3811 (1984), no. 107.
12. D. Bradshaw, 'Europe warms to energy management', *Financial Times* (12 January 1989), p. 28.
13. BS 3811 (1984), no. 706.
14. *Financial Times* (12 January 1989), p. 28.
15. MTM is a widely used predetermined motion time standard. This form of measurement is covered extensively in Chapter 11. Suffice here to say that with MTM, predetermined times for operations are used which have been built up through research and analysis, and issued as tables.
16. Universal maintenance standards (UMS) are described in detail in L. Mann, *Maintenance Management* (Lexington: Lexington Books, 1976), pp. 76–95. Also refer to P.D. Guy, 'Measurement of maintenance', *Works Management* (February 1973), 5–9 for examples of UMS applications.
17. Department of Industry, Committee of Terotechnology, *Management by Maintenance Ratios*, no. 1 in the Maintenance Aspects of Terotechnology series (London: HMSO, 1978), pp. 5–6.

Further reading

Husband, T.M., *Maintenance Management and Terotechnology* (Farnborough: Saxon House, 1976).

Newbrough, E.T., *Effective Maintenance Management* (New York: McGraw-Hill, 1967).

Newman, R.G., 'MRP: where M = preventative maintenance', *Production and Inventory Management*, 26, no. 2 (1985), 21—8.

Reed, R. *Plant Location, Layout and Maintenance*, Irwin Series in Operations Management. (Homewood, Ill.: Irwin, 1967).

Tersine, R.J., 'Preventive maintenance: a path to higher productivity', *SAN Advanced Management Journal*, 48 (spring 1983), 38—44.

Tombari, H.A. 'Designing a maintenance management system', *Production and Inventory Management*, 23, no. 4 (1982), 139—47.

Chapter 14

The job of work

An important responsibility falling within the operations manager's role concerns the people employed in the POM function. It embraces those people producing the product or providing the service together with a large proportion of the indirect or supporting staff who provide the necessary controls, analyses and support services.

Managing some 70−80 per cent of those employed (see Chapter 1) is a large task. In a society where the social values of people are changing at a faster rate than the values in most work situations, it is difficult to motivate people to exceed or even meet the required performance levels so as to gain a competitive market edge. Moreover, this management task is made even more difficult by three factors:

1. The number of people involved and the complex and interrelated nature of the decisions (no matter how small) to be taken.
2. The inherent inertia in the POM function due to its size, levels of existing investment, the level of disruption which could be caused by change and the relatively inflexible nature of the processes, procedures, functions and people involved.
3. The inherent inertia in organizations emanating from existing structures, roles and perceptions. Changes to reporting structures, established reponsibility/authority relationships and the perceived promotional routes for and contributions of individuals can present significant counter-arguments and obstacles to change.

Most organizations have a small percentage of self-motivated people: those for whom the work is challenging and who wish to do the tasks as well as possible. The majority of people, however, need to be induced to work well. This is not really surprising. Most people go to work for reasons based on custom and necessity. Furthermore, the job opportunities open to them rarely afford a wide choice. Many industrialized societies have created an economic situation in which it is difficult to find work other than with established organizations. There is no developed social or economic infrastructure which supports self-working practices. The opportunities open to people are, by and large, prescribed by education, experience, physical and mental abilities, personality and chance. Consequently, many take on jobs that, after a time, become repetitious and dull.

This set of circumstances creates a situation in which management needs to motivate people for the longer-term benefit of the organization. Improvements in people's work must be achieved and sustained through the line managers' belief in what needs to be done and in their present and future contribution to the redesign of work.

This chapter discusses issues and perspectives important to the operations manager, particularly regarding those people whose task it is to produce the item or provide the service. Behavioural and sociological perspectives tend to dominate the teaching and industrial debate. It is most important, however, that the difficulties, views and preferences of the managers responsible for those who work in organizations should be developed and put forward. This chapter is designed to initiate this type of thinking and contribution.

Some general definitions

It will be helpful at this stage to check the definition of some general terms used in discussing the job of work. This will serve the purpose of clarifying their precise meaning as a prerequisite to developing ideas on how to go forward.

Job content

Job content establishes the scope and depth of work. Job scope is the range of operations required to be completed in the job. Thus, a job with narrow scope means that it contains few operations and will tend to be highly repetitive. A widening of job scope implies that the range of operations to be completed is increased horizontally. This increases the variety of the work performed and reduces the monotony, but does not increase the responsibilities within the job, or the depth of the work involved.

Job depth refers to the degree of responsibility people have to plan and organize the work for which they are responsible. It concerns the level of control that they have over their own working environment. Thus if people have no influence over the planning of their work and have to carry out the plans of others, the job depth is low. Therefore the assembly line worker whose rate of working is controlled by the pace of the line and who carries out the tasks planned by others has a low job content (both low scope and low depth).

Similarly, an audio/copy typist who is required to prepare a narrow range of work to an agreed layout and format has low job content.

Job satisfaction and motivation

Job satisfaction and motivation are not synonomous. Job satisfaction reflects a person's attitude to the job and the level of interest it holds. This results more in increased organizational loyalty and commitment than in increased performance. Motivation, on the other hand, concerns the desire to perform well which could lead to increased effort and a higher performance. The distinction between aspects of work which lead to satisfaction or dissatisfaction and those which motivate people was well drawn by Hertzberg.[1] He emphasized the difference between those factors which led to dissatisfaction if not maintained (referred to as hygiene factors) and those which prompted motivation (referred to as motivators). Factors such as physical conditions, security, pay and relationships were put forward as hygiene factors, while aspects of work such as job growth, responsibility and achievement were classed as motivators. Whilst some of these examples have been criticized,[2] the important insight presented by these perspectives is the distinction between the factors which motivate people and those which make them dissatisfied. Motivation, therefore, plays an intermediate role between satisfaction and performance, for even a satisfied person will only tend to meet performance standards when adequately motivated. With regard to pay (see Chapter 15), it is important not to underestimate its motivational influence, especially for those traditionally paid by incentives.[2] It is important, therefore, to ensure that any significant change in the payment system is accompanied by organizational changes designed to replace any motivational qualities of the previous payment system which are no longer present.

Job performance

Job performance is dependent not only upon the level of motivation which exists but also upon a person's ability. For good performance standards to be achieved and sustained, it is essential that both skill and attitude form the ingredients of the work situation.

Job performance is a product of skill and attitude. It results from the job and behavioural characteristics being brought together in the work situation. Unless both these aspects are reviewed, therefore, the results will be less than adequate.

Managerial philosophies of work

Some of the principal philosophies of work which have influenced western business cultures are now outlined. It is not intended that this should be an exhaustive list but aims to provide a basis for later discussion on important features in work design.

Control through specialists

To achieve greater control, most organizations have appointed specialists. Their brief has been to improve the relevant functions of the organization by developing procedures, systems and activities within the broad area of their specialism. This, however, has often led to the activities of existing functions being separated (in particular, line functions) and housed under the control and auspices of the specialist function (see Figure 14.1).

This has taken place for several reasons: the view often held by organizations that all similar activities should be controlled by one function; empire-building by the specialist function, or a line function's preference and willingness to shed some of its task.

Some problem areas have, however, been created by the increased use of specialists:

1. Development within the specialism has often outpaced the line manager's involvement.
2. Certain tasks best performed in the line are performed elsewhere.
3. Ownership of the maintenance and development of the systems and procedures is seen to be part of the specialist function. This view is compounded by the fact that the specialist capacity necessary to complete these tasks is available only within the specialist departments. Thus, the feedback and response to changing requirements, so critical to the full and practical usefulness of specialist developments, is rarely built into the organization structure.
4. The responsibility for some aspects of the task is not adequately clarified. Hence,

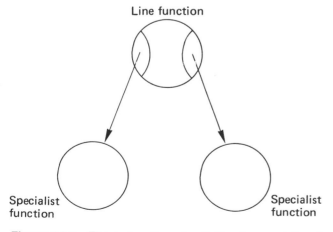

Figure 14.1 The separation of activities from existing line functions to more recently created specialist functions.

gaps appear which cause problems later on. This phenomenon tends to be inherent in the concept of functionalization.

Control of the *n*th degree

The philosophy of many organizations has been to control to the *n*th degree of detail. In the wake of this has come detailed analysis of workplace routines, procedures, systems, and controls which have been designed to specify to a low level of detail the planning and completing of tasks (see Figure 14.2).

In many organizations this philosophy has been used indiscriminately. Applications have been made without the continuous, specialist functional support to the line, the appropriate infrastructure within the line function to cope with the control or procedural issues involved, or the redesignation of tasks to bring theory into line with the requirements of reality.

Control from a distance

The third issue is that controls and procedures have too often been designed and installed from a distance. The approach has been one of 'analytical detachment' from the reality of the function or the business concerned,[3] with the solution based upon some theoretical view of what should take place rather than developing the controls and procedures around what really happens. In addition, the support, maintenance and development of the controls and procedures installed are still, in most organizatioins, too little and too late. Procedures often fall into disrepair rather than being withdrawn or subsequently modified to meet changing needs.

Specialization of labour

With increases in volumes there will be a change in process choice from jobbing through to line (see Figure 4.8). With these higher volume requirements, the basic

Figure 14.2   Control to the *n*th degree.

concept of job design has been that of labour specialization. This has resulted in jobs being broken down into sets of short duration activities each of which is assigned to one person. The investment in the process, which also underpins higher volumes, has often further reduced the technical content of the job and presented a simple, repetitive task at each workstation, with work aids provided to facilitate its completion. As a result, each person is able to complete his part of the job faster due to repetition and specialized provision.

This basic concept has been most valuable in increasing the effectiveness of processes and, without doubt, has made a significant contribution to the standard of living now available to most industrialized communities. However, the productivity gains experienced by many organizations are no longer being enjoyed.

Traditional approaches

Some of the traditional approaches employed to overcome the managerial philosophies to work described in the last section are now discussed.

Job enlargement

Job enlargement increases the scope of the job by adding to the number of operations to be performed. This increase is of a horizontal nature. The advantages of this structural change are to increase the variety of both the work to be completed and the skills to be used, and to provide the opportunity for a person to be responsible for a set of tasks which constitute, where possible, an identifiable programme of work.[4]

Job rotation

Sometimes it is not possible to enlarge jobs as a way of increasing their intrinsic interest. Also, in many service organizations certain jobs have to be performed throughout the normal day or on a twenty-four hour basis — for example, the check-out counter in a library or supermarket, and the night shift in fire, police and hospital services. In the first example the task is monotonous but does not lend itself to enlargement. In the second, although large parts of the work are similar to, and often include, areas of greater responsibility than the tasks completed during the other parts of each working day, the unsocial nature of the shift makes it undesirable to most people. In circumstances like these, job or shift rotation is used periodically to change the job assignments or times of working. In either case, the redesign of the job is not required.

Job enrichment

Whereas job enlargement widened the scope of a job, job enrichment also increases the job depth giving people a greater responsibility to organize and control the work which has to be done.[5] For meaningful control to take place, the necessary information on which to base sensible decisions must be made available to the employees now responsible for making those decisions. In addition, the organizational climate necessary for a change of this nature to take place successfully must be created by all concerned. In the early stages, at least, there will be many in the organization who will view job enrichment as including a measure of role reversal and an erosion of their own set of responsibilities.[6]

Changes in working schedules

In a society that increasingly debates the need for a reduced working week, certain part-step developments have been made as a way forward. The first of these is a working week comprising the normal weekly hours but worked over four days to allow a longer weekend. This is common practice in night-shift working. The second is the introduction of flexitime which allows employees a certain amount of freedom in selecting working hours. The basis for a flexitime arrangement is that each person is required to be at work during certain 'core' hours, but at other times an employee can choose, within certain procedural agreements, the pattern of working for a particular day or week.[7]

Participation

Employee participation in the decisions and developments within the business can be at varying levels and degrees of formality. The hallmark of a participative management style is the recognition of the valuable contribution which employees can make in many aspects of the business. At one end of the scale, employee advice is sought on job-related issues (including job design) and at each stage in the decision-making process. This can be introduced either as part of an individual managerial style or as part of the way an organization works (for example, refer to the use made of quality circles in Japanese businesses outlined in Chapter 11). At the other end of the scale, forms of industrial democracy have been developed which, amongst other changes, place worker representatives in all organizational decision-making bodies, including the board of directors.[8] Whatever degree of participative development exists in an organization, further changes will need to be made carefully and be supported by a substantial investment of time.

In recent years, employers are increasingly being urged to take action to improve employee communication and involvement. Under the Employment Act, 1982, UK employers are required to detail in annual company reports the progress being made on employee participation. Some argue that the requirement for industrial democracy should be taken further with a statutory framework for industrial democracy in the UK based on the EEC Fifth and Vredeling Directives. On the other hand, many believe that legally imposed structures will not work in practice.

Whatever stance is taken, the move towards participation is gaining momentum. Whether stimulated by demonstrated corporate improvement, responding to the changes in society or reflecting the felt need of many production/operator managers, changes are taking place. The most practical counter-argument to improvement through legislation is to demonstrate intent. One important factor, however, in establishing and developing realistic and workable improvements in participation is to place the responsibility for this activity onto those who have responsibility for it — production/operations managers.[9]

For this responsibility to be re-orientated to the production/operations function, an alternative set of views needs to be held and put forward by the managers charged with the responsibility for managing the people involved. In the past, in both manufacturing and service industries POM has delegated the responsibility for its initiatives. The outcome has been a whole series of answers which have left the problem unresolved.[10] After years of initiatives and endeavours, many organizations still do not have a committed and motivated workforce. This lies partly with the approach: specialists observe and prescribe from a distance, and their perspective is often too narrow and certainly lacks the essential touch with reality. To be successful in managing people a manager needs to start by liking them and knowing that there is real talent which has to be tapped.[11] For this reason and the pragmatic need to place the responsibility for developing this critical resource with those with executive authority then POM has to spearhead developments to meet current and future needs.

Ways forward — a POM view

The use of controls as a way of improving corporate performance has increasingly been used by organizations over the last three decades. The three to five year plan and the close monitoring of results has proved an effective way of achieving and sustaining growth and profits. However, tight control may become an effective way of killing creativity and the entrepreneurial traits in those people who comprise the organization. Also, the preferred controls will change depending upon the nature of the operations process chosen by an organization — see Table 4.4.

A centralized planning and control philosophy in many organizations goes hand-in-hand with the corporate view that a high degree of control through procedures and systems, the use of specialists, and the control of organizations from a distance is the most effective approach to achieving a high degree of control in the total business.

The experience of large Japanese corporations, on the other hand, confirms the wisdom of relying heavily on individual or group contributions and initiatives for improvement, innovation and creative energy . . . the individual employee is utilized to the fullest extent of his creative and productive capacity. . . . The whole organization looks organic and entrepreneurial, as opposed to mechanistic and bureaucratic. It is probably less planned, less rigid, but more vision or mission-driven than the western organization. The basic difference is that the Japanese company starts with people, or individual constituents, trusting their capabilities and latent potential.[12]

The real test in management is completing the task — it is the execution and not the formulation of strategy which underpins corporate success. In addition, many organizations develop corporate objectives for divisions or plants about which they have little first-hand experience. Where this approach is compounded by procedurally-based controls then the ideas and improvements which should flow naturally from the stimulus of business activity, will not be encouraged or facilitated.

Strategic issues

Many businesses have developed with too little forethought and too little cohesion the product/service range offered, the plant/facility to provide them and their understanding of how they compete in the market. This has partly been because of incremental growth and their failure to address the question of what forms the key requirement for them to be successful in the market-place. Although these issues were addressed more fully in Chapter 12, it is important when dealing with the job of work to recognize that the overall task for a plant or service facility is determined at the strategic level. How this task is then completed is partly strategic and partly tactical.

The principal perspective underlying these strategic considerations is that of facilities focus.[13] This necessitates that businesses concern themselves with identifying how they compete in the market-place, recognizing that the issues to be addressed involve the effectiveness of the whole operations organization and not just of the operators, processes and systems used. It focuses each facility on a limited set of products/services that are compatible with each other in terms of the operations task involved and the support functions required and then harnesses the process/service system and POM infrastructure to focus on a set of explicit tasks to meet predetermined market needs.[14] By doing this, organizations have set the parameters of the task and support requirements. This enables them to measure the work patterns, structure and responsibilities against these clearly defined parameters, thereby ensuring that what is decided at both the strategic and tactical levels is completed against a common set of criteria which, in turn, reflect the organizational task to be successful in the market-place.

Tactical issues

The responsibility for achieving corporate objectives lies with those responsible for the main functions in a business. The POM role is large and complex, and nowhere more so than in the people and work aspects of this function. It is essential, therefore, that the operations manager thinks through the various work structures available to ensure that the ideas reflect the practical issues involved and the reality of the work situation. Some important perspectives are now discussed which emphasize the POM issues involved.

1. In order to continue the productivity gains essential to improving living standards, the doing part of work will continue to be deskilled and simplified. Whether this reduces fatigue, boredom or skill is not important in terms of stimulating or justifying the change. Such changes are a prerequisite to productivity improvement. However, for many people, work is synonymous with the manual task. But, work is more than this: it also involves planning, organizing, controlling and monitoring activities. Therefore, the way to increase job interest in the future will be principally through the non-manual aspects of work.

2. It is important to move away from descriptions of jobs to descriptions of work. Where there is an increasing need to be flexible in both the short- and longer-term, detailed descriptions at the job level may offer improved control at a particular moment in time but be a source of inflexibility and unnecessary cost thereafter. It is important to avoid job descriptions by defining objectives to be achieved by groups, sections or departments. Although this is superficially less efficient, it provides a better environment in which ideas and improvements can be generated from the essential activity of the business and encourages a flexible response to the changing requirements of the organization (see Figure 14.3)

3. With increases in volume and the move towards functional specialisms and line assembly, the engineering view of orderliness is segregated tasks and straight lines. Thus, the enlargement and enrichment of work is difficult. It is essential, therefore, that configurations of work avoid both the unnecessary breakdown and separation of tasks and the layout of work using straight lines (see Figure 14.4).

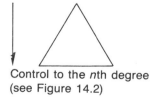

Control to the *n*th degree
(see Figure 14.2)

Control to the level of the group,
section or department with detailed
control being vested in those
responsible for the doing task

Figure 14.3 Changes in the concept of control.

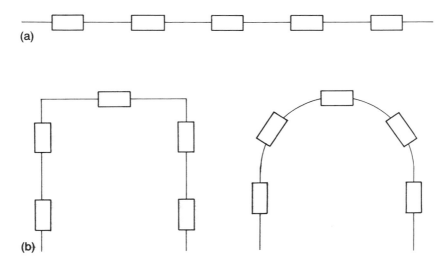

Figure 14.4 The straight-line layout and alternative solutions. (a) Straight-line layout intended to meet engineering principles of process design. (b) The same work, the revised layout of which facilitates communication and work identity.

4. The rationale for employing specialists is not only to bring in expertise but also to provide support to the line. Figure 14.1 illustrate what tends to happen in many organizations with the introduction of specialist functions. Over time, the gap between specialists and the line may widen because of their geographical separation within the plant, the value system under which they both judge the other, and the pursuit of different personal and organizational objectives. For these reasons the ownership of problems and their solutions, controls, procedures and systems tends to be seen in departmental rather than corporate terms.

As discussed in Chapter 1, one important role of operations managers is to develop the areas for which they are responsible. In corporate terms, this objective is of paramount importance due to the levels of investment and expenditure that fall within the POM function. Two important prerequisites for this to happen are time and know-how. The day-to-day pressures of the POM function at all levels and the separation of specialist inputs from the line departments tend to hinder this activity. Specialists that are put back into line functions and under the authority and responsibility of operations managers will, in turn, facilitate these important sets of cost-reduction and improvement activities.

Key work-group features[15]

In contrast to the points raised earlier (pp. 438–43), the following features in the design of work are important facets in building up groups.

The work-group

Work-groups should ideally be of between four and twenty people, self-managed but with a supervisor. The size is large enough to include a meaningful set of interdependent tasks that provides job scope, yet small enough to allow effective group working to facilitate decision-making and co-ordination.

The task

The task needs to have sufficient job scope for the activities involved to have inherent meaning in terms of the item produced or service provided. In addition, the task should include responsibility for inspection, quality control and simple maintenance, with group responsibility for initiating, arranging and introducing job improvements. This will require both training within the group and the use of specialists from within the POM function.

Planning and organizing the work

The work-group should, as far as possible, be responsible for planning and organizing its own work. This should include analysing and coping with operations problems within the group and between groups, deciding what and when to produce in line with customer requirements, the redistribution of work in cases of absenteeism and holidays, and organizing the provision of the material and other requirements to complete the tasks on hand.

Controlling and monitoring the work

The work-groups should also, as far as possible, be responsible for the day-to-day control of the activities for which they are responsible and for monitoring work performance over time. These activities should include checking the efficiency and quality of the work, analysing the results and deciding on ways to improve these activities.

Integrated specialist functions

Wherever possible, specialist support functions should be built into the group. These include maintenance and clerical capacity in order to provide the process support and analytical capability necessary to the planning, organizing, controlling and monitoring aspects of the work already described. Similarly, at the departmental level the same philosophy should be adopted. Key support functions to the operations department should be placed under the responsibility and authority of the operations manager. These include personnel, cost accounting, management services and similar functions in order to provide the capability to analyse, evaluate and report on the key investment, expenditure and people aspects of the task.

In this way, meaningful work tasks can be introduced into organizations which have, over the years, sought to reduce the technical content of the job in order to simplify the doing part of work, and hence gain the productivity improvements that higher volumes and investment in the process allow.

Combined strategic and tactical responses

Earlier sections in this chapter highlight the need to distinguish between responses at the strategic and tactical levels. Unless tactical initiatives are placed within an appropriate strategy then they will be merely panaceas which are likely to be inappropriately applied. Lacking the conceptual understanding on which these approaches are based, the organization is invariably unable to assess them in the light of the business need, to customize them as required and to provide the essential, appropriate developments over time.

At the strategic level, organizations need to recognize that, whilst sound in theory, economies of scale do not, as a rule, work in practice. The resultant size and complexity within POM creates a task which is difficult to manage, with which people are unable to identify and which attracts large overhead costs in an attempt to co-ordinate and control. The concept of focus mentioned earlier, and the plant-within-plant configurations which emanate from this approach is an essential perspective which organizations need to embrace.[16]

Within this strategic framework, businesses need to recognize the inherent advantages and strengths which go hand-in-hand with work-groups and cellular structures. However, when adopting these alternatives, organizations need to beware of the panacea syndrome. Group technology and JIT-based cells have been discussed earlier (pp. 140–5 and pp. 217–19 respectively). It needs to be recognized that their successful application is based on the degree of fit with the market need and is not a consequence of some intrinsic set of characteristics. Thus, organizations developing similar approaches need to start at the strategic level and then ensure that the structures at the tactical level link both to the strategic decisions in which they are to be placed and the market need. In addition, other facets of infrastructure treated elsewhere in this book (for example, production/operations planning and control, quality control and remuneration) need to form an integral part of this decision.

Some applications

The need for the structure of work to be coherent both in its intrinsic design and with regard to the strategic needs of the business cannot be overstressed. To illustrate the way in which developments are taking place several applications are now briefly outlined.

Shell

Between 1972 and 1985 the cost of chemical raw materials as a proportion of costs rose from 50 to 70 per cent. Even though western Europe has cut its capacity by 15 per cent since 1980, the fall in demand has left the industry in an overcapacity situation resulting in an increased level of competition. Against this background, Shell has introduced new agreements at both its chemical plant at Carrington and the Stanlow refinery.

In each instance the package involves major flexibility and efficiency initiatives, new grading structures, revised patterns of work, multi-skilled agreements, appropriate training programmes and revised manning agreements. Shell has recognized the need to manage people in a way that provides an opportunity to increase their contribution in meeting the requirements of the business.

At the Carrington chemical plant, the heart of the agreement concerns changes in working practice, the concept of multi-skilled technicians and a common union approach. From 1985, six teams of technicians complete any operating and maintenance work with support by two service groups and outside contractors. Other features of the development include new grading structures, revised shift patterns, training programmes and remuneration agreements (including redeployment assistance).

At the Stanlow refinery, the core of the agreement concerns flexibility agreements for craft and non-craft employees and its implications for grading structures, shift patterns and union representation. In addition, short, disruptive daily breaks have been replaced by five additional days of annual holiday, appropriate training programmes introduced, and changes in total remuneration concerning career progression, grading structures and redundancy/redeployment packages.[17]

Digital Equipment Corporation (DEC)

In mid-1986 at its plant in Ayr, DEC, faced with the prospect of a decline in business, recognized the need to introduce product changes and to adopt a strategic response within the business in terms of coping with the required technical change and resultant flexibility. Given the short life cycle nature of its products, the company not only needed processes that could cope with changing product specifications but also a workforce that could respond appropriately. For that reason it introduced autonomous work-groups of some twelve people who had 'front-to-back' responsibility for the product in order to create the necessary flexibility within each group. The company moved to a skill-based payment system (see pp. 472–3) which rewards people for the skills they have rather than the job they do thereby promoting the necessary flexibility within the group working arrangements. In addition, it located several support activities (e.g. material acquisition and production control) onto the shopfloor. Further ways of increasing shopfloor involvement included improved features of communication, product ownership by the groups, and appropriate training.[18]

Komatsu

Commercial pressures facing Komatsu, the Japanese construction equipment company, have forced it to set up offshore manufacturing facilities to enable it to respond more closely to particular market needs whilst avoiding trade friction and reducing the impact of fluctuating currency rates. Following factories set up in Brazil, Mexico, Indonesia and the USA, Komatsu set up its European facility in Birtley, Gateshead in mid-1987. Flexibility and teamwork were considered to be essential to meeting its market demands and these factors are, therefore, strongly evident in its agreements, part of which is given in Table 14.1.

The agreement relates to all full-time staff up to and including supervisors.[19] It contains procedures for avoiding disputes, flexibility and the use of manpower and single status employment conditions with a common pension scheme, performance review, career appraisal (see Chapter 15), sick pay arrangements, monthly pay, free medical cover and a common 39-hour week with five weeks' holiday.

Other applications

There are many other examples in the UK and elsewhere which illustrate this growing trend. They include in the UK, Trebor, Borgwarner, Rowntree Macintosh, Balfour Beatty Northern Construction Division, Blue Circle and the Austin Rover Group.[20] In the USA they include Shenandoah Life Insurance, Cummins Engines, General Motors, Procter and Gamble, Tektronix and other DEC businesses.

Service issues

The growth in the service sector, the increasing geographical base of competition and the more rapid changes in service mix are putting more pressure on organizations to adapt to changing needs. Furthermore, the upward trend in technology applications, discussed in Chapter 7, is also adding to the need to respond to these opportunities. Although the issues raised earlier in this chapter are applicable in all sectors of the economy, some of the structural features which are often more pertinent to the service task are highlighted below.

Structural features

Service businesses have a number of structural features which often facilitate the appropriate application of work structuring and other concepts described earlier.

1. *Size*. Service businesses are typically smaller in size than their manufacturing counterparts, due primarily to the way in which service provision is linked

Table 14.1   Extracts from the main agreement at Komatsu

Flexibility and use of manpower at Komatsu

Use of manpower (extract from the main agreement)
In reaching this agreement, the union recognises and supports the complete flexibility and mobility of the workforce between jobs and duties within the company and departments.

For its part, the company recognises and accepts the need for training and re-training in the broadening of skills and dealing with new technology developments to improve efficiency and profitability.

Hence the following working practices are agreed:

- Complete flexibility and mobility of employees.
- Changes in processes and practices will be introduced to increase competitiveness and these will improve productivity and affect manning levels.
- To achieve such change, employees will work as required by the company and participate in training of themselves or other employees as required.
- Manning levels will be determined by the company using appropriate industrial engineering and manpower planning techniques.

Flexibility, assignments and training (extract from the detailed terms and conditions agreement)
Complete labour flexibility, interchangeability and mobility will be practised in order to maximise productivity and correct imbalances in production flow.

It is the individual's duty to accept such interchange and mobility, to co-operate with training designed to sponsor and further this and to work up to the level of his capability without any change in pay for doing so. It is management's responsibility to allocate duties and shift patterns to individuals as best suits the operating needs of the company.

To aid flexibility it is accepted that the company may use short-term, temporary or part-time labour from time to time.

Komatsu's Advisory Council (extract from the main agreement)

(a)   The Advisory Council exists to provide a forum for the active involvement of employees and the union in regular dicussions on the on-going progress of the company. The company and the trade union support the Advisory Council as the single representative body on all matters affecting groups of employees;

(b)   The detailed role and constitution are separately defined.

    (i)   *Representation*
       The Advisory Council is to be a forum comprising elected representatives covering all employees appointed by the company, together with the union divisional organiser as an ex-officio member of the Council.

    (ii)   *Scope*
- All matters of collective interest. Issues of individual interest will not be discussed by the Advisory Council.
- Review of the operation of this agreement.
- Company investment policy and business plans.
- Company trading performance, sales and market share.
- Company manpower plans.
- Company productivity, operating efficiency and quality achievements.
- Work rules.
- Terms and conditions of employment including pay and benefits, conditions of service.
- Work environment and conditions.

Reproduced with permission.

directly to the customer. This, in turn, offers the opportunity to 'design' tasks in such a way as to incorporate appropriate work structuring ideas.

2. *Span of process*. The inherent span of process within service activities tends to be narrow, resulting in relatively few operations within a total task. This makes specialization less sensible and, conversely, makes 'whole task' approaches both achievable and desirable.

3. *Customer involvement*. One service-related issue addressed throughout this book concerns the level of customer involvement. This relates both to what is appropriate as well as what is practical. However, the outcome of these decisions will affect the definition of jobs and the practicality of structure.

4. *Level of customer contact*. One result of the decisions taken under point 3 is a recognition of the levels of customer contact embodied in different jobs. In low contact jobs, often in the back room, the approaches to work restructuring resemble those implemented in manufacturing, with similar levels of success. These include the opportunities to apply appropriate process investments and the transfer of tasks, through technology applications, to the customer (e.g. automatic teller machines or cash points).

Some firms have also restructured tasks for their higher salaried managers and professionals. By reshaping tasks, many current activities are now completed by others in the organization, thus increasing job interest for all whilst ensuring that those capacities in short supply are appropriately utilized (see p. 124).

The challenge of job restructuring in high customer contact tasks is rather more challenging. In these situations, appearance, the securing of customer interface opportunities and the need to achieve the quality levels involved are as important as the service itself. However, several organizations have reviewed the tasks involved.

With deregulation, US airlines are increasingly reshaping tasks. Delta Airlines has maintained a high level of flexibility of staff due to the lack of restrictions concerning single job rules. These developments have been taken up by other airlines, notably the People's Express. Based on non-union and employee ownership philosophies, pilots, for instance, are willing to undertake any other task (including baggage handling) once they have reached the statutory monthly limit on flying hours.

Other businesses change the structure of work and then make it a feature of the service provision. The Japanese restaurant at the Marriott Hotel (Toronto Airport) is based on the principle of the chef preparing food in front of the customers at a *hibachi*. The customer requirements and their provision are now linked, offering improved service in terms of meeting the specification, customer orientation and interface, and speed of response. For the hotel, it also reduces the level of staff required, whilst leading to an improved use of capacity in terms of the number of customers served in a given period.

Opportunities

The evolution of the service industry and the nature of the sector also provide work structuring opportunities more easily realized than in manufacturing. The development of service industries has, understandably, followed that of the manufacturing sector. Its more recent development provides some important advantages, including the absence of a history based on trade union confrontation and challenge. In addition, and partly as a consequence, trade union representation in this sector is lower than in manufacturing (non-manual representation was 48.7 per cent in 1984, compared with 70.3 per cent for manual workers — see Table 14.2). The opportunity, therefore, to develop appropriate work structures which reflect the needs of both the people and the business has been more available within the service sector.

1. *Job sharing*. The structural advantages inherent in a service organization (e.g. size and span of process) tend to offer opportunities for job sharing without impinging on the organizational tasks involved. This, in turn, offers a company the opportunity to avail itself of part-time staff to complete full-time roles, the characteristics of which are normally a better business fit in terms of the working day, organizational structure and work routines. Companies, therefore, can increase their use of this opportunity by incorporating this factor into work structuring decisions.

2. *Flexitime*. In a similar way to point 1, service organizations as a whole can utilize more fully the opportunity of flexitime arrangements than their manufacturing counterparts.[21] By taking account of this within their approach to structuring tasks, organizations can again provide more attractive working arrangements for employees without detriment to their business requirements.

3. *Home-based arrangements*. Where tasks involve low levels of customer contact, there is the possibility of these being completed on a home-based arrangement. Organizations need to be aware of the increasing opportunity for this, as mooted

Table 14.2 Trade union membership in the UK, 1980 and 1984 and percentage change in the period

Trade union membership	1980	1984	Percentage change +(−)
Manual	83.7	70.3	(16.0)
Non-manual	61.3	48.7	(20.6)

Source: P.B. Beaumont and R.I.D. Harris, 'The North—South divide in Britain: the case of trade union recognition' (Department of Economics, Queen's University of Belfast, 1988), mimeo.

in Chapter 7, in order to avail themselves not only of recruitment advantages but also of the gains associated with office space and facilities.

Conclusion

There are no panaceas to the work design problems facing many organizations. The tendency of many western industrial cultures to attempt to solve major problems by the application of techniques will suffer the fate of all simplistic approaches to complex issues and, particularly, those concerning people. It is necessary to analyse and design for each particular work situation, and to treat each situation as a separate outcome of the people and work relationship even though the basic format is common. The solutions need to be far from superficial. It is necessary to develop a comprehensive and integrated approach to work design. The essential requirement is that a complete philosophy is agreed, introduced and developed so that each facet forms part of the whole philosophy. Increased investment in the process will yield potential improvements in productivity. However, to approach these investments in theoretical, technical terms will increasingly become self-defeating. The reduction in technical skill requirements needs to be replaced by other forms of inherently interesting work. Self-directing and self-monitoring opportunities at work are amongst the most rewarding.

In addition, the needs of the market-place are changing more rapidly. It is important, therefore, to take advantage of the inherent ability of people to switch quickly between work patterns, procedures and tasks to meet changing market demands. The prerequisite for this is the motivation of the workforce to make these changes possible. This, in turn, is based upon their own response to the organization and the degree of involvement which they feel for the work activities that form their job. One of the key demands in productivity improvements is concerned with tapping the innovative resources of employees. Where the action takes place, then the stimulus for improvement is high. It is an essential POM task to ensure that these perspectives form part of tomorrow's work design. This responsibility has been given greater prominence in the 1980s with trends in the UK showing a movement away from trade union membership for both manual and non-manual workers (see Table 14.2), and also the advent of single union deals.

The opportunity to restructure work in a way which better meets current business needs, whilst providing for change in the future, is probably as good as it has been for many years. It is important, however, to ensure that changes are undertaken in a sensitive and responsible manner as these actions may well set the industrial relations scene for years to come. To increase the likelihood of successful job restructuring it is essential that it is seen as being primarily a POM task, with specialists providing an advisory role, and not vice versa. One problem holding back progress towards better people management has to do with the perceived allocation of authority and responsibility for this task.

Restructuring work, based on the principles discussed here and selected to meet the particular needs of an organization, is one important prerequisite for developing an effective, relevant and responsive workforce. This embodies a recognition of the need to base future developments on appropriate POM needs and perspectives. The second part of the approach concerns the need for a proactive style with executive leadership provided by the production/operations function. Unless this is recognized, then organizations will continue to approach decisions affecting the quality of its human resource provision and involvement as second-order issue tasks and using a reactive style. Past approaches to human resource management have contributed to past levels of competitive performance. The opportunity to change and the recognition of its contribution to the success of an organization need to be at the forefront of corporate initiatives. It is essential that increased levels of employee participation are sought and that these are company-focused and fashioned around corporate needs, cultures and requirements.

Notes and references

1. F. Hertzberg, *Work and the Nature of Man* (Cleveland World Publishing Co., 1966).
2. For instance, M. Fein 'Job enrichment: a revaluation', *Sloan Management Review*, 15, no. 2 (1974), 69–88, re-emphasizes pay as an important motivator.
3. This perspective forms part of a criticism of modern management principles put forward by R.H. Hayes and W.J. Abernathy, 'Managing our way to economic decline', *Harvard Business Review* (July/August 1980), 67–77.
4. Some of the issues involved are discussed in two papers presented at the Fourth Conference on Production Research, Tokyo, 1974, by J.R. De Jong, 'The method in work design: some recommendations based on experience obtained in job design', 931–41, and G. Salvendy, 'An industrial engineering dilemma: simplified versus employed jobs'.
5. Details of specific applications of job enrichment approaches are an increasing feature of relevant journals and other information sources. For example, American Productivity Center, 'Job enrichment, not displacement: results from office automation in Houston law firm', *Productivity Letter*, 4 (August 1984) 1–2.
6. J.R. Hackman *et al.*, 'A new strategy for job enrichment', *California Management Review*, 17, no. 4 (1975), 57–71 discusses the results of practical applications in job enrichment and proposes a new strategy for approaching the redesign of work.
7. For further details on flexitime refer to P.J. Sloane, *Changing Patterns of Working Hours*, Department of Employment, Manpower Paper no. 13 (London: HMSO, 1975); E.S. Drye, 'Flexible hours in DHSS local offices', *Management Services in Government* (February 1975); and T. Burt, 'Making the most of time with flexible working hours', *Personnel Executive* (March 1982), 37–45.
8. For a discussion on some of these developments refer to R. Harrison, *Workers Participation in Western Europe* (London: IPM, 1976); J. Crisp, *Industrial Democracy in Western Europe: A North American perspective* (New York: McGraw-Hill Ryerson Ltd, 1978); J. Hebden and J. Shaw, *Pathways to Participation* (London: Associated Business Programmes, 1977); D. Guest and K. Knight (eds), *Putting Participation into Practice* (Aldershot: Gower, 1977); and Geursten Report, European Parliament Working Document 1-862/81 (15 January 1982) concerning employee participation.
   In addition, specific applications of participation written about individual organizations provide important insights into these developments. For example, V. Kiam, 'Remington's marketing and manufacturing strategies', *Management Review* (February 1987), 43–55.

9. Peter Wilkins, *The Road to Nissan: Flexibility, quality, teamwork* (Basingstoke: Macmillan, 1987), highlights the need to give back to the production function the responsibility for managing this part of the business.
10. Some of these issues are neatly summarized by Wickham Skinner in 'Big hat, no cattle: managing human resources', *Harvard Business Review* (September/October 1981), 106–14.
11. One illustration of different attitudes to the role of people is provided by K. Matsushita in 'Why the West will lose', *Industrial Participation* (Spring 1988), 8, which was based on extracts of remarks made by him to a group of western managers.
12. K. Ohmae, 'Myths and realities of Japanese corporations', *The McKinsey Quarterly* (Summer 1981), 8–9.
13. The concept of focus was first introduced by Wickham Skinner in 'The focused factory', *Harvard Business Review* (May/June 1974), 113–31. It is more fully addressed in Terry Hill, *Manufacturing Strategy: The strategic management of the manufacturing function* (Basingstoke: Macmillan, 1985), pp. 90–140, and also in Terry Hill, *Manufacturing Strategy: Text and cases* (Homewood, Ill.: Irwin, 1989), pp. 98–112.
14. Terry Hill, *op. cit.*, (1985), pp. 100–1.
15. A set of well-developed work structuring principles has been presented in various unpublished papers, 1979–81 by P.C. Schumacher, Schumacher Projects, Church House, Godstone, Surrey RH9 8BW.
16. See Terry Hill, *op. cit.*, (1985), pp. 107–8 and (1989), pp. 105–6 for details.
17. A more detailed account of these agreements is provided in the *Industrial Relations Review and Report* (IR-RR) 358 (17 December 1985) published by Industrial Relations Services, 67 Maygrove Road, London NW6 2EJ.
18. An account of the DEC approach is given in David Buchanan, 'Job enrichment is dead: long live high-performance work design!', *Personnel Management*, May 1987, pp. 40–43.
19. Further details of this agreement are given in IR-RR 391 (5 May 1987) published by Industrial Relations Services.
20. Details of the applications of Rowntree Macintosh, Balfour Beatty Northern Construction Division and Blue Circle are provided in IR-RR 349, 360 and 366 respectively, published by Industrial Relations Services.
21. Flexitime is an arrangement which allows employees to alter some part of their working day to suit their own special and domestic needs, and personal preferences. Typical developments are built around 'core' periods of work when everyone must be present and 'flexible' periods of work which are under the discretion of each employee within an agreed set of rules, such as providing the agreed advanced notice. In addition, many arrangements allow employees the opportunity (again within an agreed framework) to accumulate time, which can be redeemed in the form of complete days off.

Further reading

Aldag, R.J. and Brief, A.P., *Task Design and Employee Motivation* (San Francisco: Scott, Foresman, 1979).

Birchall, D., *Job Design* (Aldershot: Gower, 1975).

Burrows, G., *Non-strike Agreements and Pendulum Arbitration* (London: Institute of Personnel Management, 1986).

Curson, C. (ed.) *Flexible Patterns of Work* (London: Institute of Personnel Management, 1986).

Filley, A.C. and House, R.J., *Managerial Process and Organizational Behaviour* (San Francisco: Scott, Foresman, 1969).

Hackmand, J.R. and Oldham, G.R., *Work Redesign* (Reading, Mass.: Addison-Wesley, 1980).

Kirkman, F., 'Who cares about job design? Some reflections on its present and future', *International Journal of Operations and Production Management*, 2, no. 1: 3–13.

Schumacher, E.F., *Small is Beautiful* (London: Blond Briggs Ltd, 1973).

Syrett, M., *Employing Job Sharers, Part-time and Temporary Staff* (London: Institute of Personnel Management, 1983).

Chapter 15

Remuneration

This chapter deals with the question of the work done by people in industrial and commercial organizations and the determination of a system of rewards which is seen to be fair and equitable. Conclusions highlighted over the last two decades, have pointed to the fact that money is not the only factor that will ensure the best level of performance. Other aspects such as conditions, degree of participation, job opportunities and the structure of work are some of the other important aspects which influence this situation. The danger inherent in these conclusions is that these perspectives are applicable equally to all people within an organization, no matter what their job or the nature of the system under which they are rewarded. It is important, therefore, to ensure that proposed developments are based not only on what companies wish to accomplish but also on what is appropriate for the tasks and people involved.

This chapter is concerned with pay systems at the 'operator' level — those who are concerned principally with making the product (and traditionally paid, at least in the past, on an hourly basis), or providing the service (and normally paid on a weekly basis). It will show the overall development of pay structures, outline the relevant aspects of these developments and help to clarify the importance of fitting remuneration to the particular situation. It is important in these opening remarks to stress that the research findings referred to above can only be used with great caution as a valid insight into views on pay and work, by those working at this level and paid in this way. Some reasons for this are:

1. Much of the research was completed on staff employed at higher levels than the operator level. Transfer of findings from one to the other is highly questionable.
2. The work culture of one country is different from another, and, as such, also presents problems of transferability.
3. Economic climates can change sufficiently to challenge the representative nature of the views held in times which are widely different.

4. The opportunities open to many workers are strictly limited without major attitude, philosophy and organizational changes. Such changes are not common in organizations (although the climate is improving) and so the likely opportunities are not widespread.

Although people's attitudes towards their work will be influenced by factors other than total remuneration (pay and any other benefits), non-pay aspects for hourly-paid people should be neither overestimated nor overstressed. The time and money aspects of the package are still by far the most important. This chapter concentrates on the considerations to be taken into account when deciding on the composition of pay and the options available in determining each element within the total.

The components of gross pay

What constitutes gross pay (i.e. the pay received prior to tax and other deductions) will differ from one organization to the next. Figure 15.1 illustrates the principal elements involved in most situations. Each of these elements will be discussed in some detail in the rest of the chapter. However, it is important to understand not only the components of gross pay in themselves but also the composition of these elements within the total. How a person's gross pay is made up, and the percentage

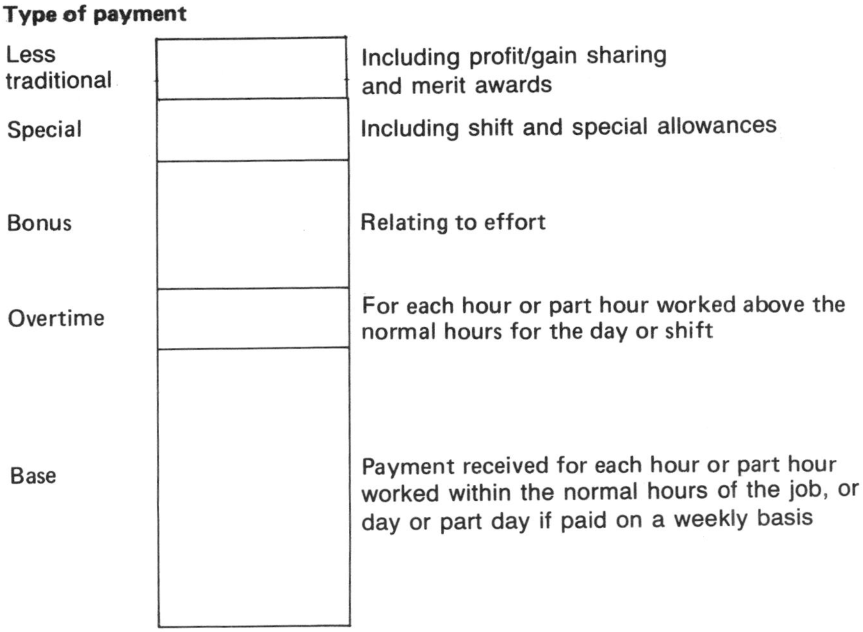

Type of payment

Less traditional	Including profit/gain sharing and merit awards
Special	Including shift and special allowances
Bonus	Relating to effort
Overtime	For each hour or part hour worked above the normal hours for the day or shift
Base	Payment received for each hour or part hour worked within the normal hours of the job, or day or part day if paid on a weekly basis

Figure 15.1   Typical components of gross pay.

that each element constitutes of the total, will affect people's views of the organization and their attitude to work. It is necessary that these components are so designed that a balance is struck between how easy the payment system is to understand by those who are remunerated by it and the sensitivity of the scheme to reflect the aspects of work which need to be stressed. Getting this balance right and then monitoring or correcting this to reflect change is an important task.

Whilst the detailed design is often the responsibility of specialists within an organization, it is most important that the operations manager understands the system of payment and contributes to its development over time. What and how people are paid is of the utmost importance to those concerned. Similarly, what aspects of work the reward system emphasizes needs to be in line with the important aspects of the operations task. In addition, it must be realized that:

1. As pay is, for hourly/weekly paid people, the most important reason for coming to work, then changes in payment systems should be seen as an opportunity to set this part of work on a sound footing.

2. Payment systems need to be designed for longer periods of time to avoid unnecessary change, and yet be able to reflect necessary changes as and when required. Major changes of direction are too often the hallmark of payment systems.

3. Management must determine its own objectives within a pay system. Typical objectives may include to:
    (a) control costs;
    (b) allow practical flexibility in the use of people;
    (c) maintain an orderly pay structure to avoid problems of differentials and instability;
    (d) increase or maintain productivity levels;
    (e) support the needs of the business.

4. It is important to recognize that workers or their representatives will also have a set of objectives which need to be considered in the design of the system. They may include to:
    (a) exert pressure to increase pay levels;
    (b) provide a stable and reliable gross pay at the end of the working period;
    (c) maintain an orderly pay structure to avoid problems of differentials;
    (d) increase the degree of participation in establishing payment systems.

It is within the background of these factors that payment systems have to be developed. How much an organization pays for each component of gross pay is, of course, a most important consideration and will be influenced by local rates, the current rate of inflation, national and local agreements and the government of the day. This chapter, however, concerns itself with the composition of pay as explained earlier and as outlined in Figure 15.1.

Basic payments

This is the fundamental component of total pay and is also the basis used when calculating other types of payment (e.g. overtime rates and shift premiums). It is also important to recognize that it forms the basic measure that employees use to judge their work and their reward. This judgement takes two forms:

1. The absolute value of the job — how much they are paid.
2. The relative value of the job — how much they are paid in relation to others in the organization.

Establishing the relative value of work can be done in different ways. In the past, the method used tended to be arbitrary. It has usually been developed over time and based on one or more formal and informal approaches, such as market conditions, local bargaining and the historical perspectives held of jobs within the organization and the local area. In such circumstances, different types of work have current relative values which may be distorted because of the *ad hoc* nature of the system used in their determination.

In recent years several important developments have occurred which have put pressure on organizations to review their grading systems:

1. Structural and organizational changes brought about by the late 1970s/early 1980s recession and the introduction of new technology have made many systems outdated and less effective. These events have often led to fewer workers, significant changes in job mix and less appropriate payment structures.
2. The 1984 'equal value' amendment to the Equal Pay Act, 1970, has focused attention on the role and relevance of grading systems and potential anomalies.
3. Trends towards the harmonization of conditions for blue- and white-collar workers are giving stimulus to the idea of single, integrated grading schemes covering all these employees.
4. Single union agreements have given further impetus to the introduction of payment systems which override existing separate structures.

For any organization, the pay structure (as outlined earlier) should meet its current and foreseeable requirements whilst satisfying the aspirations of employees (and all concerned) for an understandable and fair method of determining the relative worth of jobs.

Within this broad scenario, job evaluation can be a valuable aid to establishing and maintaining such a pay structure. It is not surprising, therefore, that many organizations are considering the introduction of a job evaluation scheme (or revision to its existing schemes) as one approach to developing a pay structure which would reflect its corporate needs whilst compensating its hourly/weekly paid employees in an appropriate way.

Job evaluation

Job evaluation is the process of determining, without regard to personalities, the worth of one job in relation to another. A scheme properly devised will:

1. Provide reliable and systematic data for working out the worth of one job compared with another.
2. Establish a logical, rather than an arbitrary, basis for arriving at the worth of jobs.
3. Ensure fairer treatment.
4. Help to determine the relative worth of a new or revised job.

Therefore, it will be concerned with:

1. The relative value of jobs and not their absolute values.
2. Establishing the relationship of one job to another using common criteria derived from the actual content of jobs.
3. Analysing the job and not the person doing the job.

The various schemes by which this procedure is carried out are known collectively as job evaluation. BS 3138 (1979) describes it as 'any method of ranking the relative worth of jobs subject to the conditions then prevailing'. The overall procedure to be adopted is as follows:

1. A job analysis is completed to find the exact content of each job being assessed and the skills required to perform it.
2. A job description is prepared to record the job characteristics in a form most suited to the method of assessment to be used.
3. Jobs are then evaluated by ranking one job against the other jobs.
4. Jobs are then arranged in progression.
5. Lastly, the job progression is related to a money scale.

This last step, as explained earlier, is independent of the job evaluation procedure outlined in steps 1–4.

The 1968 *Report on Job Evaluation*,[1] based on a survey of 8,000 companies employing 6.5 million people, revealed that some 11 per cent craft and 26 per cent non-craft employees were covered by a job evaluation scheme. Since then there has been an increase in the UK due to pressures by government incomes policies, technological changes highlighting job changes and the creation of new jobs which had to be slotted into the pay structure, drifting in payment by result and merit schemes leading to inequalities in gross pay,[2] large groups of companies wishing to create a consistent pay structure from plant to plant, and considerable publicity. A smaller survey by the British Institute of Management (1979) confirmed this increase — of 236 companies, 64 per cent operated one or more schemes and of these almost 50 per cent operated a scheme for hourly paid employees.[3] Job evaluation, whilst sometimes described as scientific and rational, is more correctly described as systemetic since all the methods used depend upon a series of judgements which are, at best, subjective. There are a number of methods of job evaluation which might be used and these are described here. They fall into two distinct types — non-analytical, which compare jobs in total to each other, and analytical, which break down the jobs in order to assess their total worth before ranking them against other jobs.

Non-analytical methods

Job ranking

Although the simplest method of job evaluation, job ranking requires a high degree of knowledge about the jobs under review. The procedure is to assess the importance of each job as a whole and in relation to all the other jobs being evaluated at that time. The jobs are not broken down to show component or separate factors, and the assessors work from their overall knowledge of each job. This knowledge is supplemented by a written job description of the duties and responsibilities involved and of the requirements necessary for an individual to undertake the work at an acceptable level. The assessors then simply compare the jobs against each other to decide whether it is as demanding, more demanding or less demanding. As a result, a list of jobs in order of importance is agreed, called the ranking list.

In a small organization one list can cover all jobs. In a larger organization it is better to prepare a list for each department or appropriate area and, when a ranking list for each area has been made, assess jobs between areas in order to equate jobs of equal worth. From this, a ranking list for all jobs is determined and a grading structure emerges.

Paired comparisons

In this method, every job is compared with every other job. If a job is considered to be 'more demanding' then it gets two points, if equal then both get one point, and if less, then no points. The scores are then totalled and a rank order is obtained.

Job grading or job classification

As in job ranking, job grading is based on the job as a whole. It differs, however, in that before any evaluation takes place the number of grading levels (i.e. levels with a monetary differential) and the criteria for determining the type of work and responsibility to meet these levels, are defined.

It is usual in this method to select one or two jobs which are typical of the stated work and responsibilities of each grading level. For these 'benchmark' jobs, job descriptions are prepared showing the duties, responsibilities and requirements necessary to fulfil them to an acceptable level of performance. It is important that the jobs so chosen are readily identifiable and universally accepted as worthy of a higher grade than jobs in the grade below. The other jobs under review are then compared with these benchmark jobs and slotted into the grading structure.

Non-analytical methods are simple and relatively inexpensive to apply and administer. However, there are difficulties. With the first two ranking methods, maintenance and control of the results is often difficult because the method used is dependent upon the assessors' detailed, personal knowledge of the job. To help overcome this it is essential to prepare job descriptions, even though it is time-consuming and expensive. On the other hand, where ranking is carried out by management and representatives of the job incumbents, judgements and values about the jobs are built into the system which help it to be accepted.

In the case of job grading, the broad levels cause practical problems. Frequently jobs are found to have certain features which fit more than one level, leading to inconsistencies in the final classification. As in the ranking methods, job grading often lacks sufficient analysis to be able to respond to changes in job content quickly and accurately. This leads to the real danger of upgrading jobs for minor additions to the task. If this goes unchecked, it will lead to an imbalance in the grading structure. In all cases, therefore, unless applied to a limited range of work these results can often prove unsatisfactory.

Analytical methods

Factor comparison
This method examines jobs in the light of the selected factors of which they are considered to be composed. For workers five factors are normally used to represent job content:

1. Mental requirements.
2. Physical requirements.
3. Responsibility.
4. Skill requirements.
5. Working conditions.

The first step is to prepare job descriptions. Benchmark jobs are then chosen on the basis that they are capable of clear description and analysis in terms of the factors chosen, they display a sufficient range of variation under each factor, and their wage rates are considered to be representative and equitable in relation to one another. These jobs are analysed against each of these factors in order to prepare a ranking list of jobs under each factor (see the example in Tables 15.1 and 15.2), thus showing the relative importance of each factor in each job.

The next step is to establish what percentage of the current wage is paid for each factor. Once determined, the money equivalent is calculated. This then leads to the development of a scale of payments for each factor showing the money range by value, with the benchmark jobs spread through the range.

The final part of the procedure is to assess all other jobs, factor by factor, against this scale. The sum of the individual factor values is the pay rate for the job. It is useful to check these aggregate values with the benchmark jobs and also to use one of the non-analytical methods described earlier as an overall check.

Table 15.1 Twelve jobs shown in rank under each factor as one step in the factor comparison method

Rank			Common factors		
	Mental requirements	*Physical requirements*	*Responsibility*	*Skill requirements*	*Working conditions*
1	Labourer	Industrial chemist	Labourer	Labourer	Industrial chemist
2	Warehouseman	Security	Warehouseman	Warehouseman	Security
3	Fork-lift driver	Assembler	Assembler	Security	Assembler
4	Assembler	Moulder	Fork-lift driver	Assembler	Storekeeper
5	Storekeeper	Fork-lift driver	Moulder	Fork-lift driver	Fork-lift driver
6	Security	Storekeeper	Storekeeper	Storekeeper	Moulder
7	Raw material mixer	Toolmaker	Security	Raw material mixer	Labourer
8	Moulder	Machine setter	Raw material mixer	Moulder	Raw material mixer
9	Machine setter	Maintenance fitter	Maintenance fitter	Machine setter	Warehouseman
10	Maintenance fitter	Warehouseman	Machine setter	Maintenance fitter	Machine setter
11	Toolmaker	Raw material mixer	Toolmaker	Industrial chemist	Toolmaker
12	Industrial chemist	Labourer	Industrial chemist	Toolmaker	Maintenance fitter

Table 15.2 Ten jobs relating to a service business shown in rank under each factor as one step in the factor comparison method

Rank			Common factors		
	Mental requirements	*Physical requirements*	*Responsibility*	*Skill requirements*	*Worker conditions*
1	Cleaner	Consultant	Cleaner	Cleaner	Consultant
2	Copy typist	section leader	Copy typist	Telephonist	Personal assistant
3	Clerk	Personal assistant	Telephonist	Copy typist	Secretary
4	Telephonist	Secretary	Clerk	Clerk	Section leader
5	Receptionist	Clerk	Receptionist	Receptionist	Receptionist
6	Secretary	Information analyst	Secretary	Personal assistant	Information analyst
7	Information analyst	Receptionist	Personal assistant	Secretary	Clerk
8	Personal assistant	Telephonist	Information analyst	Information analyst	Copy typist
9	Section leader	Copy typist	Section leader	Section leader	Telephonist
10	Consultant	Cleaner	Consultant	Consultant	Cleaner

Points rating

The points rating method is devised to achieve a higher level of accuracy by a more systematic and detailed approach to evaluation than used in other methods. Here, each job is broken down into component factors and characteristics which are evaluated separately. These factors and characteristics vary widely to reflect the nature of the work being evaluated.[4]

Job descriptions are prepared. The five specific job factors normally used are: skill requirements, range of work, physical and psychological demands, responsibilities, and working conditions. These factors do not form the basis of the system, unlike those factors chosen in the factor comparison method. Instead they serve as headings, and beneath each heading a range of characteristics common to the jobs under review are chosen. For instance, under skill requirements the characteristics often used are education, training, experience and communication. Then within each of these characteristics the degree to which that characteristic is required to do the job is assessed. To do this, five or six levels are normally used. For example, in the characteristic 'education', the degree definitions may range from 'no education required' through to 'using ingenuity and originality to solve complicated problems' (see Figure 15.2). Points for each degree, within each characteristic, are then awarded.

Each job is now analysed against each characteristic, and the degree of that characteristic needed to do a job is assessed. The relevant points are awarded, and the total for each job is calculated. Jobs are then listed in decreasing order of total points and a grading structure is established. The NBPI and BIM reports both indicated that this was the most popular job evaluation method in the UK, with about 50 per cent of all companies who use job evaluation adopting this approach.[5]

A more recent report (1983) confirmed the importance of the points rating method of job evaluation.[6] It also highlighted the prominence within manufacturing and service businesses of the 'guide chart profile' method which is described below under its full title of Hay Guide Chart Profile Method. (This method too is based on points rating principles thus clearly indicating the popularity of this basic method in terms of current applications of job evaluation.)

Other methods

In addition to the analytical approaches described above there are several proprietary methods which have been developed by consultancy companies. The principal ones are now briefly described:

1. *Hay/MSL*. This method (based on points rating principles) is known as the Hay Guide Chart Profile Method and is devised and developed primarily for executives, administrative and technical staff. In the past few years it has been extended to cover blue-collar and clerical workers. When used to evaluate jobs in the latter categories, three factors are used — know-how, problem-solving and results of work (when using this method for executive, administrative and

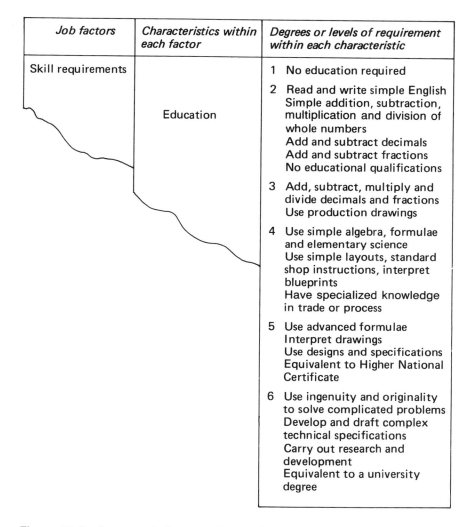

Job factors	Characteristics within each factor	Degrees or levels of requirement within each characteristic
Skill requirements	Education	1 No education required
		2 Read and write simple English Simple addition, subtraction, multiplication and division of whole numbers Add and subtract decimals Add and subtract fractions No educational qualifications
		3 Add, subtract, multiply and divide decimals and fractions Use production drawings
		4 Use simple algebra, formulae and elementary science Use simple layouts, standard shop instructions, interpret blueprints Have specialized knowledge in trade or process
		5 Use advanced formulae Interpret drawings Use designs and specifications Equivalent to Higher National Certificate
		6 Use ingenuity and originality to solve complicated problems Develop and draft complex technical specifications Carry out research and development Equivalent to a university degree

Figure 15.2 An example for one characteristic of the skill requirement factor showing the different degrees of requirement.

technical grades this latter factor is re-named 'accountability'). In addition, there is the opportunity to use a fourth factor — 'abnormal physical conditions'. Since all participating companies use the same system of points rating, results can be compared.

2. *Inbucon.* The Direct Consensus Method was developed by Inbucon in 1968. This approach builds on paired comparisons for smaller organizations and factor comparison (the so-called factor plan) for larger organizations.

Table 15.3 A synopsis of some proprietary and in-house job evaluation schemes applied to blue- and white-collar workers[7]

Major proprietary method or 'home-grown' scheme used	Application	
	Company	*Synopsis of blue-collar applications*
Price Waterhouse Urwick	United Biscuits — food and biscuit companies. Original application made in 1970	The profit method was used as the basis for blue-collar grading structures in multi-site operations. Since the initial application, the scheme has been maintained by in-house steering groups and evaluators. 11,500 people covered (1985) involving 80 broad job categories with seven grades
In-house scheme based on points weighting	Undisclosed UK company, south east. Original application made in 1978	An in-house scheme covering 140 weekly paid employees in the aerospace/defence systems and industrial product divisions of the company. It is a points-based system using eleven factors within the groupings of skill effort, responsibility and job conditions. Each individual factor is classified according to five degrees, with each of the eleven factors being specified and weighted from a total of 100 points. Each job is assessed against each factor. The initial six grades were increased to seven in 1983
Inbucon	British Airport Authority — all seven airports. Original application made in 1978	All operatives' jobs (excluding craftsmen, technicians and white-collar employees) were evaluated involving about 3,000 staff on 7 sites. A six-grade structure covering 80 jobs with 37 of these used as benchmarks. At the time of implementation, the entire evaluation committee comprised union representatives

3. *PA*. The method of developing a job evaluation system used by PA is a points rating method with factor weights determined by means of paired comparisons. Each scheme is developed to meet the individual company's needs as regards the selection and weighting of factors and the definition of factor degrees.

4. *Price Waterhouse Urwick*. The Profile Method, as it is known, was developed in the 1960s by Urwick Orr & Partners which merged with Price Waterhouse in 1984. Based on the points rating method it may be used for all types of job whether separately or in a single scheme.

5. *Wyatt*. A variation of the points rating approach, the Employee Points Factor Comparison Method was developed by Wyatt, Harris, Graham (now Wyatt Company UK Ltd). It is essentially a factor-based points rating scheme which incorporates some features of the profile method.

Table 15.3 *continued*

Major proprietary method or 'home-grown' scheme used	Application	
	Company	Synopsis of blue-collar applications
PA	The Boots Company — seven major sites. Original application made in 1979	Covering about 5,400 employees in the warehouse, production and associated areas for seven sites. The scheme identified ten relevant factors with each of the 1,100 jobs assessed against 5 or 6 levels within each factor. Each factor carries a weighting to reflect its relative importance and value. Eight grades were established based on 94 benchmark jobs
In-house scheme based on 10 factors with agreed weights ranging from 34 to 140 maximum points and totalling 1,000	Continental Can Co. (UK) Ltd, Wrexham plant. Original application made in 1980	An integrated scheme with production and clerical workers on the same grades — see Table 15.4. Provides for a single status, flexible workforce and covers 230 employees of whom 185 are in the production function. A nine-grade structure, all employees (with the exception of some senior managers) are on the same salary structure, holiday, sick pay and pension schemes
Hay/MSL (including the fourth optional factor 'abnormal physical conditions')	Pilkington, Greengate Wales, St Helens, UK. Original application made in 1982	New plant, flexible work force. Application involving ten grades covering 52 different office and factory jobs for 387 employees. Harmonized remuneration system with employees involved having the same conditions of service and all being monthly salaried. Joint review of management evaluation

6. *Arthur Young.* The Decision Board Method was originally designed by Professor T.T. Paterson and further developed by management consultants Arthur Young. Its use for blue-collar workers is not widespread. The scheme is built around six decision bands which reflect the premise that the value of the job depends upon its decision-making requirements. The method is based on the classification of jobs according to the six bands spanning the spectrum of decisions required to be made within a particular organization. Each band (except the top) is a derivative of the band above.

In addition to providing a comprehensive review of the job evaluation methods used in the blue-collar applications, an Incomes Data Services study gives examples of their application including a brief synopsis of the issues involved and approaches used in a number of different organizations.[7] A summary is provided as Table 15.3.

Grading structure

When the jobs under review have been evaluated by using one or more of the methods described in the previous sections, they are arranged in order of progression similar to the example provided as Table 15.4.[8] A glance at the details in the table will show how Continental Can involved a job evaluation approach which integrated 'blue' and 'white collar' jobs within the same scheme. A synopsis of this application is provided as part of Table 15.3.

The money scale

The final step in this procedure is to relate the grade to a money scale. As stated earlier in the chapter it is not intended to cover this aspect here; suffice to say that it is important that an organization keeps these apart in order that a clear distinction is maintained between these two facets of the total procedure.

Drawbacks to using job evaluation

Just as there are arguments favouring the introduction of job evaluation, there are also drawbacks. Some of these concern the mechanics of using these methods to help establish a pay structure whilst others concern the suitability of this approach to meet the overall requirements of an organization.

1. *Mechanics.* The two principal drawbacks experienced within this category concern the difficulty in choosing relevant factors and changes brought about by investments in technology.

The 'relevant factors' problem manifests itself, for example, where schemes are designed to embrace both blue- and white-collar workers. In some instances, factors particularly relevant to the former group (e.g. difficult working conditions and physical effort) may be inappropriate to the latter and vice versa. A review of Tables 15.1 and 15.2 illustrates this point: here, it is difficult to relate these two factors to several of the non-manual jobs included in the examples. This often leads to different combinations of factors being used resulting in a less coherent system within an organization than intended.

Organizations regularly investing in relevant, new technologies and process improvements will often find that the facets of an existing job evaluation scheme becomes unfocused requiring (often major) revisions.

2. *Suitability.* Organizations may find this approach to structuring pay less appropriate where trends are towards working groups and flexibility, and also where maintaining the system is difficult in itself and costly in practice.

Where a company has or is contemplating a form of group working, job evaluation may prove inappropriate. On the one hand there are no 'individual jobs' to evaluate, whilst on the other the tasks carried out by individuals in a group

Table 15.4 The grading structure based on an integrated job evaluation scheme adopted by Continental Can Co. (UK) Ltd at its Wrexham plant

Occupational grade structure	
Grade	*Job title*
A	Juniors Re-workers Temporary employees
B	Janitor/driver Receptionist/typist
C	Accounts clerk Clerk distribution/sales Clerk production control Operator Stores controller
D	QA inspector Secretary
E 1	Trainee production maintainer
E 2	Assistant buyer Electrician Fitter maintainer Production maintainer Tooling inspector
E 3	Lead maintainer
F	Account/supervisor Buyer Customer service engineer Personnel training/safety officer
G	Shift superintendent
H	Project engineer Shift manager
I	Electrical engineer Mechanical engineer

Note: job titles are shown in alphabetical order within each grade.
Reproduced with permission.

may relate to their particular skills, aptitude and experience. When an individual leaves, the replacement may not have the same qualities thereby necessitating a change in job content, new job descriptions and subsequent re-evaluations.

Related to the last point is the inflexibility feature which is sometimes associated with the principle of job evaluation. Where requirements change, a pay structure based on this method may prove insufficiently responsive. This in turn may result in a situation where the required level of movement is slow and restrictive or where short-term, *ad hoc* decisions are made for reasons of expediency.

Where the level of change is high, companies find that the system support costs are significant and/or the scheme operates in unacceptable, out-of-date conditions. These concern mainly the maintenance of the scheme coupled with increasing difficulties of a system where the instances of appropriate upward regrading are not matched by appropriate downward reviews.

Skill-based evaluation: paying for knowledge

The use of job evaluation as a measure of assessing the relative worth of a job supports a company's decision to use the job rather than the person as the basis for establishing the rate of pay. As explained in the previous section, job evaluation enables companies to determine the basis for establishing how much a job is worth and then to set a range of pay that an individual can get for performing that job. It also discusses some of the inherent problems associated with this approach and the internal and external pressures which are exposing these inadequacies in certain situations. Whilst some companies have purposefully reduced the impact of these effects, others have opted for approaches more suited to their requirements.

One option is paying for the skills people have. Skill-based evaluation is built on the premise that individuals should be paid for their skills and not the job they do. It uses the following approach:

1. Identify those skills that the business needs in order to provide its products/ services.
2. Determine the skills necessary to perform those tasks.
3. Establish tests and measures to evaluate whether an individual has learned and is able to perform core skills in terms of the jobs to be completed.
4. Pay an individual based on those skills that the organization needs and that they are currently able and willing to use.

The skills-based approach offers a number of advantages including:

1. Skills can be measured by the simpler and more practical method of tasks. This is considered a more accurate means than the peer assessment approaches used in job evaluation.
2. Flexibility to cover the longer-term changes in product/service mix or to facilitate scheduling to cover absenteeism, material shortage, employee turnover, training or responding to customer requirements.

3. There is increased commitment to organizational effectiveness through a broader appreciation of the whole business and its changing needs.
4. It reinforces participation.
5. It increases the opportunity for employees to undertake responsibility for the planning and evaluating aspects of work highlighted in Chapter 14.
6. It provides a means of reducing the number of existing job classifications within a company.

On the other hand there are also a number of disadvantages to the skills-based approach, including:

1. It generates higher average payments than traditional schemes as it encourages people to become 'more valuable' to the organization.
2. Training costs increase, including the provision of testing arrangements.
3. It makes pay comparisons with other organizations more difficult to arrange.
4. It creates administrative difficulties in terms of the increased frequency of pay changes, the maintenance of skill levels over time and legislating for obsolescent skills.

Although the number of skill-based applications is small (5 per cent according to a survey in the USA)[10] the growth in this approach has its roots in the movement towards management styles based on higher involvement. This is illustrated by a national survey conducted by the American Productivity Center which showed that 68 per cent of the reported 'pay for knowledge' applications had taken place since 1980.[11] For this reason too the most prominent examples are found in new plant applications based upon a more participative management culture. Moreover, the approach has been predominantly used at the operator level. However, given the current support for higher involvement structures then one way of reducing the limited upward progression for people which is inherent in this approach is to provide horizontal (as opposed to vertical) progression as a relevant means of providing job satisfaction, meeting business needs and providing a meaningful reward system.

Lastly, although the number of applications is small,[12] the participants' view of the impact on performance of 'pay for knowledge' schemes recorded an overall rating of 89% — higher than any other 'non-traditional'[13] reward system.[14] In addition, one reported feature in UK applications concerns the reduced incidence of job and pay-related disputes.

Overtime payments

The most important aspect of overtime is the control of premium time (i.e. that part of the payment for which no work is generated). It is useful to record this separately with a budget and then compare actual with budget. Premium time uplifts (e.g. time-and-a-third, time-and-a-half and double-time) are normally well established by agreements within an organization.

The reasons for choosing overtime as a way of increasing capacity are more fully discussed in Chapter 6.

Bonus payments

Bonus payments relate in the context of this section to the extra payments derived from a financial incentive scheme. (Gain sharing and profit-sharing schemes are dealt with on pp. 487–92.) Broadly speaking, financial incentive schemes are methods of encouraging people to increase their willingness to work (i.e. to use their capacity to work to the fullest extent) and reward this with a financial payment.

People's capacity to work can be increased through factors largely outside their control (e.g. improved equipment, better organization of work and improved methods) as well as by factors within their control, such as increases in:

1. The skill and effectiveness in doing the task.
2. The rate of working.
3. The amount of time spent working at the task.

It is important to realize that although some overall improvement can result from the first two, the largest increases will be derived from the third factor. It is getting a person to work more of the time that will bring with it the significant increases in labour productivity. The principle of incentives is to induce this situation by relating some part of earnings to an index over which a person has control. That person then acts to move the index upwards so as to increase earnings. If it is to be effective, then management will need to:

1. Determine the measure of influence that it seeks over the index.
2. Set appropriate objectives for the scheme.
3. Select the indices by which achievement is to be measured.
4. Enable people to achieve the level of job performance that they are capable of achieving, if they so desire.
5. Maintain and develop the system to ensure that the objectives are met and appropriate opportunities are provided.

For people who are paid partly under this type of system, the more they can influence or affect their position on the index then the greater is the inducement.

The reasons supporting financial incentive systems are that: people will tend to increase their productivity when paid incentives; it enables an organization to pay higher wages without increased unit costs, and it leads to a situation where the benefits of increased productivity and efficiency can be shared.

Support for the view that incentive schemes increase the levels of productivity achieved was provided by Flykt who studied a number of small Swedish industrial businesses with fifty or more employees.[15] His results are given as Figures 15.3–15.5 and support the claim made by many companies that when they change the pay system from one incorporating an incentive element to a fixed-rate scheme there is a fall-off in productivity of some 10–15 per cent.

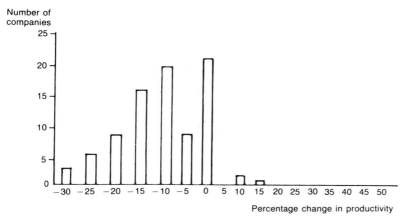

Note: the average value (−9.2) has been affected by a large group of companies which scored 0. Most of these have scored 0 because they do not now have any kind of follow-up to productivity change, and in reality may belong to the 'don't know' group

Figure 15.3   Number of companies reporting various levels of productivity change when going from an incentive to a fixed wage system (sample size = 82). With permission.

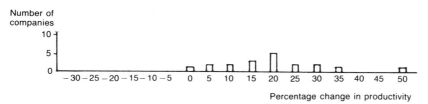

Figure 15.4   Number of companies reporting various percentage changes in productivity when going from a fixed wage to an incentive scheme (sample size = 19). With permission.

General aspects of bonus payments

Work-study-based incentive schemes

Work-study-based incentive schemes are sometimes confused with piecework. There are several major differences, as shown in Table 15.5. With piecework the payment (known as the piecework price) is usually fixed at the local level by rate-fixers, who negotiated the rate with the union or operatives concerned.

Group or individual schemes

Whilst both group and individual schemes have their place, it is important to bear in mind that the smaller the group the more effective the incentive scheme tends

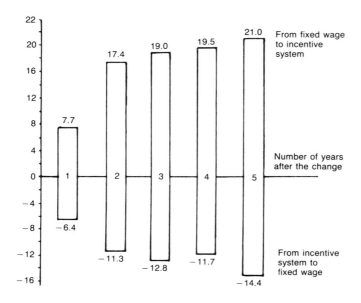

Figure 15.5 Average change in productivity for differing numbers of years after the change of scheme. With permission.

Table 15.5 Differences between piecework and work-study-based incentive schemes

Aspect	Piecework	Work-study-based incentive schemes
Unit of work established by	Rate-fixer, largely subjective	Work study, largely objective
Work method	Existing method accepted	Method study used and the best method established
Change of time standard	Can be changed each time the job is done	Value can only be changed in stated circumstances
Waiting time and breakdowns	Ignored	Allowed for
Rest allowance and personal needs	Allowed for, but arbitrarily	Allowed for, using an agreed table of rest allowances
Irregular occasional elements and contingencies	Ignored	Allowed for on a calculated basis

to be. Consequently, the ideal number is one. Other than the plantwide schemes described later in the chapter, all other schemes can be used for groups or individuals. Some factors influencing this choice are:

1. Individual schemes usually result in higher productivity. By giving a greater direct incentive, individuals are encouraged to work at their own optimum level. In groups, the faster people will often reduce their effort, for they are not prepared to 'carry' the slower members of the group.
2. Group schemes may result in disagreement within the group for reasons similar to those explained in 1 above.
3. Group schemes should be used where the work of individuals is not clearly identified or people work as a team.
4. Group schemes should be used for people performing indirect activities. This is usually because such activities relate to a number of performance factors and each individual's contribution to those factors is difficult to calculate.[16]

Structural factors

Several factors should be considered in the choice of payment systems:

1. It is important to link the nature of the operations process with the system used to reward those who are working within that process. For instance, an organization which sells a service designed to meet a customer's specific and individual requirements should not introduce a system of direct incentives related to the number of service requests which are provided. Thus, rewards and measurement must be compatible and results orientated.
2. Safeguards against quality deterioration must be built into the scheme. To place people in the ambivalent position of the output/quality dilemma is structurally unsound.
3. If there is fluctuation in the workload, then a scheme geared to output achievement has inherent problems. Where there are seasonal fluctuations, incentive schemes which are only used in the peak demand times and not during the remainder of the year, have been introduced to resolve this problem.
4. The ease or difficulty of measuring work output. If it is difficult to measure the work content, then schemes based on the time it takes to complete a task are normally inappropriate.
5. In some jobs, it is necessary that the measurements cover creativity in order not to discourage that essential part of the role.
6. Schemes need to be structured so as to facilitate future changes as part of the necessary realignment procedure.

Other aspects

1. The scheme must be designed in such a way, that those being paid under the scheme can understand how it works.

2. The scheme administration must be agreed and should include the procedure for answering queries.
3. Those parts of the scheme to cover aspects such as waiting time and unmeasured work must be determined at the outset.
4. The scheme design must minimize manipulation.

Incentive payments[17]

There are two systems of payment to be used when using the $0-100$ rating scale:

1. Payment on standard minutes (SMs) per hour.
2. Payment per SM.

Payment on standard minutes (SMs) per hour

Here the work is evaluated in SMs. If a person completes x number of task A and y number of task B, then the SMs for tasks A and B are multiplied by x and y respectively. This would give the total SMs of work achieved in the period under review. These total SMs are then divided by the time on measured work to give a ratio of SMs per hour. The time on measured work equals attendance time less any lost time, waiting time or time on unmeasured work. It is important to determine whether an 'in lieu' performance is given on these latter aspects (see (3) above), and then to agree how these are fitted into this calculation.

Tables are established to convert SMs per hour into bonus per hour on measured time (see Table 15.6). The relevant bonus rate is then multiplied by the number of hours on measured work to give the bonus payment for the period. This system is simple to understand and is the most common scheme used in work study based incentive schemes. The starting point for bonus payments can be fixed at any level of performance.

Table 15.7 (in conjunction with Table 15.6) provides an example of how a typical scheme would be applied and how a bonus payment would be calculated. Using

Table 15.6 Part of a bonus table for a straight-line proportional scheme

SMs/hour	Bonus pence/hour		Equivalent performance 0–100 scale
56	50		93
57	54		95
58	58		97
59	62		98
60	66	(standard performance)	100
61	70		102
62	74		103

Table 15.7 Typical bonus payment calculation

Products/services completed in week 9		SMs/unit	Total SMs produced
Product reference	Quantity		
110	10	16.0	160
125	4	25.0	100
016c	120	10.5	1,260
142	2	60.0	120
206	1	45.0	45
115	10	30.0	300
170	20	17.5	350
			2,335

$$\frac{2{,}335 \text{ SMs}}{60} = 38.92 \text{ standard hours}$$

$$\frac{\text{Standard hours produced}}{\text{Clocked hours}} \times 100 = \frac{38.92}{41.00} \times 100 = 95$$

Source: Terry Hill, *Small Business: Production/operations management* (Basingstoke: Macmillan, 1985), p. 169.

Table 15.6, the person to whom the calculation relates would receive a bonus payment of:

(The number of hours worked) × (bonus pence/hr relating to the average performance achieved throughout the period)

= 41 hr × 0.54 pence/hr
= £22.14

Payment per SM

This is similar in principle to piecework but with output measured in SMs rather than units. A rate per SM is established by negotiation, and work done in the period is evaluated to give the total SMs. The total SMs is converted into pay using the rate per SM.

This system is not used frequently, although it is common in certain industries, e.g. the footwear industry.

The development of work study-based incentive schemes

Earlier this century the two basic ways of paying a person for the work completed were:

1. Time rate — this applies to people who are hourly paid.
2. Piecework — in its simplest form, this refers to a scheme where rewards are based on a specified price per unit or piece of acceptable work produced regardless of the time taken. As shown in Table 15.8, nil output means no pay. This method is still often used with outworkers (people who work in their own homes).

Each of these has advantages and disadvantages which are also summarized in Table 15.8. It can be seen from this simple representation that the payment systems were providing an opposite mix of advantages and disadvantages. From these two basic systems, a hybrid was developed which combined some of the advantages of both methods as shown in Figure 15.6. Point A represents the rate of payment for any level of output or performance from zero up to point B on the horizontal axis. At point B, the rate of payment increases, as shown by the graph. On the basis of this hybrid, several further developments have taken place, as listed below.

Table 15.8   Time rate and piecework systems compared

Type of payment system	*Graphical representation*	*For the person being paird by this system the main*	
		Advantages	*Disadvantages*
Time rate	Pay ⌐ Output	Stable pay	Does not reflect the person's effort
Piecework	Pay ◿ Output	Reflects the person's effort	Instability of pay

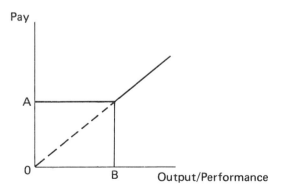

Figure 15.6   The hybrid system of payment.

Straight-line proportional schemes. In these systems, bonus earnings are directly proportional to the results achieved, subject to meeting the bonus starting point. Figure 15.7 and Tables 15.6, 15.7 and 15.9 represent, or are parts of, typical schemes. Table 15.6 shows that for every performance point increase after point B, the increase in the rate of payment is the same — hence the term straight-line

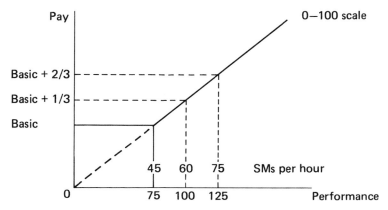

Figure 15.7 Typical straight-line proportional scheme.

Table 15.9 Typical points on a straight-line proportional scheme on a 0−100 scale

	Pay rate		*Performance level*	*SMs earned per hour*
Basic	Usually equates to 75 performance	75	That performance level expected of a person not working on an incentive scheme. Sometimes called day rate	45
Basic + $\frac{1}{3}$	The level of pay made up of basic for achieving 75 performance and $\frac{1}{3}$ of basic for achieving standard performance	100	Standard performance for which an agreed bonus rate per hour is paid. The increase in bonus rate per hour will be the same for each increase in performance from 76 to 100	60
Basic + $\frac{2}{3}$	The level of pay made up of basic for achieving 75 performance and $\frac{2}{3}$ of basic for achieving a 125 performance	125	Performance well above the average. Very fast	75

proportional. Similarly, Figure 15.7 shows typical points on a scheme of this type which are further amplified in Table 15.9. Table 15.8 illustrated a bonus calculation typical of this type of scheme. These are datum points and a person achieving a performance level from 76 to 125 or beyond would earn the level of bonus payment for that performance (see Table 15.6 as a part example and Table 15.7 as a worked example).

Gearing. In straight-line proportional schemes, the angle of the line from the performance point at which bonus earnings start is such that it would give zero pay at zero performance (see Figures 15.6 and 15.7). In geared schemes this is not so. The bonus follows a straight line but the angle is changed as shown by *a* and *b* in Figure 15.8. Examples of schemes based on the principle illustrated by *b* are the Bedaux (75/25) and the Halsey (50/50) schemes neither of which are used extensively any more in the UK.[18]

Progressive and regressive schemes. Whereas gearing is a change in the amount of bonus paid per increase in performance at a constant rate, progressive and regressive schemes move away from the principle of a straight-line relationship between an increase in performance and the amount of bonus earned.

In a progressive scheme, the rate of change in earnings rises as the results achieved rise; in a regressive scheme, the rate decreases, as the results achieved rise (see Figure 15.9).

Progressive schemes are not often used. They are constructed to encourage output and should be used only where the required quality cannot be affected by higher output levels (for example, where the manufacturing cycle is machine controlled). Regressive schemes are more widely used and have the following advantages:

1. They protect quality standards by discouraging high output levels by paying less bonus per increase in performance as output rises.

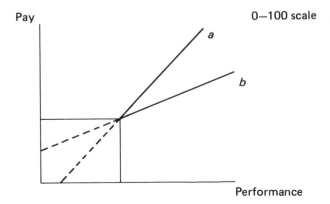

Figure 15.8   Gearing.

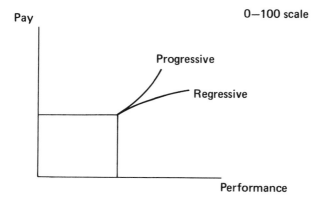

Figure 15.9 Progressive and regressive schemes.

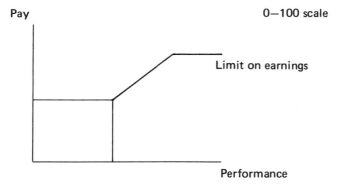

Figure 15.10 Limit on bonus earnings.

2. They stop bonus earnings from becoming very high which could happen in both progressive and straight-line proportional schemes.
3. They protect from exploitation those schemes with a significant proportion of loose time (i.e. where the issued standard time has proved to be too high or where method changes have reduced the work content but a new standard has not been developed). A well-known regressive scheme is the Rowan scheme but this is no longer in wide use in the UK.[18]

Bonus earnings limit. Another development used with incentive schemes is to fix a top level of earnings as shown in Figure 15.10. This is a usual development with a straight-line proportional scheme and the ceiling is often placed at a 125 performance (Table 15.9). Whilst this has the inherent advantage of encouraging increases in performance to a desired maximum level, the ceiling also introduces the types of advantage which go with regressive schemes, as explained above.

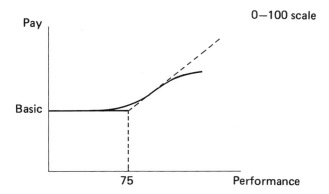

Figure 15.11   S-shaped bonus curve.

S-shaped bonus curves. Many further developments could be made by changing the path and angle of the graph. The important consideration is that any such development should be purposeful and simple to understand by all concerned. One such scheme is the S-shaped curve. Using the straight-line proportional scheme as a comparison, Figure 15.11 illustrates this type of scheme. Here the bonus earnings start earlier than a 75 performance, have the straight-line properties in the middle band of performance achievement and regressive qualities at the top end. This flattening of the earnings curve is one form of stabilizer — others are mentioned on p. 485. It can be used to encourage people on this scheme to increase their performance (the overriding aim of all incentive schemes) by paying them a bonus at a lower level of performance and is often used, therefore, in the following circumstances:

1. In the initial period after a bonus scheme has been applied (usually for a stated period of, say, three months).
2. Where the nature of the work varies because of unpredictable changes in working conditions or materials.
3. Where study work would be uneconomic leading to values of lower consistency and lower accuracy being used. In such a situation, this flattening of earnings reduces potential fluctuations.

Further developments

The bonus content has been and, in many situations still is, a significant percentage of total gross pay. This has presented those people who are paid by such a system with the problem of a fluctuating gross pay in a social climate where stability of pay is becoming more important because of increased regular expenditure commitments. Consequently, a series of developments has followed, including:

1. *Extend the bonus calculation period*. This has the result of averaging out the bonus fluctuations which arise in the shorter period (e.g. weekly as opposed to daily bonus calculation).
2. *Moving average*. The bonus is calculated as a moving average over a previous period thereby evening out shorter-term fluctuations.
3. *Consolidated time rate*. This development raises the level of payment below which a person's wage cannot fall by making a portion of the bonus payment guaranteed. Thus, part of the bonus payment is consolidated into a new rate which comprises the basic payment plus a part of the bonus payment.

However, whilst these developments help to reduce the level of instability in pay there is still the possibility of wide differences in payment from week to week. To reduce the instability/reflection of effort mix still further, other developments have taken place. In each instance, it is assumed that existing work-study-based incentive schemes, and the time standards on which they are based, exist in an organization. If they do not, then these have to be developed and the starting point in the first two examples below has to be agreed in a more arbitrary way.

Measured day-work

The main element of measured day-work is stabilized payment where the incentive element is compounded with the basic rate, thereby achieving a less fluctuating weekly wage. Under this scheme, hourly rates are set for each task through work study, and bonus tables, based upon performance, are established in the normal way. Employees then contract to work consistently at a specified level (usually their average performance over the previous, say, three month period; note that this development best follows a previous incentive scheme) over the agreed review period (usually three to six months). Actual performance is monitored and fed back to each person on a regular basis. Irrespective of actual performance, the person will be paid at the contracted performance level agreed at the beginning of the period. At the end of this contracted period, the new payment level, on which the next period's contract is based, is the average performance of the period just finished.

As far as those persons being paid under this system are concerned, measured day work provides stable and easily calculable earnings. However, it is often found that it incorporates too little opportunity to influence pay levels, and the length of period chosen is such that the person feels unable to influence average performance (i.e. the next period's pay performance). For this reason, some organizations prefer graded measured day work.

Graded measured day-work

In graded measured day-work, the performance levels are divided into a range of 5 or 10 points. For example, 90–94, 95–99, 100–104 and so on. At the start of the scheme each person is placed on this scale at the point which equates to their average performance over an agreed period (e.g. the previous three months). Rules governing the schemes allow a person to move up one level if they achieve a weekly performance in excess of their current pay band in, for example, two consecutive weeks. Conversely, if a person achieves a performance less than their current pay band for a number of consecutive weeks (e.g. three consecutive) then that person will be paid in the following week at a pay band lower than at present. The rules usually encourage upward movement as implied by the two and three consecutive week rules suggested above, and will cover situations where people may 'pull out' a good week to prevent themselves dropping a pay band.

This development, therefore, allows staff to influence their rate of payment in the short-term yet prevents fluctuations in pay due to factors outside their control. It is important, as mentioned earlier, to establish rules to cover aspects of manipulation and to include the code of discipline which would be followed.

High day rate

In high day rate schemes, fixed hourly rates for a job are established. These rates are comparable to gross payments comprising basic and incentive payments, hence the term 'high'. In instances where high day rates follow incentive schemes, the level of payment will tend to be that equal to standard performance.

As high day rate does not assist in stimulating or motivating employees to achieve desired standards of performance, it is entirely management's responsibility to secure an acceptable level of output and labour cost. To the person being paid by this method, the system offers stable, high earnings through an easily understood system. It is essential, however, that output targets are known, and the consequences of failure to meet these levels are understood and agreed by all concerned and then implemented by management.

As with measured and graded measured daywork systems, it is necessary that the organization should employ proper procedures of work measurement and labour cost controls, and should not assume that the administration and support costs will be any less than with more direct schemes.

Special payments

These can take a number of different forms. Some of the more usual ones are:

- Dirty money — an additional hourly payment to compensate people for working in worse than normal conditions.
- Danger money — similar to dirty money, this is an additional hourly payment to compensate people when working in dangerous conditions.
- Shift payments — given to compensate for the disturbance of working on shifts, which start and finish at odd hours. Shift starting times of 6.00 a.m., 2.00 p.m. and 10.00 p.m. are common examples.
- Unsocial hours — based on the rationale for shift payments, these would cover both regular and irregular working conditions especially those occurring in service businesses.

Less traditional forms of payment/remuneration

The emphasis given to various approaches to developing appropriate payment structures within the chapter has been made within the context of remuneration in its wider sense. This section aims to broaden this review through highlighting less traditional approaches to payment together with relevant non-payment features.

Merit assessment

Merit assessment concerns the systematic and regular review of an individual's performance against predetermined criteria, the results of which will form an agreed part of each person's pay. Although trade unions (particularly those representing blue-collar workers) have traditionally been, and still are, harshly critical of any form of individually assessed merit pay, a survey revealed an increase in the use of this approach for 'skilled manual workers' from 2 to 24 per cent between 1977 and 1986.[19] A further survey also recognized this trend:

> The growing sophistication in the demands being made on certain groups of manual workers — predominantly but not solely craftworkers — coupled with the trend towards harmonized terms and conditions is prompting increased interest in schemes of performance appraisal for manual employees. Increasingly the outcome of the appraisal process — despite some strongly held views to the contrary — is being linked to the pay and reward system of manual workers.[20]

On the question of trade union suspicions concerning the potential lack of fairness, favouritism and merit assessment's inherently divisive nature, the same survey suggests that the following changes in approach have helped alleviate these misgivings:

1. Union involvement and negotiation on the introduction of these schemes.
2. Open review procedures.
3. Right of individual appeal.

The Industrial Relations Services' 1987 report examines manual workers' appraisal approaches and gives details of several UK applications including BP Chemicals (Barry), Cummins Engines (Darlington, Daventry and Shotts), Digital (Ayr), Duracell (Crawley), Hewlett Packard (Edinburgh), Inmos (South Wales), Johnson and Johnson, Komatsu (North West), Metal Box (Braunstone), National Semiconductors (Greenock), Sanyo (Lowestoft), Shell (Stanlow) and several sites of the Wellcome Foundation. Although the procedures differ, Tables 15.10 and 15.11 give examples of the factors taken into account at Sanyo and details of the review agreement in place within the Wellcome Foundation.[20]

Introduced at the instigation of local UK management, the procedure at Sanyo involves an annual review leading to pay awards of ±0.5% of the annually negotiated pay increase. Although there are some four hundred manual workers employed at Lowestoft there are only three grades: operators, engineers and technicians.

Table 15.10 The factors taken into account in Sanyo's performance assessment procedure, 1986

Factors to be taken into account in each category:		
Personality/attitude	**Skill and knowledge**	**Attendance**
Reliability	Dexterity/speed	Absence
Discipline	Tech/job	Passouts
Initiative	Manager/supervision	Lateness
Co-operation	Creating/planning	
Determination		

Reproduced with permission.

Employees do not have fixed job descriptions but are expected to work flexibly within generally defined areas of responsibility. A glance at Table 15.10 shows how some of the factors chosen within the performance assessment period reflect this feature.

Table 15.11 is provided as an example of a review agreement designed to support the 'principles of harmonization, flexibility and an industrial relations climate which facilitated the acceptance of on-going change'.[21] The report identified these as common factors between the thirteen companies reviewed and summarized them as follows:

1. Largely harmonized terms and conditions for manual workers and staff.
2. Integrated pay structure, providing common or closely related pay grades for manual workers and at least some categories of staff.
3. Regular performance reviews against predetermined criteria, as a result of which individual employees are classified into a series of performance bands.[22]

A development of performance-related pay concerning merit evaluation is used by the Alliance and Leicester Building Society. Each staff member's performance is evaluated by supervisors and managers, and the level is expressed as a percentage from 0 to 200 per cent, where 100 represents the expected level to be aimed for. The factors taken into account are the previous annual appraisal discussion and reports, progress in the job, especially relating to an agreed action plan, and job experience. A performance of between 0 and 85 per cent results in no salary increase for the year, whereas above 100 leads to increases above the norm.

The continued growth in the use of merit assessment is, however, preconditioned by the care which must be exercised in its application. The usefulness of this option to help relate the needs of a business to the role of its workforce (one of its key resources) is obvious. The criteria and their application, however, are not scientifically or objectively based. Great care, therefore, has to be taken to preserve objectivity and the underlying purpose of the scheme and to avoid personal prejudices. If these payments are not used in a discriminatory way, everyone will expect a merit increase and the scheme will fall into disrepute.

Table 15.11 The Wellcome Foundation's industrial staff performance review agreement, 1986

Personnel matters

It is agreed, as part of this agreement, that those employees covered by it will be subject to individual performance reviews (on an annual basis) and remunerated in accordance with the agreed pay structures. Performance standards and the application of agreed criteria will be discussed and developed at local level. Appropriate training will be given to those who will be conducting performance reviews. Employee representatives will also receive similar training.

Performance review

Purpose
The purpose of performance review is to improve and develop the effectiveness of an employee in the job. The assessment of performance, the feedback to individuals of strengths and weaknesses in performance will be a summary of an on-going dialogue through the year. Performance review will not, therefore, take the place of day-to-day discussion, communication or counselling on specific issues, but rather will provide a formal opportunity to assess the overall picture built up during the year. It will relate to the whole job, and to the sum total of all the counselling, coaching, training and other discussions which has taken place during the year.

Performance areas

For the purpose of performance reviews the areas covered will be, where appropriate:
Job knowledge — Skills/knowledge needed to perform various tasks.
Quality of work — Degree to which work is free from error, is neat, accurate, thorough and complies with quality/departmental standards.
Quantity of work — Volume of work regularly produced.
Work behaviour — Tact, courtesy, effort, co-operation as they affect the work performance of self and others.
Attendance/punctuality — Regularity in coming to work and conforming to work hours.

Documentation

To ensure consistency of application the foregoing provisions are incorporated into a standard performance review document.

Performance assessment

There will be a broad statement of performance as a whole. This will be either: 'Meets overall standards' or 'Does not meet overall standards'.

Performance areas will only be commented on when there is a need to demonstrate and confirm specific points. The review, therefore, will not concentrate solely on performance areas. It will be a manager/supervisor's responsibility to define the standards which may be individual or group-centred. The manager/supervisor will also be responsible for ensuring that employees understand what is required of them. A section on the form will provide the opportunity for an employee to record his views. A copy of the review will be given to the employee. A more senior manager must also signify his agreement by signing the form. An employee can appeal against an unsatisfactory performance rating to his more senior manager via the company's appeals procedure.

Reproduced with permission.

Two-tier plans

In two-tier plans, recent employees are not paid at the same rate nor do they receive the same benefits (e.g. holiday entitlement) as others. This scheme is designed to reward loyalty within an organization rather than penalize the new entrant.

Companywide schemes

The principle underlying companywide schemes is that a certain percentage of profit/revenue can be allocated as an entitlement for wages. There are two distinct types of plan:

1. Profit sharing plans which provide an annual bonus or share based on the organization's profit performance. An employee's share could be paid in cash or deferred into a retirement plan.
2. Gain sharing plans which are unitwide bonus systems designed to reward all eligible members for improved performance. Gains are shared according to a single predetermined formula or target.

The two most widely known and used are the Scanlon and the Rucker Plans. Both require the establishment of the labour cost for the entire plant as a ratio, for instance of production value. A plan is then made to share with all workers the savings achieved, usually as a function of their basic rates of pay. Rules are also agreed to cover situations involving changes in prices and wage levels and relevant technological innovations. Normally, an agreed fraction of each period's bonus is paid into a pool to cover times when sales are low. Lastly, joint activities to discuss issues such as productivity, flexibility and cost reduction are instituted. These steps emphasize the participative nature underpinning these systems and the importance of sound communications. There are three major components of a gain sharing plan:

1. A management philosophy which believes that employees have more skills, contributions to make and desire to excel than is currently on offer.
2. A system for increasing the involvement of employees in all aspects of the task.
3. A mechanism to share fairly the gains between the employees and the company.

Neither profit sharing nor gain sharing plans are complete wage payment systems. Thus their effectiveness will, to a degree, depend upon the wage payment system upon which they are superimposed.

The stimulus inherent in a companywide scheme is more towards the short- than longer-term. It is important, therefore, for an organization to guard against the following characteristics in order to maintain the advantages which will accrue from this facet of a total remuneration system:

1. It is not easy for participants to link their individual performance to the global measures on which the plan is based.
2. The basis for calculating payments will be complex and, therefore, the plans will typically be difficult to:
   (a) understand and explain;
   (b) identify with in terms of an individual's contribution to overall improvements;
   (c) assess in terms of calculating the payment to which participants are entitled.
3. With rising payments, the response will be good; with falling payments the difficulty referred to above for individuals to relate their contribution to the situation often brings a lack of response.

For some of these reasons, therefore, companies must recognize the need to develop a plan over time in order to increase and maintain the fit between the objectives, participants' expectations and the outcomes.[23] A major report on American business[24] revealed that the use of both profit and gain sharing plans is increasing whilst other sources provide useful case histories.[25]

Time-off schemes

These schemes are designed to offer time off with pay once an agreed target has been met. Often known as 'job and finish' schemes, they are particularly common in situations where the tasks on hand occur on a periodic cycle (e.g. weekly). In these circumstances, earned time off is the incentive and relates mainly to tasks where additional work (and pay) is not available as an alternative/preferred remuneration arrangement (e.g. a postman delivering letters on a prescribed postal round or similarly a refuse collection crew making weekly pick-ups).

Security of employment

Although somewhat dependent upon the national culture of the workforce under review, the factor of security of employment has had an increasing amount of media exposure in the last few years. In part due to its much publicized use in some Japanese companies, this feature of a remuneration package has been gaining ground outside its traditional areas (e.g. teaching and the civil service).

Summary

A striking growth in the less traditional forms of payment and remuneration was reported in a major American report — see Table 15.12.[26] Furthermore, as Tables

Table 15.12 Use of less traditional reward systems

Type of scheme	Firms (1,598)	
	Number	Percentage
Profit sharing	507	32
Gain sharing	211	23
Two-tier	171	11
Earned time off	101	6

Table 15.13 Growth in less traditional reward systems

Type of scheme	Years in use (%)[a]				
	26+	16–25	11–15	6–10	1–5
Profit sharing	17	17	14	22	30
Gain sharing	3	1	5	18	73
Two-tier	1	1	2	8	88
Earned time off	5	14	9	22	50

[a] Percentage implemented in each period based on *n* responses to this question (*n* is variable).

Source: American Productivity and Quality Center Report (1986), pp. 8–9.

15.12 and 15.13 show, several of these plans not only enjoy high use and steady growth but their adoption has been significantly greater in recent years.

Relationship between incentive payments and labour cost

As explained earlier, incentive payment systems allow management to increase a person's remuneration whilst decreasing labour costs per unit — see Figure 15.12. This is simply because of the following:

Performance	Effect on labour cost
0–75	Labour cost will decrease with each increase in performance due to the fact that 75 performance is the normal fall-back rate.
76–125	The cost per unit will continue to fall but less steeply than previously due to the additional payments. As bonus payments are only a proportion of basic pay then the average cost still falls.
126 or more	The phenomenon described for performance between 76 and 125 would continue. Where 125 performance is a cut-off, then the average labour cost falls away more steeply with performance increases above this cut-off point.

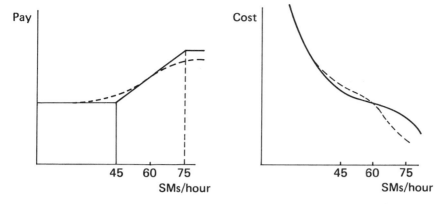

Figure 15.12   The relationship between incentive payments and unit cost.

Notes and references

1. National Board for Prices and Incomes *Report on Job evaluation*, NBPI 83 chapter 3, paras 28 and 31. Note that although 25 per cent of people were covered by job evaluation, these people were employed by only 10 per cent of all establishments included in the survey.
2. Wage drift is defined as 'a rise in the effective rate of pay per unit of labour input that is brought about by arrangements outside the control of the recognized procedure for scheduling wage rates'. See E.H. Phelps-Brown, 'Wage drift', *Economica* (1962), 339–56.
3. K. Bradley, *Job evaluation: theory and practice*, Survey Report no. 46 (London: British Institute of Management, 1979).
4. Examples of factors and characteristics used in points rating systems are given in *Job Evaluation: A practical guide*, (London: British Institute of Management, 1967), appendix 3.
5. The survey results in the 1968 NBPI report (reference 1 above) and the 1979 BIM report (reference 3 above) showed that of the schemes used for all categories of employee, the following were used:

Type of scheme	Percentage of total schemes in use		
	1968 (all)[a]	*1979 (all)[b]*	*1979 (hourly paid employees)[c]*
Points rating	47	51	50
Grading	28	12	—
Job ranking	20	22	20
Factor comparison	5	16	9
Profile (Urwick Orr)	—	7	9
Paired comparison (AIC/Imbucon)	—	12	9
Hay/MSL	—	29	1
Other	—	5	1

[a] Based on some eight hundred companies (about 10 per cent of the eight thousand questionnaires sent out in this study used a job evaluation scheme).

[b] Based on 151 companies. Percentages do not add up to 100 as some companies use more than one scheme.

[c] Based on 70 companies using a scheme for manual employees (referred to here and in the text as hourly paid employees).

6. IR-RR 310 (20 December 1983) gave the following results in terms of the number of employees covered and the number of job titles covered. With permission.

Method	Total	\multicolumn{8}{c}{*Number of staff employees covered*}
		Under 50	50– 99	100– 249	250– 499	500– 999	1,000– 2,499	2,500– 4,999	Over 5,000
Job ranking	8	2	—	4	1	1	—	—	—
Paired comparison	5	1	1	1	—	1	—	1	—
Job classification	6	—	1	1	1	1	1	1	—
Points rating	22	—	4	8	4	4	2	—	—
Profile	4	—	1	—	1	—	1	—	1
Direct consensus	3	—	—	—	—	2	1	—	—
Factor/forced pair	3	—	1	—	2	—	—	—	—
Guide chart profile	20	1	3	4	3	2	—	5	2

Method	Total	\multicolumn{8}{c}{*Number of job titles evaluated*}
		Under 25	25– 49	50– 74	75– 99	100– 149	150– 199	200– 499	Over 500
Job ranking	8	1	3	1	1	—	1	1	—
Paired comparison	5	1	1	—	1	—	—	—	2
Job classification	6	1	—	2	1	—	1	—	1
Points rating	22	1	4	5	2	3	2	4	1
Profile	4	—	1	—	—	—	—	2	1
Direct consensus	3	—	—	—	—	—	1	1	1
Factor/forced pair	3	—	1	—	—	—	2	—	—
Guide chart profile	20	—	2	1	—	2	4	5	6

7. These methods (besides an explanation of the principles of job evaluation and issues to be borne in mind in blue-collar applications) are described in some detail in the Incomes Data Service (IDS) Ltd's *Blue-collar Job Evaluation*, Study 348 (October 1985). Pages 31–42 provide a detailed overview of the applications listed in Table 15.3.
8. *Integrated Job Evaluation at Continental Can*, IR-RR 291 (8 March 1983), p. 14. Industrial Relations Services, 18–20 Highbury Place, London N5 1QP.
9. D. Grayson identifies that job evaluation schemes in many organizations are both 'under pressure' and 'in transition' in 'Job evaluation in transition', Occasional Paper 36, Work Research Unit, St Vincent House, 30 Orange Street, London WC2H 7HH. Four major sources of change affecting job evaluation systems are listed:
   1. The need to respond more quickly in a more competitive business environment.
   2. The incorporation of the 'equal pay for work of equal value' concept into the equal pay legislation.
   3. The demands of the 'flexible firm'.
   4. New technologies in both the office and factory.
10. C. O'Dell, *Major Findings from People, Performance and Pay* (American Productivity and Quality Center, 1986), table 1.1.
11. *Ibid.* figure 1.3.
12. E.E. Lawler III and G.E. Ledford, Jr, 'Skill-based pay: a concept that's catching on', *Management Review* (February 1987), 46–51 gives examples of companies that have

introduced this approach including T.R.W., Proctor & Gamble, Johnson & Johnson, General Foods and General Motors.

13. Non-traditional is the generic term used by the American Productivity Center to cover these and other types of payment approaches.

14. C. O'Dell, *op. cit.*, table 1.3.

15. S. Flykt, 'Payment systems in smaller enterprises in Sweden', *Management Decision*, 18 no. 6, (1980), 318–26, based on a paper given at the Eleventh European Small Business Seminar, Helsinki, 15–18 September 1981.

16. A discussion on the merits of these approaches is provided in 'The great gain sharing debate: group vs individual incentives?', *Productivity Letter*, no. 10 (1985), 2–3. It involves W.B. Abernathy and C.G. Thor (Senior Vice-President, American Productivity Center) and includes the former's 'ten commandments of incentive system design'.

17. Useful descriptions and outlines of incentive schemes are provided by the British Institute of Management's Information Note 81, *Financial Motivation* (September 1970) and the American Productivity Center's national survey on non-traditional reward and human resource practices, *Major Findings from People, Performance and Pay* by C. O'Dell (1986).

18. P. Long, *Performance Appraisal Revisited* (London: Institute of Personnel Management, 1986).

19. *Manual Workers' Appraisal: A growing trend surveyed*, IR-RR 398 (Industrial Relations Services, 17 August 1987), pp. 2–17.

20. IR-RR 398 (1987), pp. 4 and 6.

21. *Ibid.*, p. 5.

22. *Ibid.*, p. 3.

23. American Productivity Center, *Productivity Letter*, 6, no. 4, (1986), 1, 2 and 7 outlines the developments undertaken over a seven year period by Knoli International, manufacturer of high quality furniture.

24. C. O'Dell, *Major Findings from People, Performance and Pay* (American Productivity Center, 1986), p. 8.

25. American Productivity and Quality Center, *Productivity Letter*, 4, no. 10 (1985) provides the example of American Valve and Hydrant Manufacturing Co. In the UK the Inland Revenue's *Notes for Guidance on Profit-related Pay*, PRP2 (September 1988) proves helpful.

26. C. O'Dell, *op. cit.*, pp. 8–14.

PART IV

Cases

Adepla (A)

At the end of July 1980 Mr Millet, head of Adepla's Le Mans plant, sat back in his office reflecting on the month ahead. As was customary the plant would be closed for annual holidays but Millet knew that he had a problem to solve in August. Earlier in the year he had been instructed by the managing director of Adepla following a trip to Japan, to institute a campaign to improve the quality of his products. Currently on average 26 per cent of production was found to be defective. As a first measure he had set up a study group to investigate the problem under the leadership of Mr Goldie the plant's head of quality control. The group had now put forward a recommendation that a system of quality circles be instituted at the plant to achieve the desired result. Secondly Millet was waiting to see the effect on quality of an experimental group assembly system recently installed in which a team of workers assembling products in groups of one or two replaced production line assembly.

Background

Adepla was the French part of the heating division of a multinational group whose consolidated turnover amounted to nearly Fr.6,000 million in 1979 of which 84 per cent was linked to the automobile industry. The heating division manufactured heaters and radiators as well as ventilation and air conditioning units for the automobile industry accounting for nearly 15 per cent of the group's turnover. It was one of the leaders in the European market.

Adepla's headquarters were just outside Paris. Its principal places of production were at:

1. Tours, which was responsible for 60 per cent of Adepla's turnover.
2. Ballon near Le Mans (200 kilometres from Paris), which was responsible for the rest.

Ballon, was a small town of some four thousand inhabitants. Adepla was the main employer in the town and a large percentage of its 900-strong workforce lived within fifteen kilometres

This case study is © 1983 by CEDEP. It was prepared by Christopher Hopton, research assistant, under the supervision of affiliate professor James Teboul, as the basis for class discussion rather than to illustrate either effective or ineffective handling of an administrative situation.

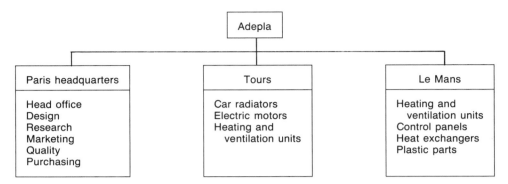

Figure 1 The Adepla organization.

of the plant. Many of such local workers expected lifetime employment with Adepla. Figure 1 summarizes the way Adepla was organized.

Adepla's main customers were the European automobile manufacturers and in particular the French constructors Renault and PSA (Peugeot, Citroën, Talbot). About 40 per cent of its products were exported mainly to the German manufacturers Mercedes, BMW and VW.

Products

The Le Mans plant manufactured components for and assembled heating and ventilation units (ACVs — Appareils de Chauffage et de Ventilation) for automobiles. Figure 2 shows a drawing of a typical ACV.

At the heart of an ACV is a heat exchanger, a stack of thin aluminium sheets through which pass a series of tubes carrying hot water. There were moulded plastic end tanks at the top and bottom. Air is drawn into the unit and either heated by the heat exchanger before passing into the interior of the automobile or expelled directly into the automobile as cold air. The speed of the air passing into the automobile can be increased with the use of a fan.

The temperature of the air and the fan speed are controlled from the control panel in the dashboard of the automobile. The temperature is varied by means of a system of flaps which either direct the air over the heat exchanger to be heated or cause the air to bypass the heat exchanger and be expelled cold. An alternative technique varying the air temperature with the aid of a tap which regulated the amount of hot water flowing into the heat exchanger was being phased out because of the slower reaction time between altering the controls and a change in the temperature of the air.

In addition to the heat exchanger an ACV consisted of various parts moulded from thermoplastic such as the outer casing, certain rubber parts and a control panel all of which were manufactured at Le Mans, an electric motor manufactured at the Tours plant and various components such as electric wiring purchased from outside suppliers. In order to ensure that the best prices possible were obtained, buying from outside suppliers was centralized at the company's headquarters.

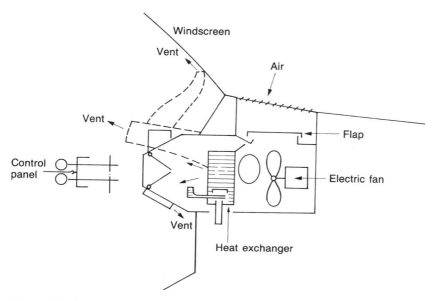

Figure 2 An example drawing of an ACV and how it operates.

The total cost of an ACV could be broken down into the costs associated with the component parts approximately as follows:

	%	
Moulded plastic and rubber parts	30	⎫
Heat exchanger	15	⎬ Manufactured at Le Mans
Control panel	15	⎭
Electric motor	10	Manufactured at Tours
Outside components	30	
	100%	

The average ex-factory price of an ACV to customers was FR.200.

No standardization of the design of ACVs had ever been achieved. There tended to be a different design for every model of automobile — Le Mans would consequently have anything up to fifty different ACVs in current production at any one time. Often the heating unit was one of the last components to be designed before production of a new automobile began and, being made essentially of plastic, it was felt to have more flexibility of design than most other components. Thus it was usually necessary to create an efficient system which would fit within the confines of the space remaining.

At the design stage of a new automobile the constructor would approach Adepla's design department at its Paris headquarters in an effort to come up with a mutually acceptable ACV design. A new ACV represented a considerable investment in new equipment, in the order of Fr.5−10 million, of which the mould for the plastic casing was normally the most expensive item costing approximately Fr.1 million. In addition the costs of design were considerable. Thus negotiations would take place with the constructor regarding the apportionment of the costs of design and new equipment.

Once the design and the necessary investment had been agreed on, pricing of the ACV would be undertaken by Adepla. This was a critical operation not only because the price fixed would be the reference for the ruling price when mass production of the ACV began some two years hence, but also because for every model of ACV a constructor would normally have two suppliers. The next stages were the planning of production methods and task organization by the industrial engineering department at Le Mans and the scheduling of production by Le Mans' planning cell. The industrial engineering department at Le Mans thus played a key part in the development of every new product. Its role was to determine the most economic fashion of production at each stage of the manufacturing process. For each product there was a technician from the department responsible for the implementation and follow up of plans. First production runs were then carried out also at Le Mans. Any production difficulties would be resolved at this time by the industrial engineering department and once all problems had been ironed out the ACV would be transferred to Tours for mass production by the methods developed at Le Mans. ACVs tended to remain at Le Mans only for about two years on average.

As already mentioned, an automobile constructor would normally ensure that despite the costs involved it had two suppliers of each model of ACV, even a constructor which had integrated backwards and had its own captive ACV manufacturer. It would thus conduct negotiations at the design stage with several of Adepla's competitors to achieve this end. Mr Millet felt that to give itself an advantage over competition Adepla needed to remain as flexible as possible on design and in particular on modifications proposed by the customer once initial production had started. This was a frequent occurrence and Millet thought that the reaction time at Le Mans was particularly good within the industry. On the contrary, if a modification was suggested to the customer by Adepla at that stage it often took as long as six months to reach agreement. In addition, Millet believed that the quality of Adepla's products was an important factor. Not only was an automobile heating unit particularly awkward to repair or replace if it went wrong, because of the difficulty of access once mounted, but also the automobile constructors tended to be very sensitive to Japanese quality levels. Their aim was to abolish the need for inspection of parts coming from outside suppliers by asking them to 'assure' quality so delivery could be made directly to the assembly line.

Production facilities at Le Mans

The site at Le Mans was divided into three production units, various workshops, stores and offices. Figure 3 shows the layout of the site. Factory A was used for moulding the various plastic parts and housed some 60 presses. Moulding was done using presses of between 50 and 1,800 tonnes hydraulic pressure into which were fitted metal moulds weighing up to 10 tonnes. Each part had its own unique mould. The cost of a 900 tonnes press was in the order of Fr.2.5 million.

A press would normally operate under the supervision of an unskilled worker called a press operator. Raw material (essentially polypropylene) was fed into the press from a hopper, heated and moulded under high pressure. The mould itself was then cooled by water to make the moulded part harden quickly. The average cycle time was one minute.

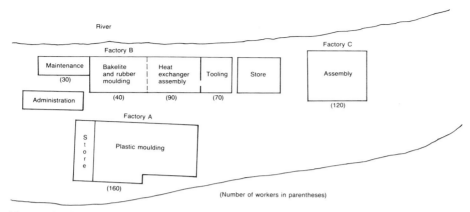

Figure 3   Le Mans plant.

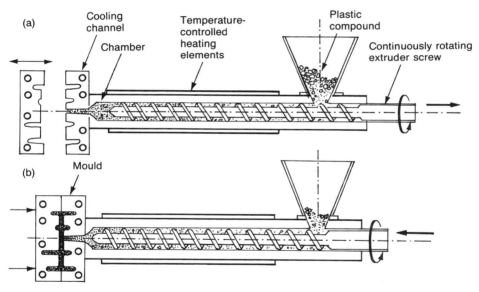

Figure 4   A typical press. **(a)** The mould opens to unload the product whilst the screw fills the chamber with molten plastic. **(b)** The screw is hydraulically pushed forward to empty the chamber into the mould; the mould is cooled before opening.

Some of the modern automatic presses only required one operator between five machines. However, the large older presses needed two operators each — Figure 4 shows the design of a typical machine.

Whenever it was necessary for a press to produce a different part the mould had to be exchanged by a set up operator (a skilled worker) in an operation taking an average of four hours. Approximately four hundred moulds would be changed during the course of each month.

The work of a press operator differed enormously from that of a set-up operator. The former was totally governed by his machine and isolated from his colleagues by the size and noise of the presses. He merely supervised the functioning of the machine, removing the plastic parts from the press as they were moulded, trimming off any rough edges and placing them in a container. If his machine needed resetting or the mould needed changing he had to wait for the more skilled set-up operator to do this job — he had none of the relevant skills to be able to assist. For many of the older press operators moulding was the only life they knew. They had never advanced beyond that level after several years in the factory and were considered unlikely to do so. Nor was it uncommon to find press operators who had never visited some of the other production facilities at the plant after fifteen years of employment.

The operation of all the presses created a very hot and noisy atmosphere in factory A which operated continuously on three eight-hour shifts. During each shift an all-male team would be working in the factory consisting of a foreman, a supervisor, six set-up operators, forty press operators, two fork-lift truck drivers and four material preparers. The foreman and supervisor had usually progressed up through the ranks of press operator and then set-up operator. The average age of the day shifts was about 45, while the night shift tended to be composed of younger men.

Le Mans was responsible for moulding 80 per cent of Adepla's plastic part requirements. Some two-thirds of the factory's production was sent to Tours for assembly. For an established ACV model the monthly production of a particular plastic part might be in the order of twelve thousand pieces. This length of run would take about ten days to complete whereupon the press in question would immediately have its mould exchanged to enable it to produce another part.

Factory B housed some fifteen older presses for moulding bakelite and rubber parts but in the main was used for the assembly of heat exchangers for ACVs. Adepla's had developed and patented its own design of heat exchangers. In consequence the majority of exchangers manufactured in the factory were of virtually standard design.

Assembly of heat exchangers was done on six production lines. Each began with a press to cut and shape the aluminium sheets, employed seven operators and could produce 185 radiators per hour. Figure 5 shows the way a production line was set up. The speed of the press governed the line's rate of production.

The factory operated two eight-hour shifts. The working conditions were rather noisy but, unlike factory A, both men and women were employed on the production lines. This contributed to a friendly atmosphere within the factory since there are no difficulties in conversing with colleagues. Thirty per cent of production was intended for the final assembly of ACVs at Le Mans. The remainder was either sent to Tours or sold to outside purchasers for assembly in their own ACVs.

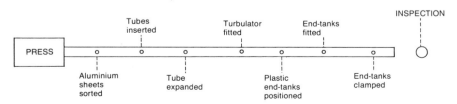

Figure 5 Production line for heat exchanger assembly.

Factory C was where the assembly of ACVs took place. Most of the assembly was done on production lines of between fifteen and twenty all-female operators depending on the complexity of the ACV. Each operator would perform three or four simple tasks with an average operating cycle of thirty seconds.

One relatively simple product was assembled using a recently introduced group assembly system where each operator performed up to thirty tasks and assembled all or part of a complete unit in a cycle averaging six minutes. Thus simple units would be assembled by one operator whilst more complicated ones would be assembled by groups of two operators. The system had been proposed by Mr Mercier, the head of the industrial engineering department at Le Mans to alleviate the boredom of repetitive work on the production lines where rotation of jobs was not the normal practice. It was set up as an experiment in place of the shortest line in the factory which only employed eight operators. Although no figures were yet available it was thought to improve the quality of products significantly. Opinions amongst the operators varied as to the merits of the new system. The majority preferred it because of the greater responsibility involved and because the fewer time constraints made possible the introduction of flexitime. However, there were those that liked the team spirit generated by a production line and preferred being able to talk to colleagues easily. Because of the greater working area required and of the need to supply each operator with all the tools necessary for assembly the additional cost of the group assembly system over production lines was estimated at Fr.6,000 per working post. In addition the operators took an average of 7,000 cycles to reach the same rate of output as achieved by a production line. Figure 6 shows the learning curve of an average operator.

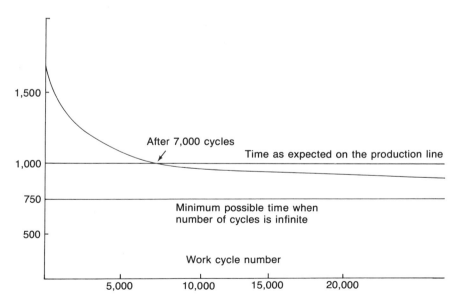

Actual time by average operator in terms of the number of cycles
Cycle of 1,000 time measurement unit with 40 per cent difficult movements

Figure 6 Learning curve.

Factory C operated one eight-hour shift. The majority of the operators working there were women possessing few qualifications. The foremen were mainly male. Working conditions were less harsh than in the other two factories being considerably less hot or noisy.

Quality control

Quality control at Le Mans was the responsibility of Mr Goldie, the head of the quality control department (see Figure 7). Each different operation at the plant had its own separate control system:

1. Moulding operations (factories A and B) used a system of control by sampling. An inspector would test six or seven pieces per hour from each press for dimensional defects to determine whether a batch should be accepted or rejected. Four per cent of production was rejected in this manner. In addition, each press operator visually checked the physical appearance of each part as it came out of the press.
2. A similar system of control by sampling was used for parts coming from outside suppliers. If any outside part was below acceptable quality but was nevertheless reparable at Le Mans the cost of such repair was noted and an invoice sent to the supplier concerned.
3. The heat exchangers assembled in factory B were individually controlled by an inspector situated at the end of each production line. They were checked both visually and with the aid of a testing device which verified that there were no leaks in the tubes which would carry hot water. In addition there was a system of control by sampling. Overall, 0.8 per cent of radiators were discarded as unacceptable.
4. In factory C the assembled ACVs were also individually controlled by two inspectors situated at the end of every production line. They would each check about sixty units per hour for such aspects as functioning, noise level, dimensions, appearance. Behind the two inspectors were situated a packer, and a repairer who would repair any units which were deemed reparable and resubmit them for inspection. This means of control was backed up by a 'super control' system in which five units per day underwent detailed testing of specific characteristics. Despite these various methods of control 1.5 per cent of ACVs were still returned by customers as unacceptable.

The average number of defective units discovered in factory C was 26 per cent with common defects being malfunctioning of flaps (20 per cent of all units produced), flaps sticking (4 per cent), excessive motor noise (3 per cent), fan vibrations (3 per cent) and bad fitting of outer casing (3 per cent). Certain units had more than one defect.

Quality levels

In 1980 Adepla estimated that the cost of 'non-quality' of its products amounted to 10 per cent of its annual turnover. The cost of 'non-quality' was defined in this context to be the difference between the actual cost of production of a product and the theoretical cost of production if there were no defects arising during or after the development, production or sale of that product. Thus the cost of 'non-quality' was made up of the cost of quality control (i.e. preventive measures and inspection) and the cost of defective pieces (i.e. repairs and rejects).

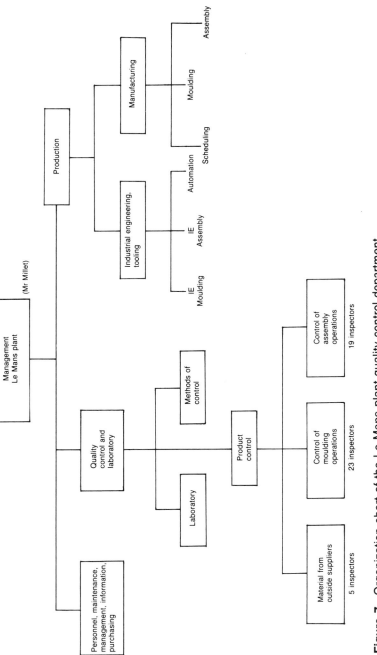

Figure 7 Organization chart of the Le Mans plant quality control department.

At Le Mans Mr Goldie and the study group found that the origin of the defects was divided between assembly operations (51 per cent[1]), moulding operations (16 per cent), defective parts received from outside suppliers (16 per cent) and design faults (17 per cent). However, the costs of 'non-quality' broke down slightly differently with 49 per cent being attributable to moulding operations, 24 per cent to assembly of heat exchangers and 27 per cent to final assembly. Figure 8 summarizes these figures.

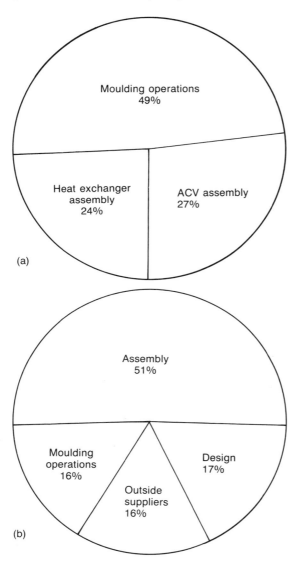

(a)

(b)

Figure 8 **(a)** Cost of non-quality at Le Mans plant. **(b)** Origin of defects at Le Mans plant.

The study group therefore set a target of cutting the average number of defective ACVs from 26 per cent to 5 per cent and of drastically reducing the costs of non-quality. It proposed therefore the creation of a system of quality circles.

Quality improvement

Mr Millet was thus faced with the problem of improving product quality at Le Mans. He had the opportunity to introduce either or both of the group assembly system and quality circles. However, he realized the risks involved of alienating the workforce by introducing new techniques without their support. A wrong decision now might effectively prevent any improvement in quality over the short or even medium term. In addition, the unions were a potential source of trouble despite their past record of co-operation. Millet felt that whilst they were likely to agree to improving quality they would possibly demand reductions in working speeds or increases of salary in return.

Millet thought quality circles had the potential not only to improve quality but also to create better communications within the plant and to improve morale through increased employee participation. However, if he decided to introduce them he first had to decide where in the plant they might be set up. He realized the composition of quality circles would be critical — who should be the members, how should they be chosen, who would be assigned to play the various roles involved? Finally, there would be the problem of introducing quality circles in a manner which did not create employee suspicion or resistance and therefore he thought a carefully designed plan of action would be needed.

Notes

1. Mr Goldie thought this figure was inflated and contained faults which might properly belong to other categories.

Applicon

Applicon was founded in 1970 by a group of venture capitalists and MIT professors. The company, which is now owned by Schlumberger, designs and manufactures computer aided engineering (CAE), computer aided design (CAD), and computer aided manufacturing (CAM) systems. In 1987 Applicon had a total of 1,000 employees and sales of approximately $150 million. All manufactured products are produced in a single facility located in Billerica, Massachusetts.

The high-end CAE products include sophisticated systems used for various analytical engineering applications. The software for these high-end systems is proprietary and runs on DEC and Sun central processing units with Applicon designed workstations. The low-end CAM systems use Applicon software, Sun and Tektronics workstations, and DEC VAX processors. Major applications of such CAM systems include robotics and numerical control machines.

Applicon's first product line, the Applicon Graphics System (AGS), was introduced in 1974. This system was successfully sold in the electronics market during the 1970s, with sales peaking in 1980. Although the AGS was a profitable product line for Applicon, it was felt in late 1980 that the electronics market at which it was aimed had become saturated. The real growth was now in the mechanical market. In this market, CAD/CAM systems were increasingly being applied by such users as the automotive industry and machine shops.

These market factors were instrumental in Applicon's decision to introduce the Series 4000, an entirely new product line targeted at the mechanical market. The Series 4000 was announced in the spring of 1981 with the first shipment made in May 1982.

Rapid change

The introduction of the Series 4000 was a major turning point for the company. Applicon had entered an extremely competitive market with a new and unproven product. Competing against such CAD/CAM system producers as Computervision, Intergraph and Autocad, Applicon faced tremendous start-up problems. One result of these conditions was a serious shortfall in actual sales as compared with forecasts. At the time, however, management did not react to the shortfall in demand. The belief was that sales would eventually increase once the introductory 'bugs' had been shaken out. Thus no action was taken and Applicon continued to build to finished inventory in anticipation of increased demand.

Another problem was the higher than expected cost of introducing and manufacturing the Series 4000. The importance of reducing product costs was quickly becoming apparent. Unlike the electronics market, the price-to-performance ratio was a critical issue to the price sensitive CAD/CAM consumers in the mechanical market.

Large product start-up costs were incurred. These included training costs of field engineers, applications engineers, and the salesforce. Frequent engineering change orders and reliability problems also contributed to the high costs of product start-up by making obsolete large amounts of finished inventories. Overhead costs were another contributing factor. Increasing costs of MIS, materials management, production management, inventory control and quality control were the norm.

Applicon was also losing its competitive edge because of an inability to respond quickly enough to changes in technology. It was not uncommon for radical hardware and software advancements to occur on an almost monthly basis in this dynamic market. Applicon had to become much more responsive to the frequent design changes characterizing the industry.

Lastly, Applicon was now dealing with a more sophisticated customer base than in previous years. These consumers had a better understanding of both the hardware and software of CAD/CAM systems. They not only developed higher expectations for price-to-performance ratios and delivery responsiveness, but also demanded a higher quality product. Applicon's quality improvements of one or two percentage points per year were not sufficient, and something needed to be done to improve quality dramatically.

The traditional factory

Under the 'traditional' mode of operation, production would build to stock in accordance to an annual build plan, as estimated by marketing. The perception was, 'if the finished items could not be sold it was a sales problem, not a manufacturing problem'.

Using the annual build plan, a master production schedule (MPS) was created for each month's production of end-items. These MPS requirements were then input into a materials requirement planning (MRP) system. The MRP system generated the work orders for the lower-level items by exploding through the bill of material (BOM), applying the 'gross-to-net' logic, and off setting for lead times. These work orders were used to schedule and control production on the floor.

Figure 1 is a simplified indented bill of materials for a typical product, the 4620 Alpha terminal. This BOM shows the in-house manufactured items that support the top-level product. The BOM also identifies the four types of manufacturing operations involved in producing the 4620; top-level assembly, lower-level mechanical assembly, cable assembly, and printed circuit board (PCB) production. Figure 2 shows the complete terminal and the three top-level assemblies that make up the terminal.

The detailed production steps and material flows for each of the manufacturing operations are shown in Figure 3. Here, the production process was initiated with the release of work orders by the MRP system. These work orders were lot sized into one month

```
4620 Terminal
        Monitor Assembly*
                Control panel†
                Control PCB§
                Swivel assembly†
                Cables‡
        Base/electronics assembly*
                Logic PCB§
                Interface PCB§
                Cables‡
                Cabinet assembly†
        Keyboard/tablet assembly*
                Keyboard assembly†
                        Agid PCB§
                        Cables‡
                        Cover assembly†
                Tablet†
                Pen†
```

Only shows *manufactured* items that go into the top-level assembly.
* Top level assembly
† Mechanical assembly
‡ Cable assembly
§ PCB production

Figure 1   Intended bill of materials (4620 Alpha terminal).

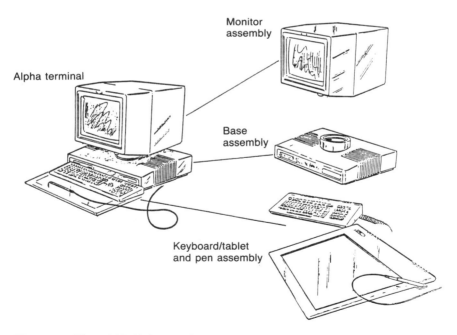

Figure 2   The 4620 Alpha terminal.

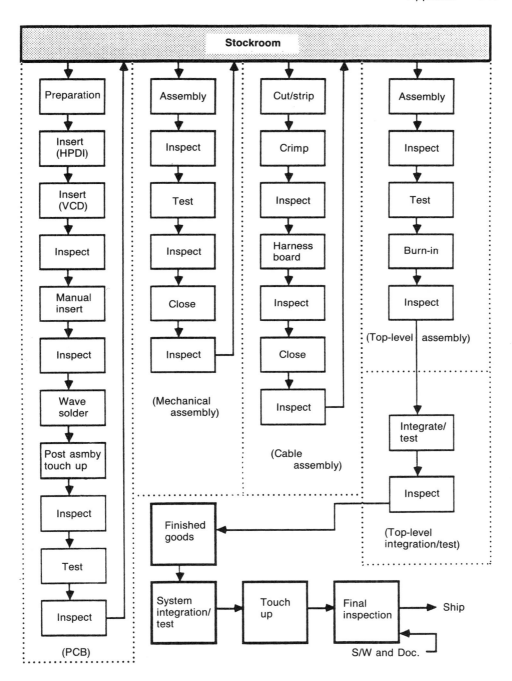

Figure 3 Production steps and material flow (traditional layout).

batches. Material for one month's worth of demand was kitted in the central stockroom for each of the subassembly (PCB, mechanical and cable) operations. These kits were then released to their corresponding production areas. Once completed, the batches, or kits, of finished subassemblies were sent back to the stockroom where they were rekitted for final assembly in the top-level assembly area. The finished top-level assemblies were then integrated and tested as a single unit in the top-level integration/test area.

Once tested, the terminals went to finished goods inventory. Upon receipt of an actual customer order, the terminals and various purchased peripherals (plotters, tape drives, etc.) were released to system integration and test. Here, the complete system was tested, and 'burned in'. After completing any necessary final touch-ups, the software and documentation were consolidated with the system. The complete order then underwent final inspection before it was shipped to the customer.

The various lead times associated with each of the processes are shown in Table 1. Figure 4 portrays the plant layout under this production system. Under this layout, the production operations (top-level) assembly, mechanical assembly, cable assembly and PCB production) and the integration activities are arranged in a functional manner.

This traditional MRP based production system was prone to a number of problems. These problems became serious when Applicon developed the Series 4000. Running the production floor to an annual build plan and ignoring actual customer orders resulted in large amounts of over-built finished inventories. By 1984, $8 million worth of products sat in finished goods (approximately four to five months' worth of demand). In addition to the large finished inventory levels, $17 million of component inventories existed, and over twenty weeks of work in process was on the floor. These inventories not only tied up working capital, but also required extensive floor space. Furthermore, millions of dollars were lost as a result of stagnant inventories being made obsolete by the constant bombardment of engineering changes and new product introductions. Reserves of $150,000 to $175,000 per month were routinely set aside for such obsolescence.

Large overhead expenses were associated with the traditional production system. The numerous transactions in stockroom kitting, shopfloor control, and the production and financial control mechanisms were key drivers of these overhead expenses. Eighty-three employees were working in materials management and 60 in quality assurance (QA), as compared to only 160 actual line manufacturing operators.

The responsiveness of the traditional production system was too slow for Applicon to remain competitive in the dynamic CAD/CAM market-place. The four to five month manufacturing lead times were much too long in a market where major product design changes were occurring on a monthly basis.

In 1982 the plug-and-play rate was 85 per cent. The plug-and-play rate is the percentage of units sold to customers that contain no manufacturing defects and can therefore be plugged in directly and used. Improvements in quality were needed to quickly get this rate into the upper 90 per cent range. Quality problems also resulted in excessive rework requirements on the shopfloor. Under the traditional system, a lot, on average, had to be completely reworked one time through each of the four manufacturing operations (PCB production, mechanical assembly, cable assembly and top-level assembly).

Quality improvements were difficult to achieve under this system because work was scheduled in lots of one month's worth of demand. Such scheduling in monthly batches caused the quality problems to be masked by inventories. Moreover, the low visibility of defects, combined with slow feedback to the source of the quality problems, did little to foster worker involvement in any quality improvement efforts.

Table 1 Lead times ('traditional' production system)

	PCB production		
Operation	*Task*	*Lot run time*	*Set-up, queue and move time*
1	Preparation	1.0	4.0
2	Insert (HPDI)	0.125	0.75
3	Insert (VCD)	0.125	0.75
4	Inspection	0.50	0.50
5	Manual insert	0.25	1.0
6	Inspection	0.50	0.50
7	Wave solder	0.50	0.50
8	Post assembly/touch up	0.50	1.0
9	Inspection	0.50	0.50
10	Test	1.0	2.50
11	Inspection	0.50	0.50
	Mechanical assembly		
1	Assembly	0.25	2.5
2	Inspection	0.50	1.0
3	Test	0.25	1.5
4	Inspection	0.50	1.0
5	Close	0.125	0.75
6	Inspection	0.50	1.0
	Cable assembly		
1	Cut/strip	0.125	2.00
2	Crimp	0.125	1.00
3	Inspection	0.250	0.75
4	Harness board	0.250	0.50
5	Inspection	0.250	0.75
6	Close	0.125	0.50
7	Inspection	0.250	0.75
	Top-level assembly		
1	Assembly	1.0	2.0
2	Inspection	0.50	0.50
3	Test	2.5	0.50
4	Burn-in	2.5	0.50
5	Inspection	0.50	0.50

	Post top-level assembly activities	
Activity	*Total lead time*	
Top-level integration/test	20	
Finished goods	2	
System integration/test	10	
Touch up	2	
Ship/inspection and consolidation	2	

Notes
1. All times are in days.
2. Run times apply to an average lot of one month's end-item demand (10 units).

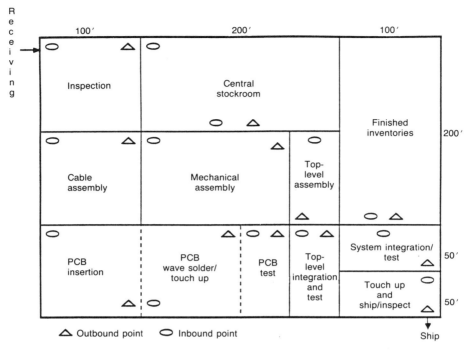

Figure 4 Original plant layout.

JIT implementation

Applicon came to realize that the manufacturing methods of the 1970s were now inappropriate for the highly competitive and dynamic mechanical market. In 1984, Don Fedderson, the company's president at the time, issued a mandate to Tom Genova, the newly promoted vice-president of manufacturing: 'Reduce costs and inventories, increase quality and responsiveness, and make Applicon competitive once again.'

Genova, being the 'radical young engineer who was put into the factory by Fedderson to shake things up', was given free rein to implement any changes deemed necessary. Genova concluded that just-in-time (JIT) production was the solution that Applicon was looking for. With the support and backing of Fedderson, Genova forced manufacturing to convert to JIT.

JIT production was first implemented on a single product model, the 4620 Alpha terminal, in May of 1984. Experience with the Alpha line then allowed for a full conversion effort, which started three months later.

This full scale conversion to JIT can be divided into three phases. Phase 1, which took place over the second half of 1984, focused on process conversion. Phase 2, which began in 1984 and lasted into the beginning of 1987, focused on resource management. Applicon is now in the third phase of implementation where major efforts are being directed towards improving vendor integration.

The conversion to JIT resulted in far-reaching changes at Applicon, many of which are still occurring. Production related changes include the layout of the shopfloor, the production processes, production scheduling and control, MRP and capacity planning, master production scheduling and order processing.

Layout and process improvements

One of the first actions taken when converting to JIT was to rearrange the equipment to achieve a smoother flow of production. In this respect the concept of work cells, in which equipment is grouped by product or similar product families, was introduced.

Concurrent with the relayout into work cells were efforts focused on process improvements. Assembly instructions were improved to help maintain the rapid flow of production characteristic of JIT. In addition, equipment and production processes were modified to reduce set-up times so that production could be scheduled in small, daily lot sizes.

The layout of today's JIT based production facility is illustrated in Figure 5. The figure also shows the flow of materials through the plant. As can be seen by comparing Figures 4 and 5, the total area dedicated to manufacturing has been significantly reduced under the new layout.

Purchased materials enter the plant through receiving and either go to inspection or, if coded as 'dock-to-stock', go directly to the using work cells. At this time, only 30% of the purchased items must be inspected upon receipt. Purchased items are designated as dock-to-stock if the QA department determines that they need not be inspected. The goal is to have all incoming parts as dock-to-stock and thus totally eliminate incoming inspection.

Parts that fail to pass inspection are sent to the material review board (MRB) area. This is a temporary holding area for 'bad' material. Here, the decision is made as to either rework the defective parts in-house, use them as they are, or send them back to the vendor.

All other parts are sent directly to the printed circuit board (PCB) production area, the final assembly (FA) work cells, A, B, C and D, or to location Kit. The production of PCBs is the first in-house production step. Components enter this production area, are built into PCBs, and then sent directly to the FA work cells. As such, the PCB area may be viewed as an in-house vendor to the FA work cells.

Work cells A, B, C and D are the final assembly areas. Work cell A produces the Alpha terminals. Cell B produces Headlight terminals and Micro-VAX workstations. Cell C is the final assembly work cell for Micro-VAX central processing units. Cell D is the Sun work cell. Work cell D is differentiated from the other FA cells in that no in-house manufactured PCBs feed into it. In each FA cell, the mechanical assembly, cable assembly, and the top-level assembly operations for a particular end-item (or similar group of end-items) are consolidated. In addition to these assembly operations, the top-level testing, burn-in, clean-up and packaging activities are also performed in the FA cells.

Also shown in Figure 5 is location Kit. Kit is a staging area for purchased, shippable products, such as printers and plotters. Kit products will eventually be packaged with the completed final assembly items in finished goods inventory (Fin).

Figure 6 illustrates the production steps that the Alpha terminal would go through. PCB production follows nearly the same sequence of operations as under the old MRP-based system. The major process differences include the elimination of the PCB preparation operation, and the elimination of all but one inspection station.

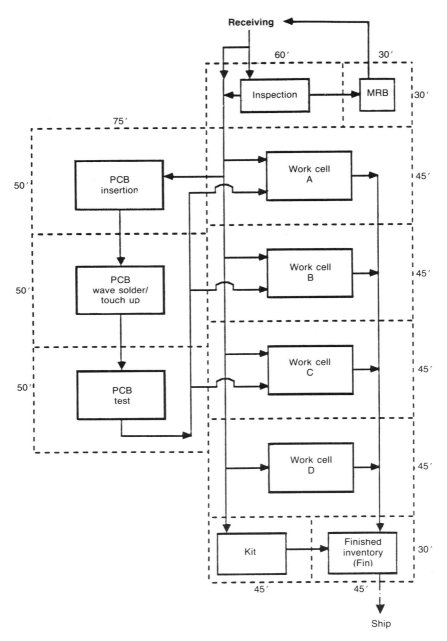

Figure 5 JIT layout and material flow.

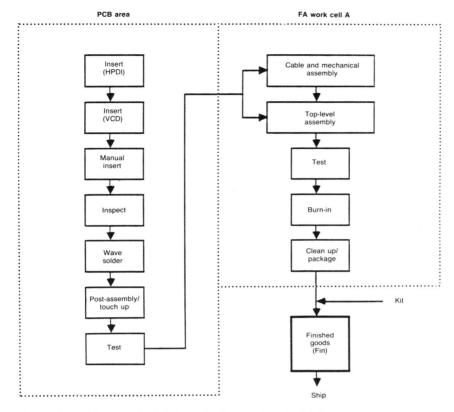

Figure 6   Alpha terminal JIT production and material flow.

The FA work cell is the consolidation of all the non PCB production related activities necessary to assemble an end-item. The cable and mechanical subassemblies are now built up in the FA work cell, rather than in their own functional areas. Purchased parts making up these subassemblies are delivered directly to the FA cell from receiving (or inspection if not coded as dock-to-stock). Typically, a minimum level (one or two) of these subassemblies is built up one day ahead of time for the next day's production of end-items. The cable and mechanical assembly processes follow the same sequence of operations as under the old MRP system except for the elimination of all the inspection tasks.

Production scheduling and control

With JIT, production scheduling is no longer done at the subassembly level. Scheduling is done only at the final assembly level. In conjunction with this fundamental change, a completely new production control system was devised.

The first step in developing this new system was to eliminate work orders generated by the MRP system. Since production was only to be scheduled at the end-item level, there would no longer be a need for the lower-level work orders. Instead, a card system, similar to the Toyota Kanban system, was used to control the flow of materials. Under this system a 'move' card was used to move material (or assemblies) between successive work centres. 'Production' cards were used to build or test materials within a work centre. These cards identified the production lot sizes, move quantities, routeings and so on. With this card system, the practice of picking materials from the stockroom was eliminated. Material inventories were now placed in bins located directly in the work cells. As a result, the central stockroom was eliminated.

The card system, however, was short-lived. It was soon realized that the use of these cards was unnecessary. Having come from an environment characterized by work orders and excessive tracking and control mechanisms, the natural tendency was to use the card system to maintain control over the production floor. Experience showed that the workers could build to the daily production quota and move items to the proper place without the cards telling them what to do. As a result, control of the shopfloor was given to the equipment operators and a new system unique to Applicon's work environment was developed.

In this system a production card initiates work at the first operation in the production process, the building of PCBs. The PCBs are scheduled on a rate per day basis and are 'pushed' through the production floor. The operators at the first process of PCB production, HPDI insertion, read the information on the production cards and build to that schedule. All subsequent PCB processes work to the same daily rate. The PCB production cards (Figure 7) are issued by the production scheduler four days before an order is due in finished inventories. The four days is the total production lead time for a completed unit.

At the other end of the production process final assemblies are 'pulled' by customer orders. Using actual customer orders, the production scheduler converts the weekly production plan into specific daily requirements. This information is posted on a status board visible to all the FA work cells. The production scheduler also places end-item build cards in a sequential pile in each corresponding work cell. These build cards (Figure 8) are used to schedule work in the final assembly work cells. They identify the customer for which a top-level unit will be assembled, and any specified options that must be built into that particular unit. A separate, individual build card is used for each top-level item. To assemble a terminal, the operators will remove the card from the top of the pile and build the terminal with the specified options. Only one terminal is assembled at a time. Thus, for example, if the status board indicates that two terminals are required for Monday, then the first two build cards on the pile will be used to assemble the customer-specific units for that day.

Under JIT, only two inventory transactions are made. The first transaction is to credit item inventory balances in one general floor-stock location (FLS) upon receipt of materials at receiving. Floor-stock includes all the areas shown in Figure 5 except for MRB and Fin. The second transaction occurs when finished products from work cells A–D, and peripherals from Kit, enter Fin. This transaction is the system 'backflush'.

Backflushing is widely used with JIT. Under the old system, inventory tracking was based on detailed transactions that were generated by the MRP system whenever materials (kits) were put into or released out of the central stockroom, or whenever the kits moved from one task to the next in the production process. Eliminating work orders and very short lead times made this system of control obsolete.

With the backflush transaction, the finished products (and any purchased peripherals) are credited to Fin upon entering finished inventories. At the same time, all the lower-level components that make up these products are subtracted from FLS. These lower-level

Production
Part number: 32820−001
Description: Fr.buffer bd.
Quantity: 3
Supplied by: Work centre A
Outbound: Wavesolder rack
Production Notes

Figure 7 PCB production card.

components are identified by the MRP system bill of materials. The MRP system has been modified to treat all non-purchased components and subassemblies in the BOM as 'phantom' parts. Thus, when backflushing, the system will work through the BOM and stop only when branches that end with purchased items are reached. The appropriate usage multiples of these purchased components are then subtracted from FLS.

MRP and capacity planning

As a result of these modifications and refinements, MRP is now limited to two major functions. The first is to generate orders for purchasing on a monthly basis.

Using the MRP system, top-level model 'family' quantities are translated into MPS

Production card: 4635B

Customer name: Applicon Deutsch

Order reference number: 8707224

Comments: To ship 8–14

	Part number	Description	Serial Number
[X]	33374–002	4635B, (220 V/50 Hz)	_____
Options			
[X]	31989–001	Macropad	_____
[X]	31362–002	25′ Sil cable	

Figure 8 Build card.

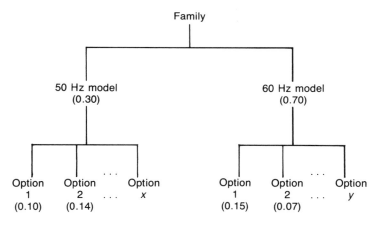

Numbers in parentheses are percentage useage figures.

Figure 9 Family bill of materials.

purchased parts requirements. This is done through a family bill of materials. An example is shown as Figure 9.

The family bills of top-level items are broken down into 50 and 60 Hz models, with each such model broken down into the various options in which it is sold, based on percentage usage figures. These figures, which are based on historical data, are the predicted fractions of the total family sold as one of the two frequency models, or as some particular option. Thus, for example, we can see from Figure 9 that if 100 units of this model family are forecast to be sold next month, then 70 units will be designated as 60 Hz, 30 units as 50 Hz, and so on.

By using family bills, the master production scheduler only schedules the top-level (family) items. The system uses the percentage usage figures to automatically convert these top-level family quantities into the various specific saleable item (option) requirements.

These requirements are used to create Applicon's MPS. The MPS is stated in saleable item terms and has standard available-to-promise capability. The MPS quantities then become the new MRP gross requirements when the system is regenerated. The necessary quantities and timings of specific purchased items can then be determined by exploding through the manufacturing bills of material, netting against the gross requirements, offsetting for production lead times, and adding a safety lead time factor.

Figure 10 illustrates how the scheduling of purchased items is carried out in the ideal case. In this example the requirement for the purchased parts is at the beginning of August. Added to this is a two week safety lead time to protect against any uncertainty in the vendor delivery date. Under these conditions, a purchase order must be released such that 1 August items are received on 15 July.

This purchase signal is transmitted to the planner-buyers, who are responsible for material inventories. The planner-buyers make the final decision as to following the recommendation of the MRP system or following some other course of action.

The second function of MRP is to generate capacity plans from the MPS quantities.

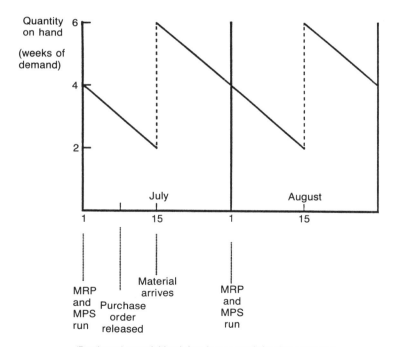

(Purchased material lead time is one week for this example.)

Figure 10 Purchased material scheduling.

These capacity projections are used as a check on labour levels, to determine if there are enough resources at each work centre, and to identify potential bottlenecks.

To generate the capacity plan, the MRP system converts the MPS quantities into corresponding quantities of the various lower-level items. Capacity projections are then calculated by combining these quantities with information from the routeings. The information used from the routeings includes the sequential operations needed to build a particular product, the work centres at which those operations are performed, and the standard production times for each work centre. The capacity projections can be output by individual work centre, by specific part number, or for the total production floor. The capacity reports are run on a weekly basis.

Figure 11 is a sample capacity status report. Here, capacity requirement projections for one month are broken out by individual work cells. The work cell capacity hours include both labour and machine hours. Seventeen work cells are used for capacity planning purposes. The first column in the report identifies the capacity planning work cell. The second column figures are the load hours. These are the projected capacity requirements that are calculated by the MRP system. The load hours can then be compared to the standard capacity hours available, to efficiency adjusted hours (adjusted standard capacity hours), or to maximum capacity hours (standard capacity hours adjusted for 10 per cent overtime).

The MRP system itself is in monthly time buckets. The system is run at the end of each week and the records updated as to that week's activities. This weekly regeneration ensures that purchased item scheduling and capacity planning are provided with accurate, up-to-date information.

06/12/87	8:12:24			Work centre Co App Dv
		Adjustment percentage 70		Date range:
Work centre	Load (std. hours)	Capacity (standard)	Capacity (adj. std)	Capacity (maximum)
ALF-A	70.03614	480.00000	336.00000	528.00000
ALF-T	5.28740	80.00000	36.00000	88.00000
HLT-A	458.36500	800.00000	560.00000	880.00000
HLT-T	85.08024	160.00000	112.00000	176.00000
MIS-A	270.60698	800.00000	560.00000	880.00000
MIS-T	14.65010	80.00000	56.00000	88.00000
MUX-A	399.27339	1120.00000	784.00000	1232.00000
MUX-T	79.47110	80.00000	56.00000	88.00000
OLD-P	81.10000	0.00000	0.00000	0.00000
PCB-A	52.24560	160.00000	112.00000	176.00000
PCB-H	44.64200	160.00000	112.00000	176.00000
PCB-I	124.91800	320.00000	224.00000	352.00000
PCB-M	441.85760	480.00000	336.00000	520.00000
PCB-P	408.79479	960.00000	672.00000	1056.00000
PCB-T	918.10800	1680.00000	1176.00000	1848.00000
PCB-V	123.24500	160.00000	112.00000	176.00000
PCB-W	56.76000	160.00000	112.00000	176.00000
Totals	3634.44134	7680.00000	5376.00000	8440.00000
		20 total workdays included		

Figure 11   Capacity status report.

Master production scheduling and order processing

With JIT, the master production schedule is still updated on a monthly basis. However, much less reliance is placed on the forecasts generated by marketing. Today's approach is to look at the past five or six months' shipment trends and at the actual orders booked. Don Hathaway, the manager of materials and logistics commented on today's production planning method: 'There is little need for any formal forecasting techniques . . . the approach is to reconcile past trends with marketing expectations, roll up the results, and get an overall plan. The accuracy in estimating overall monthly requirements within 30 days is about 95 per cent, and between 60 and 70 per cent when looking 60 days out.'

The MPS is in monthly time buckets and uses a five month planning horizon. It is stated in top-level item terms and coded by major model number. These top-level models include five processors, sixteen workstations and sixteen major peripherals. The information from the MPS is used only for planning purposes (i.e. to plan and order purchased materials as necessary). With JIT, Applicon plans to forecasts but builds only to actual customer orders. By building to orders rather than forecasts, finished goods inventory levels are kept to a minimum.

Customer orders enter the system from 'order processing'. Whenever order processing books a new order from sales, or changes the status of an existing order, a 'work order' is generated and printed the following morning in the 'new and modified sales order' report. The information from this report includes the quantity booked for the new or modified orders, and the due dates of those orders. The only orders that appear on this report are those that have been changed or booked on the previous day.

The information from the daily 'new and modified sales order' report is automatically updated into the order backlog records. From this, a weekly 'manufacturing order schedule/backlog' report is generated. This weekly report contains all the necessary information on the orders in backlog and links order processing to the shopfloor.

The 'manufacturing order schedule/backlog' report is used by the production scheduler to control PCB production. The order quantities from the report are converted into daily production rates. These daily rates are then posted on the PCB production cards. Work on the final assemblies is also scheduled from the information given by the 'manufacturing order schedule/backlog' report. In this case, the production scheduler transmits the information about a customer's order to the final assembly work cell on the end-item build cards.

The future

In September 1987, Bill King, the director of materials, Deborah Cantara, the production control supervisor, and Don Hathaway were reviewing Applicon's progress towards full JIT implementation.

One issue that needed to be addressed was production control's suggestion of modifying the MRP system to weekly time bucket. It seemed to Don and Deborah that this was a good idea, but they wondered if the payoffs would be worth the costs. The group also discussed the possibility of completely eliminating finished goods inventory. However, they needed to know what this action would entail and what the ramifications would be.

Another issue that concerned them was how to respond to corporate's evaluation of the Billerica plant's manufacturing performance. A new controller at Schlumberger corporate headquarters felt that, amongst other things, the plant had too much excess capacity and that labour and equipment were underutilized. The controller was advocating a standard cost accounting system at Billerica, and Bill King was asked to respond to this suggestion.

The group also wondered what to include in a report to the new vice-president of manufacturing concerning the benefits of JIT. In addition, the vice-president had requested an action plan of recommendations as to what should be done next. Although Bill, Don and Deborah were happy with the results that had been achieved, they wondered what new improvements were possible.... What should Applicon do next?

Barclays Bank Plc

Barclays Bank Plc is one of the major clearing banks in the UK and has worldwide activities comprising in excess of £5 billion net operating income. The UK activities use three service delivery systems:

1. Corporate division.
2. High street outlets.
3. Central retail services division.

The corporate division handles the activities of and relationships with large clients, typically multinational companies, as well as industries on a worldwide basis such as oil, automotive, retail and mining.

The responsibility for managing high street outlets is administered through a regional head office organization. This system comprises twenty-four regional offices throughout the UK. They are responsible for handling all the aspects of banking procedures and related needs.

The central retail services division is responsible for providing 'remote delivery' services such as credit and debit cards.

Regional head offices

Each main high street outlet is controlled by a branch manager. The current policy is to cluster smaller outlets around a main branch on a satellite basis. The smaller units lose their principal role and report to the main branch for an agreed service provision with staffing levels reduced to reflect this.

In turn, branch managers report to a corporate director and then to a regional director as shown in Figure 1. This gives the structure for the Birmingham region and one which

This case study is © Professor T.J. Hill (London Business School). It was prepared for teaching purposes and not as an example of good or bad management.

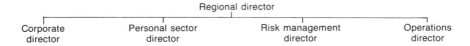

Figure 1   The outline reporting structure for the Birmingham region of Barclays Bank.

is typical of the divisional structure within this sector of the bank's activities. The principal role of each facet of the region as given in Figure 1 is as follows:

> *Corporate*: responsible for business centre branches and the corporate business of the personal sector.
> *Personal sector*: responsible for non-business centre branches.
> *Risk management*: manages the lending book regarding advances above those levels within a branch manager's discretion, whilst monitoring the latter's performance in terms of lending activities.
> *Operations*: responsible for personnel, premises and equipment.

Since March 1988, branch designations have been based on one of two prime activities, although in reality they are involved in a mix of work involving both sets of tasks:

1.   Business centres which are principally engaged in corporate business.
2.   General outlets involving the retail activities of small companies, professional and personal accounts.

Both types of outlet comprise the three principal activities of lending money, taking money and transmissions. Furthermore, each branch is graded in line with its initial outlet designation, the number of accounts and the number of managers. Staff grades range from 1 (the junior level) to 21, with a further level of executive grading above this. The largest twenty-five or so business centres are run by directors.

Coventry City Centre

Coventry City Centre (CCC) is one of Barclays' larger business centres and is managed by a senior executive of the bank carrying the designation of business centre director. As a business centre, it has a mix of work which includes that of a general outlet as well as corporate business. The current organizational structure is shown as Figure 2 and the layout for floors 1 and 2 as Figures 3 and 4. The principal activities of each section are now explained.

Floor 1 arrangements

Personal bankers
A team of nine staff (six of whom are full-time) discuss account-related issues with both existing and prospective customers. Their responsibilities comprise administration and selling the services offered by the bank.

   When opening new accounts they ensure that the customer is advised of the range of suitable options so that the appropriate account facilities can be selected. In addition,

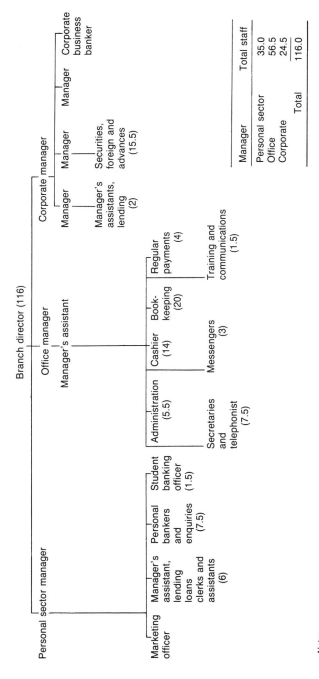

Figure 2 Organization chart showing the manning levels within each section of Coventry City Centre.

Notes
1. The numbers in brackets indicate the staff within each section and brought together in the summary table.
2. Also reporting to the personal sector manager are the three service branches at Cheylesmore, Radford and the University of Warwick with 4.4, 4.1, and 9.5 staff respectively and these are included in the 35 total given in the summary table.
3. Training and communications are undertaken by several staff as part of their overall duties with each specializing in certain aspects.
4. The staff figures include allowances for forecast levels of holidays and sickness.

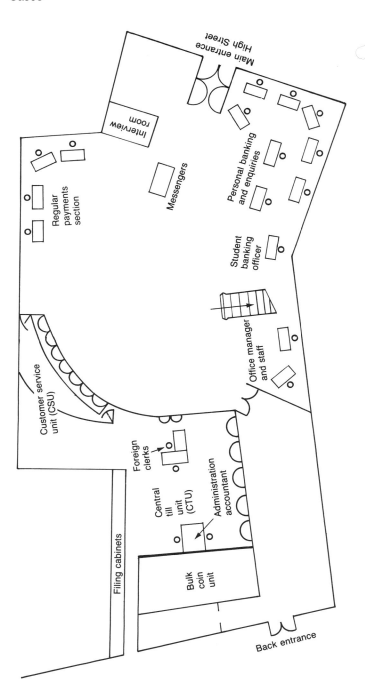

Figure 3 Layout showing the principal activities on floor 1.

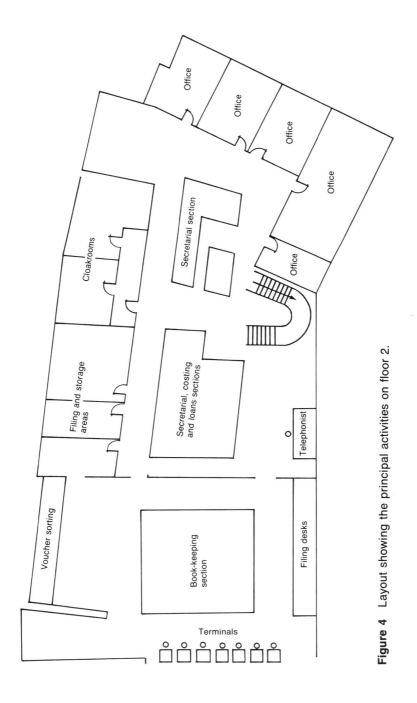

Figure 4 Layout showing the principal activities on floor 2.

they are attentive to identifying other general customer needs and to explain the relevant products/services available and to link them into specialist counsel where necessary.

Enquiries of all kinds are also handled by this section. This enquiry provision entails recording details, passing all or some of the requirements onto a relevant section or seek the answers to the questions themselves and replying to the relevant customer. Although this is very often a distraction from the other personal banking tasks it does offer economies concerning workload and manning levels.

In order to facilitate the provision of these activities, this section is located close to the main entrance on floor 1.

Student banking section
One and a part student banking officers are employed to meet the demands of further education students (primarily Coventry Polytechnic) with regard to the opening of accounts, general queries and other student-related matters.

Regular payments section
Two full-time staff are responsible for arranging and updating standing order provisions for all customers (including corporate business). Requests for changes to standing orders are received by mail, telephone and direct personal request. All requests are routed to the section together with any general queries relating to this particular service. Although direct personal requests often lead to numerous (and sometimes lengthy) explanations concerning procedures and also the provision of appropriate advice, it is recognized as being part of the overall general customer enquiry support provision.

Messenger services
In order to provide support for those activities outside the bank, three messenger/drivers are employed to carry mail, important and urgent messages, and other forms of communication within and around Coventry and to the regional and head offices in Birmingham and London respectively.

Customer service units (CSUs)
The way of handling money/cash transactions with the general public has been separated to reflect the size of the cash transactions involved. Eight CSUs are located on the right-hand side of floor 1 as customers enter the bank from the high street and some or all of these are staffed depending upon the day and time of day.

Figure 5 shows how the capacity requirements of each period are calculated and Figure 6 the way in which the necessary staff are allocated. These units handle cash transactions to a limit of £199. Transactions in excess of this are handled by the central till units.

Central till units (CTUs)
Also positioned on floor 1 are five CTUs. Located in a different area, these units provide services similar to those offered by CSUs but also specifically cater for cash transactions involving amounts of £200 or more. Typically, these units cater for the specific needs of small businesses especially local retail outlets. Figures 3 and 5 provide layout and staffing arrangement details respectively.

Foreign section
Situated in the same area as the CTUs, the foreign section has one and a part staff who, when necessary, provide the direct customer service by offering advice, giving information

BRANCH __COVENTRY, CITY OFFICE__

RECORDING PERIOD FROM 16 NOV. TO 11 DEC.

AVERAGE TRANSACTION TIME 52 SECS	MONDAY		
	CASHIERS (a)	AVERAGE TRANSACTIONS (b)	MAXIMUM TRANSACTIONS (c)
Before 9.30		–	
9.30 – 10.30	5	237	250
10.30 – 11.30	5	253	250
11.30 – 12.30	6	308	312
12.30 – 1.30	7+	392	403
1.30 – 2.30	5	253	250
2.30 – 3.30	5	246	250
TOTAL		1,698	

AVERAGE TRANSACTION TIME 52 SECS	THURSDAY		
	CASHIERS (a)	AVERAGE TRANSACTIONS (b)	MAXIMUM TRANSACTIONS (c)
Before 9.30		–	
9.30 – 10.30	3	136	132
10.30 – 11.30	4	171	190
11.30 – 12.30	4	191	190
12.30 – 1.30	5	254	250
1.30 – 2.30	4	176	190
2.30 – 3.30	4	176	190
TOTAL		1,104	

AVERAGE TRANSACTION TIME 52 SECS	TUESDAY		
	CASHIERS (a)	AVERAGE TRANSACTIONS (b)	MAXIMUM TRANSACTIONS (c)
Before 9.30		–	
9.30 – 10.30	4	184	190
10.30 – 11.30	4+	199	220
11.30 – 12.30	5	229	250
12.30 – 1.30	5+	270	281
1.30 – 2.30	4+	203	220
2.30 – 3.30	4	168	190
TOTAL		1,253	

AVERAGE TRANSACTION TIME 55 SECS	FRIDAY		
	CASHIERS (a)	AVERAGE TRANSACTIONS (b)	MAXIMUM TRANSACTIONS (c)
Before 9.30		–	
9.30 – 10.30	5+	248	253
10.30 – 11.30	5+	258	253
11.30 – 12.30	6+	292	308
12.30 – 1.30	8	383	390
1.30 – 2.30	5+	243	253
2.30 – 3.30	6	279	280
TOTAL		1,703	

AVERAGE TRANSACTION TIME 53 SECS	WEDNESDAY		
	CASHIERS (a)	AVERAGE TRANSACTIONS (b)	MAXIMUM TRANSACTIONS (c)
Before 9.30		–	
9.30 – 10.30	4	170	170
10.30 – 11.30	4+	175	198
11.30 – 12.30	4+	189	198
12.30 – 1.30	5+	240	253
1.30 – 2.30	4+	195	198
2.30 – 3.30	4+	176	198
TOTAL		1,145	

	DAY EVENING		
4.30 – 5.30			
5.00 – 5.30			
5.30 – 6.00			
TOTAL			

Cashier Scheduling Table
Service level — 80 per cent of customers queue for less than sixty seconds.
To ensure this level of service, the following activities should be in operation:
1. The cash handling system is used in full.
2. Effective supervision is exercised by both the first cashier and office manager.
3. At times of peak activity, additional cashiers must be drafted on to the counter.

Figure 5 Cashier scheduling table C.S. form 3. **(a)** Customer service units.

BRANCH __COVENTRY CITY OFFICE__

AVERAGE TRANSACTION TIME 92 SECS	MONDAY		
	CASHIERS (a)	AVERAGE TRANSACTIONS (b)	MAXIMUM TRANSACTIONS (c)
Before 9.30		98	
9.30 – 10.30	3+	82	83
10.30 – 11.30	3+	81	83
11.30 – 12.30	3+	75	83
12.30 – 1.30	2+	54	52
1.30 – 2.30	3	56	67
2.30 – 3.30	5+	144	150
TOTAL		590	

RECORDING PERIOD
FROM __16 NOV.__   TO __11 DEC.__

AVERAGE TRANSACTION TIME 84 SECS	THURSDAY		
	CASHIERS (a)	AVERAGE TRANSACTIONS (b)	MAXIMUM TRANSACTIONS (c)
Before 9.30		29	
9.30 – 10.30	2+	50	56
10.30 – 11.30	3	67	71
11.30 – 12.30	2+	49	56
12.30 – 1.30	3	59	71
1.30 – 2.30	2+	43	56
2.30 – 3.30	3+	89	88
TOTAL		386	

AVERAGE TRANSACTION TIME 99 SECS	TUESDAY		
	CASHIERS (a)	AVERAGE TRANSACTIONS (b)	MAXIMUM TRANSACTIONS (c)
Before 9.30		39	
9.30 – 10.30	2+	40	45
10.30 – 11.30	2+	38	45
11.30 – 12.30	2+	39	45
12.30 – 1.30	2+	45	45
1.30 – 2.30	2+	43	45
2.30 – 3.30	3+	71	73
TOTAL		315	

AVERAGE TRANSACTION TIME 81 SECS	FRIDAY		
	CASHIERS (a)	AVERAGE TRANSACTIONS (b)	MAXIMUM TRANSACTIONS (c)
Before 9.30		27	
9.30 – 10.30	3+	81	94
10.30 – 11.30	3	72	76
11.30 – 12.30	2+	59	60
12.30 – 1.30	3	72	76
1.30 – 2.30	3	74	76
2.30 – 3.30	4	104	111
TOTAL		489	

AVERAGE TRANSACTION TIME 87 SECS	WEDNESDAY		
	CASHIERS (a)	AVERAGE TRANSACTIONS (b)	MAXIMUM TRANSACTIONS (c)
Before 9.30		43	
9.30 – 10.30	2+	44	56
10.30 – 11.30	2	33	40
11.30 – 12.30	2	37	40
12.30 – 1.30	2	39	40
1.30 – 2.30	2+	46	56
2.30 – 3.30	3+	83	88
TOTAL		325	

	DAY EVENING		
4.30 – 5.30			
5.00 – 5.30			
5.30 – 6.00			
TOTAL			

Cashier Scheduling Table
Service level — 80 per cent of customers queue for less than sixty seconds.
To ensure this level of service, the following activities should be in operation:
1. The cash handling system is used in full.
2. Effective supervision is exercised by both the first cashier and office manager.
3. At times of peak activity, additional cashiers must be drafted on to the counter.

Figure 5   Cashier scheduling table C.S. form 3. **(b)** Customer till units.

Mon. 16 Nov.	09.30–10.30	10.30–11.30	11.30–12.30	12.30–13.30	13.30–14.30	14.30–15.30	15.30–16.00
Cashiers required	5.0	5.0	6.0	7.5	5.0	5.0	None
Full-time	2.0	2.0	2.0	2.0	0.0	2.0	
Part-time							
Val	✓	✓					
Gail			0.5	✓	✓		
Pam			✓	✓	✓	15.00	
Janice						✓	
Joan	✓	✓	0.5	✓	✓	✓	
Balance +(−)	(1.0)	(1.0)	(1.0)	(0.5)	✓	(0.5)	
Cashiers shared between CTUs and CSUs							
Linda	✓	✓	✓	0.5	✓	✓	
Glenda	✓	✓	✓	0.5	✓	✓	

Tues. 17 Nov.	09.30–10.30	10.30–11.30	11.30–12.30	12.30–13.30	13.30–14.30	14.30–15.30	15.30–16.00
Cashiers required	4.0	5.0	5.0	6.0	5.0	4.0	None
Full-time	2.0	2.0	2.0	1.0	1.0	2.0	
Part-time							
Kate	✓	✓	0.5	✓	✓	✓	
Glenda	✓	✓	✓	✓	✓		
Ingrid			✓	✓	✓		
Lesley			✓	✓	✓	✓	
Linda			✓	✓	✓		
Gail	✓	✓	✓	✓	✓	✓	
Balance +(−)	1	✓	1.5	1.0	✓	✓	
Cashiers shared between CTUs and CSUs	—	—	—	—	—	—	

Figure 6 Sample CSU staffing arrangements schedule.

and completing financial transactions at the two till units shown in Figure 3. They are responsible for providing a full range of foreign currency transactions (cash and travellers cheques) including scheduling requirements in line with customer requests, processing payments for the transactions involved and all other aspects of foreign currency provision for both business and individual customers.

Bulk coin unit
Located within the perimeters of the security area, the bulk coin unit handles the sorting of the sterling coin and notes.

Office management
Together with an assistant, the office manager is responsible for the general administration undertaken on floor 1 as well as that on floor 2 (see later) except securities, loans and secretarial/typing support.

Administration accountant
Located in the secure area, the administration accountant, together with an assistant is responsible for checking all transactions concerning money transmissions. For example, direct payments (through branch terminals, branch to branch or to other banks) and larger amounts of money such as for solicitors and house purchases, and for business companies wishing to transfer funds immediately to subsidiaries.

Floor 2 arrangements

The general layout for floor 2 is shown as Figure 4 and on this level are located the following sections.

Corporate banking
As shown in Figure 2 over 20 per cent of the staff currently employed at the Coventry city office are deployed in the corporate banking sector of its activities. With the additional and focused support of the branch director the activities of this section primarily concern business customers and range from large public companies to partnerships and sole traders.

Secretaries/telephonist
The secretarial support for all the activities of the bank is separated into that which is designated certain activities and managers and that which is classed as being a general or unallocated provision. The former is located on floor 2 in the area shown in Figure 4, with the latter on floor 3 as explained later. Although coming within the overall jurisdiction of the office manager the activities undertaken by the secretaries are, in fact, managed by the particular senior members of staff involved. Within this broad category of supporting activity is the telephone switchboard which remains the principal task of a telephonist with support throughout the day provided by designated secretaries.

Book-keeping
The book-keeping section is responsible for the input of all money transmissions into the bank's data processing systems. These are made through the office terminals into the centrally-based customer systems at Gloucester and Manchester. In addition, it links all cheques presented and credits paid into the national/international bank clearing system which is used by all major banks in the UK.

Administration

In addition to providing general administrative support, the administration section also comprises foreign transactions principally relating to business customers regarding import/export arrangements, stock exchange transactions, banker's cheques and other low-volume products/services.

Loans and overdraft sections

This section is responsible for handling queries regarding loans and overdrafts, the issue of credit cards and determining credit ratings for both individual and business customers.

Advances sections

The advances section provides statistics and other data to support a whole range of managers' analyses and decisions. This provision is to support particular requirements (as part of the assessment of a major loan application) as well as those requirements for general activities.

Secretarial support services

In addition to the secretarial support for individual managers there is also a provision of a general nature which is not permanently allocated to support particular areas of activity. Any sections requiring secretarial services, therefore, may use this provision to meet their particular needs.

Floor 3 arrangements

Most of the space on floor 3 of the current premises is leased to Abbey Life. Due to its need for more space with growth from its own activities as well as from the satellite policies described earlier, the bank has agreed to take over the lease for floor 3. This has now provided the opportunity to reorganize the bank using three floors.

Automatic teller machines

In addition to the manned services outlined above, as with all UK banks and building societies, Barclays has been increasingly investing in automatic teller machines (ATMs) at all its outlets. Referred to as 'Barclays Bank cash dispensers' (BBCDs), the ATMs are aimed at providing an improved level of customer service both in normal banking hours (between 09.30 and 15.30 from Monday to Friday) and more importantly, at all other times on every day of the year. The benefits to customers as well illustrated by the number of cash transactions completed, details of which are provided in Figure 7.

Clerical work improvement programme

Barclays Bank monitors the staff requirements within its outlets through a clerical work improvement programme (CWIP). Centrally administered, CWIP measures the staff requirements based primarily upon the volume of tasks which are undertaken. Using synthetics it establishes times for major transactions and from this can calculate the number of staff required to meet the services provided at each outlet. Figure 5 provides an illustration of this for the cashier scheduling task at this branch. Based upon a service level where 80 per cent of customers should queue for less than sixty seconds (refer to the bottom right-hand corner of Figure 5), average transaction times are calculated for each day together

Outlet	Number of transactions	Cash withdrawn (£)	Average amount of cash withdrawn (£)
Average number of transactions during a typical 24 hour period			
1. TTW/1	696	13,317	19
2. TTW/2	664	12,253	18
3. Cheylesmore	226	5,070	22
4. Station	315	7,107	23
5. Lobby	343	5,447	16
Total	2,244	43,194	19
15.30 Tues. to 09.30 Wed.			
1. TTW/1	97	3,160	32
2. TTW/2	77	3,380	43
3. Cheylesmore	60	2,230	37
4. Station	105	2,660	25
5. Lobby	No access	No access	—
Total	339	11,430	34
15.30 Fri. to 15.30 Mon.			
1. TTW/1	2,153	44,710	21
2. TTW/2	2,163	43,120	20
3. Cheylesmore	980	22,000	22
4. Station	875	24,010	27
5. Lobby	546	9,045	17
Total	6,717	142,885	21

Note: On one day when outlets 1, 2 and 5 were inoperative, the cash service units in the banking area completed 789 cash withdrawal transactions between 09.30 and 15.30 — on a similar day, the number of cash withdrawal transactions would average 275.

Figure 7   Number of cash withdrawal transactions.

with the average number of transactions hour by hour throughout each day. Both of these variables are intended to reflect the cashiers' mix of work and the varying levels of throughput involved. With these established, staffing arrangements can then be scheduled similar to those shown in Figure 6.

Marketing the bank's services

There is growing competition in those services which had in the past been traditionally within the banking sector. Not only is this coming from other financial sectors (for example building societies) but also from major department stores who have all developed arrangements for credit facilities for their customers. Barclays, like other banks, has similarly been increasing the emphasis on its marketing function. It has recognized the importance of determining the level of service offered to different types of customer. By highlighting

---

The Coventry City Centre offers a whole range of services which total over three hundred. Many of these, however, are corporate products which are at the 'top end' of the professional advice scale (for example, investment and share dealings). In addition, although supplied through a High Street branch, some one hundred of these services are, in fact, typically provided by regionally-based staff (for example, the international services branch).

The main services provided are relatively few in number and are:

- Assent
- Barclaycard
- Barclayloan
- Barclayplus
- Capital advantage
- Connect card
- Current accounts
    Interest option
    Instant option

- Deposit account
- High rate deposit account
- Standby
- Starting work package
- Student account
- Supersavers

Figure 8 Current services provided by the bank.

customers within certain salary brackets, the bank is able to personalize its approach in terms of relevant products which may better serve the particular customer. Like most banks, Barclays offers a wide range of services some of which are described in Figure 8. The bank's aim is to target those sectors of its customers in order to improve the relevance of any services it highlights by personalized mailings throughout the year. In this way it supports the product-selling objectives by appropriate mailings supported by personal contact by letter and/or telephone, as required. Internally, it has also developed a customer action procedure in order to identify customer ratings, thereby enabling it to respond with knowledge of the relevant customer details. The provision of a marketing officer to spearhead these initiatives indicates the bank's recognition of these necessary corporate changes.

Saturday opening provision

When Barclays decided to increase its times of opening to include a Saturday provision, all other major banks were quick to follow. All banks provide a similar basic structure where only key outlets open for this extra day.

In order to staff the branches concerned, the regional office in Birmingham arranges for the allocation of staff, some of whom work elsewhere in the region. Given that this is voluntary overtime working, individual members of staff are asked to indicate their own level of availability throughout a twelve-month period, identifying those Saturdays on which they are unavailable. All submissions are processed by the regional office together with the staff levels requested by each branch involved.

As with other banks, the activities are restricted to exclude all cash withdrawals and paying-in facilities normally provided by the CSUs and CTUs. Envelopes containing paying-in slips can be deposited and ATMs are, as usual, open for cash withdrawals. The principal activities concern support for discussions and receipt of applications for various products and services together with general and specific enquiries to include account balances, cheque book requests, the collection of foreign currency and travellers cheques. Queries regarding regular payments and similar activities are recorded to be dealt with at the beginning of the following week.

Coventry city business centre currently has a provision of ten staff on each Saturday working from 9.30 a.m. to 12 noon.

The summary below provides some of the key aspects which need to be taken into account when reviewing current arrangements in line with the needs of the business. Providing appropriate operations support is recognized as being a critical contribution to the overall growth and success of the bank.

Given that sales revenue, customer services and costs are the essential facets of this business, then these need to be reflected in what the staff do and where different functions are positioned. The brief explanations below are designed to reflect these.

1. Coventry City Centre is both a business centre and general outlet. It needs therefore, to meet its overall objective by improving both its corporate and general activities.

2. However, the different needs of these two tasks must be recognized and provided within the one building.

3. Personal bankers are recognized as providing a key activity both in terms of giving appropriate advice to customers and also selling services.

4. Student banking section often deals with first time or relatively inexperienced customers, this section is charged with providing an overall range of activities including advice, general enquiries and direct selling related tasks. As potentially important customers of the future, the bank considers that this provision is important to both the short- and longer-term growth of the business.

5. Regular payments section has the task of creating, maintaining and terminating regular payments for both business, professional and personal customers. The work requires (as do other transactions and transmissions) a high level of accurate recording and the need for initiative-taking in terms of cross-checks and placing instructions within this context of a client's previous records and activities.

6. Customer service and central till units form a core activity of the bank's activities. Assessing capacity requirements in order to maintain agreed levels of customer service are well recognized as illustrated in the case study narrative and Figures 5 and 6.

7. Foreign section provides a full range of activities from request through to the cash transaction. Providing a quick response in terms of the immediate needs of both business and personal customers is an important (though relatively infrequent) part of the overall service.

8. Securities section handles a range of activities as detailed earlier in the case study. It predominantly receives customer enquiries and requests by telephone and mail. In addition, some customers do call in person at the bank and are then linked to this section through enquiries. These matters are currently handled by a member of this section's staff.

9. The corporate banking section is responsible for handling the service requirements of businesses in the region. These can range from day-to-day tasks through to the negotiation of loans to a certain level. This side of the bank also links to the risk management function in the region in order to help provide its customers with professional help in line with their high level financing needs.

10. The book-keeping section is responsible for all money transmissions and fulfils the other part of the core activity described under CSUs and CTUs. Working on tight schedules and high volume transactions it needs to meet daily deadlines linked to centrally-based corporate and national clearance systems. At the moment there are occasions when the daily transmissions have not been completed on the same day. It appears that work comes into the section through both entrances and does not always feed into the start point of the system. The few that occasionally are missed are 'found' later.

11. The loans and overdraft section is responsible for providing the after-sales documentation and maintenance of existing arrangements throughout the life of an agreement.

Figure 9 Issues concerning appropriate banking arrangements.

Review of current banking arrangements

'When Graham Richardson took over as branch director some months ago', explained John Gibson, the office manager, 'he was able to replace several of the existing team partly through retirement and also by appropriate transfers within Barclays Bank as a whole. Having working for him at another large branch at the other end of the Birmingham region I was delighted to contribute towards improving existing activities and to the planned overall growth within CCC itself. Decisions concerning growth strategies and the rearrangement of small units on a satellite basis were obviously considered early on and the impact on support activities needed to be part of that review. I was also appropriately asked to look at the current banking arrangements in terms of the position of activities with regard to both the customer and other support functions within the bank.

'The overriding need in any organization is to increase sales revenue while meeting agreed customer service targets within acceptable levels of cost. A service business like ours is no exception. Given the CWIP provision then we have tried and tested times for jobs to allow us to monitor our staffing requirements as work volumes change, improvements are implemented and new equipment becomes available. Part of the initial review of our current arrangements, however, is to ensure that we are deploying our staff effectively to ensure agreed levels of customer service on the one hand and the efficient achievement of the numerous administrative and other tasks on the other. Having now settled into the routines of this branch I am now at the point of reviewing where we position activities in relation to improving sales growth, customer service and costs.' A summary of some of the key issues to be borne in mind are given in Figure 9.

Future developments

The part of floor 3 which is currently leased to Abbey Life has become available and it is intended by the business centre to retain it for its own use. The closure of two smaller branches within Coventry over the past twelve months has entailed the rescheduling of work to this main branch. In addition, a restriction on the services offered by other branches is underway and the cumulative effect of these moves together with the growth within the branch itself has necessitated an increase in floor space requirements. The opportunity to take over floor 3 has removed the space constraint which had, until this time, been a major restriction. With this change in circumstances, space is no longer a problem and the bank now has the opportunity to reconsider its service provision and the positioning of its various activities and sections in line with providing adequate customer service and yet ensuring that the branch can meet the staffing levels considered to be appropriate and to achieve the profit necessary from one of Barclays more important and growing business centres.

Berwick Carpets Plc

Berwick Carpets Plc (BC) manufactures and sells tufted and woven carpets and carpet yarn. Although part of an international group of companies, it is managed as an independent business responsible for its own marketing, manufacturing and investment requirements. It ranks about tenth in size in the industry with a turnover of £50m in 1988. In common with the remainder of the carpet industry, it has over the past fifteen years experienced a shift in the balance of sales towards tufted and away from woven carpets.

The manufacturing facilities consist of a spinning mill and both a tufted and woven carpet facility. Whilst the spinning mill is on a separate site, carpet manufacturing processes are in the same location as are the sales and other functions of the business. The tufted and woven carpets, however, comprise two separate divisions, and this case study concerns the tufted carpet division (TCD).

The products

Unlike many UK carpet companies, BC has held its sales levels for tufted carpet over the past three years. It makes a range of carpet qualities and Tables 1 and 2 show these in three grades and the average manufacturing costs of a typical product. The company's marketing strategy has been to provide products in the top segment of each of the grades shown in 1. Hence, each of the grade 1 carpets is at the top of grade 1 range, and so on.

Sales have been maintained over the past three years. Details for these up to 31 December 1988 are given in Table 3 together with the forecasts for 1989, which have been based upon the upturn in actual sales in the second half of 1988 and known orders in the first two months of 1989.

Raw materials

Each carpet is offered in a range of colours and is made from either a spun polypropylene, nylon or spun-woollen base. The colours offered and raw materials used are given in Table

This case study is © by Professor T.J. Hill (London Business School) and K.H.A. Negal (University of Bath). It is intended as the basis for class discussion and not as an example of good or bad management.

Table 1 Grades of tufted carpet

Grade	Tufted carpets
1	Marble, Grenoble, Firenza, Barcarole, Casino
2	Maltese, Gazelle, Baroque, Barbary
3	Dalmatian, Royalty, Centurian, Lotus

Notes
1. Grade 3 is the highest quality of carpet.
2. Contract carpets are one-off carpets designed to customer specification and sold direct to the customer (e.g. hotels, house and office block builders and cinema chains). Invariably, they are made from non-standard colours, and often in material qualities not used on the standard range of carpets.
3. All non-contract carpets are sold to retail shops.
4. On contract carpets, one problem is judging the required yarn delivery to meet the order. Excess yarn is difficult to use whilst under-production constitutes failure to meet a customer's contract.

Table 2 Manufacturing costs for a product which is typical of all grades of carpet

Aspect	Percentage of total manufacturing costs
Direct labour	7
Direct materials	81
Manufacturing overhead[a]	12
	100

[a] 'Other' overhead is included at a later stage in the costing procedure.

4. Both polypropylene and nylon are man-made, whilst wool is a natural fibre. Consequently, there is a relatively high incidence of faults in the spun-woollen yarn deliveries (see Table 4). Without raw material inventory in the appropriate colour, faults in a yarn delivery will lead to failure to meet a customer's delivery promise. This problem is invariably the case on contract carpets where the yarn colour(s) involved will be customer-specified. If faults go undetected and the yarn enters the process, then the additional costs associated with substandard carpet and the further impact upon delivery delay can be considerable.

Raw material inventory is valued at about £350,000 with work-in-progress standing at a further £180,000.

Production process

The process lead time is between two and five days. Each carpet goes through some of the common processes and these are shown in Table 5. Carpets can be delayed between one process and the next without affecting the quality of the carpet. All carpets are tufted (i.e. the primary backing cloth for the carpet is fed underneath a needle carrying the yarn. At predetermined intervals, the needle passes through the backing cloth and a looper on the underside retains a loop of yarn beneath the cloth). After several other processes, the carpet has its secondary back put on by the backing plant. This can be either jute cloth which is stuck to or latex foam which is applied to the reverse side of the carpet.

Table 3   Actual sales of tufted carpets in the three years to 31 December 1988 and forecast sales for the next twelve months

Grade	Carpet	Actual sales[a]			Forecast 1989 sales[a]
		1986	*1987*	*1988*	
1	Marble	1,423	1,321	1,457	1,400
	Grenoble	76	35	30	20
	Firenza	38	6	4	4
	Barcarole	24	4	2	4
	Casino	59	35	36	55
	Total	1,620	1,401	1,529	1,483
2	Maltese	42	46	45	50
	Gazelle	213	225	166	150
	Barbary	54	52	64	180
	Baroque	202	268	286	250
	Total	511	591	561	630
3	Dalmatian[b]	—	28	57	100
	Royalty	106	84	108	130
	Centurian	184	134	168	230
	Lotus[b]	—	—	16	100
	Contract	7	11	28	160
	Total	297	257	377	720
Total		2,428	2,249	2,467	2,833

[a] All figures are in square metres (000).
[b] Dalmatian was introduced in 1987 and Lotus at the end of 1988.

Spun-woollen yarn deliveries

On deliveries of spun-woollen yarn, the number of faults experienced on a delivery reduces, because of delays involved, the tufting process to about two-thirds of its standard throughput. It is estimated that for every square metre of yarn tufted there will be, on average, one yarn break due to faulty yarn.

In addition, because of the different materials (yarns) and the different carpet qualities involved, not all tufting machines can be used to make all carpets. Table 6 shows the range of tufting machines, the average weekly, potential output and the carpet types for which the machines can be used.

Dyeing and drying are processes only used on nylon yarn which is purchased as a natural shade. After tufting, nylon-based carpets are then dyed and dried, a process called 'piece dying'. The dye house currently works a forty-hour week and can produce in a single shift sufficient dyed yarn per week to make 10,000 square metres of carpet.

Table 4 Raw materials and colour range offered

Grade	Carpet	Number of colours	Spun polypropylene	Nylon	Spun-woollen
			Raw material		
	Marble	26	✓		
	Grenoble	8	✓		
1	Firenza	(see note)		✓	
	Barcarole	(see note)		✓	
	Casino	(see note)		✓	
	Maltese	(see note)		✓	
2	Gazelle	15	✓		
	Barbary	7			✓
	Baroque	12	✓		
	Dalmatian	10	✓		
	Royalty	(see note)		✓	
3	Centurian	20			✓
	Lotus	(see note)		✓	
	Contract	Unlimited	✓	✓	✓
Material delivery lead times (weeks)			2	6	6

Note
These carpets are made from nylon which is delivered in a natural colour and dyed on site to meet a whole range of colours. The dyeing process takes one day.

The shearer crops the tip of each tuft as a cylinder lawn mower trims grass. The length of yarn removed by the cut can be adjusted on the machine. The pre- and post-steaming processes take place before and after the shearer. They are, however, only used for Centurian and to ensure that the tuft is presented in the way to yield the best quality results. The shearing machine is currently utilized for about 65 per cent of its time.

The backing plant is currently running on a 24-hour basis over five days with weekend overtime where necessary. The skills required for this job are difficult to find and consequently three eight-hour shifts are not feasible. Also, an agreement with the local trade union restricts the total hours which can be worked over a twelve month period. Average output from this process is some 45,000 square metres per week. This figure takes into account average maintenance, breakdowns and changeover times. The number of working weeks available in a year is 46 when account has been taken of the annual shutdowns and bank holidays.

Labour force

Of the 220 directs employed at BC, some 70–80 work on the production processes described in the case. In total, there are about 350 employees on this site. Table 7 gives the breakdown of gross pay for a direct worker. Bonus payments are made in direct proportion to output

Table 5   Production processes by carpet quality

Grade	Carpets	Production process							
		Tuft	*Yarn dye and dry*[a]	*Repair*[b]	*Print*[c]	*Steam*	*Shear*	*Steam*[d]	*Back*
	Marble	✓					✓		✓
	Grenoble	✓					✓		✓
1	Firenza	✓	✓		✓		✓		✓
	Barcarole	✓	✓		✓		✓		✓
	Casino	✓	✓		✓		✓		✓
	Maltese	✓	✓				✓		✓
2	Gazelle	✓					✓		✓
	Barbary	✓					✓		✓
	Baroque	✓					✓		✓
	Dalmatian	✓		✓			✓		✓
3	Royalty	✓	✓				✓		✓
	Centurian	✓		✓		✓	✓	✓	✓
	Lotus	✓	✓				✓		✓
	Contract[e]								

[a]   Yarn dye and dry is only for nylon-based carpets.
[b]   Repair — all carpets are inspected after tufting. If a repair is necessary it is completed on the tufting machine except in the case of Dalmatian and Centurian where any repairs are completed on a separate frame.
[c]   This printing process is to apply dye-resistant chemicals to these carpets.
[d]   Only the top quality grade 3 carpets go through the steaming process before and after shearing.
[e]   Contract carpets go through different processes depending upon the raw material. Polypropylene is as for Gazelle; nylon, Royalty and woollen, Centurian.

and do not relate to the hours worked. The payments made vary depending upon the weekly output and are shown in Table 8. In the current pay discussions, the trade unions are requesting, amongst other things, a higher incentive payment for output. They argue that the current actual bonus earnings are reducing and that a productivity-linked payment increase through the incentive scheme would make sense all round. This line of argument is supported by the work study department as a sensible approach to resolving the pay issue and also in helping to reduce manufacturing costs.

The future

BC's marketing strategy is to continue to produce the present range of carpets and also to start to build up the business in the contracts market. Currently, 50 per cent of all contract carpets are made of spun-woollen and it is expected that this composition of sales will remain the pattern for the future. If it does change, then it is anticipated that it will show an increase in spun-woollen yarns of up to a further 10 per cent.

Table 6 Tufting machine average output

Tufting machine	Carpet type	Average weekly output (square metres)
1	Dalmatian	5,500
	Contracts	3,000
2	Casino	10,000
	Barcarole	10,000
	Firenza	10,000
3	Royalty	7,000
4	Centurian	4,000
	Lotus	4,000
5	Baroque	10,000
	Contracts	8,000
6	Marble	15,000
	Grenoble	20,000
	Maltese	10,000
7	Marble	15,000
	Grenoble	20,000
	Maltese	10,000
8	Gazelle	12,000
9	Grenoble	20,000
	Barbary	10,000

Notes
1. Centurian outputs on machine 4 can vary between 3,000 and 5,000.
2. Contracts on machine 5 can vary between 6,000 and 10,000.
3. Dalmatian on machine 1 can vary between 4,000 and 7,000.
4. Woollen contracts are completed only on machine 1 and both polypropylene and nylon on machine 5.
5. Not all tufting machines are run throughout a week. The output figures above express the potential levels of output and not the actual, as machines are run in line with sales demand.
6. The output figures above show alternative figures depending upon the carpet type. Hence machine 1 can produce either 5,500 m²/wk of Dalmatian or 3,000 m²/wk of Contract carpet.
7. Carpet types can only be made on the machines shown above. In a very few instances it may be possible to make a carpet on another machine but it would result in lower throughput figures and a significant increase in faults.

Contracts is a very cost competitive market but one where very large repeat orders may be earned by a successful supplier. BC intends that this area of the market should provide an important area of sales growth. BC's all round success, however, has been built on its growing reputation as a manufacturer of quality carpets. It recognizes quite clearly that this is the basis for both its current and future strategy in the market-place.

Table 7 Composition of gross pay for a typical direct worker

Payment	Percentage of total gross pay
Basic	75
Overtime	10
Bonus	15
	100

Table 8 Standard production hours for different carpets and bonus payments

Standard Production hours

Grade	Carpet	Standard hours to produce 100 sq. metres
	Marble	4.1
	Grenoble	3.0
1	Firenza	5.1
	Barcarole	5.1
	Casino	5.1
	Maltese	5.4
2	Gazelle	4.5
	Barbary	6.8
	Baroque	4.9
	Dalmatian	6.8
	Royalty	5.9
3	Centurian	8.5
	Lotus	4.8
	Contract	Varies depending upon the yarn

Bonus payments

Weekly output (square metres)	Bonus payment per thousand sq. metres (£)
Up to 30,000	0.35
31.000–40,000	0.45
41,000–50,000	0.55
51,000 and over	0.65

Blitz Company

The president of the Blitz Company, Alfred Jodal, was reviewing the company's position in October of its third year of existence. In the days ahead, he had to plan the next year's operations.

The market

The Blitz Company manufactured electrical circuit boards to the specifications of a variety of electronic manufacturers. Each board consisted of a thin sheet of insulating material with thin metal strips (conductors) bonded to its surface. The insulating sheet acted as a structural member and supported electrical components and fragile conductors that connected the components into an electrical network. A typical example of the products produced by the company was a circuit board consisting of a $4'' \times 2'' \times \frac{1}{16}''$ plastic plate with 18 separate conductors bonded on its surface. In the customer's plant, assemblers positioned electronic components in the holes on the board, soldered them in place, and installed the assembly in final products such as two-way radios, electronic instruments, and radar equipment. Because circuit boards reduced the labour required in assembling and wiring electrical components, lessened the chances of human errors in assembly, and reduced the size of completed assemblies, the market for circuit boards had grown rapidly since World War II.

Competitive advantages

Since the start of operations nearly three years before, the Blitz Company had specialized in making circuit boards for experimental devices and for pilot production runs. Earnings statements and a balance sheet are shown in Tables 1 and 2 respectively. Most of the company's managers were engineers with substantial experience in the electronics industry.

Table 1 Profit and loss statements

	Sept., year 3		Aug., year 3		July, year 3		Jan.–June, year 3		Year 2	Year 1
Net sales[a]	$66,402	100.0%	$69,378	100.0%	$32,178	100.0%	$157,170	100.0%	$187,674	$101,556
Direct material										
Beginning in-process inventory	16,554	24.9	9,486	13.7	7,812	24.3	6,324	4.0	5,022	2,418
From stock and purchases	11,532	17.4	24,924	35.9	9,114	28.3	45,942	29.2	51,894	28,272
Chemicals, film, and supplies	4,650	7.0	7,254	10.5	4,836	15.0	20,088	12.5	13,206	7,998
Shop wages and foreman's salary	12,462	18.5	11,718	16.9	7,812	24.3	45,384	28.9	58,032	32,550
Overtime wages	558	0.8	2,046	2.9	0	0	2,046	1.3	na	na
Other expenses[b]	2,976	4.5	2,232	3.2	1,860	5.8	12,462	7.9	14,508	7,068
Total	48,732	73.4	57,660	83.1	31,434	97.7	132,246	84.1	142,662	78,306
Less closing in-process direct material	(13,206)	19.9	(16,554)	23.9	(9,486)	29.5	(7,812)	5.0	(6,324)	(5,022)
Cost of goods manufactured	35,526	53.5	41,106	59.2	21,948	68.2	124,434	79.2	136,338	73,284
Gross profit	30,876	46.5	28,272	40.8	10,230	31.8	32,736	20.8	51,336	28,272
Company overhead										
Salaries (administration, engineering and office)	9,672	14.6	10,974	15.8	8,556	26.6	50,964	32.4	53,568	22,692
Other (rent, interest, telephone, utilities, etc.)	1,674	2.5	1,860	2.7	1,302	4.1	8,742	5.6	15,624	5,766
Profit (loss) before taxes	$19,530	29.4%	$15,438	22.3%	$ 372	1.2%	$(26,970)	(17.2)%	$(17,856)	$ (186)

[a] Recorded on day of shipment.
[b] Includes water, heat, power, payroll taxes, group insurance, and depreciation ($558 per month in year 3).
Source: Company records.

Table 2 Balance sheet, 30 September, year 3

Assets				Liabilities		
Cash		$ 26,598		Accounts payable	$ 48,360	
Accounts receivable		106,392		Commissions	12,462	
				Taxes payable	6,138	
				Notes payable	28,458	
Inventory						
Raw material	5,952					
Supplies	4,464					
In-process	13,206	23,622				
Prepaid expenses		4,650				
Current assets			161,262	Current liabilities		95,418
	Cost	*Depreciation*				
Buildings	29,760	3,906		Long-term notes		5,208
Machinery	31,062	6,324				
Small tools	4,650	4,464				
Office equipment	7,254	1,302				
	72,726	15,996				
Fixed assets			56,730			
				Net worth		
				Capital stock	127,038	
				Deficit Jan. 1, year 3	(18,042)	
				Profit for year	8,370	117,366
Total			$217,992			$217,992

Source: Company records.

Jodal and the firm's design engineer Alexander Krebs had invented several of the company's processing methods; they had also patented applications, processes and modifications of some commercial machinery. The president believed that the Blitz Company was therefore more adept than its competitors in anticipating and resolving the problems inherent in new designs and production techniques.

Manufacturing process

The manufacturing process was divided into three stages: preparation, image transfer and fabrication. In the first stage, patterns, jigs and fixtures were produced and raw material was prepared for processing. The next step, image transfer, yielded a sheet of plastic with appropriate conductors bonded to the surface. In the final stage, this material was transformed into shaped, drilled and finished circuit boards. The most common sequence of operations is shown in Table 3.

Table 3   Sequence of operations, standard times and production records for September, year 3

Operation	Standard production times (minutes)		September's production		September's total standard production			
					(minutes)			(hours)
	Set-up	Run	Orders	Circuits	Set-up	Run	Total	Total
Photograph	29	0	59	4,690	1,710	0	1,710	28.5
Inspect and shear	20	0.5[a]	60	5,740	1,200	360	1,560	26.0
Drill (location holes)	10	0.5[a]	60	5,740	600	360	960	16.0
KPR	1	10[a]	60	5,740	60	7,200	7,260	121.0
Touch up and inspect	10	3[a]	60	5,740	600	2,150	2,750	45.8
Plate	10	5[a]	52	5,616	520	3,510	4,030	67.2
Etch	10	4[a]	59	5,739	590	2,870	3,460	57.7
Shear (into circuit boards)	10	0.5[a]	56	5,828	560	360	920	15.3
Drill (location holes)	10	0.5[b]	53	5,709	530	2,855	3,385	56.4
Configuration								
Rout	50[c]	1[b]	49	2,380	2,450	2,380	4,830	80.5
Punch press	150	0.6[b]	4	3,329	600	2,000	2,600	43.3
Drill holes								
Green pantographic	50[c]	0.05/hole	8	1,879[d]	400	9,400	9,800	163.3
Manual	15	0.10/hole	40	494	600	4,940	5,540	92.3
Epoxy painting	50[c]	1[b]	8	1,000	400	1,000	1,400	23.7
Stake								
Eyelet	20	0.07/eye	14	487	280	340	620	10.3
Terminals	20	0.15/term	3	257	60	40	100	1.7
Solder	30	1.5[b]	8	1,233	240	1,850	2,090	34.8
Inspect and pack	10	1.5[b]	60	5,740	600	8,610	9,210	153.5
Total					12,000	50,225	62,225	1,037.1

[a] Per panel.
[b] Per circuit board.
[c] Includes time for jigs and fixtures.
[d] Only lots of more than 100 boards were drilled on this machine. This time is for each board; it was estimated by assuming that more than one board would be drilled at a time.
Source: prepared by casewriter from company production records and standard times estimated by Jodal.
Assumptions: 8 circuit boards per panel; 100 holes per circuit board; 10 eyelets and 1 terminal per circuit board.

Preparation stage

The pattern used in the image transfer stage was made by photographing the customer's blueprint and producing a 'panel' negative showing a number of the circuits in actual size, side by side, on a 12″ × 18″ film. This negative was then used in conjunction with a light-sensitive chemical (KPR), as described later in the case. In other preparatory steps, simple drilling jigs and fixtures and routing fixtures for the fabrication operations were made, using bench drills, a circular saw, a band saw and hand tools. Stamping dies, when required, were obtained from subcontractors.

The principal raw material used by the company was a plastic panel with a thin sheet of copper facing bonded to one surface. This material was usually purchased in sheets of desired thickness measuring approximately 48″ × 36″. In the preparation stage, these sheets were inspected visually for flaws, and were then cut on a shear into smaller panels measuring approximately 12″ × 18″. The panel's exact dimensions were chosen by the operator so that the maximum number of circuit boards could be obtained from the sheets. Location holes, used to facilitate positioning in later processes, were then drilled in each panel.

Image transfer

In the image transferring process, the panels were washed, dipped into a solution of a light-sensitive chemical (KPR) and baked. A panel negative was then laid over the KPR-coated copper surface and the assembly was exposed to ultraviolet light for two minutes. A finishing dip in a solvent removed that portion of the KPR coating not exposed to ultraviolet light because it had been covered by the dark portions of the negative. After this step, the areas of the panel's copper surface corresponding to the desired conductors remained bare.

Next the bare surfaces (conductors) were protected with a metal plating. The plater inspected each panel, touched up voids in the remaining KPR coating and removed any excess, and then inserted the panel into a 50-gallon plating tank where a 0.001″ thick coating of lead−tin alloy or other metal was deposited on the panel's bare surfaces. In the following etching operation, the plated panels were placed in rubber-coated racks and successively submerged in a coating solvent, a rinse solution, an acid bath and another rinse. The acid ate away any unprotected copper. What remained was a sheet of plastic with a pattern of plated conductors on its surface.

Fabrication

Subsequently, the etched panels were cut into individual circuit boards on the same shear used previously to cut the plastic sheet into panels. Two location holes were then drilled in each circuit board on a bench press.

Each individual board was then reduced to the desired final size and shaped either by die-stamping in a 20-ton punch press or by shaping on a routing machine. The operator of the routing machine (which was similar to a vertical milling machine) placed each circuit board on a fixture that controlled the way it was fed into the cutting tool.

On average, 100 holes were drilled in each circuit board using either ordinary bench drill presses or the company's modified Green pantographic drill press. (Occasionally, these holes were punched out in the preceding stamping operation.) An operator using the pantographic press could drill as many as three circuit boards simultaneously by stacking them on top of each other in a fixture positioned on the machine's worktable. The location of all the drilled holes was controlled by a master pattern (a plastic plate with the proper hole pattern drilled in it) mounted alongside the worktable. To position the tool and drill the circuit boards, the operator simply inserted the machine's follower stylus successively into each of the pattern's holes.

After drilling, some circuit boards were coated with an epoxy resin in a painting process to inhibit damage caused by corrosion, scratching and rough handling.

To assemble eyelets and terminals in the holes of the circuit boards, an operator sat before a simple staking machine and placed the hole to receive an eyelet or terminal on the machine's anvil. Eyelets were fed and positioned automatically and terminals were positioned manually.

In the soldering operation, each circuit was dipped into a vat of molten solder for a few seconds.

For final inspection, any production employee who had run out of his ordinary work visually checked each finished board for omitted operations, scratches and poor workmanship. Items passing inspection were wrapped in draft paper and deposited in a shipping container.

Although the work normally progressed through the entire sequence of operations, some orders bypassed two or three operations. For example, some initial operations were omitted when the customer supplied pre-cut boards or negatives; others were omitted when the customer preferred to do them in his own shop. Occasionally an order was sent ahead and then returned to continue through the normal sequence of processes.

Supervision

Supervisory responsibility for various phases of production was shared by three men: Joseph Hadler, the expediter; Alexander Krebs, the design engineer, and Michael Beck, the shop foreman. Hadler and Krebs reported to the president, Beck reported to Krebs.

Hadler had been hired two months earlier, in August. He kept track of orders in process and initiated action if an order failed to progress through manufacturing satisfactorily. When the foreman's daily progress report (showing the last operation performed on each order) indicated a delay, Hadler investigated and usually secured the missing supplies or instructions, told the foreman to start the job moving again, or called the customer and advised him of possible late delivery. On average, Hadler investigated two or three slow orders each day. In addition, he conferred with the sales manager and president to determine how many small special orders (usually having a four-day delivery date) should be sent into processing.

Krebs's primary duties were to inspect the customer's blueprints and requirements in order to locate design errors, to determine the best means of processing and to identify unusual production problems. In addition, he commonly spent ten hours a week talking with shop employees about these problems and others that cropped up in processing.

Beck, the foreman, was in charge of all other aspects of manufacturing from the time he received a shop order and blueprints until he shipped the order. In total, Beck supervised the activities of twenty production employees. Four of these were lead men who spent about 10 per cent of their time instructing people in their areas or advising the foreman on various problems.

The shop employees

The shop was non-union and employees were paid an hourly wage averaging $3.44 per hour. They used simple, manually controlled apparatus to perform light, short-cycle, repetitive tasks and commonly performed two or three different operations every week. Only the photographing, plating and etching operations were not traded among a number of workers. The photographer alone used the company's camera and darkroom to produce and develop negatives used in image application. The plater and etcher exchanged jobs between themselves, but not with other employees. The usual pattern of work was such that most workers interrupted their tasks from seven to nine times a day to secure more work from another room, to seek advice on a problem, or to deliver completed work to the foreman's desk or other storage area.

Judgement and experience were important in the photographing, plating and etching processes because the operators had to compensate for such factors as changes in the shop's temperature and the slow deterioration of the chemical action in various solutions. In the other operations, some care was required to position both tools and work-pieces accurately and to prevent scratching or marring of the circuit boards. To reduce the chance of damage in transport, panels and circuit boards were moved and stored between operations in racks that held as many as fifteen pieces.

Order processing

As the first step in the preparation of a factory order, Jodal and Krebs estimated material and labour costs. These estimates were then used in preparing a bid for the customer. If the customer subsequently accepted the bid, the Blitz Company would promise delivery in three weeks for orders of less than 1,000 boards and five weeks for larger orders. The estimate sheet and blueprint were then pulled from the files by a secretary and delivered to Krebs, who wrote out detailed material specifications (there were thirty types used by the company) and a factory order showing the delivery date, the number of circuits, the material specifications and the sequence of operations. The order was then sent to the treasurer, who required one or two days to locate the needed raw material at a low price and to order it. (The materials used in September are shown in Table 4.) A secretary then entered the order in a log and sent the blueprint and factory order to the foreman. Most orders reached the foreman about four days after the bid had been accepted.

Occasionally the president or sales manager promised delivery within four days in order to satisfy the customer's urgent need. These rush orders were expedited by Krebs. As soon as the order was received, he wrote material specifications, gave the foreman a factory order and a blueprint, and instructed the treasurer to secure material for delivery on the same or following day.

When Beck received a factory order, he used his own judgement in scheduling preparatory work. Usually, Beck delayed his scheduling decision for several days until the raw material arrived from the vendor. He then estimated the labour required in each step, examined the work in process at critical points, estimated the difficulties in meeting the new order's shipping date, weighed the sales manager's priority on orders already in process, guessed at the possibilities of these orders being held up, and then decided when to schedule the order. As foreman, Beck spent much of his time determining when to move jobs ahead of others during process and when to shift workers from one operation to another.

Until a job was shipped, the factory order and blueprints were kept by the foreman, who gave them to any worker requiring information. A ticket denoting the factory order number was kept with the first rack of material as it moved through processing.

Facilities and layout

When the company moved to its present location in January of its second year, Jodal had chosen a production layout that he felt minimized installation costs, preserved the life of expensive machines and isolated the operations' diverse environments (see Figure 1). Cost had been an important consideration because the company had committed most of its funds for equipment and had not been able to attract outside capital. The plating apparatus had

Table 4 Order size and number of orders processed in September, year 3

Order size[a]	Raw material code letters	Number of orders	Total number of circuit boards
1	A,B,D,E	7	7
2	A,B,F	6	12
3	B,D	2	6
4	A,B,C,F,H	11	44
5	A,D	2	10
6	B,C	2	12
10	B,D,E	3	30
11	D,F	2	22
12	A,J,K	3	36
14	A,E,G	3	42
20	D	1	20
40	B,K	2	80
50	C,E	2	100
60	C	1	60
84	J	1	84
100	C	1	100
113	E	1	113
136	C	1	136
140	F	1	140
154	A	1	154
200	D	1	200
229	E	1	229
252	A	1	252
800	G	1	800
1,000	D,M	2	2,000
1,050	A	1	1,050
		60	5,739

[a] Number of circuit boards in each order.
Source: Company records.

cost about $10,000, while the photographic equipment, the Green pantographic drill press, and the punch press were purchased for approximately $3,000 each. The company had paid an average of $600 apiece for the shear, eight bench-drill presses, the routing machine, band saw, and circular saw; and less than $6,000 (total) for all the other equipment.

Jodal had spent $2,000 to install the partitions for isolating the production processes. (Recent inquiries indicated that removing these and putting up six other ones would cost about $6,000.) The plating and etching processes, which released acid vapours, had been located far from the machining operations to prevent excessive corrosion of the machine tools. Similarly, the machining operations, which created dust, had been separated from the photography, KPR, plating and etching processes, which were sensitive to dust and dirt. After a year and a half, neither the machine tools nor the photographic equipment exhibited signs of corrosion. Similarly, dust from the machining areas had not contaminated other processes, although no doors had been installed to seal the passages between the process areas. In October of its third year, the company was fully utilizing the space in its existing plant. An 1,800-sqare-foot addition was due to be completed in November.

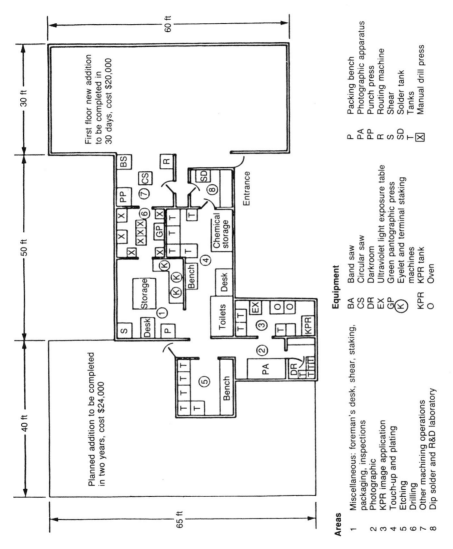

Areas

1. Miscellaneous: foreman's desk, shear, staking, packaging, inspections
2. Photographic
3. KPR image application
4. Touch-up and plating
5. Etching
6. Drilling
7. Other machining operations
8. Dip solder and R&D laboratory

Equipment

BA	Band saw
CS	Circular saw
DR	Darkroom
EX	Ultraviolet light exposure table
GP	Green pantographic press
Ⓚ	Eyelet and terminal staking machines
KPR	KPR tank
O	Oven
P	Packing bench
PA	Photographic apparatus
PP	Punch press
R	Routing machine
S	Shear
SD	Solder tank
T	Tanks
☒	Manual drill press

Figure 1 Plant layout and additions.

Current operating problems

In assessing the company's operating position, Jodal was most concerned about the current difficulties, which he described as bottleneck, performance, quality and delivery problems.

Production bottleneck

The bottleneck was perplexing because it shifted almost daily from one operation to another, without pattern. Anticipating where work would pile up in the shop on a given day had proven difficult because individual orders imposed varying work loads on each operation. These variations stemmed from difference in order size, from orders bypassing some operations, and from differences in circuit designs. Also contributing to fluctuations were the four-day rush orders (usually three a week), orders requiring rework at one or two operations, and work delayed in process pending a customer's delivery of special eyelets and terminals or a design change (one to nine a week). Approximately a quarter of the jobs delayed in process were held as a result of telephone calls from the customer's engineers who had encountered a problem. Then, any time from one day to two weeks later, the customer would relay permission to complete the order as originally specified or give new specifications. About one-quarter of the jobs were stopped as a result of processing problems or mistakes made by a specification change. These orders were held until Krebs could secure permission to deviate from the customer's original specifications.

During the past several months the foreman had found compensating for these variations increasingly difficult because he had no accurate way of predicting where work would pile up or run out, or of assessing the future effects of any corrective action. A recent Wednesday's events were typical.

Early in the morning, three men engaged in manual drilling had run out of work. The foreman shifted them to other tasks, therefore, until additional boards could be expedited to the drilling operation. In this case, the foreman decided to meet the situation by expediting two orders that required work in only one or two operations preceding drilling. By mid-morning one of the men transferred away from drilling had completed his new assignment and had to be given a different job. In the afternoon, when the expedited orders had reached the drilling operation, the foreman found that two employees assigned to certain of the steps, which the expedited orders had bypassed, had run out of work.

Only the small orders (ten circuit boards or less) seemed to pose no scheduling problems. Such orders were always assigned to a senior employee, Arthur Dief, who carried each order from step to step, doing the work himself or having someone else perform it. Dief consistently met delivery deadlines, even on four-day rush orders, and his reject rate was usually zero.

Performance and methods

Jodal realized that it was impossible to evaluate shop productivity precisely. During his daily trips through the shop, however, he had noticed that several of the machines were idle more often than he would have expected. In commenting on the summary of productive labour shown in Table 3, the president noted that total standard man-hours did not include time spent reworking or replacing circuits that failed inspection or were returned by customers. In addition, he believed that the time required to move boards from one operation to another and between elements within an operation was not adequately reflected in the standards. The time standards used in Table 3 were based in part on a synthesis of what Jodal and Krebs knew to be the standards applied in competing firms (from whom they had hired various workers and supervisors), and in part they were based on judgements made by Jodal and Krebs after long experience gained in performing and observing jobs in the Blitz Company. In preparing time estimates for bid preparation, Jodal actually used figures that were substantially above those standards.

The president felt, however, that the job methods in use were far from ideal and that the standards did not reflect improvements that could probably be made in almost any job in the shop. As a specific example, he cited the plating operation. The plater worked at a desk inspecting (touching up) panels and then carried the panels to plating tanks 18 feet away, inserted them, and returned to inspect more panels. Work at the desk was interrupted every three or four minutes to inspect the panels in one of the tanks. Krebs thought that the platers sometimes spent 15 per cent of their time simply walking between the desks and the tanks.

Jodal suspected that methods improvements were not being introduced because the current pressure for output, the constant shifting of workers from job to job, and other immediate problems inhibited experimentation with new ideas. Furthermore, job improvements often seemed, in retrospect, to have created more problems than they solved. For example, those infrequent cases in which improvements had substantially increased production at one station often resulted in work piling up at the following operations. The foreman was then forced to reschedule orders and reassign workers, thus adding to the general confusion and occasionally creating personal friction.

Quality and delivery problems

Roger Sacks, who had joined the company as the sales manager six months earlier in April, was concerned about recent failures in maintaining quality standards and in meeting promised delivery dates. Since August, customer returns had increased from 4 to about 8 per cent and shipments had averaged nine days late. Sacks felt that a continuation of these conditions would impede his hope of increasing the present sales volume and achieving the company's sales goals. The sales goals shown in Table 5 had been developed by a local consulting firm in November of Blitz's second year, after a month's study of the potential market. The sales manager predicted that volume would reach only $1,200,000 in three years if he began promising a four-week delivery on small orders, as four competitors were quoting. If, on the other hand, the company was able to regain its pre-August delivery performance, Sacks felt sales would exceed $3 million in three years. Both Sacks and Jodal believed that the company should continue to bid only for low-volume, special circuit board business. Their sales estimates, therefore, were based on an order-size profile similar to that actually produced in September of the third year (see Table 4).

Quality

Jodal was also concerned about the present inspection system in which formal inspections of raw material and finished boards were supplemented by each worker's informal examination of the units as they moved through processing. The president felt that any effort to specify quality standards more exactly and to enforce them more rigorously might

Table 5 Pro forma profit and loss statement ($000)

	Year 3		Year 4		Year 5		Year 6	
Net sales	$398	100.0%	$672	100.0%	$1,042	100.0%	$1,646	100.0%
Direct material	90	22.4	150	22.4	232	22.3	362	22.0
Chemicals, film and supplies	34	8.4	64	9.4	112	10.7	148	9.0
Wages and foreman's salary	100	25.2	176	26.3	270	25.9	428	26.0
Other expenses[a]	22	5.6	36	5.3	56	5.4	94	5.6
Cost of goods sold	246	61.7	426	63.4	670	64.3	1,032	62.6
Gross profit	152	38.3	246	36.6	372	35.7	614	37.3
Company overhead								
Salaries (administration, engineering and office)	84	21.0	112	16.6	158	15.2	260	15.8
Other overhead (rent, interest, utilities, etc.)	26	6.5	40	5.8	56	5.4	84	5.1
Profit before taxes	$42	10.8%	$94	14.1%	$158	15.2%	$270	16.4%

[a] Water, heat, power, depreciation, and so forth
Source: Company records, and prepared by Rothchilde and Rommel, Inc., management consultants, on 21 November of year 2.

not be feasible because the standards varied from customer to customer and even from order to order. For example, in one recent episode a customer's engineers had praised the quality of the Blitz Company's work on one order even though the boards were scratched and marred and had one or two holes located out of tolerance. A week later, other engineers at the same company had rejected 25 apparently perfect boards because one conductor on each had a single 0.005″ × 0.010″ nick in it.

A tenth of the boards returned were damaged or out of tolerance. The remainder were returned because the Blitz Company had failed to perform one or two required operations. These boards were reprocessed and shipped within one or two days. The company's preshipment reject rate in September amounted to 7 per cent, of which 4 per cent were total losses and 3 per cent were missing operations.

Deliveries

Jodal had always emphasized a shipping policy aimed at clearing all the work possible out of the shop prior to the end of each month. As a result, substantially fewer shipments were made in the first half of each month than in the second half (see Table 6). Actual deliveries

Table 6 Value of actual shipments in September, year 3

Date	Daily	Cumulative
1	$ 5,914	
		$ 5,914
4	(632)[a]	5,282
5	2,158	7,440
6	902	8,342
7	1,184	9,526
8	4,484	14,010
11	1,274	15,284
12	(364)	14,920
13	1,362	16,282
14	3,152	19,434
15	(78)	19,356
18	2,102	21,458
19	7,030	28,488
20	5,356	33,844
21	2,958	36,802
22	1,210	38,012
25	94	38,106
26	(706)	37,400
27	(4,242)	33,158
28	9,542	42,700
29	23,702	66,402

[a] Negative shipments, shown in parentheses, indicate that receipts returned for rework or refabrication exceeded shipments.
Source: Company records.

in August, September and the first part of October had averaged 10, 8 and 9 days late respectively. During the period, the company had continued its historical practice of quoting a three-week delivery on orders of less than 1,000 circuit boards and five weeks on larger orders. In August, when deliveries climbed to a volume of $69,400, eight new people had been added to the production force. Jodal observed that these eight workers had developed some skill by the second week in August, but believed that they would require three months to become as skilled as the company's more senior employees.

Crystalox Limited

Audun Boerve, Managing Director of Crystalox Ltd, stepped off the airplane at Heathrow airport after a quick trip to Switzerland. He had capitalized on a visit to a potential customer to stop at his alma mater, a well-known international management institute to talk with some of the faculty about recent developments at his company. He was quite pleased with the progress that had been made since he had joined the company in 1985. Sales and sales potential had been increased, for example. He had also been successful in hiring a number of people to strengthen several areas of the company and in implementing a reorganization that would help them focus their efforts. He was still concerned, however, about the company's manufacturing activities.

As a part of the reorganization, Mr Boerve had arranged to have the manufacturing activities report directly to him. In the discussions about manufacturing, Graham Young, one of the manufacturing managers, proposed that part of the manufacturing facilities be moved to another location and that a joint venture between him and Crystalox be created. Mr Young felt that this would help Crystalox and that it would help him achieve a longstanding goal of having his own machine shop. He had just submitted a detailed written proposal on the idea for Crystalox's consideration. Mr Boerve knew he would have to deal with the proposal as a part of his overall evaluation of the manufacturing activities. As he walked down the gateway, he mused, 'What can I do to improve our manufacturing effectiveness and position us for future growth?' He was already trying to prioritize the actions he would take on arriving at the office the next morning.

Background and history

Crystalox was founded in 1970 by Dr David Hukin, who holds a PhD in physics. As a specialist in crystal 'growth' techniques, he had developed equipment to produce high purity crystals while serving as head of materials preparation at Clarendon Laboratories in Oxford.

The case was prepared by Juli Dixon, Research Associate, under the direction of Professor D. Clay Whybark as a basis for class discussion rather than to illustrate either effective or ineffective handling of an administrative situation. Copyright © 1987 by IMEDE, Lausanne, Switzerland. IMD International, resulting from the merger between IMEDE, Lausanne, and IMI, Geneva, acquires and retains all rights. Reproduced by permission.

The remarkably successful use of silicon crystals for making micro chips had spurred an interest in seeking other applications of silicon and in studying the properties of other crystals. Dr Hukin's research colleagues around the world and the visitors to the laboratory convinced him that there was a large potential market for machines that could produce high purity crystals of various metals, so Crystalox was formed. (Some of the potential uses for the products which use these crystals are described in the appendix.)

The first activities of the company involved technical consulting. The character of the company as a 'problem solving' firm was set at this early stage. Dr Hukin, working closely with the customers, designed specific machines to solve their crystal growing problems. Through his personal contacts and professional reputation, Dr Hukin was able to meet many potential customers and, by the mid 1970s, he had two employees helping assemble machines from purchased and subcontracted components. Working from a small shed in Wantage, England, about thirty kilometres from Oxford, the company produced one or two machines a year, for university, government and industrial research laboratories around the world.

By 1982, the number of employees had increased to ten and Dr Hukin found the time for his professional activities squeezed by the demands of managing the company. To leave him more time for the technical activities and to raise capital for expansion, Dr Hukin sold a 75 per cent interest in the company to a local property development firm. They agreed to construct a new building and to be responsible for the day-to-day management of the company. The building was built, but unfortunately, financial and other problems plagued the arrangement nearly from the beginning. The new managers did not have experience in managing a manufacturing firm nor did they have a good understanding of the technology upon which the company was based.

During this period, Crystalox was working on a project to build a special machine for Elkem AS, a Norwegian firm that produces silicon and other basic materials, products that had not been enjoying expanding markets. The Crystalox machine was to produce large silicon crystals for solar cells that would help Elkem enter other markets. As Elkem's management became aware of the deteriorating situation at Crystalox, they considered acquiring the company to protect their interest in the project. The acquisition offered Elkem some other advantages as well. It could expand the base of the business by providing access to advanced technology in a variety of materials and by providing forward integration into other processing activities.

With this in mind, negotiations commenced and, in 1985, Crystalox became a profit centre in the Electronic Materials Division of the Elkem Group. Crystalox brought the technology to the new company, and Elkem supplied an infusion of funds plus management support. Audun Boerve, for example, had been sales manager for silicon metal in Norway before being appointed as managing director, and Per Dybwad, a member of the Elkem acquisition team, provided financial consulting services.

Mr Boerve's first activities as managing director were focused on finishing up two special machines that were in process (both of which were behind schedule when he arrived) in order to generate some cash for the company. While this was going on he spent some time identifying strengths and weaknesses of the company so he could develop a plan to position the firm for the future. During 1985, personnel were added and more contracts were sought, but the company recorded a loss. In 1986, his efforts began to pay off and the company made a profit for the first time since 1982. (See the financial statements in Tables 1 and 2.)

During 1986, it became clear that it would be necessary to restructure the organization. Because of the difficulties prior to Elkem's arrival, Dr Hukin had been spending time on

Table 1 Consolidated profit and loss statements

	Twelve months to 31 Dec. 1986 £	Twelve months to 31 Dec. 1985 £
Sales	907,775[a]	342,045
Cost of goods sold		
Purchases	274,659	107,767
Labour	236,901	147,487
Materials	33,044	20,014
Subcontracting	28,323	17,244
Manufacturing overhead	25,304	15,395
	598,231	307,907
Gross profit	309,544	34,138
Operating expenses		
Marketing expenses	89,792	54,687
General and administrative	219,720	193,889
Operating (loss)/profit	32	(214,438)

[a] Sales breakdown

Subcontracting	49,214
Special machines	614,803
Standard products	243,758
	907,775

virtually every aspect of the business, from initial customer contact to manufacturing and delivery problems. During 1986, as the size of the company increased to thirty employees, he still found it necessary to help out in a variety of areas, even though everyone realized that his contacts and technical knowledge were essential for reaching the market. At the same time, manufacturing co-ordination was becoming more complex as the volume of business increased.

The reorganization in early 1987 provided the structure for Dr Hukin to focus his attention on the technical aspects of marketing and new product development. It also provided for direct involvement in manufacturing by Mr Boerve. (An organization chart is shown in Figure 1.) Mr Boerve felt that the current organization would allow them to increase the output from the six special machines produced in 1986 to nine to eleven machines in 1987.

The market

Crystalox's products are sold worldwide to research and development laboratories in both the private and public sectors. The company estimates that there are about three thousand such laboratories in the world. For Crystalox, the key persons in these institutes are the scientists who conduct the research and the adminstrators who approve the budgets for

Table 2   Balance sheet as of 31 December

	1986 £	1985 £
Current assets		
Cash	52	(12)
Accounts receivable	132,502	10,566
Inventory	373,585[a]	185,740
Other	4,943	4,442
	511,082	200,736
Fixed assets		
Land and buildings	340,055	302,366
Plant/machinery	67,210	32,343
Other	59,117	56,240
	466,882	390,949
Intangible assets	—	3,219
Total assets	977,964	594,904
Current liabilities		
Bank note current	408,337	246,655
Accounts payable	217,724	121,465
Other	181,834	56,747
	807,895	424,867
Long-term liabilities		
Loan from Elkem	399,928	399,928
Equity	(299,859)	(299,891)
Total equity and liabilities	977,964	594,904

[a] Raw materials and supplies	11,037
Work-in-process	362,548
	373,585

equipment. The scientists form a fairly close-knit community and many gather once a year or so to exchange information at professional meetings and conferences. Dr Hukin's presence at these gatherings is an important mode of contact for the company. The administrators tend to get involved in the buying process only after the preliminary discussions on the technical aspects have taken place and the research proposals are being approved.

The buying decision often starts with a scientist who is conducting research for which crystals will be required. The scientist may involve Crystalox in answering some basic questions early in the process. For example, can a crystal that will meet the specifications for size, purity and shape of the material required be grown, and what would be the approximate cost of a machine that could do it? If it appears feasible, Crystalox may be asked to submit a quotation for inclusion in the research proposal. Then the decision process moves to the administrators involved.

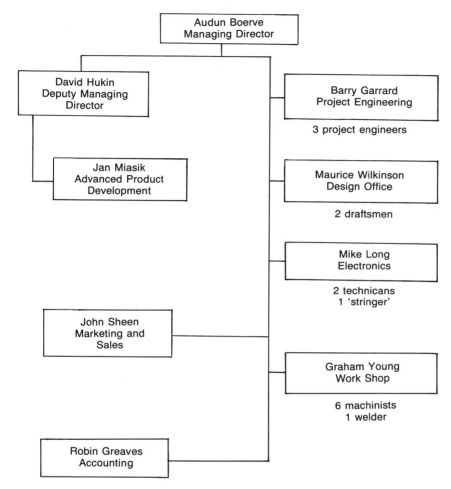

Figure 1 Organization chart.

The research proposal approval process can take a long time during which even the research scientist does not know if it will be approved. Sometimes a quote will be outstanding for a year or more before it is clear whether there will be a contract or not. Often the proposal is simply rejected. Occasionally the budget has been cut, and Crystalox is asked what they can do for a reduced amount of money. If the proposal is approved, however, Crystalox has a good chance of getting the contract for the detail design and manufacturing of the machine. In total, about 25 per cent of the quotes result in contracts.

Crystalox enjoys a unique niche in the market. Its competition is indirect, coming from firms that have different strategic objectives. There is a group of firms, for example, that sells components that the laboratories themselves can assemble into a machine. There is another group of companies, often competing on a cost basis, that make 'production' machines. They sell in lots of ten to fifty machines to companies that produce crystals commercially. There are no other companies that have the combination of scientific and other talent to offer uniquely designed 'turn-key' machines to the research community.

The market for research crystals is constantly changing as new materials attract attention or as new properties become important. The research scientists appreciate being able to work with a company like Crystalox that 'speaks their language' and understands the 'leading edge' of the technology. The ability to offer solutions or intelligent alternatives to their problems is important to this community.

The products

The product line consists of special machines that are designed and built for a specific customer and 'standard' products that were designed as components of special machines but which are now sold separately. In addition, some subcontracting is done by the machine shop for local manufacturers. The special machines provided about two-thirds of the 1986 revenue.

The special machines are built up from modules of components that perform the specific functions required to produce the kind of crystal the customer wants. All machines, however, perform several common basic functions. For example, all machines melt the material from which the crystal is to be made. This can require temperatures up to 2,000°C. They all have a means for growing the crystal. In the Czochralski process, for example, a 'seed', around which the crystal is grown, is inserted into the melt. This is then rotated and pulled from the melt in such a way that the crystal size and shape is controlled. The pulling action has given rise to the name 'crystal pullers' for machines of this type. In the Bridgeman–Stockbarger process, the crystal is grown around the seed in the melting vessel. Crystalox produces machines for both processes.

In addition to the functions performed by all machines, some may require a system for purifying the material before growing the crystal, or a vacuum system, or a means of injecting controlled amounts of additives, or even systems for surrounding the process with specific gases. Regardless of configuration, however, the whole process requires very close control. Each machine, therefore, has electronic equipment for monitoring all aspects of the process. All of the systems are connected together and mounted in cabinets. (An example product is shown in Figure 2). Most special machines fall in a price range £50,000–£200,000, with the average price currently about £100,000.

Most of the current standard products had first been designed as a component for a special machine. Many still are used on new machines, as well as being sold independently. The products range from parts like the crucible in which the material is melted or the chamber that surrounds the process, to complex electro-mechanical assemblies like the head which pulls the crystal from the melt. The Advanced Product Development group has been given the responsibility of developing new products that can be sold separately, whether or not they will be used on a special machine. Prototypes of some of these new products are being built now.

Project engineering

Much of the responsibility for co-ordination of projects for special machines rests with the project engineers. They are involved throughout the life of the project, with special

The Crystalox CGS is designed for the Czochralski growth of:

- metals
- semiconductors
- oxides
- halides

high purity, single crystals, up to 50 mm diameter.

RF induction heating is available with programmed precision temperature control.
Readout through thermocouples or pyrometer.

The CGS comprises:

Growth chamber — 500 mm
diameter   A
Vacuum system   B
Inert gas system   B
Residual gas analysis   B
RF power/temperature control   C
allowing for
Remote computer control
and
Fully microprocessor   D
Controlled:
Digital pulling head   E
Rotation and translation
Digital crucible rotation or   F
crucible load cell monitoring
ADC interface module

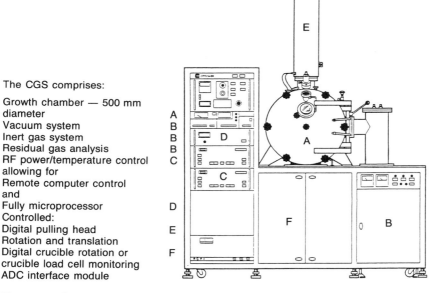

Figure 2 Sample product.

responsibilities at the beginning and the end. At the beginning, they are involved in the technical design issues and help determine the components to be purchased outside. At the end, they have responsibility for making sure the machine performs as the customer expects. In between, during design and manufacturing, they monitor, control and co-ordinate the progress of the machines.

Before 1986, there was only one project engineer, Dr Barry Garrard. During the year, Crystalox hired three more, two of whom had PhDs. Dr Garrard explained: 'The focus of the project engineer is on the machine, a sort of champion for the customer here in the shop. He constantly reviews the design to make improvements or to rectify faults. Sometimes the theory doesn't translate into practice or something was missed and changes must be made. Since he knows that he must make the machine work during final test, he wants as few surprises as possible by the time it gets there.'

The project engineer's job requires many skills. It requires technical knowledge to be able to modify and improve the design of the machine. It also requires organizational skills to perform the co-ordination needed to keep the machine on schedule. Lastly, a great deal of inventiveness may be required when problems occur in final test. The greatest amount of the projects engineer's time is spent in final test, but the general co-ordination activities take an average of ninety hours for each special machine.

General process

The general process from the receipt of a customer inquiry to the delivery of a special machine is shown in Figure 3. The activities are shown as occurring sequentially, but there is substantial interaction between all elements during the process. Each machine is assigned to a project engineer, usually at the preliminary design stage. The preliminary design is the basis for the quotation that goes out to the customer. The customer may request changes that might require more design work and negotiations with the customer. Once everything is agreed upon, the general design is finalized and the detailed drawings that are used to build the machine are completed by the design office and sent to the work shop.

The purchasing of specialized parts and components from outside suppliers is done by the project engineer. These would include such items as special vacuum pumps or gas analysers. Graham Young, manager of the work shop, is responsible for purchasing the raw material and components for making the mechanical parts of the machine. He would make, for example, the chamber which surrounds the crystal growing process, would subcontract manufacturing of some of the metal parts, and would purchase raw materials and components like sheet steel and ball bearings. Mike Long, manager of the electronics department, purchases cables and circuits, and fabricates, for example, control panels. Component testing is done in the individual departments while final testing at the end of the process involves the project engineer.

Machine design

A customer's inquiry about a special machine leads to a preliminary design meeting attended by the managers of the design office, the work shop, the electronics department, the project engineer and Dr Hukin, with others attending as needed. In this meeting, they will develop the initial design specifications. Using these specifications, Maurice Wilkinson, manager of the design office, will prepare an initial drawing of the machine, something like that shown in Figure 2. The other departments will prepare labour and purchased part cost estimates for the quotation to be sent to the customer. The quotation also states that the delivery date will be determined after the quotation is accepted.

When a quotation is accepted, the delivery date must be determined. This is influenced by the work in process and by the desires of the people involved. Discussions between the customer, Mr Boerve, the project engineer, and others are used to set the date. Generally the customer wants the machine right away, the project engineer wants to have about five months (three for manufacturing and two for final assembly and test) and Mr Boerve wants to minimize the capital tied up in work in process. Usually the delivery dates for the special machines are established for three to four months from the time the machine can be started.

In the meantime, the final design specifications are set and the overall machine drawings prepared. The last step in the design effort is the drafting of detailed drawings and the development of the final list of purchased components. Some of the manufacturing work

Responsibility   Steps

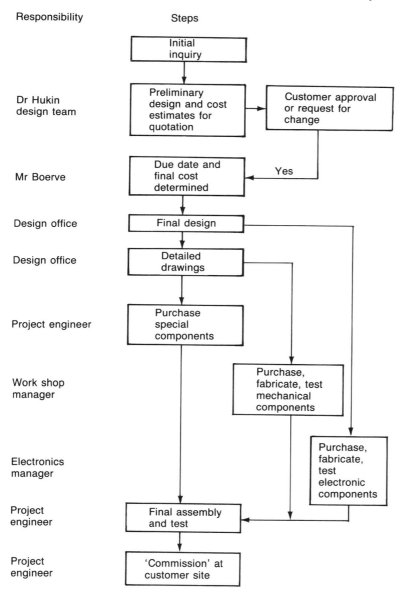

Figure 3 General process for a special machine.

can be started as soon as the first detailed drawings are done. It can continue while the remaining detailed drawings are being completed.

The special machine activities of the design office and the range of times required for each are shown in Table 3. The North American university machine was a typical product for the department. Mr Wilkinson himself does the first two steps, although he can help

Table 3 Steps and labour hours required in the design office (special machines)

		North American university machine (hours)	Range (hours)
1	Preliminary design specifications for cost estimates for quotation	25	2−100
2	Final design and drawings showing all views of the product but not detailed enough to be used to manufacture the machine	75	30−300
3	Detailing — drawings of every part of the machine and the specification of the order in which the parts must be assembled	400	200−2,000
4	Checking and correcting — ensures that parts all fit together	90	50−400
5	Bought-out list (purchasing) — lists of all components and any materials to be purchased with the names of the suppliers specified and the assignment of the person who must do the purchasing of each part	30	15−150
6	Special drawings for the customer	10	5−30
7	Modifications — drawings of changes in the design suggested by the project engineer either while the product is being built or during the testing stage	30	20−175
		660	

in any of them. 'Either of the two draftsmen can do any of the other steps', he said. 'Our job is not limited to the start of a special machine project, though. The project engineer will come to our office at any stage and ask for some changes. These may come from the customer, or the project engineer may have found a problem or a better way to do something. We also spend about ten hours a week on new product prototypes but almost nothing on the standard products. They have already been designed.'

Mechanical parts

Graham Young, the manager of the work shop, is responsible for the machine and welding shops, and for assembling and testing the mechanical aspects of the company's products. A layout of the shop is shown in Figure 4. Eight people are involved with this work. In addition to Mr Young, there are six machinists and one welder. The work-week consists of five $7\frac{1}{2}$ hour days, but they are now working about 4 hours a week overtime per person.

The special machines follow the sequence of steps and require the times presented in Table 4. (The North American university machine was typical for the workshop.) The six machinists perform all the machining (milling and lathe work) in steps 1 and 3. They can all operate each of the company's lathes and mills, so Mr Young tries to assign them responsibility for all the machining necessary to produce an order instead of assigning each person to a single milling machine or lathe. 'This helps the people understand what they are making, gives them a greater sense of satisfaction and provides broadly trained people who give me flexibility. This will be possible as long as I have enough lathes and milling machines as I do now', he explained.

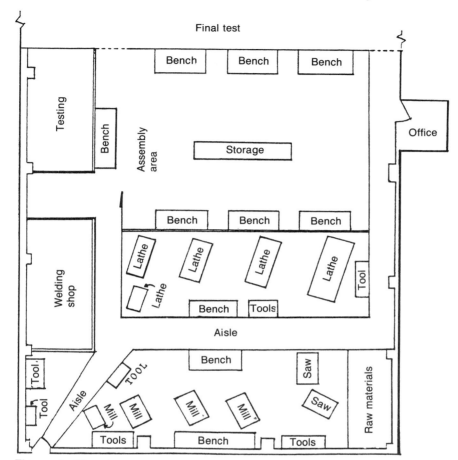

Figure 4 Shop layout.

The first machining starts with the preparation and cutting of raw materials and requires work on both the milling machines and lathes to produce parts. In the second step the parts are joined together by the welder who is the only one who does this work. Mr Young can do some welding, but rarely has time to help with any of the jobs in the shop. The second machining will be done on the welded parts. This step, like the first, requires work on both the milling machines and the lathes.

Crystalox subcontracts some of its work to outside machine shops. Some of it, like making the frames for the machines, could be done in house, while such things as bending stainless steel and anodizing aluminium cannot. There is no problem finding subcontractors, although Mr Young sometimes complains about their quality or cost. For instance, one recent set of frames was not 'true' (square) and additional time was required in assembly because things did not fit as well as they should. For purchased parts, Mr Young uses several suppliers. 'There are lots of suppliers for the common raw materials and I enjoy playing them off against one another to get the best prices', he says. 'I really don't have any trouble

Table 4 Steps and labour hours required in the work shop (special machines)

	North American university machine (hours)	Ranges (hours)
1 First machining		
Lathe	85	65–100
Mill	93	75–100
2 Welding	90	50–150
3 Second machining		
Lathe	235	180–270
Mill	257	225–300
4 Assembly	150	120–190
5 Test	60	40–90
	970[a]	

[a] In addition to these hours, the work shop manager recorded a total of 86 hours for modifications to this project. The range for modifications is 50–120 hours.

with any of my suppliers. I can get most of the common things in four to six days and I just order the long lead time items as soon as we know we are going to build a machine.'

Once all of the parts have been produced or received from suppliers, steps 4 and 5, the assembly and testing of the mechanical aspects of the machine, can be started. The steps consist of attaching the various parts to the frame and assuring that they can perform their intended function. For example, the vacuum system would be tested to see if it leaks and to see if it could reach the pressures required for the particular machine. The work is performed by two of the machinists with the occasional help of the welder.

Mr Young explained: 'We do more than build the special machines in here. We spend about eighty hours a week (fifty in machining, ten in welding, and twenty in assembly and test) on our standard products. We also have a department that is trying to develop new products. They currently require about ten hours a week of our time for making prototypes. We also make parts for other firms.

'One Saturday, quite some time ago, a fellow walked by our shop and saw our big lathe. He came in, saw what we could do and asked us to bid on some work for him. I did and we have been doing some subcontracting for him ever since. Word of mouth about our quality and reliable delivery performance has brought us other customers as well. This business turns us a nice profit and uses my extra machine time. I get an average of £25 an hour for it, though I really sock it to a guy who needs something in a hurry. I think we could get a great deal more of this work. At the moment it's only taking about thirty hours a week in the machine shop and ten in welding.'

Mr Young schedules the work shop, the outside subcontracting and the delivery of purchased components. He uses an overall estimate of 1,000 labour hours (plus 10 per cent for contingencies) of work shop time for each special machine. The schedule takes into account current work in process and the need to co-ordinate the production of some parts with the activities of other departments. The daily assignment of people to their jobs is in his head. 'I've evolved a feeling for moving people around during my fourteen years in the business', he says. 'Luckily, I was able to build up the number of people in the work shop gradually so that I could develop my systems slowly. It's already getting a bit difficult, and I'm not sure that I'd be able to continue operating as I do now if I had to add more people. Besides, I don't know where I could put them if I had to.'

He tries to adhere to the schedule but finds that it must be changed frequently. He describes the major problem as unforeseen interruptions. 'The project engineers keep wanting to make changes that just weren't in the schedule. For example, we were just asked to remake some parts for a machine that we had completed last week. There was some problem in final test, and the project engineer wanted to make some changes. Now I'll have to help install those new parts as well. What they don't realize is that for every unscheduled hour they ask for, our schedule is set back two since I can't then do the work that is slotted into that time. There is additional set up time too.

'These changes can continue right up to the moment the machine is to go to the customer. The project engineers like to keep the machines around a long time so that they can fine tune them. I'm all for getting them out as soon as possible so that we can get some money in the bank. Besides, the more times a machine comes back on the shopfloor after we think it's finished, the less interest people have in doing the work.'

Electronics

Mike Long, manager of the electronics department, attends the design discussions at the beginning of a special machine project. He describes this stage as the 'pinning down' phase, saying the project engineers must describe exactly what the machine specifications are so that we can design the control system and connections. He will do the detailed design of all the electronics himself. The project engineer will review the design and any required adjustments will be made before the detailed drawings are produced.

To schedule the electronics department's work, Mr Long works backwards from the shipment date for the machine. For this purpose he uses a figure of 300 labour hours per special machine. The department's activities take much less time than those of the work shop, but he must co-ordinate with the work shop during the process since some of the control equipment is mounted on parts produced by them. Table 5 shows the process steps in the electronics department along with the times required for each.

Table 5 Steps and labour hours required in electronics (special machines)

	North American university machine[a] (hours)	Ranges (hours)
1 Design	44.5	30−100
2 Fabrication of subassemblies	178.0	170−250
3 Assembly and test	7.5	5−80
	230.0	

[a] This project was not typical from the electronics department's standpoint. For planning purposes, the electronics manager uses 60 hours, 200 hours and 40 hours for design, fabrication and assembly/test respectively.

All subassemblies for the control system, which connect to the other systems (vacuum, heating, power, gas analysis, etc.), are produced in-house. In the electronics department, in addition to Mr Long, there is one person who is employed especially to string the wires during assembly, and two persons for fabrication of subassemblies (who can also help on the assembly and test). All of the subassemblies will be tested individually before they are connected together. The recent installation of programmable logic in the control systems has allowed Mr Long to increase flexibility and reduce the assembly time to its current value.

Mr Long keeps several suppliers on tap and has never experienced trouble with any of them. For the everyday items he can get delivery in two days, and the suppliers are very price competitive. The purchased components are tested before being installed on a machine. The suppliers have never caused a delay for the department and, as Mr Long says, 'We usually get our special machine work done ahead of schedule now. We also work about twenty hours a week in subassembly fabrication and five hours a week in assembly and test on standard products, and about an hour a week on prototypes of new products.'

Final test

The project engineer is responsible for final testing once final assembly is completed. The test involves checking the temperature profile, melt capabilities, growth mechanism and so on. Sometimes the project engineer will even grow a crystal on the machine. He also likes to make very sure everything is right at this stage, since he often must go out to the customer's site to 'commission' the machine. The average time spent in final test is about 220 hours, with a range from 100 to 600 (in addition to the 90 hours for general co-ordination). The project engineers also spend about 4 hours a week testing standard products.

According to Dr Garrard, 'The testing time we get is never as long as it should be. All the problems from design, work shop and electronics eat into the testing time. Problems often occur just because we're on the fringe of technology, and we must make changes to make the machine perform up to specifications. Often, we also find some ways to make real improvements in performance. But at times we're just squeezed. I remember one special machine that hadn't even been put up to the required temperature before the customer came for the acceptance test.

'What the shop people don't seem to understand is that we are making the changes to improve the product for the customer. These interruptions are part of our business and must be accepted.' He continued, 'The shipment date is like a brick wall. We can't usually extend it, so we get squeezed in final test.' Table 6 shows the delivery performance for some special machines and standard products.

The company has earned a fine reputation for quality products. Very rarely are there problems once they have been sent out. Most problems that do occur can usually be solved over the phone. Crystalox has occasionally sent someone out to do some work on products in the field, however. The project engineers argue that the quality image could be in jeopardy if final test continues to get squeezed for time.

Improving production

Mr Boerve has taken some initial steps in the process of improving the production activities. For instance, a time and cost reporting system has been implemented. An example of the breakdown of costs now possible is shown in Table 7 for the North American university

Table 6   Product delivery performance

	Due in final test	Arrive in final test	Shipment date	Actual shipment
Special machines				
1061	n.a.	n.a.	4 Oct. 1985	4 Oct. 1985
1098	1 Dec. 1985	19 Dec. 1985	10 Feb. 1986	10 Feb. 1986
1123[a]	5 Dec. 1986	19 Dec. 1986	19 Jan. 1987	14 Jan. 1987
1176	19 Dec. 1986	7 Jan. 1987	27 Feb. 1987	24 Feb. 1987
Standard products with project engineering				
1152	28 Sept. 1986	10 Oct. 1986	30 Oct. 1986	28 Oct. 1986
Standard products with no project engineering				
1024			9 Sept. 1986	8 Sept. 1986
1193			5 Sept. 1986	5 Sept. 1986

n.a.: not available.
[a] North American university machine.

Table 7   Costs associated with North American university machine

	£
Work shop	
Materials	4,500
Labour (at £9.43 per hour)	10,241
Parts purchased outside	11,925
Subcontracting	2,500
Electronics	
Materials	3,796
Labour (at £15.48 per hour)	3,560
Parts purchased outside	3,721
Subcontracting	4,180
Design Office	
Labour (at £13.44 per hour)	8,870
Project engineering	
Labour (at £16.25 per hour)	4,631
Parts purchased outside	27,204

[a] Revenue received for this project was £107,000.

machine. The reporting system has not helped explain the delays in getting to the final testing stage, however.

To meet the budget projections for the next year, production output will need to be increased. It would require producing about ten special machines and the standard product business would need to increase by about 20 per cent as well. Mr Boerve said, 'Production has got to produce — we have doubled the number of people in the last year, and our overheads are high. I would like to see sales increase to £1,400,000 next year to cover these increases. So production is going to have to perform.'

He is hesitant to suggest subcontracting more work to outside firms because of possible delivery and quality problems. He also feels that Crystalox has developed some special manufacturing skills, and the ability of the work shop to sell subcontracted parts seems to support this contention. Besides, he felt some production capacity was needed to support the project engineers. Dr Hukin explained: 'When a project engineer is having a difficult time with his machine in final test, he needs all the support he can get. We have a machine in final test right now that's a good example. It is right at the edge of technology and I know we can make it perform, but the project engineer is spending day and night trying to get it right. Each time he makes a change, he needs a couple of parts right away and we have to be able to supply him.'

The proposal

Mr Boerve knows that he must deal with the proposal to move the machine shop out to a different location. The proposal recommends that all the machine tools and the welding equipment be moved to a different location several miles away. Graham Young feels that having some distance between Crystalox and the shop would mean fewer interruptions by the Project Engineers. He also feels that the current level of Crystalox special machines and standard products will serve as a solid business base for the enterprise, but that there is a great deal of other general machine shop business available to them. Per Dybwad, from Elkem, was enthusiastic about the idea. 'This could be a way to absorb some of the increased overhead. We have already seen that there is a market for the service. Besides, what's wrong with filling up the extra capacity with cash generating business. Of course, Crystalox would have to have priority for production time.'

Mr Boerve mused, 'In the past our machine projects have required more brain power than machine power. But now I'm wondering if we are experiencing a shift in the type of business we are doing with more of an emphasis on the machine power and if this is putting a burden on production. Over the last year we have done some standardization, have sold some special machines similar to ones we'd made before and have introduced our line of standard products. Maybe these factors have made the manufacturing part more simple.'

'It's clear the character of the place has changed', Dr Hukin added. 'The families of the workers used to come around and see the special machines before we shipped them off to the customers. They even wanted their pictures taken with the machines. That kind of thing is happening less frequently now.'

Appendix

The crystal machines that are sold by Crystalox go into laboratories around the world. The research that is performed on the crystals that they produce is concerned with things like the electrical properties, the light transmission properties and so on. In addition to the use of silicon crystals for micro chips, other crystals have found use in night vision systems, laser beams in various wave lengths and superconductive materials. The potential for future applications of crystals of various kinds is just being discovered, hence the research interest.

The rapid and wide adaptation of glass fibre for transmission of information is an example of the potential. Lasers have great potential for transmission of energy in addition to information. The light transmitting and detecting properties of other materials have just begun to be understood. The potential uses, other than night vision systems, are still being explored, but include things like detecting various waves from outer space and transmission of great amounts of energy efficiently.

Great interest has been expressed in growing crystals in space to enhance their purity and symmetry. The space connection does not stop at increasing the purity attributes of the crystals, however. The use of ever purer crystals for detection and separation of various waves from space have great potential for improving human understanding of the universe. The military is involved, as well, looking for the strength, energy transmission, and detection capabilities of pure crystals. In some cases, particular impurities are introduced into the crystals to give them other properties. Much of the future for these kinds of materials is yet to be discovered.

Georgian Frames

Georgian Frames is a small company engaged in making and installing new Georgian style, premeasured windows to replace existing windows in the homes of its customers. Table 1 details the activities required to complete the task of removing the old and installing a new window. Although occasionally more than one window will be installed at a site, at present about 75 per cent of all jobs involve a single window installation. The critical path diagram representing this set of activities is shown in Figure 1.

The recent company sales growth has necessitated allocating more men to window installation on a full-time basis. However, there are increasingly days when it is necessary to install a window on two separate sites. Whilst Georgian Frames wishes to maintain sales growth, it needs to keep capital investment to a minimum. Therefore, it does not wish to purchase a second vehicle (necessary to transport men, tools and windows to the customer's premises) unless it is essential. In addition, it also needs to keep labour costs to a minimum in order to stay competitive, whilst maintaining acceptable profit levels.

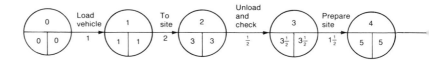

Table 1 Principal activities involved in replacing a window on site

Activity	Time units ($\frac{1}{2}$ hour) to do the task, depending upon the number of men available			Minimum number of men required to do the job
	1 man	*2 men*	*3 men*	
Load vehicle at yard and prepare	2	1	1	1
To site	2	2	2	1
Unload and check the window size	1	$\frac{1}{2}$	$\frac{1}{2}$	1
Prepare site	2	$1\frac{1}{2}$	1	1
Remove old frame	2	$1\frac{1}{2}$	1	1
Offer new frame to the opening	—	1	1	2
Load old frame to vehicle	1	$\frac{1}{2}$	(note 7)	1
Finish installation	4	3	2	1
Load tools etc. to vehicle	1	$\frac{1}{2}$	(note 7)	1
Return to yard	2	2	2	1
Load old frame and tools to vehicle	2	1	$\frac{1}{2}$	(note 7)

Notes
1. Where two windows and other items are loaded onto a vehicle with 3 men, the time taken will be the same as that for one window and other items with 2 men.
2. It is custom at this company for the vehicle driver to participate in the window installation activities.
3. The activity times given are the average for these tasks and take account of allowances for fatigue, rest and mid-morning and mid-afternoon breaks.
4. In the network diagram (Figure 1) the work throughout is carried out by two men. The men, on returning to the yard, do other work such as priming and sanding of window frames.
5. The time to travel from one site to another would take $\frac{1}{2}$ hour.
6. Activity 'remove old window frame' is not dependent upon 'prepare site'.
7. For three men, the activities 'load old window frame to vehicle' and 'load tools etc. to vehicle' are combined into the one activity 'load old frame and tools to vehicle' which takes $\frac{1}{2}$ of one time unit.

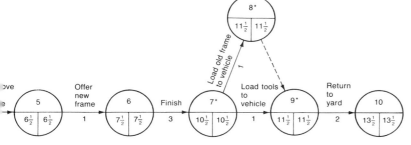

* Activities 7, 8 and 9 are shown to run in parallel. If it were decided to run these activities in sequence then the overall time taken would be the same.

Figure 1 Network diagram for the activities given in Table 1 with a two-man team.

Ghent Fireworks Plc

In March, Ghent Fireworks (GF) Plc celebrated a 100 years in the fireworks business. It had, in its time, experienced most of the growth problems of a typical manufacturing company, but was now an established name in the UK markets for its firework products.

Perhaps the most significant change in direction for the company had occurred in the late 1970s when, based upon its traditional business and reputation as a fireworks manufacturer, GF applied and gained registration on the UK Ministry of Defence's list of assessed contractors, having met the requirements as laid down in Defence Standards 05-21 to 05-29. This successful application now opened up home and export markets for all types of pyrotechnic products. Typical of these would be smoke generators in a range of colours, hand-held, ground, grenade and trip-wire flares, small arms simulators (single and multi-shot), explosion, flame and smoke simulators, thunderflashes and rocket motors.

Sales

Whilst sales for fireworks showed a steady growth, pyrotechnic sales had increased noticeably in the past three years, to the point where sales last year exceed for the first time those of fireworks; current sales are anticipated to be higher still (see Tables 1 and 2).

Fireworks

By far the biggest proportion of firework sales (value and units) was to the general public, and the trend in recent years had been to sell them in boxes through wholesale and retail outlets. GF sells boxes of fireworks in seven sizes with current retail prices up to £35.00. Other firework sales were for large orders from organizations of different types. These orders would typically comprise fireworks at the top end of the price range sold to the general public or more normally from their wide range of designs in the product categories of displays, set pieces and daylight fireworks. To fulfil these orders (which comprised some

Table 1 Actual and forecast sales

Sales (£m)		Current year minus						Current
	7	*6*	*5*	*4*	*3*	*2*	*1*	*year*[a]
Fireworks	2.1	2.3	2.3	2.6	2.7	3.0	3.1	3.3
Pyrotechnics[b]	—	0.1	0.3	0.3	0.8	2.6	3.3	3.9
Total	2.1	2.4	2.6	2.9	3.5	5.6	6.4	7.2

[a] Current year figures are forecast not actual.
[b] Exports for pyrotechnic products were 70 per cent last year and are expected to increase to 75 per cent this year.

Table 2 Types of firework, current catalogue

Firework category	Number of sizes in each category
Lights	10
Showers	16
Fountains	34
Rockets	20
Catherine wheels	7
Roman candles	18
Volcanoes	14
Shells	48
Mines	5

10 per cent of the total value of firework sales) the top end of the price range and daylight fireworks were usually taken from existing finished goods stock and the specials (i.e. displays and set pieces) which comprise four-fifths of these orders were made to a customer's specification. The range of fireworks sold currently is shown in Table 2.

About 85–90 per cent of all GF's fireworks sales are sold in line with Bonfire Night on the 5 November each year. Order are taken at the spring toy fairs at Brighton and Harrogate, or by direct order. Delivery of all these orders is made from August onwards and customers normally settle their invoices in either November or December each year.

Pyrotechnics

Sales for pyrotechnic contracts have increased significantly in the last three years and are forecast for this year at £3.9m (see Table 1). The size of contracts awarded so far has varied from £40,000 to £1.7m. The latter contract was in fact awarded last month — the previous largest contract had been for £1.2m. Contracts currently in manufacture or recently finished had values ranging from £52,000 to £650,000. Each contract received is always for one product only, such is the nature of the business. Thus, if a customer wanted a number of products it would be required to place a contract to cover each product, even if two or more contracts were placed with the same supplier. The chances of GFP receiving a contract for a product which it had made before are given in Table 3.

Table 3 Chance of GF receiving a pyrotechnic contract for a product they have made before

Number of years after receiving the first contract	Chance of receiving an order with the same product specification[a] (%)
1	Nil
2	10
3	15
4	15
5 and over	20

[a] The low chances of receiving a repeat order are attributable to the fact that the range of products required by GFP's customers is very wide, and although many of these products' specifications may not be changed, the tendency is for customers to order several years' requirements at a time. Combine this with the fact that GFP may not be asked to tender or may not get the order then the chances of receiving a contract for the same product are small.

Table 4 Inventory value by category and production type (£000)

	Raw materials/components	Work-in-progress	Finished goods[a]	Total
Fireworks	202	117	715	1,034
Pyrotechnics	107	333	—	440
Total	309	450	715	1,474

[a] The opening finished goods inventory for fireworks on 1 December last year was £0.25m (which is normal for this time of the year) and nil for pyrotechnics. The other categories of inventory have remained steady throughout these three months.

Pyrotechnic sales are the responsibility of the managing director Ray Livingstone, although the preparation of quotations and the control of the commercial side of the contracts is handled by the quotations and contracts department which reports to the commercial director as shown in Figure 1. Ray considers that this segment of GFP's sales as the area for growth within the company:

> Now that we are becoming established in this market, the opportunity to maintain current sales growth should be achievable. However, sales are not as predictable as on the fireworks side of our business for two important reasons. The first is that we are not certain which contracts, if any, we shall secure. This leads to the problem, therefore, of deciding how many and for which contracts to tender. Too few or too many orders won will bring its own set of manufacturing problems — a case in point is the £1.7m contract we have just received. Furthermore, as we are not well-established in pyrotechnics it would be ill-advised to turn down the opportunity to tender if asked. Many of our orders are for export contracts and dealing with different cultures has its own set of problems. The second reason is that not being well-established also means that we are less certain about our customers and the nature of the repeat business from them, even though this would be for different products.

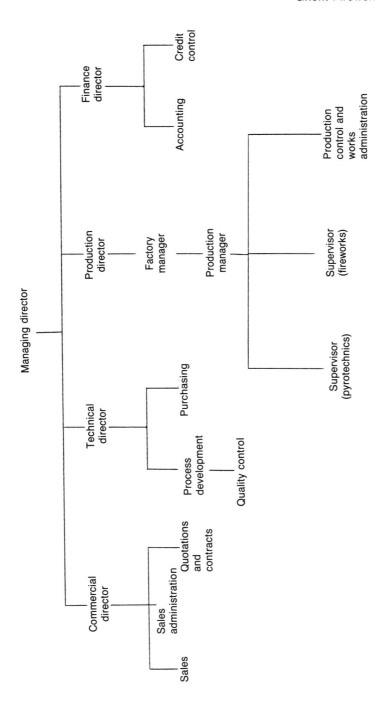

Figure 1 Organization chart.

Manufacturing

GF moved to its present site on the outskirts of Dundee in the mid-1950s. The present site is an arrangement of about thirty small production units which have been added to over the years. The limitations on the amount of explosives which can be held in a given area forces this organizational configuration onto GF and any other manufacturing company in this line of business.

GF has a total of 143 employees, of whom 104 are direct workers. Manufacturing usually works on a single shift basis from 7.30 a.m. to 4.00 p.m. except in times of high throughput. At these times extra people have been employed on a part-time basis spanning a wide range of $2\frac{1}{2}$–5 hour daytime shift combinations. Recently though, when a large contract has been going through manufacturing the company has worked two 12-hour shifts based on the full-time workforce and supplemented by part-timers and a few temporary full-timers who also worked the 12-hour shift pattern.

Fireworks

The manufacturing process for fireworks comprises four steps or stages as shown in Figure 2. Each of these main steps (except stage 3 which is completed after stage 2) is completed in a separate building because of the ruling on explosives described earlier.

All fireworks are packed into boxes or against a specific customer order. However, completion of this stage will always depend upon the appropriate mix of fireworks being available. Thus box 17 comprises seventeen different types of firework from within the categories given in Table 2, all of which have to be available before packing can commence.

Whereas the mixing and filling activities are confined to small areas, packing takes place in a larger factory area which has been designated solely to firework packing. Fireworks after stage 3 in the process are now ready for packing. On completing stage 3 they are stacked into containers and transported to the packing area.

Although fireworks are made to a written specification, the filling operation is less than exact. Typically, a bundle of fireworks are strapped together by a rubber band and the composition is poured into them. By spreading the composition by hand and shaking, the firework tubes are filled before the clay is inserted.

Pyrotechnics

The manufacturing process to complete pyrotechnic products is similar from one to the next, as outlined in Figure 3. Working to the quality requirements of Defence Standards

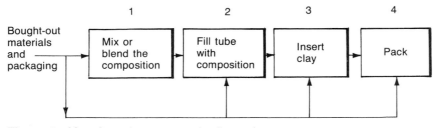

Figure 2   Manufacturing process for fireworks.

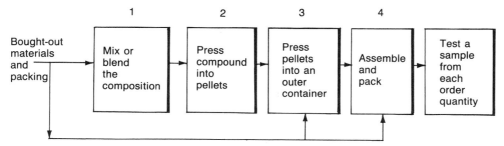

Figure 3   Manufacturing process for pyrotechnic products.

Stage
1   Mix compound to the product specification provided by the customer and specified by process development.

2   Press compound into pellets — a simple press is used.

3   Assemble or press pellets into the required outer containers — again, a simple press is used.

4   Assemble ignitor and any other components (e.g. a spike) onto the container. Paint, stencil, silk screen, heat shrink the required identification onto the container. The identification is specified by the appropriate Defence Standard and the customer. Process development specifies the process to be used to make the required identification.

5   Cap, tape flares together, pack in outer container and label.

6   Test product samples out of each order quantity processed.

Figure 4   Production stages to produce a flare.

05-21 to 05-29 (for either UK or export sales — in fact, being a Ministry of Defence registered company is almost a prerequisite to win export contracts for pyrotechnic products), the specification against which GF quoted goes first to process development (see Figure 1). This function then specifies the appropriate way in which the product should be manufactured. Once these process specifications have been established they are handed over to production who can then schedule them into manufacturing once the required components and packaging are available. A more detailed summary of the processes through which a typical pyrotechnic product goes is given in Figure 4.

Production planning and control

The production planning and control function is provided by the production control and works administration department (see Figure 1) which reports to the production manager. The procedures are outlined in Figure 5.

Fireworks

Following the peak sales in November each year, fireworks are manufactured initially in line with sales forecasts and then later in line with the firm sales orders received from spring onwards. Individual orders which are not related to 5 November sales are met as and when they are required. To keep manufacturing steady, the aim is to produce each month one-twelfth of the forecast annual sales. The procedure used is to order materials, etc. in line with these sales forecasts and then make the same quantity of the high-volume fireworks each month, and to make two months of some of the lower-volume fireworks one month, and then two months of the other lower-volume fireworks the next month, and so on. 'If we are to meet our August-onward deliveries', remarked Phil Mills, production director, 'it is essential that we make about £260,000 of fireworks each month. If we fail to do this we will find it very difficult to meet our deliveries later in the year. Based on the trade-offs and associated costs, it has been decided to adopt this method rather than any alternative.' Production schedules are established in line with stockholdings and anticipated deliveries of the required materials, components and packaging. However, the combination of the fact that the process is fairly flexible and the fireworks in work-in-progress allows the packing programme to be adjusted in line with what is available to pack and the packaging in stock. The manufacturing process before packing can also be adjusted from the laid down schedules again in line with the materials, etc. which are available in stock.

Pyrotechnics

A pyrotechnic contract has typically to be delivered within four months of GF receiving the order. Although delivery times do relate, to some extent, to the size of the contracts: the bigger the quantity involved, then the longer the delivery lead time, and vice versa. The procedure used to schedule this into production is given in Figure 5. The first step is for process development to determine the best way to manufacture the particular product. Using laboratory process facilities, process development will select from a limited number of different ways of making the product in order to meet the agreed specificaton. The increase in work in this department means that it takes on average one month to issue a process specification. The quality control department is responsible for testing the samples taken from the production order quantities which comprise a contract, and Figure 6 provides an analysis of the number of sample failures generally experienced.

The other activity which delays the start of manufacturing is the procurement of production quantities of materials, components and packaging. To meet the Ministry of Defence (MoD) standards, all suppliers must be on the MoD register, which restricts the number of suppliers from which companies such as GF may choose. It has taken up to six weeks to procure production quantities of some items (quantities sufficient for some fifty products can normally be obtained in a week by process development) but usually it takes up to three to four weeks from receipt of an order to supply production quantities.

When the first order quantity is completed, a sample is taken for 'proofing' as explained in Figure 6. However, manufacturing, under pressure to meet the delivery promise on a contract, invariably has no option but to continue to manufacture without waiting for the results of the proofing. If changes subsequently have to be made then the rework involved is completed by production as soon as possible.

Fireworks

Production planning and control is based primarily on forecast sales in the first few months of each financial year (i.e. 1 December onwards) and later (after the spring toy fairs and receipt of direct orders) on the basis of sales orders. Placing purchase orders with appropriate suppliers based on a monthly schedule, which is two months firm (i.e. a committed schedule) and two months tentative.

Production schedules are laid down against these material, component and packaging deliveries with daily adjustments made according to what combinations of materials/components/packaging are in stock and in order to minimize manufacturing disruptions. To achieve this, the production control and works administration department works closely with the relevant production supervisor.

Pyrotechnics

The procedure involved in pyrotechnic contracts is as follows:

1. *Tender*. A tender is made by the quotations and contracts department, based upon an assessment of past contracts of a similar nature and a working knowledge of the operations involved to complete the work involved. However, there is no formal feedback of information from production to quotations and contracts of actual production achievement (e.g. actual throughput times) nor is this information systematically collated by production for this purpose.

2. *Order received*. Where a tender is successful and an order is received, the specified delivery date of the tender is then triggered off on the basis of order receipt. Hence, a tender will specify that the delivery required is, say, four months from receipt of the order.

3. *Parts are ordered*. These usually take one month. However, if parts have a longer lead time then this is taken into account when setting the specified delivery time.

4. Process development is then completed on the basis of an advanced batch of some fifty sets of materials, components and packaging. These are completed in the process development department but does not normally involve production in these procedures. This department then produces a process specification to be followed by manufacturing.* However, the specification does not normally include a synopsis for production of the problems, difficulties and 'things to watch for' as experienced by the process development department. It will also include a proofing procedure which details the tests to be made and sample size to be taken from each manufacturing order quantity.

5. Production converts the process specification into a set of working instructions:
   (a) tasks involved;
   (b) safety precautions to be taken (e.g. footwear and protective clothing);
   (c) explosive limits to be adhered.

6. Materials are then issued re Defence Standard 05–21 and a record of which material was used and the supplier is kept with the order quantity of products. This is to allow all materials, etc. to be traced in case of problems later in the process or when the product is being used by the customer.

7. Each order quantity is then proofed (explained in Figure 6).

* As the process equipment and conditions of working are very different (e.g. laboratory as against high-volume manufacturing) the failure of process development to develop the suggested process specification in line with the conditions in which manufacturing will work, leads to many of the initial 'proofing' failures.

Figure 5 Production planning and control procedures.

In order to complete a pyrotechnic contract, production manufactures a number of order quantities which typically equate to two work shifts (this size of order quantity is considered sensible in terms of the explosive limits and the volume it represents going through the different processes). Each order quantity has to be 'proofed' (i.e. inspected) by the quality control department (QCD). For example (and in line with the customer specification) these will comprise vibration testing, ignition burn length and damp test. The size of sample taken from an order quantity reduces over the production runs to meet the whole contract quantity and in line with the failure rates observed. To complete the test procedures on the first sample takes at least two days and sometimes five or more. Tests on later samples take less time.

If a sample fails the proofing then manufacturing will be stopped until the problem has been checked out. This may result in an internal manufacturing process change or a rejection of a particular component(s) and discussion with the supplier(s) involved.

Order quantity	Samples taken which fail proofing by QCD (%)
1st	25
2nd	10
3rd	Occasional
4th	Rare
5th onwards	None
Source of failure	Percentage of total failure
Production process	95
Component supply	5

Figure 6 Sample failures for pyrotechnic contracts and their source.

Inventory

The results of a stock check at the end of February, earlier this year (the first quarter of the current financial year) are shown in Table 4. The stock check showed a 10 per cent loss on the evaluation of fireworks (i.e. the value of work-in-progress for fireworks was 10 per cent less than expected, based upon the materials issued). This, however, was not considered unusual and is accounted for by the material losses in the manufacturing process, especially at the 'fill tube with composition' stage. However, this check on WIP for pyrotechnics is computed at the end of each contract and normally there is little adjustment to be made.

The future

Ray Livingstone concluded:

> The increase in pyrotechnic sales in recent years has been important on two counts. Firstly, it has given us an important boost in overall sales turnover. Secondly, it has provided us with an alternative

product range in itself which also provides a balance in activities to being solely in fireworks, with the added advantages in cash flow. Fortunately, we have such a flexible workforce that we can move them from fireworks to pyrotechnics and vice versa without much disruption. Similarly, we can increase our capacity temporarily with part-time and full-time employees. In fact, winning the recent pyrotechnic contract for £1.7m has meant that we have now decided that to meet all our sales commitments in fireworks and pyrotechnics we shall have to run a second shift as we did once before with a large contract. Our permanent employees will be divided into two groups so as to form the basis for each shift. We are now recruiting temporary staff to bring the shift members up to the required level. Achieving delivery on the contracts is not only important in itself but also has significant consequences in terms of cash flow.

Production/operations control: short cases

Ash Electrics Plc

Ash Electrics Plc is a manufacturer of door bells, door chimes, switches, industrial alarm bells and a range of small transformers. Producing some five million units per year (from a 15″ diameter bell to a replacement bulb in a lighted switch) the company sells to electric wholesalers throughout the UK and abroad. One of its important selling features is to meet home orders on a same-day-as-receipt basis whilst the dispatch of export orders only waits for appropriate shipping arrangements.

The range of manufacturing activities include coil winding, simple cropping and punching and other operations such as bending, forming and crimping simple components for later assembly. The principal activity, however, is the assembly, test and packing of products from the necessary bought-out and made in-house components, mouldings and parts. In outline, the manufacturing process is shown in Figure 1. In order to reduce

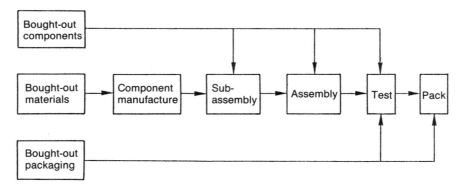

Figure 1 Outline of the manufacturing process.

manufacturing costs and WIP inventory holdings, the company has standardized many components in each of the products from fixing screws through to clips, bobbins, coils, lamps and multi-language instruction leaflets. Besides the metal bars or domes which produce the sound, the principal material used is plastic. Plastic bases, front pieces and components are brought-in from outside suppliers to meet demand forecasts for each final product.

The company works on thirteen four-week periods and the period forecast sales, by product, is provided. In addition, the forecast end-of-period finished goods inventory holding is also known. It is expected that anticipated differences between actual and forecast sales will be reflected in the production programme so that the actual end-of-period finished goods inventory is as close as possible to the forecast level. These adjustments are made at the start of each period when firm production outputs are agreed.

Hunting Swift Plc

Hunting Swift (HS) Plc manufactures a range of pumps and turbines for the petrochemical industry. The current product range consists of twenty basic units offered in a total of 110 sizes (i.e. some 5 sizes per unit) and, on average, each size can be manufactured in up to ten different materials. All products are manufactured to the very precise standards of the American Petroleum Institute in order for HS to avail itself of world export markets and the rigorous international requirements of the industry.

Typically a unit consists of some 350 parts of which about 120 require some machining. The other 230 are bought-out components which go into the final assembly. The machining processes within the company comprise 21 work-centres such as centre lathes, turners, millers, drills and borers. The machining requirements of the different parts vary greatly from as little as a single operation of 3 minutes on one work centre to as high as a total of 13 hours on some 8–10 operations spread over 7 work-centres. About 65 per cent of machined parts are common to more than one type of end-product and in a typical year there are 1,000 of these common parts, the cumulative demand for which exceeded 28,000 items (see Table 1). Once all the materials are on site, the majority of the manufacturing time is taken up in the machine shop.

HS submits tenders to the major oil companies and civil engineering contractors who

Table 1 Typical demand pattern for common parts

Demand for parts	*Number of parts*	*Number of items*
0– 10	488	1,939
10– 20	213	2,912
20– 50	168	5,112
50– 100	78	5,420
100– 200	30	3,894
200– 300	11	2,543
300– 500	7	2,757
500–1,000	5	3,653
	1,000	28,230

design and build petrochemical plants. The order quantities are small with a maximum of four similar units on any one order. Total unit sales in recent years have risen to about 280 for all pumps. A similar quantity is anticipated for the coming year. The delivery time offered to customers for a typical unit is six months with some suppliers quoting a three months delivery on castings. At the other end of the delivery spectrum some small items are held in stock or are same-day delivery.

The products supplied by HS have a long life and consequently generate a significant demand for spares. For instance, in the last full year there were 300 orders for spares. These orders were for 1,400 different parts with typically, several different parts on each order. When the order quantities for each part were totalled, they exceeded 12,000 items and accounted for some 50 per cent of the sales value. The typical delivery time for spare parts was also quoted as six months where many machining operations were required. Other parts (e.g. small components where the quantities required were high but they were either bought out or require little machining) were quoted two to three months for delivery.

Platt Green Electronics Plc

Platt Green Electronics (PGE) Plc is a small company which manufactures and assembles a small range of oscilloscopes. There is only one basic product but this is sold in four versions: mains supply, d.c. supply, battery pack (including charger) and mains pack. The oscilloscopes are also sold with or without a probe and connector. These latter items are also sold individually.

The production process involves the following principal phases: metal fabrication, printed circuit board (PCB) manufacture, PCB test, subassembly, assembly, test and pack. The policy of the company is to use outworkers to complete parts of these processes with the others being performed inside the plant as shown in Figure 1. The oscilloscope cases and drilled blanks to take the components are fabricated in the metal shop. From these, subassemblies are made which, together with other parts, are then assembled before test and packing. The component parts and subassemblies for each product are shown in Table 1.

The present workforce comprises three full-time and two part-time staff, employed at the plant with twelve outworkers who can allocate up to twenty hours per week to PGE's work. Production levels average twenty oscilloscopes per week. Probes and connectors are

Table 1 The number of components and subassemblies by product type

Product	Number of components		Number of subassemblies
	made-in	*bought-out*	
Mains	20	85	9
D.c.	32	105	10[a]
Battery pack	26	92	6
Mains pack	30	70	4
	108	352	29

[a] Eight of these subassemblies are also common to the mains version of this product.

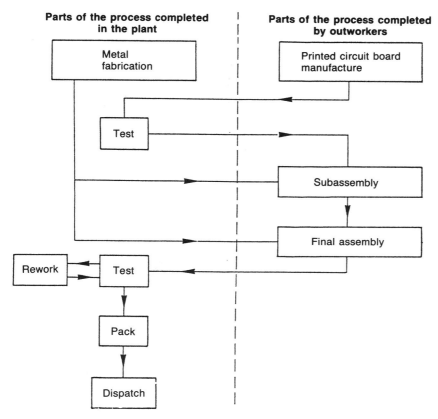

Figure 1   The manufacturing process.

bought-in and require little additional work. The products are sold as standard items to meet a range of different industrial applications.

The weekly production levels, though averaging twenty units, can vary from week to week depending upon the number of oscilloscopes requiring rework after final assembly test. The amount of time it takes to correct the faults can vary from $\frac{1}{2}$ to 6 hours. At the moment, the full-time staff are responsible for the rework activity.

Richmond Plastics Plc

Richmond Plastics produces a wide range of products which fall into three categories: items which it sells to several customers, items which are designed for one customer who calls off from a blanket order with the required notice, and items made on a subcontract basis.

The first two items are for products that typically have a number of bought-out components added to them and require specific labels and packaging before they can be assembled and packed. Whilst some subcontract items also fall into this category, others comprise products which are bulk-packed into secondhand cartons and require no labels.

The principal manufacturing processes involved are injection moulding and assembly. A typical product has one or more parts which are moulded. These then go direct to assembly or into WIP stores prior to assembly. After assembly and packing the products go into the finished goods warehouse. The injection moulding machines are grouped into one of four sizes with each mould going onto one size of machine:

Moulding machine group	Number of machines
1	29
2	14
3	10
4	4
	57

As many of the products are bulky and the volumes can total up to four thousand shots[1] per shift, it is important to keep WIP inventory to a minimum. The mould shop works on a 24 hour basis for five days per week with some weekend working on particular orders as necessary. The assembly department rarely works overtime except to meet the peak demands prior to Christmas — the normal working week is $37\frac{1}{2}$ hours. In addition, Richmond Plastics occasionally subcontracts work to one or two other moulding companies in times of high demand. When this happens, some of the products are returned to Richmond Plastics as WIP for inspection, assembly and packing whilst others (usually where quality is less critical) are assembled and packed at the subcontractor's premises and then delivered to Richmond Plastics' finished goods warehouse.

Note

1. A multi-impression mould will produce in each shot the number of components on that mould.

Spencer Thompson Plc

Spencer Thompson (ST) Plc is a firm of professional accountants which provides both accounting, finance and management consultancy services to its clients. ST has offices throughout the UK with the largest in central London.

At the central London office, there is a typing centre and proof reading department which types the majority of reports prepared for clients by staff at this office, together with internal documents, statements, reporting procedures and information papers. There is a manager, supervisor, nine typists and three proof readers employed to provide this facility. The documents received for preparation vary in length from a few pages up to 250 A4 sides or more. Estimated final extents of documents placed into typing frequently differ greatly from their actual final extents after they have been typed up and tables and diagrams incorporated.

The typists use a word processing facility comprising input and printout equipment plus a few electric typewriters. The average output of each typist is five hundred lines per day which includes both typing and corrections. The demand placed upon the typing facility varies as does the lead time required to meet client and consultancy assignment deadlines.

The process to complete a report consists of initially typing, editing if requested, proof reading, typing corrections and proof reading the corrections. The three proof readers provide the editing and proof reading capability in the process. However, in some situations the person writing the report may wish to take the initial typed document, edit or revise the text and then put it back into the process. In some cases, the revisions may be extensive.

Each proof reader averages about seventy pages of work a day. This average covers a typical mix of work and includes the checking of corrections.

Redman Company

Redman Company was a wholly-owned subsidiary of Bomat Industries. Although all its sales were internal within the group, it was judged under normal commercial rules of which one was profit performance.

Its task was to take requirements and, having discussed these in detail with the 'customer', it would prepare initial drawings to ensure that the product met requirements. On the basis of this it would agree a price and delivery schedule and then proceed to manufacture it. The principal steps involved from that stage onwards are described below and summarized in Table 1.

In order to meet the requirements of its customers, Redman Company would, in essence, prepare drawings and cost estimates in line with a customer's stated requirements and then arrange for the whole manufacturing task to be completed and delivery to the customer's premises.

With regard to manufacturing, the company would buy-in standard parts from suppliers and also seek quotations for and organize the making of any special parts from chosen subcontractors. The company would be responsible for issuing materials to both its own manufacturing unit and subcontractors. Whilst much of this material was in inventory, any other material could be purchased locally, with guaranteed short deliveries. When the component parts were received from its subcontractors, Redman would bring these together with the relevant subassemblies made in-house and complete the final assembly prior to delivery.

When placing orders for component parts with local subcontractors, the company had developed a policy of requiring estimates, the acceptance of which coincided with the placement of the order (activity 6 in Table 1).

Internal pressure to reduce costs had led the company to review its current practice. As part of this revision it had listed the activities involved and determined how long each one currently took to complete. Furthermore, it had estimated that for each day the total assembly duration could be reduced there would be a saving on each order of £100 per day. These savings were, however, not to be made without some additional costs. Details of these, together with the activities where potential reduction in time was available, are given in Table 2.

This case study is © by Professor T.J. Hill (London Business School). It is intended as the basis for class discussion and not as an illustration of good or bad management.

Table 1 Schedule of principal activities in the manufacturing task

Activity	Place at which the activity would be completed	Normal duration (days)
1 Assemble component parts and subassemblies to make the final product	Redman	10
2 Prepare final drawings	Redman	5
3 Make subassemblies	Redman	15
4 Make and deliver component parts	Subcontractor	20
5 Obtain estimates for special parts from relevant subcontractors[a]	Redman	20
6 Accept quotation and place an order on the relevant subcontractor[b]	Redman	3
7 Issue appropriate standard components and/or materials:[b]		
Internally	Redman	2
To subcontractors	Redman	5
8 Deliver to customer	Redman	4

[a] Includes the decision on whether or not to subcontract the work.
[b] Both activities 6 and 7 can start as soon as activity 5 has been completed.

Table 2 Opportunities to reduce total lead times and associated costs

Activity	(A)	(B)	(C)
1 Assemble component parts and subassemblies to make the final product	10	8	30
2 Prepare final drawings	5	5	—
3 Make subassemblies	15	11	40
4 Make and deliver component parts	20	11	80
5 Obtain estimates for special parts from relevant subcontractors	20	20	—
6 Accept quotation and place an order on the relevant subcontractor	3	3	—
7 Issue appropriate standard components and/or materials:			
Internally	2	2	—
To subcontractors	5	2	20
8 Deliver to customer	4	4	—

Column A — the normal number of days required to complete each activity as given in Table 1.
Column B — the shortest possible time (days) needed to complete each activity.
Column C — the increased costs (£) incurred for each day's reduction achieved in completing an activity (i.e. reducing the normal time taken as shown in column B towards the shortest possible duration, as shown in column C).

Riverside Press

'Casual or first time customers are likely to view high-speed copying services as commodity products', said Tom Bates, the president of Riverside Press. 'Because of this it is important that we distinguish our company, through excellent customer service and by getting jobs right the first time, in effect, by building a reputation that will distinguish Riverside Press in the eyes of the more sophisticated, repeat customers. The University Class-Note market is a good example of our ability to differentiate our services in the market-place'.

'In the past our marketing strategy for the Class-Note market has produced important sales growth for the company. As an example, our Gift Certificate programme for Class-Note customers, which encourages the early receipt of customer orders, has been quite successful in developing additional sales by moving some of the production work on Class-Note orders from the peak demand periods into the non-peak demand periods. In addition, the focused group interview sessions that we hold bi-annually with selected customers have been very helpful in identifying the critical needs of our customers.'

'We are now contemplating a relocation of our Oakley store which will provide an exciting new location adjacent to the university campus, and give us excellent visibility in the market place', continued Tom. 'This location, our highly qualified staff, and the new equipment that we are planning to install at the new Oakley store location, such as the replacement of our IBM 6000 with a new IBM 7000 high-speed copy machine, will give us an excellent advantage in the Oakley market. I plan to make a presentation on the advantages of the proposed 7000 machine for the Class-Note market at the board of directors meeting next month. It is important that we gain a speedy approval for the installation of this machine so that we can complete our plans for the new location of the Oakley store.'

Background

Riverside Press is a high-speed copying service company established ten years ago in Oakley. The business has grown substantially and now has four locations serving university

This case study is © 1990 by the University of North Carolina, Chapel Hill, North Carolina. It was prepared by Professor William L. Berry (University of North Carolina), Professor Terry J. Hill (London Business School) and Mr Cecil C. Bozarth (University of North Carolina) as a basis for class discussion rather than to illustrate either effective or ineffective handling of an administrative situation.

communities in two states. The services provided by the company range from self-service convenience copiers to more elaborate backroom work, such as litigation and architectural jobs, flyers, bound Class-Notes for university courses, and corporate training and software manuals.

The high-speed copying services offered by Riverside Press are aimed primarily at the 'internal' copying needs of a business. These 'internal' copying needs account for about 20 per cent of the total market for printed matter. The remaining 80 per cent of the market consists of business-to-business (or external) requirements. These needs include brochures, calendars, envelopes, letterheads, etc., where print quality and colour are important factors. This part of the market requires offset printing capabilities which Riverside Press does not currently provide.

There are at least thirteen companies in the immediate geographic area advertising some level of copying services, although not necessarily offering as broad a range of services as Riverside Press. The most closely matched competitors are Plaza Copy Center and Office Supply, Central Copying, and Kinko's. The latter, like Riverside Press, is open 24 hours seven days a week, and specializes in a wide range of copying services, including the Class-Note market referred to earlier.

The Class-Note market

The biggest single influence on Riverside Press's copying and sales volumes at the Oakley store is the local university and its 25,000 students. The Class-Note work accounts for approximately 40 per cent of the annual copying volume at Riverside Press and around 50 per cent of the annual sales revenue. In addition, the Class-Note sales contact with students and instructors often leads to additional copying work such as résumés and reports.

Because of the demand for Class-Notes at the beginning of the fall and spring semesters, the company's peak demand periods are August/September and December/January. The total copy volume during each two month period is approximately 3 million copies, or $1\frac{1}{2}$ million copies per month. This is roughly double the typical average volume during the eight other non-peak months. The seasonal nature of the demand puts considerable strain on the Oakley operations. The sales volume for the other business markets, aside from the Class-Note sales, decreases significantly during June and July due to a general slowdown in local businesses brought about by the exodus of students from the campus, and summer vacations.

Buying decisions

Classroom instructors from a wide variety of departments in the university use the Class-Note service which can best be described as the publication of customized textbooks. A Class-Note typically includes case studies, laboratory assignments, text material, problems and exercises, and research journal articles that are specialized to a particular university course. Class-Notes often include copyrighted material which must be cleared with the publishers as well as original material. At the beginning of the semester students pick up the Class-Notes, which usually have attractively designed soft paper covers and use a plastic spiral binding.

Riverside Press has a university marketing representative, Janet O'Neil, who is responsible for the Class-Note market. She deals directly with the instructors. Her job is to co-ordinate the timely and accurate completion of the Class-Note orders and develop new business. Riverside Press uses several marketing incentives to win business, including:

1. Free pick-up and return of originals and a complimentary instructor copy.
2. Copyright checking as well as checking for readability and continuity.
3. Typing up the table of contents and the title page.
4. Price discounts or gift certificates for instructors if the order is placed and the material is received prior to one month before the start of the semester.

The Class-Note market is unique in several respects from the other markets served by the company. First, the person who submits an order (the instructor) is not the final customer. The students are the final customers and they may or may not decide to purchase the Class-Note for a course. Because of the actual demand uncertainty, Riverside Press must decide just how many Class-Notes to produce in the first run on an order. In effect, the quantity on each customer order can be viewed as a forecast of demand for a particular Class-Note. The result is that the company can make: (1) just enough to meet the actual student demand; (2) too many in which case the extras are thrown away, or (3) too few which results in small over-runs (typically run in quantities of one or two) to fill the additional requests of the students. From an operations perspective, each Class-Note order will result in at least one long run, and perhaps several smaller ones (which frequently result in a much higher cost per unit and the loss of scarce copy machine capacity during the peak demand period).

Typical Class-Note orders

The typical order from an instructor is for 20—25 copies of a master consisting of around two hundred original pages. A representative sample of the Class-Note orders is shown in Table 1. The order winning criteria for this sample of customer orders, developed by Janet O'Neil, are shown in Table 2. As indicated in Table 1, the lead time for the Class-Note orders can vary from several months to a day or two. Factors beyond the control of Riverside Press that can affect the customer order lead time include: instructor delay in making up the Class-Note, university delays in finalizing the teaching assignments for instructors, and the extent to which the Class-Notes are new or are significantly modified.

Riverside Press uses several incentives to increase the lead time allowed for copying, and to move the production activities into a non-peak demand period. These include price discounts and instructor gift certificates from the campus bookstores. Pat Matthews, who has the production responsibility for Class-Note orders, says that 'The bookstore gift certificates have been most successful. These have produced an increase from a level of one-third to approximately one-half of the Class-Note customer orders being turned in two or more weeks before the start of the busy season.'

The most important quality characteristics of the Class-Notes are readability and continuity. Because of the importance of these two factors, Riverside Press checks the text legibility and continuity on all orders. If a problem is discovered, the company works with the instructor to resolve it.

Service operations at Riverside Press

The Oakley store has both front office (service) operations where store personnel and equipment directly interface with customers, and back room operations where Class-Note

Table 1 Customer order sample
Table 1(a)

Course		Gift cert.	Instructor name	Number masters	Number ordered	Number impress.	Date order received	Date order requested	Date order delivered	Unit price	Customer contrib./ order
Operations Mgmt	233	1	Steve Kilmon	472	42	19,824	14/12	21/01	28/12	26.57	0.66
Engineering Mec	117	1	Derrick Middleton	350	35	12,250	15/12	13/01	29/12	19.52	0.65
Agriculture	390		Craig Pippert	428	4	1,712	10/01	28/01	11/01	28.24	0.64
Biology	61		George Saad	208	23	4,784	24/01	31/01	27/01	12.33	0.73
Government	53	1	Charlotte Adams	102	180	18,360	09/01	20/01	n.a.	6.92	0.80
Stage Craft	38		Joe Plant	114	78	8,892	14/12	15/01	10/01	7.27	0.73
Agriculture	288		Ben Huggins	323	25	8,075	30/12	17/01	n.a.	18.33	0.74
Chinese	317		Cynthia Shail	349	10	3,490	13/12	17/02	16/02	19.19	0.63
Mathematics	114	1	Dwight Huller	201	25	5,025	15/02	15/01	10/01	11.95	0.66
Plant Life	228		Larry Moy	249	40	9,960	28/12	17/01	09/01	14.24	0.76
Calculus	18	1	Danny Silver	201	25	5,025	14/12	22/01	21/01	11.57	0.66
Operations Mgmt	171		George Baylin	558	10	5,580	22/12	18/01	13/01	33.76	0.67
Engineering Grap	126	1	Debra Coles	205	10	2,050	13/12	10/01	16/12	11.29	0.50
Statistics	213		Judith Hong	410	7	2,870	21/12	10/01	29/12	24.76	0.69
*Oper. Research	16		John Pitts	58	70	4,060	10/01	10/02	02/02	3.00	0.63
Civil Engineer	260	1	Steve Walston	263	25	6,575	12/12	05/01	n.a.	14.65	0.56
Stage Craft	148	1	David Coles	364	60	21,840	12/12	12/01	11/01	19.99	0.73
Statistics	197		Thalia Bratton	896	41	36,736	09/01	24/01	23/01	48.90	0.75
*Chemistry	142		Phil Anders	17	36	612	18/04	21/04	19/04	0.95	0.26
Engineering Mech	117	1	John Abbink	179	25	4,475	15/12	17/01	30/12	11.29	0.59
Plant Life	220		Julie Kraft	408	15	6,120	06/01	24/01	n.a.	23.24	0.72
*Agri Econ	176		Cindy Place	70	30	2,100	09/03	14/03	09/03	3.67	0.55
Chinese	322	1	Cynthia Shail	382	12	4,584	07/12	11/01	30/12	18.67	0.49
Chinese	2		Cynthia Shail	228	140	31,920	05/12	10/01	21/12	12.90	0.77
Plant Life	218		Fred Russ	476	22	10,472	12/01	30/01	27/01	24.88	0.71
Plant Life	158		Carl Williamson	420	15	6,300	08/01	26/01	25/01	24.52	0.73
French	576		Dorothy King	94	13	1,222	15/12	01/01	22/12	8.38	0.80
Industrial Eng	282		Ben Gordon	83	14	1,162	11/01	24/01	18/01	5.95	0.75
Mechanical Eng	64	1	Dave Curry	66	56	3,696	13/12	05/01	17/12	3.86	0.65
Operations Mgmt	216		Edie Curry	243	10	2,430	16/02	08/03	07/03	13.88	0.60
Biology	121		David Biggers	65	20	1,300	13/01	21/01	14/01	3.76	0.55
*Electrical Eng	27		Marilyn Biggers	14	70	980	05/12	10/01	10/12	0.81	0.52
Statistics	231		Carol Wilson	293	17	4,981	23/01	30/01	27/01	17.00	0.58
Chemical Eng	144	1	Mary Abram	50	30	1,500	06/11	10/01	15/12	4.05	0.20

Table 1(b)

Total sold	Pre-run quantity	Over-run	Left-over	Forecast error	Spiral binding	3-hole drill	Shrink-wrap	Number vols	Stapled	Special paper	Copywrite Days	Copywrite Hours
31	41	0	10	11		1		1				1
28	34	0	6	7	1			1				
6	4	2	0	-2	1			1				
22	23	0	1	1	1			1				1
178	152	26	0	2	1		1	1				
75	75	0	0	3	1			1				
27	26	1	0	-2	1			1				
9	10	0	1	1	1			1				
26	25	1	0	-1	1			1				
48	43	5	0	-8	1			1				
30	21	9	0	-5				1				
12	15	0	3	-2		1		1				
13	9	4	0	-3		1		1				
12	6	6	0	-5	1			1				
57	64	0	7	13	1			1	1			2
21	25	0	4	4	1			1				2
58	50	8	0	2	2			1				
50	41	9	0	-9				1	1			1
27	37	0	10	9	1			1	1	1		
21	25	0	4	4	1			1				
19	15	4	0	-4				1				
22	31	0	9	8				1				
11	12	0	1	1				1				
136	126	10	0	4	1	1		1				
23	23	0	0	-1	1	1		1				
16	15	1	0	-1			1	1				
16	16	0	0	-3				1		1		
23	14	9	0	-9	1			1				
86	54	32	0	-30	1			1				2
13	10	4	1	-3	1			1				
14	20	0	6	6			1	1	1			
74	74	0	0	-4		1		1				
11	17	0	6	6			1	1				
16	29	0	13	14	1			1				

Table 1(c)

Double-sided	Total prepare hours	6000 total run hours	6000 unit cost	5000 total run hours	5000 unit cost	7000 total run hours	7000 unit cost	Total over-run hours
2	6.26	3.39	6.25	3.70	6.59	2.67	6.12	0.00
2	5.05	2.19	4.92	2.28	5.15	1.65	4.80	0.00
2	3.96	0.93	10.26	0.59	10.01	0.51	9.65	0.22
2	2.87	0.98	3.23	0.92	3.34	0.67	3.13	0.00
2	7.54	2.72	1.41	3.61	1.50	2.78	1.40	0.67
2	4.39	1.30	1.65	1.63	1.75	1.17	1.64	0.00
2	4.31	1.74	4.76	1.70	4.93	1.26	4.62	0.06
2	3.26	0.94	6.47	0.69	6.49	0.52	6.15	0.00
2	2.94	1.06	3.07	1.02	3.17	0.75	2.97	0.04
2	4.61	2.17	3.44	2.36	3.60	1.79	3.37	0.31
2	3.13	1.35	3.07	1.28	3.13	1.05	2.96	0.46
2	5.21	1.96	8.88	1.64	9.06	1.20	8.51	0.00
2	2.15	0.73	3.65	0.58	3.65	0.48	3.47	0.21
2	4.22	1.45	7.56	1.13	7.48	1.01	7.16	0.62
2	2.64	0.59	0.93	0.71*	0.98*	0.51	0.92	0.00
2	5.05	1.31	4.41	1.27	4.55	0.92	4.29	0.00
2	8.26	3.78	5.04	4.21	5.29	3.24	4.95	0.74
2	17.03	8.48	12.44	9.07	12.96	7.11	12.13	2.04
2	1.55	0.11	0.50	0.12*	0.51*	0.09	0.49	0.00
2	3.16	0.89	2.91	0.86	3.01	0.63	2.84	0.00
2	4.68	1.84	6.50	1.61	6.60	1.29	6.23	0.41
2	1.52	0.41	1.13	0.42*	1.18*	0.30	1.11	0.00
2	3.57	1.16	6.59	0.90	6.65	0.67	6.28	0.00
2	8.78	4.52	2.91	6.03	3.12	4.49	2.90	0.58
2	5.67	2.24	7.10	2.12	7.35	1.54	6.87	0.00
2	4.12	1.63	6.70	1.39	6.83	1.01	6.40	0.11
1	1.35	0.34	1.69	0.29	1.72	0.21	1.63	0.00
2	1.56	0.47	1.47	0.42	1.49	0.36	1.41	0.19
2	3.50	1.12	1.04	1.21	1.08	1.02	1.02	0.53
2	4.27	0.90	5.12	0.73	5.13	0.61	4.92	0.25
2	1.22	0.28	1.18	0.25	1.21	0.18	1.14	0.00
1	2.21	0.16	0.37	0.20*	0.39*	0.14	0.37	0.00
2	3.08	1.12	4.64	0.97	4.75	0.71	4.46	0.00
2	1.41	0.28	0.91	0.28	0.94	0.20	0.89	0.00

Notes

1. All of the customer orders, with the exception of the four orders marked with an *, were run on the 5000. The four orders marked with an * were run on the 6000.

2. The unit cost value shown for the 5000, 6000, and 7000 copy machines includes all variable costs, e.g. direct labour, paper, and maintenance.

3. The first week of classes began on 16 January.

4. n.a. means that the data were unavailable.

Table 2 Order-winning criteria
Table 2(a)

Course		Instructor name	Length of customer relation (years)	Field sales support (faculty)	Field sales support (staff)	Gift certific. advert.
Operations Mgmt	233	Steve Kilmon	1	**	**	*
Industrial Eng	282	Ben Gordon	1			
Agri Economics	176	Cindy Place	1			
Biology	121	David Biggers	1	*		
Chemistry	142	Phil Anders	2	**		
Government	53	Charlotte Adams	3	**	**	
Biology	61	George Saad	3			
Statistics	231	Carol Wilson	3			
Calculus	18	Danny Silver	1		*	
Chemical Eng	144	Mary Abram	1	*		
Chinese	317	Cynthia Shail	1	*		
Chinese	2	Cynthia Shail	1	*		
Chinese	322	Cynthia Shail	1	*		
Eng Mechanics	117	John Abbink	1	*		
Statistics	197	Thalia Bratton	3			
Mathematics	114	Dwight Huller	3	*		
Eng Graphics	126	Debra Coles	2			
Stage Craft	38	Joe Plant	3			
Operations Mgmt	216	Edie Curry	3			
Operations Mgmt	171	George Baylin	3			
Mechanical Eng	64	Dave Curry	3	*		
Plant Life	228	Larry Moy	2		*	
Plant Life	218	Fred Russ	3			
French	576	Dorothy King	3		*	
Electrical Eng	27	Marilyn Biggers	3	*		
Plant Life	220	Julie Kraft	3			
Plant Life	158	Carl Williamson	3			
Oper. Research	16	John Pitts	2			
Agriculture	288	Ben Huggins	3			
Agriculture	390	Craig Pippert	3			
Eng Mechanics	147	Derrick Middleton	3			
Civil Eng	260	Steve Walston	3	*		
Statistics	213	Judith Hong	3			
Stage Craft	148	David Coles	3	***		

and other work is routed through a series of distinct processes. The front office personnel have a number of service tasks aside from taking orders and ringing up sales which include:

1. Order pick-up and delivery of completed copies of Class-Note and other types of order.
2. Informal customer assistance in planning layouts.
3. Copyright checking and other co-ordination tasks for Class-Note orders.
4. Assisting walk-in customers (when necessary) in using the convenience copier machines.

Typically, all Riverside Press staff providing both customer contact in the front office, and production tasks in the back room. However, an employee's customer contact role takes precedence when a customer is present either in person or on the telephone.

General advert.	Being an exist'g supplier	Delivery		Product quality	Store sales support	Location	Product features		Parking	Price
		Speed	Reliabil.				Gift certif.	Price discount		
	**		**	**		Q				Q
*										Q
*		***								Q
		*								Q
		**								Q
		*	**							Q
		****		*						Q
		*	*	*						Q
							***	*		Q
										Q
							****			Q
							****			Q
							****			Q
			*				*			Q
			*							Q
									QQ	Q
							*	*		Q
		*	*			Q	Q			Q
		*	*	*						Q
		*	*							Q
	*	*	*					*		Q
		*	*							Q
		*	*							Q
		*	*					QQ		Q
		*	*	*				****		Q
		*	*							Q
		*	*							Q
		***	**	*						Q
		***	**							Q
		*	**	*						Q
		**	**	**				Q		Q
			***				***			Q
		***	***							Q
		***	***				*			Q

Back room operations at Riverside Press

The back room operations at Riverside Press are typical of a jobbing type of process. The employees are normally responsible for handling every stage of a job, from writing up the customer order to binding the finished product. In fact, one informal scheduling rule at the company says that the shift that receives an order is responsible for completing the order. Because each order may require a different set of processes (such as copying, paper drilling, shrink-wrapping or binding) customer order flow must remain highly flexible.

Table 2(b)

Order-winning criteria and order-qualifier definitions

Field sales support — faculty	Janet's personal contact with instructors, and/or pick-up and delivery of material
Field sales support — staff	Janet's personal contact with secretarial staff, and/or pick-up and delivery of material
Gift certificate advertising	advertising the availability of the gift certificate
Advertising	advertising the availability of the Class-Note service
Existing supplier	being on an approved list of suppliers
Delivery speed	meeting a customer's stated need for a delivery lead time of 5 days or less
Delivery reliability	delivering the customer order on or before the quoted delivery date
Product quality	producing a correctly formated, complete reproduction of the manuscript with a minimum of blemishes
Product features:	
Gift certificate	receipt of a $30 bookstore certificate
Discount	a 10% student price discount
Copyright checking	provide copyright information and processing
Product knowledge	familiarity with the Riverside Press Class-Note format
System knowledge	familiarity with the Riverside Press Class-Note process
Store sales support	friendly, courteous and professional store personnel
Location	proximity to campus
Parking	available parking close to store

Notes
1. The code representing the length of the customers relationships is: 1 = new customer (first year), 2 = repeat customer (second year), and 3 = long-term custom (third or more year).
2. The code for the order-winning criteria is: **** = extremely important, *** = very important, ** = important, * = somewhat important, Q = a qualifier, and QQ = an order-losing sensation qualifier.

High-speed copying equipment
The copying machines are the most significant pieces of equipment in the back room operations both in terms of their need for skilled operators and their total cost and space requirements. Table 3 compares the major features of the high-speed copiers used by the company, i.e. the IBM 5000 and 6000, as well as information on the features of the new

IBM 7000. The 5000 machine has a large range of features including: multiple paper trays, an automatic stapler, internal collation of up to ten sets of copies, and a programming feature to control these features. The 6000 is capable of running orders with a minimum of user intervention, and provides the capability of internally collating up to fifty sets of copies. The proposed 7000 machine is a high-speed copier which has a number of automatic features that enables customer orders to be run with very little user intervention.

Binding
The binding process consists of two steps: punching and ringing. A skilled operator can bind around five thousand back-to-back copies in about fifty minutes, depending on the

Table 3 Comparison of the high-speed copiers used by the company

	Current high-speed copiers		
	6000 *(2nd gen., 1980)*	*5000* *(3rd gen., 1986)*	*7000* *(4th gen.)*

Unique features	7,200 RTS copies/hr
	50 collecting bins,
	     100+ pages/hr
	No stapler
	Excellent quality
		5,100 RTS copies/hr
		No collator, but up to
		     10 stapled copies
		     with covers
		Programmable
		Best quality
			135 imp./min vs 91
			     for 5000
			Stapler and program
			Auto-insert covers and
			     divid.
			11 × 17 back-to-back
			Option for heated tape
			     'auto-binding'

Volume	High volume:
	     200–300 K
	     normal, 1 M peak
	     periods
		Low/medium volumes:
		     200–300 K
		     normal, 500 K
		     peak during Class-
		     Note runs
			Similar to 6000

Targeted jobs	90+% Class-Note	All commercial work
		     during Class-Note
		     runs
			6000's load,
			     quality/multicolour
			     including Class-
			     Note work

Maintenance costs[a]	7.4 m, <10
	     impress.
	1.5 m, 10+
	     impress.
		6.6 m/impression	Cost structure same
			     as 6000

Flexibility	Less flexible for
	     small jobs
	     needing stapler,
	     covers
	Can run for 1+
	     hours without
	     user
	     intervention
		More flexibility and
		     faster, but needs
		     more user
		     intervention for
		     large jobs
			Similar to 5000

[a] Maintenance charges in 0.001 dollars.

size of the manual. Two-thirds of this time is spent punching the paper, the remainder of the time is spent ringing the manuals. There are two separate binding options at the company, Velo-binding and spiral binding. Velo-binding is a high quality, stiff binding and is the more expensive of the two. Similar operator skills are required for the two processes.

Shrink-wrap and three-hole drilling

Shrink-wrapping is a heat-based process that the company uses to wrap stacks of paper up to ten inches thick. Each shrink-wrapping takes about eleven seconds to perform and up to four packets can be processed at one time. Three-hole drilling takes place after the copying has been done. The drilling machine at Riverside Press can handle up to 250 sheets at a time, and a trained operator can process up to five sets in a minute.

Class-Note processing steps

Since the Class-Note orders tend to be similar with regard to the processing steps and materials requirements, the company has developed an order processing form for this market. The information on this form (shown in Figure 1) provides a means of developing a formal checklist and sequence for each Class-Note order, and includes process steps such as copyright checking, pre-checking of the master copy, and 'blue-lining' (which assures that every article starts on a right-hand page).

Packet Number _____   Semester _____

1. Co-worker logging in order _____   Date _____
2. Course (department and number) _____
3. Volume number _____
4. Instructor _____
5. Office address _____
6. Office telephone _____   Home telephone _____
7. Is this material required?   YES   NO
8. Will this material be on reserve in the library?   YES   NO
9. Do you want the pages numbered in black?   YES   NO
10. Are you providing a cover?   YES   NO
11. Do you want your packet double-sided?   YES   NO
12. How do you want the material contained?
    SPIRAL   3-Hole   STAPLE   BAG   Shrink-Wrap   3 ring binders ($1.75)
13. What special instructions do you have?
    _____
    _____
    _____
    _____
14. Do you want to approve the master before the pre-run?   YES   NO
15. Do you want us to deliver your originals and desk copies? _____
16. Where would you like these delivered? _____
17. How many desk copies do you want? _____
18. What will be the total number of students using this material? _____
19. By what date will the material be needed? _____

Figure 1   Order form.

Marketing and operations strategy

'The decision that we are now contemplating concerning the relocation of the Oakley store provides us with an excellent opportunity to review our customer needs in the various markets that we serve, starting with the Class-Note market', said Tom Bates. 'To maintain our current market position it is important that we continually review our marketing and operations strategy in each of our markets. The data that Janet O'Neil has put together on our customers in the Class-Note market (Tables 1 and 2) should help us in evaluating our marketing and operations strategy in this important market.'

Service delivery system review

In this section of the book, the information which forms the basis of analysis and class discussion is given in the classic format of a written case study. In this instance, however, the source of information is for you to collect in the field and bring with you to the scheduled class.

The orientation is a study of the service delivery system used by two organizations involved in the provision of food. In order to provide the opportunity to compare and contrast select a self-service, fast-food outlet (e.g. McDonalds, Wimpey or Burger King) and another outlet of your choice which provides a sit-down, waiter/waitress service. The latter could either be a snack/light meal or fuller meal provision.

The task is to analyse the service delivery system and other pertinent features to address the following:

1. An outline of the procedures involved and indicate any key features in terms of the operations task.
2. Select four important areas in your analysis which contrast the difference between these establishments.

Sunshine Builders, Inc.

In the five years since its founding, Sunshine Builders, Inc., had become one of Florida's largest builders of residential housing. In the opinion of the company's management, major credit for this success was attributable to customer-oriented service and guarantee policies which, in combination with good construction, reasonable prices, and on-time completions, had earned the firm an excellent reputation.

The founders of the company, Charles and Arthur Root, came to Florida six years earlier at the ages of 28 and 26, respectively, having spent the preceeding five years as owners of a retail furniture business in Chicago. Charles Root had majored in economics at college and Arthur Root in chemical engineering. Although their furniture business had been moderately successful, both brothers eventually had concluded that the potential margin of profit was becoming increasingly narrow and that the personal time and effort required was disproportionate to the return attainable. They therefore had decided to sell their furniture store and move to Florida, a state which they believe offered rapid growth and attractive business opportunities.

The Root brothers spent their first several months in Florida becoming familiar with a metropolitan area with a population of nearly 500,000 within a ten-mile radius. During this period, realizing that land was appreciating in value, the Roots purchased eight lots for speculation. Shortly thereafter, with the encouragement of their father, who had some experience in building, they decided to erect houses on the lots, subcontracting the construction work to local contractors.

Within a few weeks after completion, all eight houses had been sold at a profit. Since this initial housing venture proved successful, population growth and industrial activity in the area were accelerating, and land was relatively inexpensive, the Root bothers became convinced that the home construction business in Florida offered excellent prospects. They therefore founded Sunshine Builders, Inc. Five years later, commenting on the company's early days of operations, Arthur Root stated:

We realized at the outset — just as we realize today — that five principles represent the key to success for our firm:

1. Sunshine houses must be completely livable.
2. They must have 'eye-appeal'.
3. As builders we must have a reputation for honesty, skill and 'on-time' completions.

4. We must offer exceptional value.
5. Our houses must be properly promoted.

Below-par performance in regard to any one of these areas would hurt us badly. Our task is to do a top-flight job in all five.

Operations during the first four years

The first major move of the newly formed company was to erect a model home which displayed the type of building it was prepared to construct on customers' lots. Orders were quickly received for forty units which Sunshine arranged to have constructed by local building contractors. Under terms of the purchase agreement with the company, a customer made an initial down payment of 15 per cent of the purchase price and then made regular progress payments as the construction proceeded towards completion. With these arrangements the Roots were required to invest relatively little of their own capital. During the next two years, they were hard pressed to build enough houses to meet the sales demand.

During this period Charles Root found that his greatest business interest lay in land development. He therefore formed a separate firm, Root Land Development Corporation for this purpose, while Arthur, as President of Sunshine Builders, concentrated on home construction (their father took no active part in the management of either firm). Each brother devoted nearly all of his time to his own field of operations, assisting the other only as requested, or when major policy issues had to be decided. Later, a third corporation, Root Associates, was established to handle sales for Sunshine Builders, with Arthur serving as president. Co-operative selling arrangements also were established with local real estate firms.

The activities of all three organizations expanded steadily during the next four years. During this period management operations at all three firms, although hectic and requiring consistently long hours on the part of both brothers, had been simple in concept. With few exceptions the land on which Sunshine Builders constructed homes was already owned by the customer as a result of purchase from either the Root Land Development Corporation, or some other source. All construction work was performed by various local subcontractors who, by mutual consent, concentrated most of their efforts on work for Sunshine Builders.

During the early period of operations, Arthur Root was assisted in the construction phase of the operations by Herbert Playford. Mr Playford, who was in his mid-twenties, had known the Root brothers in Chicago and had moved to Florida at their request only a few months after Sunshine Builders was founded. Mr Playford had a high school education and, prior to joining Sunshine, had worked successively as a shipping clerk, a neon glass blower, and in his father's junk business. On arrival in Florida, Mr Playford was taken by Arthur Root to see thirteen home sites which were then in various stages of construction. He then was given immediate responsibility for their completion with the instruction, 'build them'. In carrying out this assignment Mr Playford acted as superintendent, working with and through the various contractors in scheduling, co-ordinating, and supervising the various construction activities.

As the business grew, four additional superintendents were hired at salaries that were equal to, or slightly above, the earnings that a top construction tradesman could expect in the local area. After about a year Mr Playford was 'moved into the office' to serve as expediter and co-ordinator of the four superintendents, and also given responsibility for the mounting volume of paper work associated with the firm's construction activities. One of his contributions in this new capacity had been to set up the systems of scheduling and cost control to be described subsequently.

Mr Playford's handling of many of the daily 'home-office' details relating to construction left Arthur Root free to concentrate more time on sales work, purchasing, and managing the company's finances. A few months later, a younger brother Daniel Root, 25, who had been pursuing graduate studies in history, also was taken into the firm to assist Arthur.

After spending about two years with the company, Mr Playford resigned to establish his own construction firm, Meadowlark Builders. He was aided in this move by a substantial investment which the Root brothers made in the new concern. Meadowlark was successful from the start, building approximately two hundred low-cost homes during the next twenty-four months. At the close of this period, however, Arthur Root persuaded Mr Playford to return to Sunshine as treasurer, assistant secretary, and manager of production and service, and the Meadowlark operation was discontinued.

By now, Daniel Root, who had become vice-president and secretary of Sunshine Builders, had assumed full responsibility for sales, broker relations, customer relations, advertising, and the devloping and merchandizing of new models. Arthur Root, as Sunshine's president, handled all financing and purchasing. Charles Root continued to devote his time principally to the Root Land Development Corporation.

Sunshine's construction work, under Mr Playford, now required eight subcontractors, who were responsible for the following functions:

Plumbing	Plastering
Electrical work	Carpentry
Painting	Heating
Masonry	Cleaning

Each subcontractor submitted a weekly bill to Sunshine for the wages he had paid to his crews, plus an 8 per cent override for use of equipment. Except for the masonry crew, the subcontractors' employees were not unionized, but the wages received approximated the general community average for the craft in question. The subcontractor's own time was also charged to Sunshine at an hourly rate approximately 15 per cent above that earned by the highest paid man in the crew. Material was purchased and supplied by the subcontractor at cost. Each one hired and fired as he felt necessary, but Sunshine Builders had the right to approve any wage increases. Arthur Root and Herbert Playford made it a practice to question the subcontractors on jobs on which their costs appeared out of line with previous experience. To furnish this information, total costs of each subcontractor were tabulated for each job.

The subcontractors each employed an appropriate number of crews, whose activities were scheduled by the four Sunshine superintendents. Each superintendent was responsible for all Sunshine Builders' homes under construction in the geographic territory assigned to him — roughly one-quarter of the seven-mile radial area that embraced the bulk of Sunshine's activity.

By the latter part of Sunshine's fourth year of operation, Arthur Root had become increasingly concerned about the effectiveness of this arrangement. In discussions with his brothers and Mr Playford, he advanced the following observations and criticisms of existing practices:

1. The four superintendents spent most of their time competing against each other for subcontractors' crews to work on the houses in their respective territories. It could

be argued, in fact, that the superintendents functioned merely as 'high-grade expediters', and made little or no effort to co-ordinate company-wide crew requirements.

2. Seven[1] of the subcontractors were netting $11,000 to $12,000 per year from their association with Sunshine. Actually, however, they were acting more in the capacity of foremen than of independent contractors. Foremen could be hired at a far lower cost.

3. The subcontractors were not buying new labour-saving equipment but tended instead to 'run old equipment into the ground'.

Arthur Root's net conclusions were that it should be possible to centralize controls and scheduling, and thus eliminate conflicts, delays, and the need for superintendents. After considerable discussion of these matters, a unanimous management decision was reached the previous November to absorb the subcontractors' organizations into the Sunshine firm by employing the previous subcontractors as Sunshine foremen, and placing their labour crews on the Sunshine payroll.

During the month following this decision, Arthur Root and Herbert Playford held individual meetings with the various subcontractors to explain the proposed changes. Each was offered employment as a foreman at a salary reflecting his experience and ability. The proposal also included Sunshine's offer to negotiate a fair purchase price for each subcontractor's equipment.

In spite of the fact that the salaries offered were 10–25 per cent below their recent annual earnings (the masonry subcontractor, for example, previously had been making about $12,000 and now was offered $9,250), each of the subcontractors accepted the Sunshine proposal. Arthur Root reasoned that this response reflected the fact that the salaries offered were actually higher than the earnings the men could reasonably expect to achieve if they ended their association with Sunshine. He suspected also that the men realized that their previous arrangement with the firm had been 'a gravy train and had to stop sometime'. He also believed that most of the subcontractors actually were glad to be relieved of the paperwork entailed in the payroll and other responsibilities required of them as independent contractors. Under the new arrangements the former subcontractors, in their new capacity as salaried foremen, were to continue to hire and fire crews, as necessary. The foremen also were promised possible year-end bonuses, dependent on Sunshine's annual profit.

On January 1, having reached agreement with all of the former subcontractors, Sunshine management shifted to the new method of operation and dismissed the four superintendents.[2] An additional eight construction workers, who had been in the employ of certain of the former subcontractors but engaged on other projects, were hired, thus bringing Sunshine's new construction crew to 124 men.

Operations during the current year

Initial reactions to the new organization

After the organizational change was completed, the Sunshine payroll numbered 161 persons (Figure 1). The distribution of employees amongst the various functions is indicated by the number shown in parentheses after each descriptive title. With the exception of the cleaning crew, which employed only unskilled general labour, the employees of each construction crew were divided fairly equally between skilled tradesmen and helpers.

Both Arthur Root and Herbert Playford felt enthusiastic about results achieved during the first few months under the new organization. They said that there now seemed to be

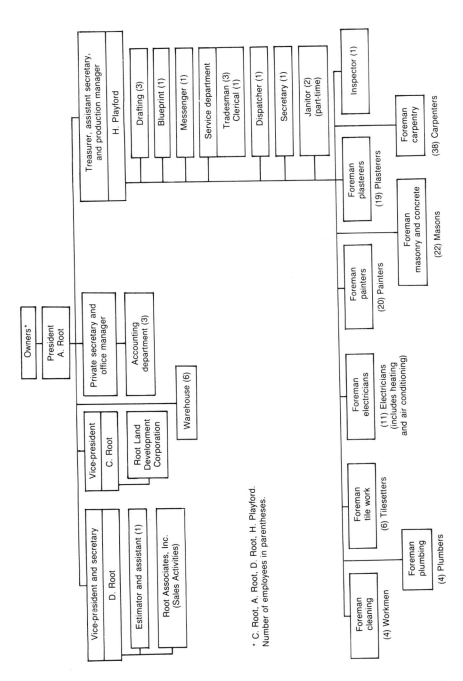

* C. Root, A. Root, D. Root, H. Playford.
Number of employees in parentheses.

Figure 1 Organization as of 1 May, current year.

'a closer, more direct line of communication between the office and the crews'. Mr Playford remarked that fewer mistakes were being made, and Mr Root believed that the foremen appeared to be taking a broader point of view, demonstrated, for example, by their now keeping the office better informed regarding the progress of each job.

Planning and control techniques

The basic approaches to planning and controlling production were essentially those that Mr Playford had established during the initial year of operation. The dispatching office had 'production boards' mounted on two of its walls. These provided the nucleus of production information. Whilst no formal scheduling was attempted, the 'boards' aided the dispatcher in keeping up-to-date regarding the status of each job. The boards themselves consisted of wallboard material on which was tacked blueprint paper divided into two-inch grids. Across the top, along the horizontal scale, were headings for the owner's name, the address where the house was to be built, the model number of the house, and the 65 individual steps, operations, or phases of the construction work required. These are described in Table 1. The houses were then listed vertically, with new homes being added at the bottom as orders were received, as shown below:

Jobs			Construction steps							
Owner	Location	Model	1 Sign clear (lot)	2 Deliver	3 Power	4 Stake	5 Dig	6 Pour	7 Order	...
E.K. Williams	14 Coral St	69								
D.W. Onan	26 Beach Rd	14								
A.T. Bovril	60 Hacienda	090L								

The company's dispatcher, Mabel Roark, aged 35, was responsible for issuing work assignments to the foremen and for keeping the wallcharts posted with current information. Although each of the foremen knew, of course, the specific operations, material and equipment required for each of the construction steps his crews had to perform, they all relied on Miss Roark to instruct them regarding the exact house, and the step, or steps, that should be undertaken next. After relaying these instructions to the foreman, Miss Roark would make note of this assignment by initialing the appropriate box on the wallchart, and writing in the date by which the foreman had promised completion of the work. Later, when the foreman reported that the particular steps had, in fact, been completed, Miss Roark would record this fact by adding the notation 'OK' to the box.

Miss Roark also employed the following coloured-pin code system to call attention to a particular box on the wall chart:

Table 1 Steps of the construction job as used on the company's production boards, including manpower and time estimates for dispatcher

Step number	Operation required	Explanation	Crew	Norm. crew no. men	Man-days of work	Elapsed time allowed (days)	Remarks
1	Sign-posted, lot cleared		Masonry	1	1	1	In typical subdivision lot already cleared
2	Deliver stakes, material and steel		Warehouse	—	—	—	
3	Power pole and water metre in	Done by utilities	Power co.	—	—	—	
4	Stake out		Masonry	3	3	2	Includes a day for checking by foreman
5	Dig footing	Footings only 12″–18″ below the surface	Masonry				
6	Pour footing		Masonry	2	1	$\frac{1}{2}$	
7	Order sliding glass doors		(Mabel)	—	—	—	
8	Lay foundation	Set reinforcing steel and pour concrete	Masonry	2	1	$\frac{1}{2}$	
9	Fill foundation	Fill and pack dirt within foundaton for slab	SC	SC*	—	1	
10	Tie-in foundation	Plumbing for water and sewer connections	Plumbing	2	5	—	Done during no. 11
11	Plumbing rough-in	Set plumbing for slab	Plumbing	3		$2\frac{1}{2}$	Includes a day for city inspection
12	Grade slab		Masonry	2	2	2	Includes a day for city inspection
13	Pour slab		Masonry	3	$1\frac{1}{2}$	$1\frac{1}{2}$	Includes a day after pouring for slab to set
14	Strip for terrazzo	Place strips for sills or sliding doors	SC	SC	—	1	
15	Pour terrazzo		SC	SC	—	$1\frac{1}{2}$	Includes a day for terrazzo to set
16	Deliver blocks, steel, sills		Vendor and warehouse	—	—	—	
17	Lay block walls		Masonry	5	10	2	

No.	Activity	Description	Crew				Remarks
18	Form and pour lintels		Masonry	2	1	$\frac{1}{2}$	Must be inspected
19	First grind, terrazzo		SC	SC	—	2	
20	Carpenter's frame	Frame up interior wall studs and roof	Carpenters	4	20	5	
21	Order cabinets		(Mabel)	—	—	—	Included in time allowance for no. 20
22	Dry-in	First layer of lumber on the roof	Carpenters	4	1	—	
23	Flue and/or duct work		Masonry	2	4	2	Done during framing
24	Set tub		SC	SC	—	$\frac{1}{2}$	Done during framing
25	Electrical rough-in	Place most of electrical wiring	Electricians	2	4	2	Done during framing (after studs in)
26	Prime cornice	Paint under overhang of roof	Painters	2	1	$\frac{1}{2}$	
27	Order lath		(Mabel)	—	—	1	One day necessary for framing and elec. inspection
28	Lath		Plaster	4	4	1	
29	Order vanity		(Mabel)	—	—	—	
30	Ceiling heat	Electrical radiant heating usually used	Electricians	2	2	2	
31	Roof complete	Pitch and gravel built up roof	SC	SC	—		
32	Scratch for tile	Preparation for tiling	Plaster	2	3		
33	Brown coat plaster and stucco		Plaster	4	4	2	
34	Second grind, terrazzo		SC	SC	—	$\frac{1}{2}$	
35	Iron work	Any decorative iron work	Carpenters	2	1	$\frac{1}{2}$	Includes a day for drying
36	Tile walls	Bathrooms and sometimes kitchen areas	Tile	4	6	$1\frac{1}{2}$	
37	Plaster and stucco complete		Plaster	4	4	1	
38	Glaze	Install window glass	SC	SC	—	1	Need two-day notice
39	Install sliding glass doors		SC	SC	—	1	
40	Insulation		SC	SC	—	1	Does not interfere with any other work

No.	Operation	Notes	Crew				Remarks
41	Clean and rough grade lot	Remove debris and grade	SC	SC	—	1	Usually done while framing
42	Front stoop		Masonry	2	1	½	
43	Form outside concrete		Masonry	2	2	1	
44	Pour outside concrete		Masonry	2	2	1	
45	Outside gravel or asphalt		SC	SC	—	2	Need good weather
46	Order trim material	Mouldings, door frames, etc.	(Mabel)	—	—	—	
47	Carpenter's trim		Carpenters	5	20	4	
48	Glaze jalousie doors		SC	SC	—	½	
49	Install cabinets		SC	SC	—	1	Done by vendor during trim operation
50	Septic tank		Plumbers	2	2	1	
51	Plumber's trim	Final plumbing work	Plumbers	2	2	1	
52	Heating	Install and (or) complete heating system	Electricians	3	6	2	Done while carpenters are trimming
53	Paint		Painters	4	16	4	Must be alone in house
54	Install operators and deliver screens	Window mechanisms	Carpenters	1	½	½	
55	Electrical trim	Install lamps, outlet plates, etc.	Electricians	3	3	1	Now done before glazing
56	Polish terrazzo		SC	SC	—	2	Must be alone in house
57	Clean windows and interior		Cleaning	2	2	1	
58	Grass		SC	SC	—	1	
59	Install screens		1	1½	½	½	
60	Painters complete, inspect		Painters	5	15	3	Includes final inspection and adjustments
61	Wallpaper and mirror		Painters	2	2	1	
62	Plumbing inspection	By city inspector		—	—	1	City inspection
63	Electrical inspection	By city inspector		—	—	1	City inspection
64	Permanent electrical connection	By power company	Power co.	—	—	1	
65	Production inspection		Co. inspector	1	1	1	Note also inspection at step no. 60

SC = subcontracted. At the present time the average house required approximately $2,500 of subcontracted work.

Pin colour	Status indicated
Black	On order.
Red	Did not arrive, or get completed, as promised.
White	Crew is there, on the job.
Yellow	Need to call foreman.
Blue	Have a question for the foreman when he calls.

Since a considerable proportion of the purchasers of Sunshine homes were new residents in the community, with many moving details to schedule, Arthur Root and his associates were convinced that any delays in house completions would be the source of extreme personal inconvenience and, thus, significantly jeopardize customer relations. He and Mr Playford were convinced that the wallchart helped identify potential delayed completions while there was still time to remedy the situation.

Since the most recently contracted houses were added at the bottom of the chart, and the construction steps were listed in sequence from left to right, the completed steps indicated by the boxes containing Miss Roark's 'OK' formed a slightly irregular diagonal line on the chart, slanting downwards from right to left. Thus, any house on which construction had fallen behind schedule showed up as an 'indent' to the left of the diagonal line of the 'OK' boxes. A quick visual check of the chart promptly identified trouble-spots. Mr Playford took pride in the fact that during the past twelve months Sunshine had completed the typical house in roughly 80 to 85 calendar days, a figure well under the 100 calendar days specified in the Sunshine construction contracts with purchasers.

In addition to assigning the work to the foremen and maintaining the production boards, Miss Roark served as a communication and recording centre for all reports and instructions. She employed the company's two-way radio system under which each foreman, Mr Playford, and the warehouse supervisor had a two-way unit in his car or truck. The system had been installed the previous year on a lease basis calling for a monthly rental of $375.

Miss Roark usually talked with each foreman by radio at least three times each day. In a typical conversation the masonry foreman might call in and tell her that the footings his crew had been constructing at the Kelly house were now completed, but that the iron work for the Kent job had not arrived and that Mr and Mrs Kent had visited the construction site that morning and asked for a change in the dimensions of their back patio from 12 × 15 feet to 12 × 20 feet. He might ask where Miss Roark wanted his crew to work the next day and also request her to check whether the Larsen house was to have a front planter and whether the plumbers had finished work at the O'Leary house thus permitting the masonry crews to lay the slab.

During a typical day's operation, Miss Roark independently made innumerable decisions regarding operations and jobs to be done next, receiving little or no aid from Mr Playford, whose office was next door. Mr Playford checked the wallcharts once or twice a week, but usually did not participate in the hour by hour job of scheduling the crews.

To prevent delays and idle crews, Miss Roark had to have a clear understanding of the various construction operations required and the relationship amongst them. It was essential, for example, for her to know that the electricians could not 'rough-in' until the studs were up, that the heating work could be done while the carpenters were trimming, that the electricians and plumbers had to work either ahead of, or behind, the painters on certain operations, but could work simultaneously with them on other jobs, and so forth.

Miss Roark said, 'I still make some mistakes, but I've learned a lot about house building during this past year.'

In scheduling the crews, Miss Roark employed the 'time and crew requirements guides' shown in Table 1. These had been prepared by Mr Playford and Miss Roark out of their combined experience regarding how many men were required, and how much time was necessary, for the completion of each construction step. They had learned, for example, that it was reasonable to expect a crew of four carpenters, working at an ordinary pace, to 'frame-up' an average house (step 20) in five days.

Purchasing and warehousing

Miss Roark's purchasing function was confined to ordering specific items from vendors previously selected by Arthur Root. Arthur Root handled all major negotiations with suppliers, including questions of prices, delivery, and payment terms. This work occupied a significant portion of his time. He regularly 'shopped' for better values in windows, fixtures, lumber, appliances and similar items, and had effected considerable standardization of purchased items.

Late in the previous year Sunshine had leased a 6,000 square-foot warehouse, thus making it possible to stock required items and to realize discounts on quantity purchases. In advocating this move, Arthur Root had predicted that once Sunshine was in a position to accept deliveries in quantities equivalent to about four months' requirements it would be possible — on an overall basis — to realize annual savings of perhaps 4 per cent on items representing roughly 75 per cent of Sunshine's dollar purchase requirements. The statistics of the leading trade journals showed that, on a national basis, construction material costs had been rising at an average rate of about 2 per cent annually over the past four years.[3] This fact seemed to Mr Root to give added significance to the purchase economies the warehouse would permit. He and his associates became convinced that Sunshine could benefit also from being able to control delivery of materials to individual housing sites.

Administrative procedures developed after the start of warehouse operations required the various foremen to submit orders direct to the warehouse for all items required by their crews, with the exception of staking-out material which Miss Roark ordered. The warehouse truck would deliver the items to the appropriate building site. If the work being done by the crew involved a standard operation, the quantity of each of the materials delivered was predetermined on a basis of 110 per cent of estimated actual need. If the work being done was non-standard in response to a customer request, the material delivered was 110 per cent of the amount that the Sunshine estimator had included in costing the work involved. In Mr Playford's judgement, this over-supply actually was economical in the long run, for it avoided the loss of labour time otherwise spent by construction crews in 'picking and hunting' for materials. Excess material left after the completion of a job was returned to the warehouse and restored to the inventory.

Operation of the warehouse (receiving, storing and delivery) required six employees. One of these, however, was a truck driver who had been required previously. The net increase in the Sunshine workforce created by the warehouse actually was only five persons.

Pricing

Sunshine houses were priced by estimating 'contruction costs'[4] and adding 5 per cent for 'expenses' and 15 per cent for selling costs and profit. The estimating was performed by

Daniel Root's assistant, an employee who had some architectural training and who spent a large portion of his time supplying customers with price quotations on construction changes they wishes to make in standard plans.

Sunshine had found that the construction costs associated with a given model tended to rise slightly as improvements of a minor nature gradually were introduced into the design or specifications. Thus far in its history, however, Sunshine never had increased the price originally quoted for a model. In this context, Arthur Root and Herbert Playford agreed with Daniel Root that Sunshine's prices could not be increased if the firm was to remain competitive. Brochures describing the least costly, and the most expensive, models in Sunshine's line are shown in Figures 2 and 3.

Customer change orders and post-construction repairs

Sunshine encouraged customers of standard model homes to make any non-structural changes they desired. In commenting on this practice, Mr Daniel Root noted, 'different models are featured in each Sunshine subdivision, thus providing a considerable range of choice for the buyer. This fact, coupled with the changes which Sunshine offers to make in its standard models at a nominal price, permits customers to acquire a home which offers considerable individuality, and yet is still moderately priced.' The nature and quantity of the exceptions and additions a customer might specify in a typical purchase contract are indicated by Figure 4.

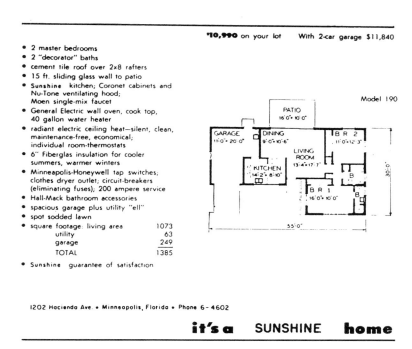

$10,990 on your lot   With 2-car garage $11,840

- 2 master bedrooms
- 2 "decorator" baths
- cement tile roof over 2x8 rafters
- 15 ft. sliding glass wall to patio
- Sunshine kitchen; Coronet cabinets and Nu-Tone ventilating hood; Moen single-mix faucet
- General Electric wall oven, cook top, 40 gallon water heater
- radiant electric ceiling heat—silent, clean, maintenance-free, economical; individual room-thermostats
- 6" Fiberglas insulation for cooler summers, warmer winters
- Minneapolis-Honeywell tap switches; clothes dryer outlet; circuit-breakers (eliminating fuses); 200 ampere service
- Hall-Mack bathroom accessories
- spacious garage plus utility "ell"
- spot sodded lawn
- square footage: living area 1073
  utility 63
  garage 249
  TOTAL 1385
- Sunshine guarantee of satisfaction

Model 190

PATIO 16'0"× 10'0"

GARAGE 11'0"× 20'0"   DINING 9'0"× 10'6"   B R 2 11'0"×12'3"

LIVING ROOM 13'4"×17'7"

KITCHEN 14'2"× 8'10"

B R 1 16'0"× 10'0"

30'0"

55'0"

1202 Hacienda Ave. • Minneapolis, Florida • Phone 6-4602

it's a   SUNSHINE   **home**

Figure 2   Model home.

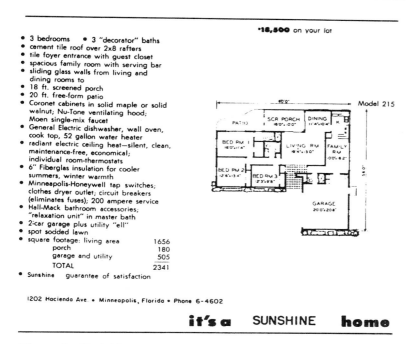

*18,500 on your lot

- 3 bedrooms   • 3 "decorator" baths
- cement tile roof over 2x8 rafters
- tile foyer entrance with guest closet
- spacious family room with serving bar
- sliding glass walls from living and dining rooms to
- 18 ft. screened porch
- 20 ft. free-form patio
- Coronet cabinets in solid maple or solid walnut; Nu-Tone ventilating hood; Moen single-mix faucet
- General Electric dishwasher, wall oven, cook top, 52 gallon water heater
- radiant electric ceiling heat—silent, clean, maintenance-free, economical; individual room-thermostats
- 6" Fiberglas insulation for cooler summers, winter warmth
- Minneapolis-Honeywell tap switches; clothes dryer outlet; circuit breakers (eliminates fuses); 200 ampere service
- Hall-Mack bathroom accessories; "relaxation unit" in master bath
- 2-car garage plus utility "ell"
- spot sodded lawn
- square footage: living area   1656
      porch   180
      garage and utility   505
      TOTAL   2341
- Sunshine   guarantee of satisfaction

1202 Hacienda Ave. • Minneapolis, Florida • Phone 6-4602

it's a   SUNSHINE   **home**

Figure 3   Model home.

Once the basic purchase contract was executed, Miss Roark and the foreman were given copies of the basic house plan, plus the blueprints for any construction changes specified. From these documents Miss Roark prepared a 'customer detail sheet' listing the original construction requirements, plus any additional requirements arising from changes negotiated subsequent to the initial contract. Any of these postcontract changes were priced by Sunshine's estimator and summarized in a 'customer request for extra work' form which was signed by the customer. The original of this document was sent to the office to be used for billing purposes, with copies going to the customer, the foreman of the work crew whose services would be required, and to Miss Roark.

Before actual construction could begin on a specific house, from two to three weeks were required to complete the 25 preliminary steps shown on the start chart (items 1 through 25 on Figure 5). Mr Playford personally performed all of these preproduction activities.

Considerable emphasis was placed on customer satisfaction after the house was completed. Sunshine's policy was that during the first year following completion of a house, the company's service department would repair, without charge, any item that the customer considered unsatisfactory. Within the Sunshine organization such jobs were referred to as 'punch work', that is, work that was to be 'punched out, without delay'. The biggest single form of punch work involved repairs to ceiling cracks. In pricing a house, about 2 per cent of the expected retail price was included in construction cost as an estimate of punch work requirements.

THIRD: All details of material and construction will be identical with those used in the model home located at
... Lot no. 4, Belle Lake Subdivision ... with the following exceptions:

1.	Model 190L.	$10,990
2.	Place wrought iron shutters, with oak leaf design on kitchen windows, front bedroom windows, and left side bedroom window. Retain stucco decoration.	90
3.	Substitute screen patio with terrazzo floor at house level, full foundation, 1 waterproof electric outlet, light fixture centered over sliding glass doors. Floor area 16′ × 10′. Roof to extend 2′ past floor area with screening to be canted toward floor. Roof to be aluminum with styrofoam insulation.	740
4.	Install glass shower door in bath no. 2.	50
5.	Substitute American Standard Bildor castiron tub for present steel tub.	n/c
6.	Erect tile wainscot in bath no. 2 to 3′8″ height.	145
7.	Install air-conditioning aperture centered under front windows to bedroom no. 1, with 220V outlet on separate circuit for same.	28
8.	Install tile backsplash above base cabinets in kitchen.	50
9.	Install gutter and downspout over front entrance, left side of bedroom wing, kitchen and garage.	50
10.	Eliminate Walltex in baths nos 1 and 2.	
11.	Install bookshelves between living room and dinette in lieu of present planter and wrought iron. Shelves to be placed at 42″, 54″, and 74″ height.	n/c
12.	Raise 1″ × 4″ pressure treated drapery hanger above sliding glass doors in living room to ceiling height.	n/c
		$12,143

n/c — no change

Figure 4   Excerpt from building agreement with customer.

Customer's name: Broker:
Address: Legal description:
Phone:

1. Contract signed or on file   ☐
2. Detail sheet no. 1 received   ☐
3. Plans ordered   ☐
4. Survey ordered   ☐
5. Detail sheet no. 2 received (if there is more than 48-hr lag between nos 3 and 5 report to A.R.)   ☐
6. Plans returned   ☐
7. Plans inspected (if there is more than a 24-hr lag between nos 6 and 9 report to A.R.)   ☐
8. Plans returned for correction   ☐
9. Corrected plans returned   ☐
10. Plans inspected for correction   ☐
11. Plans sent to   ☐
12. Plans received from   ☐
13. Building permit applied for   ☐

14. Plans and letter to customer (air mail special delivery with enclosed return envelope)   ☐
15. Send loan plans   ☐
16. Submit plans for subdivision approval (special messenger)   ☐
17. Subdivision approval received   ☐
18. Survey received   ☐
19. Notify supervisor and production to check lot for clearing and for errors in lot line   ☐
20. Customer's approval   ☐
21. Notify accounting of loan approval and of who holds the loan   ☐
22. Construction loan   ☐
23. Add name to production chart   ☐
24. Building permit picked up   ☐
25. Water meter permit picked up   ☐

Figure 5   Start chart.

Some explanatory remarks by Mr Playford

In commenting about present practices in the construction phase of the business Mr Playford made the following observations:

1. Two employees have been added to Sunshine's drafting staff since the first of the year to eliminate the subcontracting of drafting work. We find it necessary to have separate plans for every house because of the large number of construction changes requested by the typical customer.

2. Under our new organizational structure, responsibility for the different phases of construction is divided as follows:

Operation number[a]	Supervisor or foreman responsible
1– 2	Mr Playford
3	Electrical
4	Carpenter
5–10	Mason
11	Plumber
12–18	Mason
19–23	Carpenter
24	Plumber
25	Electrician
26–30	Plasterer
31	Carpenter
32–34	Plasterer
35	Carpenter
36–37	Plasterer
38–49	Carpenter
50–51	Plumber
51–55	Electrician
56–65	Inspector

[a] See Table 1.

3. In my judgment, low-cost construction is achieved when jobs are performed in a conventional manner. Cost savings are accomplished by making operations fast and smooth. In recent years Sunshine has reduced the time required for building the average home by two weeks. Eventually we should be able to cut this by still another week or two. I made a study at Meadowlark which showed that a home comparable to Sunshine's $15,000 models could be built in 52 calendar days if everything worked out well. The methods our men use for each step in every house — the block work, slab, framing, electrical work, plastering — are pretty much standardized. Our crews use only the most common tools and equipment, such as power saws and cement mixers.

By and large 'prefabbing' does not pay unless the customer is not permitted to make any changes in the house he buys. If Sunshine adopted such a policy we would lose sales. Also, the size of our line argues against our relying on prefabbing. For instance, prefabbed roof trusses, which many construction firms use, are more expensive than 'on site' construction for Sunshine because we have so many models.

A few years back I visited Classentown, New Jersey,[5] to see if I could pick up any helpful ideas on construction economies. I discovered that the Classentown people permitted customers to make no construction changes whatever. Also, by building houses block by block they were able to employ more pre-cutting and standardizing than would be possible for Sunshine since our houses are usually not adjacent.

One way we can — and do — save time is to encourage 'productivity-consciousness' on the part of our supervisors. Our masonry foreman has learned, for example, that a mason will lay blocks faster if his helper keeps a supply piled-up ahead of him. But overall, conventional methods of building — well executed — are our surest path to construction economy.

4. Our foremen hire and lay off workers as needed. They usually already know, or hear about, good craftsmen whom we might want to add to our workforce. Many of the men they hire are their friends, or have been recommended by friends. Crews work a five-day week, nine hours a day. The crew members tend to work in two-man teams, a journeyman and a helper. They also tend to specialize. For instance, a typical carpenter crew will consist of certain men whom the foreman always assigns to construct doorjambs and window frames, others for rafter cutting, others for cornices, others for general framing, and a saw specialist.

Our current wage structure is: helpers, $1.25 to $1.75 per hour; masons, $2.75; plumbers, $3.00; electricians, $2.25; painters, $2.40. We offer our construction crews no systematic job progression, no guarantee of security, and no benefits other than those required by law, that is, social security and the like, which add up to about 8 per cent over hourly rates. But Sunshine has never had to make any major lay-offs, and we have darn good crews.

5. Up until this January, Arthur Root used the six charts on my office wall to control costs. These charts, which I originally introduced, showed the dollar per square foot cost for each phase of work for each house. They were designed to reveal any overall trends, and also to pinpoint any house where costs were out of line. No trends ever appeared, however.

We have now discontinued use of the charts. They simply required too much work. Instead, about once a month we spot-check costs by studying several completed jobs quite closely and calculating the total cost per square foot on various operations, such as electrical, plumbing, and the like. Every three months I make a still more detailed check on a dozen houses randomly selected. Also, on a day-to-day basis, I, of course, control material costs by authorizing the amount delivered to each house. Arthur keeps check on supply sources.

If any costs begin to appear out of line, I talk to the foreman involved. For example, I recently noted that tile costs had increased around 15–20 per cent. Upon investigation I found a number of sources of trouble. The foreman was driving twenty miles for supplies every day; I showed him how to order in advance and to stock more in our warehouse. He had also guaranteed his crew ten hours of pay regardless of the actual time worked. And some of his crew were driving to our warehouse to pick up material instead of getting material delivered. We corrected each of these problems.

In summary, I am confident that as long as I'm out watching, and the crews are working, and Miss Roark keeps things moving, Sunshine's costs will be OK.

6. I suspect that we are still too lax in our attitude toward delays. I want more flow and speed, better customer relationships, lower work-in-process. I am getting out in the field more now that I've got things set up better in the office here, and I am keeping my eyes open for jobs where no action is taking place. Miss Roark gets along fine with the foremen, and they like her. But she is not firm enough with them, or with outsiders. She can learn to do her job even better.

7. Since our crews work a nine-hour day, this means that if on a given morning a crew starts a job that really requires only eight hours of work, the workmen will probably actually spend the full nine-hour day on it. But this practice works in the other direction, too. Ten-hour jobs are often pushed through in nine hours to make it unnecessary for the crew to return to that particular site for only an hour's work the following morning. Our instructions to foremen are to let a crew work up to one hour of overtime if this will permit them to complete a job in a given day.

Current volume of operations

As of 1 May, Sunshine's production boards listed 42 houses 'in process'. Comparable figures for the start of operations six months, and one month, earlier had been 35 and 36 houses, respectively. The 42 units now under construction were divided among 12 different models, as follows:

Number of units of a model under construction	Number of models
7 to 9	1
3 to 6	5
2 or less	6

Table 2 Operating results expressed as a percentage of sales

| | Current year minus | | | 1st four months current yr |
	3	2	1	
Sales[a]	100.00%	100.00%	100.00%	100.00%
Construction costs[b]	85.20	86.60	83.33	84.80
Gross profit	14.80%	13.40%	16.67%	15.20%
Expenses				
Sales expense	5.00	5.00	5.00	5.00
Salaries and wages[c]	3.15	3:85	5.23	5.20
Sales promotion and advertising	0.63	0.27	0.78	1.38
Depreciation	0.10	0.21	0.40	0.61
First-year house maintenance ('punch work')	0.13	0.45	0.38	0.37
Auto and aircraft expense	—	0.17	0.33	0.33
Office expenses	0.37	0.18	0.18	0.32
Radio expenses	—	—	0.10	0.19
Production office[d]	0.37	—	0.16	0.70
Equipment rental	—	—	—	0.36
Maintenance of model homes	0.07	0.10	—	0.02
Maintenance of trucks, tools and equipment	—	—	—	0.66
Legal and accounting	—	0.04	0.16	0.04
Taxes and licences	0.46	0.15	0.13	0.69
Travel and entertainment	0.10	0.08	0.20	0.34
Telephone and postage	0.08	0.09	0.10	0.14
Warehouse expense	—	—	—	0.81
Insurance	0.19	0.10	0.09	0.23
Christmas gifts to employees	0.19	0.07	0.09	0.12
Plans and designs	—	0.10	0.08	0.12
Discounts and collection fees on mortgages	—	—	0.04	0.46
Rent	0.10	0.10	0.08	0.21
Miscellaneous	0.08	0.11	0.05	0.11
Total expenses	11.02%	11.07%	13.58%	18.41%
Operating profit (loss)	3.78	2.33	3.09	(3.21)
Number of houses built	124	134	151	52
Average selling price	$13,500	$14,250	$15,000	$15,250
Average number of construction workers	94[e]	114[e]	113[e]	124

[a] Based on completed houses. A 'sale' was made only when a house was completed.
[b] Construction costs include direct labour, material, subcontracting cost, and the salaries and wages of foremen, superintendents, warehousemen, draftsmen, blueprint operators, messengers, and the service department, plus fringe benefits for those salaries and wages included.
[c] Includes all other salaries and wages not included under 'construction costs'.
[d] General-purpose production requirements, such as blueprint paper, steel tapes, forms, office supplies, small hand tools.
[e] Subcontractors' crews.

None of the 12 models in Sunshine's current product line had fewer than one unit in process. The most popular model had nine.

The six-unit increase in houses-in-process over the previous month's totals reflected an influx of orders which had begun in late March and continued throughout April. In response to the increased sales, Mr Playford gradually had increased the number of houses started into production each week from the level of three, during the first week of April, to six in the last week of April. From all indications, sales prospects for the balance of the year were excellent and Mr Playford expected to be able to continue starting five to six houses into construction each week. He said, however, that he liked to make any such change on a gradual basis in order to maintain a smooth flow of work for all crews. 'The rate of starts', he said, 'paces the whole operation.'

Operating statements for the first four months of the current year, and for the three full preceding years are shown in Table 2.

Notes

1. The eighth, the cleaning subcontractor, had been receiving approximately $5,000 per year.
2. Three of the former superintendents subsequently took positions as tradesmen on the various Sunshine crews.
3. The same sources indicated that during this period construction labour costs had been increasing at an annual average rate of roughly 4 per cent.
4. The average house constructed by Sunshine included approximately $2,500 of subcontracting.
5. A major, low-cost housing development which had attracted international publicity for its mass-production construction methods.

Copyright

Tile Products Plc

Tile Products Plc is a small company which makes fire-retardant ceiling tiles. The tiles are plaster mouldings made to any size or pattern, but the standard size is 2 feet square and the company offers a range of ten patterns. Any customer requiring either a tailor-made size or pattern, would be charged the setting-up costs which entail the production of a one-off mould from which the tiles would then be produced.

After the initial work by the founder of the company Ben Graham, upon whose ideas the tile is based, sales had begun to increase over the past three to six months. Sales for the first twelve months of business and the first six months of this second year are given in Table 1. Ben Graham is currently solely responsible for sales besides having overall control over production and the financial aspects of the business.

Production

Arthur Marshall, the production supervisor, is responsible for the day-to-day control of production. He had been with the business from the early days. As output requirements increased, the company had employed two additional moulders — Ian Yates and Maurice Coles — who were now both fully trained. For at least half his time Arthur Marshall did the production jobs of either moulding or packing besides helping, as did Ian and Maurice, to unload materials and load-up dispatches.

The working week is from Monday to Friday, 8.00 a.m. to 4.30 p.m. with half an hour for lunch. If overtime is worked it would usually be in the evening, but occasional Saturday working is arranged depending upon order volumes and delivery requirements.

The layout of the factory is shown in Figure 1 and the method of working is described in Figure 2. Although some tiles are made-to-stock, production tends to follow sales orders because of the lack of information on sales patterns and volumes. It is anticipated, however, that once sales have reached a higher level, then production will be against sales forecasts for each pattern type.

This case study © by Professor T.J. Hill (London Business School). It is intended as the basis for class discussion and not as an illustration of good or bad management.

Table 1 Tile sales in the first eighteen months of business

	Year 1	Year 2					
		Jan	Feb	Mar	Apr	May	Jun
Standard tiles							
Classic	2,050	—	1,400	—	—	—	—
Georgian	2,850	—	—	600	650	—	400
Victorian	3,800	1,000	—	—	250	1,000	500
Modern	2,400	—	—	800	—	400	100
Simplicity	2,850	—	—	900	—	300	300
Scandinavian	1,600	—	500	—	—	—	900
American	—	—	—	—	—	400	600
Scottish	—	—	—	—	500	700	300
Floral	2,800	700	—	—	—	—	600
Heraldic	750	—	100	—	300	200	300
Customer's own design	1,000	—	—	—	200	400	—
Total	20,100	1,700	2,000	2,300	1,900	3,400	4,000

Notes
1. All figures are in number of tiles produced.
2. Some designs (e.g. Heraldic) tend to be ordered as part of a ceiling pattern rather than as the main design.
3. Once moulds are available then tile process production time is the same for each design. There are some minor set-up times involved, but these are of little significance.
4. American and Scottish designs were not introduced until April of year 2.
5. Taking into account bank and other holidays, employees work for 46 weeks of each year.
Source: company records.

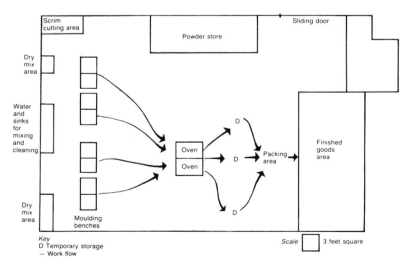

Figure 1 Existing shopfloor layout.

Moulding

A moulder mixes the dry materials in the appropriate area, moves to the water sink and completes the mixing stage. He returns to the moulding bench and pours the mixture into the mould. He then goes to the scrim cutting area, cuts scrim (a synthetic gauze to help bond the tile) to the appropriate size and returns to the moulding bench. He places the scrim into the mould and then puts down the lid of the mould. The required pattern is in the mould base and the scrim, therefore, is placed in what will be the back of the tile. At the end of the initial drying cycle, the tile is lifted from the mould, carried to the oven and hung by lugs which form an integral part of the back of the mould. The moulder returns to the mould, cleans down the mould of any excess plaster and then repeats the process. The normal practice is to cut two or three pieces of scrim at a time and place them near at hand. This saves a journey to the scrim cutting area.

Typically a moulder works three moulds and very occasionally four. A person working all the time on moulding makes, on average, sixty tiles in an eight-hour day. In addition, the moulders and Arthur Marshall unload and load vehicles besides packing tiles once they have been baked in the ovens.

Drying

The drying process is in two stages. The initial drying or setting takes place in the mould as described above. This takes fifteen minutes from pouring the plaster mixture into the mould to the time for lifting. The second drying stage takes place in the ovens. There are currently two fixed-position ovens each of which has a capacity to hold ninety tiles. When the oven has a full load (although occasionally this part of the process is started with a part-load due to delivery requirements) the heat is brought up to the required temperature of 75°C and the tile is baked for eight hours.

Packing

When the tile has been oven-dried, it is allowed to cool for a minimum time of thirty minutes. Then the ovens are unloaded and the tiles are stacked on edge between the ovens and packing area (see Figure 1). When the tiles have accumulated or delivery requirements are pressing, each tile is packed individually and then four tiles are packed into an outer carton. The packed tiles are then stored in the finished goods area, by pattern, and up to three outer cartons high (the cumulative weight restricts storage height).

Dispatch

Sales orders are met from stock (unless it is a special tile and then these are made only to order) and the finished goods are stored in such a way as to facilitate stock rotation and so ensure that the older tiles are dispatched first.

Technical Note

The materials used in making fire-retardent ceiling tiles are relatively fast setting which precludes the opportunity to make larger mixes than is the present practice. Consequently, each moulder may only mix sufficient for one moulding cycle which ensures that the required technical specification is achieved.

Figure 2   Current methods of working.

Company performance

Following a loss in the first year, the position has improved by the end of the first half of year 2 (see Table 2). Sales for the second half of year 2 are running at a level slightly

Table 2 Information on the first eighteen months of business

	Year 1	*Year 2*
Sales (£)		
Standard designs	56,000	43,900
Customers' designs	3,600	2,490
	59,600	46,390
Direct costs (£)		
Materials	13,800	9,700
Moulding labour	15,550	8,700
Packaging	3,800	2,660
Packing labour	1,200	700
Dispatch	2,000	1,400
	36,350	23,160
Manufacturing profit	21,250	23,230
Indirect costs		
Salaries	15,100	7,950
Mould and other manufacturing costs	3,500	2,100
Other overhead costs	7,100	4,000
	25,700	14,050
Net profit (loss)	(4,450)	9,180

Notes
1. 'Customers' designs' sales include the costs of moulds. These were for year 1 £600 and for the first six months of year 2, £470.
2. Salaries include the owner and 50 per cent of the supervisor.
3. Year 2 figures are for the first six months only.
4. The average selling price of a tile in year 1 was £3.00. In year 2, the selling price had averaged £3.28 and there had been some increase in direct and other costs.
5. Because of the relatively short life of a mould, these costs are treated as revenue expenditure.
Source: company records.

higher than in the first six months and the company has submitted tenders for some very large orders. Ben Graham's immediate concern is production capacity: a good moulder would produce, under current methods of working, a maximum of sixty tiles per day.

Ever since the start of the business Ben Graham's attention had been directed towards the product. It had been necessary to refine the fire-retardant qualities of the tiles and improve the other aspects of tile quality whilst trying to reduce the costs of raw materials. Considerable steps have been achieved in this direction and arrangements are now in progress to get the appropriate certification for the fire-retardant properties of this newly designed tile. Once this has been achieved, Graham's aim is to reduce the price per tile in line with the material savings available with the new design. This would enable the company to increase sales by achieving greater market penetration with the lower price tile.

Study of production methods

With the increase in sales of existing tiles and the anticipated uplift in orders following a decrease in price as described above, Ben Graham had requested a study of production methods in order to establish the facilities and labour required for these higher volumes. The initial results of this preliminary investigation are given in Table 3.

Table 3   Study of existing methods

Activity	Estimated time
Moulding	
To dry mix	0.12
Mix dry ingredients	0.27
To water and sink	0.07
Wet mix	0.20
Return to moulding bench	0.12
Pour mixture to mould	0.18
To scrim cutting area/per journey	0.15
Cut scrim/per piece	0.13
Return to mould bench/per journey	0.15
Put scrim into mould and place down lid	0.14
Initial set	15.00
Take out tile	0.55
Tile to oven	0.14
Hang tile	0.18
Return to mould bench	0.14
Clean mould	0.27
Packing	
Pack four tiles then to an outer carton and stack	4.00

Notes
1. All estimated times are in basic minutes.
2. These estimated times have been arrived at by observation and some use of synthetics.
3. Typically, a moulder works three and very occasionally, four moulds.
4. Also see the Technical Note, figure 2.

Too short, the day

Giles Chamberlain, production manager of the Playhouse Theatre, set out for work on Monday morning. Over the weekend he had drawn up a priority list of the important longer-term tasks he needed to accomplish and now took the opportunity of reviewing them. Amongst the important items was the need to find new suppliers for several high-cost materials and those materials used in large quantities in order to reduce the ever-increasing production costs. However, to help achieve this he needed to develop and agree new procedures with the administrator about planning the production of shows. This would not only help to reduce overtime working and the casual labour bill but would also mean that materials could be ordered in advance and so enable lower prices to be secured rather than the present position were sourcing was usually based upon fast delivery. In addition,

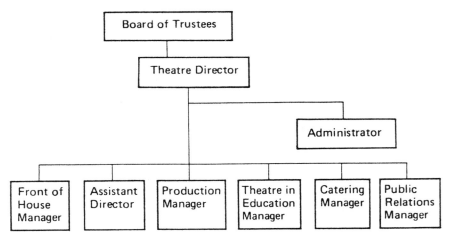

Figure 1 Playhouse Theatre organization chart.

This case study is © by Professor T.J. Hill (London Business School). It is intended as the basis for class discussion and not as an illustration of good or bad management.

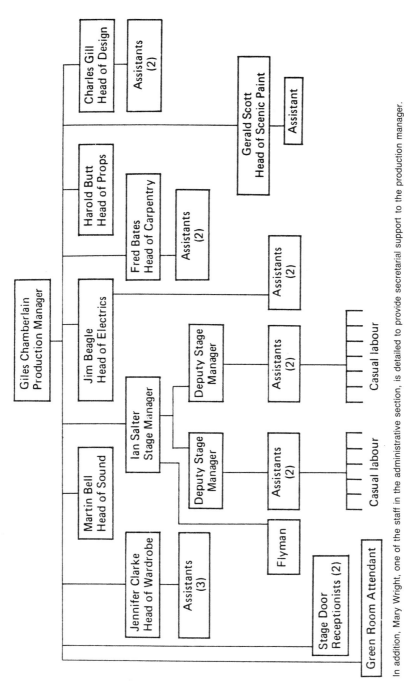

In addition, Mary Wright, one of the staff in the administrative section, is detailed to provide secretarial support to the production manager.

Figure 2 Organization chart for the production manager's responsibilities at the Playhouse Theatre.

he had been requested some months ago to draw up plans and expenditure estimates with the stage manager regarding proposals to provide new facilities on stage to offer more scope to designers and less work to provide the necessary requirements of a typical production. Lastly, he had to discuss the increased use of modular stage designs with the head of carpentry in order to reduce the timber costs and construction time to produce a show.

By the time he reached the theatre he was feeling pleased about the approaching day and anticipated taking steps towards the resolution of these tasks, some of which he had intended getting down to over the last six to nine months. As he entered the building, the stage manager Ian Salter called him and explained that he needed more casual labour than planned due to the agreed changes made last Friday to the forthcoming play 'The Sons of Light'. They discussed the proposed increases and agreed on the course of action to take. He asked Ian to advise him on the outcome and to let his secretary Mary Wright know the costs involved. In the conversation, Ian had also reminded Giles of several items which needed either purchasing or progressing from suppliers. When Giles got to his office, on his desk were some invoices and also the time sheets for the casual labour employed last week. In order not to keep the pay procedure waiting, Giles checked the wage claims, made one or two notes and authorized for payment those without queries. He then checked the invoices and telephoned the head of electrics (Jim Beagle), the head of carpentry (Fred Bates), the head of sound (Martin Bell) and head of wardrobe (Jennifer Clarke) to confirm that the items and quantities had been received. Neither Jim Beagle nor Jennifer Clarke answered so he made a mental note to ask them later in the day. He then made several telephone calls to outside suppliers in line with his earlier discussion with Ian Salter and asked for information to be put into the post.

Giles then telephoned Mary Wright to ask her to come up to his office. While he waited, he telephoned the local fire officer to check a point of detail that had come up in conversation with the assistant director late last week. Following the discussion he checked his file containing details of the local fire regulations and marked the appropriate section. Just then Mary entered. He discussed some points of administrative detail and handed over the signed invoices and authorized casual labour time sheets. Mary handed over the morning mail and explained one or two points.

After a coffee break, Giles then went down to the stage area to check on the progress being made on the alterations for the current production 'The Bottom Drawer'. He walked over to Ian Salter to ask how the work was progressing. 'The problem is fitting the rostrum onto the stage' explained Ian. 'Fred [the head of carpentry] is working on an idea I have in order to both ensure fit and to keep it stable once in position.' Giles discussed the idea with both Ian and Fred and together they came up with another possibility. Giles looked on as first one idea then the other was tried. Further discussion took place until a satisfactory solution was reached. Before leaving the stage area, Giles checked the casual labour time sheet queries with Ian, particularly about the level of overtime incurred. Giles, having listened to the reasons why this additional overtime had been worked, asked Ian to get overtime authorized in future, reinforcing the necessity to keep all costs within production budgets.

Giles then set off to see the head of wardrobe, Jennifer Clarke, to discuss the final costs of the current production and tomorrow's proposed trip to London with the head of design, Charles Gill, to buy costumes for a future production of 'Anyone for Denis?' The discussion addressed costs, costume resale policies and the budget limits for the new costumes. Before he left, Giles also checked out the invoice query he had had that morning. By the time this discussion was over and Giles had walked back to his office, it was lunchtime.

He made a few notes on points that had been made in the morning and then went off to lunch.

When he returned, there was a note from the theatre director's secretary advising him that his meeting with the director would have to be put back to 3.30 p.m. He then made a telephone call to a supplier of special effects to order a smoke gun for a future production. As he was discussing the request, Mary Wright entered with memos and letters for him to check and sign together with the second delivery of mail. Having cleared the memos and letters, Mary made one or two points contained in the letters and then left. Giles checked through both lots of mail in detail, made some notes and prepared his replies. He then telephoned Mary and asked her to come to his office at about 3 p.m.

As he got up, a telephone call came through from a company enquiring about a shower unit which it had loaned to the theatre for a production which finished earlier in the year. Giles then left the office and immediately bumped into Gerald Scott, head of scenic paint. Gerald discussed the need for some particular paints he required and asked if the request could be dealt with urgently. Giles agreed to this and continued into the stage area. He checked with Ian Salter that the earlier problem was now resolved. Ian also took the opportunity of enquiring if he could use the theatre's large van to pick up some props for the next production, to which Giles agreed. On seeing Jim Beagle he crossed over and asked him about some queries on invoices concerning the purchase of electrical equiment and consumables. Giles then continued to the carpentry shop to discuss with Fred Bates the next production in terms of deadlines for props and scenery. Fred also took the opportunity of handing over purchase requisitions for tools and timber, explaining that some of the items were urgent. On returning to his office, the administrator telephoned him about a touring theatre due the month after next. He asked Giles to note in his diary the date of a meeting he had arranged to discuss the detailed requirements with the touring theatre's agent. Just then Mary Wright entered and from then until his scheduled meeting at 3.30 p.m. he dictated letters, handed over filing and recorded dates in both diaries. Mary also asked him to call in to see the assistant director about an employee later that afternoon.

Meetings with the theatre director took place at least twice weekly. They involved discussions on a number of issues such as, like today's, an up-to-date progress report on the current production, rehearsals for the next two productions and the forward planning for both in-house and touring shows. Like most meetings, this one lasted about forty-five minutes and Giles, on leaving it, had a list of points to check out and to confirm the detailed arrangements made. This information was normally required within 24 or 48 hours and, at the latest, formed part of the next meeting's agenda.

When he left the director's office he called in to see the assistant director and checked through the terms of employment details for a new member of staff due to start next week. He also mentioned the fire regulation query and agreed to let the assistant director have sight of the relevant section. He then went to see Harold Butt, head of props, to ask about the shower unit query. Harold explained that it had been broken after the production had ended, and consequently, was thrown away some weeks ago. Giles asked some questions on detail and then returned to his office, telephoned Martin Bell and Jim Beagle and asked them to come to see him. He then called the company about the shower unit, explained the problem, asked the price involved and agreed for them to send an invoice for the replacement cost. When Martin and Jim arrived, he discussed details of the special effects required for the next two productions checked the up-to-date position and the lead times involved for those parts which were not yet ready. He noted the points and completion dates discussed in order to report back to the theatre director. He then telephoned Charles

Gill, head of design, to ask him to come up to the office. Between Jim and Martin leaving and Charles arriving, Giles telephoned a paint supplier about the artistic paints request and also made an appointment to talk to an artist's agent about the requirements for a one-man show booked into the theatre in three weeks' time. By then Charles had arrived. Giles asked for a progress report on the design implications for three future productions: 'The Resistible Rise of Arturo Ui', 'The Miser' and 'Atarah's Band'. As a result of this discussion, Giles agreed to further scheduled discussions with all those involved in these productions as time was now pressing in order to ensure that all aspects of these shows could be scheduled on time. He again made appropriate notes in order to report the detail back to the director.

Giles then went down to the stage area as he had arranged to supervise a trial fit-up for the next production. He discussed aspects with the heads of the departments involved, noted the agreements and asked them to assess the deadlines to meet the necessary changes. By the time this was finished, the scheduled stage conversion back to that evening's performance had begun. Just as he was about to leave the stage area, Giles was beckoned by the front of house manager who wanted to discuss the provision of cover for two people (one on holiday and one who was ill) for tomorrow's matinee and evening performance. Giles agreed to arrange the cover, and went back to his office. He then made a series of notes following the afternoon's discussions and, when he glanced at his watch it was 6.40 p.m. Time to go home.

Busy? he asked himself. Too busy he thought. He had, on reflection, covered all the necessary aspects of his job, and put a lot of necessary effort and pressure behind the important tasks to ensure that present and future shows would be successful productions. But, he had spent no time at all on the longer-term tasks he had set himself that morning. I seem to be doing well, he thought and both my superiors and subordinates seem to appreciate the job I do and the role I fulfil. But, what is my job? Earlier today, it all seemed so clear, but now I am not so sure.

Wilson Pharmaceuticals Plc

Wilson Pharmaceuticals had been manufacturing and selling a mouth ulcer treatment since the early 1960s. At the time of its introduction (known as Ulcercare) there had been few products in this area of health care. The product consisted of a small glass bottle, with a cork and printed label. The bottle was filled with a pink fluid (the chemical formulation for which had been derived by Wilson's own research laboratories) leaving enough room to fit a cotton bud in the neck of the bottle without inducing spillage. Twelve double-ended cotton buds were included in the pack, providing sufficient for twenty-four individual applications.

The treatment was made by dipping one end of a cotton bud into the fluid and then applying it directly to the infected area within the mouth. The package was made from rolled card tube. This tube was in three parts — a single inner and two close fitting outer tubes, each closed with a card disc which formed the top and bottom of the pack (see Figure 1). Inside the inner tube was a small card cup into which the glass bottle fitted. This cup was surrounded by corrugated paper sheet which held it firmly in the inner tube. The cotton buds fitted between the glass bottle and the corrugated paper, thus providing additional protection for the bottle. The top and bottom of the outer tube were closed by a label, and the disc of the top tube was covered by a circular label.

Over the past eighteen months, sales for Ulcercare had been declining steadily. Enquiries revealed that two large competitors had introduced their own products in this range, which were lower in price than Ulcercare. The current profit margin enjoyed by Wilson's product, though above average, was not sufficiently high to withstand a price reduction in line with the competitors' products.

As part of their review of the situation, the executives involved turned to the question of product costs details of which are included as Table 1.

This case study is © by Professor T.J. Hill (London Business School) and K.H.A. Negal (University of Bath). It is intended as the basis for class discussion and not as an illustration of good or bad management.

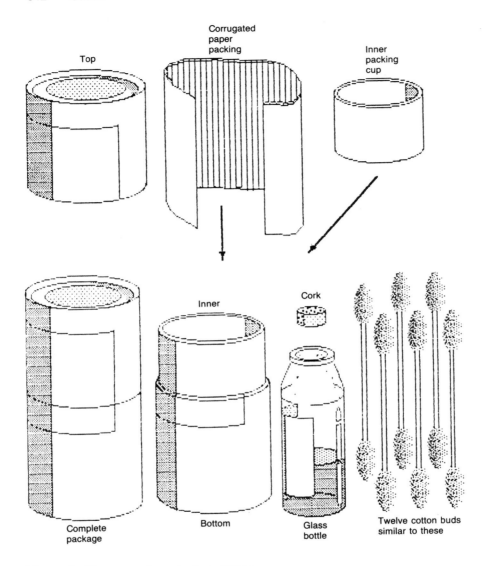

Figure 1   The current production design.

Table 1 The cost breakdown for ulcercare

Cost/100 items	Materials (£)
Ulcer Fluid	2.55
Bottle	1.85
Cork	0.95
Bottle label	0.25
Card cup	0.80
Corrugated paper	0.20
12 double-ended cotton buds (total)	1.76
Inner tube	1.05
Top tube	1.33
Bottom tube	1.33
Tube label	0.65
Disc label	0.25
Assembly and packing labour	3.86
Total materials and labour	£16.83

Yuppie Products

The Yuppie Products Company produces a line of furnishings for hotels and restaurants. Amongst the items manufactured is the Yuppie Executive Water Pitcher whose product structure is shown in Figure 1. Components A and B are manufactured by the firm's plastic moulding shop and components C, D, E and F are purchased from a supplier. The Yuppie Executive Water Pitcher is completed by the final assembly department located at the firm's plant in Geneva. (A flow diagram indicating the different manufacturing stages in the Geneva plant is shown in Figure 2.)

The firm's products are supplied to customers from stock held in the company's distribution centres which are located in Amsterdam and Rome. A distribution requirements planning (DRP) system is used to plan and schedule the replenishment of inventory at the distribution centres and the scheduling of production operations at the Geneva plant. (See

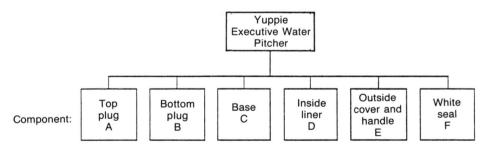

One unit of each component is required to produce one Yuppie Executive Water Pitcher.

Figure 1 Product structure.

The case was prepared by Professor William Lee Berry as a basis for class discussion rather than to illustrate either effective or ineffective handling of an administrative situation. Copyright © 1988 by IMEDE, Lausanne, Switzerland. IMD International, resulting from the merger between IMEDE, Lausanne, and IMI, Geneva, acquires and retains all rights. Reproduced by permission.

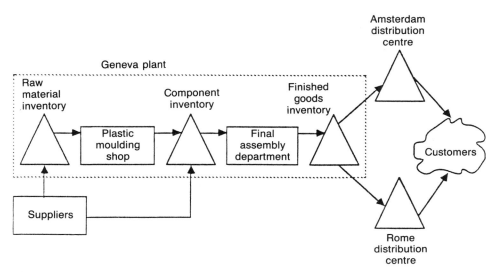

Figure 2 Manufacturing system.

Figure 3 for sample information used by the DRP System.) This information is updated daily by the company's computer system:

The DRP system

The firm's distribution requirements planning system includes four main elements:

1. Time-phased order point (TPOP) records for each end product stocked at a distribution centre (Figure 3, part A).
2. Time-phased master production scheduling records for each end-product produced by the Geneva plant (Figure 3, part B).
3. Time-phased material planning records for each component part manufactured or purchased by the Geneva plant (Figure 3, part C).
4. Shopfloor control reports used to schedule production in the various plant departments (Figure 3, part D).

A standard format is used for all of the time-phased planning records. The first row contains a weekly forecast of demand for the product item. The second row contains the delivery schedule for any orders that have been relayed for shipment to the distribution centres or for production in the plant. The third row provides a projection of the closing inventory each week, and the fourth row indicates planned orders that are scheduled for release so that inventory shortages are not incurred. The schedule for the planned orders takes into account the order quantity, lead time and safety stock information for each item as shown below the item record.

The DRP system co-ordinates the planning of operations in the distribution centres, the plant and the suppliers (as illustrated by Figure 4). For example, the planned order

Part A: Distribution centre planning records

Yuppie Executive Water Pitcher
Amsterdam distribution centre

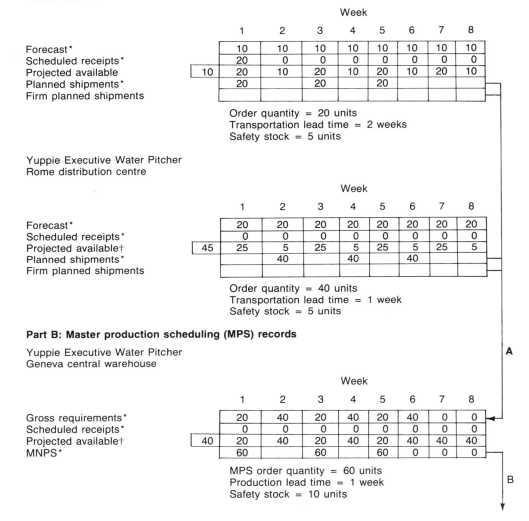

Week

		1	2	3	4	5	6	7	8
Forecast*		10	10	10	10	10	10	10	10
Scheduled receipts*		20	0	0	0	0	0	0	0
Projected available	10	20	10	20	10	20	10	20	10
Planned shipments*		20		20		20			
Firm planned shipments									

Order quantity = 20 units
Transportation lead time = 2 weeks
Safety stock = 5 units

Yuppie Executive Water Pitcher
Rome distribution centre

Week

		1	2	3	4	5	6	7	8
Forecast*		20	20	20	20	20	20	20	20
Scheduled receipts*		0	0	0	0	0	0	0	0
Projected available†	45	25	5	25	5	25	5	25	5
Planned shipments*			40		40		40		
Firm planned shipments									

Order quantity = 40 units
Transportation lead time = 1 week
Safety stock = 5 units

Part B: Master production scheduling (MPS) records

Yuppie Executive Water Pitcher
Geneva central warehouse

A

Week

		1	2	3	4	5	6	7	8
Gross requirements*		20	40	20	40	20	40	0	0
Scheduled receipts*		0	0	0	0	0	0	0	0
Projected available†	40	20	40	20	40	20	40	40	40
MNPS*		60		60		60		0	0

MPS order quantity = 60 units
Production lead time = 1 week
Safety stock = 10 units

B

row information in the distribution centre TPOP records is summarized and displayed as the gross requirements row in the master production scheduling records (see arrow A in Figure 3). Likewise, the master production schedule (MPS) row information in the master production scheduling records is used to calculate the gross requirements in the material requirements planning records for the component items, using bill of material information (see arrow B in Figure 3).

Part C: Materials requirement planning records

Item A — top plug

		Week							
		1	2	3	4	5	6	7	8
Gross requirements*		60	0	60	0	60	0	0	0
Scheduled receipts*		60	0	0	0	0	0	0	0
Projected available†	65	65	65	5	5	5	5	5	5
Planned orders*		0	0	0	60	0	0	0	0

Order quantity = 60 units
Production lead time = 1 week
Safety stock = 5 units

Item B — bottom plug

		Week							
		1	2	3	4	5	6	7	8
Gross requirements*		60	0	60	0	60	0	0	0
Scheduled receipts*		0	0	90	0	0	0	0	0
Projected available†	35	−25	−25	5	5	35	35	35	35
Planned orders*		0	90	0	0	0	0	0	0

Order quantity = 90 units
Production lead time = 3 weeks
Safety stock = 5 units

Item C — base

		Week							
		1	2	3	4	5	6	7	8
Gross requirements*		60	0	60	0	60	0	0	0
Scheduled receipts*		0	0	120	0	0	0	0	0
Projected available†	15	−45	−45	15	15	75	75	75	75
Planned orders*		0	120	0	0	0	0	0	0

Order quantity = 120 units
Purchasing lead time = 3 weeks
Safety stock = 10 units

Part D: Shopfloor control reports

Plastic moulding department scheduling report

Shop order number	Component item	Order quantity	Order due date*	Machine time (in days)‡
10-XXY	A	60	week 1	3
10-XZV	Z	20	week 1	1
10-XXX	G	45	week 2	2
10-XYZ	B	90	week 3	4

* As of the beginning of the week.
† As of the end of the week.
‡ The plant works five single-shift days per week.

Figure 3   Distribution requirements planning worksheet.

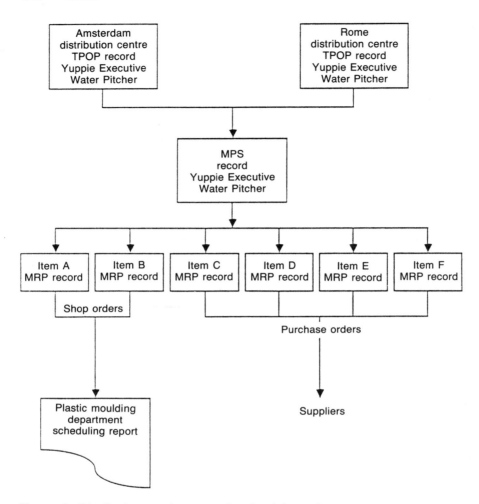

Figure 4   Distribution requirements planning information system.

Finally, information in the material requirements planning records is used to establish priorities for the scheduling of production in the plant. Orders are scheduled in sequence according to their due date. The due dates for open shop orders contained in the scheduled receipts row of the material requirements planning records is shown on the scheduling reports for individual departments in the plant. For example, the due date of week 1 for the order of 60 units for item A is shown both in the material requirements planning record for this item, and on the scheduling report for the plastic moulding department in Figure 3, part D. Currently, two open shop orders for Yuppie Executive Water Pitcher components are waiting to be processed in the plastic moulding department — items A and B. All of the

Part A: Distribution centre planning records

Yuppie Executive Water Pitcher
Amsterdam distribution centre

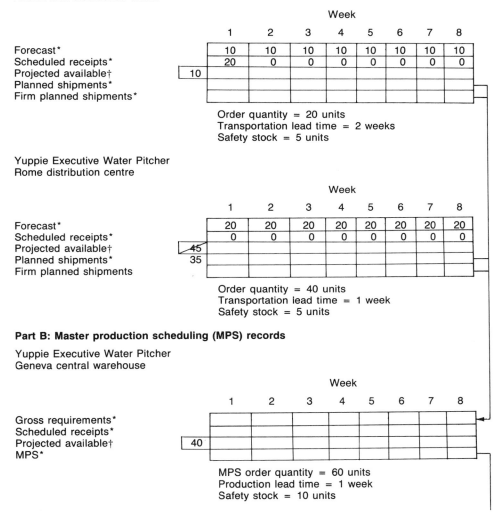

	Week							
	1	2	3	4	5	6	7	8
Forecast*	10	10	10	10	10	10	10	10
Scheduled receipts*	20	0	0	0	0	0	0	0
Projected available†	10							
Planned shipments*								
Firm planned shipments*								

Order quantity = 20 units
Transportation lead time = 2 weeks
Safety stock = 5 units

Yuppie Executive Water Pitcher
Rome distribution centre

	Week							
	1	2	3	4	5	6	7	8
Forecast*	20	20	20	20	20	20	20	20
Scheduled receipts*	0	0	0	0	0	0	0	0
Projected available†	45							
Planned shipments*	35							
Firm planned shipments								

Order quantity = 40 units
Transportation lead time = 1 week
Safety stock = 5 units

Part B: Master production scheduling (MPS) records

Yuppie Executive Water Pitcher
Geneva central warehouse

	Week							
	1	2	3	4	5	6	7	8
Gross requirements*								
Scheduled receipts*								
Projected available†	40							
MPS*								

MPS order quantity = 60 units
Production lead time = 1 week
Safety stock = 10 units

orders shown on the plastic moulding department scheduling report are made complete in one operation, and are subsequently ready for the final assembly department.

The material requirements planning record for item C, the base, is shown in Figure 3, part C; this item is produced by a plastic moulding company in Taiwan. Because of lengthy overseas shipment times, the purchasing lead time for this item is a firm three weeks and the current open order of 120 units will not be received until the beginning of week 5.

Part C: Materials requirement planning records

Item A — top plug

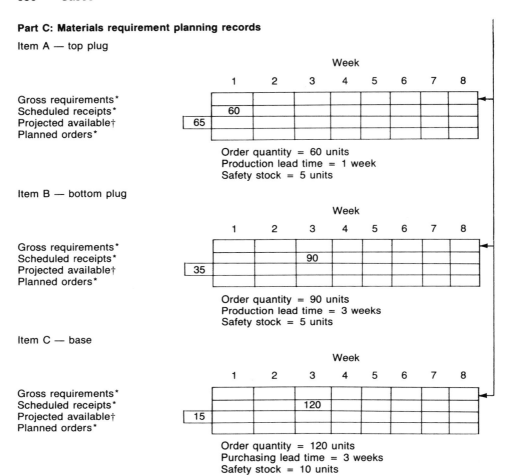

	Week							
	1	2	3	4	5	6	7	8

Gross requirements*
Scheduled receipts*
Projected available†
Planned orders*

65 | 60

Order quantity = 60 units
Production lead time = 1 week
Safety stock = 5 units

Item B — bottom plug

	Week							
	1	2	3	4	5	6	7	8

Gross requirements*
Scheduled receipts*
Projected available†
Planned orders*

35 | 90

Order quantity = 90 units
Production lead time = 3 weeks
Safety stock = 5 units

Item C — base

	Week							
	1	2	3	4	5	6	7	8

Gross requirements*
Scheduled receipts*
Projected available†
Planned orders*

15 | 120

Order quantity = 120 units
Purchasing lead time = 3 weeks
Safety stock = 10 units

Part D: Shopfloor control reports

Plastic moulding department scheduling report

Shop order number	Component item	Order quantity	Order due date*	Machine time (in days)‡
10-XXY	A	60	week 1	3
10-XZV	Z	20	week 1	1
10-XXX	G	45	week 2	2
10-XYZ	B	90	week 3	4

* As of the beginning of the week.
† As of the end of the week.
‡ The plant works five single-shift days per week.

Figure 5   Distribution requirements planning worksheet.

Index

M.G